DIPLOMACY
of
POWER

DIPLOMACY
of
POWER

Soviet Armed Forces as a Political Instrument

STEPHEN S. KAPLAN

with

MICHEL TATU

THOMAS W. ROBINSON

WILLIAM ZIMMERMAN

DONALD S. ZAGORIA *and* JANET D. ZAGORIA

PAUL JABBER *and* ROMAN KOLKOWICZ

ALVIN Z. RUBINSTEIN

DAVID K. HALL

COLIN LEGUM

THE BROOKINGS INSTITUTION
Washington, D.C.

Copyright © 1981 by
THE BROOKINGS INSTITUTION
1775 Massachusetts Avenue, N.W., Washington, D.C. 20036

Library of Congress Cataloging in Publication Data:

Kaplan, Stephen S
   Diplomacy of power.

   Bibliography: p.
   Includes index.
      1. Russia—Armed Forces—History—20th century.
   2. Russia—Foreign relations—1945–   3. Russia—
   Military policy.   4. World politics—1945–
   I. Title.
   UA770.K28   327.1'17'0947   80-25006
   ISBN 0-8157-4824-8
   ISBN 0-8157-4823-X (pbk.)

   9 8 7 6 5 4 3

TO MY FAMILY

THE BROOKINGS INSTITUTION is an independent organization devoted to nonpartisan research, education, and publication in economics, government, foreign policy, and the social sciences generally. Its principal purposes are to aid in the development of sound public policies and to promote public understanding of issues of national importance.

The Institution was founded on December 8, 1927, to merge the activities of the Institute for Government Research, founded in 1916, the Institute of Economics, founded in 1922, and the Robert Brookings Graduate School of Economics and Government, founded in 1924.

The Board of Trustees is responsible for the general administration of the Institution, while the immediate direction of the policies, program, and staff is vested in the President, assisted by an advisory committee of the officers and staff. The by-laws of the Institution state: "It is the function of the Trustees to make possible the conduct of scientific research, and publication, under the most favorable conditions, and to safeguard the independence of the research staff in the pursuit of their studies and in the publication of the results of such studies. It is not a part of their function to determine, control, or influence the conduct of particular investigations or the conclusions reached."

The President bears final responsibility for the decision to publish a manuscript as a Brookings book. In reaching his judgment on the competence, accuracy, and objectivity of each study, the President is advised by the director of the appropriate research program and weighs the views of a panel of expert outside readers who report to him in confidence on the quality of the work. Publication of a work signifies that it is deemed a competent treatment worthy of public consideration but does not imply endorsement of conclusions or recommendations.

The Institution maintains its position of neutrality on issues of public policy in order to safeguard the intellectual freedom of the staff. Hence interpretations or conclusions in Brookings publications should be understood to be solely those of the authors and should not be attributed to the Institution, to its trustees, officers, or other staff members, or to the organizations that support its research.

Foreword

THE Soviet Union has often used military power to attain political objectives outside its borders without going to war. Since the Second World War the Soviet armed forces have grown stronger and more capable of influencing developments in areas far beyond the USSR's periphery. Thus their significance as a political instrument has increased.

In this book, Stephen S. Kaplan identifies 190 incidents since World War II in which the Soviet Union employed ground, sea, or air forces to help attain foreign policy goals. This history and analysis of Soviet use of military diplomacy thus complements the earlier work by Kaplan and Barry M. Blechman, *Force without War: U.S. Armed Forces as a Political Instrument* (Brookings, 1978), a historical record of U.S. military operations in support of American diplomacy in the postwar era.

In part 1 Kaplan examines the political context of the Soviet military operations he has identified, the types of armed force involved, and the actions taken. His analysis also explores the willingness of Soviet leaders to accept the risks of using military power as a foreign policy instrument. In part 2, the authors of eight sets of case studies analyze incidents in Eastern Europe, along the Sino-Soviet border, on the Korean peninsula, in Southeast Asia, in the Middle East, and in Africa to assess the effectiveness of Soviet military diplomacy and its implications for the United States. Kaplan concludes in part 3 that Soviet armed forces were an uncertain tool for achieving results abroad. Success varied greatly and depended upon immediate circumstances. Even when specific objectives were achieved by resort to Soviet forces, more general Soviet interests were not necessarily well served.

Stephen S. Kaplan is a member of the Brookings Foreign Policy Studies program and coauthor (with Philip J. Farley and William H. Lewis) of *Arms across the Sea* (Brookings, 1978) and (with Barry M. Blechman) of *Force without War: U.S. Armed Forces as a Political Instrument* (Brookings, 1978). The case studies were written by academic and other specialists working as members of the Brookings associated staff: David K. Hall is assistant professor of political science at Brown University; Paul Jabber is associate professor of political science at the University of California, Los Angeles; Roman Kolkowicz is professor of political science and director of the Center of International and Strategic Affairs at the University of California, Los Angeles; Colin Legum is a correspondent for *The Observer;* Thomas W. Robinson is professor of international relations at the National War College, National Defense University; Alvin Z. Rubinstein is professor of political science at the University of Pennsylvania; Michel Tatu is on the staff of *Le Monde;* Donald S. Zagoria is professor of political science at Hunter College; Janet D. Zagoria is teaching adjunct at Mercy College; and William Zimmerman is professor of political science at the University of Michigan.

The research upon which this book is based was supported by the Defense Advanced Research Projects Agency (DARPA) of the U.S. Department of Defense under Contract N00014-77-C-0479. Brookings and the authors are grateful for this assistance and for the personal support of Stephen J. Andriole and Judith Ayres Daly, director and program manager, respectively, of the DARPA Cybernetics Technology Office. A report as well as a computer tape and manual prepared for researchers wanting to use the data collected for this study were submitted to the Cybernetics Technology Office in 1979.

Brookings and the authors thank Alexander L. George, Robert Legvold, and Helmut Sonnenfeldt for evaluating the manuscript and for making valuable suggestions. Barry M. Blechman, Edward Tufte, Bradford Dismukes, James M. McConnell, Charles C. Petersen, Richard B. Remnek, Stephen S. Roberts, Robert G. Weinland, and Kenneth Weiss also provided helpful comments and criticism.

At Brookings, advice and assistance were received from A. Doak Barnett, Robert P. Berman, Richard K. Betts, Raymond Garthoff, Henry Owen, and John Steinbruner. Christine K. Lipsey provided research assistance during the study; she was helped by Linda Corbelli, Elizabeth U. Karzon, John J. MacWilliams, Cynthia Weisman, and Alexandria Williams. Faith Thompson Campbell compiled an initial data base. Elizabeth H. Cross and Jean Rosenblatt edited the manuscript; Clifford A. Wright verified its factual content; Delores Burton, Ruth Conrad, Jeanane Patterson, and Julia Sternberg provided secretarial assistance; and Diana Regenthal prepared the index.

The views and conclusions expressed in this book are the authors' alone and do not represent the official policies, expressed or implied, of the Defense Advanced Research Projects Agency or the U.S. government; nor should they be ascribed to the trustees, officers, or other staff members of the Brookings Institution.

BRUCE K. MACLAURY
President

October 1980
Washington, D.C.

Contents

PART THREE: CONCLUSIONS

Appendixes

Tables

Figure

CHAPTER ONE

Introduction

ALTHOUGH the most important functions of Soviet armed forces are to deter aggression against the Soviet Union and to defend the homeland of the USSR, military power has also been a critical instrument of Soviet foreign policy. It has been used to expand and preserve Soviet authority in adjacent areas and to influence other Communist regimes, to respond to Western and Chinese actions and unsettling domestic developments in neighboring nations that Moscow has perceived as threatening to Soviet security, and to create favorable relations with new nations emerging from colonial empires.

As the Kremlin has become less anxious about the USSR's military security, the significance of Soviet armed forces as a foreign policy instrument has loomed larger. Not too long ago the reach of Soviet military diplomacy was restricted to territories neighboring or not far beyond the periphery of the USSR. The development of an increasingly competent oceangoing navy and of a strategic airlift capability allowing the rapid movement of troops and matériel over great distances has extended Moscow's reach to distant waters and regions. The backing of strategic nuclear forces has allowed Kremlin leaders to use conventional armed forces as a foreign policy tool with increased confidence.

Since the Cuban missile crisis Soviet armed forces have been used to intervene in Afghanistan, suppress political change in Czechoslovakia, coerce China, and constrain the behavior of neighbors such as Rumania and Japan. Moscow also placed more than 20,000 military personnel in Egypt to provide air defense against Israel; Soviet air force, naval, and airborne units played important roles in the 1973 Middle East war; Soviet naval forces were active in the 1970 Jordanian crisis and in the 1971 Indo-Pakistani war; and Soviet air and naval operations influenced the

1

outcomes of the 1975–76 civil war in Angola and the 1977–78 Ethiopian-Somalian conflict. Soviet combat aircraft also participated in civil wars in Yemen, Sudan, and Iraq, and Soviet naval vessels were on the scene during the 1973 "cod war" between Great Britain and Iceland, the 1974 Cyprus crisis, the 1979 China-Vietnam conflict, and little noticed internal crises in Somalia, Sierra Leone, and other nations.

There is nothing extraordinary about a great nation using armed forces to attain political objectives abroad without going to war. U.S. policymakers have turned to the military as an instrument of coercive or cooperative diplomacy on more than 200 occasions since the Second World War. Such action has ranged from sending a single ship to visit a foreign port as a symbol of American support, to the crisis deployment of major ground, air, and naval units and the alert of strategic nuclear forces.[1] France, Great Britain, and a host of other countries have also practiced military diplomacy to achieve political objectives.[2] This study focuses on the use of Soviet armed forces as a discrete foreign policy instrument—that is, on Soviet military operations designed to achieve specific objectives abroad at particular times.

The goals of this book are to: (1) present a historical record of discrete political-military operations by Soviet ground, sea, and air forces since the Second World War, focusing on the political context of incidents and related uses of Soviet armed forces; (2) examine the Soviet Union's readiness to use military power in the pursuit of foreign policy objectives and its willingness to accept risks in doing so; (3) evaluate the effectiveness of coercive diplomacy in protecting Soviet interests and achieving foreign policy goals; and (4) assess the implications of Soviet coercive diplomacy for U.S. interests and behavior.

Soviet Armed Forces and International Relations

Before pursuing the relatively limited subject of this study, it is appropriate to examine the wider influence of Soviet armed forces on interna-

1. See Barry M. Blechman and Stephen S. Kaplan, *Force without War: U.S. Armed Forces as a Political Instrument* (Brookings Institution, 1978).

2. Nor is the use of armed forces for purposes other than war a post–World War II phenomenon. Nations have used armed forces demonstratively throughout the ages. Xerxes spared the spies of Greece so that they could report the awesome power marshaled by the Persians, and the Athenians sought to coerce the Melians. Herodotus, *The Persian Wars,* trans. George Rawlinson (Modern Library, 1942), pp. 553–54; *The Complete Writings of Thucydides: The Peloponnesian War,* trans. John H. Finney, Jr. (Modern Library, 1951), pp. 330–37.

tional relations and the military's multidimensional role in Soviet foreign policy. To overlook the importance of the normal state of Soviet armed forces and their routine activities risks implying that they play a role in international relations only when they are called on to do something out of the ordinary. The opposite is true. A prominent Soviet defense intellectual has said of the daily significance of Soviet armed forces to Moscow's international interests:

The Soviet Union and other socialist countries, by virtue of their increasing military potential, are changing the balance of forces in the international arena in favor of the forces of peace and socialism. This is exerting a very sobering effect on extremist circles in the imperialist states and it is creating favorable conditions for achieving the Soviet foreign-political goals in the international arena.[3]

The following pages summarize the routine Soviet military developments and activities since the Second World War that have influenced Soviet foreign relations.

The Foundation: Strategic Nuclear Forces

The Soviet Union is recognized globally as a great nuclear power, equaled only by the United States in its ability to wreak destruction upon the planet. The Soviet nuclear arsenal, which affords the USSR superpower status, is the principal foundation of the Soviet Union's international position. Without nuclear armaments, Moscow would not be able to orchestrate conventional armed forces with confidence, and Moscow's diplomacy would not be taken as seriously as it is by the United States, China, Western Europe, Japan, and other nations.[4]

Evaluating the strategic nuclear balance between the United States and the Soviet Union in the late 1970s, Secretary of Defense Harold Brown's judgment was that "a rough strategic nuclear equilibrium exists between the two superpowers at the present time. Neither country enjoys a military advantage; neither is in a position to exploit its nuclear capabilities for political ends. The situation is one of standoff or stalemate. Mutual strategic deterrence and essential equivalence are in effect."[5] However, be-

3. V. M. Kulish and others, *Military Force and International Relations*, JPRS Report 58947 (Moscow: U.S. National Technical Information Service, 1972), p. 170.

4. Soviet strategic forces in 1979 included 90 submarines able to launch 1,028 missiles, about 1,398 ICBMs (intercontinental ballistic missiles), 710 IRBMs and MRBMs (intermediate- and medium-range ballistic missiles), and 850 long-range and medium-range bombers. International Institute for Strategic Studies, *The Military Balance, 1979–1980* (London: IISS, 1979), p. 9.

5. *Department of Defense Annual Report, Fiscal Year 1979*, p. 4.

cause of this rough strategic parity, the United States' preparedness to use nuclear weapons against the Soviet Union in retaliation for Soviet aggression against American allies became a subject of considerable disagreement; U.S. policymakers seemed to many more fearful of conventional military confrontation with Moscow; and the United States reluctantly accepted a greater Soviet role in international affairs. U.S. allies grew doubtful about what they could expect from the United States in crises, Soviet allies became more confident, and all nations accorded Soviet positions increased respect.

Throughout most of the post–World War II era the Soviet Union has presented itself to the world as a nuclear power and derived political advantage from this stature. The USSR carried out its first atomic weapon test in 1949 and detonated a thermonuclear device in 1953. Although bomber aircraft (the MYA-4 Bison and TU-20 Bear) able to make round-trip flights to the United States became available only in 1956–57, medium-range Soviet aircraft—able to make one-way journeys to North America as well as round-trip flights to Europe and Japan—were deployed beginning in 1948.[6] The threat of nuclear war directed at U.S. allies in Eurasia was further reinforced by Soviet deployment of medium-range ballistic missiles (MRBMs) beginning in 1955.[7]

Moscow's end to the U.S. nuclear monopoly and nuclear threat to Western Europe caused or reinforced Western defense decisions in the early and mid-1950s that had major foreign policy and other political implications.[8] At this time, when the United States still retained a large lead over the USSR in strategic capability, anxiety developed that "the two nuclear forces would now deter each other and cancel each other out—while Soviet ground forces were free to roll westward."[9] Western concern was further increased by analyses suggesting, "on the basis of existing production rates and expected expansion of industrial capacity," a two-to-one Soviet advantage over the United States in long-range

6. Robert P. Berman, *Soviet Air Power in Transition* (Brookings Institution, 1978), pp. 26–27.

7. Edward L. Warner III, "Soviet Strategic Force Posture: Some Alternative Explanations," in Frank B. Horton III, Anthony C. Rogerson, and Edward L. Warner III, *Comparative Defense Policy* (Johns Hopkins University Press, 1974), p. 313; Thomas W. Wolfe, *Soviet Power and Europe, 1945–1970* (Johns Hopkins Press, 1970), p. 183.

8. George H. Quester, *Nuclear Diplomacy: The First Twenty-five Years* (Dunellen, 1970), pp. 59–87.

9. Ibid., p. 62.

bombers by the end of the 1950s.[10] These fears—accentuated by the
launch of *Sputnik I* in October 1957, succeeding Soviet space shots, and
Moscow's claims about the progress of its intercontinental ballistic missile (ICBM) program—were, in the end, overplayed by Nikita Khrushchev. But in the interim—between 1957 and the Cuban missile crisis in
1962—Soviet diplomacy benefited mightily from the improved image of
USSR military power brought about by these achievements and accompanying Soviet rhetoric. With the United States widely perceived to be
five years behind the USSR in space and missile technology, the Soviet
Union seemed to many to have gained the upper hand in the cold war.
Western Europeans saw the USSR gaining great military advantage over
the United States, and Americans worried about the "missile gap."[11]
Western governments, although less pessimistic than their citizens, behaved less confidently. Horelick and Rush wrote of the U.S. reaction:

> Being uncertain about the strategic nuclear balance, the West found it diffi-
> cult to assess the aims of particular Soviet moves. Whereas the Soviet leaders
> could plan their initial moves with confidence that they ran no risk of pro-
> voking war, the United States leaders were uncertain as to the risks involved
> in various alternative countermoves and therefore felt constrained to respond
> cautiously. This caution, in turn, strengthened Soviet reliance on American
> restraint in the cold war and increased the USSR's confidence that it could
> control the risk of war stemming from its actions.[12]

The sag of morale in the West buoyed the confidence of Soviet allies and
friends in the third world.

The perception of USSR-U.S. strategic parity in the 1970s developed
principally as a result of the USSR's continuing deployments of ICBMs
and missile-carrying submarines after the United States set limits on the
size of its own strategic forces. Just after the Cuban missile crisis, in
early 1963, 44 percent of those interviewed in a poll in Britain believed

---

10. The quotation is from Allen Dulles, *The Craft of Intelligence* (Harper and
Row, 1963), p. 162. See also Quester, *Nuclear Diplomacy*, pp. 126–29; Jerome H.
Kahan, *Security in the Nuclear Age: Developing U.S. Strategic Arms Policy* (Brook-
ings Institution, 1975), pp. 30–31.

11. Wolfe, *Soviet Power and Europe*, pp. 84–89; Arnold L. Horelick and Myron
Rush, *Strategic Power and Soviet Foreign Policy* (University of Chicago Press,
1966), pp. 63–64; Leo P. Crespi, "Trend Measurement of U.S. Standing in Foreign
Public Opinion," paper prepared under the auspices of the United States Informa-
tion Agency; Robert B. Mahoney, Jr., "The Superpower Balance, Military Policy
and Public Opinion in the United Kingdom, France, and the Federal Republic of
Germany," in Donald C. Daniel, ed., *International Perceptions of the Superpower
Military Balances* (Praeger, 1978), pp. 102–03.

12. Horelick and Rush, *Strategic Power and Soviet Foreign Policy*, p. 110.

the Soviet Union was "equal" to or ahead of the United States in "strength in nuclear weapons"; in mid-1971 40 percent believed this. The respective percentages in similar polls taken at these same times were, in France, 49 and 36 percent, and in West Germany, 37 and 35 percent. By contrast, in early 1977, 63 percent of those polled in Britain, 58 percent in France, and 60 percent in West Germany perceived the USSR as being "equal" to or "ahead" of the United States in nuclear strength. This change in public opinion, together with perceptions of increased Soviet conventional military power, no doubt heightened North Atlantic Treaty Organization (NATO) concern about U.S. readiness to defend Europe. Another question asked in polls was, "How much trust do you feel we can have in the United States to come to our defense?" Between 1968 and 1975 the percentage of those who had a "great deal" of trust fell in polls taken in Britain from 39 to 22 percent, in France from 18 to 9 percent, and in West Germany from 22 to 13 percent. Japanese confidence also declined.[13] Moscow, for its part, demanded that increased attention be paid to its views and interests on the basis of its improved strategic position.

The Conventional Military Storehouse

It is also recognized within the USSR that "international relations have . . . been greatly influenced by conventional armed forces."[14] Soviet military men entered the postwar world with a favorable reputation. The retreat before the Wehrmacht in 1941–42 to the suburbs of Moscow and the Volga, following the poor performance of the Red army in the 1939–40 war with Finland, showed Stalin's military to be poorly led, ill-equipped, and disorganized, and stirred memories of the Russian performance in the face of Napoleon's onslaught of 1812. But unlike Napoleon's men, the German army did not enter Moscow and then unravel of its own accord. It was halted in battle and then driven back to Berlin with a vengeance. Stalingrad provided a mighty land counterpart to the battles of Midway and the Coral Sea, as did Kursk and the great Russian

13. Poll data is from Crespi, "Trend Measurement," tables 15, 16, and 26. The term "strength in nuclear weapons" was not defined in any specific way. On Moscow's diplomatic use of improved Soviet strategic capabilities beginning in the early 1970s, see John Newhouse, *Cold Dawn: The Story of SALT* (Holt, Rinehart and Winston, 1973), pp. 57–58.

14. Kulish, *Military Force and International Relations*, p. 172.

summer offensive of 1944 to the island-hopping by U.S. Marines in the Pacific war and the Allied landing at Normandy and breakout in France.

Despite the 7½ million Soviet combat casualties suffered by the war's end,[15] the Soviet army obtained an image of tenacity and resilience in homeland defense approaching legend; on the offensive, the army was fearsome. Nor was the army's reputation harmed by the August 1945 Far Eastern campaign, Soviet suppression of the revolt in Hungary in 1956, and the 1968 intervention in Czechoslovakia.

Since the Second World War the continued large size and high quality of the Soviet army and, more recently, of Soviet tactical air forces, have greatly affected Europe and Asia. Before the Korean War, Moscow's demobilization left between 4 million and 5 million Soviet citizens in arms, while U.S. armed forces were reduced to about 1.4 million.[16] In the late 1970s Soviet armed forces totaled roughly 3.7 million.[17] Soviet military power grew stronger in Eurasia after the August 1968 intervention in Czechoslovakia and clashes with China in 1969. New Soviet armies were permanently deployed in Eastern Europe and the Far East; Soviet divisions were enlarged; new tanks and other armored vehicles were deployed in large numbers; and mobility was enhanced generally. This reinforcement in personnel, firepower, and ability to move rapidly afforded Moscow a force more closely aligned to its military doctrine, which has emphasized high-speed offensive operations led by heavy armor and mobile artillery.[18] While the West embarked on a policy of détente in the first half of the 1970s, Moscow's continuing buildup of Soviet ground and air forces in Europe and Asia eventually led NATO to regroup politically, strengthen its armed forces, and become more unyielding in East-West relations—developments decidedly not in the USSR's interest.

The size and deployment of the Soviet army and its supporting air forces in Europe is the foundation on which the status quo there and relationships within the Atlantic world have been erected. If routine Soviet military power were absent in Europe, it is hard to believe that either Eastern or Western European nations would continue to behave

15. J. David Singer and Melvin Small, *The Wages of War, 1816–1965: A Statistical Handbook* (Wiley, 1972), p. 67.

16. Wolfe, *Soviet Power and Europe,* pp. 10–11.

17. IISS, *The Military Balance 1979–1980,* p. 9.

18. Jeffrey Record, *Sizing Up the Soviet Army* (Brookings Institution, 1975), pp. 12–16; Barry M. Blechman and others, *The Soviet Military Buildup and U.S. Defense Spending* (Brookings Institution, 1977), pp. 9–10.

as they do toward the Soviet Union, the United States, and each other. In the East, meanwhile, China's fear of both nuclear and conventional conflict with the Soviet Union seems to have been the most important factor in China's ending its posture of isolation and pursuing friendly relations with the West. This, in turn, has influenced Western relations with the Soviet Union. Japan, too, has been influenced by Soviet military deployments. Soviet armed forces in Asia have always concerned Japan and influenced its foreign policy. The Soviet buildup that began in the late 1960s and continued in the 1970s (in large part related to the Sino-Soviet conflict) reinforced relations between the United States and Japan, gave Tokyo reason to welcome a closer relationship with Peking, and pushed Japan to more seriously consider the adequacy of its defense program.

While the Soviet army and its supporting tactical aviation have long marked the USSR as a great power in Eurasia, the forward deployment of major naval forces and production of long-range transport aircraft have extended the USSR's military reach to more distant places. Until the mid-1960s Soviet surface warships were restricted to coastal waters with few exceptions. Operating out of USSR ports, Soviet submarines were of little value politically. The USSR gained new credibility in the third world and weakened the political currency of Western naval forces when Moscow established a continuous surface navy presence in the Mediterranean, permanently deployed forces in West African waters and the Indian Ocean, and inaugurated regular naval appearances in the Caribbean. Moscow's use of these forces in later crises changed perceptions even further.

The modernity of the Soviet navy is also significant. Although a number of older gun cruisers and destroyers have been retained, a large proportion of those vessels that first appeared on the high seas in the late 1960s were newly constructed and missile-armed. The Soviet navy's credibility and political influence were dramatically reinforced in October 1967 when a missile-firing Egyptian patrol boat, supplied by the Russians, sank an Israeli destroyer. Commissioned just months earlier was the *Moskva,* the USSR's first helicopter carrier. Five years later the *Kiev,* able to accommodate vertical or short takeoff and landing aircraft, was launched. These Soviet ships have given the impression of a burgeoning sea-based air capability, even though they appear to have been designed mostly for antisubmarine warfare and cannot project significant power ashore—unlike U.S. aircraft carriers, whose principal mission is tactical air support. The deployment of newer classes of Soviet aircraft carriers will have even greater impact on global perceptions.

The size of the Soviet navy has also enhanced its credibility. In the 1970s many observed that the Russians had more major operational surface combatants than did the United States, although this discrepancy was largely related to the block retirement in the late 1960s and early 1970s of U.S. warships built during World War II and the counting of inferior Soviet vessels.[19]

Soviet naval leaders have not been unaware of the political use of warships. Commander in Chief and Admiral of the Fleet Sergei G. Gorshkov has written and spoken frequently about the peacetime value of navies, the Soviet navy in particular. In a major treatise published serially in 1972–73, he wrote, "The Navy possesses the capability to vividly demonstrate the economic and military might of a country beyond its borders during peacetime. . . . The Soviet Navy is a powerful factor in the creation of favorable conditions for the building of Socialism and Communism, for the active defense of peace, and for strengthening international security."[20]

Soviet military power and the USSR's ability to exert influence in distant areas has also been strengthened by the development of long-range heavy-lift air transport. Into the mid-1960s the Soviet Union lacked the ability to airlift sizable amounts of personnel or equipment any significant distance. Production of the first Soviet tactical airlift plane, the AN-8 Camp, did not begin until 1956. The more advanced AN-12 Cub, able to carry 100 troops or 20 tons of cargo and available beginning about 1959, had a range of only 1,500 miles.[21] Much earlier the United States had developed the C-130 Hercules, which could carry similar loads over twice the range. In 1967 the Soviet air force began receiving the AN-22 Cock, able to carry a load of about 88 tons a distance of 3,000 miles.[22] Although only relatively few of these aircraft were produced, as compared, for example, with the U.S. C-141 Starlifter, which began to enter the U.S. Air

19. *Annual Defense Department Report, Fiscal Year 1978,* p. 24; "The Trend in the Naval Balance: A Fact Sheet," Office of Rep. Les Aspin, July 1976, p. 6.

20. Sergei G. Gorshkov, *Red Star Rising at Sea,* trans. Theodore A. Neely, Jr. (United States Naval Institute, 1974), pp. 115, 134. This essay originally appeared in 1972 as a series of articles in *Morskoi Sbornik.*

21. Berman, *Soviet Air Power in Transition,* pp. 34–35; William Green and Gordon Swanborough, *The Observer's Soviet Aircraft Directory* (Frederick Warne, 1975), pp. 36–37; John W. Taylor, ed., *Jane's All the World's Aircraft, 1977–78* (New York: Franklin Watts, 1977), p. 422.

22. Figure calculated by Robert P. Berman, Brookings Institution.

Force inventory in 1965, the AN-22 enabled Moscow to impress the world with its possession of a powerful and growing strategic airlift capability.

In the mid-1970s Soviet airmen began to take delivery on a new long-range transport aircraft, the IL-76 Candid. This plane, although in a class with the U.S. C-141 Starlifter rather than the more capable C-5 Galaxy, has been produced in large numbers. Soviet airlifts to Egypt and Syria during the 1973 Middle East war, Angola in 1975–76, and Ethiopia in 1977–78 reinforced international consciousness of the USSR's ability to move large amounts of troops and military equipment by air intercontinentally. Between 1965 and 1977, the aggregate lift capacity of Soviet Military Transport Aviation more than doubled.[23]

Armed Forces Activities

Aside from their character, size, equipment, and deployment, the activities of Soviet armed forces also influence Soviet foreign relations. A military exercise may be used to support coercive diplomacy during a crisis and in other instances to inform foreign nations of the seriousness of a specific claim or commitment. Most exercises, though, are carried out for more general purposes: to improve the talents and techniques of soldiers, sailors, and airmen for war, and to teach them the strengths and weaknesses of doctrine and equipment; and to impress upon foreign observers the credibility of commitments or to gain recognition as a power to be reckoned with.

Soviet ground and air exercises regularly show off the capabilities of Soviet forces and their preparedness for conflict in Europe and Asia. The combination of field exercises in Eastern Europe, European Russia, Central Asia, and the Far East, together with more specialized logistics and air defense and staff maneuvers, reinforces respect for the USSR and keeps alive the image of Soviet armed forces as ever ready for action and of the USSR as a great power. Communist party leader Leonid Brezhnev, commenting on exercises held in the USSR in 1970, declared that "at the present time no question of any importance in the world can be solved without our participation, without taking into account our economic and military might."[24]

23. Berman, *Soviet Air Power in Transition*, p. 36.
24. As quoted by Foy D. Kohler, in *The Soviet Union: Internal Dynamics of Foreign Policy, Present and Future*, Hearings before the House Subcommittee on Europe and the Middle East of the House Committee on International Relations, 95 Cong. 1 sess. (Government Printing Office, 1978), p. 33.

The joint exercises and other cooperative activities of Soviet and Eastern European military personnel are used not only to practice for conflict and deter the West, but also to maintain strong bonds between the armed forces of the USSR and other Warsaw Pact nations and to portray the USSR as all-powerful in Eastern Europe and committed to defending it against the West—particularly West Germany.[25] The late Soviet defense minister and Politburo member, Marshal Andrei A. Grechko, wrote:

Joint troop and command and staff exercises play a large role in strengthening military cooperation. By accomplishing common missions in the course of such exercises, the soldiers of fraternal armies come to know each other more closely, learn together the art of modern combat, understand better their international duty, and become imbued even more deeply with a feeling of friendship and respect, and of mutual trust and understanding. It can be said with complete justification that joint exercises are a genuine school of inviolable friendship and combat comradeship of soldiers of the fraternal armies. They demonstrate the growing defensive might of the socialist states and motivate personnel of the allied armies to defend the revolutionary achievements of the peoples.[26]

To offset the imperial appearance of Soviet armed forces in foreign countries, maneuvers in East Germany, for example, typically include Polish as well as Soviet units; those in Poland include East German and Czechoslovakian troops; and so forth. Joint exercises directed by a home country commander are another device often used to downplay Soviet dominance.

The Soviet Union also conducts joint naval exercises with East Germany and Poland to strengthen alliance bonds. Soviet navy commander in chief and Admiral of the Fleet Gorshkov has commented:

The development and deepening of combat cooperation between Soviet military sailors and sailors of the allied fleets are promoted by the improved coordination of actions among the naval forces at all operational levels and by the holding of joint voyages and exercises, which have become a good school of international education.[27]

25. On the creation of the bonds between Soviet and East German military personnel, see G. Jokel and others, "The Development of Combat Cooperation Between the GDR NPA [National People's Army] and the Soviet Army During the 1970s," *Voyenno-Istoricheskiy Zhurnal* [*Military Historical Journal*], no. 7 (July 1978), pp. 65–71. Reprinted in *Soviet Press: Selected Translations,* distributed by the Directorate of Soviet Affairs, U.S. Air Force Intelligence Service (December 1978), pp. 341–50.

26. A. A. Grechko, *The Armed Forces of the Soviet State: A Soviet View,* 2d ed., translated and published under the auspices of the U.S. Air Force (GPO, 1976), p. 341.

27. *Pravda,* July 31, 1977 (translated in U.S. Foreign Broadcast Information Service [FBIS], *Daily Report: Soviet Union,* August 4, 1977, p. V4).

After the first large-scale Soviet naval maneuvers in open waters—the Norwegian Sea—in 1961, the Soviet navy began conducting such exercises every other year. In 1965 and in 1968 larger maneuvers were held in the Atlantic area, and as the Soviet squadron in the Mediterranean expanded, it too established a prominent exercise pattern. In 1970 and 1975 worldwide exercises were held, the 1975 ones including operations by 200 ships in the Atlantic, Pacific, and Indian oceans and in adjacent seas, as well as flights by long-range naval reconnaissance aircraft based in the USSR, Cuba, Guinea, South Yemen, and Somalia. The attention paid to large Soviet naval maneuvers adds to the USSR's credibility as a sea power.[28] Of course, naval exercises, like ground maneuvers, new procurements, and forward deployments, may stimulate defense spending and greater unity among nations hostile to or anxious about Soviet foreign policy.

Sending warships to distant ports to show off the reach of a nation's military power and the state of its technology has long been used to impress foreign peoples. The visit, the welcoming of host nationals aboard ship, and organized good deeds by sailors going ashore have been used to create or reinforce friendly bilateral relations. In addition to visiting Warsaw Pact nations, Soviet naval vessels are reported to have visited about seventy-five different countries between 1953 and 1974.[29] At first Soviet ships were seen primarily in northern European and a few Mediterranean ports. Then, following the forward deployments by surface groups into the Mediterranean, the Atlantic and Indian oceans, and West African waters in the 1960s and 1970s, the Russians began visiting nations along the Mediterranean coast, as well as ones in sub-Saharan Africa, the Caribbean, the Persian Gulf, and South Asia. In 1977 Soviet warships paid more than 600 visits to foreign ports.[30] The purpose of this

28. Donald C. Daniel, "Trends and Patterns in Major Soviet Naval Exercises," in Paul J. Murphy, ed., *Naval Power in Soviet Policy,* vol. 2 (GPO, 1978), pp. 222–24; Bruce W. Watson and Margurite A. Walton, "Okean-75," *United States Naval Institute Proceedings,* vol. 102 (July 1976), pp. 93–97; *Fiscal Year 1977 Authorization for Military Procurement, Research and Development, and Active Duty, Selected Reserve and Civilian Personnel Strengths,* Hearings before the Senate Committee on Armed Services, 94 Cong. 2 sess. (GPO, 1976), pt. 10: Tactical Air Power, pp. 5316–27.

29. Anne M. Kelly, "Port Visits and the 'Internationalist Mission' of the Soviet Navy," in Michael MccGwire and John McDonnell, eds., *Soviet Naval Influence: Domestic and Foreign Dimensions* (Praeger for the Centre for Foreign Policy Studies, Department of Political Science, Dalhousie University, Halifax, N.S., 1977), p. 511.

30. *Pravda,* July 30, 1978 (in FBIS, *Soviet Union,* August 3, 1978, p. V4).

Soviet presence is to support the USSR's foreign interests. In Admiral Gorshkov's words:

Our warships are calling with continually greater frequency at foreign ports, fulfilling the role of "plenipotentiaries" of the Socialist countries. . . . The friendly visits of Soviet navymen make it possible for the peoples of many countries to become convinced with their own eyes of the creativity of the ideas of Communism, and of the genuine equality of all nationalities in the Soviet state, and to gain a concept of the level of development and culture of representatives of the most varied regions of our immense Motherland. They see warships embodying the achievements of Soviet science, technology, and industry, and establish friendly contacts with representatives of the most diverse strata of population of our country. Soviet navymen, from admirals down to seamen, are bearing the truth about the first Socialist country in the world, about Communist ideology and culture, and about the Soviet way of life to the masses of peoples of other states. They are clearly and convincingly spreading the ideas of the Leninist peaceloving policy of the Communist Party and the Soviet government through many countries of the world. It is impossible to overestimate the significance of this ideological influence.[31]

Occasionally, Soviet military aircraft or delegations have also visited foreign nations on missions of goodwill.[32] In addition to trips to countries such as Cuba and Vietnam and to third world nations that buy armaments from the Soviet Union (Libya and Algeria, for example), ranking Soviet military personnel periodically visit countries not so attached to the USSR.[33] Each year Soviet military men themselves play host to foreign naval vessels and sometimes to air force units, as well as hundreds of military and civilian guests invited to observe exercises, examine military installations, discuss subjects of mutual interest, celebrate holidays, and so forth.[34] While Moscow uses military interactions at home and abroad to impress allies and nonaligned and antagonistic countries, visits by Soviet military personnel to Western nations (and by Western military

31. Gorshkov, *Red Star Rising at Sea,* p. 119. For some insights into the local reception of Soviet naval visits in third world nations, see Heidi S. Phillips, *Host Press Coverage of Soviet Naval Visits to Islamic Countries, 1968–73,* CRC 283 (Arlington, Va.: Center for Naval Analyses, 1976).

32. FBIS, *Soviet Union* (September 19, 1978), p. E3.

33. For example, in 1977 first deputy defense minister, General S. L. Sokolov, led a delegation to Jordan, and in 1978 Admiral Gorshkov visited Sweden. The object in both instances presumably was to promote better bilateral relations. *Krasnaya Zvezda,* November 20, 1977 (in FBIS, *Soviet Union,* November 23, 1977, p. F12, and September 11, 1978, p. E3).

34. For example see ibid., August 8, 1977, p. V4; January 12, 1978, p. F7; April 12, 1978, p. N3; September 8, 1978, p. H4; March 7, 1979, p. N1; and *Washington Post,* October 27, 1977.

representatives to the USSR) may also have a stabilizing and even civilizing political influence. An invitation to visit can be used to signal willingness to improve a relationship, and the number and quality of interactions with a country may indicate the state of a relationship. In addition, military exchanges may render antagonistic behavior less acceptable.

Besides playing host to foreign delegations, Soviet military schools and other facilities also train foreign military men. About the training given to military men from other Communist states, Marshal Grechko wrote: "While successfully mastering comprehensive ideological-theoretical, military and technical knowledge within the walls of Soviet military academies, the officers of fraternal countries are imbued with a feeling of profound respect for the heroic past of the Soviet people and its armed forces, and with a spirit of military friendship and comradeship."[35] No doubt such objectives have also applied to students from less developed nations who have been attending military schools in the USSR since the mid-1950s.[36] Soviet military assistance teams are also sent to Communist nations and the third world.[37] Still, military advisers and special delegations sent abroad as well as training and hospitality within the USSR, although meant to obtain goodwill and exert influence, are uncertain instruments. Hosts to Soviet military personnel and foreign military visitors in the USSR have sometimes found Soviet behavior and methods, and the USSR as a nation, less than appealing.

Discrete Political-Military Operations

Because this study concerns the use of Soviet armed forces to help achieve specific foreign policy objectives at particular times rather than the diffuse influence of Soviet military power, the focus is on situations between war and the routine in which Soviet military units have been

35. Grechko, *Armed Forces of the Soviet State*, p. 342.

36. Between 1955 and 1978 an estimated 43,790 military personnel from several dozen third world countries received training in the Soviet Union. By the end of 1978 about "1,900 LDC nationals were in the USSR . . . for specialized training." U.S. Central Intelligence Agency, National Foreign Assessment Center, *Communist Aid Activities in Non-Communist Less Developed Countries: A Research Paper*, ER 79-10412U (CIA, 1979), pp. 3, 5.

37. Through 1978 the USSR had delivered $25.3 billion in armaments to less developed countries. Almost 10,800 Soviet military personnel were abroad to instruct third world military personnel in 1978, when about $3.8 billion in arms deliveries were made. Ibid., p. 3.

called on to do something out of the ordinary. The range of these incidents has been diverse in both political context and use of Soviet armed forces. In some instances an important Soviet interest has been suddenly and seriously threatened with only a brief time allowed for a response. In other instances Soviet leaders have gradually become aware of an opportunity to influence Soviet interests favorably with either a relatively large probability of success or with minimal risk. To deal with these situations and others, the Kremlin has used a single warship, arrayed a fleet, used naval and air forces in combination, and so forth, as circumstances have warranted and military capabilities have allowed. The activities of Soviet armed forces in political-military operations have included new deployments, reinforcements, special exercises and visits, the transport of foreign personnel, occasional violence, and other politically motivated behavior.

A Political Use of Armed Forces

The following definition clarifies the basic concept under study:

A political use of the armed forces occurs when physical actions are taken by one or more components of the uniformed military services as part of a deliberate attempt by the national authorities to influence, or to be prepared to influence, specific behavior of individuals in another nation without engaging in a continuing contest of violence.[38]

A political use of armed forces was inferred if four elements were present in a situation.

1. A physical change in the disposition (location, activity, or readiness) of one or more component units of the armed forces had to have occurred. Mere references by Soviet leaders to the military (verbal threats or statements of support) did not qualify as a use of the armed forces. Military activities were taken to include: use of firepower; establishment or disestablishment of a permanent or temporary presence abroad; a blockade; an exercise or demonstration; escort or transport of another actor's armed forces or matériel; a visit by a military unit to a foreign location; reconnaissance, patrol, or surveillance operations that were not routine; or a change in readiness, including changes in alert

---

38. This definition was developed for an earlier examination of discrete political-military operations carried out by U.S. armed forces. The following elaboration on this definition and part of the format of this study parallel that earlier effort. See Blechman and Kaplan, *Force without War*, pp. 12–16.

status, the mobilization of reserve forces, and the movement of units toward or away from specific locations.

2. Behind this activity there had to have been a consciousness of purpose aimed at achieving some specific outcome abroad. A use of Soviet armed forces had to have been directed at influencing particular behavior in a discrete situation, or at least to have occurred because of concern about specific behavior. Of course in some instances the Kremlin had in mind multiple objectives that differed in both importance and attainability. But Soviet leaders had to have had at least one concrete goal in mind for an event to be considered an incident.

3. Soviet decisionmakers must have tried to attain their objectives at least initially by gaining influence in a target state rather than physically imposing their will. Generally speaking, armed forces may be used either as a political or as a martial instrument. When used as a martial instrument a military unit tries to seize an objective (occupy territory) or destroy an objective (defeat an army). In both cases, attainment of the immediate objective satisfies the purpose for which the force was used. When force is used as a political instrument, the objective is to influence the behavior of another actor—that is, to cause an actor to do something that he would not otherwise do, or not to do something that he would do otherwise. Thus, the activity of the military units themselves does not attain the objective; goals are achieved through the force's effect on decisions made by the actor.

4. Soviet leaders must have tried to avoid a sustained contest of violence. Although a war may result from a use of armed forces that otherwise meets the terms of the definition, initiation of war must not have been the intent of the action.

The delineation of political uses of Soviet armed forces examined in this study may be further clarified by listing types of military activity excluded by the definition.

1. Actions by Soviet armed forces to definitively terminate a foreign threat to the USSR or a Soviet position abroad were not considered political operations. Since the Second World War Soviet fighter aircraft have often fired at or near foreign aircraft claimed to be flying in the airspace of the USSR or one of its allies. Some of these aircraft were shot down or forced to land; some simply disappeared; others were fortunate enough to reach a hospitable destination. In most of these instances Soviet action did not appear related to any specific foreign policy goal, but rather seemed meant to end the intrusion. The most Soviet leaders

seemed to have had in mind by these actions—aside from rigorously protecting their sovereignty—was to demonstrate the effectiveness of the USSR's defenses and deter similar approaches by foreign aircraft in the future.[39]

Also excluded from this examination is the large number of seizures by Soviet patrol ships of foreign—usually Japanese—fishing vessels operating in or said to be overfishing waters claimed or protected by the Soviet Union.

Outside of any particular political context, Soviet troops in Eastern Europe—particularly East Germany, Berlin, and Austria before the end of the occupation there—have enforced rigorous transit checks on travelers going abroad, shot and arrested would-be escapees, and otherwise tried to prevent people from fleeing to the West. In one instance in 1949, 500 Soviet soldiers swarmed onto a Vienna soccer field to prevent several members of a Hungarian soccer team from defecting; in another, almost twenty years later to the day, Soviet aircraft tried to prevent an aircraft hijacked by East German youths from landing in West Berlin.[40] In the late 1940s and early 1950s Soviet troops were also used to arrest regime opponents in Eastern Europe and to conduct break-ins and kidnappings in West Berlin. In virtually all of these incidents the Soviet objective lay in the action itself and in discouraging other individuals in occupied lands from acting similarly.

2. Also excluded were the continued presence of forward deployed forces, nondiscriminating political deployments, and operational deployments. The ongoing presence, as psychological reinforcement only, of Soviet units in a foreign nation or distant sea is not considered as a political incident. Although Soviet garrisons in Eastern Europe and the Fifth Eskadra's continuing display of the flag in the Mediterranean, for example, may be important to Soviet foreign policy, these deployments do not constitute discrete political-military operations. Establishment of a permanent deployment seemingly aimed at a region generally and not calculated to influence specific behavior does not constitute a political operation either. Thus, while creation of the West Africa Patrol in 1970 in response to a Portuguese attack on Guinea is considered a discrete

39. The majority of these incidents occurred during the cold war. Since the early 1960s such incidents have occurred rarely, notwithstanding the dramatic attack and forced landing near Murmansk of a South Korean airliner in 1978. *Washington Post*, April 21 and 22, 1978.

40. *New York Times*, October 18, 1949, and October 20, 1969.

political operation, establishment of a Soviet naval presence in the Indian Ocean in 1968 is not.

Also excluded from the definition were deployments of newly developed weapons and force changes aimed either at strategic nuclear deterrence or the improvement of war-fighting capabilities—for example, the siting of land-based intercontinental ballistic missiles, the launching of ballistic missile submarines, the deployment of surface combatants in the North Atlantic, and the modernization of ground forces in Europe. I have also made a distinction between placing forces abroad to support a foreign nation and acquiring a military base to improve the operational effectiveness of Soviet armed forces. Thus, for example, the Soviet air defense of Egypt in the early 1970s is considered an incident, but the use of a Cuban airfield by Soviet long-range naval reconnaissance aircraft (thereby enhancing Soviet surveillance of the Atlantic Ocean) is not.

3. Routine military activities conducted to maintain or improve combat abilities and not to achieve measured political objectives at definite times were excluded. Also excluded were Soviet monitoring and harassment of Western naval operations on the high seas; airborne, seaborne, and satellite intelligence gathering; flights over foreign territory to test readiness and defenses; and approaches to foreign military and civilian aircraft in international airspace.

4. Goodwill military diplomacy, including most "friendly unofficial" visits by Soviet warships to foreign ports, was not included. Such visits imply a general expression of friendship and are meant to facilitate Soviet diplomacy and bilateral relations.[41] Their purpose is not geared toward influencing particular foreign behavior or a specific situation abroad. Not included either were "business" visits to foreign ports aimed at increasing the cost-effectiveness of Soviet forward deployments. Also not considered were disaster relief operations by Soviet military men, who have assisted in the wake of natural calamities in Eastern Europe and who flew aid to Peru after the 1970 earthquake there. Humanitarian interests aside, these actions may be carried out with political intent—the establishment or reinforcement of friendship and a positive image of the USSR. Still, they are not meant to achieve specific foreign policy goals.[42] Neither are

41. See Kelly, "Port Visits and the 'Internationalist Mission' of the Soviet Navy," pp. 513–14.

42. Moscow's memory for this assistance is long. In 1978 a Soviet destroyer paid an official visit to the Sicilian city of Messina to help commemorate the 70th anniversary of an earthquake there in which Soviet navy men played a role in rescue operations. *Krasnaya Zvezda*, October 4, 1978 (in FBIS, *Soviet Union*, October 11, 1978), p. E3.

most arms transfer agreements and the sending abroad of military training teams, staff advisers, skilled technical personnel, and construction
directors, which dates back to Lenin's day when military assistance was
given to Ataturk and the Kuomintang, as well as to Iran and the German
Reichswehr.[43] An arms transfer is not an operation carried out by an
armed forces unit; nor, in this context, are military assistance activities of Soviet military personnel. This discussion concerns actions by
Soviet operational combat and combat support units.

5. Nonmilitary operations also were not considered in this study. Excluded, therefore, were covert activities in foreign nations, the transport
of armaments and foreign military personnel by civil aircraft and merchant vessels, and actions such as the illegal 1956 landing in the Shetland
Islands of thirty Soviet herring fishermen looking for one of their number
seeking political asylum in Great Britain.[44]

6. Also excluded as incidents were statements about Soviet military
power. Kremlin leaders and the Soviet media often refer to Soviet military
power in statements of warning to antagonists and in support of friends.
Nikita Khrushchev often practiced such "rocket-rattling," as it was called
during the cold war. Although Soviet statements about the USSR's military power generally have not been as strident during the Brezhnev era—
as much the result, perhaps, of the USSR's real increase in military capabilities as of a deliberately changed style of diplomacy—references to
Soviet armed forces continue to be made by Moscow routinely as well as
in crises.[45] Of interest here is the coupling of a verbal or written statement
about Soviet military power with a discrete military operation aimed at
achieving specific foreign policy objectives.

The Incidents: Caveats and Sources

Although the forms of Soviet behavior just discussed do not constitute
discrete political-military operations as defined in this study, virtually all

43. Uri Ra'anan, "Soviet Arms Transfers and the Problem of Political Lever-
age," in Uri Ra'anan, Robert L. Pfaltzgroff, Jr., and Geoffrey Kemp, eds., *Arms
Transfers to the Third World: The Military Buildup in Less Industrial Countries*
(Boulder, Colo.: Westview, 1978), p. 131.

44. See *Keesing's Contemporary Archives* (July 19–26, 1958), p. 16303.

45. Warned routinely, for example, are nations that house important U.S. military facilities. Hence in 1978, when Turkey decided to allow the United States to
once again use various military installations, the Soviet military newspaper *Krasnaya
Zvezda,* quoting a Turkish newspaper, warned: "In the event of another world war
Turkey, where a substantial number of U.S. military installations are located, could
undergo the tragedy of Hiroshima." In FBIS, *Soviet Union* (October 25, 1978), p. B5.

of these types of activity are examined to some extent as necessary background or in relation to specific political uses of Soviet armed forces. Occasionally a type of activity normally excluded was taken to constitute an incident—for example, visits of Soviet military units to foreign nations, Soviet attacks on Western aircraft, imposed special transit controls, or the seizure of Japanese fishermen—when it constituted a particular foreign policy campaign aimed at achieving specific goals abroad.

Also treated as political incidents are several instances when Soviet naval ships were used to clear blocked waterways in third world countries after a major military conflict. Moscow seemed to have relatively specific foreign policy goals in these situations as compared, for example, with relief operations following natural disasters.

At the other end of the spectrum, the suppression of dissidence in East Germany in 1953 and in Hungary in 1956 also are considered as political incidents. Although the USSR eventually did impose its will by physical force in these actions, it did not enter into a war or a sustained contest of violence with foreign armed forces. The Kremlin probably also hoped that the initial appearance of Soviet troops or relatively small doses of violence would suffice and later used firepower as a warning to areas of East Germany and Hungary not in revolt. Since Moscow did use the military to influence behavior in these two instances, they are included in the study.

The list of incidents compiled using the definition and guidelines is presented in appendix A.[46]

A wide variety of sources was used to determine the occurrence of incidents, including studies of Soviet foreign relations and crisis behavior, histories of Soviet military actions, regional and national political histories, surveys and chronologies of international events, memoirs by political and military leaders, and unclassified and declassified U.S. government records. Appendix B presents a complete bibliography of sources and supportive data. It is difficult to know whether Soviet political uses of the military other than those determined to have occurred have gone unrecorded, are recorded only in classified documents, or did not appear

46. In several instances difficult decisions had to be made about whether an action qualified as an incident. Interpretations of Soviet activity may vary; I believe, however, anyone repeating this research using similar guidelines would compose a similar, although not necessarily identical, list of incidents. A computer file and referencing codebook including extensive descriptive data about each of the incidents listed in appendix A has been stored with the U.S. Department of Defense, Defense Advanced Research Projects Agency, Cybernetics Technology Office.

in the materials examined. The effort expended in the incident search and the variety and number of sources examined may give readers confidence that a large portion of those incidents recorded in unclassified materials has been identified.[47]

In instances of uncertainty about the accuracy of essential data—for example, an unsupported newspaper story written while an incident was purportedly breaking—scholars and other analysts known to be acquainted with the event in question were contacted for advice. In this way several events were either validated as incidents or judged to have been partly fictional or as falling outside definitional bounds. Hence I did not include as incidents, for example, reports about Soviet submarines carrying arms to Hukbalahap insurgents in the Philippines early in the cold war, participation of Soviet combat pilots in fighting between North and South Yemen in 1972, a series of ICBM tests across Soviet Asia just before a visit by Secretary of State Henry Kissinger to China in 1973, or Soviet electronic warfare against Egypt during the brief conflict between Libya and Egypt in 1977.[48]

If some incidents have been missed, they were probably small military operations that, although meant to be meaningful, were mistakenly perceived as routine or normal actions having no specific foreign policy objective. It seems unlikely that the USSR used armed forces in a crisis or a crisis occurred in which Soviet military units played a role and that that information has gone unreported. Also missed, perhaps, were a few incidents in which the sole Soviet military activity was military air transport and the numbers of aircraft and flights involved were small. A brief deployment abroad of a few ground troops or airmen may also have gone undetected.

In many instances I was not confident about the accuracy of information providing specific numbers of Soviet naval, ground, and aircraft units. Often the data available were estimates based on partial observations and calculation rather than actual numerical counts. Some reports were contradictory and many were inconsistent. In still other instances data were puzzling or implausible. Such information was sorted out as much as possible through detective work, advice from others, and judgment. For

47. Research assistants spent roughly four work years identifying Soviet political-military operations.

48. *New York Times,* April 3, 1949, and September 1, 1951; *Baltimore Sun,* October 4, 1972; *New York Times,* February 17, 1973; *New York Times,* August 1, 1977.

the purpose of aggregate analysis, the incidents were divided into categories. For example, incidents were divided into ones involving no more
than one air regiment and ones in which more than one air regiment was
used; actions including the participation of no more than one battalion,
more than one battalion but no more than one division, or more than one
division; and so forth.

One hundred ninety incidents were identified in which Soviet armed
forces units were used as a discrete foreign policy instrument between
June 1944 and August 1979. The Second World War ended in Europe
in May 1945 and officially in the Pacific area four months later. By
then the Soviet army had occupied all or part of a dozen countries; Joseph
Stalin used this presence to influence political developments in these
nations and to obtain from them territorial and economic concessions. It
seems clear that Stalin had these objectives in mind before Soviet troops
set foot outside the USSR and that they became important to Moscow in
bilateral relations as soon as foreign areas were cleared of Axis military
forces. Because it is extremely difficult to determine when Soviet forces
in a country turned from fighting to a more political role, I use as the beginning dates of incidents the month and year in which Soviet troops first
appeared to gain a hold in a foreign country. Using this guideline, Soviet
military diplomacy was first practiced after the Second World War in
Eastern Europe in 1944. In June 1944 the Soviet army secured parts of
prewar Poland and Finland, soon to become sovereign USSR territory.
August 1979 is an arbitrary cutoff date imposed on the study.

Organization of the Study

Part 1 presents the historical record. Chapter two provides an aggregate analysis of the 190 incidents identified within the period examined
and summarizes the circumstances in which discrete Soviet political-
military operations occurred, the types of armed forces used by Moscow,
and the activities of those units. Chapters three through five contain a
narrative history of Soviet coercive diplomacy since the Bolsheviks seized
power in 1917. Experiences in these earlier years made a powerful impression on Soviet citizens as well as the political and military elite and
influenced Soviet behavior in later years. This perspective partially explains why it is useful to study Soviet military diplomacy since World War
II. I believe that memories of experiences in recent decades will influence

Soviet behavior in the future and that relationships observed between past variations in the political use of Soviet armed forces and the context of particular incidents may be useful in understanding future Soviet behavior.

Previous examinations of discrete Soviet political-military operations have been theoretical or have considered only a relatively short time period, a small number of selective cases, a particular region, a single branch of the Soviet armed forces, or some combination of these dimensions.[49] Informative as this writing has been, it has left a large information gap. Part one identifies and elaborates on a more complete empirical record of discrete uses of the Soviet military as a foreign policy tool.

The case studies in part 2, done by specialists, examine the phenomenon in depth and provide a foundation for reaching conclusions about, first, the effectiveness of discrete political-military operations in protecting Soviet interests and achieving foreign policy objectives, and second, the implications of this diplomacy for U.S. interests and behavior abroad. Each analyst was asked to examine and compare two or more incidents, focusing on: (1) the concerns and objectives of Soviet policymakers; (2) their use of armed forces and other kinds of diplomacy; (3) the concerns and objectives of the foreign targets of this Soviet diplomacy; (4) the role of third parties; (5) outcomes of incidents and their relationship to the USSR's use of armed forces; and (6) implications for Soviet and U.S. interests and foreign and defense policies.

The eight sets of incidents examined were selected for their diversity in political context and structure and in the use of Soviet armed forces. Incidents chosen include situations containing direct threats to the security of the USSR (the Sino-Soviet border conflict) and to Soviet authority in Eastern Europe (crises in Hungary, Poland, and Czechoslovakia); situations in which major U.S. armed forces participated (the Korean and Vietnam wars; the *Pueblo,* EC-121, and 1976 crises on the Korean peninsula; and the 1967 and 1973 wars in the Middle East); and third world situations in which U.S. armed forces did not play a role (the Egyptian-Israeli conflict in 1969–70, insurgencies in Sudan and Iraq in the early 1970s, the Angolan civil war and Ethiopian-Somalian conflict,

49. As far as I know, the only other major empirical work published on the use of Soviet armed forces as a political instrument is Bradford Dismukes and James M. McConnell, eds., *Soviet Naval Diplomacy* (Pergamon, 1979). My own writing and that of several of the authors of the case studies in this book have benefited from the research and analysis presented in *Soviet Naval Diplomacy,* which focuses on the period between the 1967 Middle East war and the Angolan civil war.

and two West African crises in the late 1960s and early 1970s). These different sets of incidents are also diverse in regional setting, level of initial local violence, and the kinds of Soviet armed forces used and their activities.

Another concern in the case studies was to focus on incidents in the post-Khrushchev era. Exceptions were made for the Korean War and the 1956 revolts in Hungary and Poland to allow comparisons with important events that came later—the Vietnam War and the 1968 intervention in Czechoslovakia, respectively. An understanding of the USSR's use of force in these earlier incidents is also relevant to similar types of crises that might occur again in those same places.

Although the sets of cases were selected because of their diversity, the individual cases in each set are comparable in circumstances of important interest, location, the use of Soviet armed forces, and so forth. Conclusions are drawn at the end of each of the case studies on the basis of two or more similar incidents.

Finally, part 3 evaluates the effectiveness of Soviet political-military operations—their utility in satisfying Soviet foreign policy objectives—and considers implications for U.S. interests and foreign and defense policies.

The Historical Record

CHAPTER TWO

An Aggregate View

THE 190 incidents in which Soviet armed forces were used as a political instrument between June 1944 and August 1979 include crises that riveted world attention and situations that few were ever aware of. Their political context differed and the military units used by Moscow varied enormously, ranging from a visit by a single ship to improve relations with another nation—as, for example, when the cruiser *Sverdlov* joined the naval procession celebrating Queen Elizabeth's coronation in June 1953—to actions such as those in response to the Hungarian revolution in 1956, tension along the Sino-Soviet border in 1969, and the 1973 Middle East war.

This chapter presents an overview and aggregate analysis of Soviet military diplomacy during the thirty-five-year period examined. What kinds of circumstances elicited the 190 operations identified? What types of armed forces were used, and how large were these units? What did Soviet armed forces do? What did the United States do when the USSR engaged in military diplomacy? To understand the discrete use of armed forces as an instrument of Soviet foreign policy, it is useful to begin with a historical synopsis.

The Evolution of Soviet Military Diplomacy

In the summer of 1944 the Soviet army stormed across prewar Soviet frontiers in the west in pursuit of the Third Reich's retreating armies. Between then and March 1946, when the Soviet Union withdrew its military from Iran, China, and Bornholm Island (Denmark) and tempered its

27

claims to territory in eastern Turkey and its demand for joint control of the Dardanelles, Soviet armed forces were used principally to expand the USSR and Communist community. In Eastern Europe as well as in south-western and northeastern Asia Stalin sought territorial concessions and political control and used military power to support this design.

Moscow also used the Soviet army in Europe and Asia to achieve further specific objectives. Of great importance to Stalin was the with-drawal of U.S. military forces from countries neighboring the USSR's sphere of influence. Stalin refrained from attempting to establish puppet governments in Germany, Austria, Czechoslovakia, and China immedi-ately after the war. Instead, Soviet troops were withdrawn jointly with U.S. troops from Czechoslovakia in December 1945, from China in early 1946, and from Austria in 1955. In Germany, where Soviet interest was strongest, Stalin decided only in 1947–48 on a course of full control and imposition of Soviet-style orthodoxy.

In the next seven years—framed at the outset by the containment thesis taking hold in the United States and Moscow's acceptance of the "two camps" line, and by Stalin's death in March 1953—the Soviet mili-tary primarily supported security objectives in Central Europe, consoli-dation of the USSR's expanded sphere of influence, and the defense of that realm. Moscow's concern focused first on Germany's future relation-ship between East and West (the 1948–49 crises) and then on the pros-pect of West Germany's rearmament (incidents in 1950–53).[1] Shows of Soviet force were also directed at Denmark, Sweden, Yugoslavia, and Iran when those nations appeared drawn toward alliance with the United States and sought U.S. armaments.

Within Moscow's own sphere during the late 1940s, the Soviet army watched over the sovietization of Eastern Europe and North Korea. In February 1948 Soviet troops massed on Czechoslovakia's borders in support of the Communist seizure of power in Prague. Moscow also found out, though, that it would have to defend positions if it wanted to keep them. Although Stalin chose not to invade Yugoslavia after the 1948 break with Josip Broz Tito and the Soviet military did not accompany North Korean troops in their invasion of South Korea in 1950, Soviet military power was evident in both of these instances: Moscow threatened intervention in Yugoslavia in 1949 and, after the onset of the Korean

1. In two incidents, one in September 1950 and the other in January 1951, Soviet troops attempted to seize small pieces of the French and British sectors in West Berlin.

War, placed ground forces in China and later air and ground units in North Korea. Internal threats to regimes in Czechoslovakia and Albania in 1951 also activated Moscow to reposition Soviet military units.

A partial softening and diversity in Soviet policy aimed at weakening the strategic military posture of the United States and "the cohesion and momentum of the Western alliance," as Marshall Shulman observed,[2] was apparent in the early 1950s. But it was Stalin's successors who directed a forceful peace offensive at the West; hence most of the operations that were orchestrated between June 1953 and September 1956 were friendly. For example, military controls were relaxed in Austria, a special naval visit was paid to Sweden, and in 1955 Soviet troops withdrew from Austria and Porkkala (Finland).

To improve or reinforce relations with independent-minded Communist nations, Soviet military men also were withdrawn from Port Arthur and Dairen (China) and naval visits were paid to ports in Yugoslavia, Albania, and China for the first time. Moreover, of six coercive actions in this period, three were to maintain positions of authority (East Germany and Bulgaria in 1953, and Poland in June 1956). In no instance did the Kremlin provoke a crisis during these years.

In June 1956, three years after the first popular uprising in Eastern Europe (in East Germany in 1953), workers demonstrating in Poznań demanded political change in Poland and an end to Soviet domination. A month later, in the Middle East, President Gamal Abdel Nasser nationalized the Suez Canal. The surface outburst in the Polish streets was suppressed without much difficulty, and for three months negotiations went on over the future of the Suez Canal. The ferment in Poland and elsewhere in Eastern Europe continued to increase, however, as did Great Britain's and France's frustration in dealing with President Nasser. Those eruptions in Poland and Hungary in October 1956 and the British-French-Israeli attack on Egypt that same month marked a hardening in Soviet attitudes toward heterogeneity among Communist nations, an increased Soviet involvement in the third world, and, consequently, increased hostility between East and West. These developments were closely reflected in the Kremlin's use of armed forces.

Between late 1956 and 1958 the Kremlin devoted considerable effort to reinforcing its positions in Eastern Europe. The withdrawal of troops from Rumania in mid-1958 signaled Moscow's confidence that Soviet

2. Marshall D. Shulman, *Stalin's Foreign Policy Reappraised* (Atheneum, 1966), p. 259.

authority was satisfactorily restored. The Kremlin then attempted to use military power to affect developments in the West, particularly West Germany's future relationship with the North Atlantic Treaty Organization (NATO), the emplacement of nuclear weapons on West German soil, and Western access to and control of West Berlin. All of these probes, including the 1958–59 and 1961 Berlin crises and the Cuban missile crisis, were intended to reinforce Soviet security in relation to the United States and NATO. In contrast to the earlier "peace offensive" years, the Soviet Union did not direct friendly political-military gestures toward the West during this time of high cold war.

Also during these years the Kremlin for the first time began to use military power to gain influence in the third world. Notwithstanding Moscow's threats during the Suez crisis, no Soviet military action to support Egypt was taken at that time. Moscow first used supportive military action in the third world during the Syrian crisis in 1957. During the next six years Soviet military units also responded to crises in Lebanon, Indonesia, the Congo, Laos, and North Yemen.

After the Cuban missile crisis and until the Middle East crisis in the spring of 1967 that led to the June war, Soviet leaders turned to the military as a coercive instrument infrequently. Only one small action in the third world was recorded after the autumn of 1962, and the only hostile Soviet probe of NATO—related to the 1964 Cyprus crisis—was a minor one. More noteworthy was a timely Soviet naval visit to France in 1966 coinciding with President Charles de Gaulle's weakening of French ties with the United States and courting of Moscow. Infringements on Western access to Berlin in these years were essentially reactions to what Moscow perceived as provocations—for example, the Bundestag's meeting in West Berlin in April 1965. More important were Soviet actions in the east in response to the USSR's worsening relations with China and, in particular, to Peking's questioning the demarcation of the Sino-Soviet border and provocation of violent border clashes.

In the late 1960s and early 1970s the outbreak of the 1967 Middle East conflict together with the threat to Soviet authority in Czechoslovakia and the further intensification of the Sino-Soviet conflict heightened Soviet political-military activity. Eastern Europe and China were of greatest concern. The August 1968 invasion of Czechoslovakia by the USSR and its allies followed a number of Soviet-led shows of force. Thereafter Moscow also saw fit on several occasions to threaten Rumania over its independent behavior. Serious demonstrations in Poland in 1970 over price increases caused further concern and political-military activity in the name of defending orthodoxy in Eastern Europe. Conflicts between the United States and Communist nations—North Korea and North Vietnam—also occasioned political-military diplomacy by Moscow, and in 1969 Moscow inaugurated regular naval visits to Cuba as a show of Soviet support.

After restoring its authority in Prague and placing Bucharest on notice, the Kremlin responded forcefully in early 1969 to provocations by Peking along the Sino-Soviet border. Following a Chinese ambush of Soviet troops in the Ussuri River area in March 1969, the USSR provoked a series of clashes and ordered a large buildup of Soviet forces in the Far East that did not crest for about five years.

Related to the increased possibility of conflict with China and induced by political change in West Germany in 1969, Soviet political-military operations directed at the West in the late 1960s and early 1970s were largely salutary. Rather than provoke a crisis after the United States learned in 1970 that a Soviet strategic nuclear submarine base was being established in Cuba, Moscow quickly withdrew the offending submarine and related personnel. The only hostile military actions in the West were minor ones directed at Iran (1973) and Yugoslavia (1974) and attempts to weaken relations among NATO nations, as during the 1973 "cod war" between Great Britain and Iceland and the 1974 Cyprus crisis. Small demonstrations hindering Western access to Berlin followed what Moscow again considered provocations by Bonn.

This period was distinguished by the USSR's widespread and sustained military involvement in the third world. The Middle East was again the focal point. Unlike Soviet behavior in the Syrian and Lebanon crises a decade earlier, Moscow's interventions included powerful actions in situations of intense violence, representing a strong Soviet commitment to allies and greater confidence in dealing with adversaries. A sizable number of operations also were implemented in or adjacent to the Persian Gulf, the Horn of Africa, South and Southeast Asia, and West Africa. Such interventions were more serious and greater in number than earlier forays in the Congo, North Yemen, and Laos.

In the mid-1970s Soviet political-military activity let up. No operations occurred in Eastern Europe or the Far East and there was a sharp drop in the frequency of incidents in the third world, where only Moscow's intervention in the Angolan civil war in late 1975 and early 1976 was noteworthy. Airlifts to the USSR's Angolan ally in early 1975 and to

Algeria to support the Polisario rebels in 1976 were small affairs, and a 1976 naval presence complementing a U.S. appearance off the coast of Lebanon during the civil war in that nation was strictly pro forma. What was dramatic about the Kremlin's involvement in the Angolan conflict in 1975–76 was Moscow's logistical and other support of thousands of Cubans fighting in Angola while the United States remained militarily apart from the conflict.

A new surge of activity at the end of the 1970s occurred, not in third world countries, where the danger of Soviet military intervention was perceived as serious by many in the West, but in support of the ruling regime in Ethiopia in particular and in East Asia, where the Kremlin responded militarily to a number of Chinese initiatives. Soviet involvement in the Horn of Africa in 1977–78, like the intervention in Angola two years earlier, constituted a singular discrete action not complemented by similar behavior elsewhere that could be perceived as a pattern of Soviet resort to coercive diplomacy in the third world. Following the winter of 1977–78, during which Soviet personnel also engaged in air defense activities in Cuba while more Cuban troops were being sent to Africa, the focus of Soviet political-military diplomacy shifted to East Asia and Afghanistan in response to: (1) Peking's anti-Soviet diplomacy aimed at forming alliances against the USSR; (2) worsening relations between China and Vietnam, a Soviet ally; and (3) the growing weakness of Moscow's ally in Kabul in the face of insurgency.[3] The Soviet intervention in Afghanistan in December 1979, which took place after the period examined in this study, is excluded from the following analysis.

Political Context and the Use of Force

Soviet military personnel were used coercively in 158 incidents, or more than four-fifths of the 190 incidents investigated. In the remaining 32 incidents Moscow practiced cooperative military diplomacy. Soviet armed forces were used coercively to deter an antagonist from certain behavior or to compel the performance of some action—such as the exercises and other operations in the spring and early summer of 1968

3. In another coercive action in early 1978, Moscow increased the number of Soviet patrols in West Berlin following a refusal by the United States, Great Britain, and France to curtail their patrols in East Berlin. *New York Times,* January 29, 1978.

to intimidate the Dubček government of Czechoslovakia into cutting short and even reversing the political change it was shepherding there. At the same time, and often more important, coercive military activity may have reinforced or improved relations with a friend that perceived the activity to be supportive, as in the way the East German and Polish regimes viewed Soviet pressure on Czechoslovakia in 1968.[4] The provision of Soviet missile crews and pilots to Egypt in 1970 to defend against deep-penetration raids by Israeli aircraft was meant to reinforce Moscow's relationship with Cairo and the Arab world generally as much as to compel Israel to end these attacks.

Occasionally, though, the Kremlin used military units cooperatively, to improve relations with another nation or to obtain other foreign policy objectives without using coercion. Thus, particular military visits—such as the one by a Soviet MIG squadron to France in 1971 before a state visit by Party Chairman Brezhnev and Premier Aleksei Kosygin, and that by the guided missile destroyers *Boyki* and *Zhguchy* to Boston harbor in 1975 to strengthen détente—were intended as highly visible signs of regard and friendship. Along with expanded trade, cultural exchange, and other means of diplomacy, these operations frequently helped support the retention or development of favorable relations. A similar purpose was served by a number of withdrawals of occupation forces, while other Soviet withdrawals were designed to achieve the retrenchment of Western armed forces.

The imbalance in the numbers of coercive and cooperative Soviet political-military operations is explained by several factors. First, there are fewer alternatives to the armed forces as a coercive instrument than as a cooperative means of diplomacy. Economic aid, special trade arrangements, personal visits, and other forms of diplomacy in addition to military diplomacy have been not only available to Soviet leaders for the improvement of foreign relations but also perceived to be more meaningful as expressions of friendship. Second, routine military activities have not been considered incidents in this study. Hence the many Soviet naval visits paid to foreign ports each year that support Kremlin policy objectives in a general way, disaster relief operations, and several other types of political-military operations in nonconflict situations are excluded by definition.

4. Philip Windsor and Adam Roberts, *Czechoslovakia 1968: Reform, Repression, and Resistance* (Columbia University Press for the Institute for Strategic Studies, 1969), pp. 28–30.

Table 2-1. *Coercive and Cooperative Political-Military Operations,*
by Subject of Soviet Concern

Number of incidents; percentages of total in parentheses

Subject of Soviet concern	Form of political-military diplomacy	
	Coercive[a]	Cooperative
Expansion of territory or political authority	26 (16)	. . .
Maintenance of fraternal Communist regime	43 (27)	8 (25)
Security relations	45 (28)	19 (59)
Third world influence	41 (26)	5 (16)
Other	3 (2)	. . .
Total incidents	158	32

a. Percentages do not add to one hundred due to rounding.

The foreign policy purpose or concern of the USSR in using armed
forces provides a foundation for analyzing the 190 incidents. In this context the 190 operations may be categorized, for the most part, by
whether they were aimed at: (1) expanding Soviet authority around the
periphery of the USSR; (2) maintaining fraternal Communist regimes;
(3) ensuring the security of the USSR vis-à-vis independent neighbors
and other major antagonists; or (4) reinforcing Soviet influence in the
third world. Table 2-1 presents the numbers and percentages of incidents
in terms of these categories and the type of military diplomacy used.

Expanding the USSR and Soviet Authority

Attempts to enlarge the USSR or gain new political authority in neighboring lands by military diplomacy occurred immediately after World
War II. More than half of these twenty-six actions took place in the context of closing wartime operations in 1944–45; nine-tenths occurred by
the end of 1948. Only one such incident, of secondary importance, was
identified as happening after 1951.[5] Soviet postwar expansionary activity
was not restricted to a single region. Stalin's interest in filling vacuums of
power and testing the will and support of Soviet neighbors was felt around
the full perimeter of the USSR, including Northern and Eastern Europe,
Southwest Asia, and Northeast Asia.

Moscow's prime military instrument was the Soviet army, which was

5. This incident was a subtle show of force in 1975 in the form of a missile test
in the Barents Sea aimed at Norway.

usually used in force. Ground units of more than a division played a role in twenty of the twenty-five early postwar incidents; in four of the other five incidents, smaller ground units were active. Combat air elements took part in at least ten and perhaps as many as three-fourths of these twenty-five incidents. Naval forces definitely played a role in only one small action (the seizure of Haiyang Island in the Korea Bay in 1947) and were perhaps active in three other incidents. Although Soviet ground forces did engage in violence and several other diverse activities in a few incidents, in almost all instances they achieved Moscow's goals by virtue of their initial emplacement or continuing occupation and by the fear they inspired.

The United States was politically active in roughly three-fourths of these incidents, but U.S. armed forces took part in only six incidents, or one-fourth of the total. In none of these six incidents did a U.S.-Soviet military confrontation take place.

Maintaining Fraternal Communist Regimes

Maintaining allied Communist regimes in foreign nations is particularly important to the USSR. These regimes have offered Moscow positions of hegemony, influence, and special friendship, crucial to Soviet interests and the advancement of further foreign policy objectives. These friends form an inner protective circle around the USSR and are accorded a special place in Soviet thinking.

Soviet coercive actions aimed at maintaining fraternal allied regimes have been in response to four types of developments: (1) disloyalty to the USSR by an orthodox Communist regime—that is, unwillingness to accept Soviet tutelage in domestic affairs or to adopt Soviet foreign policy positions (nine incidents); (2) internal attack upon the legitimacy of an orthodox Communist regime (thirteen incidents); (3) external political pressure on a fraternal ally (fifteen incidents); and (4) external military attack on a fraternal ally (six incidents).

While those operations aimed at expanding Soviet territory and authority were in response to the immediate postwar perception of opportunities—the combination of mammoth Soviet conventional military power, weak neighbors, and doubts about Western preparedness to seriously oppose the USSR—the forty-three actions that may be categorized as ensuring the loyalty, orthodoxy, and security of fraternal Soviet allies were in response to grave danger to Soviet positions abroad. Soviet behavior in these instances was motivated not by a prospect of making new gains but by concern for holding on to gains made earlier.

All the violent external attacks on Communist allies to which the USSR responded militarily occurred in Asia. All the incidents related to regime disloyalty or internal threat to communist orthodoxy took place in Eastern Europe, as did twelve of fifteen actions precipitated by political threats from abroad. Two of the other three actions related to Cuba; the third concerned North Korea. No Soviet ally in Eastern Europe was ever the victim of military attack like North Korea (1950–53), North Vietnam (1965–72), and Vietnam (1979). However, Moscow's Communist allies outside Eastern Europe did behave independently without stimulating Soviet coercive diplomacy aimed at terminating their heterodoxy. Clearly, the Kremlin was more dedicated and able to maintain its positions in Eastern European countries than it was in Communist nations elsewhere.

China, as Vietnam's most recent antagonist, was the source of external military danger to a fraternal ally in Asia in three incidents in which Soviet military units played a role, all in the late 1970s. The United States presented the military threat in the other three incidents. The United States also was an actor in twelve of the fifteen instances of external political pressure. In sharp contrast to the high frequency of U.S. involvement in incidents including external danger to Communist allies, the United States played a role in only two of the twenty-two situations in which Soviet armed forces responded to internal developments.

The Soviet army participated in all twenty-two operations focusing on domestic developments in Eastern Europe, and more than a division was called upon in every one of the operations for which force size could be assessed. Air units were called upon in only five such incidents. Combat aircraft were used in four and perhaps all five of these instances; transport units were used twice. Air units were always used in strength: more than one regiment of combat aircraft and of transport aircraft were used in each operation.

Naval units were also called on in five incidents, but in varying strength and more symbolically. One and two vessels, respectively, were used to warn Yugoslavia in 1949 and Poland in 1956. Much larger were the naval forces used in 1968 in the Atlantic to warn off the West before the Soviet Union invaded Czechoslovakia and to intimidate Rumania in 1968 and again in 1971. The Czech-related operation was partly intended to alert the West to the seriousness of the Prague heterodoxy, the USSR's expanded military capability, and Soviet determination to deal with the crisis without outside intervention. The use of large naval forces against Rumania in 1968 and 1971 is less interesting since the USSR (and Russia before it) has always maintained a large Black Sea fleet.

Quite different was Soviet force use in political operations supporting Asian Communist nations threatened by military attack. While air and naval units were used in five and three of these six incidents, ground forces were used only twice (both times during the Korean War). Further, transport and reconnaissance, not combat, aircraft were called upon in three of the five operations in which Soviet aviation played a role, and the two combat aircraft actions occurred in the Korean War. Soviet military units did not support China in the 1954–55 Tachen islands crisis or the 1958 Quemoy crisis, North Vietnam during the war in Southeast Asia, or North Korea after a U.S. Navy EC-121 aircraft was shot down in 1969 or during the 1976 crisis related to the murder of two U.S. army officers in the Korean demilitarized zone. Soviet military support of North Korea during the 1968 *Pueblo* crisis was untimely, and the only Soviet combatants active in the 1979 Sino-Vietnamese war were at sea. With the exception of Soviet support given China during the Korean War, the Soviet Union expended minimal military effort on behalf of Communist allies in Asia facing the threat or reality of attack by the United States or China.

The pattern of Soviet readiness to use ground forces in Eastern Europe and the use of air and sea units elsewhere is reinforced by how Moscow responded to external political threats to Communist allies. All nine of the Soviet ground force operations related to external political threats were in support of East Germany; outside Eastern Europe only air or sea units were used.

Table 2-2 shows what Soviet armed forces actually did to help maintain fraternal regimes. Ground exercises or other demonstrations were used most frequently to warn against regime disloyalty and often in response to internal regime threats. Sometimes, however, threats were followed by the intervention of Soviet ground units and the sealing off of the straying nation. All seven of the blockade-type operations in response to foreign political danger concerned West Berlin. Ground forces resorted to violence in response to internal developments in several instances, but never when the threat was external. Air units engaged in violence as well

Table 2-2. *Coercive Activities of Soviet Armed Forces to Maintain Fraternal Communist Regimes*
Number of incidents[a]

	Type of incident			
Type of force and activity	Regime disloyalty	Internal threat to regime	External political threat	External military threat
Ground units				
Firepower	1	2	...	...
Blockade	1	4	7	...
Emplacement of forces	1	7	...	2
Retention of forces	1	1	...	...
Exercise or demonstration	7	6	3	...
Other coercive action	...	2	...	...
Air units				
Firepower	...	1	1	1
Harassment of other aircraft	...	...	2	1
Emplacement of forces	...	1	5	2
Exercise or demonstration	...	...	1	...
Transport of equipment to actor	...	...	...	2
Naval units				
Harassment or seizure of other ships	...	...	...	1
Establishment of presence at sea	2	...	...	2
Visit to foreign nation	...	...	1	...
Transport of foreign forces	...	...	...	1
Exercise or demonstration	2	...	...	1

a. Excludes alerts; forces may perform more than one activity in an incident.

as harassment in the latter type of situation on five different occasions, however. Air units also were deployed in a number of these incidents. The use of naval units primarily consisted of mere presence and sea exercises.

Moscow sought to maintain loyalty to the USSR not only by coercion but also by cooperative military diplomacy. Toward this end Soviet warships paid special visits (Albania, 1954; Yugoslavia and China, 1956); ground units were withdrawn from fraternal nations (Port Arthur and Dairen, 1955; Rumania, 1958); and aggressive urban patrols were curtailed in Czechoslovakia in 1969.[6]

6. Moscow directed an eighth cooperative act, at the United States, after a U.S. Navy EC-121 aircraft was shot down in 1969.

Security Relations

Actions intended to enlarge the USSR, obtain hegemony in neighboring lands, and maintain fraternal Communist regimes clearly concerned Soviet security. So, too, did several Soviet political-military operations in the third world. If the word *security* is defined broadly enough, virtually every international act of Soviet policymakers may be said to bear on the USSR's security interests. What I mean by Soviet political-military operations pertaining to security relations are uses of force in response to hostile behavior aimed at the USSR by a nonallied neighbor or a NATO member; other actions to weaken or intimidate a nonallied neighbor or a NATO nation; and operations in response to the development of unstable conditions in or among neighboring nonallied nations. But because it is difficult to determine which category accurately describes which instance of Soviet military diplomacy, I used political geography as a basis to further analyze security-related coercive Soviet actions.

If pins were placed on a map where these forty-five incidents occurred, they would outline the perimeter of the USSR and its dominion in Eastern Europe. Moscow sought to intimidate neighbors or reacted to perceived threats presented by neighboring nations in Northern Europe, Central Europe, Southern Europe, Southwest Asia, and Northeast Asia. In other words, no region bordering the USSR has been exempt from Soviet coercive diplomacy in the postwar era. Two major centers of attention were West Germany (thirteen incidents) and China (seven incidents). Of the remaining twenty-five incidents, twelve took place in Europe, eleven took place in Asia, and two were focused on Cuba. Through these actions Moscow essentially sought to limit the political evolution of West Germany and its role within NATO; to deter antagonistic Chinese behavior and drive a hostile Peking into a more conciliatory posture toward the USSR; and to press other neighbors to accept closer relations with the USSR or to deter them from embracing closer relations with the United States or China. In a number of instances the Kremlin also supported relatively friendly NATO nations or neighboring governments in Asia against local antagonists.

Over time, the focus of this coercive diplomacy shifted from trying to shape relationships with neighbors at large after the Second World War to grappling with the emergence and growing confidence of West Germany, and then to manipulating NATO members against each other and moderating a hostile China. Thus the last probe aimed at West Germany occurred in 1962 and the first action directed at Mao's China took place in 1965; and while the Kremlin acted militarily in the 1940s and 1950s to restrict European and Asian relationships with Washington, in the 1970s Moscow sought to restrict its neighbors' relations with Peking. Of relatively secondary significance in the West after the Cuban missile crisis were a number of subtle Soviet actions, following the onset of military crises between NATO members, aimed at sowing further discord and gaining favor with individual participants. Quite different, though, was the USSR's support of the new government in Afghanistan after a coup in Kabul in 1978; in this neighboring nation Moscow had to worry about the ouster of an ally perceived to be wholly dependent on the USSR and its replacement by a virulently anti-Soviet regime.

The Soviet army was used in three-fourths of the incidents in Europe and in an equal proportion of the actions in Asia. Ground units were rarely directed at Northern European targets or Japan, however. In incidents involving ground units, more than a division was called on in more than four-fifths of the incidents in Europe and in half of the actions in Asia. Every operation in Asia including such a large force was directed at China. Air units were used somewhat less regularly, being called on in three-fifths of the incidents in Europe and in the same proportion of actions in Asia. Combat aircraft were active in three-fifths of the incidents focused on West Germany and in the same proportion of the operations directed at China but were used in only a third of the other European-centered incidents and in only a fifth of Asian incidents focused on countries other than China. Transport aircraft were used occasionally in both Europe and Asia; helicopter units and reconnaissance aircraft were used in several Asian actions. Naval units were used in only a fifth of the incidents in Europe and a fourth of those in Asia but played a role in three of four operations aimed at Japan and in roughly half of the actions directed at Northern and Southern European nations.

A pattern emerges. When China was the Soviet target, large ground and combat air forces were used; but otherwise, in Asia, Moscow often used smaller ground units, nontactical aircraft, and naval vessels. Large ground forces were the norm in Central and Southern Europe; combat air forces were most frequently used in incidents related to West Germany; and naval units were active around countries on the Eurasian Cape.

Table 2-3 lists the activities of Soviet armed forces in the forty-five coercive incidents involving security relations. In dealing with West Germany, Soviet ground units were frequently ordered to restrict access to

Table 2-3. *Coercive Activities of Soviet Armed Forces Concerned with USSR Security Relations*

Number of incidents[a]

Type of force and activity	West Germany	Others in Europe	China	Others in Asia	Cuba
Ground units					
Firepower	...	...	3	2	...
Blockade	10	1	...	...	...
Emplacement of forces	1	3	5	2	1
Retention of forces	...	1	...	...	...
Exercise or demonstration	2	2	4	4	...
Air units					
Firepower	1	1	...	1	...
Harassment of other aircraft	5	...	...	...	...
Emplacement of forces	1	1	4	1	1
Exercise or demonstration	6	3	1	4	...
Transport of equipment to actor	...	...	...	1	...
Naval units					
Harassment or seizure of other ships	...	...	...	1	...
Establishment of presence at sea	...	3	...	1	1
Exercise or demonstration	1	1	1	2	...

a. Excludes alerts; forces may perform more than one activity in an incident.

Berlin while air units harassed Western commercial aircraft in the corridors between West Germany and West Berlin or carried out exercises. The only uses of firepower in the West were two sets of actions by fighter aircraft against Western commercial aircraft. While the Soviet army never engaged in violence in Europe, it did against China. More usually, though, when military force was aimed at Peking, Soviet ground and air units were redeployed and ground force maneuvers were conducted. Elsewhere in Asia, ground and air exercises were most frequent, but ground force violence was resorted to there as well.

Despite Moscow's focus on Europe and Asia, two incidents involving Cuba cannot be overlooked. These were the emplacement of nuclear missiles and of ground and air forces in Cuba in the summer of 1962 and Soviet behavior after the missile crisis erupted. While the deployment of missiles and nuclear-capable bombers to Cuba was unique, the deployment of ground forces to Cuba represented one of only three instances when Soviet army men were deployed outside Europe or Northeast Asia.

(The other two deployments were to Egypt in 1970 and Afghanistan in 1979.) After the missile crisis erupted, Moscow raised the alert status of its strategic forces and of the Warsaw Pact forces and redeployed Soviet submarines in the Atlantic. Chapters 3 and 4 examine Soviet military diplomacy in these incidents.

The United States acted in nine-tenths of the European-related incidents (as well as in the two Cuban-focused actions) but played a role in only two-fifths of the Soviet-initiated incidents in Asia. Moreover, while U.S. armed forces were definitely called upon in two-fifths and may have been alerted in another three-tenths of the actions in which the United States participated in Europe, U.S. military units were used in only two of the eight Asian incidents in which the United States was involved.

Moscow also used Soviet military units cooperatively on nineteen occasions to improve relations with nonallied neighbors or NATO members or to achieve third-party military withdrawals from neighboring nations. More than four-fifths of these actions occurred in Europe, principally in Northern and Southern Europe, where, most typically, Soviet surface vessels paid special visits to individual countries. Since five of six cooperative ground actions were immediate postwar withdrawals and because the cooperative use of air units has been rare, it is clear that the navy has been the primary instrument of cooperative military diplomacy in the modern era.

Relations with the Third World

Moscow did not use armed forces coercively in the third world until 1957; and of forty-one such actions thereafter, only one-fourth took place between 1957 and 1966, and three-fourths occurred between 1967 and 1979. The onset of the 1967 crisis in the Middle East was a turning point for Soviet political-military diplomacy in the third world.

Half of the Kremlin's military interventions in the third world were in support of one sovereign nation against another. The other half related to domestic situations. Moscow supported regimes against internal opposition and supported regime opponents with equal frequency. In violent domestic situations, the Kremlin opposed insurgencies in eight incidents and supported them in ten. Two-fifths of Moscow's third world interventions related to the southern littoral of the Mediterranean. The remaining Soviet coercive actions were more evenly divided between the Persian Gulf–Horn of Africa area, sub-Saharan Africa, and Southern Asia.

Table 2-4. *Coercive Activities of Soviet Armed Forces in the Third World*

Number of incidents[a]

Type of force and activity	USSR supports third world nation against another	USSR supports third world regime	USSR opposes third world regime
Ground units			
Firepower	1	...	...
Emplacement of forces	1	...	...
Exercise or demonstration	2	...	1
Air units			
Firepower	1	2	1
Emplacement of forces	4	5	2
Exercise or demonstration	5	2	1
Transport of equipment to actor	4	2	3
Transport of foreign forces	1	3	4
Other coercive action	3	...	...
Naval units			
Harassment or seizure of other ships	1	...	1
Establishment of presence at sea	8	...	2
Visit to foreign nation	5	6	...
Transport of foreign forces	1	...	1
Exercise or demonstration	1	...	1
Other coercive action	1	...	1

a. Excludes alerts; forces may perform more than one activity in an incident.

In the period between 1957 and 1966 forces already deployed in-theater were available in only a third of the incidents. In 1967–79 in-theater forces were used alone in a third of the incidents and played a role with out-of-theater units in another two-fifths. The proportion of incidents in which in-theater units were not available at all for use dropped from two-thirds to one-fourth. Those operations requiring both in- and out-of-theater deployments almost always took place in response to interstate crises. In-theater or out-of-theater units tended to be used alone in response to intrastate situations, which generally required lower levels of force. The interstate incidents did not necessarily present greater opportunities or threats to Soviet interests, but they clearly required more military effort.

Table 2-4 shows the kinds of Soviet armed forces used and their activities in the third world. In contrast to Moscow's frequent use of ground and supporting tactical air forces in nations surrounding the USSR and in Eastern Europe, naval forces were used most often for coercive diplomacy in the third world. Naval units were used alone in two-fifths of the incidents, and air units were used alone in one-third; ground units were never used alone. While warships were used in a total of two-thirds of the third world incidents, air units were called on in half and ground units played a role in less than one-fifth. Only once were Soviet ground forces emplaced in a third world nation (Egypt, 1970), and those forces comprised only air defense units. (The ground force emplacements in Cuba in 1962 and in Afghanistan in 1979 are discussed above in the category of Soviet security relations.) Otherwise Soviet army units in the USSR either exercised or had their alert status raised. Although used infrequently, the ground units turned to in these incidents were of larger than divisional size. Airborne and naval infantry units became a part of the picture beginning in the late 1960s. All but one of the ground involvements related to situations of interstate conflict between third world nations.

Of twenty-two air involvements, only two-fifths included combat aircraft, and in only two instances was more than one air regiment used. More frequently employed in the third world were transport aircraft, which were used in three-fourths of the incidents involving air units. Combat air units were used more frequently after 1967 than in earlier years—in one of eleven third world actions before 1967 but in a quarter of the operations afterward. As table 2-4 indicates, air units carried out a range of activities in each of the three basic situations considered. Moscow positioned aircraft abroad and engaged in aerial demonstrations on behalf of sovereign regimes and supported insurgencies by airlifting cargo and troops.

Surface warships were used in nine-tenths of the incidents involving the Soviet navy. In nine-tenths of the incidents in which five or more warships were used, the conflict was interstate rather than domestic. Submarines were used in only a fourth of the total naval involvements, but in two-fifths of the interstate incidents. In interstate conflict situations Soviet warships typically established a presence at sea or visited an allied port. Port visits were always the chosen form of support given a regime facing domestic opposition.

Through at least the 1970s, the Soviet navy did not obtain aircraft carriers of the type used by the U.S. Navy since the Second World War. Vessels combining the characteristics of a cruiser and carrier, capable of handling only vertical or short takeoff and landing aircraft and helicopters, were first deployed in the late 1960s. These *Moskva*-class and

Table 2-5. *Percentage of Incidents by Region and Force Type*

	Region			
Type of force	*Middle East-North Africa*	*Persian Gulf-Horn of Africa*	*Sub-Saharan Africa*	*South and Southeast Asia*
Naval	81	70	56	33
Air	50	40	67	67
Ground	31	...	...	17
(Total number of incidents in region)	(16)	(10)	(9)	(6)

Kiev-class ships played a role in only two incidents, both in the third world. One incident was coercive—the shadowing of U.S. Sixth Fleet vessels covering the evacuation of American nationals from Lebanon in June 1976. The other was a cooperative gesture—helping clear the Suez Canal.

Table 2-5 shows the different kinds of forces used in different third world regions. The longer-term Soviet naval deployment in the Mediterranean and the importance and frequency of interstate conflict in the Middle East would seem to explain the USSR's naval and ground unit involvement there. Distance and the special utility of Soviet transport air support to allies in Africa and southern Asia explain the imbalance of air activity in these regions.

The United States acted in two-thirds of the incidents and invariably used military force. But while the United States was a party in four-fifths of both the interstate situations and incidents in which the USSR used military force against a regime in power, U.S. participation was evident in only one-fourth of the incidents when the Soviet Union engaged in military diplomacy in support of a regime against domestic opposition. The United States regularly gave military support to sovereign U.S. allies threatened by Soviet-supported nations or domestic opponents but rarely responded with military force when the Soviet military was used to support a regime in power. All the U.S. actions directed at regimes hostile to the United States took place between 1959 and 1962—that is, at the height of the cold war. This pattern has been constant. The view that in the 1970s, as compared with times past, the United States did not become militarily involved in the third world when a sovereign ally was threatened by a nation receiving military support from the USSR is not supported by the evidence. There is some evidence supporting the view that the U.S.

was less willing in the 1970s to become militarily involved when the USSR militarily supported an insurgent group in domestic conflict.

General Observations about Soviet Political-Military Operations

The remainder of this chapter examines in geopolitical terms the Soviet Union's use of conventional and strategic nuclear forces and U.S. behavior when Moscow practiced military diplomacy.

Conventional Forces

In Europe and Northeast Asia the Kremlin invariably turned to large ground and, frequently, supporting tactical air forces, whereas in the third world and in other distant conflicts the navy and noncombat aircraft were used more frequently. Figure 2-1 shows the overall participation of Soviet conventional forces in the 190 incidents.

GROUND FORCES. More than nine-tenths of the incidents in which ground forces were used related to the occupations growing out of World War II, the loyalty and security of fraternal Communist regimes, and Soviet security relations. Virtually all of these incidents took place in Europe, Northeast Asia, and Southwest Asia (Turkey and Iran). Soviet ground forces were used in countries adjacent to the USSR or were aimed at countries adjacent to ones in which Soviet army troops were stationed.

Land-based ground units were used in 107 incidents. In almost all these actions, the participating troops were drawn from the Soviet army. Exceptions were several instances in the decade after World War II in which the units may have comprised naval infantrymen. Ship-based troops, made up of either Soviet army men or naval infantry, rarely played a role. They were definitely used apart from land-based units only once and together with them on only three occasions.[7]

When turning to ground forces, Soviet leaders regularly used units of more than one division; such was the case in nine-tenths of the incidents for which data were available.[8] To determine the fate of Eastern Europe

7. Ship-based ground units may have been used alone or in conjunction with land forces in an additional six incidents, five of which occurred after 1967.

8. Ground force size was estimated for 13 percent of the incidents about which force size data were obtained. Half of the thirty-nine incidents for which data were insufficient to afford estimates concerned actions related to West Berlin.

Figure 2-1. *Number of Incidents in Which Ground, Air, and Naval Forces Participated*[a]

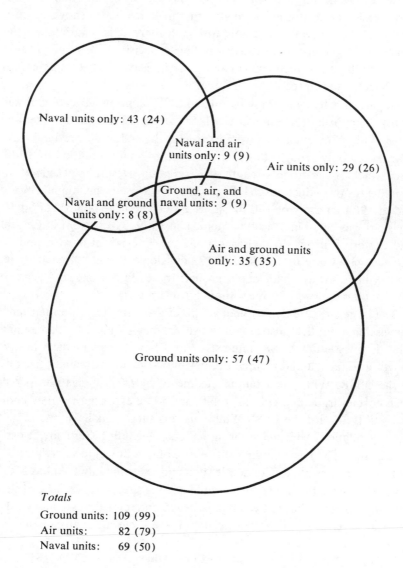

Naval units only: 43 (24)

Naval and air units only: 9 (9)

Air units only: 29 (26)

Ground, air, and naval units: 9 (9)

Naval and ground units only: 8 (8)

Air and ground units only: 35 (35)

Ground units only: 57 (47)

Totals
Ground units: 109 (99)
Air units: 82 (79)
Naval units: 69 (50)

a. Figures in parentheses refer to coercive incidents only. Ground, air, and naval units may have been used in an additional five, seventeen, and eighteen incidents, respectively. Eighteen, including fourteen of those related to air units, pertain to incidents that occurred between 1944 and 1948.

and Northeast Asia after World War II, actively suppress the rebellions in Hungary in 1956 and Czechoslovakia in 1968, and deal with the threat presented by China in the late 1960s, the use of large armed forces is easily understood. But in the many other instances when shows of force were meant to threaten or cajole foreign leaders, it is plausible that instead of using more than a division, Soviet decisionmakers might have used a battalion, a regiment, or only one division.[9] What explains this penchant for such large shows of force?

In part, this tendency may be related to the continuous availability in Europe and Asia of massive Soviet land forces. An estimated 12 million to 15 million Soviet citizens were in arms at the end of the Second World War. Peace only brought this number down to about 5 million by 1948, after which Soviet troop strength was increased. Despite a decade of intermittent force reductions that began in 1955, Moscow maintained by the end of 1964 an army of 140 divisions. After 1965 the number of Soviet divisions was again increased to include, in 1979, 31 divisions in Central and Eastern Europe, 46 divisions along the Sino-Soviet border, and 96 divisions elsewhere in the USSR—173 divisions all told.[10] Hence Soviet leaders have always had ample ground forces in Europe and Asia to carry out large shows of force without great strain.

The large size and deployment of Soviet ground forces and their massive use as a political instrument, however, may be more fundamentally related to essential USSR interests. First, Soviet leaders have always sought to establish and maintain in neighboring nations regimes friendly to the USSR. What the Kremlin has meant by *friendly* has not merely been normal trade and cultural relations and an absence of claims upon or hostility toward the USSR. Stalin and his successors have interpreted friendly relations with neighboring nations (including Germany, Yugoslavia, and Japan) as including an absence of non-Soviet foreign influence and, when necessary, Soviet domination and control. Only then has Moscow felt assured that a neighbor would not act against it. Because of this mentality Moscow has felt easily threatened and tended to see any weakening or reversal of the Soviet position in adjacent lands as calamitous.

---

9. At full strength, a Soviet motorized rifle division includes 13,000 personnel; armored and airborne divisions include 11,000 men and 7,000 men. International Institute for Strategic Studies, *The Military Balance, 1979–1980* (London: IISS, 1979), p. vii.

10. Ibid., p. 10; Thomas W. Wolfe, *Soviet Power and Europe, 1945–1970* (Johns Hopkins Press, 1970), pp. 10–11, 39–40, 164–69.

Moreover, the Kremlin has seen any opportunity for gain as necessary to Soviet security. The Romans were willing to deploy a full legion to besiege a few hundred rebels at Masada in the Judean desert (A.D. 72–73); Moscow has done no less to maintain its dominion.[11] Moscow's use of relatively large forces to achieve objectives is not so surprising insofar as it has always viewed the stakes as high.

Also, in Europe and Asia the targets of Soviet coercive activities have been either nations fielding large armies with modern weapons or domestic movements capable of obtaining widespread support and mobilizing large numbers of citizens. The Kremlin has considered the use of substantial forces necessary to make its point and coerce its opponents. This certainly also may be said about Soviet ground force actions related to the Middle East: the enemy in these instances was Israel, whose air and armored forces are among the finest in the world.

AIR FORCES. Air units were used in eighty-two incidents, though rarely alone and in virtually all instances as a coercive instrument. Combat elements—fighter or bomber units—played a part in almost one-third of the incidents and in two-thirds of those operations in which aircraft were called upon. The other most frequently used aircraft were transport planes (twenty-six incidents). Moscow seldom used reconnaissance aircraft and helicopters as foreign policy instruments. The use of air units was not nearly as restricted to Europe and Northeast Asia as was the use of ground forces. Whereas nine-tenths of the ground force actions occurred in these two regions, only three-fifths of the air operations were carried out there. A quarter of the Soviet political-military operations in which aircraft or helicopters played a role took place in the third world.

The use of noncombat aircraft or small combat units in third world areas in contrast to the more frequent use of fighter and bomber aircraft in Europe and Northeast Asia indicates lesser commitment to third world countries and Moscow's careful calculation in approaching operations there. Combat aircraft involvements in Europe and Northeast Asia were usually large because of the availability of forces, the frequent perception of considerable threat or opportunity, and the capabilities of antagonists.

NAVAL FORCES. The navy was the preeminent instrument of Soviet coercive military diplomacy when the Kremlin looked beyond nations contiguous to the USSR and Central Europe. Naval vessels participated

11. On the significance of the Roman siege of Masada, see Edward N. Luttwak, *The Grand Strategy of the Roman Empire* (Johns Hopkins University Press, 1976), pp. 3–4.

in two-thirds of these incidents. The navy was also the principal tool of Soviet cooperative military diplomacy. Communist and third world nations with which the Kremlin was attempting to improve relations were the targets on a number of occasions, but the most frequent focus of cooperative actions—usually a port call by one to three warships—were Western European nations when Moscow sought to improve relations at important crossroads or to otherwise cultivate special relationships. Discernible in each of these instances was a Soviet interest in weakening NATO unity or relations between a neutral nation and NATO.

Surface combatants provided the usual expression of coercive naval diplomacy. Cruisers, frigates, destroyers, or other escorts were involved in four-fifths of these incidents. The typical operation took one of two forms: a visit or offshore presence by one or two such vessels, often accompanied by a submarine, minesweeper, amphibious craft, oiler, or other type of ship in a situation where violence was not immediately present; or an offshore presence or naval demonstration by many surface combatants supported by other vessels. No coercive operation involving more than three surface warships took place before 1967.[12]

Warships other than surface combatants—for example, submarines—were used much less frequently and almost never alone. No doubt Soviet leaders believed that surface warships would make a greater visible impression on foreign leaders than other types of vessels; after all, it was perceptions that they were trying to influence. Two important developments beginning in the late 1960s were the use of amphibious vessels to transport foreign forces and military equipment and, in several instances, to raise the specter of Soviet ground units being landed ashore; and the new availability to Soviet leaders of *Moskva*-class and *Kiev*-class carriers. These vessels, although geared for antisubmarine warfare operations and not, like U.S. aircraft carriers, for projecting air power ashore, present a greater visual image of military power than other types of Soviet surface vessels.

Like the significance of the availability of ground and air forces in Europe and Northeast Asia, Moscow's frequent coercive use of warships beginning in 1967 may be related in part to the forward deployment of the Soviet navy and the consequent readiness of naval vessels for participation in these operations. A continuous Soviet naval presence was established in the Mediterranean in 1964; in 1968 Soviet warships ap-

12. Information was unavailable on the number of surface combatants used in thirteen incidents, five of which took place before 1967.

peared in the Indian Ocean; and beginning in 1970 they were regularly in West African waters. The Soviet naval presence in the North Atlantic and the Pacific also was enlarged during these years.[13]

At least in the past, Soviet naval forces, like ground and air units, were procured essentially for deterring attack on the USSR and missions of war, not discrete political operations.[14] Their primary targets are U.S. ballistic missile and attack submarines and U.S. aircraft carriers, to prevent a nuclear attack on the Soviet Union and to increase the security of Soviet nuclear submarines. The presence of U.S. carriers and submarines in the North Atlantic, Pacific, and the Mediterranean drew large Soviet deployments to these seas. These deployments provided familiarity, confidence, and a readily available military option to Soviet policymakers. Psychologically and logistically it was easier to call upon and reinforce units already deployed than to send out warships from home waters to seas where a Soviet naval presence had not been established. No doubt Moscow's confidence was further strengthened by the improved quality of Soviet warships in the late 1960s over those of the Soviet navy a decade earlier.[15]

In many instances the use of only a few naval vessels seemed tailored to the situation at hand. For example, the deployment of only two warships near the coast of Ghana in 1969 after that West African nation seized two Soviet trawlers was probably better suited to achieving the release of those vessels than a large show of Soviet naval power would have been. In other instances, though, the small size of the Soviet naval presence at the scene of a crisis reflected lesser capabilities—for example, the deployment near Cuba of only six submarines during the 1962 missile crisis—or the Kremlin's wish to not overcommit itself or act unnecessarily provocative in distant arenas; note, for example, the Soviet deployment of only two surface combatants in West African waters during the 1975–76 Angolan conflict.

Naval actions, though, imply less concern and greater hesitation than

13. Robert G. Weinland, "Soviet Naval Operations: 10 Years of Change," in Michael MccGwire, Ken Booth, and John McDonnell, eds., *Soviet Naval Policy: Objectives and Constraints* (Praeger for the Centre of Foreign Policy Studies, Department of Political Science, Dalhousie University, Halifax, N.S., 1975), pp. 375–81.

14. Barry M. Blechman and others, *The Soviet Military Buildup and U.S. Defense Spending* (Brookings Institution, 1977), p. 11.

15. Barry M. Blechman, *The Changing Soviet Navy* (Brookings Institution, 1973), p. 3.

does the emplacement of ground and air forces, which afford less flexibility and appear to be a firmer pledge. In the third world, in supporting distant Communist regimes, and in taking advantage of rifts within NATO Moscow was willing to show off Soviet military power, increase the risk to antagonists, and sometimes commit itself by the forward deployment of ground or air units (as when it provided Egypt's air defense in the early 1970s). Usually, though, Soviet leaders sought to retain flexibility, which was best provided by naval units since they could indicate definite interest without necessarily signaling commitment.

The rare use of ship-based infantry, even in crises, is a further indication of Soviet desire to retain as much flexibility as possible when dealing with distant situations. The USSR maintained in the late 1970s five naval infantry regiments, one each with the Northern, Baltic, and Black Sea fleets and two with the Pacific Fleet.[16] Most of these troops were based in the USSR or aboard ships in home waters. Unlike the United States, which deployed one Marine Battalion Landing Team (BLT) aboard amphibious vessels in the Mediterranean and two in the western Pacific, the USSR maintained no units approaching this size far from its own waters. Nor have sizable Soviet naval infantry units been deployed at the outset of crises to prepare for landing in support of an ally. When Israeli forces rapidly surrounded the Egyptian Third Army on the west bank of the Suez during the 1973 Middle East war and Cairo desperately pressed Moscow for help, the Kremlin's ground force choices were to alert airborne forces in the USSR or actually fly those units to Egypt. Moscow did not have a credible naval infantry option. Not wanting to abandon its ally, but also seeking to hold its cards as closely as possible, Moscow alerted units in the Soviet Union.

Major Combined Operations and Confrontations

In what context did the most substantial displays of Soviet political-military power occur? Besides considering Moscow's use of ground, air, and sea units in various circumstances, it is also valuable to look at incidents including only large combined operations, defined here as actions in which two of the three following forces participated: a ground force larger than one division; a combat air unit larger than one regiment; and a naval force including more than five surface combatants. These three

16. IISS, *The Military Balance, 1979–1980,* p. 11.

Table 2-6. *Major Coercive Actions by USSR Forces since Stalin's Death*

Crisis in Hungary	November 1956
U.S. intervention in Lebanon	July 1958
Western presence in Berlin	July 1961
Cuban missile crisis	October 1962
Border dispute with China	? 1965
Border dispute with China	February 1967
Relations with Czechoslovakia	July 1968
Relations with Czechoslovakia	August 1968
Relations with Rumania[a]	August 1968
Security of regime in Czechoslovakia	October 1968
Border dispute with China	March 1969
Security of Egypt	February 1970
West Germany-USSR treaty[a]	October 1970
Relations with Rumania[a]	June 1971
Arab-Israeli war (1)	October 1973
Arab-Israeli war (2)	October 1973
Cyprus conflict	July 1974
Relations with China[a]	April 1978
China-Vietnam War[a]	February 1979

a. Definitional criteria possibly met.

force elements are not equivalent; rather each represents a large combat potential in its own terms.

Soviet combined military operations meeting the above definition were conducted in a fifth of the 158 coercive incidents and may have taken place in an additional 10 percent. More than four-fifths of these forty-four actions were directed at Europe or contiguous territories in Asia, and three-fifths occurred before Stalin's death. The last were aimed largely at expansion in the context of the end and immediate aftermath of the Second World War. Other operations during this period focused on defending new positions and attempts to influence the Western allies' policies toward Germany.

Table 2-6 lists the incidents that took place after Stalin died. The difference between the operations that took place in Stalin's era and more recent ones lies in the prominence after Stalin's death of actions to maintain Soviet authority in Eastern Europe, the need beginning in the 1960s to respond to threats presented by China, and Soviet willingness beginning in the late 1960s to become militarily engaged in the Mediterranean area in support of allies in conflict with U.S. friends. The Berlin crisis and the Cuban missile crisis—the great probes of the Khrushchev era—are now two decades in the past and do not seem likely to recur. The demonstration of support of East Germany in 1970 following the signing of the Treaty of Moscow, rather than being perceived as a Soviet threat, was actually a reaffirmation of the alliance between East Germany and the Soviet Union and indicated more the cold war's ending than anything else. What remains from the past are continuing hostile relations between the USSR and China, the likelihood that periodically the Kremlin will be faced with challenges to its authority in Eastern Europe, and a number of conflictive relationships between U.S. and Soviet friends in the third world.

Strategic Nuclear Forces

On many occasions, but particularly during the Khrushchev era, Soviet leaders verbally raised the prospect of using nuclear weapons against foreign nations. Yet in only one instance were data found confirming that the USSR had actually raised the alert status of forces presumably included in plans for nuclear attack upon the United States, Europe, or China. That incident was the Cuban missile crisis.[17] No information was discovered that would indicate that the USSR has ever redeployed strategic bomber units during a crisis. To be sure about these matters is impossible, however.[18]

What can be said about publicly unknown demonstrative uses of Soviet strategic forces during crises, though, is that first, the Kremlin did not attempt to draw foreign attention to these actions (if they occurred), unlike U.S. leaders who on a number of occasions since the Second World War made it clear by the alert and deployment of stategic forces that the United States might resort to the use of nuclear weapons. Second, if the targets of such possible Soviet moves perceived them at all, they did

17. Richard E. Neustadt and Graham T. Allison, Afterword, in Robert F. Kennedy, *Thirteen Days: A Memoir of the Cuban Missile Crisis* (Norton, 1971), p. 113.

18. No useful information was located about (1) actual crisis communications between Soviet political leaders, military commanders, and the operators of missile-laden submarines, land-based missiles, and nuclear-capable bombers; (2) activities at Soviet air or submarine bases during periods of tension that might indicate an increased or unchanged alert status; or (3) numerical counts of strategic submarines and aircraft at specific locations during crises. Considering this ignorance, it would not be shocking to learn that at least some Soviet strategic units had their alert status raised or were redeployed during the 1961 Berlin crisis or the crisis with China in 1969, or that Soviet strategic units were redeployed during the missile crisis. Other incidents in which such actions would not have been incredible are the 1973 Middle East war, the 1968 Czechoslovakia intervention, the 1958 Offshore Islands crisis, the 1956 Suez crisis, and the 1956 intervention in Hungary.

not make that information public. Valuable classified files about these matters are undoubtedly available within the United States and perhaps other governments. Whether even these files are definitive is impossible to tell from the outside.

It is certainly plausible that Soviet strategic forces were used as a political instrument in only the Cuban missile crisis. Political leaders in Moscow may historically have been more concerned than U.S. policymakers with the problem of command and control. The normal levels of alert of Soviet strategic forces are much lower than those of U.S. strategic forces, and in crises Soviet leaders may have been very anxious to restrict the risk of accident or unauthorized action. As related elsewhere, "Something is far more likely to go wrong when forces are spring-loaded for action than when they are at rest. An unauthorized or accidental launching of nuclear weapons à la *Dr. Strangelove,* is more likely in a force at high readiness than in one at low readiness."[19]

Also, when the strategic position of the USSR was one of gross inferiority and mutual assured destruction was not certain, Soviet leaders may have considered the orchestration of nuclear forces during the Suez, Quemoy, and Berlin crises, for example, profoundly dangerous insofar as the United States might have been provoked to carry out a preemptive first strike. In addition, if a discrete use of strategic nuclear units failed to deter or compel Western behavior in an era of Soviet nuclear inferiority, what then? Insofar as the Kremlin perceived its behavior over Berlin and the shelling of Quemoy and Matsu islands by the People's Republic of China as probes, almost certainly it anticipated the possibility of having to back off in the face of strong U.S. responses. To blink after escalating to the nuclear level was to brook an incomparable diplomatic disaster— as Khrushchev learned in the Cuban missile crisis. The Soviet Union instead wanted to keep the focus on its conventional capabilities in Europe and Asia.

Before the full-scale suppression in Hungary in 1956 and the August 1968 entry into Czechoslovakia, Moscow was given strong reason to believe that these acts would not evoke a Western military response. The Kremlin may have considered the alert or deployment of strategic forces concurrently with these interventions as provoking the West unnecessarily. Besides being unwilling to go to the nuclear level on behalf of Egypt following the U.S. nuclear alert during the 1973 Middle East war,

19. Joseph J. Kruzel, "Military Alerts and Diplomatic Signals," in Ellen P. Stern, ed., *The Limits of Military Intervention* (Sage, 1977), p. 89.

the Kremlin may have also perceived such escalation as unnecessary to its immediate objectives and interests. That the USSR did alert or deploy strategic forces during the 1969 Sino-Soviet crisis (when Moscow raised this threat—at least verbally) is more plausible.

The United States as an Actor

The United States did not participate in incidents between the USSR and the People's Republic of China and tended to steer clear of Kremlin actions to maintain its authority in Eastern Europe. The superpowers most frequently confronted each other on the periphery of Soviet power in the west, when fraternal Communist regimes outside Eastern Europe were endangered, and in the third world. Although the stakes may have been high and the United States or the Soviet Union were often prepared to become more heavily engaged if necessary, small military confrontations or dual appearances on the scene of U.S. and Soviet military units occurred much more frequently than did situations in which Moscow and Washington ordered the deployment or alert of very large forces. East and West Germany and the Middle East were the places of most heated contact.

The postwar occupations were established by mutual agreement. Notwithstanding their suspicion of each other, the entry of both U.S. and Soviet troops into Germany, Austria, Czechoslovakia, China, and Korea at the end of World War II did not lead to direct confrontation. Later, moreover, it was only in Europe that the USSR or the United States led the way toward confrontation. Both sides viewed their behavior in Europe as necessary to critical security interests. Elsewhere the superpowers tended to be drawn in by regional antagonists, as in Asia by North and South Korea, India, and Pakistan, and in the Middle East by the Arab-Israeli conflict and strife between allies in the Arab world.

Washington and Moscow were also enticed into a number of internal conflicts, including the civil war that resumed in China after Japan's surrender, and ones in Lebanon, Indonesia, Laos, and the Congo in the late 1950s and early 1960s. In these instances, however, the USSR and the United States did not confront each other militarily as they did in interstate crises. The tendency in internal situations was for one or both of the superpowers to play only a supportive role or to orchestrate a show of force in a way implying their intention not to be drawn into a military confrontation.

The superpowers did not both use their armed forces in response to internal crises after the early 1960s. One reason for this was perhaps the heightened opposition within the international community to intervention in the domestic affairs of third world nations. A recognized government could obtain the military backing of one superpower, but it became increasingly costly for the other superpower to back its internal opposition overtly. If an internal crisis developed into one between nations, as the 1970 Jordan crisis did when Syrian armored units crossed the Jordanian border, the barrier to military involvement by both the United States and the USSR was lowered insofar as the conflict became one between client states. Moreover, while covert action could weaken a regime, the prospect that a discrete political-military operation could bring down a regime was almost always slight. When appropriate, military aid and superpower armed forces support given to an established government was more effective.

Military involvement by both superpowers was more likely in an internal crisis when no recognized government existed, as in Angola in 1975–76. But even in that instance the USSR became heavily involved militarily only after it was clear that the United States would not and when the Kremlin's client already had the upper hand politically in the international community. That the United States did not use military force in Angola and that the USSR waited as long as it did also revealed the difficulty nonstate actors have in gaining superpower support. Playing a further role after the early 1960s were the greater caution of Khrushchev's successors and the increased opposition in the United States (related to the Vietnam War) to new foreign entanglements. Backing a fraternal ally, alliance member, or nation with which there existed longtime ties of interest or friendship entailed minimal risk; using military force to support only a potential friend was not quite so safe.

After the Cuban missile crisis neither the United States nor the USSR attempted to make gains at the expense of the other by provoking the other directly with military means. Concomitantly, there occurred no crisis confrontations between the North Atlantic and Warsaw Pact nations. While the superpowers became entangled supporting friends elsewhere, their European allies, although interested bystanders, continued improving relations with one another.

U.S. military men participated in a dozen incidents in which the Kremlin coercively used forces in large combined operations (as already defined) and in another eleven in which ground, sea, or air units alone of a size large enough to meet the criteria were used. For the most part, these twenty-three incidents—listed in table 2-7—included joint occupations at the end of the Second World War, the major crises of the cold war, and conflicts between U.S. and Soviet allies in the Middle East.

Except for the incident in Southeast Asian waters in May 1972, every confrontation after the Cuban missile crisis represented an entrapment of the superpowers; neither the USSR nor the United States planned or initiated these incidents. Even in the Cyprus crisis, when the USSR did act in a way to add further to NATO's disarray, Moscow had images to protect—as a power to be reckoned with in eastern Mediterranean regional affairs and as a Warsaw Pact ally (of Bulgaria). Compared with the other incidents listed in table 2-7 since the missile crisis, this incident and that in May 1972 were the ones in which the sense of superpower military confrontation was weakest. Although both the Soviet Union and the United States used armed forces to signal interest and concern during these years, the prospect of violent conflict between the superpowers was minimal.

Large Soviet and U.S. naval forces played a role in all but one of the incidents listed in table 2-7 following the Cuban missile crisis. The threat of major Soviet ground unit involvement arose in three of these incidents; Soviet combat air units were deployed in none. Thus, generally speaking, after 1962 superpower military confrontations—at least in terms of the nearness of military units to each other—took place at sea. This was heavily related to the responsive rather than initiatory character of the USSR and U.S. involvements in these situations and Moscow's and Washington's desire to retain maximum flexibility while issuing political-military signals. The Cuban missile crisis seemed to teach the superpowers that direct provocation could be extremely dangerous, that the course of such a crisis could not be planned, and that withdrawal could be exceedingly difficult. A lesson of the October war was that friends could create or get themselves into a situation where one or both superpowers felt compelled to lend a hand and go far beyond a point where they felt secure.

After the Cuban missile crisis serious U.S.-Soviet confrontations became less frequent because of easing tensions in Europe, Moscow's shift in attention to the threat of China coupled with U.S. unwillingness to play a military role in the Sino-Soviet conflict, and U.S. restraint when the USSR unilaterally engaged in coercive military diplomacy in defense of sovereign third world regimes. The Cuban missile crisis signaled an end

Table 2-7. *Incidents in Which U.S. and Major USSR Armed Forces Were Used*[a]

Issue over political future of Czechoslovakia	January 1945
Issue over political future of Germany	January 1945
Issue over political future of Austria	March 1945
Issue over political future of China	August 1945
Issue over political future of Korea	August 1945
Attempt to gain economic influence in Manchuria	November 1945
Maintenance of security of Port Arthur and Dairen	February 1946
Dispute over Turkish provinces and Dardanelles	March 1946
Future of West Germany and Berlin	June 1948
Maintenance of security of China during Korean War	Late 1950
Maintenance of security of North Korea during Korean War	? 1951
U.S. intervention in Lebanon	July 1958
Western presence in Berlin	July 1961
Emplacement of missiles in Cuba	July 1962
Cuban missile crisis	October 1962
Egypt-Israel political crisis	May 1967
Arab-Israeli war	June 1967
Seizure of U.S.S. *Pueblo* by North Korea	January 1968
Jordan-PLO-Syria conflict	September 1970
U.S. response to North Vietnam Easter offensive	May 1972
Arab-Israeli war (1)	October 1973
Arab-Israeli war (2)	October 1973
Cyprus conflict	July 1974

a. Major USSR armed forces included ground units of more than one division, at least six major surface combatants, or more than one air regiment.

to a period of Soviet probes aimed directly at the West to which the United States regularly responded because of deeply felt security interests. In the next several years the USSR did not use military power provocatively in either Europe or the third world and chose not to respond seriously to the deepening U.S. involvement and then full entry into the war in Southeast Asia. With the exception of the fighting in Yemen, a new war did not occur in the Middle East until 1967. Although the Kremlin may well have become deeply involved in a serious Arab-Israeli confrontation had one occurred before then, Moscow was not prepared to become engaged in more distant situations in South Asia, the Persian Gulf, or sub-Saharan Africa, let alone in the Caribbean.

When the USSR responded to threats presented in Eastern Europe and by China in the late 1960s, the United States determined to steer clear of these incidents. At the same time, the lack of hostile Soviet behavior toward Western Europe and the dramatically improved relationship between the USSR and West Germany obviated superpower confrontation over the Eurasian Cape. Those superpower confrontations that did take place were occasioned by interstate crises in the Middle East and South Asia and Moscow's increased, though still very limited, support of Communist allies outside Eastern Europe. The United States did not, however, militarily challenge the Soviet political-military operations directed at supporting third world regimes against internal threats.

After the early 1970s the Middle East and South Asia were relatively quiescent; and while the United States withdrew completely from Indochina, the USSR showed itself unwilling to support provocative behavior by North Korea. When U.S. and Soviet military forces did appear together on the scene of a conflict in the third world, the potential for serious confrontation was minimal, certainly as far as U.S. objectives and intentions were concerned. When the Kremlin airlifted armaments to Algeria in early 1976 to help the Polisario rebels in the former Spanish Sahara, the U.S. response was to send the Sixth Fleet flagship *Little Rock* to visit Morocco; and when U.S. and Soviet warships appeared together in the eastern Mediterranean in June 1976, the occasion was the U.S. evacuation of American nationals from Lebanon. When the Carter administration did decide to show U.S. interest in the Somalian-Ethiopian conflict in 1978, the means chosen was a very small naval presence in the Red Sea. Although the United States would probably have acted forcefully in any serious Arab-Israeli confrontation and have opposed Cuban military actions in the Caribbean area, U.S. willingness to become militarily engaged elsewhere in the third world appeared minimal.

CHAPTER THREE

The Expansion and Defense of Communism

THE NEXT THREE CHAPTERS narrate the history of Soviet coercive diplomacy since the Bolsheviks seized power in 1917. Chapter 3 examines both Soviet expansionary operations and ones aimed at maintaining fraternal Communist regimes; chapter 4 focuses on actions concerning Soviet security relations with other neighbors and major antagonists; and chapter 5 examines Soviet military diplomacy in the third world.

I have chosen a narrative presentation of Soviet coercive diplomacy as history rather than a highly analytic approach for several reasons. First, a narrative approach gives this research documentary value as a historical record and accommodates a large amount of the descriptive data collected. (The value of a computer-based file is limited since complex events are not easily broken down into elements that electronic manipulation can transfer into copies of the original.) Second, despite the amount of information that was collected, its limitations must be respected; a heavily analytic presentation would risk misleading readers. The narrative makes analytic points that can be supported by the data with some confidence about (1) circumstances leading to and restraining Soviet coercive diplomacy; (2) the significance of broad international and domestic developments and changing military capabilities to Soviet political-military thinking and force use; and (3) Soviet prudence and risk-taking. Third, the narrative format offers a way to communicate the climate of a time—an important variable—and elucidates the complex interrelationships between incidents.

Early Operations

Leon Trotsky did not believe a socialist society could be constructed in Russia without revolution occurring elsewhere in Europe. By the mid-1920s, though, the dominant line was Stalin's belief that "socialism in one country" was possible—the Soviet Union could make it on its own. With one exception, the spread of communism abroad remained a distant goal until the incorporation of territories to the west between 1939 and 1941.

The exception was Outer Mongolia, where the USSR gained dominion in 1921. At the end of the Russian civil war, Red Army troops and a Mongol force, together numbering about 13,000 men, defeated a White Russian army in the area near Kiakhta. Soviet troops then remained in Outer Mongolia until at least 1925 to support the consolidation of power by the new People's Revolutionary Government. The Soviet military developed the Mongolian People's Revolutionary Army in its own image and continued to serve this new Red Army (as it was renamed in 1930) as advisers and staff officers.[1] In 1932 and 1934 Soviet troops helped suppress internal rebellions against the Mongolian People's Republic, setting a precedent for later interventions in Eastern Europe.

The Red Army was unable to extend the boundaries of communism in the west during the civil war years. In the winter of 1917–18 Red Finns supported by Bolshevik troops and the Baltic Fleet sought to gain power in Finland. From their island fortress of Suomenlinna and their ships near the shore of the Finnish capital, Red sailors dominated Helsinki until they were immobilized by ice and then forced by advancing German forces to withdraw. In 1920 Lenin also took advantage of a revolt against the shah of Iran. Bolshevik soldiers and naval vessels supported the insurgents, and a Soviet republic of Gilan was established in northern Iran. A withdrawal was ordered only when it became clear that a very large Soviet intervention would be necessary to obtain success. The only major battle fought by the Red Army in the west was in Poland, where Bolshevik troops wheeled as far as the gates of Warsaw before they were driven back by forces led by Józef Piłsudski. Before this retreat a Polish

---

1. Peter S. H. Tang, *Russian and Soviet Policy in Manchuria and Outer Mongolia, 1911–1931* (Duke University Press, 1959), pp. 370–76, 395; O. Edmund Clubb, "Armed Conflict in the Chinese Borderlands, 1917–50," in Raymond L. Garthoff, ed., *Sino-Soviet Military Relations* (Praeger, 1966), pp. 15–16, 20.

Provisional Revolutionary Committee was established briefly in Bialystock.[2]

On August 23, 1939, German foreign minister Joachim von Ribbentrop and his Soviet counterpart, Vyacheslav M. Molotov, signed a Treaty of Nonaggression Between Germany and the Union of Soviet Socialist Republics. Thus Hitler ensured that the invasion of Poland, beginning on September 1, would lead to war only with Britain and France, and not also with Russia. Stalin wanted Germany to spend its energy in the west to give the USSR time to strengthen itself further. A "Secret Additional Protocol" to the alliance between the USSR and Germany offered the following material incentives:

1. In the event of a territorial and political rearrangement of the areas belonging to the Baltic states (Finland, Estonia, Latvia, Lithuania) the northern boundary of Lithuania shall represent the boundary of the spheres of influence of Germany and the USSR.

2. In the event of a territorial and political rearrangement of the areas belonging to the Polish state the spheres of influence of Germany and the USSR shall be bounded approximately by the line of the rivers Narew, Vistula, and San. The question of whether the interests of both parties make desirable the maintenance of an independent Polish state . . . can only be definitely determined in the course of further political developments.

3. With regard to Southeastern Europe attention is called by the Soviet side to its interest in Bessarabia.[3]

On September 17, 1939, while the Polish armed forces were being destroyed by the Nazi onslaught from the west, the Red Army crossed the Polish frontier on a broad front extending from Latvia to the Carpathians. Eastern Poland was occupied within days. An additional secret agreement between Berlin and Moscow traded Lublin Province in eastern Poland to Germany in return for the cession of Lithuania to Soviet dominion, whereupon Moscow forced "mutual trade and aid agreements" upon Estonia (September 29), Latvia (October 5), and Lithuania (October 10). The establishment of Soviet military bases in these nations— allowed by the agreements—undermined completely their ability to resist formal annexation to the USSR less than a year later.[4]

2. On these events, see Thomas T. Hammond, ed., *The Anatomy of Communist Takeovers* (Yale University Press, 1975), pp. 8, 90–92, 98–105.

3. See text of the Treaty of Nonaggression Between Germany and the Union of Soviet Socialist Republics in Alvin Z. Rubinstein, ed., *The Foreign Policy of the Soviet Union,* 3d ed. (Random House, 1972), pp. 136–38.

4. C. E. Black and E. C. Helmreich, *Twentieth Century Europe: A History,* 4th ed. (Knopf, 1963), pp. 537–39, 545; Alexander Werth, *Russia at War, 1941–*

Finland's turn was next; but Helsinki was not bullied by Soviet threats. The USSR finally declared war on its northern neighbor on November 29, 1939. After a heroic defense, the Finns ended their resistance in March 1940. The terms of surrender included the cession of Finnish territory adjacent to Lake Ladoga near Leningrad, Hanko, and large tracts along the central and northern portions of Finland's border with the USSR.[5] Moscow's adherence to the secret protocol of the Nazi-Soviet pact was total when, following an ultimatum on June 23, 1940, Rumania offered up Bessarabia and northern Bukovina to Red Army occupation. This Rumanian coda and the incorporation of Estonia, Latvia, and Lithuania into the USSR just days earlier were precipitated by the unexpectedly quick fall of France.

The tactics of Soviet political-military action in advancing the USSR's position during this period were sophisticated. Difficulty occurred only when Moscow turned to its armed forces as an instrument of force rather than for influence—that is, in the Winter War with Finland.

Gains after the Second World War

Immediately after World War II Soviet geopolitical influence increased dramatically. The Soviet army played a major role in this development by occupying Poland, Hungary, Rumania, Bulgaria, eastern Germany, and northern Korea and by standing behind local Communists in Yugoslavia and Czechoslovakia. Moscow exploited the circumstances in which the war ended by establishing across the USSR's frontiers Communist regimes that satisfied both ideological and statist objectives.

Stalin was flexible in his use of military power, however; the Soviet army did not support local Communists in all circumstances. Soviet troops withdrew from China, Iran, and Czechoslovakia; a Communist regime was not established in Austria; and a coup was not attempted in Finland. Stalin was also willing to back off after probing for weakness in Turkey.

1945 (Dutton, 1964),. pp. 54–65; Adam B. Ulam, *Expansion and Coexistence: Soviet Foreign Policy, 1917–1973,* 2d ed. (Praeger, 1974), pp. 280–87.

5. Werth, *Russia at War,* pp. 66–79; Ian V. Hogg, "Border Clashes: The Winter War," in S. L. Mayer, ed., *The Russian War Machine, 1917–1945* (London: Arms and Armor, 1977), pp. 73–79; Kurt Dittmar and G. I. Antonov, "The Red Army in the Finnish War," in B. H. Liddell Hart, ed., *The Soviet Army* (London: Weidenfeld and Nicolson, 1956), pp. 79–92.

Eastern Europe

After first entering Rumania in April 1944, Soviet troops over-whelmed Bulgaria and surged into Yugoslavia. Then, with its flanks covered, the Red Army began its great march westward through Hungary, Czechoslovakia, and Poland, into Austria, and finally into Germany and Berlin. Poland lost its three provinces east of the Curzon line. Finland was again forced to offer up the territories it had lost during the Winter War and to lease to the USSR for fifty years the naval base of Porkkala on the Gulf of Finland. Rumania was forced to cede northern Bukovina and Bessarabia to Soviet sovereignty, and Czechoslovakia had to give up sub-Carpathian Ruthenia. Germany's loss to the Soviet Union was the northern half of East Prussia.

Aside from the Baltic states, which were formally incorporated into the USSR in 1940, Moscow's other gains in 1939–40 were legitimated by agreements signed with the Allies or former Axis nations.

The military occupation of these territories was critical to obtaining them, however. To some extent the agreements reached with the USSR recognized what many saw as legitimate Soviet demands for reparations for damage suffered during the war and insurance of the USSR's future security. But essentially these warrants were signed in acknowledgment of Soviet military power and to foreclose further Soviet demands. Not to have come to such terms risked infuriating Stalin and possibly causing the Kremlin to gobble up even more territory.

The agreements at Tehran, Yalta, and Potsdam all supported the establishment of postwar regimes in Eastern Europe that were "democratic and friendly" to the USSR.[6] Stalin diligently established "people's democracies" in the occupied nations, which were joined by Czechoslovakia in February 1948. Significant and perhaps crucial to the successful finale of the Czechoslovakian drama was the massing of the Soviet army just across Czechoslovakia's borders. Although the Czechoslovak Communists held or controlled the most important government positions and even obtained the support of the army chief of staff, much of their influence and support may be attributed to Czechoslovak recognition of and sensitivities about contiguous Soviet military power.[7]

6. Zbigniew K. Brzezinski, *The Soviet Bloc: Unity and Conflict* (Harvard University Press, 1960), p. 32.

7. Morton A. Kaplan, *The Life and Death of the Cold War* (Nelson Hall, 1976), pp. 124–28. Several Soviet divisions, intended to help suppress underground activity, were reported in Czechoslovakia in early 1951. *New York Times,* February 26, 1951.

The continued deployment of the Soviet army in Eastern Europe and purges in the late 1940s of Eastern European Communists whom Moscow did not consider loyal enough guaranteed Eastern Europe's sovietization. One-half million to one million Soviet troops remained in Eastern Europe after the war. The Group of Soviet Forces Germany included twenty-two divisions and supporting tactical aircraft. Up to eight divisions and supporting aircraft were placed in Poland, Hungary, Czechoslovakia, and Rumania. And behind these formations were the fifty to sixty divisions in the USSR's western military districts.[8]

The Balkans

The use of Soviet military power in the Balkans presents an interesting contrast to the pattern followed in Eastern Europe proper. The Soviet army entered Yugoslavia only briefly. In 1944–45 Stalin felt strong ties with and, no doubt, the ability to dominate the Yugoslav Communists, who, as a result of their leading role in the partisan movement, were domestically well rooted and able to gain quick control in the wake of the German army's retreat. Hence the Soviet army did not occupy Yugoslavia after the liberation of Belgrade but was directed toward other prizes.[9] Stalin was correct about the Yugoslav Communists' ability to consolidate their position by themselves, but he was mistaken about their willingness to accept the USSR's lead in decisions affecting Yugoslavia.

The Soviet army bypassed Albania, which Moscow considered within Yugoslavia's sphere of influence; Stalin half expected that Belgrade would incorporate the country as the Baltic states had been made part of the USSR earlier. Milovan Djilas has reported that Stalin suggested this as late as January 1948.[10] At a February 1948 meeting in Moscow, Stalin expressed a different view, however, and vigorously opposed Belgrade's deployment of an air force fighter regiment and plans to dispatch two divisions to Albania. (The issue, of course, was Yugoslavia's exhibition of independence in foreign policy, not Albanian sovereignty.)[11]

Beginning in July 1948, Tirana used the crisis in Soviet-Yugoslav re-

8. Thomas W. Wolfe, *Soviet Power and Europe, 1945–70* (Johns Hopkins University Press, 1976), pp. 10–11, 39–40; Charles M. Murphy, "U.S. Military Strengths by Country of Location Since World War II, 1948–1971" (Congressional Research Service, Foreign Affairs Division, February 29, 1972), pp. 6–7.

9. George W. Hoffman and Fred Warner Neal, *Yugoslavia and the New Communism* (Twentieth Century Fund, 1962), pp. 107–08.

10. Milovan Djilas, *Conversations with Stalin,* trans. Michael B. Petrovich (Harcourt, Brace and World, 1962), p. 143.

11. Ibid., pp. 171–80.

lations that had erupted in March to denounce Belgrade's influence in Albania. Yugoslav economic, military, and other missions were forced to withdraw, and various bilateral agreements were terminated. Albania then sought Soviet military and other aid to ensure its independence.[12] To increase Soviet influence in Albania and isolate Belgrade, Stalin poured arms, equipment, and advisers into Albania, and the Albanian armed forces were remodeled in the Soviet image.[13]

As in Yugoslavia and Albania, the Bulgarian Communist party enjoyed a degree of popularity and the USSR was not concerned about nationalist, anti-Russian sentiments there, as it was in Poland, Hungary, Rumania, and what became East Germany. However, purges and more brutal means of eliminating opposition were still necessary before local Communist control was consolidated.[14] This accomplished, though, Soviet military units were withdrawn from Bulgaria in December 1947.[15] Moscow has had no reason to regret this withdrawal, unlike that from Rumania in 1958. The Bulgarian Communist party has remained the most loyal ruling Communist party in the world.

Korea

As long as the war lasted in Europe, Stalin was pleased to abide by the terms of the Japanese-Soviet Neutrality Treaty signed in Moscow on April 13, 1941. But on April 4, 1945, with the end of the war in Europe in sight, Stalin denounced the pact and during the next four months redeployed thirty-nine Soviet divisions to the Far East, doubling the Soviet army's size in that theater to about 1.6 million men. On August 9, 1945, three days after Hiroshima and three months after VE-Day (as Stalin had promised at Yalta), a massive Soviet offensive was mounted against Japanese forces in Manchuria and Korea.[16]

12. *New York Times,* July 4, 7, 10, and 11, 1948.

13. Stavro Skendi and others, *Albania* (Atlantic for the Mid-European Studies Center of the Free Europe Committee, Inc., 1957), pp. 116–18.

14. Brzezinski, *The Soviet Bloc,* pp. 15–16; Hugh Seton-Watson, *The East European Revolution* (Praeger, 1951), pp. 91, 211–19.

15. *New York Times,* December 4, 16, and 18, 1947; Seton-Watson, *The East European Revolution,* p. 218. Air units were deployed to Bulgaria in 1953 following a buildup of air power in Greece and Turkey, both NATO members. Soviet ground force units were reported to have returned temporarily to Bulgaria in November 1956 as a precaution while the uprising in Hungary was being suppressed. *New York Times,* October 12, 1953, and November 19, 1956.

16. Raymond L. Garthoff, "The Soviet Intervention in Manchuria, 1945–46," in Garthoff, *Sino-Soviet Military Relations,* pp. 60–62; Ulam, *Expansion and Coexistence,* pp. 394–95.

Making the most of their careful preparations, their overwhelming superiority, and the weakened state of the enemy, Soviet armed forces occupied in approximately eleven days all of Manchuria, Korea south to the 38th parallel, and the southern part of Sakhalin Island.[17] The purpose of this offensive was only partly to ensure the defeat of Japan; it also afforded the USSR influence over the political future of East Asia. Moscow used the opportunity to establish a Communist regime in Korea and to support the Chinese Communists' quest for power.

Soviet troops occupied northern Korea in accordance with prior Allied agreement. Unlike in China, however, where Moscow sought only to strengthen the position of the local Communists, Soviet military power in Korea was used to guarantee the establishment of a full-fledged Communist regime under the leadership of Kim Il-Sung. Like a number of others who formed the leadership of what eventually became the Korean Workers party, Kim had earlier fought with the Soviet army in Europe and entered Korea in the uniform of a Soviet officer.[18]

A Communist regime in Korea was established in stages. Despite the facade of a coalition government composed of Korean nationalists and Communists, real power rested with Soviet authorities, who used the occupation to confirm control by Kim and his associates. In 1946 a new socioeconomic order got under way, and in 1947 a Communist-dominated North Korean People's Assembly was elected. A constitution was ratified in July 1948, and in September the formation of the Democratic People's Republic of Korea was formally announced. This final step accomplished, Stalin felt confident enough to withdraw Soviet troops from North Korea. The withdrawal was completed in late 1948.[19] By this time the Nationalists had also been driven out of Manchuria, and Chiang Kai-shek's forces had begun to crumble. So the regime created in Pyongyang offered a buffer to Soviet (and, almost immediately, Chinese Communist) security in Northeast Asia as well as an extension of Soviet influence.

17. Garthoff, "The Soviet Intervention in Manchuria," pp. 67–68; J. M. Mackintosh, "The Soviet Army in the Far East, 1922–1955," in Hart, ed., *The Soviet Army,* pp. 178–79; Ian V. Hogg, "The War Against Japan," in Mayer, *Russian War Machine,* pp. 238–42.

18. Gregory Henderson, *Korea: The Politics of the Vortex* (Harvard University Press, 1968), pp. 325–26; Rinn-Sup Shinn and others, *Area Handbook for North Korea* (Government Printing Office, 1969), pp. 54–55; Robert R. Simmons, *The Strained Alliance: Peking, P'yongyang, Moscow, and the Politics of the Korean Civil War* (Free Press, 1975), pp. 25–28.

19. *New York Times,* December 31, 1948.

Withdrawals and Failures

Stalin also attempted to use his military forces in China and Iran after the war to establish regimes holding Marxist-Leninist ideals, supportive of Soviet interests, and amenable to Moscow's direction. As in Germany and Korea, the Soviet army occupied substantial portions of China and Iran and supported local Communist parties. In the end, though, Soviet troops withdrew from these countries without Communist regimes able to stand on their own having been established.

In Manchuria the Soviet military command under Marshal Rodion Ya. Malinovsky began to support the Communists almost immediately after hostilities ended, despite the Treaty of Friendship and Alliance between the Republic of China (the Nationalists) and the USSR signed on August 14, 1945. Within three months, more than 200,000 Chinese Communist troops were able to infiltrate the area. These forces were given captured Japanese arms and allowed to recruit among former Manchurian army personnel and enlist as local police. Moscow also facilitated organizational efforts of the Chinese Communist party.

Uncertainty about whether the Chinese Communists would triumph and concern about U.S. actions in Northeast Asia led Moscow to allow Nationalist troops to be airlifted to Manchuria in November 1945. At the same time, an attempt was made to wrest long-term economic concessions from the Chiang Kai-shek government. As in Germany, a massive amount of industry in Manchuria was stripped. That the Nationalists were allowed to gain control over south-central Manchuria before the Soviet withdrawal—finally achieved in March–April 1946—and the fact of the withdrawal itself appears linked to the landing of more than 100,000 U.S. troops in northern China and Soviet concern that the United States might become more directly involved than it had been in deciding China's future. With the situation in China fluid and a Communist triumph uncertain, Moscow seems to have concluded that a favorable outcome was more likely or that an unfavorable outcome was less likely if Soviet and U.S. forces were withdrawn.

Stalin also had to consider the security of the Soviet naval base at Port Arthur and special rights in Dairen, formally obtained in the Yalta agreement and further sanctified in the friendship treaty with the Nationalists. In late 1945 and early 1946 U.S. aircraft flew quite near and in some instances over these Soviet positions. In early March 1946, just before the Soviet withdrawal, these positions were reinforced and over-flying U.S. military aircraft were fired at.[20]

Another possible reason for Soviet military withdrawal from Manchuria in the midst of ongoing conflict in China was the fact that Moscow's relationship with the Maoist forces was not especially close. Moscow had given the Maoist forces little support in the past, and the ideological distance between the two was considerable. Not surprisingly, the Russians at different times tried to help the more loyal Communist group led by Li Li-san.[21] After the Soviet withdrawal the Kremlin gave Mao Tse-tung little military support during the Chinese civil war, going only so far as to occupy in 1947 Haiyang Island (which the USSR may have wanted to hold onto anyway) and to harass Chinese Nationalist aircraft at the end of the war—after it was clear that the United States would not militarily oppose a Communist triumph in China.[22]

At almost precisely the same time that the 300,000 Soviet troops occupying Manchuria were withdrawn, Moscow recalled its 60,000 troops placed in northern Iran. The Soviet army had originally entered Iran in 1941, in joint agreement with Britain, to safeguard oil fields and to ensure the security of the southern supply route to the USSR. Moscow used the opportunity to create the Communist-led Tudeh party and to establish, in December 1945, the Autonomous Republic of Azerbaijan and the Kurdish People's Republic. Moscow did not intend to recall the Soviet army in accordance with the agreement made at Tehran in 1943 until these republics were made firm. Of considerable economic importance to the USSR, moreover, was the extraction of oil concessions from Iran. So in October 1945, fresh Soviet forces were sent into Azerbaijan, and in November Iranian troops in Tabriz were given the choice—really an ultimatum—of either moving south or joining a new Azerbaijani army. When an Iranian relief force then moved toward Tabriz, it was halted by Soviet army units.[23] What made Stalin back off only a few months later was a sudden and strong interest taken by the United States. Later Presi-

20. *New York Times*, March 2, 3, 4, 1946.

21. Garthoff, "The Soviet Intervention in Manchuria," pp. 71–76; O. Edmund Clubb, *China and Russia: The "Great Game"* (Columbia University Press, 1970), pp. 349–58; Ulam, *Expansion and Coexistence*, pp. 476–79.

22. *New York Times*, March 24, 1947, and October 23, 1948.

23. Firuz Kazemzadeh, "Soviet-Iranian Relations: A Quarter-Century of Freeze and Thaw," in Ivo J. Lederer and Wayne S. Vucinich, eds., *The Soviet Union and the Middle East: The Post–World War II Era* (Hoover Institution Press, Stanford University, 1974), p. 57.

dent Harry S. Truman went so far as to say, "The Soviet Union persisted in its occupation until I personally saw to it that Stalin was informed that I had given orders to our military chiefs to prepare for the movement of our ground, sea and air forces. Stalin then did what I knew he would do. He moved his troops out."[24]

Taken together, the decisions to withdraw from both China and Iran seem to have resulted from a desire to limit U.S. hostility toward the USSR while it was securing Eastern Europe and an unwillingness to risk Soviet prestige or security in crises with the United States over these territories.

A third event in what was a substantial retrenchment of its position in Asia while Moscow was consolidating power in Eastern Europe was the failure to obtain territory from Turkey and joint control of the Dardanelles. On the basis of the 1939 Nazi-Soviet pact, the Allies' agreements at Yalta and Potsdam, the Soviet-Chinese treaty of 1945, and the postwar peace treaties, the USSR expanded to include the Baltic states, the eastern half of prewar Poland, chunks of Finland, Rumania, and Czechoslovakia, the southern half of Sakhalin Island, the Kurile Islands, naval bases in Porkkala (Finland), and Port Arthur, special rights in Dairen, and joint control of the Manchurian Railway. Considering these concessions, Turkey's lack of support of Soviet interests during the war, Britain's weakness, and the United States' apparent lack of interest, it is not surprising that in 1945 Moscow tried to compel Ankara to give up the provinces of Kars and Artvin and allow the USSR a naval base in the area of the Dardanelles.[25]

To support these demands Moscow concentrated large numbers of troops along with armor and aircraft on the Bulgarian and Iranian frontiers with Turkey in early and mid-March 1946; at the same time Moscow announced its retention of Soviet military units in Iran.[26] Shortly thereafter, though, Stalin backed off, and on April 5 the U.S.S. *Missouri*

24. *New York Times,* August 25, 1957; George Lenczowski, *The Middle East in World Affairs,* 2d ed. (Cornell University Press, 1956), pp. 176–83.

25. Considering this environment, Khrushchev's claim that Beria goaded Stalin into demanding the Turkish provinces of Kars and Artvin may bear some truth. Nikita S. Khrushchev, *Khrushchev Remembers: The Last Testament,* trans. Strobe Talbott (Little, Brown, 1974), pp. 295–96. On Turkey's behavior during World War II, see Ivar Spector, "The Soviet Union and the Muslim World, 1917–1958" (University of Washington, 1958), pp. 134–36.

26. U.S. Department of State, *Foreign Relations of the United States, 1946,* vol. 7: *The Near East and Africa* (GPO, 1969), pp. 342–43, 818–19; *Current History* (April 1946), p. 366.

docked in the harbor of Istanbul in a symbolic show of U.S. military power and interest in Turkey.[27] Stalin did not want to provoke a serious crisis with the United States over Southwest Asia.

Regime Security and Loyalty to the USSR in Eastern Europe

The permanent deployment of the Soviet army has guaranteed the existence of Communist regimes in Eastern Europe and, to a considerable degree, their continued allegiance to the USSR. Large units of the Soviet armed forces have often been called on to respond to undesirable political developments in the region, although mere disloyalty by Communist regimes in Eastern Europe has not been enough to bring about violent Soviet military action. The Soviet army forcefully intervened in East Germany in 1953, in Hungary in 1956, and in Czechoslovakia in 1968, but Moscow only made shows of force when it responded in 1949, 1951, and 1974 to Yugoslavia's independent course; in 1956 to the Poznań demonstrations and Poland's "October," and to the 1970 demonstrations in Poland; and in 1968 and 1971 to Rumania's heterodoxy.

Insurrection in the Streets

In late May 1953, three months after Stalin's death, the East German government raised production standards in several industries to improve economic efficiency. East Berlin workers responded angrily and on June 16 staged large demonstrations. Quickly the fervor in the streets led to verbal and physical attacks on Communist officials, the hauling down of the red flag from public buildings, and a siege of the government. The next day three Soviet mechanized divisions sealed off the city, seized key points within it, and systematically ended the insurrection by force, killing or wounding perhaps a thousand people.[28] Similar scenes were repeated in Magdeberg, Leipzig, Dresden, and other East German cities to which news of the East Berlin insurrection had spread. Moscow was as mortified by these events as Walter Ulbricht's East German regime.

Only Soviet military power could ensure a loyal Communist regime in

27. Log of the U.S.S. *Missouri;* Department of State, *Foreign Relations of the United States, 1946,* p. 822; Stephen G. Xydis, "The Genesis of the Sixth Fleet," *U.S. Naval Institute Proceedings,* vol. 84 (August 1958), pp. 41–50.

28. J. M. Mackintosh, *Strategy and Tactics of Soviet Foreign Policy* (Oxford University Press, 1963), pp. 77–78.

East Germany. Not until 1952 had the USSR begun to create a real East German army out of the Garrisoned People's Police. The transition to a regular army was incomplete when the June riots erupted, and the East German units called out on the first day of the uprising could not be depended on to suppress the rebellion.[29] Also, although Moscow liked to view the Soviet army in the German Democratic Republic (GDR) as a guest come to protect East Germany against Western aggression, the USSR and not the Ulbricht regime held legal rights in Berlin, which remained under four-power control. In the event of a major disturbance in West Berlin, the Western allies almost certainly would have used their military power to restore order.

Moscow responded to popular demonstrations in Poland in 1956 and in 1970 quite differently. In June 1956, after a delegation from a large Poznań engineering enterprise failed to obtain satisfactory concessions on wages and benefits from the government, the factory workers called a strike and took to the streets, where they were joined by other citizens. Protest then turned into an apparent uprising against the regime. The crowd opened a prison, attacked the headquarters of the security forces, and chanted slogans such as "we want bread," "down with the Soviet occupation," "down with communism," and "down with dictatorship."[30] The Polish regime, led by Edward Ochab and Jozef Cyrankiewicz, ordered Polish armored units to do what Soviet tanks and troops had done three years earlier in East Germany, though it meant killing or wounding several hundred Poles. The effectiveness of Warsaw's response obviated any need for Soviet military units to openly intervene. During the rebellion the Soviet army mercly patrolled the Polish–East German border to apprehend demonstrators seeking escape through the GDR to the West.

Fourteen years later a government economic decision was again responsible for setting off violent unrest in Poland. Just before Christmas 1970 the Gomulka regime publicized a broad range of price increases that were expected to add 20 percent to the average family food bill and boost fuel and clothing costs. The day after the announcement, on December 14, 1970, rioting broke out in Gdansk and spread to nearby towns in

29. Walther Hubatsch and others, *The German Question*, trans. Salvator Attanasio (Herder Book Center, 1967), pp. 184–85. Also see David Childs, *East Germany* (Praeger, 1969), p. 230.

30. *Keesing's Contemporary Archives* (July 7–14, 1956), p. 14967; *New York Times*, June 30 and July 2, 1956.

the Baltic area. The Communist party headquarters, other public buildings, and a Soviet merchant ship were set afire, political authorities were
attacked, and barricades were erected. Meanwhile, in other major Polish
cities, workers forced industrial slowdowns and engaged in other forms
of demonstration.[31]

Though embarrassed and forced to revoke its economic pronouncements, the leadership in Warsaw responded firmly to restore order. Two
Polish divisions sent north with large police formations suppressed the
disturbances forcefully, causing hundreds of casualties. A Danish journalist saw the "brutality at least as great as that used by the Nazi militia in
Copenhagen during the war."[32] If Moscow did not like this citizen outburst, at least it had no cause to doubt Warsaw's overall control and
competence to restore local authority. As in 1956, Soviet army units acted
only to seal off Poland's western border. It also appears that Soviet military units in East Germany were moved north toward the Baltic area as
a further precaution. It is reasonable to suppose that in response to the
turmoil in Poland in both 1956 and 1970 Soviet military units elsewhere
in Eastern Europe or in the USSR were placed on alert for possible deployment.

In each of these three cases of popular outburst, the local Communist
regime perceived the situation as a threat to its authority and followed a
course of action that satisfied Soviet interests. What brought about overt
Soviet intervention in East Germany in 1953 but not in Poland in 1956
or 1970 was the GDR government's inability to rapidly restore control.

Assertions of Independence

Quite different circumstances were presented to the Kremlin by Yugoslavia in the late 1940s, by Poland and Hungary in the fall of 1956, and
in later years by Rumania, Czechoslovakia, and again Yugoslavia. The
Kremlin reacted to developments in Yugoslavia, Poland, and Rumania
with threats and military demonstrations, and to Hungary and Czechoslovakia with military suppression. Security concerns and ideology would
have justified interventions to end Yugoslavia's independent course, Poland's "October," or Rumania's heterodoxy as much as those actions in
Hungary and Czechoslovakia. What then explains the USSR's differing
behavior? The decisive factors seem to be the degree of local regime con-

---

31. *Keesing's Contemporary Archives* (January 16–23, 1971), pp. 24389–90.
32. Ibid., p. 24390; *New York Times,* December 20, 1970.

trol over its populace and over the course of domestic events; the degree
of regime adherence to Marxist-Leninist political precepts and maintenance of political distance from the West; and the capacity and will of
the regime to resist Soviet intervention by force. About the last point
Christopher D. Jones has written:

> An East European Communist who has obtained control of his party and
> his country by taking a stand as both a nationalist and a socialist can deter a
> Soviet military intervention if he makes three things clear to Moscow: (1) his
> army and people will go to war in defense of their national sovereignty; (2)
> the party members who collaborate with the Soviets will be charged with
> treason; (3) the East European Communists under attack will continue their
> resistance underground or in exile.[33]

Yugoslavia: The One That Got Away

In June 1948, after exchanging harsh polemics for months, the Soviet-
controlled Communist Information Bureau (Cominform) finally expelled the "Tito clique" from the world Communist movement and the
bloc. At the same time, Bulgaria and Albania began to provoke border
incidents with Yugoslavia, apparently to intimidate Belgrade and ex-
haust its defense forces. After withstanding this pressure, Yugoslavia
was subjected in 1949 to what seemed to be an ultimatum signed by
Vyacheslav Molotov and the presence of up to nine Soviet divisions
on Yugoslavia's borders. These forces were supplemented by Rumanian
and Bulgarian (and perhaps Hungarian) military formations.[34]

Yugoslavia's original sin lay in its unwillingness to accept Soviet dicta-
tion of its domestic affairs and intrabloc behavior. What appears to have
prompted Moscow's show of force in 1949 was Belgrade's request for a
U.S. Export-Import Bank credit. President Truman acceded to this request in August, and in September a loan of $20 million was announced.
More loans were arranged in October from the International Monetary
Fund and the World Bank.

33. See Christopher D. Jones in *The Soviet Union: Internal Dynamics of Foreign Policy, Present and Future,* Hearings before the Subcommittee on Europe and
the Middle East of the House Committee on International Relations (GPO, 1978),
p. 163.

34. Vladimir Dedijer, *The Battle Stalin Lost: Memoirs of Yugoslavia, 1948–
1953* (Viking, 1970), pp. 212–14; Philip Windsor, "Yugoslavia, 1951, and Czechoslovakia, 1968," in Barry M. Blechman and Stephen S. Kaplan, *Force without War:
U.S. Armed Forces as a Political Instrument* (Brookings Institution, 1978), pp. 442,
446.

Nevertheless, Stalin could have had little doubt that Tito was a committed Communist or that he and his colleagues intended to maintain a "dictatorship of the proletariat." Indeed, Yugoslavia had, in Zbigniew Brzezinski's words, "the most orthodox, the most Stalinist, the most Soviet type of regime in East Europe."[35] Tito persecuted non-Communists as well as Cominform Communists. Previously Belgrade had been at the forefront within the bloc, denouncing imperialism and taking hostile initiatives against even the United States—as when it shot at and forced down two U.S. aircraft, threatened to seize Trieste by force, and tried people accused of being imperialist agents. Moscow also might have understood that it had driven Yugoslavia into economic relations with the West.

The Yugoslav comrades, though, unlike other orthodox Communists in Eastern Europe, were homegrown and had rapport with the populace. As a result of his wartime leadership, Tito himself was an immensely popular figure. He also appeared to have the means and intent to resist Soviet intervention, first by organized combat in the field and then by guerrilla warfare, such as the German army was subjected to during World War II. Stalin was unwilling to incur the cost of major fighting and casualties, the prospect of serious long-term resistance, and the risk that the United States would airlift military aid to Yugoslavia. The West had just recently defeated the Berlin blockade, and in April 1949 the North Atlantic Treaty had been signed. As U.S. diplomats had reported, Stalin was prepared only for a "war of nerves."[36]

A new threat was directed at Yugoslavia in September 1951 when Tito announced that Soviet bombers painted with Yugoslav markings had massed near Yugoslavia's borders.[37] This action might have been a response to recent high-level visits exchanged by Washington and Belgrade —including the Yugoslav chief of staff and U.S. mutual security administrator W. Averell Harriman—and the beginning of U.S. military aid to Yugoslavia. Because the Soviet army was not then concentrated on Yugoslavia's borders, no Soviet threat to actually invade was evident.

Twenty-five years later, after several cycles of Soviet-Yugoslav relations, large Soviet and Hungarian troop movements were reported close to Yugoslavia's border with Hungary, apparently meant as a caution to

35. Brzezinski, *The Soviet Bloc*, p. 55.
36. U.S. Department of State, *Foreign Relations of the United States, 1949*, vol. 5: *Eastern Europe; The Soviet Union* (GPO, 1976), pp. 940–41.
37. *New York Times*, September 25, 1951.

Belgrade, which then had on trial a group of alleged "Cominformists" (pro-Soviet Communists).[38] Tito could infer from these movements a warning by the Kremlin that an anti-Soviet campaign in Yugoslavia would lead to dangerous tension between the two nations—a possibility highly undesirable to the aged marshal, who wanted to lessen the likelihood of Soviet intervention following his death. Belgrade thereafter sought to smooth its relations with Moscow and its Eastern European neighbors and to dispel the sense of confrontation that had developed.[39]

Poland's "October" and the Hungarian Revolution

As the pathway to and from Germany and the Soviet Union's immediate neighbor to the west, Poland—and important political developments there—have always been very significant to the USSR. So the Kremlin was horrified to learn in October 1956 that a majority of the Polish Communist party politburo intended to resurrect Wladyslaw Gomulka and oust the Stalinist hard-line and pro-Soviet minority members—the so-called Natolinist faction, including Polish defense minister and military commander Konstantin Rokossovsky, a Soviet marshal of Polish ancestry. Gomulka, who had been a victim of Stalin's purges in the late 1940s and who had languished in prison because he championed national communism in the late 1940s, was to be elected to the Polish politburo and first secretary of the party.[40]

A Soviet delegation that included Soviet Politburo members Nikita Khrushchev, Anastas I. Mikoyan, Vyacheslav Molotov, and Lazar Kaganovich, the commander in chief of the Warsaw Pact, and ten other Soviet generals flew to Warsaw to head off this election.[41] While the Kremlin leaders raged at their Polish counterparts, ominous Soviet military movements, which had begun earlier, reached a climax. Since October the number of Soviet divisions in Poland had been increased from three to

38. *Keesing's Contemporary Archives* (October 28–November 3, 1974), p. 26788.

39. *New York Times,* September 29 and October 4, 1974.

40. On the events leading to the October crisis in Poland, see Richard Hiscocks, *Poland, Bridge for the Abyss? An Interpretation of Developments in Post-War Poland* (Oxford University Press, 1963), pp. 170–209.

41. Material on Soviet political and military actions during this crisis is drawn from Michel Tatu's extended analysis in chapter 6 of this study; also see ibid., pp. 210–21, and Raymond Garthoff, *Soviet Military Policy: A Historical Analysis* (Praeger, 1966), pp. 155–62.

seven—three of these additional units entering Poland from East Germany and the fourth from the USSR. Meanwhile, those Soviet divisions normally stationed in western Poland moved east, toward Warsaw. Soviet warships also appeared in the Gulf of Danzig. It is unlikely that Soviet units in the western USSR were not then in a state of high alert.

Like the Yugoslavs, the Poles did not behave like lambs, however. The 50,000-man Polish internal security force was mobilized, factory workers were armed, and Gomulka threatened to make a dramatic radio speech calling on the Polish people to resist Soviet intervention as strongly as possible. Moscow also could not count on the Polish armed forces, notwithstanding their Soviet and pro-Soviet commanders. They might well have turned on the Russian forces if Gomulka had asked them to; Polish air force units provided Warsaw with regular reconnaissance data on the movements of Soviet troops. The determination of Gomulka and his supporters was apparent perhaps most strongly when Polish troops standing before a Soviet tank column outside Warsaw stopped its advance and other Polish units fired on a Soviet regiment attempting to enter Poland from East Germany.[42]

Gomulka, though, offered the Kremlin delegation important assurances: the complete authority of the party was going to be maintained; movement toward liberalization was not going to be allowed to proceed; and anti-Soviet sentiments were not going to be tolerated. Warsaw did not disagree with the USSR about security or foreign policy; the Poles simply wanted greater control over their domestic affairs. Gomulka presented the image not of an anti-Soviet democrat or liberal Communist but of a tough Marxist-Leninist who promised that strong Polish-Soviet ties would continue on a firmer foundation. Although probably unconvinced, the Soviet leaders left Warsaw willing to give Gomulka time to prove himself: they did not want to risk the prospect of Soviet forces meeting fierce resistance and incurring the hatred of the Polish people. In the end, the new Polish leadership did not disappoint Moscow.

Only three days after the Khrushchev-Gomulka standoff in Warsaw and military confrontation near the capital, the Kremlin faced a political explosion in Hungary. The people of Budapest took to the streets on October 23, prompted by events in Poland but probably more because of the previous destalinization within Hungary, a poor economy, and

---

42. Frank Gibney, *The Frozen Revolution, Poland: A Study in Communist Decay* (Farrar, Strauss and Cudahy, 1959), p. 13; Garthoff, *Soviet Military Policy*, p. 158.

the despised pro-Soviet government's political irresolution in dealing with demands by workers, intellectuals, and students. By day's end the great statue of Stalin had been toppled, several demonstrators had been shot, the people were obtaining arms, and Hungarian troops, sent to quell the disturbance, had joined the demonstrators. With the situation out of control and the rebellion spreading, three Soviet armored divisions were called on to restore order. On October 20–22 and probably in response to earlier student activism in Budapest, floating bridges had been assembled on the Soviet-Hungarian frontiers, Soviet officers on leave in Rumania had been recalled, and Soviet forces in western Hungary had begun to move toward Budapest.[43]

Because it was then unwilling to engage in full combat, Moscow was forced to endure a standoff in the Hungarian streets, as the dissidents attacked Soviet tanks with Molotov cocktails and responded to Soviet fire by erecting barricades and otherwise entrenching themselves. After several days of street fighting Moscow allowed First Secretary Ernö Gerö to be replaced by János Kádár and permitted Imre Nagy to form a new government. Like Gomulka in Poland, Nagy had been a Stalin purge victim and had substantial public support. After control was somewhat restored, Soviet forces began to withdraw from the capital.

As it did in Poland, the Kremlin probably decided to stand back and wait and see—to give the new Hungarian leadership a chance to show that it could restore Marxist-Leninist order before Moscow imposed a definitive military solution. But Nagy, who quickly emerged as the dominant figure in Hungary, was not a Hungarian Gomulka, and the street situation in Hungary was radically different from that in Poland. Worker, provincial, and military councils flourished, workers and students did not give up their arms, the security police were subjected to violent popular repression, and demands rose for a proclamation of neutrality and the withdrawal of all Soviet troops from Hungary. Unable to control these developments and being sympathetic to them himself, Nagy abolished the one-party state and, after new movements by Soviet troops were reported, announced Hungary's withdrawal from the Warsaw Pact.

43. Data on Soviet behavior during the Hungarian revolution are drawn from chapter 6 of this study as well as from Mackintosh, *Strategy and Tactics,* pp. 165–78; Noel Barber, *Seven Days of Freedom: The Hungarian Uprising 1956* (Stein and Day, 1974); Melvin J. Lasky, ed., *The Hungarian Revolution: The Story of the October Uprising as Recorded in Documents, Dispatches, Eye-Witness Accounts, and World-wide Reactions* (Praeger for the Congress for Cultural Freedom, 1957).

Within days 200,000 Soviet troops and 2,000–2,500 tanks began suppressing Hungary's movement toward independence. Divisions drawn from the USSR, Rumania, and Poland reinforced those units already in the country. Soviet air strikes supported the ground forces, which, after sealing Hungary off from the West, used whatever violence was necessary to destroy the opposition. At least several thousand Hungarians were killed and many thousands more were wounded during the week of fighting that began on November 4. Pointed acts of violence to instill fear among the people were also employed.

While facing this crisis, Moscow was also concerned that Poland's "October" and the uprising in Hungary might spread to other Eastern European nations. As a precaution, the Kremlin deployed Soviet armored units to Bulgaria, from which the Soviet army had withdrawn in 1948; additional forces to East Germany; replacement divisions for those sent to Hungary to Rumania; and twenty to forty divisions to crossing points on the Soviet-Polish border.[44]

Prague's Spring and the Rumanian Coda

Unlike that of Hungary in 1956, the threat Czechoslovakia presented to the USSR in 1968 evolved over many months. The Dubček government, moreover, retained more control over developments than did Imre Nagy, and no street demonstrations or other forms of popular insurrection took place. The slow evolution of events in Prague, the lack of popular violence, and the absence of anti-Soviet sentiments expressed by the Czechoslovak government explain the Kremlin's hesitancy to use Soviet military power definitively in the months preceding its August invasion of Czechoslovakia.

In January 1968 the pro-Soviet and Stalinist Antonín Novotny was replaced in his position as first secretary of the Czechoslovak Communist party by Alexander Dubček. Two months later a free press emerged. Then in April, Prague issued the "Action Program," a document that legitimated other political parties and called for the rehabilitation of Stalin's purge victims and a general humanization of the Communist regime. There was also talk of Prague seeking a major loan from West Germany. This was particularly threatening to the East German government; both the Gomulka regime in Poland and East Berlin feared that their own

44. *New York Times,* October 27–November 19, 1956.

citizens would see Czechoslovakia's liberalization as an example to follow.[45]

The Kremlin was willing to abandon Novotny and countenance some reform in Czechoslovakia, but the free rein that the end of censorship allowed and the movement toward a multiparty state was profoundly upsetting. Moscow wanted the Czechoslovak leadership to return to censorship, which had been formally abandoned in June, to prohibit the expression of anti-Soviet sentiments, and to strictly control the activities of the liberal radicals who were pushing for further reforms. No less upsetting were periodic calls in the Czechoslovak media for a Czechoslovakian position of neutrality in world affairs. Perhaps most infuriating to the Kremlin was the August 10 publication in *Rude Pravo* of draft party statutes ending democratic centralism within the Czechoslovak Communist party. At the Fourteenth Extraordinary Party Congress scheduled for September in Czechoslovakia, pro-Soviet central committee members were expected to be ousted and replaced by Dubček followers who would then validate the political change that had taken place.[46]

The Kremlin had good reason to believe that its influence and control over events in Czechoslovakia had eroded and were about to end. Another Yugoslavia or Rumania might have been tolerable; a Czechoslovakia resembling Poland almost certainly would have been. But Czechoslovakia in August 1968 resembled Hungary in 1956, without the street chaos after Imre Nagy had become premier. Leninist party principles were being abandoned. It was reasonable to conjecture that, if allowed, Czechoslovakia would eventually be coopted to the West. Despite all this political danger, Prague did not threaten to forcefully resist military intervention by the USSR and other Warsaw Pact members; nor did the Czechoslovaks seem to be covertly preparing to do so. Thus the Kremlin had reason to believe that it could abort the grave political dangers it perceived without major violence. The real danger was the impact of such action on the

45. Philip Windsor and Adam Roberts, *Czechoslovakia 1968: Reform, Repression, and Resistance* (Columbia University Press for the Institute for Strategic Studies, 1969), pp. 18–37.

46. Jiri Valenta, "The Bureaucratic Politics Paradigm and the Soviet Invasion of Czechoslovakia," *Political Science Quarterly*, vol. 94 (Spring 1979), p. 66. On the course of political developments in Czechoslovakia and Soviet and Eastern European reactions, see Windsor and Roberts, *Czechoslovakia 1968*, pp. 37–104; Robin Alison Remington, ed., *Winter in Prague: Documents on Czechoslovak Communism in Crisis* (MIT Press, 1969), pp. 141–287.

USSR's international image and other relationships. But this was not a deterrent.

On August 20 Soviet and allied armed forces of about 400,000 men (twenty-nine divisions) began crossing Czechoslovakia's borders. The troops were supported by a Soviet tactical air-army and transport aircraft that brought an airborne division into the country on the night of the invasion. The Soviet divisions were equally drawn from the USSR and elsewhere in Eastern Europe; no Soviet forces had been permanently garrisoned in Czechoslovakia before the intervention. Poland and East Germany each provided no less than two divisions; Hungary and Bulgaria provided less than division-size units.[47] Although it was prepared for contingencies, this invasion force met no conventional or guerrilla resistance and quickly and easily secured its military objectives. The USSR and its allies built up toward this intervention for many months, however, not only in their increased frustration and verbal diplomacy, but also in their use of military diplomacy.

In March, just after liberalism had begun to flower in Prague, Soviet and East German troops exercised on short notice near the East German–Czechoslovak border while Dubček was being told at the meeting of Warsaw Pact leaders in Dresden then taking place that things were going too far in Czechoslovakia.[48] After Prague published its Action Program, it was reported that Soviet army units in East Germany and Poland were moving toward Czechoslovakia.[49] And at the end of May, while the Czechoslovak central committee discussed further reforms, Warsaw Pact staff exercises were held in Czechoslovakia. In early June, in preparation for full field exercises, Soviet, Polish, and East German units began entering Czechoslovakia. It was in the midst of these exercises, which began on June 20, that Czechoslovak newspapers printed the Two Thousand Words manifesto. This document, signed by a number of prominent people, called for a faster-paced democratization and resistance to Soviet pressure.

Although the field exercises in Czechoslovakia ended on July 2, it was not until early August that the participating Soviet units were completely withdrawn. Moscow also orchestrated, beginning in late July, Exercise

47. On the tactics of the intervention and for further details see Michel Tatu's discussion in chapter 6. Also see Wolfe, *Soviet Power and Europe,* p. 469.

48. Ibid., p. 479; Windsor and Roberts report "two main items of discussion at Dresden: the co-ordination of economic planning among the members of the Comecon, and the confrontation of Western Germany." *Czechoslovakia 1968,* p. 25.

49. *New York Times,* May 10 and 11, 1968.

"Nemen." Billed as the "largest logistical exercises" in Soviet history, these joint air and ground maneuvers by Soviet, East German, Polish, and Hungarian forces spanned these four nations' borders with Czechoslovakia.[50] Among this exercise's special touches were simulated nuclear operations and the Kremlin's calling up of reservists. Also in July, Admiral Sergei G. Gorshkov commanded joint naval operations, including Polish and East German vessels, in northern European seas and the North Atlantic. This exercise has been seen as "a part of a larger Soviet effort to deter Western intervention (or counterintervention) in Czechoslovakia . . . one part of a widespread and unusually blatant influence attempt."[51] Finally, immediately following the "Nemen" exercise, which ended on August 10, new maneuvers were begun in the USSR, Poland, East Germany, and several days later in Hungary. These were the countdown and cover for the invasion.

As soon as Czechoslovakia was secured the Kremlin warned Rumania to watch its step. Bucharest had begun acting independently five years earlier and had irritated Moscow by its diplomacy in the Sino-Soviet dispute, the Arab-Israeli conflict, and other matters, including earlier developments in Czechoslovakia. Before the invasion, Rumanian party leader Nicolae Ceausescu had been warmly received in Prague and the Rumanian example had given the Czechoslovaks strong moral support. Bucharest had also refused to take part in any of the Soviet Union's exercises or the invasion.

So the Rumanians may not have been too surprised in the last days of August when Soviet forces in Bessarabia were reinforced and a military buildup in Bulgaria was reported. Why was Rumania spared from invasion, though? Part of the answer has been summed up by Philip Windsor:

Rumania had never challenged the "leading role of the Party"; on the contrary, it ceaselessly reaffirmed it. Rumania did not threaten, as Czechoslovakia had threatened, to make nonsense of the principles by which political life in the USSR and the states of Eastern Europe was conducted, by showing that socialism could be achieved without the totalitarian apparatus of state and party control. On the contrary, it ceaselessly reaffirmed the necessity for such control. [Even farther,] the original Rumanian quarrel with the USSR dated

50. Wolfe, *Soviet Power and Europe,* p. 480.
51. Robert G. Weinland, "The State and Future of the Soviet Navy in the North Atlantic," in Michael MccGwire and John McDonnell, eds., *Soviet Naval Influence: Domestic and Foreign Dimensions* (Praeger for the Centre for Foreign Policy Studies, Department of Political Science, Dalhousie University, Halifax, N.S., 1977), p. 419.

from the *Soviet* decision to de-Stalinize. . . . the Rumanian challenge was based on an ultramontanism more papist than the Pope.[52]

Bucharest also made it known that it would fight if Warsaw Pact forces entered the country. A week before the Czechoslovak invasion Ceausescu reported that Rumania was strengthening its military capability, and on the day of the invasion the Rumanian armed forces minister, Colonel-General Ion Ionita, ordered his forces to be ready to defend the nation "at a moment's notice."[53] Rumania's independent course presented the Kremlin and its Eastern European allies with a fundamentally different and less serious political threat than did Czechoslovakia, and Bucharest, unlike Prague, added to this the threat of military resistance to intervention.

The Kremlin also had to consider the ramifications of intervention in Rumania. Yugoslavia would probably not have given Bucharest practical support in the face of aggression; it is also difficult to believe the United States would have done much. But Soviet intervention against a resistant Rumania would have ignited a much more serious international crisis than did the occupation of Czechoslovakia, and one that Moscow could not be as certain about controlling. In a speech on August 30, President Lyndon B. Johnson, after suggesting that the intervention in Czechoslovakia might soon be repeated elsewhere in Eastern Europe, warned, in words paraphrased from Shakespeare's *Julius Caesar,* "Let no-one unleash the dogs of war."[54] The risk and uncertainty may have further reinforced Soviet hesitancy about suppressing Bucharest's insolence and independence.

The Kremlin used military power to caution Rumania again in 1971. What particularly upset Moscow this time were new initiatives by Bucharest in its relations with China and the belief that Rumania might be entering into an informal Balkan federation hostile to the USSR. It was disclosed in April that Rumanian diplomacy had been directed at promoting improved relations between the United States and China. Bucharest had also recently improved its relations with Albania, causing speculation about a Belgrade-Bucharest-Tirana axis. Thus in early June, while Ceausescu was visiting China, the USSR mounted a major military exercise near Rumania's borders. For twelve days ten Soviet divisions (including one airborne division) and the Black Sea Fleet carried out ma-

52. Windsor, "Yugoslavia, 1951, and Czechoslovakia, 1968," p. 483.
53. Quoted in ibid., p. 491.
54. *New York Times,* August 31, 1968.

neuvers that could only cause anxiety in Rumania, as did a request to allow three Soviet divisions to pass through Rumania to Bulgaria to conduct maneuvers there. Then in August Soviet, Hungarian, and Czechoslovak troops conducted exercises in Hungary near the Rumanian border. These unusual maneuvers coincided with a Warsaw Pact conference in the Crimea from which Rumania was excluded, an action unprecedented since the Bratislava meeting in 1968 before the occupation of Czechoslovakia. The Crimean conference communiqué condemned "right-wing and left-wing opportunism"—that is, Rumania and Yugoslavia on the one hand and China on the other.[55]

Afterward the Soviet, Polish, Czechoslovak, and Hungarian media launched a major campaign against Rumania, which, unlike Yugoslavia and Albania, the Kremlin had not written off. Moscow was made more anxious by reports in mid-August of a visit in the fall by Chinese Premier Chou En-lai to Rumania as well as to Yugoslavia and Albania. In the end, though, the Kremlin accepted Bucharest's further quest for independence, mollified perhaps by Chou En-lai's not visiting the Balkans after all and by President Tito's arguments when Soviet party leader Brezhnev visited Yugoslavia (with a reported one month's notice) in September. Soviet maneuvers—the first in five years—scheduled to be held in Bulgaria were canceled at this time. This seemed to signal an end to the tension that had been building up.

The Brezhnev Doctrine

Treaties signed in the 1940s with the USSR by Eastern European nations did not sanction Soviet intervention into their domestic affairs or other intrusion upon their sovereignty. Rather these treaties stressed national independence and the equality of the parties.[56] The Brezhnev doctrine was an attempt to legitimate Soviet military intervention in Czechoslovakia and elsewhere in Eastern Europe. "Sovereignty and the International Duties of Socialist Countries," printed in *Pravda* on September 26, 1968, contained the following passage:

The weakening of any of the links in the world socialist system directly affects all the socialist countries, which cannot look on indifferently when this happens. Thus, with talk about the right of nations to self-determination the

55. *Keesing's Contemporary Archives* (November 13–20, 1971), p. 24933–34; *New York Times,* November 28, 1971. Also see Henry Kissinger, *White House Years* (Little, Brown, 1979), p. 767.

56. Brzezinski, *The Soviet Bloc,* p. 110.

anti-socialist elements in Czechoslovakia actually covered up a demand for so-called neutrality and Czechoslovakia's withdrawal from the socialist community. However, the implementation of "self-determination" of that kind or, in other words, the detaching of Czechoslovakia from the socialist community would have come into conflict with Czechoslovakia's vital interests and would have been detrimental to the other socialist states. Such "self-determination," as a result of which NATO troops would have been able to come up to the Soviet borders, while the community of European socialist countries would have been rent, would have encroached, in actual fact, upon the vital interests of the peoples of these countries and would be in fundamental conflict with the right of these peoples to socialist self-determination.[57]

Brezhnev told the Fifth Polish Party Congress on November 12, 1968:

When internal and external forces, hostile to socialism, seek to reverse the development of any socialist country whatsoever in the direction of the restoration of the capitalist order, when a threat to the cause of socialism arises in that country, a threat to the security of the socialist commonwealth as a whole—this already becomes not only a problem of the people of the country concerned, but also a common problem and the concern of all socialist countries.[58]

That the Soviet military command saw intervention into the domestic affairs of Eastern European nations as an institutional mission was made clear by Soviet Politburo member and Defense Minister Andrei A. Grechko. "Soviet Armed Forces," he affirmed in a 1971 treatise,

keep vigilant watch over the aggressive intrigues of the imperialists, and are ready at any moment with all their might to come to the defense of the socialist victories of the allied states. Giving international aid to Czechoslovakia . . . was a clear manifestation of the fraternal unity of the socialist nations and their armies.[59]

In Czechoslovakia this "watch" was confirmed by the establishment of a Soviet Central Group of Forces of five divisions—as it was in Hungary after 1956, when the Soviet garrison there was increased from two to five divisions.[60]

57. S. Kovalev, "Sovereignty and the International Duties of Socialist Countries," *Pravda,* September 26, 1968 (in Rubinstein, *Foreign Policy of the Soviet Union,* p. 303).

58. Robin Edmonds, *Soviet Foreign Policy, 1962–1973: The Paradox of Super Power* (London: Oxford University Press, 1975), p. 74.

59. A. A. Grechko, *On Guard for Peace and the Building of Communism,* JPRS Report 54602 (U.S. Department of Commerce, National Technical Information Service, 1971), p. 79.

60. Malcolm Mackintosh, *The Evolution of the Warsaw Pact,* Adelphi Paper 58 (London: International Institute for Strategic Studies, 1969), pp. 4, 16.

Defending Communist Regimes against External Threats

Soviet leaders have always seen the USSR as the first state and beacon of the Communist world. The other members of this community frequently have been pleased to claim Moscow's succor and to allow the Kremlin to feel responsible for their security.

Until at least 1965, though, what Soviet leaders said about their commitment to the security of other Communist nations was not a good measure for predicting Kremlin behavior. Between the end of the Second World War and the mid-1950s Soviet leaders probably understated their commitment to Eastern Europe, while in the next decade, into the Vietnam War, Moscow's willingness to militarily support Communist regimes outside Eastern Europe was overstated. Whatever the rhetoric, the use of Soviet military units to support fraternal nations was always prudent when there was risk of conflict with the United States or China. Rhetoric and military action finally coincided in 1965 when Nikita Khrushchev's successors responded to the air war against North Vietnam initiated by the United States.

The Special Importance of Eastern Europe

The Soviet security commitments in the friendship treaties Moscow signed between 1943 and 1948 with various nations in Eastern Europe were directed at future aggression by Germany, which was a divided and occupied nation after World War II.[61] Soviet statements after the war avoided making military commitments to the new Communist regimes in Eastern Europe. Marshal Ivan S. Konev, for example, said on Armed Forces Day, 1951: "The Soviet Armed Forces reliably protect the peace which has been won, the sacred frontiers of our motherland, and the state interests of the USSR."[62] The term *state interests* might have warned those who would irritate the Kremlin, but the statement did not imply a commitment to anything specific.

61. The December 1943 treaty signed by Edward Beneš, then head of the Czechoslovak government in exile, remained in effect after Czechoslovakia was liberated and after the 1948 coup. The Federal Republic of Germany was established in 1949 and joined NATO in 1955.

62. *Pravda,* February 23, 1951 (translated in *Current Digest of the Soviet Press* [*CDSP*], vol. 3, April 7, 1951, p. 27).

U.S. demobilization and domestic political circumstances made it impossible for the Truman administration to contemplate threatening war against the USSR except upon severe provocation by Moscow in a region not considered a part of the Soviet sphere—for example, Western Europe or perhaps the Middle East. Except for the Berlin blockade, Stalin did not offer such provocation, and Soviet statements of commitment to the nascent Communist regimes in Eastern Europe were restrained. The commitment the USSR expressed in 1955 in the Warsaw Treaty was not gratuitous, however, being motivated largely by the United States' decision to rearm West Germany. In fact, both Moscow and Europeans generally were concerned that a rearmed Federal Republic of Germany might act aggressively to upset the de facto postwar settlements in Central and Eastern Europe. Eastern Europeans appreciated article 4 of the Warsaw Treaty, which declared:

In the event of armed attack in Europe on one or more of the parties to the Treaty by any state or group of states, each of the Parties to the Treaty . . . shall immediately . . . come to the assistance of the state or states attacked with all such means as it deems necessary, including armed force.[63]

Discrete Soviet political-military operations in Eastern Europe have been mounted only in response to systemic political changes and the pursuit of disloyal policy courses by these nations. The West has not directed specific military threats at Soviet allies in Eastern Europe. The closest things to exceptions occurred in 1946, when the United States responded to Yugoslavia's shooting and forcing down of several Western aircraft and to incidents over the sovereignty of Venezia Giulia and Trieste by deploying a number of B-29 nuclear bombers to Europe, where they flew along the border of Soviet-occupied territory.[64] Yugoslavia was then considered to be under Stalin's thumb. The only manifest use of Soviet military power in response to unprovoked Western military action during the past thirty years has been the attack on and shooting down of single NATO aircraft intruding into Eastern European airspace. There were also reports in 1951 of several dozen Soviet aircraft being sent to Albania to help intercept planes carrying émigré guerrillas and leaflets.[65]

63. Mackintosh, *The Evolution of the Warsaw Pact,* pp. 1–4; Robin Alison Remington, *The Warsaw Pact: Case Studies in Communist Conflict Resolution* (MIT Press, 1971), pp. 10–23, p. 203.

64. Although Moscow did not respond to this U.S. show of force, it was also clear that the United States had nothing further in mind as long as Belgrade exercised restraint, which it did.

65. *New York Times,* March 31 and December 28, 1951; Skendi, *Albania,* pp. 116–18.

Supporting Other Fraternal Allies

Moscow has not given direct military support to Communist movements seeking power in the third world. Since the 1948 coup in Czechoslovakia six nations have acquired Communist regimes: China (1949), North Vietnam (1954), Cuba (1961), and South Vietnam, Cambodia, and Laos (1975).[66] The support given the Chinese Communists in the 1940s has already been described. Soviet military units did not aid the Vietminh against the French or assist the seizure of power by Fidel Castro, who did not declare himself or begin to adhere to Marxist-Leninist precepts until after he was in office. Nor was such help given to North Vietnam, the Khmer Rouge (Cambodia) or the Pathet Lao (Laos) in support of their actions in the former Southeast Asia Treaty Organization (SEATO) protocol states.

The closest the Kremlin came to providing direct military support to a Communist movement in the third world occurred in the early 1960s when supplies were air transported to the Pathet Lao and their North Vietnamese mentors in Laos. This aid was first given to the non-Communist Kong Le–Souvanna Phouma government in Laos, however. The similar help given the Pathet Lao–North Vietnamese forces in Laos took place after that government was driven out of Vientiane by the U.S.-supported forces of General Phoumi Nosavan. Motivated by a continuing interest in countering Chinese influence and weakening the U.S. posture in Southeast Asia, Soviet policy was then directed at restoring a neutralist government in Laos rather than establishing a Communist regime there.[67]

Serious external threats have been presented to North Korea, China, Cuba, and North Vietnam. Each of these nations has been subjected to the danger or reality of attack by U.S. armed forces, and Vietnam has also been invaded by China. When these allies faced danger the USSR gave them armaments, economic aid, and technical support; but Soviet armed forces were used only in limited ways and then with extreme caution.

In the Korean War, the Quemoy and Cuban missile crises, the Vietnam War, and the Sino-Vietnamese conflict, Moscow was more concerned about avoiding conflict with the United States and China than it was about protecting the sovereignty and security of its allies, who, if they may not have expected the USSR to go to war on their behalf, did seem to expect

66. As of the end of 1979 the USSR did not consider the regimes in Afghanistan, Angola, Ethiopia, Mozambique, or South Yemen as Marxist-Leninist or "socialist."

67. This incident is discussed in chapter 5.

the Kremlin to do more than it did, particularly during the Khrushchev era in light of Soviet rhetoric then.

The Korean War

When the Soviet army left North Korea in the fall of 1948 it left behind, in the words of a U.S. National Security Council memorandum, "a well organized 'People's Army,' officered in part by Soviet citizen Koreans who formerly served in the Red Army, and advised by Red Army personnel attached to the Soviet 'Embassy' in north Korea."[68] Thereafter the USSR provided Pyongyang with a large amount of armaments and advisory assistance, and at some point in 1949–50, Khrushchev implied, Soviet combat air units were redeployed to North Korea.[69]

But while Stalin allowed Kim Il-Sung the means for war against the South, shortly before this enterprise was launched the USSR withdrew all of its "advisors who were with the North Korean divisions and regiments, as well as the advisors who were serving as consultants and helping to build up the army."[70] Khrushchev wrote that when he questioned this action Stalin "snapped back at me, 'It's too dangerous to keep our advisers there. They might be taken prisoner. We don't want there to be evidence for accusing us of taking part in this business.' "[71]

If Khrushchev's report is true, it is nevertheless difficult to determine whether the Soviet pilots and aircraft deployed to North Korea earlier were also withdrawn before the North's invasion of the South or were pulled back shortly after the conflict began; they were gone by the time the U.S.-led United Nations forces entered North Korea after the successful landing at Inchon. It also seems certain that Soviet pilots never flew over territory not held by North Korean ground forces; no Russian airmen were ever shot down over UN-held territory. Also, Soviet ships and submarines never interfered with U.S. naval operations in the Sea of Ja-

68. Department of State, *Foreign Relations of the United States, 1949,* vol. 7: *The Far East and Australasia,* pt. 2 (GPO, 1976), p. 974.

69. Khrushchev, *Khrushchev Remembers,* p. 369. It is also possible that Soviet air force units remained in North Korea after the Soviet army was withdrawn in 1948.

70. Ibid., p. 370. With the official U.S. Army history in mind, this statement by Khrushchev leads to the conclusion that up to 3,000 Soviet military men were withdrawn. Alexander L. George and Richard Smoke, *Deterrence in American Foreign Policy: Theory and Practice* (Columbia University Press, 1974), p. 175, note 35.

71. Khrushchev, *Khrushchev Remembers,* p. 370.

pan or the Yellow Sea; Moscow did not respond militarily to the accidental U.S. bombing of a Soviet airfield near Vladivostok in October 1950; and UN forces were allowed to overrun North Korea in the fall of that year.[72] Such evidence strongly supports a view that the USSR was anxious to avoid provoking a U.S. attack on the Soviet Far East and worried that Soviet military intervention in North Korea would lead to a third world war.

Pyongyang could have viewed the presence of Soviet airmen in North Korea when Kim launched his attack as an important sign of Moscow's commitment to at least defend North Korea, even if this presence might not have deterred the United States, since it was so well masked. On the other hand, the U.S. Air Force did report Soviet aircraft in the Shanghai area at this time, presumably there to deter and defend against bombing by Chinese Nationalist aircraft coming from Taiwan.[73] If Soviet aircraft had been in North Korea and had not been masked, the United States might have reconsidered excluding South Korea from the announced U.S. "defense perimeter." Presumably, Stalin expected North Korea to triumph in a conflict with the South and believed, on the basis of previous U.S. public statements and other behavior, that if the USSR did not intervene the United States would stand aside. Pyongyang may also have begun fighting one or even two months earlier than had been planned, before an also previously scheduled withdrawal of Soviet air units.[74]

Chinese, not Soviet, ground forces entered the war after UN forces had routed the North Koreans and gained control of the entire Korean peninsula. Only after the UN forces were pushed back and a new front was formed did Soviet air units reenter the picture. Sometime in 1951 the USSR deployed about two air regiments to North Korea, rotating these squadrons frequently thereafter. Again, though, it is impossible to say much about their activities. Moscow never advertised this presence, and no Soviet pilots were ever brought down over UN-held territory. While perhaps as many as 1,000–1,500 Soviet pilots were rotated through these units, it appears that their role at most was to fly defensive actions. Soviet ground forces also were deployed after the front was stabilized and U.S. objectives were announced to be limited. It has been reported that in late 1951 U.S. intelligence sources estimated the total number of Soviet mili-

72. *New York Times,* October 10 and 20, 1950.
73. U.S. Department of State, *Foreign Relations of the United States, 1950,* vol. 7: *Korea* (GPO, 1976), p. 159.
74. Simmons, *The Strained Alliance,* pp. 119–24.

tary men in North Korea at up to about 25,000, including a 5,000-man artillery division and 7,500 antiaircraft artillery personnel.[75]

To protect Soviet security interests, Stalin was probably willing to take military action in the event of a Western attempt to wrest control of northeast China. It may not have been coincidental that a Soviet aircraft fired on a UN fighter patrol in September 1950 just after an airfield in Manchuria was strafed by a U.S. fighter. Before China entered the war U.S. intelligence reported "Soviet-type jet aircraft" in Manchuria, along with fifteen Soviet army divisions (including or excluding—the presentation is unclear—46,000 Mongolian army troops and 40,000 Soviet artillerymen in Chinese military attire). Soviet air units in Manchuria later engaged U.S. aircraft in several defensive operations, and in one instance unmarked Soviet aircraft operating out of the USSR clashed with U.S. Navy aircraft. Soviet sources have referred to the transfer of "several Soviet air divisions to China's Northeastern provinces" and claimed that "in the ensuing air battles Soviet flyers shot down scores of U.S. aircraft."[76]

All things considered, Soviet military activity during the Korean War was designed first to avoid provoking a war between the USSR and the United States; second, to avert a neighboring U.S. military threat to the Soviet Far East; third, to maintain a strong alliance with Communist neighbors; and only last, to ensure the security of those neighbors. Soviet behavior during the Korean War was cautious and prudent. The use of air units in combat in 1951–53 appears to have been allowed only after General Douglas MacArthur was fired and the Truman administration made absolutely clear its intention to wage only a limited war and its willingness to accept something close to the status quo ante. It is doubtful whether China perceived Soviet military support as adequate; it is even more unlikely that the North Koreans were satisfied.

75. Robert P. Berman, *Soviet Air Power in Transition* (Brookings Institution, 1978), p. 60; and other materials acquired by Robert P. Berman. Also see General William W. Momyer, USAF, Ret., *Air Power in Three Wars* (U.S. Department of the Air Force, 1977), p. 114. The 1951 U.S. intelligence estimate is taken from Simmons, *The Strained Alliance,* p. 202.

76. U.S. Department of State, *Foreign Relations of the United States, 1950,* vol. 7, pp. 1025, 1189; Roy E. Appleman, *South to the Naktong, North to the Yalu: United States Army in the Korean War,* U.S. Department of the Army, Office of the Chief of Military History (GPO, 1961), pp. 486–87; *New York Times,* January 18, 1951; *Pravda,* April 7, 1979 (in U.S. Foreign Broadcast Information Service [FBIS], *Daily Report: Soviet Union,* April 9, 1979, p. B2); B. Ponomaryov and others, *History of Soviet Foreign Policy, 1945–1970* (Moscow: Progress Publishers, 1973), p. 196.

In the dozen years following the Korean War, China, Cuba, and North Vietnam faced major danger from the United States and needed strong Soviet political-military support. Notwithstanding its rhetoric, the USSR behaved cautiously in these instances, too. In each case the Kremlin allowed no military activity that might have brought about open U.S.-Soviet conflict. The limit to which Moscow appeared willing to go in supporting its allies was air defense.

Soviet aircraft able to reach the United States with nuclear weapons and then return to the USSR were flight tested in 1954. On Armed Forces Day, 1955, Marshal Konev stated that in addition to defending the USSR, the Soviet army was "the defender of the interests of the working people of all countries." Although this did not represent any specific commitment, Konev also mentioned that the USSR had "atomic and hydrogen weapons at its disposal."[77]

The USSR expressed willingness to use military power to defend its allies only after the 1957 launching of the first Sputnik. Nonintervention by the West in the 1956 political crises in Poland and Hungary and active U.S. opposition to Britain and France in the Suez crisis that autumn probably added to Moscow's confidence. On May Day, 1958, Marshal Malinovsky said, "The Soviet Army, Air Force and Navy are strong enough to thwart any attempts of imperialist reaction to disrupt the peaceful labor of our people or the unity and solidarity of the socialist camp."[78]

The Offshore Islands Crisis

In August 1958 Chinese Communist artillery batteries began a heavy and continuous bombardment of the Quemoy and Matsu islands held by Taiwan. At first this barrage seemed just another turn in the unyielding confrontation between Peking and Taipei. However, when the shelling did not stop after a time, the belief arose in Taiwan and in the United States that Peking meant not only to demonstrate these islands' vulnerability, but also to actually blockade them. Of further concern was Peking's possible intent to invade the islands and even attack Taiwan proper.

Anticipating some new violence in the ongoing Chinese civil war, U.S. military forces in the Pacific area were placed on an alert status in mid-July, and in early August additional U.S. aircraft were deployed to Tai-

77. *Pravda,* February 23, 1955 (in *CDSP,* vol. 7, April 6, 1955, p. 4); Arnold L. Horelick and Myron Rush, *Strategic Power and Soviet Foreign Policy* (University of Chicago Press, 1966), pp. 17–18.

78. *Pravda and Izvestiya,* May 2, 1958 (in *CDSP,* vol. 10, June 11, 1958, p. 17).

wan and two U.S. Navy ships began patrolling the Taiwan Strait. After
the shelling from the mainland began, Washington redeployed as many
as seven aircraft carrier task groups, several of which carried nuclear
weapons. More U.S. aircraft were sent to Taiwan and into the Pacific
area and, on September 7, U.S. warships were ordered to escort Nationalist supply ships to their docking point at Quemoy.[79]

There is no evidence of Soviet political-military operations during
an earlier Taiwan Strait crisis in 1954–55. But to what extent did Moscow
support China in 1958? Khrushchev wrote that during the planning stages
of that crisis additional Soviet military advisers were sent to China and
that the Chinese turned down Moscow's offer to deploy Soviet "interceptor squadrons on their territory."[80] Even if this is true, though, it does
not negate the fact that Soviet behavior was exceedingly prudent. The
Soviet Pacific Fleet played no role throughout the crisis; nor was there a
suggestion of any other related Soviet military activity.[81] Moreover, the
Kremlin watched developments for a week before promising Peking on
August 31 "moral and material aid" and before warning against the view
that U.S. hostilities against China could be contained from "spreading . . .
to other regions."[82] On September 5 *Pravda* did state: "The Soviet Union
cannot remain indifferent to events on the border or territory of its great
ally. . . . The instigators and organizers of this latest military venture in
the Far East should not calculate that a retaliatory blow will be confined to the Taiwan Strait and no less the offshore islands. They will receive a crushing rebuff which will put an end to U.S. military aggression
in the Far East."[83]

By then, however, it was clear that the United States would consider
military acton only if China went further in its military activity, which it
did not do. Moscow may well have been assured before the *Pravda* pronouncement, which could be interpreted as threatening only to Taiwan.
The crisis seemed to have peaked when the USSR offered stronger words

79. Data on U.S. military activities are drawn from U.S. Navy Historical Center,
Operational Archives, "Short of War" Documentation; and M. H. Halperin, *The
1958 Taiwan Straits Crisis: A Documented History,* RM-4900-ISA (Santa Monica,
Calif.: Rand Corp., 1966).

80. Khrushchev, *Khrushchev Remembers,* pp. 261–62.

81. John R. Thomas, "The Limits of Alliance: The Quemoy Crisis of 1958," in
Garthoff, *Sino-Soviet Military Relations,* p. 142.

82. *Pravda,* August 31, 1958, cited in Halperin, *The 1958 Taiwan Straits Crisis,*
p. 167; *New York Times,* August 31, 1958.

83. In Halperin, *The 1958 Taiwan Straits Crisis,* p. 219.

in a letter from Khrushchev to President Dwight D. Eisenhower on September 8: "An attack on the Chinese People's Republic, which is a great friend, ally and neighbor of our country, is an attack on the Soviet Union. True to its duty, our country will do everything in order together with People's China to defend the security of both states, the interests of peace in the Far East, the interest of peace in the whole world."[84] This front was maintained in a second letter to the President on September 19: "Those who harbor plans for an atomic attack on the Chinese People's Republic should not forget that the other side too has atomic and hydrogen weapons and the appropriate means to deliver them, and if the Chinese People's Republic falls victim to such an attack, the aggressor will at once suffer a rebuff by the same means."[85] The Eisenhower administration rejected this second note, denouncing it as "abusive and intemperate" and containing "inadmissible threats."[86]

U.S. intelligence reported no overt political-military operations to reinforce these Soviet statements or any preparations for war in the USSR. No related ground, air, or naval demonstrations were staged; nor were any Soviet military deployments observed in conjunction with the crisis. The USSR's rhetoric, although strong, was not meant to compel U.S. behavior and represented something less than deterrence. With Peking carefully controlling its actions, Moscow only committed itself to respond to a U.S. attack on China, which the Eisenhower administration showed early would not occur as long as the Chinese Communists did not attempt to wrest the offshore islands from Taiwan. Nor was it clear that the United States would respond even in this circumstance. Moscow did not commit itself to do anything if the United States responded militarily to a Chinese air or sea attack in a way that avoided an attack on the mainland. In 1963 an official Chinese government statement said:

In August and September of 1958, the situation in the Taiwan Straits was indeed very tense as a result of the aggression and provocations by the U.S. imperialists. The Soviet leaders expressed their support for China on September 7 and 19 respectively. Although at that time the situation in the Taiwan Straits was tense, there was no possibility that a nuclear war would break out and no need for the Soviet Union to support China with its nuclear weapons. It was only when they were clear that this was the situation that the Soviet leaders expressed their support for China.[87]

84. Ibid., p. 315.
85. Ibid., p. 324.
86. Ibid., p. 402.
87. In A. Doak Barnett, *China and the Major Powers in East Asia* (Brookings Institution, 1977), p. 344, note 38.

The outcome of the Quemoy crisis gave Moscow no cause for hedging about USSR solidarity with its allies, however. The crisis ended in a standoff in which Taipei retained control of the offshore islands and Peking suffered no punishment for its bombardment and retained the prerogative to continue shelling the area at will. Shortly before Armed Forces Day, 1959, Soviet Marshal Vasily I. Chuikov related:

We have the people and the means to rap the knuckles of those who dare to reach for the sacred borders of our Soviet homeland and to violate the peaceful labor and security of our great people and our faithful friends—the peoples of the socialist camp countries![88]

A year later, with additional confidence resulting from Khrushchev's visit to the United States, Marshal Malinovsky asserted even more plainly:

The Soviet Army's mighty nuclear rocket equipment enables us to guarantee more securely and dependably than ever before the invincible defense of the land of Soviets and the other socialist countries.[89]

The Missile Crisis

The conclusion to the 1962 missile crisis perceived in the United States —the forced Soviet withdrawal of missiles and bombers from Cuba—did not affect the USSR's rhetoric, since Moscow chose to focus on President John F. Kennedy's declaration that, in return for Soviet withdrawal, the United States would not invade Cuba.[90] However, the USSR had not introduced missiles and bombers into Cuba or used its armed forces during the crisis to ensure the security of Castro's regime. In these events Cuba's security was only a secondary objective.[91] (The Soviet Union's primary objective, related to Soviet security relations with the United States and West Germany, is discussed in chapter 4.)

Accompanying the strategic armaments sent to Cuba were surface-to-air and antiship cruise missiles, advanced fighter aircraft, and four regi-

88. *Izvestiya,* February 22, 1959 (in *CDSP,* vol. 11, March 25, 1959, p. 12).
89. *Pravda,* February 23, 1960 (in *CDSP,* vol. 12, March 23, 1960, p. 14).
90. See Aleksei Kosygin's 1962 Revolution Day report, *Pravda,* November 7, 1962 (in *CDSP,* vol. 14, December 5, 1962, p. 7); and R. Ya. Malinovsky, *Vigilantly Stand Guard Over the Peace,* JPRS Report 19, 127 (U.S. Department of Commerce, Office of Technical Services, 1963), p. 29.
91. See Ulam, *Expansion and Coexistence,* pp. 668–69; Michel Tatu, *Power in the Kremlin: From Khrushchev to Kosygin,* trans. Helen Katel (Viking, 1969), pp. 230–33; and Andrés Suárez, *Cuba: Castroism and Communism, 1959–1966* (MIT Press, 1967), pp. 163–64.

mental-size armored units. Although it seems certain that the Russians did not send these forces to Cuba independently but as part of a package with the missiles, it is impossible to be sure that Moscow deployed all these essentially defensive units to deter and defend against a U.S. attack aimed at destroying Soviet strategic forces in Cuba. Some of these units may have been sent to appease a Castro demand for concurrent conventional Soviet forces to ensure Cuba's general security. Soviet leaders probably did not think these deployments would add to the risk being undertaken. Not expecting a strong response to the installation of strategic missiles in Cuba, Khrushchev was also freer with words before Kennedy's dramatic pronouncement on October 22.

On September 7, 1962, President Kennedy asked Congress for standby authority to call up 150,000 reservists "to permit prompt and effective responses as necessary, to challenges which may be presented in any part of the free world." Khrushchev correctly perceived that Washington's concern was Cuba and, in a letter on September 1, retorted that "one cannot now attack Cuba and expect that the aggressor will be free from punishment for this attack. If such an attack is made, that will be the beginning of the unleashing of war."[92]

Khrushchev did not reaffirm this commitment in his response to President Kennedy's announcement of the quarantine and demand that Soviet strategic forces placed in Cuba be removed. When the President "ordered the armed forces to prepare for any eventualities," the Soviet government denounced this action as "a step towards unleashing a thermonuclear war," but went only so far as to "issue a serious warning to the U.S. Government that . . . it is assuming a grave responsibility for the fate of peace and recklessly playing with fire."[93] Even while massive U.S. ground and air forces were being marshaled in the southeastern United States for the possible invasion of Cuba, Soviet volunteers were not promised nor was any other signal given that a U.S. attack on Cuba would bring about a Soviet attack on the United States. Khrushchev did not threaten the similarly exposed Western position in Berlin either. The Kremlin meant to avoid risking the USSR's security on Castro's behalf. President Kennedy's promise not to invade Cuba did not satisfy the Soviet purpose in deploying missiles to Cuba; it merely provided Moscow with a face-saving excuse to withdraw its weapons.

92. *Keesing's Contemporary Archives* (November 3–10, 1962), pp. 19057–58.
93. Ibid., pp. 19060–61.

The Vietnam War

Vietnam, not Cuba, exposed and ended Khrushchev's empty rhetoric that the Soviet military guarded the security of the USSR's fraternal allies. Such bluster continued to have value and seemed to risk little well into 1964, helping Moscow to maintain respect as the self-proclaimed guardian of world socialism, a matter of particular importance as the rift with China widened. Peking could attack Kremlin revisionism and proclaim its own way as the path of righteousness, but the USSR had the might and was on record as being ready to use its military power to protect Communist gains.

A U.S. Military Assistance Command, Vietnam, was established and U.S. Army transport helicopter companies began to support South Vietnamese forces in 1962. By mid-1964, 16,500 U.S. military personnel were in South Vietnam.[94] Although Washington castigated North Vietnam regularly and demanded that Hanoi cease supporting the Vietcong, the North remained an untouched sanctuary, much as China had been during the Korean War. Moreover, the U.S. forces in South Vietnam in 1964 compensated poorly for the inabilities of the Saigon forces. The Kremlin probably expected this situation to continue and saw victory coming soon.

After all, despite the South Vietnamese forces' poor performance in the field, it seemed that President Johnson did not intend to send U.S. servicemen to fight in Vietnam. The Kremlin might also have noticed that Senator Barry Goldwater was suffering in the polls, partly because of his bellicose position on the war. Even if the United States was going to take some stronger action before accepting Saigon's defeat, Moscow did not expect the course taken in early 1965, only weeks after the President's inauguration.

The Johnson administration's response to the attack on the U.S. destroyers *Maddox* and *Turner Joy* in August 1964 took Moscow aback. Although the Kremlin had an image to protect, it did not intend to provide Hanoi with anything more than economic and military assistance. A Tass statement revealed nervousness and caution, and the Kremlin showed interest in a negotiated settlement.[95]

---

94. Herbert Y. Schandler, *The Unmaking of a President: Lyndon Johnson and Vietnam* (Princeton University Press, 1977), p. 352.

95. "Aggressive Actions by U.S.A. in Gulf of Tonkin," *Pravda*, August 6, 1964 (in *CDSP*, vol. 16, September 2, 1964, pp. 25–26); Donald S. Zagoria, *Vietnam Triangle: Moscow, Peking, Hanoi* (Pegasus, 1967), pp. 43–45.

Only after the limits of the U.S. response had become clear did Moscow resume a tough stance in its rhetoric. The USSR gained new confidence when in October the United States decided not to retaliate against the North after a Vietcong attack on the air facility at Bien Hoa, which caused a number of U.S. casualties and the damage or destruction of thirteen B-57 bombers. Even more significant was the lack of a forceful U.S. response in September to what may have been a North Vietnamese action against the U.S. destroyers *Morton* and *Edwards* in the Tonkin Gulf.[96] The new team in the Kremlin—Khrushchev was ousted in mid-October 1964—also may not have wanted to publicly break with the past too quickly, especially when this might offend the military. Thus on Revolution Day in 1964 Leonid Brezhnev told citizens that Soviet military power provided "a reliable guarantee that the security of the USSR and the other socialist countries is dependably assured."[97] The new men in the Kremlin seized power, however, partly out of discontent with the impetuousness and high-stakes political gambling of their predecessor. They preferred to first obtain and then work from a position of strength, avoiding false hopes and illusions.

Moscow's official response to the U.S. bombing of Donghoi and other points in North Vietnam, following the early February 1965 Vietcong attack on the Pleiku air base in which more than one hundred Americans were killed or wounded, revealed a new style and lexicon. The message to the United States was that its action would hinder "the establishment of normal relations with the U.S.A. and their improvement." Rather than go out on a limb for Hanoi, Moscow informed the United States that the USSR "will be forced to take further measures to guard the security and strengthen the defense capacity" of the Democratic Republic of Vietnam (D.R.V.). No allusion was made to the use of Soviet armed forces to support this fraternal ally, however. Moscow was referring rather to its willingness to provide as much economic and military assistance as Hanoi might need.[98]

The new Soviet leaders' reluctance to back North Vietnam militarily in any serious way was confirmed on Armed Forces Day, 1965, by Mar-

---

96. *The Pentagon Papers: The Defense Department History of United States Decisionmaking on Vietnam,* Senator Gravel ed. (Beacon Press, 1971), vol. 3, pp. 133–34, 194–95.

97. *Pravda,* November 7, 1964 (in *CDSP,* vol. 16, November 18, 1964, p. 8).

98. Soviet government statement, *Pravda,* February 9, 1965, and *Izvestiya,* February 10, 1965 (in *CDSP,* vol. 17, March 3, 1965, p. 7).

shal Malinovsky. After a week of more U.S. air strikes against the North, in response to a Vietcong attack on the Qui Nhon barracks in which many U.S. military personnel were killed or wounded, Soviet military power was announced to be only "at the service of socialist interests and social progress."[99] In short, by March 1965, when the United States shifted from "retaliatory" to "graduated" bombing, thereby initiating the air war against North Vietnam, Moscow had changed its position. An editorial in *Pravda* on March 10 confirmed that the rhetoric of Khrushchev's decade was over. "The Soviet people," it concluded, "together with the peace-loving peoples of the entire world, angrily condemn the new U.S. acts of aggression in South Vietnam. The international public expresses full solidarity with the heroic struggle of the Vietnamese people for the freedom and independence of their homeland and *has faith* that this struggle will end in complete victory."[100]

Between 1965 and 1968 and again in 1972 North Vietnam was subjected to heavy U.S. bombing. Soviet airmen did not aid in the defense against these onslaughts. Nor did the USSR provide North Vietnam with as much ground-based air defense assistance as it did Egypt in 1970. Moscow gave Hanoi armaments and other military equipment but in the way of Soviet military men only advisers and perhaps some surface-to-air missile crews. This is not to suggest that these Soviet army men did not give Hanoi important support; they did, particularly in the air defense effort and communications fields. These defense and communications personnel also deterred U.S. political leaders from bombing certain military sites. Washington tried to avoid the inference that it was ordering attacks on Russians.[101] Wearing Soviet uniforms and speaking Russian, East German missilemen also may have assisted North Vietnamese efforts. The USSR did not deploy regular Soviet army or air combat units to North Vietnam, as it did to Egypt later. Only about 1,000 Soviet military personnel were reported in North Vietnam between 1968 and 1972 —far fewer than the 20,000 or so Soviet military personnel placed in Egypt during the early 1970s.

99. Moscow Domestic Service, FBIS, *Daily Report: USSR and Eastern Europe* (February 23, 1965), p. CC7.

100. *Pravda,* March 10, 1965 (in *CDSP,* vol. 17, March 31, 1965, p. 23); emphasis added. Also see Communist party Chairman Brezhnev's statement on Victory Day in *Pravda,* May 9, 1965 (in *CDSP,* vol. 17, May 26, 1965, pp. 3–12); and William E. Griffith, *Sino-Soviet Relations, 1964–1965* (MIT Press, 1967), pp. 70, 74.

101. William B. Ballis, "Relations Between the USSR and Vietnam," *Studies on the Soviet Union,* vol. 6, no. 2 (1966), p. 55; *Pentagon Papers,* vol. 3, pp. 280, 284, 286.

In November 1965 Edward Crankshaw cited in the London *Observer* a letter purportedly from the Chinese central committee to the Soviet party and government that included the following lines: "You wanted to send via China a regular army formation of 4,000 men to be stationed in Vietnam without first obtaining her [Hanoi's] consent" and "under the pretext of defending the territorial air of Vietnam you wanted to occupy and use one or two airfields in southwestern China and to station a Soviet armed force of five-hundred men there."[102] If Moscow had really wanted to deploy a motorized rifle or support regiment to North Vietnam, it could have done so by sea, but it never did. Assuming the letter's legitimacy, though, Peking might merely have meant "personnel" and might not have meant to imply anything more than 4,000 military *advisers*. It is possible, of course, that at one time the USSR had several thousand of such personnel in North Vietnam.

The most important argument against a literal interpretation of the words "regular army formation" in the Crankshaw story, though, is the common perception of Khrushchev's successors. The Soviet political leaders who succeeded Khrushchev were prudent, sober-minded, businesslike, and not given to emotional or romantic excess when Soviet security might be at risk. Rather than gamble and risk loss of control and large setbacks, they seemed to prefer to build positions of strength and more certain gains. Sending personnel to advise the North Vietnamese and, perhaps, in some instances to engage in ground and air defense operations increased the effectiveness of their ally's military forces but still was unlikely to bring about a full-scale military confrontation between the superpowers.

Deploying a motorized rifle regiment or a large air defense force to North Vietnam might have made the Kremlin look weak if those units did not openly engage in combat, which might have led to further escalation of the war and risk to the USSR. The mere deployment of an army formation could not have been counted upon to coerce the United States to stop the bombing. Possibly the Johnson administration would have desisted if Soviet missile crews had been placed in force; yet the Kremlin could not dismiss the possibility, for example, of a U.S. attack on Soviet merchantmen making war deliveries in Haiphong harbor. Acceptance of such risk on North Vietnam's account was not in keeping with the new leadership's character.

102. *The Observer* (London), November 14, 1965. For confirmation that some proposal was put forward, see the comment in 1978 by a *Pravda* political observer (in FBIS, *Soviet Union,* September 6, 1978, p. C3).

Peking's purported comment about a deployment of Soviet aircraft to China might have served Moscow's objectives in the Sino-Soviet dispute well and, assuming those planes would not have been used to defend North Vietnam, would also have been risk-free. While the presence of Soviet aircraft in southern China would have made Peking appear weak and have allowed the USSR to present itself as deterring U.S. hostilities against the People's Republic, the Kremlin could have been confident that the United States did not intend aggression against China.

Finally to be considered are Secretary Brezhnev's statement in late March 1965 about Soviet citizens who were "expressing readiness to take part in the Vietnamese people's struggle" and a Soviet–North Vietnamese declaration in April that said: "If the U.S. aggression against the D.R.V. is intensified, the Soviet government, if need be and if the D.R.V. government so requests, will give its consent to the departure for Vietnam of Soviet citizens who, guided by a sense of proletarian internationalism, have expressed the desire to fight for the just cause of the Vietnamese people."[103] The timing of these statements does lend authenticity to the reported letter from Peking to Moscow. But given the fact that the United States did send more than 500,000 troops to South Vietnam and continued the air war against the North for three years (with some stops and starts), the United States probably did go at least as far as Moscow and Hanoi imagined in the spring of 1965. If so, then all the Kremlin had in mind in these carefully worded statements was to send to Vietnam a sizable number of military advisers. Otherwise, these words would seem a bluff directed at the United States or a cynical attempt to curry favor with Hanoi. The Kremlin may have been prepared to seriously consider providing Hanoi with a Soviet-manned ground and air defense system if the United States had further escalated the attacks and the North Vietnamese proved unable to use Soviet equipment effectively.[104] In any case, Moscow's commitment was ambiguous and the Kremlin behaved cautiously throughout the conflict.

103. *Pravda,* March 24, 1965 (in *CDSP,* vol. 17, April 14, 1965, p. 15); *Pravda,* April 18, 1965 (in *CDSP,* vol. 17, May 12, 1965, p. 13).

104. This would fit in with John Erickson's suggestion in *Soviet Military Power,* Report 73-1 (Washington, D.C.: United States Strategic Institute, 1973), p. 112. Also, at the twenty-third CPSU Congress in March–April 1966 General of the Army A. A. Yepishev told listeners that "the personnel of whole [Soviet military] units, are reporting their readiness to go to Vietnam." Had this remark complemented other rhetoric in this line, it might have implied more than requisite enthusiasm by the chief of the Soviet armed forces' Main Political Administration. The remark

Concordance in Rhetoric and Action

Moscow's relatively cautious words after 1965 showed the degree to which the grey men in the Kremlin, increasingly dominated by Brezhnev, were willing to go in supporting fraternal allies. Eastern Europe continued to be the only region within the USSR's explicit defense perimeter. Delivering a report on Revolution Day, 1966, Politburo member Arvid Ya. Pelshe affirmed only that "the Soviet Union, in cooperation with the other socialist countries of Europe, stands firmly on guard of peace and the security of the European continent." This statement was made with Vietnam clearly in mind, for it directly followed the phrase, "the United States proceeds farther and farther along the path of extending the aggression against one of the states of the socialist community."[105]

In relation to its interests in Eastern Europe and the importance of détente with the United States, Moscow's concern about North Vietnam remained small; hence the Kremlin's weak responses to the two U.S. bombings of Hanoi and Haiphong and the mining of Haiphong harbor in response to North Vietnam's 1972 Easter offensive and, in December 1972, to the bombing of Hanoi and Haiphong again (including the Nixon administration's first use of B-52s), while Washington pressed for better terms on which to end the war. Soviet leaders made denunciations and demands but did not issue ultimatums or stage any serious shows of force. Former Secretary of State Henry Kissinger has written that in reference to the spring 1972 U.S. bombings, Brezhnev said to him during an April meeting in Moscow before President Richard M. Nixon's summit visit, "Unfortunately it so happens that events in the recent period— shortly before this private meeting between us—dampened the atmosphere somewhat." Kissinger comments that "it was not much of a statement of support for an ally . . . being bombed on a daily basis."[106]

Six surface combatants (a cruiser and five destroyers) and five sub-

---

stood alone, however. The operative policy of the USSR was presented at the congress in the form of a cautiously worded "Statement . . . Concerning U.S. Aggression in Vietnam." See "Address to the XXIII Congress of the CPSU" by General of the Army A. A. Yepishev, in William R. Kintner and Harriet Fast Scott, eds. and trans., *The Nuclear Revolution in Soviet Military Affairs* (University of Oklahoma Press, 1968), p. 294; and *23d Congress of the Communist Party of the Soviet Union* (Moscow: Novosti Press Agency, 1966), pp. 425–28.

105. Moscow Domestic Service, FBIS, *USSR and Eastern Europe* (November 7, 1966), p. CC14.

106. Kissinger, *White House Years*, p. 1144.

marines were positioned about 500 nautical miles from U.S. forces in the Gulf of Tonkin for a few days in response to the spring bombing.[107] Although some of these ships were apparently returning to the USSR from routine deployment in the Indian Ocean, this presence was not routine. Almost certainly it was occasioned by the damaging of four Soviet merchant ships in the U.S. bombing of Haiphong harbor. In response to this bombing, in which one Soviet seaman was killed, the USSR upbraided the Nixon administration for "gangster activities" and warned it would take "all appropriate steps" to protect its ships "wherever they would be."[108] The presence of Soviet warships in the South China Sea was probably meant to supplement this relatively mild diplomatic protest. Deploying these ships was also perhaps the least the Kremlin felt it could do in light of its decision to proceed with the Moscow summit and SALT I. But this Soviet naval presence provided small comfort to Hanoi. It was probably calculated to cause the United States little anxiety about bombing North Vietnam and to avoid provoking a U.S.-Soviet crisis. The Moscow summit conference and SALT I were not sidetracked, and no Soviet military action was taken in response to the December U.S. bombing of Hanoi and Haiphong.

After the Paris agreement on Vietnam was reached in January 1973, Moscow expanded only minimally the image of Soviet armed forces as guarantor of the security of its Communist allies outside Eastern Europe. "A rebuff to an aggressor, if he dares to infringe on the interests of any country of the socialist community, can now be organized not only by its own forces but also the forces and means of all the socialist states," related the first deputy defense minister, Army General S. L. Sokolov, on Armed Forces Day, 1973.[109] Despite the improbability of renewed U.S. military action in Southeast Asia, Defense Minister Grechko was only slightly more assertive on Revolution Day, 1973, when he told his audience that Soviet military men "are always ready to fulfill their sacred duty in the defense of our motherland and, alongside the soldiers of fraternal

107. Abram N. Shulsky and others, "Coercive Naval Diplomacy, 1967–1974," in Bradford Dismukes and James M. McConnell, eds., *Soviet Naval Diplomacy* (Pergamon, 1979), p. 134; *New York Times*, April 29, May 10, and May 17, 1972; Michael MccGwire, "Changing Naval Operations and Military Intervention," *Naval War College Review*, vol. 29 (Spring 1977), p. 21.

108. Richard M. Nixon, *RN: The Memoirs of Richard Nixon* (Grosset and Dunlap, 1978), pp. 591, 607.

109. *Izvestiya*, February 23, 1973 (in FBIS, *Soviet Union*, February 27, 1973, p. M6).

socialist armies, to defend the great gains of socialism."[110] This ambiguous formulation was reiterated with minor variations and flourishes throughout the remainder of the 1970s.[111]

Provocations by North Korea

The one sizable, although still cautious, military action allowed by the Brezhnev leadership to show support for a Communist regime threatened by the United States followed the seizure of the U.S.S. *Pueblo* by North Korean patrol boats. In response to the North Korean action the Johnson administration deployed Strategic Air Command bombers to the western Pacific and massed in the Sea of Japan three aircraft carriers and sixteen other surface combatants—the largest display of U.S. naval power since the Cuban missile crisis. Two Soviet ships on patrol in the Tsushima Strait harassed the U.S. ships and provoked a number of small incidents. A harsh statement in *Pravda* and deployment to the area of nine additional warships and several other vessels followed along with surveillance and harassment by land-based naval aircraft.[112]

Again, though, Moscow did not go out on a limb. The Kremlin deployed its reinforcements only after it was clear that the U.S. deployments were symbolic and not in preparation for violent retaliation against North Korea. By then the Johnson administration was also in the midst of responding to the Tet offensive in South Vietnam.

110. Moscow Domestic Service, FBIS, *Soviet Union* (November 7, 1973), p. P18.

111. In 1977 see, for example, Defense Minister Ustinov's statement on the anniversary of the end of the Great Patriotic War, *Pravda,* May 9, 1977 (in FBIS, *Soviet Union,* May 13, 1977, p. R5). Also see A. A. Grechko, *The Armed Forces of the Soviet State: A Soviet View,* 2d ed., translated and published under the auspices of the U.S. Air Force (GPO, 1976), p. 30. In 1979, see Ustinov's Armed Forces Day order while Chinese forces were in Vietnam, published in *Krasnaya Zvezda,* February 23, 1979 (in FBIS, *Soviet Union,* February 28, 1979, p. V1); and also, "The Great Community," an editorial in *Krasnaya Zvezda,* November 1, 1979 (in FBIS, *Soviet Union,* November 13, 1979, p. BB2).

112. Shulsky and others, "Coercive Naval Diplomacy," pp. 119–23; *Chronology of Naval Events, 1968* (Naval Historical Center, Operational Archives, continuing); *The United States Air Force in the Pacific* (U.S. Air Force, Pacific Air Forces, Historical Division, February 1969); *Naval and Maritime Chronology: Compiled from Ten Years of Naval Review* (Naval Institute Press, 1973), pp. 158, 169; James Cable, *Gunboat Diplomacy: Political Applications of Limited Naval Force,* Studies in International Security 16 (Praeger for the Institute for Strategic Studies, 1971), p. 142; *New York Times,* February 8 and 27, 1968.

The Soviet Union's naval deployment was wholly symbolic and virtually free of risk. It also may have been staged reluctantly; Moscow may have been worried that to ignore North Korea would reinforce the USSR's Vietnam-related image of being unwilling to defend its non-European allies against the United States. Sino-Soviet competition for the allegiance of Communist states may also have been significant.

A year later North Korean aircraft shot down a U.S. Navy EC-121 aircraft, and a U.S. task force of four aircraft carriers and twenty other warships, in addition to land-based combat aircraft, was deployed to the area. The naval force was met only by a Soviet surveillance group of three destroyers and three intelligence-gathering vessels. Before this U.S. arrival in the Sea of Japan two Soviet destroyers had been deployed to assist the U.S. search and rescue effort.[113] Soviet naval reconnaissance aircraft keeping watch over the U.S. warships did not engage in harassing activities. Aside from wanting to show Pyongyang that the USSR would not allow itself to be regularly entrapped, Moscow may have been particularly anxious to maintain reasonable relations with the United States at this time. The Ussuri River clashes with China had occurred just a month earlier and the USSR did not want to chance a superpower crisis. The USSR also relaxed its military control in Czechoslovakia during this period. Soviet military units did not make any show of force to aid Pyongyang in 1976 after North Korean soldiers murdered two U.S. Army officers in the demilitarized zone and the United States built up forces in Northeast Asia and threatened North Korea.[114]

Air Support for Cuba

The USSR has directed a political-military demonstration at the United States on behalf of a Communist ally outside Eastern Europe once since the 1968 *Pueblo* crisis. This action was a low-key transfer of a number of Soviet pilots to Cuba in early 1978, when Cuba and the USSR were heavily involved in the Ethiopian-Somalian conflict.[115]

By spring 1978 Cuba had deployed in Africa (principally in Ethiopia and Angola) about 39,000 military personnel, more than one-fifth of its

113. Press release, ·Office of the Assistant Secretary of Defense, April 21, 1969; *New York Times,* April 16, 1969; *Chronology of Naval Events, 1969.*

114. *New York Times,* August 20, 22, and 25, 1976; press release, U.S. Department of State, September 1, 1976; *Chronology of Naval Events, 1976.*

115. *Christian Science Monitor,* April 25, 1978; International Institute for Strategic Studies, *The Military Balance, 1977–1978* (London: IISS, 1977), p. 69.

armed forces. Cuban ground forces in Ethiopia were supported by Cuban pilots flying Soviet-supplied aircraft.[116] The appearance of Soviet pilots in Cuba showed Soviet solidarity with the Castro regime and helped reinforce Havana's alliance with Moscow and Cuba's willingness and ability to intervene in distant regional arenas. It was also a highly visible symbol for Castro and the Cuban people, who may have felt somewhat exposed because of the shortage of Cuban military men in Cuba and the United States' increased hostility resulting from Havana's African adventures. In addition, Castro and the Kremlin may have wanted to deter a U.S. show of force in the Caribbean or, anticipating one, reduce its impact on Cuban attitudes.

In 1979 U.S. intelligence analysts concluded that the USSR had in Cuba a brigade-type formation of up to about 3,000 troops, including one tank, one artillery, and two motorized rifle battalions and an associated ground-based air defense force. It is not clear when the force arrived; some believe that it evolved from units deployed to Cuba in 1962 which, contrary to U.S. belief, did not return to the USSR as part of the finale to the missile crisis. Whatever their origin, these troops are important to Soviet foreign policy objectives related to Cuba, including Cuban deployments in the third world. Like the Soviet pilots in Cuba, Soviet combat troops reassure Havana that it is not alone and can count on the USSR for backing against the United States.

Defending an Ally against China

The U.S. threat to Cuba and other Communist allies of the USSR in the late 1970s was minimal compared to the danger China posed to Vietnam. After the anti-Communist regimes in Cambodia and South Vietnam collapsed in 1975, Hanoi moved into even closer alliance with Moscow for support against China, and Phnom Penh leaned toward Peking to oppose a united Vietnam. Moscow could appreciate Hanoi's domination of Laos and prospective influence in Southeast Asia as a strategic weight

116. In July 1969 a seven-ship Soviet naval squadron visited Cuba for a week to show Soviet-Cuban solidarity after a period of difficult relations between the two nations. This deployment included exercises in the Gulf of Mexico and preceded by less than two weeks a visit by President Nixon to Rumania. But the deployment was not related to any current confrontation or new hostility directed at Cuba by the United States. Thereafter Soviet naval vessels paid regular visits to Cuba. On the 1969 visit, see *New York Times*, July 8, 1969.

on China, but it did not relish the outbreak of heavy fighting between Vietnam and Kampuchea in late 1977. Conflict between "two fraternal peoples" was exceedingly distasteful, and Moscow worried that only the United States and China would gain from the violence that continued into early 1978.[117] Although Soviet statements plainly favored Vietnam, the Kremlin avoided a show of military support for Hanoi and sought a peaceful resolution of this "dangerous situation."[118]

The fighting did not end quickly, however. Instead of suing for peace or accepting a Hanoi proposal for a settlement after Vietnamese troops withdrew from Kampuchea in early 1978, Phnom Penh ordered attacks on border areas in Vietnam. Relations between Vietnam and China deteriorated even further when Peking gave its full support to Kampuchea. As a result, ethnic Chinese were forced to leave Vietnam, and Hanoi acquired more Soviet aid and full membership in Comecon and finally signed a Treaty of Friendship and Cooperation with Moscow. In retaliation, Peking cut off aid to Vietnam, curtailed freight shipments from the USSR to Vietnam through China, and began sending fighter aircraft into Vietnamese airspace. Chinese forces in the Sino-Vietnamese border area were also built up, and increasingly serious clashes ensued between Chinese and Vietnamese military units.

Despite the Kremlin's strong political backing and material support of Hanoi, Soviet armed forces remained out of the picture through 1978, with two exceptions. First, in early June, following reports of fighting between Vietnamese and Chinese border troops, a Soviet task force including two cruisers and two destroyers exercised in the Bashi Channel between Taiwan and the Philippines.[119] This may have been a long-scheduled maneuver unrelated to current events. Some in Tokyo believed the task force was meant as a warning to Japan against signing a treaty normalizing relations with China. At the same time, Soviet forces were carrying out an apparent political-military action in the Kuriles, and the Bashi Channel was a good place from which to illustrate the vulnerability of Japanese commerce with Eurasia. Peking, though, linked the naval maneuvers to its conflict with Vietnam. Besides appearing as a general warning to Peking and show of support to Hanoi, the maneuvers also may have been intended to deter a Chinese seizure of the Vietnamese-

117. Tass report (in FBIS, *Soviet Union,* January 5, 1978, p. L1; Moscow Radio Peace and Progress (ibid., January 7, 1978, p. L5).

118. *Pravda,* January 8, 1978 (ibid., January 12, 1978, p. A2).

119. *Christian Science Monitor,* June 9, 1978.

held Spratley Islands or the unauthorized evacuation of overseas Chinese from Vietnam.

Then in mid-August, following a further escalation in the border strife, Moscow mounted an airlift to Vietnam that included a number of flights by military transport planes.[120] Staged from Soviet Russia across Afghanistan, Pakistan, and India, these flights did not provide a major resupply of Vietnamese civilian or military stores. However, they did further demonstrate Soviet alliance with Vietnam to both Hanoi and Peking.

After Vietnamese forces took over Kampuchea in 1978–79, Peking prepared to invade Vietnam. If Moscow had taken strong measures to deter Peking against any military action directed at Vietnam, war with China would have been a serious possibility. Even if such a war could have been contained and stopped quickly, it would have destroyed many Soviet global relationships. The West might then have moved into even tighter alliance with China, NATO might have been revitalized, Japan might have rapidly rearmed, and SALT II might have been killed then; nor would the third world have been pleased—all this in addition to the possibility of large-scale conventional, or even nuclear, war. Moscow was not interested in risking so much on behalf of such an independent ally.

Meanwhile, Peking was attuned to Moscow's interest in Vietnam and believed it could provoke the USSR by incautious behavior. But Soviet armed forces were orchestrated to achieve two limited objectives in order to reinforce or at least retain Hanoi's confidence in its alliance with the USSR. First, Soviet forces were used to signal to Peking Moscow's insistence that an incursion by Chinese forces should not reach as far as Hanoi and should be limited in its duration. Second, Moscow provided Hanoi with practical military support during the conflict, which bolstered Vietnamese self-confidence.

Had Moscow tried to deter Peking from taking any military action against Vietnam it might have issued a blunt or other serious verbal warning—that is, an ultimatum—or begun extensive exercises in Soviet Asia, or both, before China struck. It did neither. Instead, about ten days before Peking attacked Vietnam, Moscow concentrated fifteen Pacific Fleet naval vessels, including two cruisers and a number of intelligence gatherers, in the Gulf of Tonkin and the South China Sea. Besides being a

120. *Washington Post,* September 2, 1978.

visible sign of support to Vietnam, these ships were able to gain electronic intelligence for Vietnamese commanders and warn China against actions aimed at severing Vietnam's sea links or grabbing the Spratley Islands. This presence was more a preparation for coming conflict than a general deterrent to Peking.

Article 6 of the November 1978 Treaty of Friendship and Cooperation between the USSR and Vietnam reads: "In case either party is attacked or threatened with attack, the two parties signatory to the treaty shall immediately consult each other with a view to eliminating that threat, and shall take appropriate and effective measures to safeguard peace and the security of the two countries."[121] On February 18, the day after China attacked Vietnam, a Soviet government statement announced that the USSR would "honor" its obligations and called on Peking "to stop before it is too late."[122] The government statement also said, though, that "the heroic Vietnamese people, which has become victim of a fresh aggression, is capable of standing up for itself this time again."[123]

In short, Vietnam was on its own for a time. During the next several days this last pronouncement was confirmed in a number of private comments by Soviet officials to Western and Asian diplomats. The USSR did not intend to engage in conflict or even a military confrontation with China as long as it could assume that the hostilities would remain limited and that Peking would not attack Hanoi and would soon order a withdrawal.[124]

However, to demonstrate its concern and continuing support for Hanoi, a few days after China launched its attack the Kremlin took a number of low-key military measures: the *Admiral Senyavin,* flagship of the Pacific Fleet, was dispatched from the Sea of Japan to the South China Sea; naval aircraft began long-range reconnaissance flights to the area of fighting; and a small airlift was carried out from the western USSR by way of Turkey (or Iran), Iraq, and India. Although Japanese reports of Soviet troop movements in Mongolia and areas bordering Sinkiang remained unconfirmed, they were not implausible.[125] China was

121. *Pravda,* November 4, 1978 (in FBIS, *Soviet Union,* November 6, 1978, p. L9).

122. See Tass report, February 18, 1979 (ibid., February 21, 1979, p. L1).

123. Ibid.

124. *New York Times,* February 23, 1979.

125. *Wall Street Journal,* February 23, 1979.

not likely to react violently to such Soviet action, and Moscow did want to confirm Peking's original intent to act with constraint. In fact, Peking was quite willing to assuage Moscow's anxiety. When asked on February 21 about the duration of China's military action, Chinese Vice Premier Keng Piao responded: "About another week, maybe a little more but not very much more."[126] Two days later Teng Hsiao-p'ing reiterated that Chinese troops would withdraw from Vietnam once "the objectives of the counter-attack have been attained."[127]

Ten days after the Chinese intervention Moscow did show signs of exasperation, but its intent to avoid conflict with China remained firm. Speaking in Minsk on February 26, Foreign Minister Andrei A. Gromyko said: "The Soviet Union resolutely demands that the Beijing [Peking] leadership end before it is too late *and I repeat, before it is too late,* the aggression against the Socialist Republic of Vietnam."[128] The italicized words were omitted in the reported version of the speech. Also interesting is that a major statement carried by Tass on February 28 did not include the litany "before it is too late."[129] Moreover, the *Pravda* version used the words "China's incursion" in place of "China's aggression."[130] The Tass communication was filed ten hours after an Agence France Presse report of remarks by Teng Hsiao-p'ing in which the vice-premier said: "We estimate that the Soviet Union will not take too big an action, but if they should really come, there's nothing we can do about it, but we are prepared against that."[131] At this point Moscow may have wanted to avoid comments that might draw the USSR into a serious confrontation with China.

Several days later, however, a threatening stance was taken in an article in BILD (a Hamburg tabloid) by Victor Louis, a journalist who is widely regarded as a conduit of official Soviet thinking. "Will the Soviet Union intervene militarily in Indochina to help its ally Vietnam against the Chinese?" Louis asked rhetorically. His answer: "In my opinion there is hardly any doubt that the Soviet Government will not let the matter

126. Agence France Presse, February 23, 1979 (in FBIS, *Daily Report: People's Republic of China,* February 26, 1979, p. A6).
127. Ibid., p. A7.
128. See FBIS, *Soviet Union* (Supplement), March 20, 1979, pp. 52, 56; emphasis added.
129. See ibid., February 28, 1979, p. C1.
130. Ibid., March 1, 1979, p. C1.
131. FBIS, *People's Republic of China* (February 27, 1979), p. A7.

rest with sharp words and threats unless China ends the war as quickly as possible."[132] If Moscow was signaling its readiness to take stronger action if a withdrawal was not ordered, it was still giving Peking several more days to act and only went as far as to say it would intervene in *Indochina*. No special Soviet military activity in the Sino-Soviet border area was reported at this time, and a new Soviet government statement that day (March 2) was ambiguous. "The Soviet Union," it read,

considers it necessary to state with all certainty: China's actions cannot leave indifferent those who have a genuine interest in insuring the security of peoples and preserving peace.

Chinese troops must immediately be withdrawn from the confines of Vietnam and military demonstrations on the borders of Laos and preparations for an incursion into this country must be stopped. The Chinese aggressors should know that the more crimes they commit, the more severely they will have to pay for them.[133]

Moreover, a major speech given by General Secretary Brezhnev that day was exceedingly constrained.[134] It implied that the USSR remained unwilling to take any violent action against China. The Louis article and the government statement were probably meant to remind Peking of the risk it would run if it did not stick to its schedule for withdrawal and to caution Peking against substituting Laos as a scene of conflict or widening the conflict into that nation. Peking reassured Moscow the following day and ordered a withdrawal two days later.[135]

After Chinese troops began to leave Vietnam a Soviet landing ship capable of carrying several hundred troops and a destroyer arrived there. About a week later, the landing ship and Soviet transport aircraft redeployed Vietnamese troops and equipment from southern to northern Vietnam.[136] Visits by a Soviet cruiser, submarine, and intelligence-gathering vessels to Da Nang and Cam Ranh Bay also were reported, and for the first time maritime reconnaissance aircraft landed in Vietnam. Although the Soviet navy had good reasons to use facilities in Vietnam, these activities may have been meant to warn Peking against directing more violence at Vietnam, for Hanoi had not given way to Peking on the issues between them.

132. FBIS, *Soviet Union* (March 5, 1979), p. C2.
133. Tass (ibid., p. C1).
134. For these comments by Brezhnev, see Tass text (ibid., p. R5-6).
135. See comment by Vice Foreign Minister Ho Ying, on March 3, 1979 (in FBIS, *Soviet Union,* March 5, 1979, p. A5).
136. *New York Times,* March 7 and 16, 1979.

In light of past Soviet behavior and particularly Hanoi's own experience during the second Indochina war, when the United States was the enemy, it would be foolish to conclude that the Vietnamese were shocked by the absence of Soviet political-military action aimed at deterring a Chinese attack. Even if Hanoi had hoped for greater support, it must have recognized that, as in the past, the general threat of the USSR and uncertainty about Soviet behavior did influence Peking and was of continuing importance to Vietnam's security.

CHAPTER FOUR

The Security of the
Revolution and Homeland

MOSCOW has often used military diplomacy to forestall or otherwise respond to threats to the security of the USSR posed by foreign powers. The
Kremlin's anxiety about its security and corresponding Soviet behavior
cannot be understood properly without knowing some early Soviet history
and the impact of World War II on the USSR. These experiences and the
ideological beliefs of the Bolsheviks and their successors have made national defense especially important to the USSR.

Things might be different if Russians could be told only about invasions by Teutonic knights and Tartars in the thirteenth and fourteenth
centuries, Poles in the seventeenth century, and Napoleon's invasion—
destructive wars not within modern memory. But the First World War,
the Russian civil war, and World War II instilled in Soviet citizens the
belief that their nation could also be invaded and destroyed in modern
times. Also frightening and influential were threats presented along the
Chinese border in the 1920s and 1930s and Japan's aggressiveness against
the Soviet Far East before the Second World War. Soviet leaders have
retained these memories and used the fear they have inspired to justify
unyielding attention to the Soviet armed forces' most important mission
—the defense of the revolution and homeland.[1]

1. A small but enlightening example of how the Russians use these memories
for socialization and policy justification is the story in *Izvestiya* on August 18, 1978,
about certain clashes in the Chinese borderlands that took place fifty years ago.
U.S. Foreign Broadcast Information Service (FBIS), *Daily Report: Soviet Union*
(August 23, 1978), p. C1.

Early Experiences

Soviet history, as it is known in the USSR, begins with the October Revolution of 1917 and the civil war that ensued almost immediately.[2] One of the Bolsheviks' first objectives after seizing power was a peace agreement with Germany and withdrawal from the First World War. The Treaty of Brest-Litovsk in March 1918, which ended hostilities on the eastern front, resulted in the intervention of the western members of the Entente—principally Great Britain and France, but also including the United States—in support of the Bolsheviks' antagonists—the Whites—in the civil war that lasted into the 1920s. In addition to sending arms, ammunition, and other war matériel, thousands of Western troops fought or otherwise cooperated with the Whites in virtually all theaters of the conflict. Although the Allies' stated goal was to reopen the eastern front, Western military units did not withdraw or end their support of anti-Bolshevik forces when World War I ended in November 1918.[3]

The Bolsheviks and their successors have always believed that the civil war was fought against counterrevolution and world imperialism. Politburo member, defense minister, and marshal of the Soviet Union, Andrei A. Grechko, wrote not long before his death in 1976: "The young Republic of Soviets was in a fiery ring of fronts . . . the chief danger was foreign military intervention. . . . All reactionary forces united under the banner of anti-Sovietism . . . [with] a common goal of crushing the power of the Soviets, and restoring capitalism in Russia."[4] Leonid Brezhnev recalled in 1979 that "Soviet Russia was invaded by some fifteen countries, including the United States, in order to strangle the revolution and restore the old order."[5]

2. Russians are not ignorant of the civilization formed around Kiev in the Middle Ages, the profound impact of Peter the Great, or other important events in their country's past. However, Soviet citizens are taught to think of these developments as a prologue to the critical juncture of the October Revolution of 1917.

3. On allied intervention in the civil war see Richard H. Ullman, *Anglo-Soviet Relations, 1917–1921:* vol. 2, *Britain and the Russian Civil War* (Princeton University Press, 1968); George F. Kennan, *Soviet-American Relations, 1917–1920: The Decision to Intervene* (Princeton University Press, 1958); and E. Léderrey, "The Red Army During the Civil War, 1917–1920," in B. H. Liddell Hart, *The Soviet Army* (London: Weidenfeld and Nicolson, 1956), pp. 33–44.

4. A. A. Grechko, *The Armed Forces of the Soviet State: A Soviet View,* 2d ed., translated and published under the auspices of the U.S. Air Force (Government Printing Office, 1976), pp. 15–16.

5. Tass, January 15, 1979 (translated in FBIS, *Soviet Union,* January 16, 1979, p. B2).

Following the civil war and particularly the Allied intervention, the new rulers of Russia felt encircled, isolated, and under siege in an alien and hostile world.[6] Soviet leaders believed that they could not afford to relax, that to remain on guard was a necessity, and that to assume that the new Soviet state could ever be accepted by a capitalist world was a delusion. To believe otherwise was to invite aggression. "Never . . . forget we are surrounded by a capitalist world," Joseph Stalin advised.[7] Ninety percent of the regular army, or about a half-million troops, continued to guard Soviet frontiers after the civil war ended.[8]

A new threat to the Soviet Far East emerged after the warlord government in north China was overthrown in 1928 and Manchuria allied itself with the Nationalist government of Chiang Kai-shek in Nanking. The Chinese began to question Russian imperial privileges obtained by the czars and moved troops up to the Soviet-Manchuria border. In response, Moscow reinforced its position and established a special Far Eastern Army headquartered at Khabarovsk. Late in 1929, after Soviet troops in the area had been increased from 34,000 to 113,000, Soviet ground and air units and the Amur River flotilla destroyed the Chinese military threat in northern Manchuria. This victory and the continuing threat of Soviet forces to Manchuria compelled the Chinese to sign in December 1929 a protocol accepting the Soviet position.[9]

The Mukden incident in 1931 and Japan's establishment of the puppet state of Manchukuo a year later increased the Soviet Union's security worries in Central Asia and the Far East. In 1934 Soviet ground and air units fought a Japanese-supported Chinese force in Sinkiang; Soviet units penetrated hundreds of miles into Chinese territory in this instance. (Later, in 1937, Soviet military men helped quell a revolt in Sinkiang.)[10] In 1935 Moscow also reinforced its military position in Outer Mongolia.

6. Merle Fainsod, *How Russia is Ruled* (Harvard University Press, 1953), p. 398.

7. This quotation is from Stalin's report to the Eighteenth Party Congress in March 1939, as presented in *Khrushchev on the Shifting Balance of World Forces: A Selection of Statements and Interpretative Analysis,* special study presented by Senator Hubert H. Humphrey to U.S. Congress, 84 Cong. 1 sess. (1959), p. 1.

8. Fainsod, *How Russia is Ruled,* p. 400; J. M. Mackintosh, "The Red Army, 1920–1936," in Liddell Hart, *The Soviet Army,* p. 55.

9. O. Edmund Clubb, "Armed Conflict in the Chinese Borderlands, 1917–50," in Raymond L. Garthoff, ed., *Sino-Soviet Military Relations* (Praeger, 1966), pp. 20–24.

10. Ibid., pp. 25–26; Geoffrey Wheeler, "Sinkiang and the Soviet Union," *China Quarterly,* no. 16 (October–December 1963), p. 58.

Not only did Tokyo seem ready to take over this country, but Japanese military forces, it was feared, were also prepared to cut the Trans-Siberian railway and attack the Soviet Far East. Finally, in August 1939, after a number of small battles, a Soviet-Mongol force led by General Georgy K. Zhukov defeated a large Japanese-Manchukuon force, the latter sustaining perhaps as many as 55,000 casualties. This action followed skirmishes between Japanese and Soviet divisions in the USSR-Manchukuo-Korea border area around Changkufeng, where the Soviet military and political position proved dominant.[11]

Between August 1937, when the USSR and the Nationalist government in China signed a treaty of nonaggression, and 1941 Moscow gave military support to China in its war against Japan. In addition to sending arms and advisers, Stalin also provided China with combat air support including, by the end of 1939, more than 1,000 aircraft and the talents of perhaps more than 2,000 Soviet pilots.[12] This participation in conflict against Japan ended only after Tokyo and Moscow signed their own nonaggression pact in 1941.

The Creation of West Germany

The Great Patriotic War of 1941–45 is clearly the most significant event in Soviet history besides the Revolution and the civil war. Between June 1941, when Hitler launched Operation Barbarossa against Russia with a force of 3.3 million men, and May 1945 more than 20 million Russians were killed, and more than 70,000 towns and villages and 1,700 cities were subjected to the destruction of war.[13] No nation, except perhaps Poland, suffered so much.

Not surprisingly, the Soviet Union focused its principal geostrategic interest after World War II on Eastern and Central Europe. In late 1945, in conjunction with the U.S. Army's withdrawal, the Soviet army withdrew from Czechoslovakia, where the local Communist party was pop-

11. An agreement ending these hostilities was reached on September 16, 1939. Clubb, "Armed Conflict in the Chinese Borderlands," pp. 30–39.

12. James C. Bowden, "Soviet Military Aid to Nationalist China, 1923–41," in Garthoff, *Sino-Soviet Military Relations,* pp. 54–55. Also see Moscow radio broadcast to China, April 5, 1979 (in FBIS, *Soviet Union,* April 10, 1979, p. B4).

13. V. D. Sokolovskiy, *Soviet Military Strategy,* 3d ed., ed. and trans. Harriet Fast Scott (Crane, Russak for the Stanford Research Institute, 1975), p. 176.

ular. Elsewhere in Eastern Europe, Soviet military power remained steadfast and was used by Stalin to guarantee the consolidation of Soviet
influence. Stalin's provocation of the first great crisis of the cold war (the
Berlin blockade) over the future of Germany, and the use of the Soviet
military during the next twenty years to influence developments in West
Germany and the status of West Berlin, were efforts to control a nation
capable of again threatening the USSR's security. Russians were also
alarmed when West Germany became the client and ally of the United
States, which after World War II was perceived in the USSR to be the
new world leader of anti-Soviet forces.

A clear picture emerges of Soviet military diplomacy during the transition between World War II and the Berlin blockade. The Soviet army
occupied vast amounts of territory around the USSR's frontiers in order
to defeat Germany and Japan. A longer-term political goal was to establish spheres of influence that satisfied Soviet security and ideological interests. Europe was the primary area of interest. Asia and the Near East
were of only secondary importance, judging from the withdrawals from
Iran and China and the easing of pressure on Turkey, all following first
signs of serious U.S. resistance.

Even in Europe, Stalin was cautious. Satellites were developed over
several years; the Soviet army withdrew from Czechoslovakia; and Yugoslavia was able to break away. The one significant attempt to compel
Western behavior—that is, the Berlin blockade—was carefully designed
and controlled and concerned Germany, the country most important to
Soviet security. Stalin chose not to bring under Soviet control the sector
of Austria held by the Soviet army and did not press Finland for anything beyond neutrality and acceptance of the territorial losses suffered
in 1941 after the Winter War. The goal of a neutral Central Europe and
the maintenance of Sweden's nonaligned status, respectively, might explain these acts of restraint.

The blockade of Berlin was prompted by the Allies' insistence that
their zones of occupation in Germany and Berlin undergo economic rehabilitation. But more deeply at issue was the future relationship of Germany to East and West and the existence of a Western enclave within the
Soviet sphere of influence. The firm alignment of France and Italy with
the West in the spring of 1948—manifested by the electoral defeat of the
Italian Communist party in April 1948 and France's support of the U.S.
and British position on Germany—probably motivated the Kremlin to try

to prevent the unification of western Germany and to obtain Western acceptance of a strong Soviet voice and even veto of the Allies' zonal policies. The more limited objectives of the blockade were to demonstrate the USSR's control over Berlin and possibly gain the cession of the city's western sectors.

Stalin built up to the blockade slowly. Moscow first threatened to oust the West from Berlin in January 1948. Along with a verbal threat, Soviet troops forced the return of a train carrying Germans from Berlin to the British occupation zone. Then from late March into April, Western air, rail, road, and barge traffic was harassed. In response to these actions, Washington deployed a number of B-29 nuclear bombers to Germany as a signal of resolve and U.S. military power. The lack of a strong reaction in the West to the coup in Czechoslovakia may have spurred Stalin on, however, despite the bombers. In early June new curbs on Western traffic with Berlin were imposed. The complete surface blockade was inaugurated in mid-month.

In imposing the blockade Stalin left the next move to the West. An airlift allowed the West to evade the blockade, and the concurrent Western military buildup in Europe may have cautioned Stalin against further provocative action.[14] No attempt was made to seriously interfere with the airlift, which the Russians almost certainly had expected. In fact, they may have been pleased about this activity at first, perceiving it to be a safety valve allowing the West to come around slowly rather than be shocked by a sudden loss of all physical communication with West Berlin. What surprised Moscow was the size of the airlift and its effectiveness. Stalin was careful not to threaten the West with war: no Soviet divisions were massed on frontiers, nor were Soviet forces in Germany heavily reinforced. Despite the West's success in holding onto West Berlin, the crisis ended without the West having gained well-defined ground access to the city.

Although the Soviet Union did not seriously threaten West Berlin and West Germany again until 1958–59 and 1961, several minor confrontations occurred in the interim. Not too long after the blockade was abandoned in spring 1949 the West began to discuss the subject of West

14. Alexander L. George and Richard Smoke, *Deterrence in American Foreign Policy: Theory and Practice* (Columbia University Press, 1974), pp. 117, 119; W. Phillips Davison, *The Berlin Blockade: A Study in Cold War Politics* (Princeton University Press, 1958), p. 281.

German rearmament. This talk upset many of Bonn's Western European neighbors and mortified the Kremlin. In Adam Ulam's words: "To the Soviet Union, West German rearmament was the main danger to her post-war positions, and the prevention of such a contingency was a principal aim of her foreign policy. In retrospect it is not too much to say that a rearmed West Germany was considered a greater danger than the American monopoly or superiority in atomic weapons."[15]

One way that the Kremlin coped with the rearmament discussion, which ended affirmatively in 1954, was to pressure West Berlin. Western aircraft were buzzed by Soviet aircraft in the corridors between West Berlin and West Germany; autobahn, rail, and barge traffic was harassed and at times blocked; threatening military deployments were made; and pointed exercises were held. Like the blockade, these actions were carefully controlled. In the summer of 1951 a squadron of Soviet jet aircraft flew over the airport in West Berlin after Chancellor Konrad Adenauer disclosed his government's plan to establish a 250,000-man army and after Bonn signed a proposal for a European army that included provision for Germany equality.[16] Five months later the enclave experienced a series of infringements on its traffic with the West, seemingly in response to (1) President Harry S. Truman's and Prime Minister Winston Churchill's backing of the European Defense Community (EDC) and its inclusion of German military power; (2) a North Atlantic Treaty Organization (NATO) agreement to support the development of a 1,000-plane West German tactical air force; and (3) Chancellor Adenauer's demand for West Germany's full inclusion in NATO.[17] Finally, in March 1953, just after Stalin's death, Soviet fighter aircraft attacked British military and civilian aircraft. France was then delaying action on the EDC, while Britain was supporting it; the Bundestag was preparing to vote on the EDC the following week.[18] The new Soviet leadership then directed a peace program at the West, which gave a respite to West Berlin and the Western presence there.

15. Adam B. Ulam, *Expansion and Coexistence: Soviet Foreign Policy, 1917–73,* 2d ed. (Praeger, 1974), p. 504.

16. *New York Times,* August 16, 1951.

17. *New York Times,* January 10 and 17, and February 5, 1952.

18. The attacks included the shooting down of a British Lincoln bomber and a mock attack on another British plane on March 12 and firing on a third British plane the following day. *New York Times,* March 13 and 14, 1953. Of further note, on March 10 two Czechoslovak MIGs shot down a U.S. Air Force F-84 aircraft over West Germany. *New York Times,* March 11, 1953.

The Soviet Union Encircled

When the great wartime alliance finally unraveled and the cold war began in earnest, the USSR became anxious that the United States and its European allies would gain influence over the formerly more neutral nations surrounding the Soviet empire. To deter these neighbors from allying with the West, Stalin threatened them with military power.

Stalin must have been anxious about the direction Tehran would take after he withdrew the Soviet army from northern Iran in early 1946, under U.S. pressure. Stalin also may have hoped that the withdrawal would encourage Iran to ratify a major oil agreement with the USSR and improve relations between the two countries.[19] But after a U.S. agreement to sell arms to Iran was reported in spring 1947, Tehran asked the USSR for compensation payments for its earlier occupation. In addition, Premier Ahmad Qavam es-Sultaneh reformed his government to include several more pro-Western members. Finally, when Iran balked at signing the oil agreement, the Kremlin reportedly deployed 3,000 Soviet troops with armor and artillery to the Iranian-Soviet border and attempted to subvert the country.[20] When Tehran further reinforced its ties with the West in 1948 and 1949, Soviet troops and aircraft began attacking Iranian frontier posts.

Stalin massed troops on Iran's border again in June 1951. Earlier that spring the Western-favored premier, General Ali Razmara, had been assassinated; the Majlis (Iran's parliament) had voted to nationalize the Western-controlled oil fields; and the nationalist Mohammed Mossadegh became premier. Accompanying these events were Communist-led riots in the Anglo-Iranian oil fields in Khuzistan and a massive rally in Tehran on May Day, held by the Communist-dominated Tudeh party. These developments surely caused the Kremlin to rejoice. In this context the Soviet troops on Iran's border probably had three purposes: to encourage the Communists in Iran; to intimidate the Iranian government so that it would not take harsh action against the Tudeh party; and to deter Britain and the United States from intervening militarily. Fear of Soviet interven-

19. George Lenczowski, *The Middle East in World Affairs,* 2d ed. (Cornell University Press, 1956), pp. 182–83.

20. *New York Times,* August 18, 1947; U.S. Department of State, *Foreign Relations of the United States 1947,* vol. 5: *The Near East and Africa* (GPO, 1971), p. 963.

tion in northern Iran did influence Britain not to intervene, although there were reports of British naval movements in the Persian Gulf. The Truman administration opposed taking military action, as long as the Soviet army left Iran alone.[21]

Moscow also reacted to the growth of ties between the United States and Scandinavian nations in 1947–49. Earlier, when the United States had tried to obtain naval and air facilities in Iceland, the USSR made known a desire for bases on the Norwegian island of Spitzbergen; Moscow also then delayed its withdrawal of troops from Denmark's Bornholm Island, which had been invaded by Soviet forces after German units there refused to surrender at the end of the war. This Soviet occupation lasted until spring 1946, when the Russians insisted that only Danish military units reoccupy the island.[22] Moscow probably was worried about the British troops then in Denmark. The Soviet withdrawal might have been meant to reduce Scandinavia's fears and to avoid driving them closer to the United States. That this withdrawal occurred at the same time as those from Iran and China also suggests that it was part of a broader strategy to retrench and allay Western anxiety about the use of Soviet military power to extend Soviet frontiers and control indiscriminately.

By 1948 the competition between the Soviet Union and the United States in Scandinavia was intense. When the Kremlin pressed Finland to sign a treaty of friendship and mutual defense pact, the United States sent a task force to visit Norway in anticipation of a Soviet diplomatic drive to gain Oslo's acceptance of a similar treaty.[23] And when Denmark sought arms from the United States during the Berlin blockade and seemed to be drawing closer to the West, Soviet naval and air forces demonstrated Moscow's displeasure by repeatedly violating Copenhagen's sovereignty over Bornholm Island during exercises in September 1948.

Sweden chose to remain neutral, unlike Norway and Denmark, which became charter signatories of the North Atlantic Treaty. After the Korean War began, though, Sweden did not remain immune from the heightened tension in Europe and, like the West, increased its defense spending and prepared to defend itself against Soviet aggression. Soviet

21. *New York Times,* May 13–June 24, 1951.
22. *Keesing's Contemporary Archives* (March 16–23, 1946), p. 7791; *New York Times,* November 19, 1945.
23. *New York Times,* April 6 and May 3, 1948.

embassy activities and espionage by Swedish Communists pushed Stockholm toward closer relations with the West, which included a symbolic visit to Washington by Premier Tage Erlander.[24] In apparent disapproval of Sweden's change in attitude, Moscow ordered two Swedish air force planes shot down in mid-June 1952, when the Swedes were beginning a major espionage trial.[25]

Soviet military threats to Yugoslavia in 1949 and 1951 were at least partly related to improved relations between Belgrade and Washington. One month after the attack on the Swedish aircraft and two days after the United States announced its intention to send jet aircraft, tanks, and heavy artillery to Yugoslavia, a Soviet jet fighter aircraft flew into Yugoslav airspace.[26]

In 1952 the Kremlin used political-military diplomacy to express dissatisfaction to Japan when it accepted an alliance with the United States. The United States effectively countered Moscow's attempts to influence political developments in Japan after the war ended in the Pacific. Stalin wanted Japan to assume a posture of neutrality and to enter into close relations with the USSR and, later, with the People's Republic of China. Since the Kremlin probably expected North Korea to defeat the South, it also probably believed, when the Korean War began, that a neutral Japan would preclude Western influence in Northeast Asia and allow the Soviet Union to dominate the region.

Soviet hostility toward Tokyo increased when Japan became the command and supply center for U.S. military operations during the Korean War and when the United States and its allies signed a peace treaty with Japan and Tokyo entered into a bilateral defense pact with Washington in 1951. Moscow refused to sign the peace treaty, and when the security agreement was ratified by the U.S. Senate and declared effective by President Truman in April 1952, the Soviet ambassador to the United States declared it illegal.[27]

After Moscow rejected the peace treaty and Prime Minister Shigeru

24. Former Central Intelligence Agency (CIA) Director William Colby has hinted at the development in these years of covert U.S. intelligence links with Sweden. See William Colby and Peter Forbath, *Honorable Men: My Life in the CIA* (Simon and Schuster, 1978), p. 103.

25. *New York Times,* June 18, 1952.

26. *New York Times,* July 14 and 16, 1952.

27. Donald C. Hellmann, *Japanese Foreign Policy and Domestic Politics: The Peace Agreement with the Soviet Union* (University of California Press, 1969), p. 31; *New York Times,* April 29, 1952.

Yoshida informed the USSR that Japan no longer recognized the Soviet mission in Tokyo, Soviet warships and aircraft carried out military exercises near the eastern tip of Hokkaido.[28] The final straw for Stalin was Tokyo's recognition of Nationalist China and rejection of ties with the People's Republic. Moscow recalled its representative in Tokyo, Major General Andrei P. Kislenko, and within the next several weeks began a campaign of regular intrusion by fighter aircraft into Japanese airspace and over Hokkaido.[29] These violations went on for six months and let up only after the United States reinforced its air presence in Hokkaido and had F-86 aircraft intercept Soviet MIGs. To deter Moscow from renewing its hostile activities, General Mark Clark, U.S. military commander in the Far East, was allowed to publicly direct his pilots "to shoot, if and when they contacted Communist MIGs."[30]

The Problems of West Germany and West Berlin

The events in Poland and especially in Hungary in the fall of 1956 made the Kremlin anxious about West Berlin's appeal to East Germans. Embedded in East Germany and next to its capital, West Berlin was, in effect, an outpost where Eastern Europeans could catch a glimpse of the West and leave the paradise of socialism. It also offered a haven to political refugees. In late 1956 Soviet troops began to delay and closely inspect trains and military convoys going between West Berlin and West Germany and to demand more transit documentation.[31] When East Germany changed its currency in October 1957, the border was completely closed, and in January 1958 U.S. army trains were halted in a dispute over procedures for crossing into West Berlin.

More important to Moscow, though, was West Germany's role within NATO and the extent of its rearmament. The U.S. proposal in 1957 to send tactical nuclear weapons and intermediate-range ballistic missiles to Europe and to train non-U.S. NATO military men to use them prompted new Soviet anxiety and a diplomatic offensive against the West. The NATO Council resolution in December 1957 to place ballistic

28. *New York Times,* June 7, 1952.
29. Martin E. Weinstein, *Japan's Postwar Defense Policy, 1947–1968* (Columbia University Press, 1971), p. 70; *New York Times,* June 28, 1952.
30. Weinstein, *Japan's Postwar Defense Policy,* p. 72.
31. *New York Times,* November 25–December 7, 1956.

missiles in West Germany especially concerned the Kremlin because it wanted not only to bar the possibility of Bonn's gaining access to nuclear weapons but also to obtain West Germany's neutralization.[32] Moscow also wanted the West to recognize the East German regime and East Germany's borders and wanted to end the problems West Berlin was causing East Germany.[33] By fall 1958 over 10,000 people were leaving there for the West each month.[34]

Moscow's first course was to support the proposal made by Polish Foreign Minister Adam Rapacki in the fall of 1957 for a nuclear-free zone in Central Europe (East and West Germany, Poland, and Czechoslovakia). In January 1958 Moscow called for nuclear-free "zones of peace" in Europe, conventional force reductions, and measures to prevent surprise attack in Europe. Unilateral Soviet troop reductions were also announced at this time. The Kremlin then proposed a summit conference and threatened to deploy ballistic missiles to East Germany, Poland, and Czechoslovakia if NATO would not agree to Soviet proposals. When all of these actions failed, Khrushchev prompted the 1958–59 Berlin "deadline" crisis.

The Berlin Crisis of 1958–59

In a speech on November 10, 1958, Nikita Khrushchev declared it time "to renounce the remnants of the occupation regime in Berlin" and announced Moscow's intention to hand over its powers in Berlin to East Germany, thus forcing the West to recognize and deal with the regime of Walter Ulbricht.[35] When the West failed to react, Soviet troops detained several U.S. Army trucks for eight and a half hours on the autobahn outside Berlin.[36] Finally, on November 27, the Kremlin announced that if, in the next six months, it could not reach an agreement with the West mak-

32. Ulam, *Expansion and Coexistence*, p. 620; J. M. Mackintosh, *Strategy and Tactics of Soviet Foreign Policy* (Oxford University Press, 1963), p. 205; also see Stockholm International Peace Research Institute, *Tactical Nuclear Weapons: European Perspectives* (London: Taylor and Francis; New York: Crane, Russak, 1978), pp. 14–15.

33. Nikita S. Khrushchev, *Khrushchev Remembers: The Last Testament* (Little, Brown, 1974), pp. 453–54.

34. Robert M. Slusser, "The Berlin Crises of 1958–1959 and 1961," in Barry M. Blechman and Stephen S. Kaplan, *Force without War: U.S. Armed Forces as a Political Instrument* (Brookings Institution, 1978), p. 347.

35. The quotation is from Mackintosh, *Strategy and Tactics*, p. 212.

36. George and Smoke, *Deterrence in American Foreign Policy*, p. 406.

ing West Berlin a demilitarized city within a sovereign East Germany, the Kremlin would sign a separate accord with East Germany. This ultimatum generated great consternation and diplomatic activity among Western leaders and to some degree succeeded in turning NATO members against one another. In the end, Khrushchev accepted a proposal for a foreign ministers' conference at Geneva and withdrew the deadline.

Moscow used minimal military force throughout this crisis. The autobahn incident of November 14 was small, apparently meant to remind the West of its tenuous position in West Berlin. For the same purpose a U.S. Army truck convoy from Berlin had been halted in early February and U.S. transport aircraft flying at high altitudes (signaling U.S. readiness for a new airlift) had been buzzed in Berlin air corridors.[37] Although Soviet leaders made many claims about the USSR's development and production of intercontinental ballistic missiles and its achievement of strategic parity with the West, the Soviet army and air forces in East Germany and elsewhere in Eastern Europe were not reinforced and Western aircraft were never fired upon; nor was a blockade established.[38] The real threat was presented verbally and applied to the future: if the West used force against East Germany after the Ulbricht regime took action to isolate and gain control of West Berlin, which was expected to follow a Soviet–East German accord, then the USSR would fulfill its military commitment to East Germany as a Warsaw Pact ally.[39]

Although restrained, U.S. military activity during the crisis was more noteworthy than Soviet military actions: In a move designed to go unobserved publicly but be seen clearly by Soviet intelligence, U.S. combat and support units in Europe were filled out; U.S. transport planes prepared for an airlift; and in May, as the deadline approached, U.S. aircraft carriers laden with nuclear weapons were redeployed in the Mediterranean and marines were alerted for rapid movement to West Berlin.[40]

37. Slusser, "The Berlin Crises of 1958–59 and 1961," pp. 358, 375–76.

38. Regarding Soviet rhetoric on strategic weapons development, see Arnold L. Horelick and Myron Rush, *Strategic Power and Soviet Foreign Policy* (University of Chicago Press, 1966), pp. 50–53.

39. Ulam, *Expansion and Coexistence,* p. 620.

40. Dwight D. Eisenhower, *Waging Peace, 1956–1961: The White House Years* (Doubleday, 1965), p. 340; Rear Admiral J. C. Donaldson, Jr., Director of Fleet Operations Division, U.S. Department of the Navy, "Memorandum to Director of Naval History and Curator for the Navy Department" (Operational Archives, Naval Historical Center, Department of the Navy, August 20, 1969); *A Chronology of the United States Marine Corps,* vol. 3 (U.S. Marine Corps, 1971), p. 41.

After the deadline crisis Khrushchev sought his objectives in Central Europe through personal and traditional diplomacy. He might have exerted heavy pressure on West Berlin beginning in spring 1960 had he not then been engaged in conflict with the United States about developments in Cuba, the Congo, and Laos; the disarmament negotiations in Geneva; and the RB-47 incident.[41] Khrushchev was also under intense domestic pressure within the party and constrained by the public emergence of the USSR's rift with China. Under these circumstances he probably concluded that the risk of losing control was too great if he were to prompt a new Berlin crisis. In addition, having already failed with Dwight D. Eisenhower, Khrushchev was prepared to wait until a new president was in office.[42]

In October 1960 Khrushchev threatened a new crisis for April 1961 if the new administration did not agree to a summit meeting by then. In September, just before Khrushchev had left for the UN General Assembly session, East Germany had demanded that West Berliners obtain special police permits to travel in East Berlin. When the Western allies retaliated in kind, a Soviet fighter aircraft buzzed a British airliner, almost causing it to crash.[43]

The 1961 Berlin Crisis

Khrushchev launched his new offensive in early June 1961 at the Vienna summit meeting. Unless the West agreed to the "normalization" of Berlin, the Soviet leader told President John F. Kennedy, the USSR would sign a unilateral accord with East Germany. The President was also given an aide-mémoire calling for East and West Germany to sign within six months either a reunification agreement or separate treaties with each of the four powers. Berlin was to become an unoccupied city with access controlled by East Germany. In mid-June Khrushchev made these demands public and in early July announced an increase in Soviet defense spending and suspension of planned troop cuts. President Kennedy announced in a televised speech a recommitment to Western rights in Berlin and his intention to ask Congress to authorize (1) an increase in de-

41. On July 1, 1960, two months to the day after the U-2 piloted by Francis Gary Powers was shot down over Russia, Soviet fighter planes shot down an RB-47 reconnaissance aircraft over the Barents Sea.
42. Khrushchev, *Khrushchev Remembers,* pp. 487–91.
43. *New York Times,* September 17, 1960.

fense spending of $3.2 billion; (2) an increase of 217,000 people in military manpower; (3) expanded draft calls; (4) a call-up of reserves; (5) the retention or reactivation of ships and aircraft slated for retirement; and (6) an increase in civil defense spending.[44]

During the next three months Soviet armed forces were used to help the Ulbricht regime seal off West Berlin from East Germany and to respond to the consequent U.S. military buildup in Europe. After the Kennedy administration had announced that it would not abandon West Berlin the Kremlin agreed to support action by East Germany both to stop the exit of East Germans through West Berlin (this flight had increased dramatically after the crisis began) and to end the powerful influence West Berlin exerted on East Germans. When East German border police moved on August 12–13, 1961, to seal off West Berlin, two Soviet divisions surrounded the city in a show of support.

The United States responded only symbolically: between August 14 and 21 a U.S. Army battle group of 1,500 men was sent to West Berlin, tours of duty for 26,800 U.S. naval personnel were extended, and 113 reserve and National Guard units were alerted. The USSR held military maneuvers in the USSR and on August 23 sent notes to Washington, London, and Paris threatening to close off their access to West Berlin by air. On the previous day East Germany had closed off all but one of the West Berlin border crossing points open to foreigners, including Western occupation troops, and had established a one-hundred-meter no-man's-land around the enclave. No Soviet military moves accompanied these actions by East Germany or the USSR's threat, which, unlike the sealing off of West Berlin from East Berlin and East Germany (formally, four-power authority still existed in Berlin), could not be justified legally. A series of Soviet military activities began on August 29—part of a tit-for-tat game with the United States that followed the strong U.S. military reaction to the USSR's threat.

The day after the Soviet notes were delivered, 1,000 U.S. troops, with tanks, were deployed along the border between East and West Berlin; on August 25, 76,500 U.S. reservists were called up. On August 29 and 30 the Kremlin announced that it would keep on active duty personnel that were to have been released into the reserves and that it would resume its testing of nuclear weapons. The United States also resumed nuclear testing (underground), deployed airborne troops to Greece and

44. Slusser, "The Berlin Crises of 1958–59 and 1961," pp. 412–13, 421–22.

Turkey, held exercises in the Mediterranean area, called up two National Guard divisions and 249 smaller reserve and guard units, and sent U.S. Air Force fighter squadrons to Europe. Meanwhile, the USSR had begun holding naval exercises in the Barents and Kara seas. The only Soviet action interfering with Western air access to West Berlin was the harassment in mid-September of several U.S. airliners by Soviet fighters.

Military activity by both sides slowed down in late September. When Khrushchev realized that the Berlin Wall was the most that could be achieved without seriously risking war, and with the six-month period given in his June aide-mémoire approaching an end, he used the forum of the Twenty-second Congress of the Communist Party of the Soviet Union (CPSU) to lift the deadline.

What explains, then, the confrontation on October 26 between U.S. and Soviet tanks at the Friedrichstrasse crossing in Berlin? According to Khrushchev, the Kremlin believed that the United States was preparing to use bulldozers, tanks, and infantry to tear down certain portions of the newly established wall; so Soviet units were deployed to deter that action.[45] A second explanation is that each side wanted to inform the other that it would not tolerate a change in the status quo after local tension had built around this crossing point. Although neither side might have intended to act aggressively, each could have perceived its action as one of successful deterrence. A third and more complex explanation ties the confrontation to developments at the Soviet party congress and Khrushchev's need to regain lost authority while demonstrating that the United States could not be finessed out of West Berlin. Facing attacks by the Chinese and Soviet party hawks, Khrushchev may have provoked the confrontation to demonstrate his personal will and to test the West's commitment. If the United States reacted strongly, he would be able to identify internal Soviet opposition to ending the crisis as courting war.[46]

The Missile Crisis

Khrushchev's last attempt to resolve or at least obtain greater leverage for dealing with the threat posed by West Germany and West Berlin to

45. Khrushchev, *Khrushchev Remembers*, pp. 506–07.
46. On Khrushchev's domestic position, see Robert M. Slusser, *The Berlin Crisis of 1961: Soviet-American Relations and the Struggle for Power in the Kremlin, June–November 1961* (Johns Hopkins University Press, 1973), pp. 339–461.

East German and Soviet security precipitated the Cuban missile crisis.[47] After the 1961 campaign failed—Bonn's role within NATO continued to grow, and West Berlin remained a Western enclave within East Germany —Moscow did not try a similar campaign, but neither was it willing to let the West become too confident. In early December 1961 Soviet military men again delayed a U.S. Army convoy outside Berlin, and in February and March 1962 Soviet planes flew through the Berlin air corridors and dropped chaff to confuse Western radars. Still another U.S. Army convoy was blocked in May. Rather than pursue this futile line, however, Khrushchev appears to have concluded that he could attain his objectives by placing strategic nuclear forces in Cuba and trading this deployment for an acceptable settlement on Germany or using it to coerce the United States into an acceptable agreement. As Michel Tatu has observed:

The objective of the manoeuvre was clearly Berlin. Ever since Khrushchev had raised the issue in 1958, the Russians had tried all possible tactics: first pressure (the six-month ultimatum), then smiles (at Camp David), then pressure again and even the fist-banging session (during Khrushchev's summer offensive of 1961). Everything had been in vain. In the spring of 1962 an entirely fresh approach was needed. Khrushchev's prestige was largely at stake and his adversaries in the communist camp were using the issue as a weapon against him.[48]

The deployment of missiles to Cuba was also a quick response by the Kremlin to the U.S. refutation in fall 1961 of the "missile gap."[49] Khrushchev knew that during the next several years a huge U.S. lead in intercontinental ballistic missiles would be revealed. Since lesser-range Soviet missiles in Cuba might have been perceived as equaling U.S. intercontinental-range missiles, Moscow surely preferred to keep them there rather than bargain them away. So Khrushchev probably hoped to use the missiles in Cuba to force the United States to accommodate to Soviet objectives in Central Europe rather than as a bargaining chip.

Moscow sent to Cuba in the summer and fall of 1962 the following arms: medium-range (1,100 nautical miles) and intermediate-range (2,200 nautical miles) ballistic missiles (MRBMs and IRBMs); IL-28 (Beagle) bombers capable of carrying up to 6,000 pounds of nuclear or

---

47. Ulam, *Expansion and Coexistence,* pp. 668–69; Michel Tatu, *Power in the Kremlin: From Khrushchev to Kosygin,* trans. Helen Katel (Viking, 1969), pp. 230–33.

48. Tatu, *Power in the Kremlin,* p. 232.

49. Horelick and Rush, *Strategic Power and Soviet Foreign Policy,* pp. 83–84, 136–38; Herbert S. Dinerstein, *The Making of a Missile Crisis: October 1962* (Johns Hopkins University Press, 1976), pp. 155–56.

nonnuclear ordnance; cruise and surface-to-air missiles (SAMs); missile patrol boats; and MIG-21 fighter aircraft. With these weapon systems came 22,000 military personnel and technicians including, in addition to missile operators and presumably pilots, four regimental-size armored units equipped with T-54 tanks, surface-to-surface tactical nuclear rockets, and antitank missiles.[50]

The military mission of the IRBM, MRBM, and IL-28 units was to pose an increased nuclear threat to the United States. The other forces may have been sent to deter U.S. military action against the nuclear strategic forces and to defend them. It is possible, however, that at least some of these defensive forces were sent only at Castro's insistence, to add to Cuba's general security.

When President Kennedy demanded that the missiles be removed from Cuba, the Kremlin refrained from provocative military activities. Moscow even allowed Soviet submarines joining Russian freighters en route to Cuba to suffer U.S. Navy harassment. Khrushchev did not directly threaten West Berlin again, as Washington had half expected it would. The only really provocative military action directed against the United States during the crisis was the shooting down over Cuba of a U-2 aircraft by a SAM missile, almost certainly directed by a Russian. This action may have been meant as a signal to Washington that Soviet military units in Cuba would be used to defend the offending missiles against a U.S. attempt to destroy them.

Maintaining the Status Quo and Détente

After the USSR withdrew from Cuba the Kremlin provoked no new crises over West Germany or West Berlin. Thereafter Soviet military actions were almost always in response to actions by Bonn that Moscow believed were politically threatening to East Germany and Soviet rights in Berlin. Harassment in the air corridors and the delay of military convoys in spring 1963 followed an increased number of escapes from East Berlin, bombings along the wall and of the Soviet Intourist office in West Berlin, and the announcement that President Kennedy would visit West Berlin in June. Moscow also believed Bonn was trying to extend its jurisdiction to West Berlin.[51] In April 1965, after Bonn held a Bundestag ses-

50. Graham T. Allison, *Essence of Decision: Explaining the Cuban Missile Crisis* (Little, Brown, 1971), pp. 104–05.
51. *New York Times,* April 24, 1963.

sion in West Berlin, Soviet jets flew over the city and Soviet and East German troops closed and paraded on the autobahn. Four years elapsed before Moscow again used the military to harass West Berlin, this time protesting the West German Federal Assembly's meeting to elect a new president. Forthcoming visits by Prime Minister Harold Wilson and President Richard Nixon gave Moscow further cause to jam Western aircraft communications and radars, close the autobahn, and order troop maneuvers and aircraft reinforcements.

Regularly during the cold war, Soviet citizens and military men were warned that world capitalism was waiting only for the right moment to strike at the USSR. Although the acquisition of nuclear weapons, long-range bombers, and intercontinental ballistic missiles enabled the USSR to devastate the West if necessary, these weapons did little to allay Soviet fears about Western hostility toward Communist nations. The "ruling circles of the United States" were expected to do everything possible "to preserve the old, thoroughly decayed foundations of the capitalist world, to stem the progressive evolution of human society."[52] Given the chance, Moscow believed, the United States would use violence against the USSR. "The threat of . . . preventive war by American imperialists against the Soviet Union and the other countries of the socialist camp is quite real," Marshal V. D. Sokolovsky wrote.[53] The Soviet Union also remained obsessed about West German "revanchists" and NATO aggression in Europe.[54]

Soviet perceptions of Western intent began to change only after the elections in West Germany in September 1969, which led to the formation of a government led by Chancellor Willy Brandt. In November 1969 West Germany signed the Treaty for the Nonproliferation of Nuclear Weapons, and in December the Brandt government responded positively to Moscow's long-standing call for a final peace conference to ratify the national borders that had existed in Central Europe since the end of the Second World War.

The USSR's increased deployments of Soviet ICBMs, the development of missile-armed nuclear submarines, and the movement toward

52. From the Revolution Day speech by A. N. Kosygin, shortly after the Cuban missile crisis. *Pravda,* November 7, 1962 (translated in *Current Digest of the Soviet Press* [*CDSP*], vol. 14, December 5, 1962, p. 6).

53. Sokolovskiy, *Soviet Military Strategy,* p. 62.

54. See, for example, L. I. Brezhnev, *Pravda,* November 4, 1967 (in *CDSP,* vol. 19, November 22, 1967, p. 16); and K. T. Mazurov, *Pravda,* November 7, 1968 (in *CDSP,* vol. 20, November 27, 1968, p. 7).

strategic parity with the United States further increased Moscow's confidence about its ability to deal with the West. President Nixon wrote in early 1970: "An inescapable reality of the 1970's is the Soviet Union's possession of powerful and sophisticated strategic forces approaching and, in some categories, exceeding ours in numbers and capability."[55] Moscow received with satisfaction President Nixon's opposition to "sharp increases" in the development of U.S. strategic weapons and to any attempt to reverse the movement toward strategic parity—his decision to seek only "sufficiency" for the U.S. strategic weapons arsenal.[56]

In August 1970 Bonn signed the Treaty of Moscow, thereby recognizing the frontiers between East and West Germany and between East Germany and Poland. Also that summer East and West exchanged memoranda on the agenda of a European security conference. The purpose of the large Warsaw Pact exercises held in East Germany in October 1970 under the command of an East German general was to reassure East Germany as much as it was to caution the West that "East Germany is and will be an integral part of the East bloc," according to one Eastern European diplomat.[57] Traffic holdups by Soviet border guards in January 1971 seemed less related to Soviet objectives concerning Berlin than a response to pressure on the USSR by East Germany to uphold its interests. It became clear that the Kremlin wanted to avoid provoking any serious confrontation with the United States when in fall 1970 Moscow withdrew a submarine tender and halted construction of a ballistic missile submarine base in Cienfuegos, Cuba, after the United States claimed that the USSR was violating the Kennedy-Khrushchev agreement that ended the Cuban missile crisis.[58]

In 1971 the Quadripartite agreement on Berlin was signed, and the

55. *U.S. Foreign Policy for the 1970's: A New Strategy for Peace,* report to the Congress by Richard Nixon, President of the United States, on February 18, 1970 (GPO, 1970), p. 119.

56. Ibid., pp. 121, 123.

57. *New York Times,* October 13, 1970.

58. The Nixon administration was apparently prepared to enter into a major crisis over the submarine base. In a note to Secretary of State Henry Kissinger, President Nixon wrote: "I want a report on a crash basis on: (1) What CIA can do to support any kind of action which will irritate Castro; (2) What actions we can take which we have not yet taken to boycott nations dealing with Castro; (3) Most important, what actions we can take, covert or overt, to put missiles in Turkey—or a sub base in the Black Sea—anything which will give us some trading stock." Richard M. Nixon, *RN: The Memoirs of Richard Nixon* (Grosset and Dunlap, 1978), pp. 486–89; also see Marvin Kalb and Bernard Kalb, *Kissinger* (Little, Brown, 1974), pp. 209–12.

United States and the Soviet Union signed the Agreement on Measures to Reduce the Risk of Outbreak of Nuclear War. Finally, in 1972 a SALT agreement was reached, and the United States and the Soviet Union signed the Joint Declaration on Basic Principles of Relations. This détente helped reduce Soviet suspicions about Western intent and aggressiveness. Stalin had assumed that war was inevitable as long as the two different ideological camps existed; Georgi M. Malenkov and Khrushchev had concluded that war in the nuclear age was no longer a sane policy choice; and in the early 1970s Soviet political authorities began to believe that the West might be willing to accept not only the USSR as it was but also the existence of Communist regimes in Eastern Europe (including East Germany) and the USSR's continued domination over it. The Final Act of the Conference on Security and Cooperation in Europe signed in Helsinki in 1975 culminated what the Russians perceived to be a period of progress.

Although Moscow remained anxious about the possibility of nuclear war with the United States and regime change in West Germany, Soviet leaders appeared increasingly to think of the danger in terms of Western military capabilities—U.S. strategic nuclear weapons and NATO—rather than in terms of a capitalist and revanchist world waiting for the right moment to attack or undermine the USSR and its empire. Military preparedness became more a matter of prudence than a panic-driven necessity. Marshal Dimitri F. Ustinov observed on Revolution Day, 1977, "The defensive potential of the Soviet Union is maintained at such a high level that no one would risk disturbing our peaceful life."[59] General Secretary Brezhnev expressed this thought more positively: "People look into the future with a growing hope."[60]

As a result of the agreements reached between 1969 and 1975, the continued growth of Soviet strategic and conventional military capabilities, and Moscow's new view of the West, the USSR did not aim any political-military operations directly at the West. Soviet behavior in late 1977 and early 1978, after the Western allies turned down a request to curtail their military patrols in East Berlin, showed how much conditions had changed in Central Europe. The Kremlin responded not by taking action against the Western presence in Berlin but by increasing the number of Soviet military patrols in West Berlin, as was its legal right.

Nevertheless, although Moscow did not engage in coercive diplomacy

59. Moscow Domestic Service, FBIS, *Soviet Union* (November 7, 1977), p. P4.
60. Tass, June 21, 1977 (in FBIS, *Soviet Union,* June 22, 1977, p. E5).

to resolve disagreements between the Warsaw Pact nations and NATO, it did between NATO nations, presumably to undermine Western unity. From the Soviet perspective, "although the threat of war has been pushed back, it has not yet been eliminated. Imperialism was and remains a source of military danger."[61] Many Russians also continued to view the USSR as an island in a hostile sea. For example, *Pravda* told readers that "the American military's bases encircle the territory of the Soviet Union and the other Socialist community countries in a solid ring."[62]

Efforts to Weaken NATO

To counter the continuing danger posed by the West and to improve the USSR's ability to influence it, about ten Soviet ships and an equal number of submarines exercised in Icelandic waters in May 1973, in the midst of the "cod war" between Britain and Iceland. Soviet warships had recently completed a major exercise in the North Atlantic and Norwegian Sea; a portion of this exercise had been conducted near the area entered by Soviet warships during the cod war. A new exercise in these waters so soon afterward was unusual. Another exercise area could have been found if the USSR had wanted to avoid appearing as if it were intervening in the conflict between Britain and Iceland. But since the Soviet exercises also occurred after a reported request to the USSR by Iceland's minister of fisheries for a gunboat to strengthen Iceland's coast guard, and just after London ordered British warships into the area, Moscow probably intended the exercises to signal Iceland that it did not have to face Britain alone and to show Britain that it might have to contend with a super- power.[63]

61. Marshal D. F. Ustinov on the thirty-second anniversary of the end of the Great Patriotic War, *Pravda,* May 9, 1977 (in FBIS, *Soviet Union,* May 13, 1977, p. R4).
62. T. Kolesnichenko, "Why are the Bases Needed?," *Pravda,* May 6, 1977 (in FBIS, *Soviet Union,* May 10, 1977, p. B10). For a naval complement, see interview with Admiral S. G. Gorshkov, *Pravda,* July 30, 1978 (in FBIS, *Soviet Union,* August 3, 1978, p. V3).
63. Robert G. Weinland, "The State and Future of the Soviet Navy in the North Atlantic," in Michael MccGwire and John McDonnell, eds., *Soviet Naval Influence: Domestic and Foreign Dimensions* (Praeger for the Centre for Foreign Policy Studies, Department of Political Science, Dalhousie University, Halifax, N.S., 1977), pp. 418–21; *The Times* (London), May 19, 1973. Soviet warships do not appear to have entered the scene until after Brezhnev had visited West Germany and returned to Moscow.

That the dispute between Britain and Iceland could undermine NATO became apparent when Reykjavik, responding to London's deployment of frigates to protect British trawlers, denied Royal Air Force planes landing rights at the NATO airfield in Keflavik. Withdrawal from NATO also became a subject of discussion in Iceland.[64] Soviet naval planners may have hoped that the Icelandic government would hinder the important NATO antisubmarine warfare operations that depended on use of the Keflavik air base. Continued NATO use of this base was already an issue in Icelandic politics.[65]

Moscow also practiced military diplomacy during the 1974 Cyprus crisis. Immediately after the coup against President Makarios led by insurgents supported by the Greek government, a Soviet task group including cruisers and destroyers moved toward Cyprus, and the Soviet Mediterranean fleet was reinforced. Moscow was reported (by U.S. Defense Department officials) to have also placed its seven airborne divisions on alert, and Soviet AN-12 and AN-22 transport aircraft were prepared for action.[66]

Since these actions occurred before constitutional government had been restored in Athens, they could have been interpreted as supportive of Turkey. The Kremlin had cultivated Ankara for some time, and Turkey was deeply disturbed by the Cyprus coup; Turkish military intervention in Cyprus and Greek-Turkish conflict were plausible. Moscow's naval deployments also may have been meant to counterbalance a concurrent U.S. naval presence and to demonstrate continued support for Makarios, who, after fleeing to Malta, went on to London. The United States had been close to the Greek government and had always had trouble dealing with Makarios, who had kept his distance from Washington.[67] Many supposed that the Greek government had directed the coup and had Washington's

64. *The Times* (London), May 24, 1973; *New York Times,* May 21–22, 1973.

65. *The Times* (London), May 24, 1973. On the use of the Keflavik base and the importance of Iceland to NATO defense, see Congressional Budget Office, *The U.S. Sea Control Mission: Forces, Capabilities and Requirements* (GPO, June 1977), pp. 54–55; and Frank Leary, "The Anti-Ship Submarine," *Space/Aeronautics,* vol. 46 (July 1966), p. 61.

66. *New York Times,* July 17, 20, and 21, 1974; *Washington Post,* July 17, 1976; R. J. Vincent, *Military Power and Political Influence: The Soviet Union and Western Europe,* Adelphi Paper 119 (London: International Institute for Strategic Studies, 1975), p. 10.

67. This trouble was despite flights by U.S. U-2 aircraft out of Britain's Akrotiri air base and radio monitoring by the CIA's Foreign Broadcast Information Service on Cyprus. Lawrence Stern, *The Wrong Horse: The Politics of Intervention and the Failure of American Diplomacy* (New York Times Books, 1977), pp. 66–73, 100–102.

support. At any rate, the United States did not condemn the coup and expressed no interest in the return of Makarios.[68]

The Soviet airborne alert and reported troop movements in Bulgaria were probably precautions against the possibility of war breaking out between Greece and Turkey in Thrace, adjacent to Bulgaria (a Warsaw Pact ally).

Security Relations with China

Moscow's retreat from confrontation with the West over West Germany and West Berlin after the Cuban missile crisis was related to more than the disastrous outcome of the placement of missiles in Cuba, the disposition of Khrushchev's successors, and growing resignation about West Germany's place within NATO. Also significant was the USSR's increasingly hostile relations with China and the development between 1963 and 1969 of a situation that threatened to end in war between the two Communist giants.

Relations between Moscow and Peking began to deteriorate after Khrushchev's destalinization speech at the Twentieth Party Congress in early 1956. The Chinese believed that destalinization undermined the legitimacy of Communist regimes everywhere as well as the struggle with the West. The gulf widened further when Moscow, unimpressed by Peking's demands for more militant action against capitalism, accepted Mao's thesis that "the east wind prevails over the west wind" only to a limited degree and remained steadfast in its call for "peaceful coexistence." In addition, although Khrushchev was willing to probe the West to satisfy important Soviet security objectives, he was unwilling to help the Chinese develop nuclear weapons. The two countries parted even further when Moscow refused to help build up China's navy; when the Chinese abandoned the Soviet economic model in favor of a radical domestic course; and when the Kremlin adopted a stance of neutrality in China's border dispute with India.[69]

Peking Raises the Border Issue

In the early 1960s Peking gave up hope of cajoling the Kremlin into accepting China's course. Mao Tse-tung then expressed China's long-held

68. Ibid., pp. 112–13.
69. See A. Doak Barnett, *China and the Major Powers in East Asia* (Brookings Institution, 1977), pp. 32–39.

desire for large territorial adjustments of the Sino-Soviet border. In March 1963 Peking indicated its intention to lay claim to southeastern Siberia, the Maritime Territory, and a half-million square miles of Soviet Central Asia, all obtained by czarist Russia in the nineteenth century through what the Chinese called "unequal" treaties. Precipitating this threat was Peking's strong objection to Moscow's handling of the Cuban missile crisis and Khrushchev's point to the Chinese in this exchange that the USSR had recognized U.S. nuclear power just as China had sensibly recognized the existence of British Hong Kong and Portuguese Macao.[70] Of further significance was the occurrence of several border incidents and the exodus of many Kazakhs and Uighurs from China to the USSR in 1962. Aside from Peking's material interest in the disputed territories, the border issue placed the USSR on the defensive and showed the world that Moscow followed the imperialist path of the czars and the West.

After the Korean War Soviet military strength in the Far East had been reduced from about thirty to twelve to fourteen divisions. But in 1965, following inconclusive talks on border and territorial issues, new assertions by Peking, more border incidents, and the onset of nuclear testing by China, Moscow began to slowly build up its military position in the area. Units were filled out and rotated with more capable Soviet troops then deployed in Central and Eastern Europe, surface-to-surface nuclear weapons and other advanced armaments were sent eastward, and forces were moved closer to the border.[71] Moscow also went out of its way to reaffirm its alliance with Mongolia. Accompanied by Defense Minister Rodion Ya. Malinovsky, Leonid Brezhnev signed in January 1966 in Ulan Bator a new twenty-year mutual assistance pact. Soviet troops were then deployed to Mongolia for the first time in a decade.[72]

When relations with Peking continued to deteriorate, the USSR re-

70. See Tai Sung An, *The Sino-Soviet Territorial Dispute* (Westminster Press, 1973), pp. 74–77.

71. Also sent to the frontier area was equipment for monitoring Chinese missile and nuclear weapon tests. Thomas W. Wolfe, *Soviet Power and Europe, 1945–1970* (Johns Hopkins Press, 1970), p. 467, note 27; Institute for Strategic Studies, *Strategic Survey, 1969* (London: ISS, 1970), p. 66; Thomas W. Robinson, "The Sino-Soviet Border Dispute: Background, Development, and the March 1969 Clashes," *American Political Science Review*, vol. 66 (December 1972), pp. 1185–86; Barnett, *China and the Major Powers in East Asia*, p. 44; *New York Times*, November 22, 1966.

72. Soviet troops had been withdrawn from Mongolia in 1956 after twenty years. Wolfe, *Soviet Power and Europe*, p. 467, note 27; *New York Times*, March 16, 1966.

inforced its military position further. Red Guard activity in Sinkiang province, the violence of the Cultural Revolution elsewhere in China (for more than two weeks in early 1967 the Soviet Embassy in Peking was besieged), and continued nuclear testing (a thermonuclear device was exploded in June 1967) all made Moscow increasingly anxious that, despite China's overall military inferiority to the USSR, Peking might either provoke a crisis by, for example, deploying intermediate-range missiles to Albania or, even more irrationally, try to restore by violence some portion of the so-called lost territories.[73] Boldly facing the thought of a joint Soviet-American attack on China, Foreign Minister Chen Yi wrote: "We are not afraid . . . . The Chinese people are ready for war and confident of final victory. We now have the atomic bomb and also rockets . . . all the nuclear bombs that fall on China will be returned with interest."[74] For the first time since the Great Patriotic War Moscow confronted the possibility of an unprovoked or preemptive military action against the USSR and saw its territorial security in serious jeopardy.[75]

After a slow beginning in 1965–66, the Soviet military buildup proceeded swiftly in 1967–68. Divisions in Eastern Europe continued to be rotated with divisions in the Far East, and Soviet forces began to enter Mongolia. In November 1967 Soviet tank units paraded in Ulan Bator in a public demonstration of warning to China and a show of commitment to Mongolia. By mid-1968 there were estimates of up to six Soviet divisions in Mongolia, and in the summer of that year, at the same time the USSR was threatening Czechoslovakia, large-scale Soviet maneuvers were held in Mongolia.[76] Additional divisions were deployed to Soviet Central Asia. Peking also had to consider the improved state of Soviet-U.S. relations at that time, the August 1968 agreement between the USSR and Japan for their joint development of Siberia, the invasion of Czechoslo-

73. Tai, *The Sino-Soviet Territorial Dispute*, pp. 84–88. Harold C. Hinton, *China's Turbulent Quest: An Analysis of China's Foreign Relations Since 1949*, rev. ed. (Indiana University Press, 1972), pp. 134–36, 153–56, 160. *New York Times*, November 22, 1966, and August 12, 1967.

74. Statement published on December 11, 1967, and quoted in *Keesing's Contemporary Archives* (May 20–27, 1967), p. 22045.

75. As John Newhouse has observed, "By 1969, there was general acceptance that the real purpose of the Soviet Galosh ABM [antiballistic missile] was to protect Moscow from primitive Chinese nuclear weapons, as distinct from high-performance American missiles." John Newhouse, *Cold Dawn: The Story of SALT* (Holt, Rinehart and Winston, 1973), pp. 164–65.

76. Robinson, "The Sino-Soviet Border Dispute," p. 1186; Institute for Strategic Studies, *The Military Balance, 1966–1967, 1967–1968,* and *1968–1969.*

vakia, and the Brezhnev doctrine. The Soviet military deployments and activities directed at China constituted a serious warning to Peking within an ominous strategic environment.

The 1969 Clashes and Soviet Threats

The increasingly tense situation between the USSR and China came to a head between March and September 1969. A Chinese ambush of a Soviet patrol on Damansky Island in the Ussuri River on March 2, 1969, led to a Soviet action there on March 15, which included artillery exchanges, the use of Soviet tanks, and infantry battle that lasted for about nine hours and resulted in about sixty Russian and eight hundred Chinese casualties. Violent interchanges in other border areas continued intermittently until August. In April 1969 the scene of violence shifted westward to territory near Chuguchak, where the Sinkiang-Uighur Autonomous Region of China fronts the Kazakh Soviet Socialist Republic. While clashes continued in this area, fighting broke out in May and June in the Amur River border area in the east again. Finally, on August 13, 1969, near the Dzungarian Gate, the ancient trade and invasion route between Sinkiang and Kazakhstan, a major clash erupted. Peking claimed that Soviet tanks, helicopters, and several hundred troops entered Sinkiang to provoke this battle. Indeed, after the initial clash on March 2, the Soviet Union appeared to be responsible for the hostilities that followed.[77]

Soviet objectives after the first Damansky Island incident were to (1) persuade Peking to begin new talks to "normalize" the border situation—that is, to establish a diplomatic framework that would allow the USSR to retain the territory the czars had taken from China; (2) deter Peking from further military action against Soviet personnel and territory; and (3) be prepared for war with China. Soviet border provocations were aimed at attaining the first two of these goals; the action on March 15, an exhibition of Soviet determination, was also aimed at the international Communist movement and catered to Russian nationalism and a desire for revenge.[78] The last concern—to be prepared for war—as well as the first two were further served by a number of other political-military actions, including the transfer of six additional Soviet army divisions to the Far East; the expansion of airfields in the east; a call-up of reserves and

77. ISS, *Strategic Survey, 1969,* pp. 66–69; Tai, *The Sino-Soviet Territorial Dispute,* pp. 105–06.
78. Robinson, "The Sino-Soviet Border Dispute," p. 1199.

general expansion of the Soviet army from 140 to 148 divisions; and major exercises in the Amur River area and the Transbaikal military district. About the latter exercise, the Soviet military newspaper *Krasnaya Zvezda* proclaimed that Soviet forces had scored "a convincing victory" after "courageously and decisively *attacking* the enemy."[79]

In late summer the Kremlin appeared to lose patience with Peking, which, in spite of its agreement in May to have the Sino-Soviet Commission for Navigation on Boundary Rivers meet, had not backed down in its propaganda or in its demands for satisfaction by the USSR as a precondition for more fundamental border talks. Moscow was unable to translate military superiority into political recognition of its case, as Peking remained unwilling to enter into serious direct negotiatons. The Kremlin dealt with its frustration by provoking the Chinese on August 13 and by threatening China with nuclear war.

In early August Colonel General Vladimir F. Tolubko, a Soviet army missile specialist and author of an article published on August 6 commemorating the 1929 outbreak of conflict between the USSR and China, was appointed to command the Soviet Far East Military District. When this appointment—meant as a warning—and the August 13 provocation failed to produce the desired effect, a *Pravda* editorial hinted to Peking that adherence to "absurd territorial claims against the Soviet Union" courted nuclear war. "If a war were to break out under present conditions, with the armaments, lethal weapons and modern means of delivery that now exist, no continent would be unaffected," the Kremlin warned Peking and advised the West.[80] Earlier, Henry Kissinger has reported, "A middle-level State Department specialist in Soviet affairs, William Stearman, was having lunch with a Soviet Embassy official when, out of the blue, the Russian asked what the U.S. reaction would be to a Soviet attack on Chinese nuclear facilities."[81] Observed in late August, according to Kissinger, was

a standdown of the Soviet air force in the Far East. Such a move, which permits all aircraft to be brought to a high state of readiness simultaneously, is often a sign of a possible attack; at a minimum it is a brutal warning in an intensified war of nerves.[82]

79. Quoted in *New York Times,* May 9, 1969; emphasis added. Also see Wolfe, *Soviet Power and Europe, 1945–1970,* p. 467; *New York Times,* September 12, 1969.

80. *Pravda,* August 28, 1969 (in *CDSP,* vol. 21, September 24, 1969, pp. 3–5).

81. Henry Kissinger, *White House Years* (Little, Brown, 1979), p. 183.

82. Ibid.

Moscow also circulated among Eastern European governments and among foreign Communist parties a letter raising the possibility of a pre-emptive nuclear strike against China.[83] In addition, Soviet Deputy Defense Minister Matvey V. Zakharov suggested the possibility of a surprise attack against China, and Victor Louis wrote in the *London Evening News:*

Some circles in Eastern Europe are asking why the doctrine (i.e., the Brezhnev Doctrine) that Russia was justified in interfering in Czechoslovakia's affairs a year ago should not be extended to China. Events in the past year have confirmed that the Soviet Union is adhering to the doctrine that socialist countries have the right to interfere in each other's affairs in their own interest or those of others who are threatened.

The fact that China is many times larger than Czechoslovakia and might offer active resistance is, according to these Marxist theoreticians, no reason for not applying the doctrine. Whether or not the Soviet Union will attack Lop Nor, China's nuclear center, is a question of strategy, and so the world would only learn about it afterwards.[84]

Since the Louis article was published just after a hastily arranged meeting between Aleksei Kosygin and Chou En-lai at Peking's airport on September 11, where Chou agreed to resume border negotiations with the USSR, the piece may have been meant only to confirm Moscow's seriousness and to extract a formal statement from Peking renouncing violence as a way to alter the existing border arrangement. On October 7 Peking announced that it was willing to reopen negotiations with the USSR and that the issue should be "settled peacefully." The Chinese declared, "Even if it cannot be settled for the time being, the status quo of the border should be maintained, and there definitely should be no resort to the use of force."[85]

The Continued Buildup of Soviet Power and Additional Incidents

Although the border talks that began in October 1969 quickly proved fruitless and Sino-Soviet relations remained stormy, the Kosygin-Chou meeting, the Chinese statement of early October, and new negotiations

83. *New York Times,* September 18, 1969; Harold C. Hinton, *The Bear at the Gate: Chinese Policymaking Under Soviet Pressure,* special analysis 21 (Washington, D.C.: American Enterprise Institute; Stanford, Calif.: Hoover Institution on War, Revolution and Peace, Stanford University, 1971), pp. 29–30.

84. As quoted in Tai, *The Sino-Soviet Territorial Dispute,* p. 107; *New York Times,* September 18, 1969.

85. Quoted in Tai, *The Sino-Soviet Territorial Dispute,* p. 109.

gave Moscow and Peking a long enough pause to step out of their drift toward war. But the two sides kept up their heated diplomatic battle. Despite each one's effort not to provoke new border incidents, an atmosphere of military confrontation continued. The Soviet Army's presence in the border areas (the Transbaikal and Far East Military districts and Mongolia), which increased from fifteen divisions in 1968 to twenty-one divisions in 1969, rose to thirty divisions in 1970 and to more than forty divisions in 1973. Soviet air power deployed in the east was also increased during this time. Although Peking moved forces closer to the border to counter Soviet deployments there, the number of Chinese divisions in these areas was maintained at about thirty-three until 1972–73, when Peking increased the number of its divisions on the border to match the Soviet presence.[86]

Additional evidence of Moscow's anxiety was a proposal made in July 1970 by Vladimir S. Semenov, head of the Soviet SALT delegation in Vienna, calling, in effect, for a U.S.-Soviet alliance against other nuclear powers—that is, China. Moscow suggested that when the USSR and the United States discovered a plan for a "provocative" action or attack they would act together to prevent it; failing this, they would retaliate jointly against the third party.[87] About this time China was beginning to emplace its first intermediate-range ballistic missiles.[88] The Kissinger and Nixon visits to China and the general movement toward Sino-American rapprochement that ensued in 1971 alarmed Moscow even further.

After increasing dramatically the number of Soviet military divisions in the east, the number leveled off at about forty-three until the late 1970s.[89] A reported Sino-Soviet military clash in the Mongolian border area in November 1974, perhaps provoked by Moscow to push Peking into new negotiations, was not followed by a renewed military buildup,

86. International Institute for Strategic Studies, *Strategic Survey, 1973* (London: IISS), p. 67. As Barnett has observed, however, "estimates of forces on the border vary depending on the area on both sides of the border considered." Based on interviews with Western intelligence specialists, he conjectures that thirty-nine Soviet divisions have been "close to the Chinese border" since 1974. Barnett, *China and the Major Powers in East Asia*, pp. 77–78, 355, note 37. In January 1976 the number of Soviet aircraft deployed near the Sino-Soviet border was reported to have doubled since 1968. Secretary of Defense Donald H. Rumsfeld, *Annual Defense Department Report, Fiscal Year 1977*, p. 126.

87. Newhouse, *Cold Dawn*, pp. 188–89.

88. IISS, *The Military Balance, 1971–1972*, pp. 40–41.

89. IISS, *The Military Balance, 1975–1976*, p. 9; and IISS, *The Military Balance, 1977–1978*, p. 9.

and a new round of negotiations began in Peking in early 1975. A somewhat similar sequence of events occurred a year later, when, shortly after the report of a large increase in Soviet tactical missiles and armored vehicles in the Far East, China released a Soviet helicopter crew captured in 1974. Having earlier accused the crew members of espionage, Peking called their story credible upon their release.[90] Whether this change of mind was a response to Soviet military pressure is difficult to tell.

On April 1, 1978, a long *Pravda* editorial again rejected China's preconditions for further border negotiations. Advised the Kremlin: "A joint statement to the effect that the sides will build their relations on the basis of peaceful coexistence, firmly adhering to the principles of equality, mutual respect for sovereignty and territorial integrity, noninterference in each other's internal affairs, and the nonuse of force, could advance the matter of the normalization of our relations."[91] Four days later Soviet party leader Brezhnev and Defense Minister Ustinov watched Soviet ground and air exercises in the Far East near Khabarovsk, about twenty-five miles from the Sino-Soviet border. Brezhnev was reported to have thanked the troops for their "high state of preparedness" and to have been assured by them that they would continue to "vigilantly defend our socialist motherland."[92]

A month later approximately thirty Russian soldiers, supported by a helicopter and military river boats, were reported to have crossed the Ussuri River into China for a short time. Moscow said the incursion was a mistake that occurred when Soviet border guards had pursued "a dangerous and armed criminal" at night; Peking accused the USSR of an "organized military provocation."[93] Since the incident took place just after a visit to North Korea by party chairman Hua Kuo-feng, a week before a visit to China by Rumanian leader Nicolae Ceausescu, and two weeks before a visit to China by U.S. National Security Adviser Zbigniew Brzezinski, it is plausible that Moscow intended this action as a caution to Peking to restrain its anti-Soviet activity and to keep the dispute between them within existing bounds. Because the Soviet troops ended up in Yueh Ya in Hulin county, Heilungkiang province, it is also possible that Moscow meant to caution North Korea against endorsing China's position in the Sino-Soviet conflict.[94]

90. "Quarterly Chronicle and Documentation," *China Quarterly,* no. 65 (March 1976), p. 197. *Keesing's Contemporary Archives* (March 25, 1977), pp. 28261–62.
91. *Pravda,* April 1, 1978 (in FBIS, *Soviet Union,* April 5, 1978, p. C1).
92. Khabarovsk Domestic Service, ibid., p. R1; *Washington Post,* April 6, 1978.
93. *Washington Post,* May 12 and 13, 1978; *New York Times,* May 12, 1978.
94. *Far Eastern Economic Review* (May 26, 1978), p. 15.

Implications of China's Diplomatic Offensive

Despite a new border buildup to forty-six divisions and supporting aircraft, in the late 1970s Moscow appeared less anxious about a sudden Chinese attack on Soviet territory in the Far East than about Peking's diplomacy aimed, as Moscow saw it, at forming "an anti-Soviet alliance, to undermine the unity of the socialist states, to torpedo the attained level of European détente based on the principles of peaceful coexistence."[95] Moscow believed that the deterioration of relations between the USSR and the United States in spring 1978 was related to a nascent entente involving the United States, NATO Europe, and China. Moscow's evidence consisted of presidential adviser Zbigniew Brzezinski's expressions of concern about Soviet behavior during his May 1978 visit to China, journeys to the People's Republic of China by West German and British general officers just before Brzezinski's trip, the reported support by the Carter administration for Chinese arms purchases in Western Europe, and the U.S. decision to sell China advanced technology items (U.S. high technology sales to the USSR were viewed more coolly).[96]

The treaty of peace and friendship that China and Japan signed in August 1978—days before Chinese party chairman Hua Kuo-feng was to visit Rumania and Yugoslavia—added further to the Kremlin's belief that China was making headway in shifting the global balance of power to the USSR's disadvantage. The treaty included an article opposing third party attempts to establish in any part of the world a position of "hegemony," a code word in Peking's lexicon denoting Soviet imperialism. In accepting this "pivotal provision," Tokyo, according to Moscow, had "capitulated" in the negotiations in which Peking's objective had been the "undermining [of] Soviet-Japanese neighborliness."[97] Earlier, Moscow had warned Japan repeatedly against signing an agreement with China. At one point, when Japan and China were preparing for a new round of negotiations, Moscow staged naval, amphibious, and ground maneuvers in the Kurile Islands, which Tokyo demanded back from the USSR when Japan regained its sovereignty after World War II. Soviet maneuvers in this area

95. *Pravda,* August 24, 1978 (in FBIS, *Soviet Union,* August 24, 1978, p. C3); International Institute for Strategic Studies, *The Military Balance, 1979–1980* (London: IISS, 1979), p. 10.

96. *New York Times,* May 18, 23, 24, and 28, 1978; Tass (in FBIS, *Soviet Union,* June 19, 1978, p. B1); Michael Ledeen, "How the Russian-Chinese War Will Be Fought," *New York,* vol. 11 (June 19, 1978), p. 52.

97. *Pravda,* August 25, 1978 (in FBIS, *Soviet Union,* August 30, 1978, p. M1); *Izvestiya,* August 25, 1978 (ibid., p. M4).

had been common at one time, but no military exercises had been held there since 1970.[98] A Soviet buildup of forces on the islands from about 2,000 to 10,000 troops in 1978 and 1979 suggested that the Kremlin wanted to deter not only the development of strengthened Chinese-Japanese relations but also any thoughts in Tokyo about regaining the islands by force.[99] The Kremlin saw that the United States and Japan were receptive to Peking's overtures and concluded that Washington and Tokyo were actively seeking to strengthen their own bilateral alliance as well as their relationships with China. Military leaders in the USSR perceived the construction of "a NATO for Asia."[100] Before the 1979 conflict between China and Vietnam the Kremlin also worried about the prospect of improved relations between China and India, including the acceptance by New Delhi of Peking's world view. In addition, friendly relations between China and North Korea were apparent. So Moscow not only warned New Delhi of the danger posed by a powerful China but also reminded Pyongyang that it was Peking, not the USSR, that sought the retention of U.S. forces in the Pacific area, including South Korea.[101]

Coda in Afghanistan

In April 1978 the regime of Mohammad Daoud in Afghanistan was overthrown and replaced by a government tied closely to Moscow, but the new regime soon faced a large insurgency. Fortified by base camps in Pakistan and considerable popular support, the rebellion became so serious that Moscow had to turn to Soviet armed forces to keep in power the new regime led by Noor Mohammad Taraki. Arms were airlifted to Afghanistan, several thousand military advisers were dispatched to advise Afghan units, and in the summer of 1979 Soviet pilots began to operate advanced helicopter gunships against the insurgents. A Soviet ground force of several hundred men was also sent to guard the airbase used by incoming Soviet transport aircraft.[102]

This support proved inadequate, however. In the fall of 1979 the

98. *Washington Post,* June 8, 1978.
99. *New York Times,* October 3, 1979.
100. Colonel A. Leontyev, "A NATO for Asia," *Krasnaya Zvezda,* December 17, 1978 (in FBIS, *Soviet Union,* December 19, 1978, pp. A7–11).
101. For example, see *Izvestiya,* December 16, 1978 (in FBIS, *Soviet Union,* December 20, 1978, p. C1).
102. *Washington Post,* October 9, 1979.

Afghan armed forces crumbled and President Taraki was deposed. In late December, airborne units were airlifted into Afghanistan to overthrow the new leadership of Hafizullah Amin, and motorized rifle divisions were sent into the country to further ensure Soviet control. Soviet fighter aircraft regiments were also deployed into Afghanistan, and additional Soviet army divisions were massed just inside the USSR.[103]

Because Afghanistan is adjacent to the USSR and because Moscow was able to exert considerable military and civilian influence in Kabul after the 1978 coup, it is plausible that the Kremlin engaged in limited political-military diplomacy before the December 1979 invasion to obtain firm dominion over Afghanistan and not just to secure a friendly regime there. However, what was possibly an attempt at expansion (with an eye toward the Persian Gulf) certainly included a strong element of security maintenance.[104] Because Moscow had committed itself so heavily to the Taraki regime in what was formerly a neutral nation, it had to worry about the attitude and policies of a succeeding regime triumphant after a bloody civil war in which the enemy had depended on Soviet armaments and military men. Concern about Soviet security, moreover, may have been why the USSR helped to overthrow the Daoud regime in the first place: Selig Harrison has suggested that, at the time, Moscow may have feared that Kabul would be drawn away from its attentiveness to Soviet interests and be led into an Iranian-dominated entente with the West.[105]

103. At the time of this writing, the best available information had been provided by daily newspaper reports.

104. *New York Times,* April 13 and May 4, 1979; *Washington Post,* May 10, 1979; *L'Express* (April 13, 1979), pp. 128–30.

105. Selig S. Harrison, "The Shah, Not Kremlin Touched Off the Afghan Coup," *Washington Post,* May 13, 1979.

CHAPTER FIVE

The Third World

DURING STALIN'S RULE Soviet policy toward noncommunist nationalist movements and governments ran in cycles. From the end of the Russian civil war through the mid-1920s the Bolsheviks sought to accommodate the major European powers and to identify Soviet views with the aspirations of Asian nationalism. But from about 1928 through the early 1930s a more radical line prevailed. Moscow attacked nationalists in the colonial areas as well as European socialists, and the USSR isolated itself from the major powers.

After a brief transition following the 1933 elections in Germany, the cause of revolution was shelved as Moscow threw its support behind popular front governments in Europe and sought alliances to reinforce Soviet security. This course remained dominant until 1947, when again the world was divided into two camps. As in the late 1920s and early 1930s, the "national bourgeoisie" in the underdeveloped nations were considered part of the camp of "capitalism, imperialism, and nationalism." Although Moscow did soften its posture a bit in the early 1950s, it was left to Stalin's heirs to accommodate the newly independent nations and nationalist movements in the third world.[1]

1. Roger E. Kanet, "The Soviet Union and the Colonial Question, 1917–1953," in Roger E. Kanet, ed., *The Soviet Union and the Developing Nations* (Johns Hopkins University Press, 1974), pp. 1–26; Wladyslaw W. Kulski, *Peaceful Co-Existence: An Analysis of Soviet Foreign Policy* (Chicago: Henry Regnery, 1959), pp. 188–228. Richard B. Remnek, *Soviet Scholars and Soviet Foreign Policy: A Case Study in Soviet Foreign Policy Toward India* (Durham, N.C.: Carolina Academic Press, 1975), pp. 5–11.

Early Experiences: China and Spain

Throughout Stalin's years in power Soviet military men were called on only twice to support policy not dominated by the needs of Soviet military security or efforts to establish or maintain Communist regimes in adjacent lands. These two instances were an intervention in China in the mid-1920s and in Spain during the Spanish civil war. Both took place during the two periods of Soviet accommodation to the non-Communist world.

In the early 1920s the new Bolshevik government had difficulty establishing relations with the "legitimate" warlord government in Peking because of Soviet interest in Outer Mongolia and in recovering a concession in the Chinese Eastern Railway (lost at the time of the Russian revolution) and because of the hostility of the powers holding concessions in China. Thus in 1923 Moscow began to support the Nationalist government of Sun Yat-sen in Canton and his political organization, the Kuomintang, or Nationalist party.[2] From the Soviet Union's point of view, in the short term, Sun and his followers—who included Chiang Kai-shek—were the group in China willing to deal with the new Soviet regime and reach an understanding with Moscow; in the longer term, a Nationalist government promised to weaken the British, Japanese, and other foreign positions in China and to allow greater opportunity for the growth of communism.

A Sino-Soviet alliance was formed by an agreement signed by Sun and Adolph A. Joffe in January 1923 in Shanghai. In 1924–25, the National Revolutionary Army and Whampoa Military Academy were established in Canton with the support of Soviet military advisers led initially by P. A. Pavlov and then by General Vasily K. Blücher, who became Chiang Kai-shek's chief of staff. Sun Yat-sen said at the ceremony opening the Whampoa Military Academy:

Six years ago Russia started a revolution and at the same time organized a revolutionary army. This army developed by stages and was able to destroy the old forces and external dangers and achieved great successes. Opening this academy, we follow the example of Russia. In the academy the principles of the building of the Red Army of the Soviet Union will be studied.[3]

2. O. Edmund Clubb, *20th Century China* (Columbia University Press, 1964), pp. 88, 114–22; Allen S. Whiting, *Soviet Policies in China, 1917–1924* (Columbia University Press, 1954), pp. 201–04.

3. Quoted by James C. Bowden, "Soviet Military Aid to Nationalist China, 1923–1941," in Raymond L. Garthoff, ed., *Sino-Soviet Military Relations* (Praeger, 1966), p. 46.

Soviet arms and other matériel were also forthcoming, and the number of Russian military advisers providing training and staff support and who took part in Nationalist military expeditions rose quickly to more than 1,000.[4] Soviet assistance, which also included the training of Chinese military men in the USSR, continued until 1927, when the Chinese Communists were expelled from the Kuomintang and became subject to violent repression at the hands of the Nationalists.[5]

Moscow did spur political change in China during the mid-1920s, and the Kuomintang did become the dominant force in China, at least for a time. The end result, though, greatly disappointed Stalin and spurred the Soviet shift to the ultraleft line that prevailed into the 1930s. This disappointment after giving military support to a nationalist government was to be repeated often in later decades.

Stalin's other military adventure between the world wars was in Spain, where the USSR sought to counter Hitler's and Mussolini's support of the Nationalists during the Spanish civil war. As in China, Soviet objectives were limited and operationally did not include the takeover of Spain by Communists loyal to Moscow. Most important was that the Republicans not be defeated by forces identified with fascism that were receiving major assistance from Germany and Italy. However, Stalin also wanted to maintain good relations with France, which had previously signed a nonaggression pact and a mutual assistance treaty with the USSR. Nor did Stalin want to antagonize Great Britain, which, like France, favored the illusion of the Non-Intervention Agreement signed by Britain, France, Germany, Italy, and the USSR shortly after the Spanish civil war began.[6] Because of the purges then being pressed in the USSR, the Soviet Union was completely unprepared for general war in Europe.

Choosing to keep a low profile, Stalin sent no Lenin Battalion to Spain

4. Ibid., pp. 45–53; John Gittings, *The Role of the Chinese Army* (Oxford University Press, 1967), p. 100; Joseph E. Thach, Jr., "Soviet Military Assistance to Nationalist China, 1923–41," pt. 1, *Military Review,* vol. 57 (August 1977), pp. 72–82; Clubb, *20th Century China,* p. 124.

5. Clubb, *20th Century China,* pp. 135–40. For extended analyses of Soviet policy toward China in the early and mid-1920s, see Whiting, *Soviet Policies in China, 1917–1924;* and Conrad Brandt, *Stalin's Failure in China: 1924–27* (Harvard University Press, 1958).

6. Adam B. Ulam, *Expansion and Coexistence: Soviet Foreign Policy, 1917–73,* 2d ed. (Praeger, 1974), pp. 243–45; Hugh Thomas, *The Spanish Civil War* (Harper, 1961), pp. 260–61; see also G. M. Gathorne-Hardy, *A Short History of International Affairs, 1920–1939,* 4th ed. (London: Oxford University Press, 1950), pp. 434–37.

to match the Ernst Thälmann, Abraham Lincoln, George Dimitrov, and other international contingents that formed the international brigades supported by the Comintern. Nor did Stalin send to Spain a Russian equivalent to the German 7,000-man Condor Legion, not to mention the 50,000 Italian military personnel who fought for the Nationalists at one time. Cautiously, Stalin sent several hundred tanks and aircraft along with personnel to operate them; a relatively small number of advisers to provide senior-level staff support; and instructors to train Loyalist troops in the use of Soviet military equipment, which was provided in quantity.[7]

The relatively small Soviet contribution of military personnel was not trumpeted, and no acknowledgment was made of their participation in combat, although it was plain that they did engage in a number of actions. Stalin also was not willing to escalate the level of Soviet involvement once it became clear that the Republicans would be defeated. As in China, the intervention in Spain ended in failure. Stalin probably never had much hope in Spain after he recognized that Britain, France, and the United States would not restrain Germany and Italy or support the Loyalists in any practical way. The provision of Soviet military men, matériel, and financial aid to the Republicans first offered a way to buy them time and then became a necessary sacrifice. The experiences in China and in Spain could not have persuaded Stalin that military intervention in distant lands was effectual.

Developing Soviet Diplomacy in the Third World

Between the end of World War II and the beginning of the cold war, Moscow looked favorably upon nationalist movements in India, Indonesia, and elsewhere, despite the "national bourgeoisie" leadership in these countries. By late 1947, however, the view of two camps struggling for world supremacy was dominant in the Soviet Union. As in the late 1920s and early 1930s, only true believers in the communist ideal were acceptable; cooperative relations with the leaders of other workers' organizations and bourgeois nationalist leaders were again condemned. During the next few years Moscow considered only Communists as being worthy of leading the masses in underdeveloped countries. Jawaharlal

7. Thomas, *The Spanish Civil War*, pp. 304–05, 320–22, 337, 346, 525, 634–43; Dante A. Puzzo, *Spain and the Great Powers, 1936–1941* (Columbia University Press, 1962), pp. 136–40; Ulam, *Expansion and Coexistence*, p. 244.

Nehru, Sukarno, and others like them were thought to be serving imperialism.[8]

This tough stance began to change late in 1951, but it was only after Stalin's death in March 1953 and during the new "peace offensive" that a new line was pursued boldly. In August, Georgi M. Malenkov, party chairman and head of the Council of Ministers, spoke favorably about developments in India and Burma, and in September the USSR signed a five-year trade agreement with India. By 1955 the Russians were giving strong support to the Bandung Conference, and Nikita Khrushchev and Soviet Premier Nikolai Bulganin were visiting India, Burma, and Afghanistan. The two "camps" were replaced by two "zones"—a "zone of peace" that included the "peace-loving" Communist and non-Communist nations and the "war zone" of Western nations.[9] The previous Stalinist line was recognized as self-defeating. Soviet policy now identified the interests of neutral countries with Soviet objectives. The Kremlin also looked favorably on nationalist movements in colonial areas.

Leaders of the new nonaligned states were pleased to be courted by Moscow. They had rejected the European colonial powers and been put off by U.S. Secretary of State John Foster Dulles's lack of sympathy with their aspirations and by U.S. orthodoxy and insistence—akin to the earlier Soviet line—that a third way, between East and West, did not exist.

Soviet bloc trade with the underdeveloped nations, which had plummeted in the late 1940s and early 1950s, increased dramatically in the mid-1950s. Playing a large part was the bloc's extension of credits, which totaled $1.1 billion between 1953 and 1957.[10] In September 1955, for

8. Kanet, "The Soviet Union and the Colonial Question," pp. 16–24; David J. Dallin, *Soviet Foreign Policy After Stalin* (Lippincott, 1961), pp. 290–95.

9. For example, see Lazar M. Kaganovich's 1955 Revolution Day speech, *Pravda,* November 7, 1955 (translated in *Current Digest of the Soviet Press* [*CDSP*], vol. 7, December 7, 1955, p. 8); and Khrushchev's Twentieth Party Congress speech, in Leo Gruliow, ed., *Current Soviet Policies—II: The Documentary Record of the 20th Communist Party Congress and Its Aftermath* (Praeger, 1957), pp. 32–34; and in Dallin, *Soviet Foreign Policy After Stalin,* pp. 294–321.

10. Credits to Yugoslavia, amounting to $444 million, are not included in this figure. Joseph S. Berliner, *Soviet Economic Aid: The New Aid and Trade Policy in Underdeveloped Countries* (Praeger for the Council on Foreign Relations, 1958), pp. 56–58, 84–87. Through 1978 Soviet and Eastern European credits and grants to less developed nations totaled $26.2 billion. U.S. Central Intelligence Agency, National Foreign Assessment Center, *Communist Aid Activities in Non-Communist Less Developed Countries, 1978: A Research Paper,* ER 79-10412U (CIA, 1979), p. 7.

the first time in the postwar era, Moscow ventured the open sale of arms to a non-Communist nation—Egypt—by way of Czechoslovakia. This sale was prompted by the January 1954 treaty between Turkey and Iraq and Western diplomatic activities leading to the Baghdad Pact. In response, the Kremlin had tried to obtain Soviet allies in the Middle East. President Gamal Abdel Nasser of Egypt, who bitterly opposed the Baghdad Pact and was unable to obtain arms from the United States, was an obvious choice to receive bloc arms.[11] Prague's intermediary role was not wholly new; Czechoslovakia had provided Israel with weapons to support Israeli independence in the late 1940s and had delivered arms to the Arbenz government in Guatemala in 1954. Shortly after the agreement with Egypt was announced, the USSR made known its direct sale of major armaments to Syria.

So began the flow of Soviet arms to the nonaligned states, complemented by the dispatch of Soviet military advisers and the training of third world military men in Warsaw Pact nations. Through 1978 the USSR and its Eastern European allies signed arms agreements valued at approximately $32.9 billion with at least three dozen underdeveloped nations and brought 49,755 military personnel from these countries to the USSR and Eastern Europe for training. At the end of 1978 roughly 12,070 Warsaw Pact military advisers and technicians were in the third world.[12]

However, kind words, visits, trade, aid, and arms were not enough for new nations wanting to eliminate the vestiges of colonialism or facing violent crises with neighbors. Soon Moscow's new allies sought the support of Soviet military power. These nations seized on the USSR's display of long-range jet bombers in 1954–55, the launching of *Sputnik I* in October 1957, and effusive Kremlin oratory as implicit warnings to antagonists and as reasons to expect strong Soviet backing when it was needed.

11. On the events leading to the Egyptian arms deal, see Uri Ra'anan, *The USSR Arms the Third World: Case Studies in Soviet Foreign Policy* (MIT Press, 1969). On Nasser's attempts to obtain arms from the United States during this period, see Mohamed Hassanein Heikal, *The Cairo Documents: The Inside Story of Nasser and His Relationship with World Leaders, Rebels, and Statesmen* (Doubleday, 1973), pp. 31–55.

12. CIA, *Communist Aid Activities in Non-Communist Less Developed Countries, 1978*, pp. 2, 4–5.

An Era of Pretense

The USSR's new allies in the third world did not fail to notice that in crises until the late 1960s, Moscow provided them scant support beyond rhetoric. Crises over the Suez Canal (1956), Jordan (1957), Syria (1957), Lebanon (1958), the Congo (1960 and 1964), Cuba (1961), and Laos (1959–62) included small or no exhibition of Soviet military forces. The basic reasons for this relative noninvolvement probably included the strong stance taken by the United States in most of these incidents, the clearly apparent strategic nuclear inferiority of the USSR to the United States (except for a time between 1957 and 1961), and Moscow's inability to project conventional military power to places not adjacent to the USSR.

The Suez Crisis

The attack by Israel, Britain, and France on Egypt in October 1956 occasioned the first call for help to the USSR by one of the Kremlin's new associates. Mohamed Heikal has written that when Syrian President Shukri al Kuwatly, who went to Moscow during the crisis, told his hosts that they must intervene, Marshal Georgi K. Zhukov "unfolded a map in front of him and said: 'Mr. President, here is the map, look at it, how can we intervene?' "[13] Of no practical value to Cairo, Soviet support during the fighting included only condemnation of Egypt's aggressors and appeals to Nehru and Sukarno to mobilize the Bandung nations as a political force in the crisis.[14] Nor did the USSR react effectively when British and French naval units closed the eastern Mediterranean during the conflict.

Only after waiting until it was clear that the United States would not support military action against Egypt and that Britain, France, and Israel were internationally isolated did Moscow issue threats. Thus it was a week after hostilities began that Egypt's aggressors were told in letters from Soviet Premier Bulganin that they were vulnerable to "rocket weap-

---

13. Heikal, *The Cairo Documents,* pp. 111–12. The same perspective is presented by Egyptian President Anwar Sadat, *In Search of Identity: An Autobiography* (Harper and Row, 1978), pp. 145–46.

14. O. M. Smolansky, "Moscow and the Suez Crisis, 1956: A Reappraisal," *Political Science Quarterly,* vol. 80 (December 1965), p. 588.

ons," and it was several days after hostilities had ceased before Soviet "volunteers" became available. The Soviet and Czechoslovak military advisers in Egypt meanwhile had been withdrawn to Sudan.[15]

The letters from Bulganin made world headlines and were given serious consideration in London, Paris, and Tel Aviv, but they did not determine the direction of events. However, they did create enough uncertainty in London and Paris to throw Britain and France firmly into the hands of the United States, whose price for supporting them in the face of the USSR was the end of their hostilities toward Egypt.[16] Moscow did not respond to the military alert declared by the Eisenhower administration, in which U.S. Strategic Air Command aircraft were deployed to forward bases and aircraft carriers bearing nuclear bombers were moved toward closer striking range of the USSR.

Despite its limited role in determining the outcome of the Suez crisis, the Kremlin took credit as Egypt's protector and savior and its stock rose enormously among Arab peoples. President Nasser and other Arab leaders who knew what had happened were less elated; they understood that the decisive element behind Egypt's rescue had been the Eisenhower administration's strong opposition to France, Britain, and Israel. Later Nasser clearly implied that Egypt was more indebted to Washington than to Moscow, and in 1959 he said of the USSR's support during the conflict: "We had not the slightest intimation of support from any foreign state, even the Soviet Union."[17]

15. Various false reports about Soviet military activity may have been more important. For the texts of the Soviet letters that were sent to Anthony Eden, Guy Mollet, and David Ben-Gurion, see *CDSP,* vol. 8 (December 19, 1956), pp. 23–25. Also see Anthony Eden, *Full Circle* (Houghton Mifflin, 1960), pp. 620–21; Harold Macmillan, *Riding the Storm, 1956–1959* (Macmillan, 1971), pp. 165–67; Moshe Dayan, *Diary of the Sinai Campaign* (London: Weidenfeld and Nicolson, 1966), pp. 184–86; Kennett Love, *Suez: The Twice-Fought War* (McGraw-Hill, 1969), pp. 612–14; Michael Brecher, *Decisions in Israel's Foreign Policy* (Yale University Press, 1975), pp. 284–90; Jon D. Glassman, *Arms for the Arabs: The Soviet Union and War in the Middle East* (Johns Hopkins University Press, 1975), pp. 15–20; and Hans Speier, "Soviet Atomic Blackmail and the North Atlantic Alliance," *World Politics,* vol. 9 (April 1957), pp. 318–28. In my judgment, the unusual Soviet military activity in the western military districts of the USSR before and during the Suez crisis was related to developments in Eastern Europe, not the Middle East. For a different view, see Ferenc A. Váli, *Rift and Revolt in Hungary: Nationalism versus Communism* (Harvard University Press, 1961), p. 358n.

16. Smolansky, "Moscow and the Suez Crisis," p. 599.

17. Smolansky, "Moscow and the Suez Crisis," pp. 596–97; Heikal, *The Cairo Documents,* pp. 147–48; Sadat, *In Search of Identity,* p. 146; Love, *Suez,* p. 611.

The Syrian Crisis

Less than a year later the Syrian crisis erupted. In August 1957 the United States was accused of fomenting a coup against the Soviet-leaning government in Damascus, and three U.S. embassy personnel were expelled. The Eisenhower administration then supported a series of actions that appeared designed to bring about political change in Syria by another route. The actions included the massing of Turkish troops along the Syrian border, a show of force by the U.S. Sixth Fleet, and highly publicized airlifts of arms to U.S. allies in the Middle East. The crisis went through several phases and finally ended in late October.[18]

There had been no Soviet military response to the spring crisis in Jordan when allies of President Nasser in Amman had attempted to overthrow King Hussein. Moscow's support of Damascus was the first instance of Soviet political-military support of a third world nation. In late September the cruiser *Zhdanov* and destroyer *Svobodin* visited the Syrian port city of Latakia for ten days, and in October the Black Sea Fleet staged exercises. However, the timing of these actions showed Moscow's willingness to take advantage of a situation more than its willingness to undertake risks on behalf of an ally, even though Syria had moved closer to an alliance with the USSR than any other third world nation not engaged in war since the October Revolution of 1917.[19]

Parts of the U.S. Sixth Fleet appeared in the eastern Mediterranean in late August; the U.S. airlift and Turkish military activities began in early September. To these the Kremlin responded on September 10 in the form of a letter signed by Premier Bulganin to Turkish Premier Adnan Menderes. Moscow warned that should hostilities break out between Turkey and Syria, "the danger of violation of the peace would not be limited to that area alone." Turkey was risking "great calamities," the Kremlin announced. The letter asked, moreover, "how the Turks would feel if foreign troops were being concentrated on their borders."[20]

Turkey did not pay much attention to Moscow's threats because

18. Patrick Seale, *The Struggle for Syria: A Study of Post-War Arab Politics, 1945–1958* (Oxford University Press, 1965), pp. 293–306; J. M. Mackintosh, *Strategy and Tactics of Soviet Foreign Policy* (Oxford University Press, 1963), pp. 225–29; Robert Stephens, *Nasser: A Political Biography* (Penguin, 1971), pp. 266–67.

19. Walter Z. Laqueur, *The Soviet Union and the Middle East* (Praeger, 1959), p. 254.

20. Quotations are from the text, as reprinted in the *New York Times,* September 14, 1957.

Soviet troops were not concentrated on Turkish borders and because the two Soviet warships that were to visit Syria did not arrive until September 21, having first visited the Yugoslav port of Split.[21] Moreover, between the U.S. and Turkish military actions and the Soviet arrival at Latakia, King Saud of Saudi Arabia had begun to mediate the crisis. By the middle of September Saud was reported to have sent a message to President Dwight D. Eisenhower calling for U.S. moderation, and Jordan had announced its noninvolvement, declaring Syria "independent and entitled to do what she likes in her own interests."[22]

By the end of September it seemed unlikely that violence would be directed at Syria. However, on October 4 the USSR launched *Sputnik I*. Although this event caused consternation in the West, it was greeted with jubilation by Soviet allies, particularly those in the Arab world. Moscow reopened the Syrian situation, realizing the potential for propaganda and the fact that by this time the risk of war was near zero. In an interview given on October 9 to James Reston of the *New York Times,* Chairman Khrushchev threatened that Turkey "would not last one day" in the event of war. The U.S. Department of State responded immediately that the USSR "should be under no illusion that the United States . . . takes lightly its obligations under the North Atlantic Treaty."[23] Several days later, Secretary of State Dulles said that in the event of an attack on Turkey the United States would not conduct a "purely defensive operation" and that the USSR would not be treated as "a privileged sanctuary."[24] Following this exchange neither Khrushchev nor any other Soviet Politburo member made any further noteworthy statements, although Moscow sought additional Arab praise through rhetoric and military exercises carried out by forces in the Transcaucasus and by the Black Sea Fleet (which probably had been scheduled long before). When Arab appreciation was thoroughly milked, Khrushchev ended the crisis by making an unexpected grand appearance at a Turkish embassy reception in Moscow.

21. Laqueur, *The Soviet Union and the Middle East,* p. 258.

22. See Seale, *The Struggle for Syria,* p. 303.

23. Ibid., pp. 303–06; also see George S. Dragnich, "The Soviet Union's Quest for Access to Naval Facilities in Egypt Prior to the June War of 1967," in Michael MccGwire, Ken Booth, and John McDonnell, eds., *Soviet Naval Policy: Objectives and Constraints* (Praeger for the Centre for Foreign Policy Studies, Department of Political Science, Dalhousie University, Halifax, N.S., 1975), pp. 243–45; *Keesing's Contemporary Archives* (October 19–26, 1957), p. 15812.

24. *Keesing's Contemporary Archives* (October 19–26, 1957), p. 15812.

The Syrian crisis gave the Russians an opportunity "to leap to Syria's defence, to reiterate their claim to a voice in Middle Eastern affairs, and to denounce the 'interventionist fever' of 'American imperialism.' "[25] Throughout the crisis Soviet statements and military activities were timed to gain the maximum propaganda advantage with the least possible risk.

Lebanon and Jordan, 1958

The July 1958 coup in Iraq against King Faisal was warmly received by Arab nationalists and raised hopes that similar political changes were close at hand in Lebanon and Jordan. But when the United States placed 15,000 soldiers and marines in Lebanon and Britain placed 2,000 soldiers in Jordan, the Kremlin quickly recognized Washington's intentions and, well aware of U.S. strategic power and conventional military capabilities in the Mediterranean area, took pains not to act provocatively. President Nasser, who had been visiting Yugoslavia, went to Moscow for help. Khrushchev responded to his request with prudence, saying, "We are not ready for a confrontation. We are not ready for World War III." Khrushchev probably had in mind the worldwide U.S. military alert and, in particular, the U.S. Strategic Air Command. Hence the Soviet leader refused to issue an ultimatum to the United States and told Nasser that he would only increase the size of planned maneuvers on the Bulgarian-Turkish frontier, adding, "Don't depend on anything more than that."[26]

Despite harsh Soviet rhetoric directed at the United States, Moscow was careful not to do anything that would lead Washington to believe that the USSR would intervene militarily or take any other forceful action. The Soviet maneuvers, which included joint Soviet-Bulgarian operations, Soviet army and air activities in the Turkestan and Transcaucasian military districts, and Black Sea Fleet exercises, were perceived correctly in Washington as sops to Moscow's Arab allies and were ignored. In response to a letter from Khrushchev that referred to the situation as "extremely dangerous" and fraught with "unpredictable consequences," President Eisenhower replied that he was "not aware of any factual basis

25. Seale, *The Struggle for Syria*, p. 301.
26. Heikal, *The Cairo Documents*, p. 134; Mohamed Heikal, *The Sphinx and the Commissar: The Rise and Fall of Soviet Influence in the Middle East* (Harper and Row, 1978), pp. 99–100; Margaret M. Bodron, "U.S. Intervention in Lebanon —1958," *Military Review*, vol. 56 (February 1976), p. 74; *Keesing's Contemporary Archives* (July 26–August 2, 1958), p. 16308.

for your extravagantly expressed fear."[27] Both Moscow and Washington understood Soviet military activity during the crisis as nothing more than playacting.

Earlier, in May and June 1958, when tension had again begun to rise in the Middle East, Moscow had threatened to dispatch "volunteers" if the United States and Britain intervened, and in previous months Khrushchev had frequently mentioned the developments and capabilities of Soviet strategic weapons.[28] The USSR's Arab friends had been impressed by Soviet behavior during the Syrian crisis and had begun to place stock in Moscow's ability and willingness to militarily intervene on their behalf. Events like the launch of *Sputnik III* the day after the United States had announced a temporary doubling of its U.S. Marine force in the Mediterranean could only have encouraged these allies. When Soviet naval units had moved westward through the Baltic in June while U.S. and British naval units were showing their flags in the eastern Mediterranean, the Egyptian news media had presented the Soviet action as one "to maintain the balance of power"—an effective counter to the Western naval forces in the Mediterranean. Actually, the Soviet naval action had been related to a Northern Fleet exercise.[29]

The U.S. and British landings in Lebanon and Jordan had a sobering effect on President Nasser and others in the Middle East sharing his views.[30] Moscow's inability to prevent these interventions was a bitter disappointment and forced radical Arab leaders to recognize the global military power of the United States.[31]

The Congo, Laos, Indonesia, and North Yemen

Thereafter Soviet relations with Egypt declined, and the cold war shifted to Africa and Southeast Asia. Premier Patrice Lumumba was Moscow's chosen instrument when the Congo crisis broke out in July 1960, following the mutiny by the Force Publique against its Belgian officer corps and the secession of the mineral-rich provinces of Katanga and Kasai. The Soviet Union's first use of transport aircraft outside the bloc

27. *Keesing's Contemporary Archives* (August 16–23, 1958), pp. 16341–42.
28. *New York Times*, June 20, 1958; Arnold L. Horelick and Myron Rush, *Strategic Power and Soviet Foreign Policy* (University of Chicago Press, 1966), pp. 42–49.
29. Dragnich, "The Soviet Union's Quest," p. 246.
30. Sadat, *In Search of Identity*, p. 153.
31. Dragnich, "The Soviet Union's Quest," p. 16.

area in a crisis took place when the Kremlin provided several dozen aircraft (and perhaps 100 trucks and 200 technicians) to Lumumba.[32]

Moscow ran no risk in this action, which was carried out under the guise of international aid to the beleaguered Congo. Many other nations, including the United States, also provided military support to hold that newly independent country together. However, the Soviet position was weak. When Lumumba was ousted from power in September 1960 and the United Nations Command closed the Leopoldville airport to prevent Soviet aircraft from flying troops loyal to Lumumba back to the capital, Moscow was virtually helpless to do anything to support its client. Lumumba demanded that UN forces leave the Congo and threatened that if they did not, Soviet forces would "brutally expel the UN from our Republic."[33] The deposed premier also asked the USSR to intervene against his internal opponents and the secessionist provinces. Moscow ignored these appeals. In December 1960, after Lumumba was taken prisoner in the Congo, UN units again prevented Soviet aircraft from flying supplies to the Lumumbist forces in the Stanleyville area.

The Soviet Union also transported arms by air to Laos beginning in December 1960 and continuing with stops and starts into 1962, first to the Kong Le-Souvanna Phouma government and then to the Pathet Lao and North Vietnamese in Laos. Despite the Kremlin's desire to restrict Peking's influence in Southeast Asia and to weaken U.S. influence in the third world, Soviet leaders in this instance did not seem willing to raise the stakes and risk deeper involvement. When Moscow initiated the use of Soviet transport aircraft, it took pains to communicate that "whereas two or three months ago the U.S. government made some effort to camouflage its . . . actions in Laos, the United States . . . has recently become to all intents and purposes a party to military operations . . . against . . . the government of Laos."[34] After the Kennedy administration threatened military intervention in Laos in April 1961, the USSR supported the establishment of a cease-fire. And when 5,000 U.S. soldiers and marines and an accompanying aircraft carrier task force were sent to Thailand in 1962, the only hope Khrushchev could offer to Hanoi and

32. Colin Legum, *Congo Disaster* (Penguin, 1961), pp. 106, 141.
33. Ernest W. Lefever, *Crisis in the Congo: A United Nations Force in Action* (Brookings Institution, 1965), p. 46; *New York Times,* January 1, 1961; Brian Urquhart, *Hammarskjold* (Knopf, 1972), p. 444; "Evolution de La Crise Congolaise, de Septembre 1960 a Avril 1961," *Chronique de Politique Étrangère,* vol. 14 (Septembre–Novembre 1961), p. 658.
34. *New York Times,* December 12, 1960, and November 7, 1962; *Pravda,* December 14, 1960 (in *CDSP,* vol. 12, January 11, 1961, p. 17).

the Pathet Lao was that "the Americans may fight fifteen years if they want to, but it will not help."[35]

Also in 1962 Soviet military men were active in Indonesia, supporting President Sukarno's campaign to wrest control of West Irian (Dutch West New Guinea) from the Netherlands. As a leader of the new bloc of nonaligned nations, Sukarno had been assiduously cultivated by Stalin's successors after Moscow's shift in policy toward the third world. Moscow had lavished high-level official visits, trade, aid, and armaments on Djakarta and had not backed away when a major rebellion in West Sumatra broke out in 1958. Sukarno's campaign against the insurgency had been supported by Soviet arms deliveries that included fighter and bomber aircraft and an assortment of naval vessels; a naval visit by warships from the Soviet Pacific Fleet; economic aid; and, in February 1960, a visit by Nikita Khrushchev.[36]

Moscow felt strongly about supporting Indonesia in the confrontation over West Irian. In early 1962 Sukarno had adopted a "two-camp" concept of international relations. Among "newly emerging forces" were Indonesia and other underdeveloped lands, as well as the socialist nations; opposing their interests were the "old established forces"—the West.[37] Sukarno had also supported the Indonesian Communist party (PKI). When Moscow learned that Indonesia might be defeated in the conflict with the Dutch after violence had begun, the Kremlin, we are told by Khrushchev, provided Sukarno with the services of Soviet pilots and submarine officers.[38] However, the Kremlin knew that the United States did not support The Hague in this conflict. In fact, Washington was then attempting to persuade Sukarno to slow his movement toward, if not reverse, alignment with the East and was pressing the Dutch to capitulate.[39]

35. Quoted by David K. Hall, "The Laotian War of 1962 and Indo-Pakistani War of 1971," in Barry M. Blechman and Stephen S. Kaplan, *Force without War: U.S. Armed Forces as a Political Instrument* (Brookings Institution, 1978), p. 152.

36. On Soviet-Indonesian relations, see Justus M. van der Kroef, "The Soviet Union and Southeast Asia," in Kanet, *The Soviet Union and the Developing Nations*, pp. 99–101; and Justus M. van der Kroef, "Soviet and Chinese Influence in Indonesia," in Alvin Z. Rubinstein, ed., *Soviet and Chinese Influence in the Third World* (Praeger, 1975), pp. 54–58.

37. Quoted in Guy J. Pauker, "The Soviet Challenge in Indonesia," *Foreign Affairs*, vol. 40 (July 1962), p. 613.

38. Nikita S. Khrushchev, *Khrushchev Remembers: The Last Testament* (Little, Brown, 1974), p. 327; also see Ide Anak Agung Gide, *Twenty Years: Indonesian Foreign Policy, 1945–1963* (The Hague: Mouton, 1973), pp. 294–98, 395.

39. Arthur M. Schlesinger, Jr., *A Thousand Days: John F. Kennedy in the White House* (Houghton Mifflin, 1965), pp. 532–36.

Nevertheless, the Kremlin sought to keep its military involvement secret. Moscow's objective was not to visibly threaten The Hague with Soviet military power but to bolster Sukarno's forces and reinforce Indonesian political confidence. The Russians did not want Washington to view the situation as one of East-West confrontation. When the Indonesians leaked word to the United States of Soviet assistance, Moscow worried about the exposure of its weak military position in Southeast Asia.[40]

Still another operation in this era of minimal Soviet involvement in the third world was a small airlift of Egyptian troops to North Yemen after civil war broke out following the coup and establishment of a Republican government in Sanaa in September 1962.[41] Although the Kremlin quickly acceded to Cairo's request for air transport, Nasser apparently withheld the request until the Cuban missile crisis had ended, so that Moscow would be able to claim that it was supporting a regime in power rather than lending military support to insurgents. Indeed, the airlift may have taken place after the United States recognized the new government in Sanaa in mid-December. The USSR's support of Egypt and the Republicans against the Royalists and their patron, Saudi Arabia, a U.S. ally— despite the uncertain relationship between Moscow and Cairo—gave new weight to the perception of Soviet identity with Arab nationalism, a perspective of considerable value to the Kremlin in its relations with Cairo and other Arab capitals.

Between these involvements in 1962 and the 1967 Middle East war, Moscow used Soviet armed forces to support non-Communist governments or national liberation movements only once: to airlift small arms to Congolese insurgents in December 1964. The flights were reportedly made from Algeria and Egypt to the Sudan, where the rebels operated after they were driven out of Stanleyville.[42] Moscow ended its minimal effort quickly when it proved futile.

Of Soviet political-military support of third world nationalism in the late 1950s and early 1960s, the following may be said: (1) Moscow lacked strategic confidence in the face of the United States and, militarily, did nothing of serious consequence during major crises; (2) the ability of the USSR to project conventional military power into the third world was

40. Khrushchev, *Khrushchev Remembers*, p. 327.

41. Heikal, *The Sphinx and the Commissar*, p. 118.

42. *New York Times*, December 6 and 7, 1964. It is possible that this effort was an entirely Arab-African affair.

minimal; and (3) the USSR's most practical contribution was to provide friends in power with small transport airlifts.

Forward Deployment and Challenge

Small task forces of Soviet surface combatants briefly ventured into the Mediterranean in the mid-1950s, and in 1958 Soviet submarines began to use a support facility in Vlonë, Albania. This regular access to a Mediterranean port was lost in 1961, however, as a casualty of the Sino-Soviet rift. Also at this time, the small number of surface combatants present became erratic. The USSR initiated a continuous naval presence in the Mediterranean in 1964 and by 1966 maintained an average of twelve ships there.[43] These vessels were more capable than Soviet warships deployed in earlier years, both in ship-to-ship and ship-to-air combat. Less visible was the development in these years of a Soviet naval infantry and airborne capability.

Russia has always been a great land power, and for the last several hundred years it has also maintained one of the world's largest navies. After the Second World War Stalin continued to support a diffuse naval construction program including large balanced fleets of heavy and light cruisers, destroyers, submarines, and, later, aircraft carriers.[44] When Stalin died this program was in midstream; for example, the carriers had not yet been built. Nikita Khrushchev reversed Stalin's course dramatically, firing Admiral N. G. Kuznetsov, commander in chief of the navy, and scrapping or delaying plans for procuring surface warships and submarines. Khrushchev said later: "Gone were the days when the heavy cruiser and the battleship were the backbone of a navy. It still made a beautiful picture when the crew lined up smartly at attention on the deck of a cruiser to receive an admiral or call on a friendly foreign port. But such ceremonies were now just an elegant luxury. . . . So we relegated our surface fleet to an auxiliary function, primarily for coastal defense."[45]

43. Robert G. Weinland, "Soviet Transits of the Turkish Straits, 1945–70," in Michael MccGwire, ed., *Soviet Naval Developments: Capability and Context* (Praeger for the Centre for Foreign Policy Studies, Department of Political Science, Dalhousie University, Halifax, N.S., 1973), pp. 335–38; Robert G. Weinland, "Land Support for Naval Forces: Egypt and the Soviet Escadra, 1962–1976," *Survival*, vol. 20 (March–April 1978), p. 74.

44. Robert Waring Herrick, *Soviet Naval Strategy: Fifty Years of Theory and Practice* (United States Naval Institute, 1968), pp. 59–65.

45. Khrushchev, *Khrushchev Remembers*, pp. 30–31.

Believing that the principal threat to the USSR was surprise nuclear attack and constrained by other budgetary demands, Khrushchev and his new navy chief, Admiral Sergei G. Gorshkov, supervised a revamped construction program that focused heavily on nuclear-propelled, missile-armed submarines and light surface warships and on land-based naval aviation. The increased range of U.S. carrier-borne aircraft and the U.S. deployment of ballistic missile submarines (SSBNs) prompted the forward deployment of the Soviet navy, which had been decided on in principle by the early 1960s. Concern about U.S. submarine development also led to the *Moskva*-class helicopter-carrier program. Also in the early 1960s, Admiral Gorshkov convinced the Kremlin that a much larger surface navy was necessary after all, to counter the threat presented by seaborne U.S. nuclear strike forces. So when the USSR did begin to deploy its navy forward in the mid-1960s, its forces were increasingly modern and well-equipped to deter and defend against U.S. nuclear attack, which was their essential mission.[46]

The USSR also reconstituted a naval infantry force in the early 1960s. In the mid-1950s Khrushchev had disbanded the navy's amphibious landing units (comparable to the U.S. Marine Corps) and had virtually eliminated sea-based ground forces. Their reinstatement a decade later was partly a result of "the personal intervention of Admiral Gorshkov (himself an amphibious commander during World War II), a low-keyed 'revolt of the admirals' against the downgrading of the Soviet Navy's role in amphibious warfare, linkage between the Naval Infantry and Sino-Soviet and Warsaw Pact relations, a Soviet trend toward strategic flexibility, changed Soviet views on the utility of amphibious operations in the nuclear era, and Soviet ambitions in the Third World."[47]

The Soviet naval infantry included about 6,000 men in the mid-1960s

46. On naval planning and procurement during the Khrushchev era, see Herrick, *Soviet Naval Strategy*, pp. 67–79; and Michael MccGwire, "Naval Power and Soviet Oceans Policy," in *Soviet Oceans Development*, Committee Print, prepared for the Senate Committee on Commerce and National Ocean Policy Study (Government Printing Office, 1976), pp. 81–85. For a concise listing of the delivery dates and capabilities of Soviet warship classes and submarines during the 1950s and 1960s, see Michael MccGwire, "The Structure of the Soviet Navy," in MccGwire, ed., *Soviet Naval Developments*, pp. 151–58.

47. Charles C. Pritchard, "Soviet Amphibious Force Projection," in Michael MccGwire and John McDonnell, eds., *Soviet Naval Influence: Domestic and Foreign Dimensions* (Praeger for the Centre for Foreign Policy Studies, Department of Political Science, Dalhousie University, Halifax, N.S., 1977), p. 250.

and grew to 12,000 by the end of the decade.[48] In the late 1970s, regimental units and amphibious lift ships were assigned to each of the USSR's four fleets (two regiments were serving with the Pacific fleet). These elements participated in regular Soviet naval exercises and occasionally were deployed outside of home waters. The units' great shortcoming in carrying out distant operations was always a lack of accompanying air support. (The *Moskva-* and *Kiev*-class carriers have been equipped principally for antisubmarine warfare.)

Soviet airborne forces, always a part of the Soviet army, were fully maintained during Stalin's rule and were not cut back during the Khrushchev years, although the USSR's military airlift capability remained limited throughout the 1950s. The introduction into the air force inventory of the AN-12 medium transport in the early 1960s and then the AN-22 heavy lift aircraft in about 1967 improved Moscow's ability to quickly transport ground forces and large amounts of military matériel long distances.[49] During the 1960s the Soviet Union also placed greater emphasis on airborne operations in Soviet exercises and procurement of new models of air mobile artillery, armored vehicles, and antitank and other weapons.[50] However, the lack of tactical air support in noncontiguous areas was a severe military deficiency when airborne units or transport aircraft were expecting violent resistance.

In many instances, however, Moscow could conclude that the likelihood of Soviet armed forces units being fired on, even in conflicts, was small or nonexistent since friendly territory could be overflown and landing areas were secure, or other nations did not want to antagonize the USSR because of its nuclear forces, ability to interdict shipping, and the possibility of at least the temporary forward deployment of Soviet fighter aircraft. When only equipment was being airlifted, the risk of violent resistance was minimal. Real danger to Soviet military men was expected only when they were ordered to take part in actual military operations.

48. Thomas W. Wolfe, *Soviet Power and Europe, 1945–1970* (Johns Hopkins Press, 1970), p. 450.

49. Graham B. Turbiville, Jr., "Soviet Airborne Troops," in MccGwire and McDonnell, *Soviet Naval Influence*, p. 283. Also see Robert P. Berman, *Soviet Air Power in Transition* (Brookings Institution, 1978), pp. 34–35.

50. Wolfe, *Soviet Power and Europe, 1945–1970*, p. 449; M. Gareyev, "Ever Guarding the Achievements of October," *Voyenno-Istoricheskiy Zhurnal* [*Military Historical Journal*]. Reprinted in *Soviet Press: Selected Translations,* distributed by the Directorate of Soviet Affairs, U.S. Air Force Intelligence Service (April 1978), p. 110.

Also in the 1960s, Soviet military thinkers began to question the assumption that any violent conflict between the United States and the USSR would inevitably escalate into nuclear war. "Obviously," wrote Colonel-General Nikolai A. Lomov, "the probability of the development of limited war into world nuclear war, in the event of the involvement in local conflicts of nuclear powers, is always great and, under *certain conditions,* it may become inevitable."[51] One implication of this perspective was that there were circumstances in which escalation to world war was *not* inevitable. Marshal M. V. Zakharov's perspective contained a similar inference: "Escalation is more likely with the participation in the local war of states having nuclear weapons, and especially when the vitally important interests of these states are enfringed upon in such a war."[52]

In the last (1968) edition of *Soviet Military Strategy,* Marshal V. D. Sokolovsky wrote that the "USSR will render, when it is necessary, military support . . . to people [third world nations] subject to imperialist aggression."[53] Clearly the marshal and his colleagues were not welcoming an opportunity for nuclear conflict; nor could the reference have been meant to refer only to Soviet military assistance, which had been given to third world nations for more than six years before this book's first publication in 1962. The Russians concluded that they could now provide much more in the way of military support to their third world allies without necessarily having to engage the United States in combat.[54] Departure from the idea that the USSR could choose only between capitulation and nuclear war enabled Moscow to respond more flexibly to developments in the third world.

These changes in capabilities, force deployments, and attitudes about conflict between the superpowers created an environment more conducive to Soviet military involvement in foreign conflicts than had existed in the past. The June war marked a major change in Soviet willingness to use armed forces to support third world nations. Moscow's strong rela-

51. This paragraph represents the research and analysis of James McConnell, "Doctrine and Capabilities," in Bradford Dismukes and James McConnell, eds., *Soviet Naval Diplomacy* (Pergamon, 1979), p. 24. The quotation is from William R. Kintner and Harriet Fast Scott, eds. and trans., *The Nuclear Revolution in Soviet Military Affairs* (University of Oklahoma Press, 1968), p. 156; emphasis added. McConnell uses a slightly different translation.

52. Quoted in McConnell, "Doctrine and Capabilities," p. 24.

53. *Soviet Military Strategy,* 3d ed. (Crane, Russak, 1968), p. 184. Also see Wolfe, *Soviet Power and Europe, 1945–1970,* pp. 451–56.

54. George E. Hudson, "Soviet Naval Doctrine and Soviet Politics, 1953–1976," *World Politics,* vol. 29 (October 1976), p. 109.

tionship with Egypt, Syria, and other Arab nations and Israel's preemptive attack on Egypt and Syria in June 1967 brought the Kremlin over a hurdle; afterward the USSR began using military power to influence events on the Horn of Africa and in the Persian Gulf and then in South Asia and West Africa.

The June War

Between early May 1967 and the end of the 1967 war in the Middle East on June 10, the number of Soviet surface combatants in the Mediterranean increased from three to thirteen, and the number of Soviet naval vessels there increased to approximately forty ships. During the conflict Soviet warships—for the first time in a crisis—took up positions extremely close to U.S. carrier groups and to a British carrier force also in the Mediterranean. At one point Soviet ships also reportedly harassed a U.S. aircraft carrier task force. On the last day of the war, when Israeli forces moved toward Damascus, Premier Aleksei Kosygin warned that if the Israelis continued to advance, the Soviet Union would take "necessary actions, including military."[55]

Although Soviet behavior was generally circumspect and restrained in light of the enormous disaster that befell the Arab side in the June war, Soviet actions did show that the USSR was willing to consider a combat deployment during a crisis distant from the USSR and to counter a major U.S. military presence. What Moscow might have done if the Israelis had actually moved on Damascus will never be known. However, in contrast to President Eisenhower's virtual dismissal of Soviet threats during the Suez crisis, the Johnson administration viewed Premier Kosygin's message gravely and believed that Soviet airborne units would have intervened if the Israelis had continued toward Damascus.[56]

Nevertheless, the general view in the immediate aftermath of this conflict was that the value of U.S. aid to Israel had been much greater than

55. Lyndon Baines Johnson, *The Vantage Point: Perspectives of the Presidency, 1963–1969* (Holt, Rinehart and Winston, 1971), p. 302; Jonathan Trumbull Howe, *Multicrises: Sea Power and Global Politics in the Missile Age* (MIT Press, 1971), p. 117.

56. Anthony R. Wells, "The June 1967 Arab-Israeli War," in Dismukes and McConnell, eds., *Soviet Naval Diplomacy*, p. 166. It has been suggested that the Kosygin message, coming as it did at the end of the conflict, was perhaps no more than a grandstand attempt to recoup lost Soviet prestige. See Glassman, *Arms for the Arabs*, pp. 57–58.

the value of Soviet aid to the Arabs. While President Nasser found it expedient to blame the Arab defeat on U.S. support of Israel, going so far as to say that U.S. aircraft took part in the initial air strikes, it was more widely observed that Moscow did not have the ability to prevent or in any case permitted its clients to suffer major losses of territory and an overwhelming political disaster. This image of the USSR did not endure, however.

The USSR followed up its actions in the 1967 war by not immediately withdrawing the additional forces it had sent to the Mediterranean, increasing the size of its permanent naval deployment there, sending a squadron of TU-16 bombers to Egypt on a visit, sending several thousand Soviet advisers to rebuild the Egyptian and Syrian armed forces, and resupplying Egypt and Syria with arms. By early July Soviet AN-12 aircraft had made approximately 350 flights to the Middle East.[57] Even more important, the Kremlin continued to intervene militarily on behalf of these allies.

In July 1967 Soviet warships began a series of visits to Egypt's port cities of Alexandria and Port Said, seemingly to deter Israeli attacks, and in October, when an Egyptian *Komar*-class patrol boat supplied by the Russians sank the Israeli destroyer *Eilat,* Soviet ships paid an immediate visit to Port Said to demonstrate support for Egypt and to deter Israeli retaliatory action. In fact, the Soviet navy established a virtually permanent presence in Egyptian waters.

The sinking of the *Eilat* was perceived by many as a dramatic demonstration of the capabilities of Soviet warships and military technology. The U.S. presence in the Mediterranean area lost some of its impact as questions arose about the vulnerability of Sixth Fleet carriers and other U.S. surface warships to missile-equipped Soviet cruisers and destroyers. Moscow increased its prestige even higher in December by sending another squadron of TU-16 bombers to Egypt, where they flew over Cairo and carried out live bombing demonstrations.[58]

The USSR's military image in the Middle East was also boosted by the establishment in Egypt of extensive shore facilities for replenishing and

57. Richard B. Remnek, "The Politics of Soviet Access to Naval Support Facilities in the Mediterranean," in Dismukes and McConnell, eds., *Soviet Naval Diplomacy,* p. 388.

58. Glassman, *Arms for the Arabs,* pp. 66–68; Lawrence L. Whetten, *The Canal War: Four-Power Conflict in the Middle East* (MIT Press, 1974), p. 61; Dragnich, "The Soviet Union's Quest," p. 267; *Middle East Record, 1967,* pp. 25–26.

repairing Soviet ships and submarines and as bases for patrol and reconnaissance aircraft. As explanation for this new Soviet-Egyptian relationship, President Nasser of Egypt reportedly had concluded that

it was to the advantage of the whole non-aligned world for Russia's naval presence in the Mediterranean to be strengthened. He hoped that some sort of parity might be reached between the Soviet fleet and the American Sixth Fleet. By this means the Mediterranean would cease to be an American lake, and if, bearing in mind the claim once made by [Prime Minister of Israel Levi] Eshkol that the American navy in the Mediterranean was Israel's strategic reserve, Egypt and other Arab governments tried at a later date to urge a reduction in America's naval strength there, they would have some cards in their hands. Balanced reductions by both superpowers would have some attraction for the Americans, whereas as long as they enjoyed a virtual monopoly there was no inducement for them to cut down.[59]

These developments fostered a new perspective, decidedly less generous to the U.S. military presence and more favorable to the Soviet presence. In the Middle East, American military dominance was no longer taken for granted. Instead, the question was asked whether U.S. forces could defend themselves in a conflict, much less provide adequate support to allies and friends as these forces had done in the past. The image of a balance of power between American and Soviet forces developed, misleading as the term *balance* may be in relation to the missions of the two forces and their actual capabilities.

Egypt, Syria, and other Soviet friends were delighted with the USSR's new image, which they helped to cultivate by publicizing the theme that Soviet military forces were a deterrent to aggressive U.S. behavior and that a balance did, in fact, exist. For example, two days after the 1969 coup in Libya, Tripoli radio announced that what was otherwise regarded as a coincidental Soviet naval presence nearby had deterred British intervention on behalf of the deposed regime.[60] Israel also worried about these new perceptions, although Israelis did not seem to doubt that U.S. forces in the region were still the strongest.[61]

---

59. Mohamed Heikal, *The Road to Ramadan* (Ballantine, 1975), p. 47.

60. James Cable, *Gunboat Diplomacy: Political Applications of Limited Naval Force* (Praeger for the Institute for Strategic Studies, 1971), pp. 146–47.

61. See report on statement by Deputy Prime Minister Yigal Allon in the Knesset, October 30, 1968. U.S. Foreign Broadcast Information Service (FBIS), *Daily Report: Middle East and North Africa* (October 31, 1968), p. H1.

Air Support and the Defense of Egypt

While the Soviet naval presence in the Mediterranean was being built up further and gave Egypt and Syria some protection against Israel, Soviet airmen became directly engaged in fighting in North Yemen. At the Khartoum Conference in August 1967 President Nasser agreed to withdraw the Egyptian servicemen fighting on the side of the Republicans, and King Faisal of Saudi Arabia promised to curtail aid to the Royalists. When the fighting did not end, the USSR gave the Republicans in November 1967 the assistance of several Soviet combat aircraft and pilots, and armaments and other supplies were airlifted to Hodeida. Soviet military advisers were sent to aid Republican ground troops.[62]

Similar Soviet interventions apparently occurred in 1970–71 in Sudan and Ceylon and in 1973–74 in Iraq.[63] Each of these efforts was aimed at helping a government in power suppress a domestic insurgency. In Sudan, Soviet tactical aircraft and helicopter pilots and ground advisers reportedly took an active role against non-Arab separatists. Soviet-piloted aircraft and helicopters also appear to have been sent to Ceylon in support of the Bandaranaike government's suppression of a rebellion by the militant People's Liberation Front. In Iraq, Soviet bomber and reconnaissance aircraft aided the effort against the Kurdish minority.[64]

In January 1970 the USSR provided Egypt with a complete air defense system, which by the end of the year included the services of more than 200 pilots and 12,000–15,000 missile crewmen. These personnel manned approximately 150 fighter aircraft and between 75 and 85 surface-to-air missile (SAM) sites and took control of six airfields in Egypt. What prompted this involvement was the Egyptian armed forces' inability to prevent deep penetration bombing raids by Israeli aircraft and the

62. *Keesing's Contemporary Archives* (February 24–March 2, 1968), p. 22548; *New York Times,* December 13, 1967; Wolfe, *Soviet Power and Europe, 1945–1970,* p. 341; William J. Durch, Michael D. Davidchik, and Abram N. Shulsky, "Other Soviet Interventionary Forces—Military Transport Aviation and Airborne Troops," in Dismukes and McConnell, *Soviet Naval Diplomacy,* pp. 336–51. Syrian and perhaps other non-Soviet personnel appeared to replace Soviet pilots within a few months. *New York Times,* March 15, 1968.

63. It is unclear whether Soviet pilots took part in fighting between North Yemen and South Yemen in late 1972. *New York Times,* October 7, 1972; *Baltimore Sun,* October 4, 1972.

64. *New York Times,* January 5 and February 22, 1971, and October 30, 1973; *Washington Post,* December 17, 1974; International Institute for Strategic Studies (IISS), *Strategic Survey, 1971* (London: IISS, 1972), p. 89.

Kremlin's recognition that both the political survival of President Nasser and the Soviet position in Egypt and the Arab world were at risk. From another perspective, Egypt's plight appeared to offer Moscow the opportunity to heighten its influence in the Middle East. By mid-1972, when President Anwar Sadat ordered the expulsion of Soviet operators and advisers, the number of Soviet personnel in Egypt had risen to 21,000.[65]

Soviet army missile crews were almost certainly responsible for shooting down several Israeli planes. By mid-April 1970, Egypt's strengthened defenses and the fact that Russians rather than Egyptians would have to be fired on led Israel to end its deep penetration raids. Thereafter the Israeli air force attacked Egyptian ground targets only as far as the Suez Canal battle area. Egyptian military men also showed greater confidence and improved tactical abilities after the Soviet presence was established.[66] Meanwhile, the Nixon administration, although it perceived Soviet aid to Egypt as a challenge, did not back up Israel to offset the USSR's increased support of Egypt.[67] In March Washington decided to postpone the delivery of F-4 Phantom jets to Israel, partly to slow down the arms race in the Middle East but also to avoid strengthening Egypt's dependence on the USSR. Secretary of State Henry Kissinger was anxious about the growing Soviet military presence in Egypt and how it would affect the utility of American military power in the Mediterranean area.[68]

Moscow might have stopped exposing Soviet military men to air combat after several Russian-piloted aircraft were shot down in late July 1970. The cease-fire in the Middle East in early August and then the forward movement on Egyptian territory of SAM sites left this unclear. What Moscow did not expect was the attitude of President Sadat, who succeeded Nasser after his death in October 1970. Sadat was less grateful for what the Soviet military had done for Egypt's defense than he was forceful in demanding that the USSR provide Egypt with more armaments. In July 1972 Moscow discovered that it had merely satisfied Cairo's needs momentarily rather than forged a strong alliance with Egypt.

65. Heikal, *The Road to Ramadan*, pp. 78–84, 177–78; Sadat, *In Search of Identity*, p. 197; IISS, *Strategic Survey, 1970*, pp. 47–48; Durch, Davidchik, and Shulsky, "Other Soviet Interventionary Forces."

66. Heikal, *The Road to Ramadan*, p. 85; Whetten, *The Canal War*, pp. 95–96.

67. Richard M. Nixon, *RN: The Memoirs of Richard Nixon* (Grosset and Dunlap, 1978), p. 479.

68. Marvin Kalb and Bernard Kalb, *Kissinger* (Little, Brown, 1974), pp. 192–93; Nixon, *Memoirs*, p. 480.

The Ali Sabry affair (Ali Sabry had been accused of an attempt to overthrow Sadat), the Communist-attempted coup in Sudan in 1971, and the Russians' heavy-handed dealing with Egypt in its time of need infuriated Sadat and other Egyptians who had great national pride and who opposed increased Soviet influence in the Arab world generally. Although Soviet warships were allowed continued access to Egyptian ports for several years thereafter, in 1972 Cairo took over the uncompleted Soviet naval base at Mersa Matruh and ordered the withdrawal from Egypt of the Soviet naval reconnaissance, antisubmarine, and air-to-surface missile launching aircraft, despite the importance of these planes to Soviet naval operations in the Mediterranean.

Soviet Political-Military Thinking in the Early 1970s

In March 1971 the Twenty-fourth Congress of the Communist Party of the Soviet Union convened in Moscow. Restored control in Czechoslovakia, improved Soviet relations with the United States, West Germany, France, and other North Atlantic Treaty Organization (NATO) nations, military stabilization of the Sino-Soviet border, the Communist victory foreseen in South Vietnam, and increased Soviet strategic and conventional military capabilities all contributed to Soviet aggressiveness in the third world. The United States had seemed to be starting to accept parity in strategic armaments and had withdrawn 100,000 U.S. troops from Europe in the 1960s to meet Southeast Asian needs. This was followed by gradual U.S. withdrawal from South Vietnam. U.S. warships built during World War II were then being retired en masse, and U.S. defense budget authorizations for strategic, general purpose, and mobility forces were rapidly declining. The Kremlin may have seen in these developments a weakening of U.S. willingness to intervene in the third world and thus a chance for the USSR to gain new positions there.

In early 1971 the Soviet position in the third world was improving. Close relationships were being developed with India and Ceylon; the USSR had become more popular in Africa; Soviet prestige in the Middle East was high; and the Allende government was in power in Chile. This state of affairs contrasted with that of the mid-1960s, when the USSR's position was weak in Africa and uncertain in the Middle East and South Asia. During this time there were also U.S. military interventions in Southeast Asia and the Dominican Republic, and the Soviet Union suffered important setbacks in Indonesia, Algeria, and Brazil.

Leonid Brezhnev reported to the Twenty-fourth Party Congress that "imperialism is being subjected to ever greater pressure by the forces which have sprung from the national liberation struggle." He said that "quite a few countries" in Asia and Africa "have taken the noncapitalist way of development," while in Latin America "great changes" were perceived to be "taking place in a number of . . . countries" (Chile, Peru, and Bolivia).[69] At the Twenty-third Party Congress in 1966 Brezhnev had affirmed only a very vague "continued all-round support of the people's struggle for final liberation from colonial and neo-colonial oppression."[70] In 1971 the Soviet party leader promised to pursue "a line in international affairs which helps further to invigorate the worldwide anti-imperialist struggle" and "the active defense of peace."[71]

The marshals of the USSR remained cautious about (1) trumpeting this renewed political confidence about developments in the third world and (2) the greater openness within high party circles to increasing Soviet involvement there. Soviet Defense Minister Grechko discussed developments in the third world only perfunctorily in a book published after the congress. The "national liberation movement" was said to be "growing and broadening," and a "significant number of states were perceived to be on "the non-capitalist path of development." To these states Grechko offered in writing at this time only "the sympathy of all the progressive forces."[72] In discussions of airborne and air transport units, no suggestion was made about sending them to formerly colonial lands. Given its context, nothing could have been made of the statement that Soviet military aviation could ferry "troops and heavy military matériel great distances."[73] About the navy Marshal Grechko said, "It honorably represents our nation on the expanses of the world ocean and has repeatedly demonstrated its increased combat capabilities with great conviction."[74] General of the Army A. A. Yepishev, head of the Main Political Administration of the armed forces, did relate Soviet military power

69. *24th Congress of the Communist Party of the Soviet Union: March 30–April 9, 1971, Documents* (Moscow: Novosti Press Agency, 1971), pp. 23, 25.

70. *23rd Congress of the Communist Party of the Soviet Union* (Moscow: Novosti Press Agency, 1966), p. 41.

71. *24th Congress*, pp. 29, 36.

72. A. A. Grechko, *On Guard for Peace and the Building of Communism*, JPRS Report 54602 (U.S. Department of Commerce, National Technical Information Service, 1971), p. 8.

73. Ibid., p. 35.

74. Ibid., p. 37.

to political change in underdeveloped nations explicitly, in an article published in May 1972. However, he emphasized the significance of newly capable Soviet forces to the environment of the third world, not the active use of military units to achieve specific objectives. Yepishev wrote:

It must be seen that socialism's military might objectively assists the successful development of the revolutionary, liberation movements and that it hinders the exportation of imperialist counterrevolution. In this lies one of the most important manifestations of the external function of the armed forces of a socialist state.[75]

Navy Commander in Chief Gorshkov, though, seized on the thoughts drawn out at the Twenty-fourth Party Congress to argue that the Soviet navy could support Soviet interests in distant lands in times of peace as well as war. In February 1972 the Soviet navy journal *Morskoi Sbornik* began a series of eleven articles by Admiral Gorshkov called "Navies in War *and Peace*." The Soviet navy was said to be "making a significant contribution to improving mutual relations between states and peoples and to strengthening the international influence of the Soviet Union."[76] One article, "Navies as Instruments of Peacetime Imperialism," informed readers that the navy, "while representing a formidable force in war . . . has always been an instrument of policy of the imperialist states and an important support for diplomacy in peacetime."[77] Gorshkov wrote, "It would be difficult to find an area on our planet where U.S. leaders have not used their pet instrument of foreign policy—the Navy—against the progressive forces of the peoples of various countries." The Soviet navy, he concluded, "is a powerful factor in the creation of favorable conditions for the building of Socialism and Communism, for the active defense of peace, and for strengthening international security."[78]

In the minds of Soviet naval leaders—"Navies in War and Peace" is assumed by many to have been a group effort—the use of sea power as a political instrument did not detract from the USSR's larger responsibility for national defense. Naval diplomacy was accepted as an important

75. Quoted by Foy D. Kohler in *The Soviet Union: Internal Dynamics of Foreign Policy, Present and Future,* Hearings before the Subcommittee on Europe and the Middle East of the House Committee on International Relations (GPO, 1978), p. 34.

76. Sergei G. Gorshkov, *Red Star Rising at Sea,* trans. Theodore A. Neely, Jr. (United States Naval Institute, 1974), p. 119; emphasis added.

77. Ibid., p. 115.

78. Ibid., pp. 117, 134.

mission finally able to be fulfilled as a result of the Soviet navy's increased capability. These articles did not argue for more ships and resources for the navy. The series intended to describe how a navy can advance state interests in peacetime by its ability "to vividly demonstrate the economic and military might of a country beyond its borders, . . . to suddenly appear close to the shores of different countries, . . . to support 'friendly states,' " and "to exert pressure on potential enemies without the direct employment of weaponry."[79]

One issue of debate in the West following the publication of these articles was whether they represented naval advocacy (an attempt to influence discussion among nonnaval political authorities about the navy's requirements and roles in war and peacetime) or "what the Soviets refer to as a 'concrete expression of doctrine,' i.e., a work rationalizing particular tenets of military doctrine that apply to the navy."[80] About the navy's role as a political instrument in peacetime, it is also possible that Gorshkov was merely trying to educate and lead an open-minded audience inclined to support policies also favored by Soviet naval leaders. From this perspective, Gorshkov was not so much arguing as he was attempting to show the way.

Soviet military and civilian intellectuals were also thinking about the use of armed forces as a political instrument. In a study conducted in 1971–72 under the auspices of the Institute of World Economics and International Relations of the Academy of Sciences of the USSR, Vasily M. Kulish, the study director, concluded that "military force is one of the most important foreign-political means available to states."[81] "At the present time," it was argued elsewhere in the monograph,

the principal means for restraining imperialist aggressors in all regions of the world is the ability of the USSR to deliver nuclear missile weapons to any point on the earth's surface. This method for restraining imperialist military expansion is extremely important from the standpoint of preventing an all-out nuclear war. However this form will not always be effective in those situations

79. Ibid., p. 115.
80. The quotation is from James McConnell, "Military-Political Tasks of the Soviet Navy in War and Peace," in *Soviet Oceans Development*, p. 183. See also ibid., pp. 109–209; and Robert G. Weinland and others, "Analysis of Admiral Gorshkov's 'Navies in War and Peace,' " in MccGwire, Booth, and McDonnell, eds., *Soviet Naval Policy*, pp. 547–72.
81. V. M. Kulish and others, *Military Force and International Relations*, JPRS Report 58947 (Moscow: 1972; U.S. Department of Commerce, National Technical Information Service, 1973), p. 171.

that could develop into limited wars, even though the interests of the Soviet Union and other Socialist Bloc countries might be directly involved.

In connection with the task of preventing local wars and also in those cases wherein military support must be furnished to those nations fighting for their freedom and independence against the forces of internal reaction and imperialist intervention, the Soviet Union may require mobile and well trained and well equipped armed forces. In some situations the very knowledge of a Soviet military presence in an area in which a conflict situation is developing may serve to restrain the imperialists and local reaction, prevent them from dealing out violence to the local populace and eliminate a threat to overall peace and international security. It is precisely this type of role that ships of the Soviet Navy are playing in the Mediterranean sea.[82]

Explicit statements of this sort were not forthcoming from Brezhnev or other members of the Soviet ruling circle because they did not want to endanger accommodations being sought from the West. Although it is clear that détente did not mean to the Kremlin an end to struggle with the West for position and influence, Moscow wanted to avoid military confrontations with the United States and controlled its rhetoric to support détente.[83] The Kremlin continued to shun provocative remarks and gratuitous boasting.

Beyond the Mediterranean

Forward deployment of the Soviet navy continued to be pressed through the late 1960s and leveled off in the early 1970s. An average of thirty Soviet ships were deployed daily to the Mediterranean by 1968. The number increased to forty-five by 1970 and fifty-six by 1973.[84] Ships also began cruising in the Indian Ocean in 1968, the average daily number of ships there being roughly three in 1968, ten in 1970, and twenty-five in 1973.[85]

The deployment of Soviet warships in distant waters not only strengthened the USSR's image as a great power and elicited the appreciation of nations wanting to use a close relationship with the Soviet Union to sup-

82. Ibid., p. 103.

83. Dimitri K. Simes, *Detente and Conflict: Soviet Foreign Policy, 1972–1977,* The Washington Papers 44 (Sage for the Center for Strategic and International Studies, Georgetown University, Washington, D.C., 1977), p. 20.

84. Weinland, "Land Support for Naval Forces," p. 74.

85. Figures are calculated from Robert G. Weinland, "Soviet Naval Operations: 10 Years of Change," Professional Paper 125, in MccGwire, Booth, and McDonnell, eds., *Soviet Naval Policy,* pp. 377–79.

port their own foreign policies. The deployment of warships also gave Moscow the prerogative to quickly appear at the scene of a crisis or other event without having to get permission for aircraft overflight or refueling. After the experiences of the 1967 Middle East war and later naval support of Egypt, the Kremlin used the instrument of port visits and naval presence frequently to support friends in the third world.

In 1968, when Soviet Pacific Fleet warships first began cruising the Indian Ocean, several ports along the littoral were visited. One port visit to Aden in South Yemen, which had recently celebrated its independence, took place just after the outbreak of a rebellion by extreme left-wing elements of the ruling National Liberation Front.[86] Although the visit probably had been planned in advance, the timely presence of a Soviet cruiser, destroyer, submarine, and oiler was most likely well received by the government of President Qahtan as-Shaabi as a symbol of recognition and support by the USSR, which had earlier provided this new nation with armaments. It is difficult to believe that Soviet authorities were unaware of the potential significance of this visit to South Yemen's beleaguered government: it was to the USSR's advantage to be on the scene, displaying its military support of the as-Shaabi regime, thereby increasing the prospect of strengthened relations with South Yemen.

Between 1962 and 1969 Moscow helped construct a deepwater port in Somalia and in 1965 initiated arms aid and training assistance. A period of instability followed the Somali army's seizure of power in October 1969 after the assassination of President Abdirashid Ali Shermarke. While a new regime, led by President Mohammed Siad Barre, consolidated power, a Soviet cruiser and destroyer began a series of visits to Somali ports to show the USSR's friendship toward the new order and, perhaps, to deter hostility toward Barre's regime. Soviet ships also paid unusually long visits to Somali ports in 1970 and 1972. The first began ten days before an announcement that a countercoup had been thwarted; the second began just before and ended just after a UN Security Council special session on African colonialism in Addis Ababa, Ethiopia's capital. Dismukes reports that during this period UN Security Council delegates and UN Secretary-General Kurt Waldheim visited Mogadishu, Somalia's capital. The 1972 visit appeared to be a demonstration of Soviet

86. *Keesing's Contemporary Archives* (July 12–19, 1969), pp. 23451–52; Geoffrey Jukes, *The Indian Ocean in Soviet Naval Policy,* Adelphi Paper 87 (London: IISS, 1972), pp. 12–18, 25.

support for revolutionary governments (for example, Somalia) and movements of national liberation (for example, in Mozambique and Angola).[87]

In the spring of 1973 Soviet warships demonstrated support for Iraq in its border dispute with Kuwait. After Iraq seized a piece of Kuwaiti territory around its port and naval base at Umm Qasr in late March other Arab states mediated the dispute and played a decisive role in resolving it. (Baghdad was eventually forced to withdraw its claim.) Meanwhile, a four-ship Soviet naval squadron and the navy commander in chief, Admiral Gorshkov, visited Iraq in early April, supposedly to commemorate the signing of a treaty of friendship and cooperation by the USSR and Iraq the previous year.[88] Gorshkov's visit was not announced until just a few days before his arrival, and the Soviet warships arrived without prior announcement.

Although it is possible that these visits had been planned in advance, it seems that the Kremlin was at least willing to appear supportive of Baghdad; earlier a Tass statement had broadcast the official Iraqi version of events, blaming Kuwait for the situation.[89] But the USSR did not encourage Baghdad or try to intimidate Kuwait and its supporters. Behind the scenes the Kremlin seems to have pressed Iraq to accommodate Kuwait. Moscow probably wanted above all to maintain the fragile front of Arab unity. The planned Arab offensive against Israel, originally scheduled for May 1973, may also have contributed to Moscow's restraint.[90]

Directly related to Arab solidarity and, it would seem, the preparations for war against Israel was the Soviet sealift of Moroccan troops from Oran in Algeria to Syria in April.[91] The two Soviet amphibious ships carrying out this operation may also have been escorted by Soviet warships or submarines. The sealift not only served the Arab cause but also ensured the safe arrival of the Arab troops. Soviet ships sealifted additional Moroccan troops to Syria in early summer 1973, after the planned offensive against Israel had been delayed. Also in 1973 Soviet vessels

87. Bradford Dismukes, "Soviet Employment of Naval Power for Political Purposes, 1967–1975," in MccGwire and McDonnell, eds., *Soviet Naval Influence,* pp. 486–90.

88. Anne M. Kelly, "The Soviet Naval Presence During the Iraq-Kuwait Border Dispute," in MccGwire, Booth, and McDonnell, eds., *Soviet Naval Policy,* pp. 287–306.

89. Ibid., pp. 289–90.

90. Sadat, *In Search of Identity,* p. 241.

91. See Dismukes, "Soviet Employment of Naval Power," pp. 491–93.

transported South Yemeni troops on their way to support the Dhofar rebellion in Oman.[92]

In the early 1970s the USSR began to engage in naval diplomacy on behalf of friends in West Africa. Warships were initially used to support Soviet interests in West Africa in 1969 while Soviet and Ghanaian authorities were negotiating the release of two Soviet fishing trawlers and their crews, who had been accused of smuggling arms to opponents of the regime in Accra.

In mid-February 1969 two Soviet missile destroyers, a submarine, and an oiler paid an official visit to Conakry in Guinea, the first Soviet visit to a sub-Saharan West African port and one that followed a serious turn in the Ghanaian investigation of the trawlers' activities. These ships then took thirteen days to travel to Lagos, Nigeria (the trip normally takes four days), where they paid a visit on short notice. It is not certain whether the movements of these Soviet ships—first south to West African waters and then the lingering trip between Conakry and Lagos—influenced the Ghanaian authorities, but Moscow apparently meant them to do so.[93]

A close Soviet relationship with Guinea had developed after Guinea had gained its independence in 1958 and rejected continued close relations with France. Conakry had received military assistance from the USSR as early as 1960. In November 1970, Portugal mounted an amphibious attack on Conakry, partly because President Sekou Touré supported the African Party for the Independence of Guinea and Cape Verde Islands (PAIGC), which was also headquartered in the Guinean capital. Off the coast of West Africa Moscow immediately established a small naval presence, which, whatever the initial intention, became a permanent deployment. This deployment deterred Portuguese military action directed at Guinea and protected the PAIGC.

Five months later Soviet military power was again invoked in West Africa, this time in Sierra Leone, where the government of President Siaka Stevens was infirm. After avoiding a planned coup, this regime had faced considerable uncertainty for a time. Previously Sierra Leone had accepted

92. Abram N. Shulsky and others, "Coercive Naval Diplomacy, 1967–1974," in Dismukes and McConnell, eds., *Soviet Naval Diplomacy*, p. 137.

93. See David Hall's discussion in chapter 12; also Dismukes, "Soviet Employment of Naval Power," pp. 485–86. Of further note, in early 1973 PAIGC leader Amilcar Cabral was murdered in Conakry. The assassins were then seized in West African waters by a Soviet warship in the area.

"positive neutralism" and the Stevens regime had given neighboring Guinea strong support after the Portuguese attack on Conakry. The instability in Sierra Leone, in turn, led quickly to the deployment there of Guinean troops and the signing of a defense treaty by Conakry and Freetown. Consequently, in May 1971 a Soviet destroyer visited Freetown to reinforce the legitimacy of the government there and to strengthen relations between Sierra Leone and the Soviet Union.[94]

These visits to South Yemen, Somalia, Iraq, Guinea, and Sierra Leone were not made in the midst of ongoing major violence or any U.S. military effort or serious political involvement. Although the local parties benefiting from the visits were perhaps made more secure, the USSR did not incur any military risks or political costs. In each action the USSR supported the recognized government of a sovereign nation (as it did in Egypt between the 1967 and 1973 wars and in Sudan, Ceylon, and Iraq during these years). In addition to strengthening Soviet relations with these governments, Moscow's support helped it gain access to foreign installations, which was important for satisfying the Kremlin's broader military interests. In Egypt, Somalia, Guinea, South Yemen, and Iraq, Soviet warships were able to use shore facilities; and Soviet naval aircraft were based in the first three of these countries at least intermittently for reconnaissance operations, thereby making Soviet military capabilities in the Atlantic, Indian Ocean, and Mediterranean more efficient and effective. In late 1978, one year after the USSR lost its military position in Somalia as a result of Moscow's support of Ethiopia in the ongoing Ethiopian-Somali conflict, Soviet naval reconnaissance aircraft began to make flights from South Yemen. (They had done so once before in 1975). Such flights were also made from Angola after the USSR had intervened in 1975–76 in that nation's civil war.

The sealifts of Moroccan and South Yemeni troops in 1973 were not noticed; the risk of hostile action by regional actors was minor; and the United States was uninvolved. That these Soviet actions offended Israel, Oman, or Saudi Arabia presumably did not concern Moscow much. Although the USSR showed support for Baghdad in the 1973 Iraq-Kuwait imbroglio, Moscow handled that situation in a way that caused little disturbance in the Arab world.

94. Ibid., pp. 488–89; B. Pilyatskin, "Objective Necessity," *Izvestiya*, April 28, 1971 (in *CDSP*, vol. 23, May 25, 1971, pp. 42–43); James M. McConnell, "The Soviet Navy in the Indian Ocean," in MccGwire, ed., *Soviet Naval Developments*, p. 398.

Superpower Confrontations

Unlike the incidents just discussed, the Jordanian crisis (1970), the Indo-Pakistani war (1971), and the 1973 Middle East war included serious interstate conflict and a potential for or actual superpower confrontation. A pattern of U.S. and Soviet behavior emerged from these situations in the third world. It appeared "permissible for one superpower to support a friend against the client of another superpower as long as the friend is on the defensive *strategically*; the object must be to avert decisive defeat and restore the balance, not assist the client to victory. The issue of who began the war is not central; it is the strategic situation of the client at the time of the contemplated intervention that counts."[95]

What also became apparent was the USSR's increased willingness to support its allies militarily and to take risks on their behalf and a relative decline in U.S. willingness to militarily support its allies in crises between superpower clients. The change in U.S. behavior may partly be related to the Vietnam War and consequent American disillusionment about the use of military power as a foreign policy instrument. U.S. policymakers confronting the USSR in crises beginning in the late 1960s and continuing into the 1970s were also increasingly more impressed by the Kremlin's strategic and conventional military capabilities than were their predecessors. Soviet military activities in the 1967 Middle East war and the air defense of Egypt have already been considered. Following are discussions of the other third world crises in the early 1970s including major involvement by both superpowers.

THE JORDANIAN CRISIS. In September 1970, when the Jordanian military encountered stiff resistance while attempting to end the armed Palestinian presence in Jordan, Syrian armored units intervened in the fighting. The Nixon administration believed that the Kremlin had led the Syrians to do this (Soviet military advisers accompanied Syrian formations to the

---

95. James M. McConnell and Anne M. Kelly, "Superpower Naval Diplomacy in the Indo-Pakistani Crisis," in MccGwire, ed., *Soviet Naval Developments*, p. 449. The significance to coercive diplomacy of asymmetries of motivation (unequal motivation) was initially explored in Alexander L. George, David K. Hall, and William E. Simons, *The Limits of Coercive Diplomacy: Laos, Cuba, Vietnam* (Little, Brown, 1971), pp. 22–26, 218–20. James M. McConnell developed a thesis on this subject and the defense of the status quo, which he presents in "The 'Rules of the Game': A Theory on the Practice of Superpower Naval Diplomacy," in Dismukes and McConnell, eds., *Soviet Naval Diplomacy*, pp. 240–80. My analysis owes much to these works.

Jordanian border and perhaps into Jordan), or at least had supported Damascus in its decision. In either case Moscow was considered responsible since Washington believed that Syria would probably not have invaded Jordan without Soviet approval.[96]

Eventually, King Hussein's position became desperate enough for the United States and Israel to contemplate military intervention. By this time the United States had moved two aircraft carriers and an amphibious task force into the eastern Mediterranean. A third aircraft carrier and a second marine force were also steaming toward the Mediterranean; U.S. Air Force tactical and transport aircraft had been moved to Turkey; and U.S. Army units in Europe and in the United States had been alerted for rapid deployment. While a Soviet destroyer tracked the third aircraft carrier, two Soviet task groups formed around the first two; the U.S. amphibious ships also were watched closely. In the June war only one Soviet warship had tracked each U.S. carrier. It has been suggested that the Soviet ships were "in excellent position to launch a surprise attack" and had "a reasonable chance of taking significant offensive action before a U.S. counterattack could have had full effect."[97] Still, Moscow sought to contain the situation. Between the beginning of the crisis and the withdrawal of Syrian forces from Jordan, only three additional surface combatants were redeployed into the Mediterranean; a cruiser on its way from the Caribbean to the Mediterranean was made to proceed at a leisurely course; while some submarines entered the Mediterranean, others left; naval air reconnaissance by aircraft then in Egypt was not carried out; and no airborne units in the USSR were ever alerted.[98]

When Hussein's forces alone were unable to reverse the course of battle, Israel prepared to intervene in their behalf, Washington having assured the Israelis that if the USSR or Egypt took military action against Israel the United States would enter the conflict.[99] The growing certainty that President Richard Nixon would not allow Hussein's regime to be

96. Nixon, *Memoirs,* p. 483; William B. Quandt, "Lebanon, 1958, and Jordan, 1970," in Blechman and Kaplan, *Force without War,* pp. 265, 267; Kalb and Kalb, *Kissinger,* p. 201.

97. Abram N. Shulsky, "The Jordanian Crisis of September 1970," in Dismukes and McConnell, eds., *Soviet Naval Diplomacy,* pp. 170–75. The quotation is from page 175.

98. The number of Soviet warships in the Mediterranean increased further after the crisis peaked. Ibid., pp. 171–72.

99. Nixon, *Memoirs,* p. 485; Kalb and Kalb, *Kissinger,* p. 206.

turned out by Syrian military force led the Kremlin to inform U.S. officials that it was calling on the Syrians to withdraw from Jordan, which they did.[100] The Kremlin had reason to fear the prospect of conflict between Israel and Syria and possibly Egypt. If Syria and Egypt were defeated again by Israel, the USSR's position in the Arab world would become untenable. If Israel were defeated, the United States would probably intervene, thereby also threatening the Soviet position. To threaten Israel would mean either risking the exposure of a Soviet bluff or fighting a regionally powerful U.S. ally. Compelling the United States to cease its military support of Israel also would mean either having a bluff exposed or actually attacking U.S. armed forces. The Kremlin preferred Syrian withdrawal and the defeat of the Palestinians. The purpose of Soviet naval operations during this conflict was to give Moscow the appearance of deterring U.S. military action against Syria and Egypt, which Washington had not even contemplated.

THE INDO-PAKISTANI WAR. Soviet armed forces acted somewhat similarly during the Indo-Pakistani war in December 1971. Some months before, the Soviet Union and India had signed a friendship treaty. Adding to Moscow's interest in India was China's hostility toward India, China's support for Pakistan, and the burgeoning relationship between China and the United States.[101] The United States also was committed to Pakistan, a member of the Southeast Asia Treaty Organization (SEATO) and the Central Treaty Organization (CENTO) and the nation through which Secretary of State Kissinger had recently passed on his way to Peking.

Several days after the fighting between India and Pakistan began, a Soviet task group was dispatched from the Pacific Fleet, seemingly to counter the presence in the Indian Ocean of a British aircraft carrier and a commando carrier. A second Soviet surface group was deployed into the Indian Ocean in the wake of a U.S. task force including the aircraft carrier *Enterprise*. These two Soviet squadrons reinforced the ships already stationed in the Indian Ocean and countered the Western military presence

---

100. Henry Kissinger, *White House Years* (Little, Brown, 1979), pp. 616, 627–29; Kalb and Kalb, *Kissinger*, pp. 205–07; William B. Quandt, *Decade of Decisions: American Policy Toward the Arab-Israeli Conflict, 1967–1976* (University of California Press, 1977), pp. 124–25.

101. "The Indian-Pakistani Conflict and Peking's Anti-Sovietism," *Pravda*, December 8, 1971 (in *CDSP*, vol. 23, January 4, 1972, pp. 2–4); V. Kudryavtsev, "Flames Over South Asia," *Izvestiya*, December 12, 1971 (in *CDSP*, vol. 23, January 11, 1972, pp. 8–9).

there. About fifteen Soviet MIG-21 and TU-16 aircraft deployed in Egypt at that time were also reportedly sent to India in response to the transfer of U.S.-built combat aircraft from Jordan and Libya to Pakistan.[102]

Although Pakistan's defeat clearly was a disaster for the government in Islamabad and the Nixon administration was outraged by the Indian offensive, the United States favored independence for East Pakistan. Thus Washington was not disposed to militarily intervene on East Pakistan's account. Nixon argues that the deployment of the *Enterprise* was prompted by intelligence suggesting that India might attack in the west. Nixon and Secretary Kissinger also wanted China to perceive the United States as being militarily capable and responsive to the interests of friends.[103]

Ominously, though, the Soviet ambassador to India, Nikolai M. Pegov, told New Delhi, according to the Central Intelligence Agency, that the USSR "will not allow the Seventh Fleet to intervene" and "would open a diversionary action" in Sinkiang if China intervened against India.[104] The movement of Soviet troops closer to the Sino-Soviet border during the war could have had no other purpose than to divert Chinese forces and deter Peking from intervening on Pakistan's behalf.[105] On the other hand, U.S. intelligence also indicated that the Kremlin did not really expect either the United States or China to intervene in the conflict. The Kremlin probably made a strong verbal commitment to New Delhi because the Nixon administration could only sensibly deploy enough military power to the Indian Ocean for a demonstration of force rather than actual combat. Moscow might also have been willing to offer New Delhi a commitment as long as India did not intend to initiate military operations against West Pakistan. From the outset of the conflict, Soviet diplomacy sought a cease-fire and recognition of East Pakistan's independence.

The United States was, in fact, unable to do very much for Pakistan militarily. The moral ambiguity of the East Pakistan issue disallowed a sense of defending Pakistan as a nation; in the west, the scene of potential

102. McConnell and Kelly, "Superpower Naval Diplomacy in the Indo-Pakistani Crisis," pp. 443–44; Elmo R. Zumwalt, Jr., *On Watch: A Memoir* (New York: Times Books, 1976), pp. 367–68; *Africa Diary*, vol. 12 (April 29–May 5, 1972), p. 5945.

103. Nixon, *Memoirs,* pp. 527–28; Kalb and Kalb, *Kissinger,* pp. 260–61. For other considerations of the Nixon administration that may have motivated U.S. policy, see McConnell and Kelly, "Superpower Naval Diplomacy in the Indo-Pakistani Crisis," p. 446.

104. Quoted by Jack Anderson, "Bay of Bengal and Tonkin Gulf," *Washington Post,* January 10, 1972.

105. Nixon, *Memoirs,* p. 526.

fighting was far inland, and the U.S. carrier group was quite alone in the Indian Ocean. Had India actually attacked the west and had U.S. aircraft been ordered to support West Pakistan—without attacking India—it is doubtful that a Soviet military attack on the *Enterprise* group would have taken place.

But as things worked out, India had good reason to be pleased with Soviet behavior. India, which held the upper hand over Pakistan throughout the war, did not want to provoke the West more than it had to; hence New Delhi could not have minded that Moscow sent ships to the Indian Ocean only after British naval units and U.S. warships had been deployed there. Soviet actions on the Sino-Soviet border also increased New Delhi's confidence and sense of command over the situation.

To further improve the Soviet Union's position in South Asia, Moscow offered the help of Russian sailors to the new government in Bangladesh after the conflict to clear port areas made inaccessible during the fighting.[106]

THE OCTOBER WAR. The 1973 war in the Middle East vividly portrayed how far the USSR had come during the previous decade in military capability and willingness to support friends in the third world during crises, despite the fact or prospect of serious U.S. military involvement. Clearly Moscow had foreknowledge of the Arab attack on Israel and was not caught unaware by the outbreak of hostilities.[107] This does not mean that the Kremlin looked favorably on the Arab attack. It did not, for major conflict between important U.S. and Soviet allies such as Israel, Egypt, and Syria jeopardized the aura of détente, which Brezhnev wanted very badly, and several agreements with the United States sought by Moscow. But when Egypt and Syria decided to go to war to regain their lost territories, Moscow felt obliged to ensure this effort's success. Not to do so risked the destruction of Soviet standing in the Arab world. The USSR, therefore, followed a course of relations with the Arabs that included both support and restraint.

Before the conflict began, surface-to-surface missiles had been sent to Egypt to reinforce Arab strategic deterrence; additional armaments had

106. Soviet minesweepers and salvage ships began this work in April 1972. See Charles C. Petersen, "The Soviet Port-Clearing Operations in Bangladesh," in MccGwire, Booth, and McDonnell, eds., *Soviet Naval Policy,* pp. 319–40; also Charles C. Petersen, "Soviet Mineclearing Operations in the Gulf of Suez, 1974," in MccGwire and McDonnell, eds., *Soviet Naval Influence,* pp. 539–62.

107. Robert G. Weinland, "Superpower Naval Diplomacy in the October 1973 Arab-Israeli War," Professional Paper 221 (Arlington, Va.: Center for Naval Analyses, 1978), pp. 3–13.

been sealifted and airlifted; Moroccan units had been sealifted to Syria; and the Kremlin had begun strengthening Arab unity at the diplomatic level. After the fighting started, it was the USSR, not the United States, that began airlifting military supplies to its clients. The Soviet navy's essential mission was to keep close account of the U.S. Sixth Fleet and offset any influence it might attempt to exert on the course of the war. Major choke points in the Mediterranean were kept under close watch, and Soviet warships and submarines were concentrated near U.S. aircraft carriers and amphibious units. Between the outbreak of the war on October 6 and the U.S. "Defcon 3" alert on October 24, the number of Soviet surface combatants deployed from the Black Sea to the Mediterranean rose from seventeen to twenty-six. Deployments of additional submarines and support ships brought the total number of Soviet naval vessels then in the Mediterranean to eighty.[108]

In the week following the U.S. alert, the Soviet naval force grew to ninety-six units, including thirty-four surface combatants and twenty-three submarines. The U.S. chief of naval operations observed later: "I doubt that major units of the U.S. Navy were ever in a tenser situation since World War II ended than the Sixth Fleet in the Mediterranean was for . . . [that] week."[109] At the same time, seven Soviet airborne divisions were on alert—three had been alerted earlier in the war—and transport planes, which previously had been airlifting armaments to Egypt and Syria, appeared in a state of readiness to airlift troops.[110] Of further concern to the United States was the establishment of a Soviet airborne command post over southern Russia and the entry into the port of Alexandria of a Soviet freighter with cargo emitting neutrons, implying the possible delivery of nuclear warheads for Egypt's SCUD missiles.[111]

During the conflict Soviet pilots made 934 flights to Arab nations, transporting in AN-12 and AN-22 aircraft some 15,000 tons of matériel. Several times this volume was sealifted by Soviet freighters. The U.S. airlift that began on October 13—the Soviet sealift had been initiated at the start of hostilities and the Soviet airlift on October 10—included 566 trips

108. Ibid., p. 47; Stephen S. Roberts, "The October 1973 Arab-Israeli War," in Dismukes and McConnell, eds., *Soviet Naval Diplomacy*, p. 193.

109. Zumwalt, *On Watch*, pp. 446–47.

110. Nixon, *Memoirs*, p. 937; Kalb and Kalb, *Kissinger*, pp. 481, 488; Glassman, *Arms for the Arabs*, pp. 161–62; William B. Quandt, *Soviet Policy in the October 1973 War*, R-1864-ISA, prepared for the Office of the Assistant Secretary of Defense/International Security Affairs (Santa Monica, Calif.: Rand Corp., 1976), p. 33.

111. Quandt, *Soviet Policy in the October 1973 War*, pp. 30–31.

by Air Force C-5 and C-141 aircraft and the delivery of about 23,000 tons of supplies.[112]

The Kremlin also tried to contain and end the conflict—not to protect the Arabs but to minimize Arab demands on the USSR and the risk of a confrontation with the United States. Moscow began to support Arab war planning only after Egypt and Syria had scaled down their objectives considerably and had established a strategy of first using military means to achieve limited territory and then exerting political pressure on Israel. But the Kremlin was not enthusiastic about even these plans. Moscow continued to hope for a peaceful settlement in the Middle East.[113] Indeed, at San Clemente in June 1973, Brezhnev may have tried to warn President Nixon of the likelihood of war if political developments favorable to the Arabs did not take place immediately.[114]

Within hours of the Arab attack, Soviet representatives began asking Egypt and Syria to halt their offensive. Although Cairo and Damascus would not do this, Moscow continued to press for a cease-fire, thus antagonizing President Sadat and straining Soviet-Egyptian relations.[115] Cairo was already displeased by the Kremlin's earlier refusal to transfer MIG-25 aircraft and certain other armaments to the Egyptian armed forces and by the evacuation of Soviet nationals from Egypt several days before the Arab offensive; indeed, President Sadat was infuriated by this lack of confidence. Sadat also believed that the USSR did not resupply Egypt with enough armaments during the conflict and was angry about Soviet unwillingness to provide Egypt with satellite reconnaissance.[116]

As he had in the 1967 war, Algerian President Hoari Boumedienne went to Moscow to press the Kremlin for strong support. The Tass description of these talks as having taken place in a "friendly, *frank* atmosphere" suggested significant differences between Arab demands and Soviet supplies.[117] One important consequence of this Arab dissatisfaction was the conclusion reached by President Sadat and to a lesser extent by President

112. Ibid., p. 23; IISS, *Strategic Survey, 1973,* p. 27. For different figures, see Durch, Davidchik, and Shulsky, "Other Soviet Interventionary Forces," p. 340.

113. Galia Golan, *Yom Kippur and After* (Cambridge University Press, 1977), pp. 41–60.

114. Nixon, *Memoirs,* p. 885.

115. Golan, *Yom Kippur and After,* pp. 74–78; Vladimir Petrov, *U.S.-Soviet Détente: Past and Future* (American Enterprise Institute, 1975), pp. 32–33.

116. Sadat, *In Search of Identity,* pp. 218–31, 246–47, 252–53, 259, 263–64, 317–27.

117. FBIS, *Daily Report: Soviet Union* (October 16, 1973), p. F1; emphasis added.

Hafiz al-Assad of Syria that dependence on the USSR and hostility toward the United States did not serve Egypt's and Syria's interests. Another consequence was the expulsion of the Soviet military from Egypt in 1976, at which time President Sadat also terminated the 1971 Soviet-Egyptian Treaty of Friendship and Cooperation.

Moscow's military actions were nevertheless critical to Soviet standing in the Arab world. While the Soviet naval actions provided a counter to the Sixth Fleet, the Soviet airlift and particularly the alert of several airborne divisions appear to have been prompted by the first signs of Arab retreat and Israel's bombing of Damascus.[118] Moscow issued a direct warning to Israel on October 12 after Israel intentionally bombed Soviet transport aircraft in Syria and sank a Soviet merchant vessel in the port of Tartus. This, a Tass statement announced, the USSR "cannot regard indifferently"; the "continuation" of such acts, the statement went on, "will lead to grave consequences for Israel itself."[119] Earlier Moscow had let slide the bombing of its cultural center in Damascus with mere condemnation and a walkout from a UN Security Council meeting by Soviet Ambassador Yakov A. Malik. Even while the USSR was threatening Israel, however, Moscow was trying to establish a cease-fire. Moreover, the Russians went out of their way to say that "no one in the Soviet Union, including the government, has anything against Israel as a state."[120]

Brezhnev and Kissinger personally hammered out a cease-fire agreement in Moscow on October 20–21, after the Russians had gotten Cairo to agree to direct talks between Egypt and Israel. Sadat finally agreed to this only after Brezhnev assured him that, if necessary, the USSR would act unilaterally to ensure Israel's observance of the cease-fire.[121] By October 24, though, Israel had violated two cease-fires and had entrapped Egypt's Third Army on the west bank of the Suez Canal. On that date Moscow alerted four additional airborne divisions, and Brezhnev delivered this message to President Nixon: "If you find it impossible to act together with us in this matter, we should be faced with the necessity urgently to consider the question of taking appropriate steps unilaterally."[122] (Previously the Kremlin had sought a joint Soviet-American

118. Golan, *Yom Kippur and After,* p. 86.
119. FBIS, *Soviet Union* (October 15, 1973), pp. F1–2.
120. Ibid., p. F7.
121. Kalb and Kalb, *Kissinger,* p. 485.
122. Ibid., p. 490.

intervention against Israel.) On October 23d Moscow had warned Israel again "of the gravest consequences."[123]

In the end, Moscow did precipitate the situation it most sought to avoid: a military confrontation between the United States and the USSR. Such a confrontation weakened détente and endangered important Soviet political objectives in East-West relations. Moscow went as far as it did, however, not as a result of eagerness to demonstrate Soviet military power or to undermine U.S. credibility among American allies, but to protect its credibility in the Arab world. When Brezhnev sent his message to Nixon, Cairo was in a state of panic and the Russians were in the position of having helped to arrange an Arab military disaster. Moscow may have worried further that the Israelis would advance toward Cairo after their encirclement of the Third Army. Not to give Egypt practical support at this time was also to play into Peking's hands.

The Kremlin's behavior after the second cease-fire violation was not reckless, but highly calculated. The Soviet objective on the 24th was not to send ground forces to Egypt to fight against Israel, although Moscow was open to the idea of a joint Soviet-American intervention essentially directed against Israel. Rather the Kremlin wanted to signal the United States that it could not allow any greater degree of Arab defeat and that the United States either had to make Israel realize this or itself force Israel to observe the cease-fire. From the Soviet perspective, if the United States did not do this it was either acting with duplicity or would have to accept unilateral USSR intervention. The U.S. nuclear alert coupled with U.S. diplomatic behavior was aimed at satisfying Moscow's objective.[124]

It is important that Moscow did not relish its behavior in this crisis and did not act out of ideological passion, sympathy, or vindictiveness. However, in spite of the Kremlin's efforts to end the conflict and in spite of Arab disappointment with Moscow, Soviet military support of Egypt and Syria was substantial. The Kremlin did choose to risk détente and face the

123. Tass, October 23, 1973 (in FBIS, *Soviet Union,* October 24, 1973, p. F2).

124. Of note, "the American military command structure did not appear to consider that the actual use of strategic forces had become a serious possibility. Elaborate decentralized preparations—the preliminary tuning of forces for combat— were not triggered. The response to the alert order was minimal and *pro forma*." John Steinbruner, "An Assessment of Nuclear Crises," in Franklyn Griffiths and John C. Polanyi, eds., *The Dangers of Nuclear War* (University of Toronto Press, 1979), p. 43.

United States firmly rather than lose all credibility with the Arabs and perhaps with other third world clients as well.

After the October War

After the 1973 war in the Middle East, Soviet military leaders became more confident about the USSR's ability to use military power to successfully influence events in the third world. In early 1974 Marshal Grechko took up the theme of "expansion of the internationalist functions of the Soviet armed forces." "At the present stage," he wrote for the journal *Questions of CPSU History,*

the historic function of the Soviet armed forces is not restricted merely to their function in defending our motherland and the other socialist countries. In its foreign policy activity the Soviet state actively and purposefully opposes the export of counterrevolution and the policy of oppression, supports the national liberation struggle, and resolutely resists imperialist aggression in whatever distant region of our planet it may appear. The party and Soviet Government rely on the country's economic and defense might in fulfilling these tasks. . . .

The development of the external functions of the socialist armies is a natural process. It will continue.[125]

These lines closely resembled passages in Defense Minister Grechko's book *The Armed Forces of the Soviet State,* which was first published in 1974.[126] Grechko's statements did not indicate greater commitment to third world allies but did imply that within the Kremlin the use of Soviet armed forces in distant lands was no longer considered exceptional or tenuous; Soviet capabilities thus were fully recognized. It was perhaps for this reason as well as out of consideration for détente that Grechko did not discuss in these writings the peacetime roles of individual services or types of forces but considered only their combat capabilities.

On the other hand, Admiral Gorshkov, only a Central Committee member, with a more specific interest than Marshal Grechko (a full Politburo member), was not at all silent about the navy's role in supporting Soviet foreign policy. Building on "Navies in War and Peace," he, and

125. A. A. Grechko, "The Leading Role of the CPSU in Building the Army of a Developed Socialist State," *Voprosy Istorri KPSS* [*Questions of CPSU History*], no. 5, April 1974 (in FBIS, *Soviet Union,* May 30, 1974, pp. A7, A10).

126. See A. A. Grechko, *The Armed Forces of the Soviet State: A Soviet View,* 2d ed., trans. and published under the auspices of the U.S. Air Force (GPO, 1976), pp. v, 99–100.

presumably members of his staff, wrote *Sea Power of the State*, published in 1976 and honored by a nomination for the M. V. Frunze prize. This honor and the relatively large number of books printed indicate that the views expressed in this volume, particularly those on the navy as a policy instrument, either represented the thinking of Soviet political leaders or were acceptable to them. Gorshkov touted

the specific features of the navy as a military factor which has been used in peacetime for demonstrating the economic and military power of the state beyond its confines, and the fact that, of all the branches of the armed forces, the navy is best capable of operationally ensuring the state interests of the country beyond its borders.[127]

Gorshkov viewed the Soviet navy as graphically representing to the world Soviet military and technological prowess and as being supportive of USSR friendship with other nations through routine visits and as being especially useful for achieving political objectives in discrete situations. "Demonstrative actions by the fleet," wrote the admiral, "in many cases have made it possible to achieve political ends without resorting to armed struggle, merely by putting on pressure with one's own potential might and threatening to start military operations."[128] He had in mind particularly the third world. Gorshkov went on: "It is hard to find in the world an area where American politicians have not employed their navy against progressive forces." The Soviet navy was an instrument for "cutting short the aggressive endeavors of imperialism, restraining military adventurism, and decisively countering threats to the safety of the peoples from the imperialist powers."[129]

Despite the significant use of Soviet aircraft as a political instrument in the 1970s—particularly tactical combat and strategic transport planes—senior airmen remained silent about the peacetime contribution made by Soviet air forces to the USSR's foreign policy. Perhaps P. S. Kutakhov, deputy defense minister and chief marshal of aviation, said the most that could be said when, on Aviation Day, 1979, he related that "in peacetime, as in war, Soviet airmen, on finding themselves in a complex situation, show courage, bravery and high moral, political and psychological qualities."[130] Unlike the navy, Soviet air forces have had no continuous peace-

127. S. G. Gorshkov, *The Sea Power of the State* (Naval Institute Press, 1979), p. xii.
128. Ibid., pp. 247–48.
129. Ibid., pp. 250–51.
130. Interview with Chief Marshal of Aviation P. S. Kutakhov, *Pravda,* August 20, 1978 (in FBIS, *Soviet Union.* August 31, 1978, p. V2).

time roles except in routine deployments in Eastern Europe and along the Sino-Soviet frontier. Since air units have been turned to only intermittently for policy support in the third world, senior airmen may not consider their role as important as navy men consider theirs. This is probably changing, however.

After the Middle East war, Soviet political leaders remained reticent about their armed forces' activities in the third world. Statements like those by Defense Minister Grechko and Admiral Gorshkov would have served no useful purpose had they been articulated by Chairman Brezhnev or other Soviet political leaders. Although the USSR wanted to strengthen its position in the third world and felt strong competition with China, the Kremlin also wanted friendly relations with the West. Soviet armed forces might continue to support foreign policy objectives in Africa and the Middle East, but boastful remarks about Soviet military capabilities and activities in the third world would have made arms control, trade, and other important negotiations with the United States and Western Europe even more difficult.

Moscow also probably did not want to raise expectations among its clients too much, so that it could pick and choose carefully where it might become engaged heavily without suffering recriminations from misled friends.

Marshal Grechko's statements did not appear in *Pravda, Izvestiya, Krasnaya Zvezda,* or as a Tass interview; nor were they part of any verbal announcement. They appeared in a specialized journal and were deeply embedded in *The Armed Forces of the Soviet State.* They were probably not meant as announcements to the world but as parts of a treatise on the role of the armed forces in the Soviet state and in the USSR's international relations, prepared for those in the USSR particularly attentive to Soviet defense policy.

General Secretary Brezhnev, in his report to the Twenty-fifth Party Congress in 1976, stated no new military commitment to third world allies; he promised only "support to peoples who are fighting for their freedom."[131] Rather than welcoming a contest of will and power with the West in influencing the course of the new nations, he exhorted "strict observance of the principles of noninterference in the affairs of other states, respect for their independence and sovereignty . . . [as] one of the im-

---

131. Text of Brezhnev's report to the 25th Party Congress, Moscow Domestic Service (in FBIS, *Soviet Union,* February 25, 1976/Supplement 16, p. 12).

mutable conditions of detente," which was viewed as "a way to create more favorable conditions for peaceful socialist and communist construction." Brezhnev continued, "Detente and peaceful coexistence are concerned with interstate relations. This means primarily that quarrels and conflicts between countries should not be decided by war, use of force or the threat of force. Detente does not in the slightest way abolish, and cannot abolish or change the laws of class struggle."[132]

On Armed Forces Day, 1978, Brezhnev referred to the Soviet military "together with the allied armies" only as "a reliable guard for the peaceful labor of the Soviet people and the other peoples of the socialist community." No mention was made of internationalist functions or other commitments to the third world.[133] Perhaps Brezhnev's strongest words in the late 1970s were contained in his 1977 Revolution Day speech, when he said:

The socialist countries are staunch and reliable friends of . . . [third world] countries and are prepared to give them utmost assistance and support in their development along the progressive path. This means not only moral and political, but also economic and organizational support, including assistance in strengthening their defenses.[134]

The phrase "including assistance in strengthening their defenses," while clearly implying arms transfers and military training, was at most a vague allusion to military support that might be provided by Soviet armed forces units.

After the 1973 Middle East war, Moscow did not use military units to support offensive behavior by third world allies. Not evident either was a consistent pattern of Soviet military support of friends in power suffering from internal political difficulties. For example, no Soviet airmen or seamen were sent to aid, by their presence or military skills, the short-lived success of revolutionaries in Portuguese Timor, the seizure of power by insurgents in Mozambique, or the governments of India, Sierra Leone, or Jamaica following declarations of states of emergency in these nations. Rather the Kremlin used military units occasionally to support friends in the third world when a vacuum of legitimate rule was created by the rapid withdrawal of a colonial power, as in Angola and Spanish Sahara in 1975–76, and when the USSR was able to help defend a third world nation's

132. Ibid., pp. 27–28.
133. Moscow Domestic Service, FBIS, *Soviet Union,* February 23, 1978, p. V3.
134. Moscow Domestic Service, FBIS, *Soviet Union,* November 2, 1977, p. P11.

sovereignty or territorial integrity, as in Iraq in 1973–74, in the Lebanese civil war, and in the 1977–78 Ethiopian-Somalian conflict. In all of these actions, moreover, Moscow avoided military confrontation with the United States.

The Soviet intervention in Iraq in 1973–74 resembled the USSR's involvement in Sudan in 1970–71. In both instances Moscow helped a friendly regime suppress an insurgency by an ethnic minority. Whereas the Anyanya in southern Sudan, who were backed by Ethiopia, Zaire, and Uganda, had sought to throw off the yoke of Khartoum, Baghdad in the early 1970s faced a new Kurdish rebellion backed by Iran and, more indirectly, the United States and Israel. In each instance Moscow's aid consisted of unannounced air support. While many in the world sympathized with the plight and objectives of the insurgent minorities, neither old nor new nations were prepared to make much issue of the conflicts, if only because of their own interest in principles of national sovereignty.

In Lebanon Moscow supported the Palestinians and opposed Syria's intervention into the civil war, but the USSR did not intervene in these events militarily. Soviet warships appeared nearby in June 1976 only because the Sixth Fleet was evacuating Americans and Europeans from Lebanon. The Soviet naval presence, which included a helicopter carrier, was meant to counteract the image of U.S. military power projected by the aircraft carrier, helicopter carrier, and supporting warships present during the evacuation. It was also customary for Soviet vessels to keep close watch of major U.S. warships when they entered the eastern Mediterranean. Although Moscow could not be sure that U.S. military forces would not be used as they had been in Lebanon in 1958, Moscow was fairly confident that this would not happen, considering the political climate in the United States, the absence of other U.S. military preparations, and the Ford administration's rhetoric at the time. Nevertheless, the Soviet squadron was a reminder that aggressive U.S. military action in the eastern Mediterranean could not be taken without risking military confrontation with the USSR.

The Soviet actions in Iraq and off the coast of Lebanon caused the United States little anguish. In neither case was Soviet military behavior directed at establishing a new regime. The situations in Angola and in the former Spanish Sahara in 1975–76 were different, however. Also disturbing was the extent of Soviet military activity in Ethiopia in 1977–78 and the intervention, with critical Soviet support, of thousands of Cuban combat troops in both Angola and Ethiopia.

Angola and the Horn of Africa

Soviet aid to Angolan insurgents initially took the form of arms and other matériel deliveries by sea and air to the Popular Movement for the Liberation of Angola (MPLA) led by Agostinho Neto. At least as important to the USSR as its inclination to support anticolonial movements was Peking's support of the National Front for the Liberation of Angola (FNLA) and the National Union for the Total Independence of Angola (UNITA). Chinese arms began to flow to Angola in 1973, and in 1974 Peking began sending military advisers. The FNLA and UNITA were also favored by the United States. Moscow announced renewed support of the MPLA—Soviet aid had been suspended after a leadership split in the MPLA in 1973—one month after the Central Intelligence Agency began to fund the FNLA in mid-1974.[135] Soviet transport aircraft began airlifting armaments to Brazzaville for the MPLA in March 1975. The United States began transporting arms into the area in July.[136] This U.S. aid to the MPLA's opponents may have played into the hands of Soviet leaders opposed to any trade-off that sacrificed Soviet support for national liberation movements to the altar of détente with the West. Moscow considered its matériel support of the MPLA quite legitimate in the summer of 1975. Politburo member Mikhail Suslov was not viewing things boldly when he said: "The principle of peaceful coexistence between states with different social systems, as is well known, has nothing in common with class peace between the exploiters and the exploited, the colonialists and the victims of colonial oppression, or between the oppressors and the oppressed."[137]

Cuban military men able to use the sophisticated equipment being delivered from the USSR began to take part in combat operations in late spring 1975. In the fall, after South African military units and Zairian troops entered Angola to fight against the MPLA, large Cuban ground

135. IISS, *Strategic Survey, 1975*, pp. 31–32; Colin Legum, "The Soviet Union, China, and the West in Southern Africa," *Foreign Affairs*, vol. 54 (July 1976), pp. 751–52. William J. Durch, "The Cuban Military in Africa and the Middle East: From Algeria to Angola," Professional Paper 201 (Arlington, Va.: Center for Naval Analyses, 1977), p. 39; John Stockwell, *In Search of Enemies: A CIA Story* (Norton, 1978), pp. 67–68.

136. Stockwell, *In Search of Enemies*, pp. 57–59. Also see Nathaniel Davies, "The Angola Decision of 1975: A Personal Memoir," *Foreign Affairs*, vol. 57 (Fall 1978), pp. 110–17.

137. *Kommunist*, July 21, 1975 (in FBIS, *Soviet Union*, September 11, 1975, p. R4).

forces were fielded. To equip the Cuban forces an emergency airlift by Soviet military transport aircraft (about seventy flights) was carried out beginning in late October. Transport for the Cuban buildup was provided initially by Cuban troopships and aircraft.[138]

MPLA forces in Angola obtained the services of several hundred Soviet military advisers only after Angola's independence day (November 11, 1975), the entry into Angola of South African troops, and several battles between South African and Cuban units. Aeroflot IL-62s began flying Cuban troops to Angola in January 1976, but only after Havana's shorter-range Bristol Britannias were denied refueling by Barbados and Portugal (in the Azores). The Soviet aircraft were able to fly nonstop to Guinea, where fuel could be obtained. By the time the airlift ended in late January, about 11,000 Cuban soldiers were in Angola.[139] In conjunction with the increase in arms deliveries by sea and air and then the airlift of Cuban troops, a Soviet amphibious ship, destroyer, and oiler—the West African patrol—took up a position off the coasts of the Congo and Angola, and a Soviet cruiser and perhaps submarine escort were deployed from the Mediterranean to a position south of Guinea. These ships probably were sent to deter an attack by Zaire on Soviet aircraft and cargo vessels and to provide incoming transport planes command control and communications support. The first vessel to arrive—an *Alligator*-class amphibious landing ship—may also have been intended to provide for the evacuation of Soviet military advisers if that had become necessary.[140]

These Soviet actions were neither politically nor militarily dangerous. South Africa's earlier entry into the conflict had resulted in strong support for the MPLA from previously neutral African nations. At the emergency Organization of African Unity (OAU) meeting in Addis Ababa in mid-January 1976, twenty-two OAU members recognized the MPLA as the legitimate government of Angola; other members sought only a compromise "government of national unity."[141] In Washington, Secretary of

138. Charles C. Petersen and William J. Durch, "Angolan Crisis Deployments (November 1975 to February 1976)," in Dismukes and McConnell, eds., *Soviet Naval Diplomacy,* pp. 144–45; Durch, "The Cuban Military in Africa and the Middle East," pp. 41–48; Stockwell, *In Search of Enemies,* p. 163.

139. *New York Times,* January 30, 1976. The number of Cuban military personnel in Angola in 1976 reached between 15,000 and 18,000 men. Durch, "The Cuban Military in Africa and the Middle East," p. 49. Equatorial Guinea also has been cited as a stopover for the airlift.

140. Petersen and Durch, "Angolan Crisis Deployments," pp. 146–47; Durch, "The Cuban Military in Africa and the Middle East," pp. 48–49; MccGwire, "Naval Power and Soviet Oceans Policy," p. 143n.

141. IISS, *Strategic Survey, 1975,* p. 36.

State Kissinger warned in November 1975 that "the United States cannot remain indifferent" to Soviet and Cuban military intervention in Angola and that "continuation of an interventionist policy must inevitably threaten other relationships." He said, "We will never permit détente to turn into a subterfuge of unilateral advantage."[142] However, popular sentiment in the United States did not favor U.S. intervention in the conflict, and in December the Senate voted fifty-four to twenty-two to end covert U.S. military assistance to the FNLA and UNITA.[143] President Gerald Ford responded to this by saying: "The issue in Angola is not, never has been, and never will be a question of the use of U.S. forces. The sole issue is the provision of modest amounts of assistance to oppose military intervention by two extra-continental powers, namely the Soviet Union and Cuba."[144] In early January the President ruled out the withholding of American grain shipments in retaliation for Soviet behavior in Angola. Hence when the USSR initiated the airlift of Cuban troops to Angola and even when the first Soviet warship was deployed toward the scene of the conflict at the end of November, Moscow had good reason to expect the Ford administration to content itself with denunciation only.

The USSR knew to be false a London *Observer* and United Press International story that reported the U.S. aircraft carrier *Independence* as "operating in waters off Angola, possibly providing tactical support for air strikes in the Angolan war"[145]—the *Independence* was visible in the Mediterranean. The Kremlin also knew that the aircraft carrier *Saratoga*, which had left Florida on January 7, was heading for the Mediterranean, not the South Atlantic. Ever cautious, however, and anxious to avoid any possibility of U.S. intervention, a *Pravda* editorial stated: "The Soviet Union does not seek anything in Angola—neither economic, military nor other gain. Any assertions concerning the Soviet Union's intention to establish military bases there and about Soviet military expansion in Africa in general, are unfounded."[146] But, just in case the Ford administration did decide to deploy ships to the South Atlantic, Soviet warships were ready to quickly blunt the political impact of that deployment. In

142. *New York Times,* November 25, 1975.
143. In January 1976 this amendment to the Defense Department appropriations bill received an equally one-sided vote in the House. *Congressional Quarterly Almanac, 1975,* vol. 31 (Washington, D.C.: Congressional Quarterly, 1976), pp. 885–86.
144. *Keesing's Contemporary Archives* (April 6, 1976), pp. 27661; also see statement by Secretary of State Henry Kissinger, *New York Times,* December 24, 1975.
145. For example, see the *Boston Globe,* January 11, 1976.
146. *Pravda,* January 3, 1976 (in FBIS, *Soviet Union,* January 5, 1976, p. H1).

position near the Strait of Gibraltar, after being redeployed from the eastern Mediterranean and Northern Fleet, were two Soviet cruisers and a destroyer, and an intelligence-collecting vessel had been redeployed to the mid-Atlantic. This Soviet readiness dissolved any remaining U.S. thoughts about the value of establishing a major naval presence in West African waters.[147]

The Soviet Union's involvement in the Angolan civil war did not mean that the Kremlin was willing to accept serious risk in the use of military power in third world conflicts. Moscow simply took advantage of extremely easy pickings. Moreover, considering U.S. operations in Angola earlier and the clear desire of the Ford administration to intervene more heavily in late 1975 and thereafter, the Kremlin may also have considered its behavior within the bounds of détente from a U.S. perspective. Soviet leaders may have reasoned that the Ford administration's limitations, imposed by internal forces reacting to the outcome of the Vietnam War, were not a legitimate cause for USSR restraint, although some in the Kremlin may have worried about the effects of the Cuban intervention and Soviet airlift on Soviet-American relations and future U.S. defense efforts. Balancing these doubts, however, was the attractive image of the USSR acting strongly against South Africa, concern about Chinese influence in Africa, relations with Cuba, and the opportunity to show the world that the Soviet Union could project military power globally. The Kremlin was unwilling to pass up this opportunity.

The Angolan conflict illustrated a strong Soviet-Cuban alliance and Havana's willingness to support friends militarily. Insofar as Cuba could not have mounted the operation it did in Angola without Soviet logistics and other support, the USSR was responsible for this intervention. However, Cuban military men were active in Africa at least as early as 1961, when Havana established a permanent military mission in Ghana. Also at that time, Cuba gave military support to Algeria. In the mid-1960s Cuba established a military presence in Congo-Brazzaville (now called the People's Republic of the Congo) and Guinea and, in the early and mid-1970s, military missions in six other African countries, Angola among them. A detailed analysis of these involvements and of Cuban-Soviet relations shows that Havana was interested in African affairs quite apart from prompting or promises by the USSR.[148] The Kremlin's role was to make Cuban military intervention both possible and effective.

147. Petersen and Durch, "Angolan Crisis Deployments," p. 148.
148. Durch, "The Cuban Military in Africa and the Middle East," pp. 1–38.

While Soviet transport aircraft were airlifting Cubans to Angola in January 1976, a substantial amount of Soviet armaments that arrived in Algeria—a major stopover point for Soviet arms destined for Angola—was apparently given to the Algerian-backed Polisario guerrillas disputing the division of the former Spanish Sahara by Morocco and Mauritania. There is reason to believe that the continued U.S. attacks on Soviet behavior in Africa in February were related to this situation in North Africa. Earlier, in mid-January, the Sixth Fleet cruiser *Little Rock* had been sent to Casablanca, and in several statements thereafter Secretary Kissinger referred to Soviet-Cuban intervention in the third world generally. Upon his departure for Moscow in late January for strategic arms limitation talks, Kissinger had said: "I am going to make clear to my hosts that the United States will not accept intervention in other parts of the world."[149] Aside from speculation about Algerian leverage over the USSR, Moscow's general sympathy for movements like the Polisario, and the cover provided by the airlift to Angola, it is difficult to know what else may have prompted the unannounced unloading of Soviet arms in Algeria.

Almost two years went by between the Soviet airlifts of Cuban troops to Angola and of arms to Angola and Algeria in early 1976 and the next Soviet military action in the third world.[150] In 1977–78 Cuban and then Soviet military personnel were sent to Ethiopia to help government armed forces fighting with Somali forces in the Ogaden area in the southeast and Eritrean secessionists in the north. Soviet military assistance, after first being sent by sea, was then also transported in a large airlift in late 1977. The Soviet airlift capability, as demonstrated in the 1973 Middle East war, the Angolan civil war, and the Ethiopian-Somalian conflict, was the product of continued development of long-range transport aviation. Between 1965 and 1977 the aggregate lift capacity of Soviet military transport aircraft had grown by 132 percent.[151]

149. *New York Times*, January 21, 1976; *Boston Globe*, February 15, 1976.

150. In mid-1977 President Sadat alleged that helicopters of the Soviet carrier *Moskva* had practiced electronic countermeasures against Egyptian forces during the conflict between Egypt and Libya that had erupted that year. The *Moskva*, however, was in the Black Sea at the time. The basis for Sadat's accusation could be explained by an Egyptian technical mistake or an unreported Libyan military capability. Of course, Sadat might have made the accusation simply to gather support for his final expulsion of the Soviet military from Egypt in 1976 and his increased hostility toward Moscow thereafter. *New York Times*, August 1, 1977; FBIS, *Soviet Union* (August 9, 1976, p. F1). The Soviet statement reported in the latter source was confirmed.

151. Berman, *Soviet Air Power in Transition*, p. 36.

Eventually the number of Soviet advisers in Ethiopia rose from about 100 to about 1,000. In early spring 1978 between 16,000 and 17,000 Cuban soldiers were reported in Ethiopia, as compared with 50 a year before and 2,000 in January 1978.[152] A number of South Yemeni military men were also on the scene. While Cuban pilots flew tactical aircraft into combat on behalf of Addis Ababa, Soviet personnel were reportedly piloting helicopters in the Ogaden area and then in Eritrea. The specific timing of Moscow's military diplomacy in Ethiopia beginning in 1977, Moscow's argument that it was simply supporting national sovereignty in Ethiopia, and the risk the Kremlin ran of losing its position in Somalia, which had been nurtured for a long time, indicated prudence and calculation among Soviet leaders about using armed forces coercively in the third world. There was probably discussion and argument in Moscow about Soviet operations in Ethiopia, positing, on the one side, interest in outdistancing the United States and China and obtaining positions of influence for the USSR and, on the other, a desire not to trigger renewed U.S. activism or to undermine important negotiations with the United States and European nations.

The Soviet airlift to Ethiopia was begun only after President Siad Barre finally expelled the incongruous Soviet and Cuban military presence from Somalia. Soviet involvement in the conflict escalated slowly, and Somalia received no practical Western support. The Kremlin may have calculated that the fighting could be ended before Mogadishu reached its limit of tolerance and that, in the end, the USSR would not only obtain a strong position in Ethiopia but also be able to retain or regain its military facilities in Somalia. Presumably, however, the Kremlin viewed Ethiopia as being more important strategically than Somalia. Certainly the Ethiopian government of Mengistu Haile Mariam seemed more susceptible to Soviet influence.

During this conflict Moscow had no reason to expect a military confrontation with the United States. Opposition within the Congress and among the American public to new foreign entanglements remained strong; further, when exiled Lunda tribesmen had invaded Shaba province in Zaire in early 1977, the Carter administration had been willing to send the Mobutu government only "nonlethal" equipment. When the USSR and Cuba had become involved in Ethiopia, the United States had done nothing to support Somalia, except to hint at the possibility of a small

152. *Washington Post,* December 16, 1977, and January 6 and 13 and April 3, 1978; *New York Times,* December 14 and 17, 1977.

security assistance program. In February 1978, when the Ethiopians—
with Cuban and Soviet support—took the offensive, the USSR reportedly
had twenty-seven ships in the area. No U.S. aircraft carrier was in the
Indian Ocean at the time, and only three U.S. Navy destroyers were
nearby. Washington never suggested that the United States might become
militarily engaged in these events. As in Angola, Moscow perceived a
relatively clear field.

Even strong proponents of détente in the USSR considered it unreason-
able for the United States to view Soviet behavior in Ethiopia as being in
violation of détente. Said Georgi Arbatov, head of the USSR's Institute for
the USA and Canada and a reported confidant of Brezhnev: "In undertaking the large and laborious work of improving Soviet-American relations
the two sides could not but understand from the very beginning that they
are separated both by radical ideological and social differences and by
their approaches to many international questions."[153]

These words did not mean that the USSR intended to use its armed
forces frequently to promote Soviet foreign policy objectives. Rather the
Kremlin's rhetoric and behavior after the 1973 Middle East war indicated
that it was prepared to take advantage of extremely favorable circumstances—in particular, when it could intervene on behalf of a principle of
international law, supported by a large number of third world nations, with
little likelihood of military confrontation with the United States, and with
an otherwise large prospect of rapid success. Moscow also appeared ready
to substitute covert U.S. involvement, Western military activity, and previous military action by enemies of large groups of third world nations (for
example, South Africa) for the legitimacy provided by international law.

153. *Pravda,* March 28, 1978 (in FBIS, *Soviet Union,* March 29, 1978, p. B3).

PART TWO

Case Studies

CHAPTER SIX

Intervention
in Eastern Europe

MICHEL TATU

THE CRISIS in Poland in October 1956, the Soviet suppression of the Hungarian revolution in November 1956, and Warsaw Pact intervention in Czechoslovakia in 1968 were quite different, but they had at least two points in common.

First, the local starting point was political and social turmoil, which brought about sweeping changes and a pronounced weakening of the leadership in the face of growing unrest of the population. The combination of these two elements—a succession crisis at the top and what the Russians call *stikhiinost* (spontaneous demonstrations) by the population—is traditionally perceived in Moscow—in fact, in every Communist system—as the main danger to the system, the only one that could produce a total collapse.

Second, internationally, the Soviet Union was a factor in each case, though to a different degree. Its role was maximal in Hungary and minimal in Poland in 1956, but in each case it was a real or potential threat, which the different local factions tried to use for their own purposes.

Before comparing the Soviet role in these cases, I shall briefly set down the history leading up to and the main events of these crises.

Historical Background

The events in Poland and in Hungary in 1956 had a common starting point: the Twentieth Congress of the Communist Party of the Soviet

Union (CPSU) in January and February 1956, which officially launched the destalinization campaign. The effect of this on other Communist parties could only be a further destabilization of leaderships already weakened by the first departures from the dictator's policies. In Hungary, for example, the ups and downs of Imre Nagy's political fortune between 1953 and 1956 closely followed the struggle for power in Moscow, with the Russians arbitrating the fight between Stalinist hard-liner Mátyás Rákosi and Nagy, the future head of the counterrevolutionary government, who was at that time only a "consumerist" reformer. The July 18 decision to fire Rákosi was conveyed by Soviet Politburo member Anastas Mikoyan, who came from Moscow with a direct order from Nikita Khrushchev. The same thing happened in Poland, where the replacement of the deceased Boleslaw Bierut, first secretary of the Polish party under Stalin, was presided over by Khrushchev personally in March 1956.

Another starting point for Poland was the Poznań riot at the end of June 1956. In a Communist system, such a localized, brief riot does not lead to a crisis and may even have little political significance under a united leadership since it presents no challenge to the authority of those in charge. The picture is quite different if the leadership is divided, when each contending faction will find in the riot, in the way it was handled by the authorities and explained to the public, an argument to be used in its struggle. That is what happened in Poland in 1956, though two observations must be made.

First, the uprising, though violent, did not spread to other cities. In the months that followed it, the authorities, even though they were changing, remained in control.

Second, the Poznań riot was suppressed by exclusively Polish forces— police and army. This helped keep the Soviet Union out at that stage and allowed the Polish leaders to resist Moscow's pressure later. At the same time, it limited popular anti-Soviet feelings, making the riot and its aftermath more manageable. This was not true of the Hungarian situation.

Politically, the Poznań riot further isolated the Stalinist hard core of the party leadership (discredited by awkward attempts to portray the riot as counterrevolutionary) and helped the irresistible rise of Wladyslaw Gomulka. Formerly head of the party (he had been elected in 1943, without formal Soviet approval due to wartime conditions), Gomulka was purged in 1949 as "deviationist," jailed, set free in 1954, but kept out of any political activity until the fall of 1956. But after the Twentieth Congress of the CPSU and the riot, he appeared to be the only man capable of leading a destalinized, more liberal, more nationalistic party. An important factor, indeed unique among the three cases under study, was that many previous leaders genuinely accepted the necessity for this new course.

Nevertheless, Gomulka's opponents remained a powerful group. They attempted a coup, which included plans to arrest hundreds of liberal Communists, among them Gomulka, and was intended to prevent the meeting of the party's Central Committee, scheduled for October 19, that was to bring Gomulka back as party leader. At the same time, Soviet troops began to move on Warsaw. On top of that, Khrushchev and a high-level Soviet delegation arrived in Warsaw the same day.

The showdown ended on the morning of October 20, after a full night of tough talks, with an apparent capitulation by Khrushchev, who made major concessions to the Poles: not only was Gomulka duly elected to head the party, but the demand of the new leadership for the removal of Soviet-born Marshal Konstantin Rokossovsky from the post of defense minister was accepted by Moscow some weeks later.

The situation was very different in Hungary, where the crisis culminated in a total collapse of the party leadership, an outbreak of prolonged and uncontrolled violence, and finally a brutal crushing by Soviet forces of what had become a national revolution typical of the nineteenth century. The main culprits in this tragedy, apart from the Russians, were undoubtedly the pre-October leaders in Budapest—Ernö Gerö for the party and András Hegedüs for the government (the latter was later found to be a revisionist, though many years after these events). Both men, unlike Edward Ochab and others in Poland, climbed to power not only without regard for popular aspirations for change, but also oblivious of the winds from Moscow, which favored a "reasonable" destalinization. Imre Nagy, the symbol of reformer's communism and the Hungarian equivalent of Gomulka, was readmitted to the party on October 10, 1956, only ten days before his nomination as head of the government.

Nagy's return to power occurred after a huge Hungarian demonstration of solidarity with the Poles, on October 23, had turned into a riot. Gerö was still in power (he was not ousted until October 25, after Mikoyan and Mikhail Suslov made a trip from Moscow to Budapest), preventing the new prime minister from acting effectively during two crucial days. In addition, the previous leadership had asked the Soviet forces in Hungary to suppress the riot. This immediately turned the riot into a general uprising, with a definite and violent anti-Soviet orientation. On November 1 Nagy proclaimed the neutrality of Hungary and its withdrawal from the Warsaw Pact, and officially requested the departure of all Soviet troops from the country. I will discuss later whether this move was responsible for the subsequent Russian intervention or was merely an attempt to escape Soviet action already decided upon. In any case, the crushing of the Hungarian revolution, which started the morning of November 4, was announced by the sudden defection, on the evening of November 1, of János Kádár, first secretary of the party, who could be found three days later at the head of a "revolutionary worker-peasant government" imposed by Russian troops.

The repression was brutal (the total number of executions is estimated at 2,000, including that of Nagy himself and of his minister of defense, Pál Maléter, in the summer of 1958), but the process of normalization developed in the long run along much more liberal lines than in Poland.

In Czechoslovakia in the spring of 1968, the Soviet Union faced a situation midway between the Polish and Hungarian crises of 1956. It differed from Poland in that military intervention was decided upon, and from Hungary in that Soviet troops did not fight. It exemplifies a combination of military preparation and heavy, long-standing political pressure. It started in January 1968 with the eviction of Antonín Novotny, an old-time Stalinist leader, from his post of first secretary of the Communist party and his replacement by Alexander Dubček, head of the party in Slovakia. Behind the change were dissatisfaction with the conservative Novotny's rule, Slovak nationalist aspirations, and a growing push by intellectuals for more political freedom. (Unlike in Hungary and Poland, the role of the workers was limited until the very last days of the crisis and at no point was there an outburst of popular violence.) The main features of the Prague spring were an audacious program of political reforms (notably the "action program" in April), the lifting of the censorship of the press (de facto in March, de jure in June), and a vigorous campaign to correct bureaucratic and police excesses of the past, which further isolated the dogmatic pro-Novotny elements. It was expected that the latter would be purged by a party congress due to convene on September 9. This was prevented by the Russian intervention in August.

The Soviet leaders did not consider it necessary to save Novotny from his opponents: Brezhnev was invited by Novotny in December 1967 to Prague to be an arbiter but refused to get involved in the quarrel, saying to the Czechoslovaks: "It is your business." But, early in 1968, they began to express to Dubček their fear that the liberalizing process was going too far. A meeting in Dresden on March 23, 1968, was the first official expression of this dissatisfaction and at the same time the first grouping against Dubček of the five Warsaw Pact countries (the USSR, Poland, East Germany, Hungary, and Bulgaria), which were to take part in the military intervention five months later.

After many months of military and political pressure, a long meeting of Soviet and Czechoslovak leaders in Cierna-nad-Tisou at the end of July led to a temporary conciliation. But Dubček was unwilling or unable to take tough measures against the liberals in Prague. A few days after the return of the Soviet leaders to Moscow, the decision to act was made. During the night of August 20–21, Czechoslovakia was occupied by a large contingent of Soviet forces, supplemented by sizable groups of Polish, East German, Hungarian, and Bulgarian troops.

There was no violent resistance, but the political crisis dragged on for more than eight months. The Soviet planners were unable to impose a Hungarian-style "worker-peasant government." Major roles were played in the first days by the nonviolent but effective resistance of the population, encouraged and coordinated by a wide network of radio stations, and by President Ludvík Svoboda, who refused to cooperate with Moscow as long as Dubček and other legitimate leaders were unable to resume their functions. Once this was achieved, however, Svoboda pushed for the compromises that would lead to capitulation. The Moscow "protocol," signed on August 26, was followed by a treaty legalizing the stationing of Soviet troops in Czechoslovakia (October 16), by the breaking up of the hard core of the liberal leadership with the removal of Smrkovsky from the parliament's chairmanship (January 7, 1969), and finally by the replacement of Dubček with Gustav Husák as head of the party after a direct threat from Marshal A. A. Grechko, Soviet defense minister, of a new military intervention (April 17, 1969). Although it was a year before the August invasion was officially approved by the new Prague leadership (September 1969), the slow but growing repression of liberal tendencies led to a regime that is now one of the most tightly controlled in Eastern Europe, much more so than those in Hungary and Poland.

Soviet Behavior in the Three Crises

Poland, 1956

The behavior of the Soviet leaders toward Gomulka in 1956 was similar to their attitude toward Dubček in Czechoslovakia in 1968, with the difference that it was demonstrated before the new party leader came to power, not after, as in Prague. Basically, the Russians were disappointed that their candidate for the Polish leadership after Boleslaw Bierut's death, Zenon Nowak, was not elected in March 1956. They were not openly hostile to the selection of Edward Ochab, a middle-of-the-road man, but they continued to encourage their most dedicated supporters, the members of the "Natolin group" (named after a Warsaw suburb where they had formerly met), and watched with great anxiety the rise of what they perceived to be a nationalist-revisionist trend centered around Gomulka. In that respect, the public demand that Rokossovsky, the Soviet marshal put in command of the Polish army by Stalin, be sent back to Moscow was seen as the beginning of a dangerous "desatellization." During the fall of 1956, the growing independence of the Polish press and its anti-Soviet overtones were another cause for concern: Moscow had good reason to consider that this would be worse if Gomulka, the hero of the liberal Communists, came to power.

At that time, there was certainly no unity in the Soviet Politburo. Nikita Khrushchev, first secretary for only three years, had antagonized the Soviet Stalinist faction consisting of Vyacheslav Molotov, Lazar Kaganovich, Kliment Voroshilov, and others by his revelations at the Twentieth Party Congress. In this fight, which was to culminate in June 1957 with the defeat of the Molotov faction, Khrushchev had an interest in supporting some degree of reform in Eastern European countries and in putting some distance between the old Stalinist guard and himself. But he needed a guarantee from Gomulka that basic Soviet interests would be preserved in Poland.

The Soviet objectives in the crisis were communicated in a most direct manner. At first, Khrushchev wanted the whole Polish politburo to come to Moscow for a discussion on October 17, two days before the Central Committee meeting scheduled in Warsaw, to decide the change of leadership. The "invitation" was turned down by Ochab, so Khrushchev decided to go to Warsaw without being asked on the very day of the plenum, with Molotov, Kaganovich, Mikoyan, Marshal Konev, commander in chief of the Warsaw Pact countries, and eleven generals. All accounts of these talks agree on some basic facts: Khrushchev refused to shake hands with Gomulka, asking, "Who is this man?" According to Gomulka in what may be considered his autobiography, "every time I spoke up he turned his head away and started to talk with Mikoyan. He listened only to what Ochab was saying. . . . When he was told that the comrades actually intended to promote me to the function of first secretary, he turned so red that we thought he would blow up any minute. But he restrained himself and did not say a word."[1] Gomulka adds that Khrushchev "wanted to shout us down," that "several times he pounded the table with his fists," and that "he was particularly angry about what the Polish press wrote at that time on the Soviet Union: 'You are giving free hand to counterrevolutionary agitation,' he shouted, 'that is open treason!' "

The other accounts stress the same points. According to Frank Gibney, the Soviet leaders wanted "an immediate stabilization of the Politburo, substantially as it then was. Gomulka could join, they conceded, as long as the basic balance of the membership remained the same, i.e., pro-Soviet."[2] Nicholas Bethell, a biographer of Gomulka, quotes from a speech given by Gomulka on October 29, 1956, to Polish press editors, the text of which was published later in Paris. According to Gomulka, the Russians had pointed out that "the preparations and changes connected with the 8th Plenum [the Central Committee meeting of October 19] would lead to a breach of the Warsaw Pact, would lead to a break-off of Soviet-Polish relations."[3] A milder version was given in a Warsaw publication, which quoted from a speech delivered by Polish politburo member Aleksander Zawadzki: the "Soviet comrades, it is said, were interested in the construction of our new leadership. They pointed to the fact that the proposed leadership is now generally known, but that we gave the Soviet comrades no information about it, in spite of the relationship between us."[4]

These themes were supported by public attacks. On October 20, *Pravda* published a long article under the headline: "Anti-socialist articles in the Polish press," with numerous quotations purporting to show that the Warsaw newspapers had fallen under the control of reactionary forces. This kind of public warning is particularly important in Communist diplomacy, since it commits the Soviet leadership to achieve results.

1. *Nowiny Kurier*, April 16, 1973. This Polish-language weekly published in Tel Aviv presented in fourteen installments, from April 16 to July 13, 1973, what is described as a number of conversations held between Gomulka and an unidentified writer between March and July 1971, a few weeks after Gomulka was ousted from power. Despite the unauthenticated character of this document, there are strong reasons to believe that Gomulka actually used this means to give his own assessment of his long career, as Khrushchev did after his retirement.

2. Frank Gibney, *Frozen Revolution; Poland: A Study in Communist Decay* (Farrar, Straus, 1959), p. 12.

3. Nicholas Bethell, *Gomulka: His Poland and His Communism* (London: Penguin, 1972), p. 210.

4. *Nowe Drogi* (Warsaw), October 1956.

Another kind of pressure, more covert but ominous, came from the Soviet military. Normally the contingent of Soviet troops stationed in Poland, known as the Northern Group of Troops, was made up of three divisions, under the command of General Galicki, with headquarters at Legnica, in the western part of the country, between Wroclaw and the East German border. Beginning in early October, these 30,000 troops were reinforced by four more divisions (three coming from East Germany, one from the Soviet Union), which joined the Legnica group. At the same time, General Galicki ordered his troops to move east, toward Warsaw, and established operational headquarters near Lodz, within striking distance (by a good highway) of the capital.[5] According to Gibney, "This brought the total available inside Poland to seven divisions, with many times that number ready to move in (from the U.S.S.R. and G.D.R.). Warships had been sighted in the Gulf of Gdansk."[6]

The preparations of the Polish army, under the command of Marshal Rokossovsky and Natolinist high commanders such as Kazimierz Witaszewski, are less clear. According to Philippe Ben, the army had been put on a state of alert two weeks before the October 19 plenum, clearly to support a tentative coup prepared by the Natolinists to prevent Gomulka's rise to power. Garthoff reports that on the night of October 18–19 a Polish army force was stopped thirty miles from Warsaw by internal security units loyal to Gomulka.[7]

In any case, the combination of the Soviet show of strength and the intrigues of the Natolin group with the tacit support of the Polish army culminated in a very high degree of pressure on October 19 with the arrival of the Soviet leaders in Warsaw. Why did Khrushchev, after a night of tense discussions with the Polish leaders, decide to back down from his threats and depart early in the morning on October 20, leaving the Polish Central Committee free to elect Gomulka as its head (which took place the same day)?

In fact, the meeting was not conclusive and, though a catastrophe was avoided, the danger was not over. As Gomulka notes, Khrushchev had not made up his mind. On October 19, "the plans for intervention were ready and preparatory work began. The only thing which had to be done was to issue the order. There was no agreement precisely on that point

5. Philippe Ben, *Le Monde* (Paris), October 24, 1956.
6. Gibney, *Frozen Revolution,* p. 10.
7. Philippe Ben, *Le Monde,* October 21 and 22, 1956; Raymond L. Garthoff, *Soviet Military Policy: A Historical Analysis* (Praeger, 1966), p. 157.

(among the Soviet leadership) and Khrushchev flew in to make a decision on the spot, depending on the actual situation." A day later, the situation was not very different: "They did not give up at all the idea of intervening. They merely came to the conclusion that at that moment an intervention was not desirable or necessary. They simply decided to wait and see what would happen. That was all that we achieved."[8]

Things began to improve a few days later, but another important trial was still to come. On October 22 or 23 (accounts differ on this point), Gomulka had a telephone call from Khrushchev in Moscow. The tone was friendlier than at their last meeting. The Soviet leader invited his Polish counterpart to Moscow and made a friendly gesture by announcing that he had ordered General Galicki to move back to his headquarters in Legnica on October 25.[9] In the same manner, the Soviet naval units that were showing the flag not far from Polish Baltic ports were withdrawn. These returns to normalcy must actually have taken more time than expected, since large movements of Soviet troops across Poland to East Germany were reported at the beginning of November.[10]

Gomulka had agreed to go to Moscow on October 26 but decided to postpone the trip until November 14, fearing that the situation in Poland was not sufficiently under control to prevent anti-Soviet demonstrations. Khrushchev had made in advance the important gesture of yielding to the Polish demand for Rokossovsky's removal. Together with a group of Soviet military advisers, the Soviet marshal left Warsaw on November 14. It had become difficult to keep him in Poland anyway, since in the October 20 election of the new politburo he had received only 23 votes out of 75. A victim of Stalin's purges just before World War II, Rokossovsky had said that he was "fed up with the Polish mess" and was glad to accept the post of Soviet deputy defense minister. Nevertheless, this important concession, made only a few days after the crushing of the Hungarian uprising and at a moment when the situation in Poland was far from stabilized, must have been the subject of controversy in Moscow.

When Gomulka and two other Polish leaders (Jozef Cyrankiewicz and Aleksander Zawadzki) arrived in Moscow on November 14, the attitude of Khrushchev, who had ordered the repression in Hungary, was considerably tougher. According to Gomulka, the Soviet leader started, as on October 19 in Warsaw, by sharply attacking liberal and anti-Soviet demon-

8. *Nowiny Kurier,* April 16, 1973.
9. *Le Monde,* October 25, 1956.
10. *New York Times,* November 3, 1956.

strations in Poland (these were particularly important after the Russian action in Hungary): "He said that if those riots do not stop, he would order his tanks to move. . . . It was not a bad start of negotiations, was it not?"[11]

Khrushchev's previous actions in Poland show that these tough words were probably a bluff and that he preferred to avoid the use of force while keeping this option open. The point is that Gomulka said exactly what the Soviet leader wanted to hear. Dubček in 1968 had tried to explain to Brezhnev that things in Czechoslovakia were not that bad, but Gomulka chose the opposite line: "I stated that I knew that things were bad in Poland, that maybe they were worse than comrade Khrushchev would admit. Counterrevolutionary elements had an upper hand, the authority of the Party was very hard hit. . . . in other words, we were at the threshold of anarchy. But since it is a fire, it could not be extinguished by using tanks. We needed time, said I, so that gradually, step by step, we could introduce socialist order in Poland."[12] Khrushchev, having accepted this reasoning, became "completely satisfied, solicitous and friendly" and agreed to discuss all the problems of Soviet-Polish relations, including compensation for the low coal prices paid by the Soviet Union to Poland over the years. There were no more real problems between the two men except in 1964, when the Soviet leader tried, opposed by Gomulka, to normalize relations with West Germany.

Khrushchev's surprising turnabout in a few weeks from open hostility to nearly complete confidence in a foreign leader has to be explained by the Polish situation at that time, which imposed limits on Soviet actions, and by Gomulka's success in convincing Moscow of his goodwill and capacity to maintain "socialist order"—that is to say, an authoritarian and pro-Soviet system—a not unpleasant task since he was genuinely hostile to liberal ideas. To be sure, he did not intend to be a puppet of Moscow, and his program on certain issues—notably on rural collectivization —was very different from the Soviet model. But this could be considered a secondary problem and, given the conditions in Poland at that time, he undoubtedly seemed the only man capable of maintaining a tolerable state of affairs. One wonders, nevertheless, if another leader in Moscow— Molotov, for example—would have been as tolerant. After all, Gomulka was, after Tito, the first Communist leader in Eastern Europe who was not totally subservient to Soviet interests.

11. *Nowiny Kurier,* April 16, 1973.
12. Ibid.

Hungary, 1956

Though the same Soviet leadership faced this crisis only a few days later, its behavior was more complex. The conflict was violent and could not be settled by negotiation, as in Poland, and it covered a longer period, which may be divided into two phases: from October 23 to October 31, Moscow tried to adapt itself to the new situation, without a firm commitment to a definite course of action; on November 1, the decision to use force was made and Soviet behavior changed perceptibly.

The first phase presented the Russians with a problem almost the reverse of what they had found in Poland three days earlier: in Warsaw they opposed a change of leadership fostered by the political elite with the backing of the population; in Budapest they had to rescue a leadership that they did not strongly support from a population yearning for reforms they had at least partially supported. Unlike in Poland, they had no initiative in the crisis and tried, in the first phase, to make the best of it without a clear-cut strategy.

One may question why the Kremlin answered so readily the request of the Gerö-Hegedüs government, the night of October 23–24, that troops be sent to suppress the riots. Without proper preparation, this first intervention had little result other than to stir the anti-Soviet feelings of the population without solving the political problems, thus helping bring about a true revolution and the collapse of the system. Probably in this case the Soviet Politburo took the same position it had in 1953, when a popular uprising exploded in Berlin: it decided it had no other option than to respond to the request of the local leaders.

According to the report of the United Nations Special Committee for Hungary, two divisions of Soviet troops were already in Hungary before these events, the 2d and 17th mechanized, forming the so-called Southern Group of Troops. These forces, which consisted of roughly 20,000 men and 600 tanks, were stationed mainly around Szolnok, their headquarters, and none were closer to Budapest than forty-five miles. To be sure, the Soviet high command, aware of the rising tension in Hungary, had taken some precautionary measures. According to Noel Barber, by October 21 and 22, "all Soviet officers in Russia who spoke Hungarian or German were recalled from leave."[13] In any case, the reinforcements came quickly: at 1 a.m. on October 24, a few hours after the outbreak of violence in

13. Noel Barber, *Seven Days of Freedom: The Hungarian Uprising, 1956* (Stein and Day, 1974), p. 46.

Budapest, Russian troops began to enter Hungary from Rumania. This probably happened even before the Hungarian government's request for help reached Moscow.

But taking these precautions did not indicate a desire to act. The action in Budapest on the first day, October 24, involved probably no more than a few thousand troops and less than a hundred tanks, a force clearly secondary to that of the Hungarian political police (AVH), which had 30,000 men in the whole country and was the main instrument at the disposal of the government. The Soviet troops moved to protect the party headquarters, the Parliament House (which was also the seat of the government), the bridges, and the Soviet embassy. Though they incurred casualties—a dozen tanks were destroyed by insurgents armed with Molotov cocktails—they tried to avoid fighting. There were many cases of friendly talks between the people and Soviet soldiers. According to Miklos Molnár, a Soviet officer, General Sharutin, went so far as to proclaim the "neutrality" of his troops in Kecskemét. Molnár concludes from these observations: "We must believe that their inactions were the result of orders from above. . . . Such an attitude expressed some reluctance in Moscow's attitude with regard to Gerö's stalinist team."[14]

This behavior was maintained until October 29, when, in exchange for a cease-fire negotiated by Imre Nagy, the Soviet Union agreed to remove its troops from the Hungarian cities. The scale of the commitment was slightly increased, since on October 26, according to Western estimates, there were 50,000 to 75,000 troops in Hungary and some 150 tanks in Budapest.[15] But the degree of participation remained the same, with the Russians patrolling the main streets of the cities, leaving the side streets to the rebels and fighting only if attacked.

Behavior at the political level followed the same pattern. On October 24 Anastas Mikoyan and Mikhail Suslov arrived in Budapest; a low-level team compared to the Soviet delegation to Warsaw four days earlier. These two men had presided over the replacement of Rákosi by Gerö in July; presumably they were not only specialists on Hungary, but also a reflection of the grouping in the Soviet Politburo at that time. Since Mikoyan was clearly aligned with Khrushchev, it is possible that Suslov, at that time a junior member of the ruling group (he had been promoted to Politburo membership a year earlier), represented the tougher line of the Molotov group.

14. Miklos Molnár, *Budapest 1956: A History of the Hungarian Revolution* (London: Allen and Unwin, 1971), p. 36.
15. *New York Times,* October 26, 1956.

But the circumstances were not ripe for repressive action across the board. Instead, the Soviet representatives tried to bring about an accommodation by pushing the reforms that the Rákosi-Gerö team had prevented for so many months. Not only did they not object to Nagy's promotion to prime minister (unlike Gomulka, Nagy had been placed in that position by Khrushchev in 1953), but they supported the popular demand for the removal of Gerö, who resigned on October 24 but persuaded his Soviet bosses to announce the change a day later. This delay, which prevented Kádár, his successor, and Nagy from taking control when their actions might have been helpful, contributed to the escalation of the uprising.

There are conflicting views about Soviet intentions in the period that followed. Some Hungarians said after the intervention that the Russians were against their revolution from the very beginning and were just looking for an opportunity to suppress it. Other observers take the opposite view, for example, Molnár: "All the decisions made by Nagy between October 27th and 31st seemed to have been ratified by Moscow, including the re-establishment of former political parties and the withdrawal of troops."[16]

To be sure, the Soviet Union certainly expected a return to a normalized situation with an acceptable degree of socialist order and pro-Soviet subservience. But that does not mean that a military intervention was considered necessary or feasible to achieve this. If it had been, Moscow had only to step up its first intervention, bring in more troops, and commit them more decisively against the insurgents. The opposite happened: it not only limited Soviet troops' participation in the fighting but also agreed on October 29 to withdraw them from the Hungarian cities.

This conciliatory mood was confirmed by Mikoyan and Suslov, who made another visit to Budapest on October 29 and 30, bringing with them the text of the official Soviet statement that was published October 30 and became famous as the "new chart" of the relations between the Soviet Union and other Communist countries. The document expressed the wish to correct Stalin's mistakes and to establish more equality. As far as Hungary was concerned, the statement asked the "peoples of the Socialist countries" not to "permit foreign or domestic reactionary forces to shake the foundation of the people's democracy system" and added: "The defense of socialist achievements by the people's democracy of Hungary is *at the present moment* the chief and sacred duty of the workers, peasants,

16. Molnár, *Budapest 1956*, p. 68.

intelligentsia and all the *Hungarian* working people" (emphasis added). In other words, the fear of counterrevolution was expressed, but it was admitted that the Hungarians could deal with it by themselves, as Nagy wanted. Even though the phrase "at the present moment" implied ominously that this could change, the goodwill was confirmed by the following statement: "The Soviet government is ready to enter into relevant negotiations with the government of the Hungarian People's Republic and other participants of the Warsaw Pact on the question of the presence of Soviet troops on the territory of Hungary."

Although this statement brought considerable détente in Hungarian-Soviet relations, it is nevertheless necessary to qualify the optimism expressed by Molnár in the quotation above. In my view, the Soviet Union had no intention, even at the last moment, of withdrawing its troops from Hungary altogether. The statement of October 30 expressed only the wish to *negotiate* a withdrawal, with the participation of other Warsaw Pact countries, which meant at best a long process. This was confirmed by Mikoyan, who said to the Hungarian leaders on October 30: "The Soviet troops which are not in Hungary by virtue of the Warsaw Pact will be withdrawn,"[17] meaning that while some troops could leave, the others would stay. In fact, Moscow was not ready to abandon the only means it had of keeping the troubled situation in check and wanted to keep three options open.

First, if Nagy (later Kádár) had managed to get the upper hand and to establish a satisfactory degree of control over the Communist party, the Soviet Union might have acted as promised in its statements, stopped its reinforcement, and progressively loosened its grip on the country. A protracted negotiation on complete withdrawal might have accompanied this process, though it is doubtful that even this result would have been achieved. After all, a satisfactory normalization, in Moscow's eyes, meant that the Hungarian leaders would prefer the presence of Soviet troops and drop their demand for withdrawal.

Another option was to use the confusion created by the withdrawal/no-withdrawal game to maintain pressure and try to extract more concessions from the Hungarian leadership. The regrouping of forces implied complicated military moves that might be used as a threat.

The third option was to step up the second option and use the movement of troops not only to threaten but to prepare for an actual, and this time decisive, intervention.

17. Ibid., p. 70.

The first option was clearly impracticable in view of the chaotic conditions in Hungary. To be sure, the country was beginning to stabilize by the end of October, but in a way that was clearly not satisfactory to Moscow, with too limited a role for the Communist party and the nationalistic feelings of the population running high. The second option was probably considered when the offer of withdrawal talks was made by Mikoyan, but not for long.

It is hard to say at what moment the Kremlin decided to move from the second to the third option; but it was probably after October 30, when Mikoyan and Suslov, back in Moscow, reported on the situation. Certainly it was before the evening of November 1, when János Kádár, the party chief, disappeared from his home and defected to the Russians.

What decisions of the Hungarian government were considered beyond the threshold of acceptability? On October 30 Nagy announced that he was returning to a government "based on the democratic cooperation of a coalition of parties, as it was in 1945." He set up a new cabinet with only three representatives of the Communist party (Kádár, Pál Losonczi and himself), two of the Smallholders party, one of the National Peasant party, and one of the Social Democrat party (which refused the offer). But most of the actual power was in the hands of the workers' councils created in most regions, which established on October 31 a "parliament" for all the country. At the same time, the leaders of the insurgents, who had agreed to a cease-fire but were retaining their arms, publicly demanded the complete withdrawal of Soviet troops, the denunciation of the Warsaw Pact, and the proclamation of Hungarian neutrality. Last but not least, Communist supporters of the old regime and members of the ΛVH were subjected to repressive measures in the last days of October. Cases of lynching and summary executions were reported (215, according to a white book published later by the Kádár government).

All these measures and actions were in any case difficult for Moscow to swallow, even before Imre Nagy decided, on November 1, to accede to popular demand and withdraw from the Warsaw Pact. To be sure, recorded public statements support the view that this move made Moscow decide to intervene. *Pravda* on November 1 headlined its story on Hungary, "Budapest is back to normal" and expressed no criticism of the situation there; and a day later, it reprinted a critical comment of Belgrade's *Politika,* warning against any idea of restoring the bourgeois regime. (The tone was harsher on November 3 and 4, mentioning "anticommunist atrocities" in Hungary.) But the fact is that the proclamation of neutrality by Nagy was a desperate move in response to the growing threat of a military intervention that was, if not definitely decided upon, at least being actively *prepared* for by the Soviet Union.

The first turnabout of Soviet forces—which were supposed to leave the country, but actually remained and even came back by other roads—was reported on October 30 to Nagy by Maléter. From that day on, according to a UN special committee report, "troops were employed to encircle the Hungarian military aerodromes, ostensibly to ensure the safe evacuation of Soviet citizens, but in fact paralysing the Hungarian air force." At the same time, huge reinforcements were brought in from the Soviet Union and Rumania. According to Barber, "By the Wednesday [October 31], the roads leading into Hungary from the East were choked with Soviet military traffic, not only at Zahony [the crossing point from the Soviet Union], but at the frontier village of Nyirbator near Satu Mare in Rumania and at Battonya near Arad in Rumania."[18] Some figures give an idea of this buildup: while the number of Soviet tanks in Hungary on October 30 did not exceed 400, according to the UN report, the estimated force ready to crush the rebellion on the eve of November 4 included 2,000 to 2,500 tanks. As far as manpower is concerned, there were 200,000 Soviet troops in Hungary on November 4, ten times as many as at the beginning of the crisis on October 23, and as early as November 2 eight Soviet divisions, seven of them armored, were in Hungary.[19] The following day, the Soviet Union sealed off the Hungarian-Austrian border.

Another indication of the Soviet determination to act is the change in their behavior on November 1. There was no longer any question of Mikoyan and Suslov visiting Budapest. Imre Nagy tried without success to telephone Mikoyan or Khrushchev to get an explanation of the Soviet military buildup. The only person he could find to talk to was the Soviet ambassador in Budapest, Yuri Andropov, with whom he had five conversations—on the phone or directly—the same day. But at that level, it is traditional Soviet behavior to use communications mainly for stalling for time and for deception. There were a number of examples of this behavior in the last three days of Hungarian "independence."

The only answer Andropov gave to Nagy's questions about the Soviet troop reinforcements was that "troops of the Interior Ministry [MVD] were sent to protect the evacuation of the regular army." And the only aim of the occupation of Hungarian aerodromes was to "supervise the evacua-

18. Barber, *Seven Days of Freedom*, p. 148.
19. *New York Times,* November 3, 1956.

tion of wounded and sick people."[20] Since Andropov proposed at the same
time to create two committees—one political, the other military—to discuss relations between the two countries, including the complete withdrawal of troops, the Hungarians may have felt that the situation was not
that bad.

The first meeting of the Soviet-Hungarian military committee to discuss
the withdrawal of Soviet troops was scheduled for November 3, a day
before the Soviet attack. The Soviet delegation, headed by General Malinin, went to the parliament building at noon. Everything went smoothly.
The Russians produced a plan of gradual withdrawal. Their insistence on
discussing details, including the organization of a military ceremony at the
end of the process, made a very good impression on the Hungarians, who
agreed without objection to a second meeting the same day, this time at
Soviet headquarters on Csepel Island in Budapest. At 10 p.m. General
Pál Maléter, who that day had become Hungarian defense minister, was
greeted there by General Malinin with full military honors. One hour later
he telephoned his office to say that everything was in order. At midnight,
the meeting was interrupted by the sudden entrance of Soviet General Ivan
Serov, head of the KGB, with an armed escort. After asking Malinin to
leave the room, he placed Maléter and his group under arrest. At approximately the same time, Soviet tanks began to move all over the country to
crush the new Hungarian regime.

This particularly crude example of deception must be regarded as a
pattern of conduct decided at the highest level to achieve a specific result
(in this case, the elimination of a man who might have played a crucial
role in organizing the resistance) by whatever means available. It did not
involve the men immediately concerned, like Malinin, who was reportedly
upset by this violation of military ethics and probably was not informed
about the upcoming incident. It was repeated later with Colonel Sándor
Kopácsi, head of the Budapest police, who was invited, after the intervention, by a Russian "friend" to come to the Soviet embassy to discuss a
possible truce; there he was arrested and interrogated by Serov personally.
Last but not least, Imre Nagy, who had taken refuge on November 4 in
the Yugoslav embassy with an important group of his followers, left the
embassy on November 22 after he and the Yugoslavs had received Kádár's
written guarantee of their safety. No sooner had he reached the street than
he was taken away by a Russian military convoy, despite the protests of
the Yugoslav diplomats present at the scene.

20. Barber, *Seven Days of Freedom,* p. 162.

The military operations that began on November 4 were conducted ruthlessly, unlike the rather passive conduct of the Soviet forces during the first intervention on October 24 and the following days. The objective this time was to take full control of everything in Budapest and to crush any resistance. At 8 a.m. on November 4, Parliament House was occupied after an ultimatum to surrender had been delivered (during the first intervention, Soviet forces had satisfied themselves with "protecting" the building from outside). In all other places, the answer to isolated fire was radical. According to Barber, "If one lone sniper fired a single bullet, retribution was swift and inevitable. Half a dozen tanks rolled to the building from where the shot had been fired and obliterated it."[21]

In these circumstances, resistance was possible only in a few more or less fortified places. One was the Kilian Barracks in Budapest (a stronghold of the rebellion during the first fighting in October) and at the Csepel metal factory in the southern part of the city, where the Russians had to use twelve battalions of troops, heavy artillery, and bombers. A week after this second intervention, the last resistance was crushed, but the casualties were heavy. According to official sources quoted by Molnár, "between October 23 and December 1st, 12,971 wounded received treatment in the hospitals, dispensaries and provisional aid stations."[22] Molnár puts the number of deaths at 2,000 in Budapest and 700 in the provinces, Barber at a minimum of 4,000 in Hungary. But these figures did not cover Soviet victims, whose number has never been officially revealed.

By the same token, there was no room for negotiations, even with the new "worker-peasant government" formed under the leadership of Kádár in support of the Soviet intervention. In fact, Kádár seems to have remained the first few days in Szolnok at the headquarters of the Soviet command in Hungary, from which his appeal was broadcast; he was not brought to Budapest until November 8. During these four days, orders were given directly to the population by Soviet General K. Grebennik, commander of the Soviet forces in the capital. Actually, Kádár did not have even the appearance of authority for many weeks, even months. Nagy was arrested by Soviet troops; and on December 4 and 5, a month after the Soviet intervention, Soviet tanks, not Hungarian troops, were stationed in front of the U.S. legation in Budapest to prevent an attempted demonstration.

Soviet attempts to legitimate their actions were more limited than their

21. Ibid., p. 182.
22. Molnár, *Budapest 1956,* p. 220.

efforts twelve years later in support of their intervention in Czechoslovakia. The main theme of the propaganda was a description of "anticommunist atrocities," riots, and disorder, which made it imperative, as the Soviet delegate to the United Nations put it, "to protect Hungary against subversion." Curiously enough, Hungarian denunciation of the Warsaw Pact was less often mentioned as the prime cause of the Soviet action. This would have run counter to Khrushchev's "anti-bloc" diplomacy of the time. After all, Nikolai Bulganin, the Soviet prime minister, had explicitly "allowed" Hungary to make this move when he stated at the Geneva summit conference a little more than a year before: "Should any nation desiring to pursue a policy of neutrality and non-participation in military groupings . . . raise the question of having their security and territorial integrity guaranteed, the great powers should accede to these wishes."

Czechoslovakia, 1968

The Soviet objectives in Czechoslovakia were very similar to what they had been in the two previous crises. Moscow wanted to maintain or restore the highest possible degree of socialist orthodoxy of the Soviet type: a monopoly of power by the Communist party, and, inside the party, a predominance of pro-Soviet friends and as little influence as possible for the liberals. Last but not least, it wanted the press strictly censored to prevent the expression of liberal and anti-Soviet views. The last was probably the most powerful single motivation for the military intervention. It is likely that some compromises would have been possible on other issues (notably on economic reforms) if Dubček had been willing and able to bow to this demand.

But the achievement of these goals was made difficult by several considerations. First, unlike Poland, where the Soviet leadership had first opposed Gomulka and then trusted him, Brezhnev had decided to abandon the previous leader, Antonín Novotny, to his fate and to accept the change of leadership. He did not select Dubček, but he did not object to his appointment and chose to live with him, at least for a certain time.

Second, unlike Hungary, where the violent riots and the collapse of the Communist power structure demanded a quick decision, there was no spontaneous disorder at any time during the Czechoslovak spring. Dubček and his colleagues could legitimately claim that they were in command of the situation, that no direct threat to Soviet interests was apparent, and that all the changes took place inside the Communist party and in conformity with the party's statutes. Moscow could not have been satisfied with those explanations but must have found it difficult to define the point beyond which the situation became unacceptable. After all, it was embarrassing to decide on armed intervention because of an unpleasant article in the Prague press.

Finally, the Soviet Union had no troops in Czechoslovakia as it did in Hungary and Poland in 1956. It thus lacked one instrument of pressure that had been used in these two countries—military moves inside the country, reinforcements, maneuvers. Either troops had to be moved into the country, with all the political and diplomatic consequences of such a radical action, or the military pressure had to be exercised from outside the borders, which made it considerably less effective.

To be sure, the Soviet Union tried to correct this situation by introducing troops into Czechoslovakia at the end of May 1968 on the pretext of Warsaw Pact "staff maneuvers." Though these troops remained in the country for more than two months, their number was insufficient and their effectiveness as a political deterrent nearly nonexistent. In fact, one can argue that a steady reinforcement of this contingent similar to what took place in Hungary on October 30 to November 1, 1956, might have been another course of action. The maneuvers could have evolved into a creeping invasion of the country with the same outcome as the August intervention but with less dramatic overtones. But the Soviet leadership was probably not ready at the time to choose this option.

It is nearly impossible to keep track of all the meetings, communications, and exchanges between Soviet and Czechoslovak leaders in this period. Between January and early August 1968 there were no less than six "summits" between Dubček and Brezhnev, two of which were in the broader setting of Warsaw Pact meetings. When Soviet demands (decisive actions against the liberal elements, censorship of the press) were not met, the pressure was increased in two areas: public criticism and military preparations.

Public criticism, as demonstrated by the two previous crises, is generally counterproductive. It may have an effect on the leaders of the target country by compelling them to offer some kind of reassurances. But when it is aimed at a populace that is enjoying a newly acquired freedom of expression, unilateral and frequently awkward propaganda outbursts in Soviet official media can only inspire anti-Soviet feelings and lead to a polemic in which the free writers of the target country easily get the upper hand. Nevertheless, Communist leaders cannot help but air their views publicly when their hostility to a given situation exceeds a certain degree of intensity and extends over a period of time. In the case of China and Albania, the period of patience lasted two or three years but eventually ended with devastating consequences.

Czechoslovakia being a softer target, the probation period was much shorter. By the end of March the East German press had started to criticize the dangerous rise of antisocialist forces in Czechoslovakia. In May East Germany went one step further by denouncing "counterrevolutionary forces," implying by that term a comparison with the 1956 Hungarian crisis and its crushing. Soviet criticism came later but a Central Committee meeting in March heard tough statements against "bourgeois reaction" and advocated tight ideological control in all socialist countries. On June 27 Gromyko stated in front of the Supreme Soviet that the "strengthening of the commonwealth of socialist countries" is "the Soviet Union's primary duty in foreign policy": "Those who would like to break even one link in the chain of the socialist commonwealth are vain and short-sighted. This commonwealth will not permit it."[23] Receiving Kádár in Moscow on July 3, Brezhnev mentioned the intervention in Hungary in 1956 as an illustration of the fact that "the Soviet Union can never be indifferent to the fate of socialist construction in other countries, to the common cause of socialism and communism in the world."[24]

The main charge was to come on July 14 at a conference of the USSR, GDR, Poland, Hungary, and Bulgaria in Warsaw when Dubček, for the first time, refused to attend. The so-called Warsaw letter brought into the open all the accusations against hostile forces supposedly at work in Czechoslovakia, described the situation there as "absolutely unacceptable for a socialist country," and stated: "This is no longer your concern alone. . . . The frontiers of the socialist world have shifted to the center of Europe, the Elbe and the Sumava mountains. We shall never consent to the endangering of these historic achievements of socialism. . . . The danger to the basis for socialism in Czechoslovakia threatens also the common interests of other socialist countries. . . . Each of our Parties has the responsibility not only to its own working class and its people, but also towards the international working class and the world communist movement and cannot avoid the obligations that flow from this."[25] There was no mention of a *military* intervention, but a witness, Gomulka's inter-

23. *Izvestiya,* June 28, 1968.
24. *Pravda,* July 4, 1968.
25. An English translation of the Warsaw letter is given in Philip Windsor and Adam Roberts, *Czechoslovakia 1968: Reform and Resistance* (Columbia University Press, 1969), p. 150.

preter, states that at least one participant, Bulgarian party chief Zhivkov, stressed the need of delivering any help to the "sound forces" in Czechoslovakia "not excluding military help."[26]

Thus the "Brezhnev doctrine" was formulated even before the August intervention, if only to legitimate the direct interference in Czechoslovak affairs brought about by this unusual letter. According to my information, no definite decision was made in Warsaw about a military action. It was left up to Moscow to decide if and when such action was necessary. Although the Czechoslovak public answer to the Warsaw letter was certainly not satisfactory to the Kremlin, Brezhnev and his colleagues decided to make another and last attempt at negotiation. This was done at the end of July at the Cierna meeting. It was a most unusual meeting, at which the Soviet leaders insisted on having the whole Czechoslovak politburo in front of them, and even asked that everyone, according to former Czechoslovak foreign minister Jiří Hajek,[27] speak in his own name. In addition, private meetings were arranged, first between Brezhnev and Dubček, then, on the third day, between two smaller groups: Brezhnev, Podgorny, Kosygin, and Suslov from the Soviet side; Dubček, Svoboda, Cerník, and Smrkovsky for the Czechoslovaks. According to Pavel Tigrid, the best-informed writer on the political developments of the crisis, this new setting brought about a notable improvement: "The greatest surprise of all was a moderate and appeasing statement by Suslov, who went so far as to call the Czechoslovak January policy (the changes made after Novotny was ousted) a renaissance of Marxism in a certain sense" and to agree that "the Czechoslovak question must be settled by agreement if great harm is not to ensue for the international communist movement and its unity."[28] The meeting ended with an equivocal compromise. The Czechoslovaks claimed that they did not concede anything essential, and the Russians promised that they would stop the polemics and withdraw the troops that remained in Czechoslovakia after the "staff exercises" of the early summer.

This result was confirmed by a new meeting of the five in Bratislava on August 4. The statement signed with Dubček, to be sure, hinted at the Brezhnev doctrine ("It is the common internationalist duty of all socialist countries to support, strengthen and protect the socialist gains"), but did

26. Erwin Weit, *Dans l'Ombre de Gomulka* (Paris: Robert Laffont, 1971), p. 282.
27. Jiří Hajek, *Dix Ans Après—Prague 68–78* (Paris: Editions du Seuil, 1978), p. 101.
28. Pavel Tigrid, *Why Dubček Fell* (London: McDonald, 1971), p. 86.

not actually mention the situation in Czechoslovakia and, to all intents and purposes, "forgot" the Warsaw letter.

It is important to examine how the various Soviet leaders viewed the situation and what the Cierna-Bratislava compromise was intended to accomplish: was it a deceptive trick to weaken the vigilance of the Czechoslovak people and of the outside world before an intervention that had already been decided upon, as some Czechoslovaks stated later, or a provisional but genuine attempt to find a peaceful solution? I support the latter view, if only because there are sufficient indications that the decision was not easily made. As Gomulka explains in his memoirs: "The Soviet comrades obviously were very disturbed by what was happening in Czechoslovakia. . . . However, to intervene in a socialist country is not a simple or easy matter. . . . It was necessary to weigh very carefully on the scale the pros and cons of the situation. Even in the Soviet leadership itself there was no unanimity as to the final balance of that account. I will tell you very frankly that the scale was tipping both ways until the last minute."[29]

All reports indicate that the most vociferous opponent of the Prague spring among the Soviet leaders was Pyotr Shelest, Politburo member and first secretary of the Ukraine. Responsible for a territory adjacent to Czechoslovakia, he was reportedly particularly sensitive to the danger that liberal ideas might contaminate his own kingdom. It may be said generally that the regional leaders in the Soviet apparatus are more conservative than the top figures with central responsibilities, the latter being compelled to take into account broader, international considerations.

A major figure in the latter area was Suslov, a man with a long experience in international affairs, who was trying at the time to organize a new conference of the Communist movement. Two lesser figures were Boris Ponomarev and K. F. Katushev, secretaries of the Central Committee (but not Politburo members) in charge of day-to-day relations with other Communist parties. On the other hand, Aleksei Kosygin was then more powerful than later and played an important role in foreign policy; he may have been more concerned than other leaders about the effects of a military intervention on East-West relations. It is not surprising that all the indications received about Politburo divergences place those men in the role of "doves."

A few months after Suslov introduced the idea of a compromise at

29. *Nowiny Kurier,* June 15, 1973.

Cierna, I learned from Eastern European sources that Suslov, Kosygin, and Ponomarev were mentioned in a Soviet intraparty document as the ones who had "underestimated the danger of counter-revolution in Czechoslovakia." Czechoslovak Prime Minister Oldrich Cerník, reporting to his cabinet after his return from Moscow on August 26, said privately that Suslov and Aleksandr Shelepin (chairman of the Trade Union Council and Politburo member) had reservations about the military intervention.[30] Tigrid describes an even stranger episode that occurred in Budapest at the end of September 1968 during a preparatory meeting of the international Communist conference. Jozef Lenárt, who as party secretary headed the Czechoslovak delegation at this meeting, received a private visit from Ponomarev and Katushev, who both expressed "personal regret" for the month-old invasion of his country: "According to Ponomarev, those chiefly responsible were the dogmatic and semi-fascist elements in the Soviet party's politburo, mainly military men and 'centrists' of the Brezhnev type, who 'had kept their district secretary mentality.' The Czechoslovak affair had apparently been severely censored by all the 'sensible' progressives in the Soviet party leadership but they were unluckily in the minority."[31]

It is unusual for a Soviet leader to reveal to a foreigner (even a Communist) so many details of Politburo deliberations; this report must therefore be considered with prudence. At the same time, the circumstances of the time were quite unusual too: one month after the invasion the result was nearly a complete failure politically, with Dubček still in charge and the pro-Soviet conservatives in Prague more isolated than before. It is quite possible that the dovish minority of the Soviet leadership felt that their reservations were vindicated and tried, by blaming Brezhnev for the failure, to strike a bargain with the Prague ruling team.

A day after the Politburo had returned from Cierna to Moscow, a *Pravda* editorial supported the soft line ratified in Bratislava, stressing the need to solve by negotiation problems arising among socialist countries. But five days later, on August 11, new military maneuvers around Czechoslovakia were announced. On August 14, the presence of Grechko and Marshal Ivan Yakubovsky, the Warsaw Pact commander in East Germany, was mentioned. The Czechoslovaks learned later, according to my information, that both Soviet marshals had said to their troops: "You will soon enter Czechoslovakia. You won't be greeted there with

30. Tigrid, *Why Dubček Fell,* p. 96.
31. Ibid., pp. 127–28.

flowers." Also on August 14, the Soviet press resumed its attacks on Prague with an article in *Literaturnaya Gazeta*. I believe that a negative reaction of the regional party leaders, who formed, as I have said, the conservative hard core of the Central Committee, increased the pressure to reject the "rotten compromise" of Cierna-Bratislava.

The technical preparations for a possible invasion of Czechoslovakia seem to have started as early as April 1968. This view is supported by Jiří Hajek[32] and by other information I have received. For example, some people in Bratislava recognized in August, among Soviet officers of the occupation army, civilian "tourists" who had visited the city in April, probably to become familiar with the place of their future assignment. The exercises of June and July were for the same purpose. The maneuvers in mid-August on the Czechoslovak border were to serve as a cover for the important movements of troops—impossible to conceal in the middle of the tourist season—that were necessary before the intervention.

Various estimates have been given of the total number of troops engaged in the August 20–21 invasion. The Soviet armed forces had at that time a total of 3,220,000 men, including 2,000,000 in the army, which was made up of 140 divisions. In Central Europe, there were 20 Soviet divisions in East Germany, 2 in Poland, and 4 in Hungary, backed by 60 divisions in the western USSR.[33] According to a Western estimate made after the first day of the invasion, ten Soviet divisions took part in the action, seven coming from East Germany, two from Poland, and one from the USSR.[34] But these figures were soon increased. For example, the *New York Times* estimated the contingent of Soviet troops in Prague at only 25,000 men the first day and, four days later, at 50,000, with two armored divisions and one mechanized division.[35]

Later, some Czechoslovak officials gave different estimates of the overall figures. Frybert, a Central Committee member speaking on August 31 at a plenary session, said that 250,000 men, 7,500 tanks, and 1,000 planes had been involved.[36] Josef Smrkovsky, speaking to Soviet envoy Vasily Kuznetsov on September 11, mentioned a total invasion force of 500,000 men, including those of the four smaller Warsaw Pact countries that had

32. *Dix Ans Après*, p. 109.
33. International Institute for Strategic Studies, *The Military Balance, 1967–1968* (London: IISS, 1967), p. 5.
34. *New York Times,* August 23, 1968.
35. *New York Times,* August 22 and 26, 1968.
36. Tigrid, *Why Dubček Fell,* p. 107.

joined the Soviet Union.[37] Finally, General Martin Dzur, the Czecho-slovak defense minister, reportedly said on August 18 that there were at the time 650,000 foreign troops in his country.

The knowledgeable British writer Adam Roberts sums up these differ-ent estimates this way: "Possibly the true figure is about 400,000, of whom at least three quarters were Soviet, with a maximum total of sixteen Soviet divisions plus one Soviet tactical air army and transport aircraft for logistic back-up. . . . There were perhaps as many as 50,000 Polish troops, per-haps 20,000 Hungarians, roughly the same number of East Germans, and fewer than 10,000 Bulgarians."[38] I would accept the overall figure of 400,000, which corresponds to approximately twenty-nine divisions of that time, a number indicated by many observers and confirmed to me in a private conversation with the late Ion-Gheorghe Maurer, prime minister of Rumania. But it seems to me that the number of satellite country troops should be lower than Roberts' estimate and the Soviet figure accordingly higher. The Bulgarians, for example, played only a token role in Prague (protecting the airport and a few streets), the East Germans were more numerous but withdrew after a few days from their area (a small territory near their border), and the Hungarians were hardly noticed during their brief stay in Slovakia. Clearly, the Soviet Union demanded from its allies much more political than military support.

The fact remains, as Roberts puts it, that the total forces used in the operation "were very roughly twice as numerous as the Soviet forces in Hungary in 1956," and almost as many as the United States had in Viet-nam at that time (500,000). This was a sizable force, which, under the command of Soviet General Ivan Pavlovsky, vice minister of defense and commander-in-chief of the army, had prepared for a massive, quick inva-sion of "all Czechoslovak cities and regions," as Tass proudly stated in its first communiqué of August 21.

As in Hungary in 1956, the primary targets were the airports, notably Ruzyne near Prague, which was seized by deception in the first hour, 11 p.m. on August 20: an ostensibly civilian plane that had landed a few hours before was full of paratroopers who suddenly jumped out and took control of the field. This permitted a huge airlift (250 landings in the morning hours of August 21) to start operating at once. Incidentally, the airports were assigned a major role even in the later stages because of weakness of logistics in other areas. Leo Heiman, an Israeli military ob-

37. Ibid., p. 223.
38. Windsor and Roberts, *Czechoslovakia 1968*, p. 108.

server, noted that the land forces lacked trucks and other delivery systems, with the following result: "The airfields held by Soviet paratroops became the focal points of occupation. Only there did communications and logistics function properly."[39]

Though there was no fighting or attempt at guerrilla resistance, there are strong indications that the Soviet commanders were prepared for this option too. It was reported that white stripes had been painted on many military vehicles; Roberts notes that these signs "would have been useful for identification purposes if air power had been called in by the invaders to crush the Czechoslovak armed forces." By the same token, "the amount of bridging equipment brought in also suggests that it was possible that the Czechoslovaks would fight, or at least engage in violent sabotage."[40] Anti-aircraft guns were deployed in most units, including one in the middle of a crowded square in central Prague. Another milder form of Czechoslovak resistance might have been to choke the airfields with various equipment to prevent landing. They did not do this, but the Russians were prepared for it. According to Heiman, they used a number of planes capable of landing in short distances and on grass, but carrying no more than ten soldiers. The same writer also mentions the large amount of ammunition carried by the troops and adds: "Their operational deployment indicated tactical preparedness for battle on the ground and in the air."[41]

No such battles took place, and the operation was carried out without any known casualty on the Soviet side, though Soviet commanders tried, for internal propaganda purposes, to persuade their troops that counter-revolutionary snipers might at any moment fire at them ("We have two or three deaths a day," I was told in Prague at the end of August by a Soviet sergeant, but without credible evidence). On the Czechoslovak side, casualties were due to isolated incidents or accidents and may have been overestimated in the anti-Soviet climate of the time. A letter addressed to Svoboda by the government and other authorities on August 25 mentions thirty dead and three hundred wounded in Prague alone.[42] On September 13 Zdenek Mlynar, a liberal member of the Czechoslovak politburo, said in a television broadcast that "up to today there were killed . . . more than 70 of our citizens."[43]

39. Leo Heiman, "Soviet Invasion Weakness," *Military Review,* vol. 49 (August 1969), pp. 41–42.

40. Windsor and Roberts, *Czechoslovakia 1968,* p. 110.

41. Heiman, "Soviet Invasion Weakness."

42. Quoted in Hajek, *Dix Ans Après,* p. 131.

43. Quoted in Windsor and Roberts, *Czechoslovakia 1968,* p. 123.

For those reasons, the Soviet forces had a less dangerous but perhaps a more difficult task. They had to occupy in a visible way the main streets and squares of the cities and a few important buildings in Prague (for instance, the Central Committee of the party, Parliament House, the Academy of Sciences, the Writers' Union, which their regular tenants had vacated), but their role was a static one, consisting only in enduring the insults of the population. The troops in the streets behaved with discipline. A pattern of behavior followed by the commanders when hostility mounted was to order that the engines of the tanks be started, to frighten the crowd away; if this was not enough, that the troops fire into the air (the facade of the National Museum on Vaclavske Nameste in Prague was damaged this way). But morale fell to a low level after a few days. Unable to explain to the numerous questioners what they were doing there since there were no counterrevolutionaries (more precisely, violent rioters) to shoot at, the only answer the Soviet soldiers could give was, "Ask Brezhnev."

The Soviet troops did not try to assume full control or carry out police functions, as they had in Hungary. They made no arrests, except for the few leaders—Dubček, Cerník, Smrkovsky, Kriegel—whom they found at party headquarters the first night (those who had escaped before the arrival of the troops had no further problems). Their only active function was to attempt to track down the clandestine radio transmitters whose broadcasts were coordinating and encouraging the passive resistance of the population. The results were disappointing, because of both poor logistics on their side and good organization on the Czechoslovak side. As Heiman explains it, "the Soviets utilized a fleet of radio direction finding (R.D.F.) trucks, helicopter and jamming transmitters, but it took them more than a week to get the R.D.F. units into position. Their R.D.F. equipment was helpless against more modern Czechoslovak techniques such as bouncing beams, switchover relays, and frequency changes."[44]

To sum up, the behavior of Soviet forces in Czechoslovakia after August 20 was more like their behavior in Hungary during the first intervention (between October 24 and 29, 1956) than after the second one (November 4). On the latter occasion, the Soviet forces had not only a clear target—the armed insurgents, who had to be crushed—but a clear political prospect. A new government had been formed (under Kádár) to take the place of the previous one (under Nagy), which had been declared

---

44. Heiman, "Soviet Invasion Weakness."

illegal; they had to clear the way for Kádár to take office. This could not be done in Czechoslovakia for two reasons.

First, in Hungary, the original idea was to create a new pro-Soviet government which the Soviet army was to "assist." But the big difference—and the main weakness in the political planning—was that this government was not set up in advance. Subsequently, all attempts to form such a government failed. Conversely, the Soviet forces were not prepared to act alone, for example, by imposing a military government. In October 1956 Gerö received Soviet help, but in insufficient quantity and without the willingness to act that was crucial in the dramatic circumstances of the time. In Prague in 1968, the help was there, far more than necessary, but there was nobody to make use of it.

Second, when this failure became apparent, the Soviet leaders decided to bow to Svoboda's demand and bring Dubček to Moscow in order to "negotiate" with him. This restored some legitimacy and political orderliness to the process, but it did not change the ambiguous mission of the Soviet forces. Whereas before they had nobody to deal with or to put in command, now there was someone but he did not want them.

The first failure, though surprising, should not lead to the conclusion that the political framework of the intervention was completely neglected. Some observers, like Roberts, have even suggested that the military intervention was scheduled on a Tuesday night because the Czechoslovak politburo had its weekly meeting on that day. Actually, the plan was to encourage the pro-Soviet members of this body to launch a political offensive against Dubček that same evening that would put him in the minority and to name a new first secretary who would have called for (or, more precisely, welcomed) military help. The attempt was made, but could not be pushed further after the pro-Soviet elements discovered that they were a minority of four instead of the expected majority of six (out of eleven members). The politburo, instead of censuring Dubček, adopted a resolution condemning the intervention, the publication of which could not even be prevented.

This failure was largely the fault of S. V. Chervonenko, the Soviet ambassador in Prague, whose responsibility it was to inform the Soviet leadership of the different trends inside the Czechoslovak party and to maintain contact with the pro-Soviet conservative elements. At a higher level, there was apparently a certain lack of coordination during the whole crisis. Too many people were involved successively in the negotiations with Prague (mostly Brezhnev, but also Kosygin and Grechko, who made separate trips), and this may have had a demoralizing effect on the people in charge of the day-to-day management of the crisis. A permanent team, like that of Mikoyan-Suslov during the Hungarian events, would have been more effective.

After the invasion, however, and given the political mismanagement, the ball was again in the Soviet Politburo's court, as in Cierna. The negotiation, which took place in Moscow on August 23–26 between the leaders of the two countries, was one of the most peculiar in modern times. The apparent strategic predominance of the Kremlin could not conceal one major weakness: it had to deal with the very leaders it had labeled "revisionists" and needed their help to get out of the political mess the intervention had produced. To be sure, Moscow had the option of imposing a military government on Prague. This was the threat it used to persuade the Czechoslovak leaders, but it had to be mindful of the further deterioration of Soviet international prestige that such a move would have created.

Tactically, the Russians' position was strong, and they used it to advantage. The Czechoslovak delegation was virtually held prisoner and received almost no information from Prague (had they been aware of the high level of popular resistance they would have been less flexible). The Russians insisted that the delegation consist of members of their own choosing, including in it their friends Vasil Bilak and Alois Indra (though the latter was only a party secretary and not a politburo member). The "bad part" of it—Dubček, Cerník, Smrkovsky, and other leaders who had been captured in Central Committee headquarters—arrived at the end of the first day still as prisoners, unshaven and ill dressed, and were immediately insulted by Brezhnev and his colleagues.

The results of the talks fall into two parts: the public one and the classified one. For the public, the Moscow *diktat* was relatively mild (it had to be to avoid further exacerbating anti-Soviet feeling). The communiqué announced that "the troops of the allied countries that entered *temporarily* the territory of Czechoslovakia will not interfere in the internal affairs (of the country). Agreement was reached on the terms of withdrawal of these troops from its territory as the situation in Czechoslovakia normalizes." The communiqué was too vague about political matters to be impressive: "It was stated by the Czechoslovak side that all the work of Party and State bodies through all media would be directed at ensuring effective measures serving the socialist power, the guiding role of the working class and the communist Party, the interests of developing and strengthening friendly relations with the peoples of the Soviet Union and the entire socialist community."[45] This was little more than had already been stated in Bratislava, but it was only the tip of the iceberg.

The secret protocol that the Czechoslovak leaders had to sign dotted the i more carefully, which is why it specified that both parties "would consider as strictly confidential all contacts between [them] after August 20, 1968. This agreement thus also covers the talks that have just been concluded." Fortunately, the text of this document was smuggled to the West and published. It stated that the "so-called 14th Party congress" (a clandestine meeting of this body, held in a Prague factory a day after the invasion, had renewed the Central Committee and expelled from it all the conservative elements) would be considered void, and that the Central Committee (in its former composition) would meet in six to ten days to "dismiss from office all those whose continuance in their posts would not promote the imperative task of reinforcing the leading role of the working class and the communist party."[46]

For their part, the Czechoslovaks had to promise that they "would not tolerate that Party workers and officials who struggled for the consolidation of socialist positions against anti-socialist forces and for friendly relations with the USSR be dismissed from their posts or suffer reprisals." In other words, the Czechoslovaks would have to keep some of their most hated leaders, such as Alois Indra, who had supported the intervention and who had even been proposed to Svoboda as a candidate to form a new government. There was no explicit mention of press censorship (the word is considered bad taste in Communist language), but the Czechoslovaks had to promise "new laws and regulations" in this area, "measures with a view to controlling the information media," and "a reallotment of leading posts in the press, radio and TV."

In the military area, the formulation was different from that of the official communiqué. The protocol said: "A treaty concerning the stationing and the final withdrawal of the allied troops will be concluded." The contradiction in the terms "stationing" and "final withdrawal" recalls the situation in Hungary in the final days of October 1956 and may be explained the same way. Moscow was not willing at the time to openly state its objective, which was to maintain Soviet troops in Czechoslovakia per-

45. *Pravda*, August 28, 1968. For an English text, see Windsor and Roberts, *Czechoslovakia 1968*, pp. 178–81.
46. Tigrid, *Why Dubček Fell*, p. 210.

manently. This stick was imposed less than two months later, but at the moment only the carrot—the withdrawal of *other,* non-Soviet troops—was shown.

The signing of the agreement marked the beginning of a long process: the Russians knew that their partner was unreliable and that this half-measure had to be followed at a later date by what they had looked for from the beginning: the replacement of Dubček by a "better" man and the purge of the liberals in the party. For that purpose, they used different tactics simultaneously.

1. They continued the direct pressure on Dubček, as before the invasion. Other meetings were held, approximately once a month. On October 2, in Moscow, Brezhnev became very angry again, accusing the Czechoslovaks of having admitted to their Central Committee new liberal elements who might even be "Western agents." (The Central Committee meeting held at the end of August in Prague did not produce the results agreed upon in the Moscow protocol and reinforced the liberal wing in the leadership.) In a typical joke, the Soviet leader proposed to compensate for the stationing of Soviet troops in Czechoslovakia by deploying a Czechoslovak contingent to Russia—on the Sino-Soviet border. He stated that he did not care about the reaction of Western Communist parties (largely hostile to the intervention) since there was no chance of a Communist takeover in Europe "before fifty years."[47]

2. At the same time the USSR consolidated its military grip on the country. This was achieved with the treaty on the stationing of Soviet troops, signed October 16 in Prague. This document—rarely published in other Communist countries—had interesting contradictions. It stated that "the number of and places of location of Soviet troops [in Czechoslovakia] will be determined by agreement" between the two governments.[48] But since other provisions (articles 4 and 5) specified that Soviet troops and members of their families could travel both ways without passport or visa control, it made it nearly impossible for the Prague authorities to keep track of the actual number of their "guests."

This number varied considerably both before and after the treaty. According to the *New York Times,* 450,000 foreign troops remained in Czechoslovakia at the end of September, but this figure had to be reduced to 100,000 (Soviet forces only) within two months after the signing of

47. Ibid., p. 128.
48. An English text of the treaty is given in Windsor and Roberts, *Czechoslovakia 1968,* pp. 193–200.

the treaty.[49] U.S. Secretary of State Dean Rusk stated on December 1, 1968, that three to four Soviet divisions (approximately 45,000 to 60,000 men) remained in Czechoslovakia.[50] But when another push was made at the end of March to oust Dubček from the leadership, Grechko himself announced to the Prague leaders that his contingent of troops in Czechoslovakia had recently been increased by 35,000 men.[51] Actually, the Rusk estimate seems to have been low, and the actual figure of the "Central Group" (the name given to the Soviet forces in Czechoslovakia) stabilized in the following years at five divisions, about 75,000 men.[52] This was more than in Poland (two divisions) or in Hungary (four divisions).

3. The Kremlin intervened more directly in Czechoslovak political affairs. On the one hand, it tried to break down the solidarity of the ruling group in Prague by attacking certain elements and flattering others. Ludvík Svoboda and Gustav Husák, at that time head of the party in Slovakia, received only good words; Josef Smrkovsky, chairman of the parliament and a leading figure of the liberal movement, was singled out for criticism. Brezhnev himself, at a meeting in Kiev on December 11 with Dubček, Svoboda, Cerník, Husák, and Lubomic Strougal, called him "the leader of rightist forces in the [Czechoslovak] Party."[53] Despite a pledge made by Dubček, Svoboda, Cerník, and Smrkovsky in August to stick together, this tactic succeeded and Smrkovsky had to relinquish more and more of his functions.

On the other hand, a new effort was made to encourage conservative and pro-Soviet elements at all levels. *Pravda* played up any friendly demonstrations staged by "old" and "good" Communists. In Prague, Vasily Kuznetsov, first deputy foreign minister of the USSR, who had been selected to carry out a long survey of the normalization in September (paralleling the weak ambassador Chervonenko), insisted on arranging the visit of a large number of Soviet delegations, setting up sister cities in the USSR and Czechoslovakia, and so forth. These clumsy attempts to promote organized friendship could not work well in the circumstances, but they were intended to multiply the Soviet presence and help Moscow's isolated supporters overcome their shyness.

49. *New York Times,* October 1, 1968.
50. *New York Times,* December 2, 1968.
51. Tigrid, *Why Dubček Fell,* p. 160.
52. International Institute for Strategic Studies, *The Military Balance, 1969–1970* (London: IISS, 1969), p. 7.
53. Tigrid, *Why Dubček Fell,* p. 151.

This combination of pressure and "salami tactics" might already have achieved the desired result in January 1969 had not the suicide of young Jan Palach, who set himself on fire, renewed tension in the population. A visit by Konstantin Katushev (the young Soviet party secretary who seemed to have advocated a softer line two months before) on January 2, 1969, had conveyed a harsh message from Moscow, leading Dubček to speak of "crisis" and "tragic conflict." Cerník, according to Tigrid, warned privately that if there was no consolidation of the situation "the Soviets would simply stop dealing with us and would turn to others."[54]

The decisive push came at the end of March, after a victory of the Czechoslovak team over the Russians in the ice hockey championship in Stockholm had created an outburst of nationalist feeling in Czechoslovakia that led to an incident—perhaps provoked—against the Aeroflot office in Prague. Three days later, on March 31, Grechko arrived unexpectedly. According to Tigrid, he asked for "radical and immediate measures" and presented a three-part ultimatum: the Czechoslovak leadership was to put its own house in order, which included the cessation of all internal discussion, censorship of the press, and a "reinforcement of security organs"; if it could not, it was to ask the Soviet troops to do it; or the Warsaw Pact forces would intervene on their own initiative.

Because of the moral and political exhaustion of Dubček, his growing isolation in the leadership, and the new vigor of the conservative forces resulting from the preparatory work of the preceding period, the ultimatum succeeded. Two weeks later, on April 17, 1969, Husák, having been proposed by Svoboda, was elected first secretary of the party to replace Dubček. The first hard measures of normalization (ousting liberals, censoring the press and banning some publications, rehabilitating Moscow collaborators, and even approving the Soviet intervention) began in the ensuing weeks and months. It is interesting that after more than a year of pressure from so many people, the decisive result was finally achieved by Grechko, the Soviet defense minister who was not even at that time a Politburo member (he was not promoted to that function until 1973) and had never before been assigned such political negotiations. The military had to finish the job, which they had been well prepared to do at their own level in August 1968, but which had been badly mishandled by the political authorities. The rise of the military's power and support of their in-

54. Ibid., p. 152.

terests in the Soviet structure in the years that followed may have had to do at least partially with recognition of this.

The Soviet Targets

Poland, 1956

In this rare success story of resistance to Soviet pressure, nothing would have been possible without the attitude of the Polish people, almost unanimously aligned behind Gomulka and ready to oppose Soviet interference by all available means. The same popular determination existed in Hungary but only insofar as resistance to the Soviet Union was concerned; on all other matters, including support of Imre Nagy and the Communist party in its new configuration, there was no unity in the population. In Poland the regime was certain to remain socialist and led by the Communist party. The powerful Catholic Church, for example, under the leadership of Cardinal Stefan Wyszynski, supported Gomulka completely, while Cardinal Josef Mindszenty in Hungary wanted an end to the socialist regime and ignored the Nagy government.

The only Polish group supporting the USSR, the Natolinists, represented less than one-third of the Central Committee, judging from the number of votes (23 out of 75) Soviet Marshal Rokossovsky obtained in favor of his candidacy on October 20. Without Soviet support, this group would not have represented a serious threat to Gomulka and the reformers, especially since its lack of popular support prevented it from acting openly.

Gomulka had a limited group of personal supporters; since he was in jail or in political isolation until the spring of 1956, he could not develop a constituency of his own in the party. That is why, when he was coopted into the Central Committee on October 19, before Khrushchev's arrival, he was accompanied by only three people: Zenon Kliszko, Marian Spychalski, and Ignacy Loga-Sowinski.

But the crucial role was played by what might be called the "transition team," the leaders already in office, who were initially sympathetic to the Natolinists and supported by them, but who turned away from them as the destalinizing wind blew from Moscow in 1956, after the Twentieth Party Congress. A key man on this team was undoubtedly Edward Ochab, first secretary of the party, who decided, in a rare spirit of self-sacrifice, to open the way to Gomulka as his successor. Ochab was followed by Prime Minister Jozef Cyrankiewicz, a former socialist who had sacrificed his party on the Communist altar in 1948. Basically an opportunist, he followed the new course and managed to keep his post throughout the Gomulka era.

One wonders how old-time orthodox Communists faced the prospect of a confrontation with the Soviet Union, even of a fight against Soviet troops if necessary. In neither of the other cases under study can similar determination be found in such a large group of leaders. Traditional Polish patriotism and courage must have played a role. Even in Stalin's time, the Poles had managed not to show excessive zeal in copying the Soviet "model" and had avoided the torture and executions that were commonplace in most Communist countries (Gomulka and his associates, though ousted politically, were not harmed throughout the Stalinist period).

The situation in the army was particularly interesting. Theoretically, the presence at its head of Rokossovsky, with other Natolinists in important positions (notably Kazimierz Witaszewski, the deputy minister of defense), should have made it a powerful force serving the anti-Gomulka camp, but this was not the case. To be sure, the army was put on alert for a few weeks before the crisis. It might have backed the plot of the Natolinists if they had carried it out then; but, notwithstanding the irresolute column faced down on the night of October 18–19 and several other troop movements, the army was extraordinarily passive. Lower-level officers obviously sympathized with the pro-Gomulka forces and might have neutralized any attempt at violent action, which is probably why the decisive orders were never given them.

On the other side, a strong force in favor of Gomulka was composed, curiously enough, of the police and security organs, which together numbered 50,000 men. Normally, these types of forces, as was the case in Hungary, are the last bulwark of orthodox Communist regimes, but in August 1956 under the unofficial influence of Gomulka they had switched to the other side. Their new commander, General Waclaw Komar, had been jailed in Stalin's time and was actively dedicated to the cause of reform. Komar deployed his forces and agents to keep track of the Natolinists and the movements of Soviet forces; at the same time, he used contacts at lower levels of the army to neutralize Rokossovsky's possible moves.

Another major figure in the organization of the resistance was Stefan

Staszewski, party secretary in Warsaw, who discreetly mobilized the population and arranged with Komar and some army commanders to have arms distributed to factory workers. How effective this resistance would have been if the Soviet Union had decided on a military intervention is not known, but certainly such an action would have been met with guerrilla warfare. This was probably the most important single factor to deter Khrushchev from violent action.

On the crucial night of October 19–20, this determination to resist was shown to Khrushchev and his colleagues at two levels. In the talks, Gomulka, Ochab, Komar, and others, though they tried to refute Soviet accusations, refused to be impressed by Khrushchev's veiled threats. According to Bethell, Gomulka countered with a threat of his own: "Others say that Gomulka threatened to address the Polish people on the radio, tell them what was going on and call on them to fight the Soviet forces. . . . It is known that Polish radio was told to be ready for a broadcast from Gomulka on the night of October 19."[55] But there was other action. Gibney reports that on the same night "the main strength of Komar's troops was deployed around the city of Warsaw, in the way of any action from the Soviet garrisons. Early on Saturday morning (October 20), one of Komar's detachments had in fact stopped a tank column of the Soviet army at Sochaczew, . . . [just] west of Warsaw. No one fired, but the army column turned back." In at least one instance, though, Soviet units reportedly were repelled by fire. According to Garthoff, Polish internal security forces stopped a Soviet regiment, trying to enter Poland from East Germany, by firing on it. Other Soviet forces also were on the move.[56] Bethell adds that "members of the Polish air force were constantly aloft, reporting on the movement of Soviet troops. Throughout the discussion, both delegations were receiving information from their military men. . . . Workers from Warsaw factories, especially the Zeran car works, were being armed and deployed, ready to defend the capital."[57]

If the 375,000 men of the Polish army, prevented from playing an active role by the reciprocal neutralization of the two opposing forces operating on them, are excluded, the forces at the disposal of the Polish leadership were limited indeed. But their deployment was organized, action was coordinated at the political level, and they had popular support. It is fair to assume that the outcome in Czechoslovakia in 1968 might have been very

55. Bethell, *Gomulka,* p. 212.
56. Gibney, *Frozen Revolution,* p. 13; Garthoff, *Soviet Military Policy,* p. 158.
57. Bethell, *Gomulka,* p. 211.

different if Dubček, whose political situation was similar to that of Gomulka, had taken similar measures before August 20.

Finally, there was the behavior of Gomulka himself, who, unlike Nagy
and Dubček, was determined to resist the liberal trends and, unlike Dubček, was motivated by strong personal conviction. He had pleased Khrushchev in November 1956 by telling the Soviet leader exactly what he
wanted to hear. In his interview after his fall, he was quite explicit about
his allies of the time, the liberal Communists: "They were noisy fellows,
they talked without stop about democracy, about changes, about some
kind of a revolution, while what we needed was obedience and discipline;
what we had to talk about was not some kind of great freedoms but rather
something quite the opposite. I had to get rid of those people from the
party. . . . My job actually was to turn around that Polish ship 180 degrees
and sail in the opposite direction."[58]

Gomulka consequently had no difficulty in giving the Soviet leaders
the assurances they wanted about "socialist order," his only demand being
that he be able to apply this policy progressively. But he also had the
courage to state some of his positions publicly from the beginning, taking
the risk of disappointing his supporters. For example, he said on October
20, the very day of his promotion to head of the party: "We must give a
decisive rebuff to all voices and whispers that aim at weakening our
friendship with the Soviet Union. . . . If anyone imagines he will be able
to sow moods of antisovietism in Poland, he is making a deep mistake."[59]
Four days later, in a huge popular meeting in Warsaw, he opposed the
demand that Soviet forces be withdrawn from the country, stating that
their presence was "directly connected with the presence of Soviet forces
in the G.D.R." and "in accordance with our highest state interests."[60]

Hungary, 1956

There is no point in trying to keep track of all the political or social
groupings involved in the Hungarian crisis, which was much more confused than either of the other two crises described here. The non-
Communist political parties that appeared during the revolution had little
time to organize themselves. Even though some of their leaders were given
functions in the successive Nagy governments, these governments were

58. *Nowiny Kurier,* April 16, 1973.
59. Bethell, *Gomulka,* p. 216.
60. Ibid., p. 218.

powerless. Cardinal Mindszenty's role has often been described as evidence of the counterrevolutionary character of the uprising or, alternatively, of Nagy's weakness, but it must be pointed out that the cardinal made his only public statement a few hours before the second Soviet intervention, at a moment when hardly anything could have changed the Soviet decision. This is why it seems preferable to focus on three groups or forces: Nagy himself, the various armed groups involved in the crisis, and János Kádár.

1. The evolution of Imre Nagy from an old-time Communist to a true revolutionary and national hero is one important factor explaining the outcome of the crisis. His weaknesses—indecision, inability to dominate the situation, and lack of a clear-cut strategy—have been described by all observers. As Molnár sums it up: "He was always 24 hours late in reacting to public demands but nevertheless 24 hours ahead of the Party leaders."[61] It can be said in his favor that he assumed power in the worst possible circumstances, even, in the first two crucial days, being a physical hostage of Gerö, who hoped to discredit him in the eyes of the public. His main task was to restore order, and the only way to do it was to make concessions to the insurgents, since the only counterforce nominally at his disposal, the AVH, was hostile to him. This brought him into growing conflict with the Russians.

In the last days of October, he realized that Moscow's duplicity about the withdrawal of Soviet troops was the main obstacle to normalizing the situation. His proclamation of neutrality on November 1 pushed him into the camp of the revolution; at that moment only, he became a leader and moved ahead of events. Though this came too late and could only precipitate tragic consequences, Nagy made it clear even after the intervention that he did not regret his move. In a sort of political will dictated to a secretary on November 4 and quoted by Barber, he made his break with Moscow: "Today it is Hungary and tomorrow it will be the turn of other countries, because the imperialism of Moscow does not know borders; it is only trying to play for time." He later admitted that "the revolution went far beyond its aims and that is why it failed."[62] But his martyrdom was a reconciliation of his old belief with his dedication to his people. He said before his execution, "If my life is needed to prove that not all Communists are enemies of the people, I gladly make the sacrifice."[63]

61. Molnár, *Budapest 1956*, p. 154.
62. Barber, *Seven Days of Freedom*, pp. 180, 223–24.
63. Ibid., p. 231.

2. Another problem for Nagy was that he had to fight the insurgents before becoming their ally. The insurgents, who were to become famous as the "freedom fighters," were neither an organized force nor a powerful one: at the beginning, no more than 2,000 men in Budapest, mainly in the Kilian Barracks in Pest; at the end, perhaps 50,000 men including the estimated 30,000 workers who offered the strongest organized resistance to the second Russian intervention on Csepel Island. With strong leadership such as Poland had, the riot of October 23 would have been easily crushed, even with only the 30,000 men of the AVH. But other forces acted on their own and their sympathy for the insurgents contributed to the escalation.

In the first place, there was the police force, which under the command of Sándor Kopácsi, a thirty-six-year-old colonel, rose against the Gerö-Hegedüs government very early: Kopácsi reportedly ordered his personnel to help the insurgents as early as October 24. A second element was part of the army, in which two men played major roles. One was General Béla Király, commander in chief in Budapest, who from the first night of the rebellion had been aware that his troops sympathized with the insurgents and who supported Nagy. A week later, he was put in charge of the national guard, a new force combining the Budapest police and the pro-Nagy insurgents with approximately 10,000 men and Kopácsi as deputy commander. Another military hero of the revolution was Colonel Pál Maléter. As a young officer on duty in the Ministry of Defense the night of October 23, he was sent by his superiors to the Kilian Barracks to restore order. After a short hesitation, he decided to join the insurgents and became their commander. He was later named minister of defense in the last Nagy cabinet and was arrested the same day by the Russians.

The attitude of these officers does not mean that the army as a whole switched to the insurgent side or played an active part one way or the other. On the contrary, there was in Hungary, despite the violent action, the same pattern of behavior as in the other crises under study here: at the top, a division between a few pro-Soviet officers, another group of people ready to side with a popular patriotic rebellion, and a larger group of uncommitted commanders; in the rank and file, strong sympathy for the insurgents and, generally speaking, great reluctance to assume repressive functions. Add to that the presence in the upper echelons of Soviet advisers and their probable doubts about the reliability of the troops and you have a virtual neutralization of the regular army in such crises.

During the first part of the revolution, the two regiments sent by Gerö to

Budapest in October 23 had little ammunition (probably because of the distrust of the authorities) and immediately demonstrated their sympathy for the insurgents, notably in front of the radio station. A number of students at the military academies joined the rebellion, and certain units distributed their arms to the population. The opposite happened in Szeged and Kecskemét, where the army briefly attacked the insurgents. In Pécs, one pro-Gerö commander disarmed his unit to prevent it from joining the rebellion. At Szolnok, according to Molnár, "the Hungarian army kept to its barracks, although the town was also one of the most important Soviet garrison towns, with a military aerodrome."[64] The fact is that the army as such (at least no organized unit) did not fight the Soviet troops directly. Even before the decisive Soviet intervention, when the movements of troops were the only action and no shooting took place, the Hungarian army does not seem to have opposed the occupation of Hungarian airports by Soviet forces: the only such place to be held by the Nagy government was a small airport in Budaörs with two airplanes only, perhaps forgotten by the Soviet command. At the last moment, Király suggested that Nagy use it to flee abroad, but the prime minister preferred to take refuge in the Yugoslav embassy.

The neutralization of the army made the fight even more hopeless. According to Barber, Nagy's first reaction when he learned from the Yugoslav embassy on November 4 that the Russians were moving into Budapest was to order Király not to fight. A few minutes later, however, he said in his last radio proclamation: "Our troops are fighting."[65] General Király had this same day held a secret meeting with his officers in the Jesuit monastery of Manresa in Buda. According to Barber, about half of the participants proposed a cease-fire; finally a majority of them, including Király, decided to resist the invasion. But even after that, only small groups of insurgents, the Csepel factory workers, and a part of the national guard did the fighting, not the army. The Király group was the luckiest; it succeeded in holding out in Buda until November 9, then withdrew to Nagykovácsi, where it was attacked by Soviet tanks and MIG fighters on November 11. Finally, it managed to cross the border to Austria.

3. The behavior of János Kádár is another important element and probably, even now, the most mysterious. This long-time Communist (though only forty-five years old at this time, he had been a party member since 1929) who had been tortured under Rákosi, had every reason to sympa-

64. Molnár, *Budapest 1956*, p. 162.
65. Barber, *Seven Days of Freedom*, p. 177.

thize with the new course and with Nagy himself, who, as prime minister, had helped free him from prison in 1954. Until the evening of November 1, there is no indication of any serious disagreement between Kádár and Nagy. To be sure, his first statement as party first secretary on October 25 was tougher than Nagy's, denouncing the "armed aggression against the authorities of the People's democracy," which "must be repulsed by every means at our disposal."[66] But his perspective seems to have been similar to that of the prime minister, in increasingly favoring the objectives of the revolution and even turning against the Russians. On the crucial day of November 1, Kádár unquestionably supported the calls for neutrality and Soviet withdrawal; according to Barber, he said to Soviet Ambassador Yuri Andropov in the presence of a few other people: "I am ready as a Hungarian to fight if necessary. If your tanks enter Budapest, I will go into the streets and fight against you with my bare hands."[67]

But there is better evidence of his attitude in the speech he broadcast at 9:40 p.m. that same day: "Our people has shed its blood in order to show its unshakable desire to support the government's demand for the total withdrawal of Soviet forces. We no longer wish to exist in a state of dependence." At the same time, however, he expressed his concern about the situation and stated that the country was at a "crossroad": "Either the Hungarian democratic parties will be strong enough to consolidate their victory or we shall find ourselves faced with a counterrevolution. . . . The Hungarian youth did not shed its blood to see Rákosi's tyranny replaced by the tyranny of the counterrevolution." Later he mentioned "the fate of Korea" to warn against "foreign intervention."[68]

In other words, at that moment he was ready to go along with the revolution and accepted the situation as it had developed: a government with the "democratic parties" consolidating their "victory," pursuing a nonaligned neutral policy without Soviet troops or other interference. But he certainly wanted to stop there; some of the developments of the next three days, such as the open appearance of rightist parties and Cardinal Mindszenty's appeals to get rid of any "heirs and participants of a bankrupt system," would not have had his support anyway. As chief of the remnants of a party that was now only part of a broader coalition, Kádár could stay some distance from the government while Nagy, in the thick

66. Molnár, *Budapest 1956*, p. 182.
67. Barber, *Seven Days of Freedom*, p. 151.
68. Molnár, *Budapest 1956*, p. 193.

of events, was carried away by them and could not concentrate on the basic issues.

Still, Kádár's disappearance a few hours after this radio broadcast came as a complete surprise: even his wife was not informed and came to the parliament building the next day to ask about his whereabouts. Barber gives the best account of how it happened by furnishing two interesting pieces of information. The first is the account of an unidentified Western journalist who on the evening of November 1 had an interview with Ferenc Münnich, minister of the interior. During the conversation, Münnich received a telephone call in which he conversed in Russian. The topic of the talk appeared to be "an appointment in half an hour, together with Kádár." The other item is the account of a driver for the government who drove Münnich and Kádár that same night to a park near the Kerepes cemetery in a Budapest suburb. A Soviet ZIS car was waiting there, but, according to this report, Münnich had to push Kádár into it: "It appeared that Kádár was unwilling to enter the car. He looked as though he could not make up his mind."[69] The end of the story is better known. Kádár was taken to the Soviet embassy in Budapest and, an hour later, to a nearby Soviet military aerodrome where he boarded a plane that took him to the USSR; he is known to have spent a few days in Uzhgorod, the Soviet city closest to the Hungarian border, and it seems likely that he also went to Moscow to speak with Khrushchev.

Some of those details may be questionable, but it is not too difficult to reconstruct the main elements. Kádár's public speech of a few hours before shows that he was not prepared to betray Nagy and his government so soon. Clearly his sudden change was motivated by an external factor, probably a message he received—from Münnich or Andropov—that the Kremlin had decided to break with Nagy and crush the revolution. Faced with this unavoidable outcome, he chose, after some hesitation, to endorse the move in order to save what he might of the new course.

That makes it difficult to completely accept Kádár's own interpretation of his decision, which he gave, for example, to a *New York Times* correspondent twenty-two years later, saying that "there would have been virtual civil war in Hungary" and it was only "to avoid bloodshed that we asked the Soviet Union for help."[70] However, the bloodshed in Hungary was subsiding when Kádár changed sides; the Soviet intervention resulted

69. Barber, *Seven Days of Freedom*, p. 159.
70. *New York Times,* June 10, 1978.

in much greater bloodshed. Also, it is quite clear that the Soviet Union had decided to "help" before being asked, at least by him. Not surprisingly, Moscow used Ferenc Münnich, previously a socialist leader but one aligned with the Soviet Union since the late 1940s, to bring Kádár over to its side.

The behavior of Western powers after the first Soviet intervention in Hungary had clearly indicated to the Soviet Union that it need not expect much trouble from this side. The United States, the United Kingdom, and France did not ask for a meeting of the UN Security Council until October 27 (three days later) and no resolution was introduced until November 3. But on October 31, the day the Russians must have decided to take action against Nagy, British and French forces landed along the Suez canal. This offered Khrushchev the best opportunity he could have wished for to divert attention and denounce Western imperialism.

A speech by President Dwight D. Eisenhower, also on October 31, afforded Moscow further confidence. After relating that the aim of American policy in Eastern Europe had always been these nations' achievement of "sovereignty and self-government," the president added the caveat, "we could not, of course, carry out this policy by resort to force."[71] To say the least, there was strong presumption of this last fact but its public statement at this crucial moment could only impel Khrushchev further toward a solution of violent action. Eisenhower states clearly in his memoirs the dilemma he faced: "Hungary could not be reached by any U.N. or U.S. units without traversing [neutral] territory. Unless the major nations of Europe would, without delay, ally themselves spontaneously with us (an unimaginable prospect), we could do nothing. Sending United States troops alone into Hungary through hostile or neutral territory would have involved us in a general war."[72]

Since any military operation behind the iron curtain was excluded, the only action contemplated by the West to help the Hungarians was sending UN observers to Budapest. The Soviet Union rejected the request, which had been approved by the UN General Assembly on November 4; not until December did the Kádár government hint it might accept, but then it was too late. Many people thought that Secretary General Dag Hammar-

71. "Radio and Television Report to the American People on the Developments in Eastern Europe and the Middle East," *Public Papers of the President: Dwight D. Eisenhower, 1956* (Government Printing Office, 1958), p. 1061.

72. Dwight D. Eisenhower, *The White House Years: Waging Peace, 1956–1961* (Doubleday, 1965), p. 89.

skjöld should have challenged the Soviet refusal and landed in Budapest without the agreement of the local authorities. Instead, Hammarskjöld went to Egypt, encouraging the accusation of a double standard.

Another embarrassment for the U.S. administration was the behavior of Radio Free Europe, which broadcast to Eastern Europe. Quite irresponsibly, the station poured oil on the fire of the Hungarian uprising by its criticism of Nagy and its appeals to the population to continue the fighting after the cease-fire of October 29, even explaining to listeners how to prepare Molotov cocktails. Presumably, either this was done without the knowledge of the American government or a double standard was applied, because the proclaimed official policy implied a recognition of some sort of moderate communism and a willingness to cooperate with it. Secretary of State John Foster Dulles said in a speech given in Dallas on October 27, 1956: "We do not look upon these nations [of Eastern Europe] as potential military allies. . . . Nor do we condition economic ties between us upon the adoption by these countries of any particular form of society."[73]

Czechoslovakia, 1968

There were three main groups of political forces during the Czechoslovak crisis.

First, there was the conservative, or pro-Soviet, group, which was in the minority early in the spring, after the elimination of Novotny and his personal followers such as Jiří Hendrich. This group cannot be identified completely with the team of the former party first secretary, since the main figures in it were either people from the mid-level apparatus of Novotny's time who had accepted part of the "January policy" (such as Alois Indra, Oldrich Svestka, Jan Piller, Emil Rigo) or people who had been prejudiced against Novotny for nationalist reasons (such as Vasil Bilak and later Gustav Husák). The failure of Moscow in August to rely on these people may be explained by the fact that they were neither united, as the Natolin group had been in Poland in 1956, nor, certainly, as courageous and forceful as Brezhnev would have liked them to be. For example, the Soviet Politburo expected them to come forward at a meeting in Cierna against Dubček and his liberal comrades. Their behavior was undoubtedly influenced by the population's unanimous support of Dubček and awareness that the Soviet leadership itself was still largely undecided.

---

73. Address by Secretary of State Dulles, *Department of State Bulletin,* vol. 35, no. 906 (November 5, 1956), p. 697.

In July the decision not to go to Warsaw was not opposed in the party politburo (called presidency), and even Bilak is reported to have been rather shy in Cierna in supporting the Warsaw letter. Indra, a party secretary without politburo status, was considered the most reliable by the Russians, who proposed to Svoboda on August 21 that Indra form a new government. A few weeks before, nevertheless, he had supervised and had not objected to the new party statute published on August 10, which deviated greatly from the Soviet model and authorized the expression of "minority opinions."

As mentioned, the weakness of the pro-Soviet group was apparent in the politburo meeting of August 20, when the resolution condemning the invasion was supported by only three members out of eleven: Vasil Bilak, Drahomir Kolder, and Oldrich Svestka. Three other members who were expected by the Russians to join the group—Frantisek Barbirek, Jan Piller, and Emil Rigo—defected, removing any prospect of changing the leadership and creating a political framework for the Soviet action.

On August 21, some fifty members of the central committee, most of them with conservative leanings, met in a Prague hotel to discuss the situation. Curiously enough, the Russians were aware of this meeting and sent some officers to attend but no political representatives able to offer guidance or simply to raise the morale of their friends. No decision was made, and a day later the more active liberal wing of the party organized a party congress, selected a new central committee, and took the lead in the resistance to the invaders.

Other pro-Soviet "collaborators" had been informed of the intervention in advance and were to play a technical role of support, but they were too isolated to be efficient. Viliam Salgovič, a vice minister of the interior, was the main Soviet agent in the police apparatus. He tried to organize his friends and even made some temporary arrests (notably that of Cestmir Cisar, a party secretary), but his forces were clearly insufficient to counter the moves of Interior Minister Josef Pavel, who had turned the police in favor of Dubček. Miroslav Sulek, a former director of the press agency CTK, returned to his office on the night of August 20 and pretended to control all the news dispatches, but the workers did not obey his orders. Karel Hoffmann, head of Prague's communication center, succeeded in cutting off all radio stations for a few hours that night, which is why the politburo appeal against the Russian intervention could not be broadcast until 4:30 a.m. All those people were later rehabilitated and given new positions, but in the days and weeks following the intervention their fate was exactly the opposite of what they had hoped for and what the intervention was supposed to achieve—instead of assuming positions of leadership, they had to hide from popular anger.

The second group, the liberal radicals (they may be called so in the Czechoslovak context, though they would not have seemed radical in a Western system), were people actively dedicated to the reformist program of Dubček and generally eager to push it more strongly. Soviet leaders hated them most, but this hostility led them to burn their bridges and pushed them further along the liberal line. Frantisek Kriegel, for example, a politburo member in charge of the National Front (a coalition of the Communist party with smaller parties whose task was to promote candidates for parliamentary elections), is not reported to have been responsible for specific anti-Soviet actions, but he was perceived by Moscow for reasons that remain unclear (one of them reportedly being that he was a Jew) as the archenemy. Jiří Hajek, the foreign minister, though he was a moderate liberal, fell into the same category because he defended the Czechoslovak cause at the UN Security Council after the invasion—a move that was stopped by Svoboda at Brezhnev's request. Josef Spaček, a politburo member, was actually a more dangerous liberal, being the man behind the cessation of press censorship. He was one of the first to be sacked during the Husák normalization, as were the writers, journalists, and economic reformers, notably Ota Sik, who had been at the forefront of the liberals during the spring. But ahead of them was Josef Pavel, the minister of the interior, a Communist jailed in Stalin's time, who had later purged the police apparatus of Soviet agents; according to Tigrid, some 150 of them had been diverted into secondary jobs, and the many Soviet "tourists" who came to Czechoslovakia in July 1968 for intelligence gathering and subversion were watched. That is why the Moscow protocol of August 26 specified that "the activities of the Ministry of the Interior will also be examined fully. Appropriate measures will then be taken to strengthen the direction of this ministry." Not until five days later did Svoboda ask Pavel to resign "for the good of us all."[74]

Those liberal radicals were not at the top level and could not put up an armed fight, but they did their best to organize resistance of a different type. The journalists were responsible for the highly effective system of radio communications that was maintained for weeks after the invasion. No details of how it functioned have been reported, but it seems to have used about fifteen local stations, coordinating their actions and switching

74. Tigrid, *Why Dubček Fell,* p. 121.

from one to another every fifteen minutes to escape detection. The necessary technical equipment may have come from the army or the Svazarm, an organization for youth military training, which disposed of some 2,000 transmitters. The workers' militia, a paramilitary formation, had similar equipment and probably contributed too, though its leaders were supposed, at the end of the Novotny period, to support the conservatives. But some Communist organizations aimed at promoting orthodox ideology among the population may turn in an opposite direction in time of crisis.

The third group was made up of the principal leaders who may be termed "centrist," not only because of their aversion to radical moves, but also because of the neutralizing effect of their different backgrounds and temperaments. Of the "big four," only Ludvík Svoboda and Josef Smrkovsky had had the harsh experience of demotion (Svoboda) or repression (Smrkovsky) in Stalin's and Novotny's time. The other two had had relatively quiet careers in the apparatus; Oldrich Cerník in the economy, and Alexander Dubček in Slovakia and also in Moscow, where he had studied at the Soviet High Party school for two years. Dubček was not known as a liberal until the last months of 1967, when he seems to have sided prudently with the writers. This kind of alliance, as in Poland, is often a purely tactical move to increase the weight of one faction in the struggle for power.

Did Dubček intend to move further forward? The only indication that he might have had a deliberate plan is given by Gomulka in his *Nowiny Kurier* account. The former Polish party chief relates that in the first days of February 1968 he had a secret meeting with Dubček at the border between the two countries. He gives the following description of the talks: "He [Dubček] proposed that we act jointly. He wanted me to support him, to introduce in Poland several freedom reforms which were more or less radical, and that I would take the stand with him jointly with regard to the Soviet comrades. Dubček told me at that time that if I took such a step, we would also be joined by Kádár, who made a similar proposal to him, and that the three of us would represent a considerable force. It would not be easy to swallow us."[75] Gomulka adds that Dubček even tried to exert pressure on him by saying that Gomulka's acceptance of this plan would be the best way "not to be caught unprepared by events" in Poland itself.

Such a plan was never mentioned anywhere except in this account. It is hard to believe that a man like Kádár would not only endorse it, but initiate it, or that Dubček was looking so far ahead. Nothing in his subse-

75. *Nowiny Kurier,* June 8, 1973.

quent behavior substantiates the charge. His main characteristics, rather, were goodwill and sympathy for the liberals combined with indecision and political naiveté. He constantly tried to convince Brezhnev of his good intentions, and instead of saying no, he usually promised more than he could deliver. Gomulka certainly, and even Nagy, seem to have been stronger.

Ludvík Svoboda saw to it that the forms of legality were respected: his refusal to appoint Indra—or himself—head of the government, as the Russians proposed, added the final blow to the first phase of the intervention, but having achieved the liberation of the other three and consolidated his image as "father of the nation," the president stopped there. He had always been strongly pro-Soviet even during his disgrace (which was ended by Khrushchev's personal intervention); his decision to go to Moscow on August 23 was questionable, since it was a step on the road to compromise and actually helped the Soviet leaders out of their problems. Later, Svoboda was to go along with the Husák normalization line all the way to its final consequences.

Oldrich Cerník, Dubcek's prime minister, had to share the fate of the party chief, though he too bowed rather early to Soviet demands. He was notably active in negotiating, then in rallying support for, the treaty on the stationing of Soviet troops in October.

Josef Smrkovsky was probably the strongest character in this team of four and the most articulate in presenting liberal views. But the decision of the four to "stick together" in August made him a hostage to the advocates of compromise: he had to go along with them even if he had more reservations than the other three about the Moscow protocol. This did not prevent his later being dropped from this position with the tacit acquiescence of the other three. Personal interests may have played a part here, especially during the Moscow negotiations at the end of August. Had they refused to compromise, Dubcek and his colleagues knew they would be kept in detention and perhaps physically eliminated, as Nagy had been ten years earlier. On the other side, accepting the compromise meant a return to Prague and the resumption of their functions; they knew that this would happen in considerably worsened conditions but hoped to be able to lessen the Soviet pressure by promises, as they had done before.

Another weakness of this group was its failure to anticipate the intervention and prepare for it. A report by Stanislav Budin, editor in chief of the Prague weekly *Reporter,* tells about a meeting of some forty journalists on August 17, three days before the invasion, with a group of leaders that included Cerník, Smrkovsky, and Kriegel. The question of a possible armed intervention was raised, says Budin, but "they [the leaders] answered that this was out of the question, that the reason for their fears was the possibility of a provocation that would oblige them to call on the police forces."[76] In other words, the military maneuvers that were in full swing along the Czechoslovak borders with Communist countries were perceived as a meaningless exercise (except for the exertion of political pressure, to which Prague leaders were so accustomed that they largely ignored it).

After the invasion, there was no question of armed resistance. In its first proclamation, the leadership called on the citizens "to maintain calm and not to offer resistance to the troops on the march. . . . Our army, security corps and people's militia have not received a command to defend the country" (in a subsequent version, the following was added to the last sentence: "because defense of our state frontiers is now impossible").[77] Without questioning this decision (though many Czechoslovaks still think that fighting was necessary, if only for the honor of the country and its image for future generations), it must be pointed out that a more active nonviolent resistance would have been possible if the political leaders had shown stronger determination and preparedness.

For example, instead of waiting for the Russians in the central committee building, Dubček, Smrkovsky, and their colleagues might have escaped to private hideouts, from which they could have continued to govern the country, as other ministers, like Pavel, did. One effective measure taken after a few days by the population at the suggestion of the clandestine radio stations was to change all road markers, so that Soviet convoys were disoriented and lost precious time. This might have been supplemented by the destruction or obstruction of selected targets, like bridges. Such measures before the invasion, as well as the erection of roadblocks at the borders and on the airfields and a partial mobilization, could have been an effective deterrent, taking advantage of Moscow's hesitation.

To be sure, the Czechoslovak army was not reliable one way or the other. As in Hungary and Poland, the combination of pro-Soviet generals —and Soviet advisers too—at the top and a rank and file that sided with the people meant that neither faction could use the army decisively. The military did nothing to prevent the Soviet invasion or to oppose it after it began, especially since they were hampered in the latter effort by the

76. *New York Times,* August 28, 1968.
77. Windsor and Roberts, *Czechoslovakia 1968,* p. 174.

Soviet forces that often surrounded their barracks to prevent any move out of them.

The role of General Martin Dzur, Czechoslovak defense minister, remains a mystery. All indications are that he loyally supported Dubček through the spring and summer, though he avoided radical statements (unlike General Václav Prchlík, his assistant for political affairs, who stirred Russian anger by publicly calling for a change in the structure of the Warsaw Pact). But he seems to have sided with the Russians and the "normalizers" early in 1969 and played a major role in the final push against Dubček. When Marshal Grechko, the Soviet defense minister, arrived in Milovice on March 31, 1969, he first talked to a group of pro-Soviet Czechoslovak generals who were awaiting him; these included Rytyr, a friend of Novotny's, Dvořak, a deputy minister of defense, and Bedrich, the new head of the political directorate of the army. But it was Dzur who, after a meeting of the military council of the defense ministry, asked Dubček to accept Grechko's ultimatum—namely, to take "radical and immediate measures" to restore order. His reward for this move was keeping his post in Husák's time.

Gustav Husák's case may be compared to Gomulka's in that he was falsely perceived by the liberals as their ally and betrayed their hopes. Like Gomulka, he did little to change this perception; indeed, he accepted it as long as it suited his purposes. He rose to power after the intervention, using the liberal trends, which were at their highest point at this time, and coming against some conservatives who had been labeled "collaborators"; notably against Vasil Bilak, from whom Husák took the job of party chief in Slovakia. But having achieved this, he started to turn against Dubček and to take the lead against what he called "anti-socialist, liberalist and anarchistic forces." By September he had managed to attract the attention of Soviet leaders; Vasily Kuznetsov, the Soviet envoy, told Smrkovsky on September 11, "Things are a bit better in Slovakia, thanks especially to comrade Husák, but even there we are not satisfied."[78] After the December meeting in Moscow between the two leaderships, Husák moved exactly as the Russians had expected by leading the attack against Smrkovsky (under the pretext that a Slovak had to head the parliament).

The big difference was that Gomulka was in a better position to deal with the Kremlin since he had demonstrated his capacity to resist. Husák could consolidate his position only by total subservience to Moscow. He

78. Tigrid, *Why Dubček Fell*, p. 217.

thus had to accept the return of a great number of Novotny's friends and, though himself a victim of repression, a return also of past practices and of their supporters. This was radically different from the situation of Kádár, who, being more skilled at inner party manipulation, managed to follow the middle of the road and to rely on his own group of supporters.

Though Soviet action in this crisis avoided bloodshed, its repercussions on the Communist movement were greater than those from the intervention in Hungary twelve years earlier. Most Western European Communist parties, including the powerful Italian and French parties, condemned the Soviet Union. Among the socialist countries (except for Albania, which used this opportunity to officially renounce its membership in the Warsaw Pact, in which Tirana had not participated since breaking with Moscow in 1961), two must be singled out.

Yugoslavia was a vulnerable country, since the temptation to liquidate this permanent model of Communist dissidence might have arisen in Moscow. Tito reacted preemptively by stating on August 23 that his country would defend its independence. This statement was reinforced by the recall of some army reservists. At the same time the Yugoslavs were careful to avoid using harsh words that might have provoked the Russians: the intervention in Czechoslovakia was not "condemned" but met with "anxiety" and "concern."

Rumania was in by far the touchiest position. It had been rewarded for its cooperation with Moscow during the Hungarian crisis by a withdrawal of Soviet troops in 1958. But since 1964, it had developed an independent foreign policy, maintaining friendly relations with China at a time when Chinese insults to the Soviet Union were provocative, refusing to break with Israel after the six-day war, and developing contacts with Western nations. Though by no means a liberal, Nicolae Ceausescu, the leader in Bucharest after Gheorghiu-Dej's death in 1965, had viewed the Czechoslovak experiment with great hope: visiting Prague in early August, he had even hinted at a possible renewal of the prewar "petite entente" between Yugoslavia, Czechoslovakia, and Rumania to resist Soviet hegemony in Eastern Europe. This was an embarrassment to Dubček and a new reason for Ceausescu to fear Soviet intentions in the aftermath of August 20.

There are strong indications that Moscow was ready in the summer of 1968 to take action against Rumania, and Ceausescu, too. Major troop movements were reported along the Rumanian borders with the Soviet Union and Hungary, not all of them attributable to the preparation for Soviet action in Czechoslovakia. Ion-Gheorghe Maurer, the Rumanian prime minister, told me a few months later that twenty-nine divisions were concentrated in August 1968 against Rumania, in addition to the twenty-nine in Czechoslovakia.

This explains why the first Rumanian reaction to the August 20 action was forceful and strident. Ceausescu hastily convened a huge meeting in downtown Bucharest on August 21 and no less hastily formed "armed patriotic detachments of workers, peasants and intellectuals" to parade in the city. Denouncing Soviet action in Prague as a "great mistake" and "a grave danger to peace in Europe," he added: "Maybe tomorrow there will be some who say that here too, at this rally, counterrevolutionary tendencies were manifest. We answer all of them: the entire Rumanian people will not allow anybody to violate the territory of our homeland."[79] This tone was maintained for several days, until more ominous signals came from Moscow. On August 23, 1968, the Soviet press agency Tass departed from its rule not to criticize Rumania by name by stating in a commentary on "imperialist" arguments: "It is strange, to say the least, to hear exactly the same formulations from the lips of Rumanian or Yugoslav leaders. Don't they know that the Warsaw Pact was concluded not only for the purpose of defending national borders and territories of the states signing it?" This warning sounded particularly threatening to Rumania, a signatory of the Warsaw Pact. In the same period, direct criticism of Rumania appeared also in Hungarian, Polish, and other Communist press organs.

Some accommodation seems to have taken place at a meeting in Bucharest on August 25 between Ceausescu and Soviet Ambassador A. V. Basov—at least, the Rumanian leader toned down his attacks on Moscow. He stated the following day in a speech in Brasov: "We are determined to act with all our force and skill so as to contribute to a speedy liquidation of the present state of affairs" (in the relations among Communist parties). The same day, August 26, the Rumanian party organ *Scinteia* declared: "The relations should not be aggravated still more." *Izvestiya* answered with another direct criticism of Rumania, though a less threatening one: Bucharest was taken to task for not having given "a proper and immediate rebuff" to the rumors that Rumania was going to be invaded by Warsaw Pact countries.[80]

Although tension subsided somewhat, the danger was not completely over. In the last days of August, new movements of troops were reported near Rumania; according to Western estimates, fourteen divisions were

79. *Scinteia* (Bucharest), August 22, 1968.
80. *Izvestiya,* August 28, 1968.

concentrated around the country: nine in the USSR, two in Bulgaria, and three in Hungary.[81] More ominous signals were received by American authorities, moving President Lyndon B. Johnson to add to a speech he delivered in San Antonio on August 31 a strong warning to Moscow. After referring to the Czechoslovak invasion, he said: "There are even rumors late this evening that this action might be repeated elsewhere in the days ahead in Eastern Europe. So I say to you tonight and to the world, we cannot and we must not in the year 1968 return to a world of unbridled aggression. . . . So let no one unleash the dogs of war."[82]

Even now, Soviet intentions toward Rumania at that time are not clear. There is no doubt that the temptation to take violent action existed. Maybe President Johnson's warning was helpful in preventing it—the Rumanians were very grateful to him, at least—but another factor may have contributed to the Soviet "nondecision": the situation in Czechoslovakia, where the upsurge of popular resistance and the Soviet failure to achieve a tangible political result made it necessary to concentrate on the problems there, without adding the burden of another adventure.

By contrast, Soviet action in Czechoslovakia was not hampered in any way by Western reaction. Nothing was said in advance that might have made Moscow hesitate, and apparently even the possibility of a Soviet military intervention in Prague had been discarded by Washington policy-makers after the Bratislava "compromise." A week before August 20, the State Department disbanded a special unit that had been set up to keep a close watch on the Czechoslovak situation.[83] Before August, the only concern in the West was to refute anything that might have substantiated Soviet accusations about Western involvement in the Czechoslovak situation or West German revanchist intrigues. NATO military exercises planned for the end of August in West Germany near the Czechoslovak border were moved at the end of July to another location near Ulm, further west.

After the invasion, there was no question in Washington of going beyond verbal protests and recourse (known in advance to be platonic) to the United Nations. Soviet action was described by President Johnson (on August 21 in a television address) as "shocking the conscience of the world," but as Secretary of State Dean Rusk put it in a speech in New Haven on September 12: "There was little we could do, through the use

81. *New York Times,* August 31, 1968.
82. *New York Times,* September 1, 1968.
83. *New York Times,* August 21, 1968.

of military force, to assist any of those [Eastern European] countries without automatically engaging in general war with the Soviet Union."

Had this been said before the invasion to the Russians? At least one Czechoslovak leader, Zdenek Mlynar, has publicly stated that it had. According to an interview he gave the Western press after he left Czechoslovakia in 1978, Brezhnev told Dubček in Moscow a few days after the invasion that he had "received a formal assurance from President Johnson that the United States would not react militarily to an intervention in Czechoslovakia." More specifically, he had asked Johnson if the United States still recognized the validity of the Yalta and Potsdam agreements and had received a positive answer.[84] This does not mean that the American view was expressed to the Soviet leaders so bluntly, but it is fair to assume that it was substantially the same.

Though it was admitted that the presence of Soviet forces in Czechoslovakia had "obviously affected the military situation in Europe" (as the State Department spokesman acknowledged on August 31), there was no change in the plan for withdrawing 33,000 American soldiers from Europe, which had been 75 percent accomplished at the time of the invasion. The idea of a NATO summit meeting, put forward by Zbigniew Brzezinski, then an adviser to presidential candidate Hubert Humphrey, and by West German Chancellor Kurt Georg Kiesinger, was quickly abandoned. By contrast, President Johnson was somewhat reluctant to drop the plan for a meeting with Soviet leader Brezhnev. Both men were near agreement on announcing the opening of the strategic arms limitation talks. Because of the Czechoslovak invasion, the announcement and the start of the talks were postponed until 1969.

Outcomes and Conclusions

In all three cases under study, the Soviet Union achieved its objectives, though this was not always clear at the time.

In Poland in 1956, the Russians were certainly right not to intervene. Any use of force by them would have provoked a violent reaction from the Polish people and their leaders and would have pushed Gomulka into the anti-Soviet camp, perhaps with a result similar to that in Hungary with Nagy. In fact Soviet leaders made mistakes in both cases, trusting Nagy more than he deserved (from their point of view) and unduly antagonizing

84. *Die Presse* (Vienna), August 10, 1978.

Gomulka, who turned out to be their best ally in Poland, the leader most able to bring this liberal and nationalistic nation back into a system acceptable to Moscow. The purge early in 1957 of the liberal official party daily *Trybuna Ludu,* the banning of the ultraliberal weekly *Po Prostu* (summer and fall 1957), and the return to their official functions in 1959 of hard-liners and even members of the Natolin group (Eugeniusz Szyr, Tadeusz Gede, and Kazimierz Witaszewski) were the main steps along this path.

Gomulka might have used his victory of 1956 at least to develop an independent foreign policy, as Rumania did after 1963–64. This did not happen, mainly because of Gomulka's own inclination toward pro-Soviet "solidarity," but also because of anti-German feeling, traditional in the Polish elite, and uncertainty about the country's western border. The only exception was the policy toward China, where Gomulka kept some distance between himself and Moscow, refraining from attacking Peking too harshly. But the climax of the "dogmatic" line came in 1968, when ironically, Gomulka pressed forcefully for an armed intervention against Dubček, and in 1970, when he unsuccesfully asked the Russians to help put down the riots of Polish workers in the Baltic ports. His downfall followed quickly in December 1970.

In Hungary, the Soviet intervention of November 4, 1956, was probably the only means the Kremlin had at its disposal to bring back an acceptable regime and to keep the country among its satellites. Kádár was doubtless reluctant to assume the leadership in those conditions, but he managed, at the price of a tightly controlled pro-Soviet foreign policy, to make the domestic regime more flexible and amenable to the population. Beginning in 1960 with amnesty for many political prisoners, followed in 1961 by the proclamation of the Kádár principle (unique in Communist systems)—"Those who are not against us are with us"—this process brought about in 1964 a semiopening of the Hungarian borders in both directions, a higher degree of intellectual freedom than in other Communist countries, and an economic situation improved by a more flexible system of management. These results may be attributed to the following factors:

1. The personality of Kádár, who had been the victim of the worst repression under Rákosi and who was genuinely willing to get rid of the Stalinist past—more so than Gomulka, who tended to see the "Polish October" as little more than an episode in the struggle for power between different factions of the apparatus.

2. Kádár's decision to rely exclusively on his own constituency of middle-of-the-road Communists, keeping the dogmatists out of the way as strictly as the revisionists.

3. A broad consensus of the population, which realized that, given the circumstances and the unavoidable Russian domination, Kádár was the best alternative Hungary had.

4. The fact that Kádár had to deal in Moscow with Khrushchev, a man deeply involved in a fight against Stalinist and conservative elements and more likely to support his own brand of revisionism in Hungary. If Brezhnev and his comrades had been in charge in the Kremlin in the early 1960s, Kádár would have had a more difficult job. When they came to power, it was too late to impose a sudden turn, and Kádár managed to maintain at least the main elements of his line.

In Czechoslovakia, the Soviet intervention achieved the desired result, but after a rather long delay and with a substantial degree of overkill, which reduced the benefits of the operation. The preservation of the Dubček leadership and of the achievements of the Prague spring would undoubtedly have endangered Soviet hegemony in Eastern Europe. But at the same time the armed intervention in Czechoslovakia proved a greater embarrassment to the Soviet Union internationally, particularly in the Communist movement, than the action in Hungary twelve years earlier.

Furthermore, Husák's leadership and his inability to develop new ideas and a constituency of his own in the Communist party, prevented him from acting as Kádár had in Hungary or even as Gomulka had in Poland. The only road open to him led back to the Novotny era, to the Novotny people, and to the old methods. This created more frustration and a potentially unstable situation.

All three cases show that Soviet armed intervention, or the threat of it, is still an important fact of life in Eastern Europe. To be sure, it is not an easy or automatic option. Some leaders who asked for such an intervention to help them against their opponents—like Novotny in 1967—or to crush popular revolt—like Gomulka in 1970—were refused. After all, what matters for the Kremlin is not the fate of a particular leader (even that of an old and reliable friend), but the interests of the Soviet Union; that is, the preservation of a pro-Soviet policy and of an orthodox, Soviet-like socialism in the country concerned.

This being the case, Moscow will act without worrying about legality or diplomatic considerations. An official pretext, such as an appeal for help from at least some of the local leaders (like that of Kádár in 1956) is desirable, but is not considered necessary. The Czechoslovak leaders who supposedly asked Moscow for help were never clearly identified. The so-called Brezhnev doctrine, implying that international law does not apply to relations between Communist countries, was developed for this occasion. But the Hungarian intervention was carried out with even less explanation. In Poland, on the other hand, there was no intervention, though the presence of the Natolinists and their overt desire for Soviet help offered a much better pretext for it. In the future, there is no doubt that in an emergency or if it suited their interests, the Russians would invade another Communist country with even less "legitimation."

When an intervention is decided upon, it is carried out with overwhelming forces, all the way to a complete victory. In Czechoslovakia as well as in Hungary, the Soviet command managed to concentrate enough means to crush any resistance even when, as in the first case, the probability of such resistance was slight. By the same token, it may be assumed that an armed intervention against Gomulka in 1956, though a political mistake, would probably have led nevertheless, after a violent war and a long repression, to a normalized Natolinist regime, somewhere in between the types headed by Husák and Kádár. Moscow would not have stopped its action short of such an outcome.

The only exception to this typical behavior is the first armed intervention in Budapest on October 24, 1956, which was carried out with limited means and without a clear political objective. Moscow was then reluctant to support Gerö. It never repeated this kind of halfhearted action.

The deterrent effect of a Soviet threat before an actual intervention is limited, however. To be sure, the presence of Soviet forces in most Eastern European countries usually keeps intraparty struggles among local leaders from escalating into acute political crises. The leaders know from past examples that they cannot contend for power—or maintain it if they are already in command—without Moscow's backing. The more or less quiet elimination of Walter Ulbricht in East Germany and of Gomulka in Poland in 1970 and the fading away of the influence of the Moczar group in Poland in the early 1970s have no other cause.

If, however, intraparty struggle does escalate into an open crisis, especially if public opinion actively favors one faction, Soviet diplomatic and military pressure short of an actual intervention seems to have little effect. Soviet military movements did not prevent the Poles from designating Gomulka as their leader in 1956. They had little, if any, effect on Nagy in

Hungary and Dubček in Czechoslovakia before November 4, 1956, and August 20, 1968, respectively. One can see a sort of counterproductive cycle, in which the more Moscow applies pressure for an orthodox Communist leadership and a pro-Soviet climate in the target country, the stronger is the anti-Soviet mood of the population of the country, which pushes leaders toward nationalism and resistance. In Hungary Soviet reinforcements and movements of troops in late October 1956 led Imre Nagy to withdraw from the Warsaw Pact. In Czechoslovakia Soviet military preparation and maneuvers were so constant that Dubček failed to get the signal. Any new military move was perceived as another political pressure, not as a real danger.

Western reaction in all three cases did not present Moscow with problems. On the military side, there was nothing Western powers could reasonably do to prevent the Soviet Union from acting at will in areas that have clearly been in its sphere of influence since the late 1940s. This was true in Poland, a country surrounded by Communist countries, in Hungary, a neighbor of neutral Austria, and even in Czechoslovakia, the only country under study in which there were no Soviet troops and which shared a border with a NATO member.

The action in Czechoslovakia nevertheless clearly improved the East-West balance of power in favor of Moscow. It added five Soviet divisions to the twenty-six already stationed in Eastern Europe, and, more important, it permitted a territorial connection between the forces in East Germany and Poland—the Northern Group of Troops—and the forces in Hungary—the Southern Group. This new contingent, which naturally took the name "Central Group," gave the Russians direct control of an area in the heart of Europe that would be vital in a conflict. After the withdrawal of Soviet forces from Austria (1955) and Rumania (1958), it was the first move in the opposite direction, to the west. This change, coinciding with the first Soviet step toward nuclear parity with the United States (the number of intercontinental ballistic missiles was equalized in 1969) and with the beginning of a major buildup of Soviet conventional forces, substantially reinforced the Soviet military posture in Europe.

Moscow, however, had a political price to pay after each intervention. One consequence of the Hungarian operation was a return to the post-Stalin status of East-West tension, a cancellation of the relative détente introduced by the 1955 Geneva summit and the Austrian peace treaty. It took three years to organize the first high-level meeting with the United States (at Camp David in 1959). After 1968 the picture was different. In the East the Czechoslovak intervention further exacerbated the Sino-Soviet split and opened the way for China's rapprochement with the United States. Nearly everywhere in the Communist ranks, Moscow suffered a new and probably decisive deterioration of its image; this and the appearance of Aleksandr Solzhenitzyn's books led to the so-called Euro-communist deviation.

The Western governments, however, reacted more mildly. The détente process, started by France in 1966, continued nearly unimpaired after 1968, switching to Germany with the beginning of Chancellor Brandt's *Ostpolitik,* then to the United States with the Nixon-Brezhnev summits of the early 1970s. And before that, the way was opened for SALT and the Conference on Security and Cooperation in Europe.

One lesson Soviet leaders may draw from those crises is that each use of force inside their sphere of influence should be considered by them on its own merits and risks, not in terms of East-West tension or détente. The desire for dialogue in Western capitals will always be stronger than the desire to punish aggression against countries already dominated by the Kremlin.

CHAPTER SEVEN

The Sino-Soviet Border Conflict

THOMAS W. ROBINSON

SINCE the border incidents of March 1969, the Soviet Union and China have been at loggerheads militarily, and the foreign policies of both, as well as that of the United States, have changed immensely. Indeed, the policies and interrelations of the three states underwent a major reorientation as a result of those incidents and of the subsequent military buildups on both sides of the Sino-Soviet border. It is unlikely, for instance, that the rapprochement between China and the United States would have advanced so far had the decline in Sino-Soviet relations not been hastened by the 1969 events. Moreover, the entire international system has been affectcd by Sino-Soviet-American policy changes, as the fear-induced acceleration away from each other of China and the Soviet Union helped give the system post–cold war "looseness." This has meant that many states have felt no obligation to line up with either the Eastern or the Western bloc or with the Chinese.

Border strife between Russia and China has also served as a catalyst to induce the steady buildup of Soviet military strength, in every department, during the last decade. Far from causing the Soviet Union to shift its energies and attention away from the European theater and strategic nuclear competition with the United States, the border incidents reinforced the Kremlin's determination to protect itself militarily on all fronts. Moscow did not want to be forced to choose among further investments in its traditional Western front, in its strategic competition with the United States, and in its new Chinese front. Finding itself with increasing military productive capacity and the ability to control the consumer de-

265

mands of the still relatively docile Soviet citizenry, the Kremlin leadership elected to greatly increase its military investment on the Chinese front while not in the least deviating from its steady European and strategic buildup. It was this decision, taken directly (though not solely) as a result of the worsening military situation with China that began a serious arms race with the Chinese, led to the exacerbation by the mid-1970s of Soviet-American tension in many areas, and brought about significant changes in the relations of the three major powers and in Asian regional politics.

This is not to say, of course, that one event—the border clashes of March 1969—or the reaction to this event of the Russians or the Chinese was the sole cause of all the developments that followed. But it does appear to have been the final link in a long series of occurrences that persuaded policymakers in Moscow to take major corrective steps in a number of disparate spheres. Given the importance of these changes, it is desirable to understand how Moscow used its armed forces against Peking during and after 1969 and how the buildup of Soviet military capabilities was caused by—and in turn affected—the decision to confront China.[1]

The Sino-Soviet Border before 1969

Sino-Soviet border differences have a long history, stretching back to the signing of the first treaties between Russia and China in the seventeenth century.[2] In the post-1949 period of Communist rule in China, however, the border was not a problem for the two governments until after the Soviet and Chinese Communist parties had their initial falling-out in the late 1950s. Thus the border issue was not one of the underlying causes of Moscow-Peking difficulties.[3] Nevertheless, the border was al-

1. Thomas W. Robinson, *The Sino-Soviet Border Situation, 1969–1975: Military, Diplomatic, and Political Maneuvering,* HI-2364-RR (Croton-on-Hudson, N.Y.: Hudson Institute, November 1975).

2. Tai Sung An, *The Sino-Soviet Territorial Dispute* (Westminster, 1973), chap. 1; and Mark Mancall, *Russia and China: Their Diplomatic Relations to 1728* (Harvard University Press, 1971).

3. See Zbigniew Brzezinski, *The Soviet Bloc,* rev. ed. (Harvard University Press, 1967), pp. 180–84; Donald Zagoria, *The Sino-Soviet Conflict, 1956–1961* (Princeton University Press, 1962), chaps. 1–7; David Floyd, *Mao Against Khrushchev: A Short History of the Sino-Soviet Conflict* (Praeger, 1963); Alexander Dallin, Jonathan Harris, and Grey Hodnett, eds., *Diversity in International Communism* (Columbia University Press, 1963); William E. Griffith, *The Sino-Soviet Rift* (MIT Press, 1964); and William E. Griffith, *Sino-Soviet Relations, 1964–1965* (MIT Press, 1966).

ways potentially a place where Sino-Soviet differences could be expressed, and this did occur, for example, during the Cultural Revolution. Probably there was always constant, if low-level, border tension that stemmed from the differences in the two peoples, in the locations of the Russian and Chinese population and industry, in the levels of modernization on the two sides of the border, and in geography. These could be made use of— or were themselves potential for trouble—once the two erstwhile allies parted company.

There were also specific border-related problems that fed the general level of tension: differences (put aside until 1964) over the exact location of the border and ownership of certain pieces of real estate, especially of islands in the Amur-Ussuri river system; questions about the historic process of arriving at the treaties defining the border (for instance, Peking's unequal treaties argument); differences over treaty implementation; and problems of administering the border area, including river navigation questions and the special problem of island ownership and riparian rights in the Khabarovsk area.[4] All of these issues were purposely forgotten or were easily managed by the two sides until the Sino-Soviet ideological split cracked the broader Moscow-Peking military alliance irreparably. Then, all these residual problems gradually reemerged and soon became active components of serious Sino-Soviet differences. Adding the military dimension, starting in about 1966, led to an increasing concentration on the border problem. That problem, the product of the ideological turmoil of the previous decade, finally became a cause in its own right of further Sino-Soviet tension. It was only a matter of time until things took a violent turn and brought out all the hitherto dormant racial, historical, and irrationally emotional fears in both capitals that have been so evident since 1969.

Border Incidents

Border incidents occurred with increasing frequency, beginning in 1959 or 1960. The Russians allege that the number of Chinese "systematic provocations" began to increase in June 1962. By 1967 border relations had become quite bad. Not only were there reports of a clash on the

4. See Thomas W. Robinson, "The Sino-Soviet Border Dispute: Background, Development and the March 1969 Clashes," *American Political Science Review*, vol. 66 (December 1972), pp. 1178–82; and Neville Maxwell, "Why the Russians Lifted the Blockade at Bear Island," *Foreign Affairs*, vol. 57 (Fall 1978), pp. 138–145.

Ussuri in January 1967, but the Soviet Union accused the Chinese of wildly provocative behavior during the Cultural Revolution. Other incidents occurred on December 7–9 and 23, 1967, and in late January 1968 along the Amur and the Ussuri,[5] apparently continuing until the March 2, 1969, clash. The Russians gradually evolved a procedure for dealing with these incidents without violence, a procedure that was in effect at Damansky Island in March 1969.

Chinese complaints about Soviet border violations began only with an "intrusion" on January 23, 1967, at Damansky Island. Between that date and March 2, 1969, the Chinese claim, Soviet troops intruded onto Damansky sixteen times (including eight occasions during January and February 1969), eighteen times onto Chili Ching Island (north of Damansky), and on "many occasions" onto Kapotzu Island (south of Damansky), using "helicopters, armored cars, and vehicles." The Chinese accused the Russians of "ramming Chinese fishing boats, robbing Chinese fishing nets, turning high-pressure hoses on Chinese fishermen . . . kidnapping Chinese fishermen," assaulting and wounding Chinese frontier guards and seizing arms and ammunition, and violating Chinese air space by overflights. Further, the Chinese charged, the Soviet Union sent tanks, armored cars, and boats into Chinese territory, "drove out many Chinese inhabitants by force, demolished their houses and destroyed their means of production and household goods." Finally, the Chinese charged that the Russians "provoked" a total of 4,189 border incidents from October 15, 1964, when border negotiations broke down, to March 1969.[6] These referred to border reconnaissance by the USSR and to evicting Chinese from areas it considered Russian without taking lives. Soviet and Chinese charges, taken together, indicate little more than run-of-the-mill incidents between two unfriendly powers who disagree about some specifics or border demarcation and who find the border a convenient region in which to express the general tension. But each took the other's

5. Yuri Dmitriyev, "Far Away on the Border," *Trud*, March 16, 1969, p. 3 (translated in *Current Digest of the Soviet Press* [*CDSP*], vol. 21, no. 11, April 2, 1969, p. 4).

6. "Note of the Ministry of Foreign Affairs of the People's Republic of China to the Soviet Embassy in China," New China News Agency (NCNA), March 3, 1969; *Jen-min Jih-pao*, March 4, 1969, p. 1 (translated in *Survey of China Mainland Press* [*SCMP*], no. 4372, March 10, 1969, pp. 19–20); NCNA, reporting on border documentary film, April 18, 1969; "Statement of the Government of the People's Republic of China, May 24, 1969," NCNA, May 24, 1969; and "Down With the New Tsars!" *Jen-min Jih-pao*, March 3, 1969 (in *SCMP*, no. 4373, March 11, 1969, pp. 17–19).

activities more seriously as time went by. Tit-for-tat reprisals began after the January (1967) Revolution phase of the Cultural Revolution and lasted until early 1969.

Military Dispositions and the
Beginning of the Soviet Buildup

The "traditional" (long-term) disposition of forces along the border had roughly balanced numbers of men—the Chinese having an edge in the areas around Manchuria and the Russians having an edge in the Sinkiang area—and a Soviet superiority in weapons and logistics. During the decade of relative Sino-Soviet friendship that ended in 1959, the Chinese did not worry about this overall disparity nor were they in a position to challenge it, and the USSR never made much of it. In the early 1960s, when Sino-Soviet ideological separation came, force dispositions on both sides remained defensively oriented. The Soviet Union directed most of its attention to Western Europe and the United States and its military investment to the strategic arms race; China after 1960 renewed its faith in guerrilla tactics and defense in depth. The latter stationed about fourteen infantry divisions in the northeast (for example, Manchuria), five divisions in Inner Mongolia, and five more in Sinkiang. The last two areas also had two to three division-equivalents of border guards, other nondivisional support elements, and the well-known Production and Construction Corps, paramilitary units made up of military-age youths in Sinkiang and Inner Mongolia. This gave the Chinese a total of thirty-five to forty division-equivalents in the military districts along the border, or somewhere between 420,000 and 450,000 men.[7]

Such dispositions of troops were determined both by Chinese security needs and the availability of soldiers. A sizable defensive force was located in the northeast because Peking was in one of the military regions included in the northeast sector, the area was very populous, Manchuria was China's major industrial base, and the Korean situation was unsettled. For defense specifically against the Soviet Union, fourteen divisions in the Shenyang Military Region, backed up by forces in the Peking Military Region, allowed the Chinese strategic flexibility. The large troop concentrations in these regions necessarily limited the numbers of men available to serve in other locations. Hence the smaller forces in Mongolia and

7. Institute for Strategic Studies, *The Military Balance* (London: ISS), yearly issues 1960–69.

Sinkiang. In Mongolia this presented no problem, since with no Soviet presence Mongolia was no threat to China. Sinkiang, on the other hand, required some military presence, since it housed nuclear test facilities, strategic resources, and a not too friendly minority population with a history of rebellion. Fortunately, the topography—desert and mountains—allowed the more effective placement of necessarily smaller numbers of troops.

As for the USSR, European Russia was where most of the Russian population lived and where Soviet international political involvement had been traditionally directed. A weak, friendly, or neutral China (or, for most of the 1930s and 1940s, a neutral Japan) encouraged the Russians to maintain only a thin line of regular Soviet army divisions east of Lake Baikal (except during the period of Soviet-Japanese tension in 1937 and the buildup immediately before the Soviet invasion of Manchuria in 1945).[8] Until 1969 that meant only fifteen to seventeen regular divisions (of which ten were in a state of high combat readiness) supplemented with contingents of nondivisional forces and border guards. This gave the Chinese a substantial edge in numbers, since the Russians numbered only about 250,000 to 300,000 men, or twenty to twenty-four division-equivalents.

But the Soviet logistical picture was more favorable than that of the Chinese, despite long lines of communication. The Trans-Siberian Railway paralleled the Soviet-Chinese border for its entire length. Except in the northeast, the Chinese had no comparable rail line. There were major Soviet military and air bases in the area and sizable Soviet cities along the length of the railroad. Again, the converse was true in China. Further, the Russians had far better equipment than the Chinese—aircraft, tanks, artillery, armored cars, and personnel carriers—and their comparatively good surface and air mobility meant that they could bring large forces to bear at a given spot much more quickly than the Chinese, who moved largely on foot. So the Russians balanced Chinese numbers with Soviet equipment and speed. Finally, in the event of conflict, the Soviet Union could have brought substantial reinforcements from European, central, and southern Russia, and its mobilization potential for fully equipped and trained soldiers was probably greater than that of the Chinese.

Since the border incidents began in 1959 and annually increased in

8. Ibid., 1965–69; and John Despres and others, *Timely Lessons of History: The Manchurian Model for Soviet Strategy,* R-1825-NA (Santa Monica, Calif.: Rand Corp., July 1976).

number until 1969, both powers might have been expected to augment their border forces in proportion to the frequency, location, and severity of those incidents. But no large buildup occurred before 1967 on either side, nor were traditional force dispositions altered. But beginning in late 1965, the Soviet forces were brought to a higher state of readiness, equipped with better and more weaponry, and their numbers augmented, if only marginally. The Russians also began equipping their Far Eastern forces with missiles, including surface-to-surface nuclear-tipped rockets, and several divisions in Central Asia were earmarked for eventual duty east of Lake Baikal. Soviet media began to emphasize paramilitary training for citizens in border regions. Finally, the Soviet Union signed a new defense agreement with Mongolia which gave the USSR the right to station troops and maintain bases in that country.[9]

On the Chinese side, nothing of a similar scale was done. The Chinese were in the throes of debating what sort of military strategy to pursue toward the American intervention in Vietnam. Moreover, the power struggle preceding the Cultural Revolution had resulted in purges in the army, notably of Chief of Staff Lo Jui-ch'ing, and had weakened the army despite Lin Piao's efforts to enhance Chinese military prowess through learning Mao Tse-tung's thought. It is true that by 1965 the Chinese were capable of producing most armaments (excluding high-performance aircraft and sophisticated communications equipment) in sufficient quantity to supply the regular forces of the People's Liberation Army (PLA), a capability that prevented a major decline in Chinese military efficiency. But the Vietnam War directed Chinese military attention primarily to its southern flank, instead of its northern and western ones. The Chinese were thus able to counter the Soviet buildup only marginally.

The year 1967 was one of Soviet decision. Border incidents associated with the Cultural Revolution not only reached a new high but took on, in Soviet eyes, increasingly ominous overtones. They responded with a 20,000-man increase in the size of the border guard force, large enough to elicit a public complaint from Chinese Foreign Minister Ch'en Yi. Moreover, the Soviet Union launched a campaign to explain Sino-Soviet differences to its people and sent high-level military figures on inspection tours of Far Eastern troop contingents. The major aspect of the Soviet

9. The twenty-year "Treaty of Friendship, Cooperation, and Mutual Aid Between the USSR and the MPR" was signed with great fanfare in Ulan Bator on January 15, 1966. It replaced a similar treaty signed in 1946. Text in *Pravda,* January 18, 1966 (in *CDSP,* vol. 18, no. 3, February 9, 1966, pp. 7–8).

buildup, however, was the decision to station strong military units on Mongolian soil, a deployment begun sometime after the signing of the twenty-year defense pact in January 1966 and shifted into high gear in 1967. By November 1967 several divisions, armed with tanks and missiles, were occupying permanent bases in Mongolia.

In the summer of 1968 the Russians held their first large maneuvers in Mongolia and completed a rail line between Chita, a major Soviet military base, and Choibalsan, Mongolia's second largest city, where a new Soviet base was established. Soviet strength inside Mongolia was estimated at six divisions, including one tank division. The magnitude of this buildup upset the balance of power between the two states' forces. The Chinese did their best to redeploy their own forces in response. After the Soviet-Mongolian maneuvers, several Chinese divisions were redeployed to the Soviet-Mongolian border and significant numbers of artillery pieces were redeployed from the Fukien region. Finally, with the Cultural Revolution drawing to a close, the Chinese began again to stress the importance of the Production and Construction Corps. In all, the Chinese increased their capability in the northeast and in Inner Mongolia by four or five divisions, making the total forty in both areas, as against the thirty-five or thirty-six divisions in the traditional orientation. The Chinese also tightened their border security in response to similar Soviet moves.[10]

Four conclusions emerge from this analysis of comparative border strengths before 1969. First, for long periods a rough balance of forces existed in the military regions on the Sino-Soviet border, trading Chinese numerical superiority for Soviet equipment and mobility advantages, and balancing Chinese troop concentrations in Manchuria with Soviet defense bases along the Amur and in Central Asia. Second, the balance changed around 1965, when the Soviet Union began to improve the quality and, to some extent, the quantity of its forces. Third, the balance seems to have been definitely upset by the movement after 1966 of Soviet troops and equipment into Mongolia and close to the Sino-Mongolian border. Soviet

10. *New York Times,* December 11, 1966; *Washington Post,* December 11, 1966; *Krasnaya Zvezda,* January 11, February 15, and March 10, 1967; *New York Times,* January 21, 1967; *Krasnaya Zvezda,* July 31, 1968; *Dal'niy Vostok,* no. 1, 1968; articles by Harrison Salisbury, *New York Times,* January 3, 1969; *Novosti Mongoli,* November 11, 1967; *Los Angeles Times,* July 10, 1969; *New York Times,* May 24, 1969; Chiang Yi-San, "Military Affairs of Communist China, 1968," *Tsu Kuo,* no. 59 (February 1969), pp. 20–36, which quotes *Sing-tao Jih-pao,* August 3 (p. 2), October 7 (p. 1), and December 9 (p. 3), 1968; *Communist China 1967* (Kowloon: Union Research Institutes), pp. 230–31; *Japan Times* (Tokyo), March 9, 1967; *The Economist,* March 22, 1969; and *Le Monde,* April 14, 1969.

maneuvers in particular caused the Chinese to transfer additional, though still marginal, troops and equipment to Inner Mongolia and Manchuria. Last, increased patrolling by both sides and the exigencies of the Cultural Revolution caused rising tension all along the border. Although by early 1969 the impending end of the Cultural Revolution promised to subtract a disruptive and potentially dangerous element, the Soviet buildup more than offset that possibility and probably made the Chinese fear the future.

The March 1969 Military Clashes on the Ussuri[11]

The many incidents along the border after early 1969 may be divided into the very small—but important—group whose immediate cause probably can be traced to Chinese military initiatives and the much larger group that available evidence indicates were due to Soviet action. There are little data on most of those incidents after the first two in March 1969, which is unfortunate, since there is a fundamental difference between those two and most of the subsequent occurrences. Whereas the March 2 incident seems, on balance, to have been perpetrated by the Chinese and the March 15 incident by the Soviet army to punish the Chinese for the earlier "transgression," almost all subsequent actions were Soviet-initiated activities designed to support concurrent diplomatic initiatives, to test Chinese military reaction, or to pin the Chinese back during the period of Soviet military buildup. These later incidents have been relatively numerous and show the character of deliberate Soviet use of force. Yet since the data necessary to draw firm conclusions about the nature of those incidents is lacking, I shall concentrate on only the first two Sino-Soviet clashes, presuming that they have enough in common with the rest to permit extrapolation. I will also examine the imbalance and the uneven pace of the respective Soviet and Chinese military buildups and related foreign policy activities to judge the wider effects of the Soviet use of force after March 1969.

On March 2 a skirmish took place at Damansky Island between Soviet and Chinese frontier formations. More than thirty Soviet border guards and an unknown number of Chinese soldiers were killed or wounded. Tension all along the border rose quickly and both armies increased their state of readiness. On March 15 at the same location there was a second,

11. This section is based on Robinson, "The Sino-Soviet Border Dispute," pp. 1187–90.

larger clash with greater loss of life. Whereas the first battle had lasted two hours, the second took nine hours. Both sides used heavy weapons. The Chinese reportedly lost several hundred men, the Russians an unspecified number. Sino-Soviet relations entered a new and dangerous stage. Incidents, if not actual military clashes, began to be reported all along the border and lasted until the famous September meeting at the Peking airport between Premiers Chou En-lai and Aleksei Kosygin.

Damansky Island is in the Ussuri River, which forms the boundary between the Soviet Union and China, about 180 miles southwest of Khabarovsk. The Chinese claim the island was once a part of the Chinese bank, became separated by erosion of the river, and during low water in late summer can be reached on foot from the Chinese shore. The main channel of the Ussuri passes to the east of the island. The river at this point is wide and the river-arm (as the Chinese call it) or the channel (the Soviet term) appears to be nearly as wide, and may be as deep at high water, as the channel on the east. From the location of navigation markers on the two shores and the curvature of the river, ships appear to traverse the eastern channel. The island itself is uninhabited, although Chinese fishermen used it for drying their nets and both nations have done some logging on it. About one mile in length and one-third mile wide, it is flooded during the spring thaw. The island is largely wooded, with some open areas, and rises to twenty feet above the water. There is extensive marshland on the Soviet side of the river, which in winter forces Russian vehicles to detour about two miles before they can move onto the ice toward the island. In March 1969 the river was frozen nearly solid, and multiton vehicles could be driven over the ice.

The characteristics of the immediate area are similar to those elsewhere on the Ussuri: boggy marshes along both sides, low elevation though slightly higher on the Chinese side, sparse population along the river front, and poor land for agriculture. The meager Soviet population is concentrated farther inland, along the Vladivostok-Khabarovsk sector of the Trans-Siberian Railway and the road that parallels it. Chinese settlements in this area of the river are even more sparsely populated. Most of the border incidents in the area before March 2 took place on two larger and more important islands, Kirkinsky and Buyan, situated to the north and south respectively. However, Damansky had previously been the scene of several near-violent meetings between groups of Soviet and Chinese frontier guards.

The Soviet Union maintained two border outposts in the area, one just south and the other just north of the island. The southern post had the disadvantage that its line of sight did not include the island itself (although the river-arm and the Chinese bank could be seen) and thus on-the-spot patrolling was necessary to determine Chinese presence on the island. The Chinese border post, named Kung-szu after the local Chinese settlement, was located on a hillock directly across from the island.

On the night of March 1–2, a mixed group of about three hundred Chinese frontier guards and regular soldiers dressed in white camouflage crossed the ice from the Chinese bank to Damansky Island, dug foxholes in a wooded area overlooking the southernmost extremity, laid telephone wire to the command post on the Chinese bank, and lay down for the night on straw mats. Sometime early in the morning, the duty man at the Soviet outpost south of the island reported activity on the Chinese bank. Around 11:00 a.m. a group of twenty or thirty armed Chinese were seen moving toward the island, shouting Maoist slogans as they went. The Soviet outpost commander, Strelnikov, and an undetermined number of his subordinates set off for the southern extremity of the island in two armored personnel carriers, a truck, and a command car. Arriving on the island (or perhaps remaining on the ice covering the river-arm west of the island) a few minutes later, Strelnikov and seven or eight others dismounted and moved out to warn the oncoming Chinese, as they had several times previously. Following a procedure developed for such occasions, the Russians strapped their automatic rifles to their chests (reports differ: some say they left their weapons behind) and linked arms to prevent the Chinese from passing. A verbal altercation may have taken place at this point. In any case, the Chinese arrayed themselves in rows and appeared to be unarmed. But when the Chinese had advanced to about twenty feet from the Russian group, the first row suddenly scattered to the side, exposing the second line of Chinese, who quickly pulled submachine guns from under their coats and opened fire on the Russians. Strelnikov and six of his companions were killed outright. Simultaneously, from an ambush to the Russians' right, the three hundred Chinese in foxholes also opened fire, catching the entire Russian unit by surprise. Mortar, machine gun, and antitank gunfire also commenced at that moment from the Chinese side. The Chinese apparently then charged the Russians and hand-to-hand fighting ensued. The Soviet unit was overrun, and the Chinese (according to Soviet charges) took nineteen prisoners and killed them on the spot. They also carried away Soviet equipment, which they later put on display.

Seeing the battle, Senior Lieutenant Bubenin, head of the northern outpost, and nearly his entire command set out for the scene. Racing up in an armored car, he succeeded in gaining the right flank of the Chinese, forcing them to divide their fire. But he also found himself in the middle of the island in the ambush that the Chinese had prepared for Strelnikov (who had not proceeded that far). Bubenin's vehicle was hit and disabled, and he himself was wounded and shell-shocked. He managed to get into another armored car and direct the battle from it. A series of melees ensued, with charges by both sides. Finally, the Russians state, they pinned down, for a time surrounded, and then forced the retreat of the remaining fifty or sixty Chinese to their own side of the bank. The Chinese took all their wounded with them, although they left behind some equipment. The entire battle lasted about two hours, and the Russians were so shorthanded that civilians had to be pressed into service as ammunition bearers. Although both sides claimed victory, neither Russian nor Chinese forces remained permanently on the island after the battle, although the Russians periodically moved off and on at will (later, they were reported to have abandoned it altogether to the Chinese).

The battle on March 15 was somewhat different. Preparations on both sides were much more complete, forces were larger, losses were higher, and the engagement lasted much longer. There was also no element of surprise. In contrast to the encounter on March 2, it is not clear who began the battle on the 15th. Soviet and Chinese sources differ, of course, and the Soviet documentation is again more voluminous. This time the Russian case is much less convincing, and the moral overtone present in reports of the earlier battle is muted, if not entirely absent. Both sides probably had built up their forces in the intervening fortnight, intending to wrest permanent control of the island away from the other or, failing that, to deny the other side its unhindered use.

Apparently the Russians increased the frequency of their patrols of the island after March 2. They still did not station a permanent force on the island, however, lest the Chinese zero in on them with artillery and mortar. A small scouting party did spend the night of March 14–15 on the island, and it is possible that this group was used to lure the Chinese into a frontal attack. The Chinese say that the other side sent "many" tanks to the island and the river-arm ice at about 4:00 a.m. on the 15th, attacking Chinese guards on patrol. It is not clear why such a large force would be needed to attack a patrol. The Russians state that their own early-morning patrol, consisting of two armored cars, discovered a group of

Chinese, who had allegedly sneaked over the previous night, lodged on the island. Whatever the cause, the battle began in earnest around 9:45 or 10:00 a.m., with mortar and artillery fire from the Chinese bank and, by 10:30, heavy fire from three points there.

The Chinese now threw more than a regiment (around 2,000 men) into the fray, charging across the ice and gaining possession of at least part of the island. When they saw this wave of Chinese, the Russians sought to block their advance with fire from machine guns mounted on armored personnel carriers, but moved back, either off the island or to its eastern extremity, when they saw that the Chinese had more men. (Russian accounts speak of a ratio of ten Chinese to every Russian.) The Chinese directed intense artillery fire not only at the Soviet troops but also at the eastern channel of the river separating the island from the Soviet bank, hoping to slow or stop the movement of heavy vehicles over the ice. The Russians, adopting tactics used by the Americans in the Korean War, allowed the Chinese to advance, and then counterattacked with large numbers of tanks, armored cars, and infantry in armored personnel carriers. Soviet artillery, brought in since the March 2 incident, launched a fierce barrage at 1:00 p.m., raking Chinese positions as far inland as four miles. Three such attacks were mounted, each breaking through the Chinese positions. The first two faltered when ammunition was gone. The third apparently broke up the Chinese position on the island, and the Chinese retreated to their own bank, taking their dead and wounded. The Russians state that they did not follow up the Chinese retreat with large-scale garrisoning of the island, although they continued intense patrolling. The battle was over at 7:00 p.m., having lasted more than nine hours. The Russians lost about sixty men (including the border post commander) and the Chinese eight hundred, both figures probably including dead and wounded. The number of Soviet casualties was lower probably because the Russians had an advantage in tactics and armament, and had planned their movements in advance.

Soviet Strategy between March and September 1969

Beginning with the second Damansky incident, the Soviet Union put into practice a new strategy toward the Chinese. Summed up by the Western term "coercive diplomacy," the changed strategy sought to combine diplomatic and military pressure in an effort to make the Chinese see not only the desirability of settling the border problem itself, but also the possibility of using a border settlement as the basis for an all-around improvement in relations. It is true that there was an apparent contradiction in the two halves of this new policy: if by means of political-military coercion the Soviet Union drove China first to the bargaining table and then to the signing of a new border treaty, the Chinese would probably not have been disposed to take the next step of improving or even discussing the improvement of relations in other areas. Nonetheless, the Soviet leaders did make up their minds to try to push the Chinese into renewed border talks as an important goal in itself, and evidently hoped that the Chinese would see the eventual wisdom of signing a new border treaty and at least talking about other outstanding issues. Coercion along the border thus had more than one purpose: on the one hand, an attempt to solve a particular and important problem in Soviet-Chinese interstate relations, and on the other, a means of "talking" to the Chinese about the desirability of resolving other ideological and national differences. Apparently the Russians determined that "success" on the border issue (border talks leading to a negotiated treaty settlement or to a joint statement that the border issue was considered settled) was worth pursuing in its own right, even if it was achieved at a cost, in the short term, of lack of progress on other issues.

The Russians took another risk in employing coercive diplomacy. Their diplomatic moves were of necessity accompanied by punishing military actions at the border and by threats of more severe military actions to follow. They also felt it necessary to strengthen their forces along the entire length of the Soviet-Mongolian-Chinese border, not merely to give support to the new politico-military campaign but, more important, to deter and defend against any repetition of the first Damansky incident. The Russians sought to control the local situation by absolute superiority in tactical conventional forces and the strategic situation by absolute superiority in combined forces, including nuclear arms. This meant a huge buildup of forces against China in every category, which would dislocate the Soviet economy and push Peking toward the West. To preserve Soviet security in the narrow sense, then, Moscow took a chance that it could handle any long-term Chinese response and any shorter-term anti-Soviet realignment of political forces. In retrospect, that may seem not to have been a worthwhile gamble: border security was assured but at the cost of (1) China's fear and hostility; (2) its resolve to modernize its economy and military to counter the Soviet Union directly; (3) lack of the border treaty that was the secondary object; and (4) the threat of an anti-Soviet entente composed of all the other powerful states in the world headed by the United States and China.[12]

To demonstrate to the Chinese their resolve on the border question, from April on the Russians not only brought up a large volume of military reinforcements—both troops and equipment—but also began to use the military superiority created to initiate (or take advantage of) "incidents" to serve as signals to the Chinese of the seriousness of the Russian intent. A series of such incidents, amounting to a campaign supported by hints of nuclear attack and other untoward consequences, occurred during the late spring and throughout the summer of 1969 and peaked in late August. Publicly admitted clashes took place on April 16, 17, and 25, May 2, 12–15, 20, 25, and 28, June 10–11, July 8 and 20, and August 13; and the two governments charged each other with having perpetrated dozens of other incidents. By September China had charged the Soviet Union with 488 "deliberate" violations of the frontier from June through August, and the Russians had accused the Chinese of 429 violations in June and July alone.[13] Although the Chinese, unlike the Russians, did not provide details of their side of these stories—which under other circumstances would lead to the suspicion that Peking was the initiating side— Soviet accounts lacked the convincing authenticity of their portrayals of the two earlier episodes. The more interesting fact is that the publicized affairs took place in widely scattered locations along the border: some

12. Later I will discuss the Soviet Union's discovery that its enlarged, powerful border force could serve anti-Chinese policy objectives unrelated to the border question, as in South Asia in 1971 and Southeast Asia in 1978–79.

13. June 10–11: NCNA, June 11, 1969 (in *SCMP*, no. 4438, June 12, 1969, pp. 22–23); *New York Times*, June 12, 1969; *Pravda*, June 12, 1969 (in *CDSP*, vol. 21, no. 24, July 9, 1969, pp. 9–14). July 8: NCNA, July 9, 1969; *New York Times*, July 8, 1969; *Pravda*, July 8, 1969 (in *CDSP*, vol. 21, no. 28, August 6, 1969, p. 34); Radio Moscow, July 10, 1969 (translated in U.S. Foreign Broadcast Information Service [FBIS], *Daily Report: Soviet Union*, July 14, 1969, pp. A30–A32). July 20: *Pravda*, September 11, 1969 (in *CDSP*, vol. 21, no. 37, October 8, 1969, pp. 8–10). August 13: *Pravda*, August 13, 1969 (in *CDSP*, vol. 21, no. 33, September 10, 1969, pp. 3–6); *New York Times*, August 14, 15, 16, 1969; *Christian Science Monitor*, August 14, 1969; FBIS, *Soviet Union* (August 14, 1969), pp. A1–A4; *Izvestiya* (and other Soviet sources), August 16, 1969 (in FBIS, *Soviet Union*, August 19, 1969, pp. A21–A25); Tel'man Zhanuzakor, "Combat on the Border," *Qazaq Edibiyeti* (Kazakhstan), August 23, 1969 (translated by Radio Liberty Committee, n.d.); *Sovetskaya Kirgiziya*, February 24, 1974 (in FBIS, *Soviet Union*, February 28, 1974, pp. C2–C3); *SCMP*, no. 4435, p. 24; NCNA, August 19, 1969 (in FBIS, *Daily Report: Communist China*, August 20, 1969); and *New York Times*, September 9, 1969.

on the Ussuri River—scene of the March events, some on islands in the Amur River, some along the Sino-Mongolian border, and some in the Sinkiang-Kazakhstan region not far from the Chinese nuclear test site at Lop Nor and the historic Dzungarian Gates invasion route between the two countries.

Because the Chinese military were preoccupied with political and administrative matters associated with the Cultural Revolution, and because the Soviet Union not only enjoyed strategic superiority but also had hinted that it would take drastic measures if China did not cease its provocations and reconvene the border talks, it is difficult to imagine that it was the Chinese who took the military initiative. Although in some instances Chinese forces on the spot may have taken the offensive to forestall anticipated attack, it is doubtful, in view of these relative weaknesses, that this was Chinese strategy in general. Rather, the period before September 11, 1969, when Chou and Kosygin met at the Peking airport, must be seen as a textbook case of the use by Moscow of combined political, military, and propaganda means to force Peking to take an action—renew the talks—it otherwise resisted and to teach it not to attempt more surprises like that at Damansky.

These Soviet military actions accompanied a series of diplomatic notes setting forth in detail the Soviet position on the border problem and suggesting that all points of difference could be settled by agreeing upon a mutual and definitive border treaty. The Russians repeated the terms set forth in the abortive 1964 talks and parried each Chinese counterargument with historical or ideological points of their own, all the while coordinating diplomatic notes with military action.[14]

The most interesting and threatening aspect of the politico-military campaign was the Soviet hint of nuclear attack against China and its linkage in timing and publicity with a serious border incident in August and with the peak of Moscow's diplomatic campaign to bring the Chinese back to the negotiating table. The hint was conveyed indirectly by former Soviet news correspondent Victor Louis in the September 18 *London Evening News* but Western intelligence sources had known of it in mid-August. The Russians also let it be known that they had sounded out

    14. Tass, *Pravda,* and *Izvestiya,* March 30, 1969 (in *CDSP,* vol. 21, no. 13, April 16, 1969, pp. 3–5, and FBIS, *Soviet Union,* April 1, 1969, pp. A1–A7); FBIS, *Soviet Union* (April 14, 1969), p. A1; *CDSP,* vol. 2, nos. 23–27 (July 2, 9, 16, 23, and 30, 1969), and FBIS, *Soviet Union* (June 18, 1969); and *Pravda,* June 14, 1969 (in *CDSP,* vol. 21, no. 24, July 9, 1969), pp. 9–13.

their Warsaw Pact allies on the possibility of a nuclear strike. It is doubtful whether the Soviet Union had any intention of actually carrying out the threat, in view of the necessary magnitude of such a nuclear attack and its consequences for Moscow's relations with every other country, as well as the very high level of radiation-induced casualties that would have been suffered by all the other states of Northeast Asia downwind from the Chinese nuclear test facilities, missile deployment sites, and airfields.

But this carefully orchestrated mixture of threat, military action, and diplomatic initiative did have its intended effect on the Chinese: in early September they agreed, apparently under extreme Soviet pressure, to allow Kosygin to meet Chou in Peking on September 11. (Kosygin had attempted to meet Chou at Ho Chi Minh's funeral in Hanoi, but Chou deliberately left for Peking before Kosygin was due to arrive. Kosygin therefore returned to the Soviet Union, but when he landed in Soviet Central Asia on his way back, he received word from Moscow that the Chinese had finally agreed to receive him and that he should change his plans and fly to Peking.)[15] Although no official announcement was made of what transpired at the Peking airport, semiauthoritative sources report that both sides agreed to cease armed provocations along the border; immediately resume border negotiations, suspended since 1964, at the deputy ministerial level; restore diplomatic relations up to the ambassadorial level; and step up trade and economic relations. Apparently Peking agreed to these "suggestions," despite Chinese efforts to wriggle out of a resumption of talks through counterproposals on September 18 and October 6.[16] Border negotiations resumed in Peking on October 20.

Before going on to the post-September 1969 period, it is well to summarize Soviet and Chinese policies from March to September. The Russian strategy was two-pronged. Soviet diplomatic notes suggested restoring relations up to the ambassadorial level, increasing trade, opening talks on the resolution of ideological differences, and settling the border question through compromise. Resolution of these questions would obviously constitute a qualitative improvement in Sino-Soviet relations. Soviet actions, on the other hand, were threatening: continual drubbings along the border, possibly striking Chinese nuclear facilities, and the hint of detaching border provinces (particularly Sinkiang) from the Chinese body politic and turning them into Mongolias. Perhaps the Russians were not

15. *New York Times,* September 12 and 13, 1969.
16. *New York Times,* September 12, 1969, and *Le Monde,* November 10–11, 1974.

serious about major military activities, but it is much more likely that they were following a strategy of parallel military and diplomatic escalation, postponing a choice between them until forced by events.

The Russians' strategy arose from their wish to avoid facing over the long run an increasingly powerful and unfriendly China in Asia while they were immersed in managing difficult problems in Eastern Europe and sustaining strategic and crisis-management competition with the United States throughout the world. It seemed best to attempt to address the "China problem" before it became unmanageable. Since the border question was of immediate strategic concern and was the only means of influencing the Chinese directly, it was decided to force this issue—at least to do whatever was necessary to bring the situation under Soviet control. The Russians hoped that proposals for improvement in relations would take some of the bitterness out of the pill the Chinese would have to swallow, provide the basis for longer-term (that is, post-Maoist) improvement in relations, supply a propaganda cover for military action taken and contemplated, and establish a fall-back position in case the carrot-and-stick border strategy did not work.

Chinese strategy, born of weakness, was to reject, delay, or ignore both parts of the Russian strategy. Seeing the Russian buildup and feeling its effects, the Chinese undertook a policy of gradual diplomatic retreat. Their note of May 24 dropped the previous de facto opposition to negotiations (their pronouncements had always stressed the desirablity of such talks and blamed the Russians for their breakdown) and conceded that the abortive 1964 negotiations might now be resumed. Their presence at the Ussuri-Amur border talks in Khabarovsk from June to August and their willingness to sign a one-year navigation agreement with the Russians constituted two further steps toward negotiations. Finally, after the Peking airport meeting in September, the Chinese not only accepted the Soviet bid to resume full-scale negotiations but also, in their note of October 8, dropped the one condition that had been the primary obstacle to agreement in 1964—that the Russians agree on the "unequalness" of the historic series of treaties defining the border before there could be any further movement toward a new treaty. These concessions made it appear that, procedurally and substantively, little separated the two parties from quick and final agreement except horse-trading some unimportant river islands and small amounts of territory on the Sinkiang-Tadzhik border.

After the negotiations began, however, the Chinese backed away from this advanced position and threw up a further obstacle by demanding that the Russians join in mutually withdrawing military forces at least fifty kilometers from the border.[17] The trick was to convince the Russians that, through minor (but reversible) changes in the Chinese position, a negotiated solution to the border problem was not entirely out of the question. The Chinese felt they had no choice but to go along with the Soviet proposals for resuming negotiations. They concluded it was better to buy off the Russians in the short run through negotiations that, like those conducted in 1964, they had no intention of carrying to conclusion on Soviet terms.[18]

Soviet Strategy after September 1969

The Chou-Kosygin meeting in Peking signaled the successful conclusion of Moscow's strategy of coercing the Chinese back to the negotiating table and of convincing them that any further disruptive behavior along the border would be to their disadvantage. Although the talks were not productive and the Chinese could be said to have attained their own goal of preventing higher levels of Soviet violence, border incidents were no longer a major contributing factor to continued Sino-Soviet animosity. The record shows clearly that, after the talks began, publicly reported incidents declined to a frequency of one to three a year and were much less severe. Several of these were clearly associated with training exercises of one side to which the other side chose to react; others were evidently intentional probings of the opposition's defenses. With the large increase in troop dispositions along the frontier after March 1969, this steep decline in publicly reported incidents can only indicate that both sides agreed, tacitly or explicitly, to carry out the relevant clause of the Soviet proposal of September 11 (and the Chinese proposal of October 8, 1969), to maintain the status quo along the frontier until the exact location of the boundary was agreed upon and delimited, to avoid armed con-

17. FBIS, *Communist China* (May 26, 1969), pp. A1–A10, and *SCMP*, no. 4426 (May 29, 1969), pp. 24–36.

18. See *SCMP*, no. 4498 (September 18, 1969), p. 25; *Far Eastern Economic Review* (September 25, 1969), p. 759; "Statement of the Government of the People's Republic of China," October 7, 1969, in *Peking Review*, no. 41 (October 10, 1969), pp. 3–4; *New York Times*, October 8, 1969; "Document of the Ministry of Foreign Affairs of the People's Republic of China," October 8, 1969, in *Peking Review*, no. 41 (October 10, 1969), pp. 8–15, and *SCMP*, no. 4517 (October 10, 1969), pp. 30–39. For details of the Soviet and Chinese negotiating strategies from 1969 to 1976, see Robinson, *Sino-Soviet Border Situation*, pp. 28–56.

flicts, and to stop sending forces into disputed areas or to disengage forces that had penetrated those areas.

In general, the impression after September 1969 is of a border closely guarded by both sides. Each side took extreme precautions to prevent accidental local clashes and avoided escalation to the use of more destructive weapon systems and of larger numbers of men. In most cases, regular army units were not engaged, at least if one believes the Soviet accounts are accurate (the Chinese version is usually either lacking in detail or missing). The forces engaged were KGB-controlled border troops on the Soviet side and probably similar formations of Production and Construction Corps units on the Chinese side.

Relative quietude along the frontier thus stemmed from the Peking agreement (whether tacit or negotiated), the military buildup on both sides, and the safety valve of periodic border negotiations. Neither side wished to engage the other frequently, although occasional deliberate forays tested the defenses of the opposition. Each charged the other with this sort of activity—the Russians accusing the Chinese of conducting training operations only meters from the Mongolian boundary and the Chinese charging the Russians with flying aircraft several kilometers into Chinese territory—but neither seems to have reacted violently to such movements. The danger of escalation and the density of troops along the frontier were too high for punitive measures.

The small number of publicized incidents amounted to one side's putting a toe across the line (or patrolling disputed areas at times and in ways slightly different from those tacitly agreed upon) and then quickly withdrawing it. It is quite possible that the two sides agreed to suppress news of further incidents. In 1974, for instance, there were rumors and allegations of a large clash on the Sinkiang-Kazakhstan border,[19] and in November of that year both Moscow and Peking denied Western reports of five battles along the Sino-Mongolian frontier.[20] The location of reported incidents has varied. In the Sinkiang-Kazakhstan region, alleged incursions almost invariably occurred in the Dzungarian Gates area; and along the Amur-Ussuri boundary, the islands of disputed ownership were

19. Such incidents are vaguely alluded to in the Chinese periodical *Li-shih Yen-chiu* (Historical Research) of December 1974, and in the Soviet journal *Problemiye Dal'nogo Vostoka* (Problems of the Far East) of January 1975.

20. *Daily Telegraph,* December 17, 1974; *Pravda,* December 20, 1974; Reuters and *Agence France Presse,* December 17, 1974 (in FBIS, *People's Republic of China,* December 18, 1974, p. E2); Tass, December 19, 1974 (in FBIS, *Soviet Union,* December 19, 1974, p. C1).

the scene of alleged clashes, but not the shoreline. The exact location of alleged incidents on the Sino-Mongolian frontier is difficult to determine because neither side chose to publicize them.

There were a number of other specific occurrences related to border tension: the seizure and expulsion of two Soviet diplomats in Peking in 1974 on spy charges;[21] the detention in China, and later the release, of a Soviet helicopter and its crew after the Russians alleged it had lost its bearings and run out of fuel while on a medical evacuation mission;[22] Soviet refusal, until 1974, to allow Chinese ships to navigate the Kazakevichevo channel near Khabarovsk without permission during the summer low-water season;[23] a maritime accident off Hainan;[24] slowness or inability to come to agreement on the yearly river navigation agreements; and a Soviet show of force in early 1978.[25] Each of these was an additional indicator of the trouble on the border and therefore of Sino-Soviet relations in general, and a gauge of the degree of progress, or lack thereof, of the Peking border talks and of Soviet strategy.

More broadly, each side took precautions in the regions on its own side of the boundary to build up the economy and population, invest in infrastructure, cement the loyalty of local native peoples to the national government, and send out from its core area (especially in the Chinese case) large numbers of people from the dominant ethnic group. On the

21. NCNA, January 19, 1974 (in FBIS, *People's Republic of China*, January 23, 1974, pp. A3–A4); *New York Times*, January 20, 21, and 24, 1974; NCNA (in FBIS, *People's Republic of China*, January 23, 1974, pp. A1–A5); *Christian Science Monitor*, January 25, 1974; NCNA, January 24, 1974 (in FBIS, *People's Republic of China*, January 25, 1974, pp. A1–A2); *The Economist* (January 26, 1974), p. 43.

22. See *Pravda*, March 21, 1974 (in *CDSP*, April 17, 1974), p. 3; *Peking Review* (March 29, 1974), p. 5; *New York Times*, March 20, 23, and 29, May 3, 6, and 9, 1974; FBIS, *Soviet Union* reporting a wide variety of Soviet sources, March 29, 1974, p. C1, April 5, 1974, pp. C1–C2, April 29, 1974, pp. C1–C2, April 30, 1974, pp. C1–C2, May 3, 1974, pp. C1–C2, May 6, 1974, p. C1, May 7, 1974, pp. C6–C7, May 13, 1974, pp. C1–C10, May 16, 1974, pp. C5–C6, May 23, 1974, pp. C1–C2, June 10, 1974, pp. C1–C2, June 24, 1974, p. C1, June 28, 1974, pp. C1–C2, August 8, 1974, pp. C1–C4, and November 4, 1974, pp. C3–C4; FBIS, *People's Republic of China*, June 24, 1974, p. A4; *SCMP*, April 1–4, 1974, pp. 65–66; *The Economist* (June 22, 1974), pp. 27–28; *Daily Telegraph* (London), June 26, 1974.

23. *Pravda*, May 24, 1974 (in *CDSP*, vol. 26, no. 20, June 12, 1974, p. 4).

24. NCNA, April 18, 1971 (in FBIS, *Communist China*, April 19, 1971, p. A1); and Tass, March 31, 1971.

25. *New York Times*, March 29, and April 1, 6, 8, 9, and 10, 1978. See also *CDSP*, vol. 30, no. 13 (April 26, 1978), pp. 5–10, and no. 14 (May 3, 1978), pp. 1–5; FBIS, *Soviet Union*, vol. 3, nos. 61–69 (March 29–April 10, 1978), pp. R1, R1, R1–R5, R1–R6, R1, R1, R1–R4, R1–R5, and R1–R5, respectively.

Soviet side, the government offered monetary incentives to settlers willing to relocate near the boundary, began construction of the Baikal-Amur Mainline railway, placed farming communities on previously uninhabited (or fitfully inhabited) riverine islands, sought to prove that disputed areas had long been occupied by peoples now part of the Soviet Union, changed names of border towns to more Slavic-sounding ones, and in general accelerated Siberian development as much as possible.

Apparently the Soviet Union also harbored renewed ambition for making Sinkiang a buffer state like Mongolia, since there were persistent reports that the authorities were organizing a Free Turkestan movement, complete with its own military force and composed of those who had fled Sinkiang in the 1962 Ili disturbances. Based in Alma-Ata and led by, among others, General Zunun Taipov, a former Sinkiang Uigur leader of long standing, this scheme peaked in the early 1970s.[26] Thereafter it seems to have received less Soviet support, as the Chinese sent in large numbers of former members of the Red Guard, boosting the proportion of Han Chinese in the population to over half of the nearly ten million inhabitants. The Russians charged the Chinese with forcibly assimilating border minority peoples, especially in Inner Mongolia, where an uprising was allegedly quelled by the use of tanks and artillery. The Chinese also sent 150,000 former members of the Red Guard into Heilungkiang to augment the Production and Construction Corps and began a major archaelogical effort to prove that border regions historically have been part of China.

The Military Buildup

These efforts, important though they were, were second in importance to the military buildup by both sides. The forces were augmented at different times so that, in the early 1970s, the Soviet Union was able to emplace a much more powerful force than the Chinese (although not larger in number), arousing Chinese fears of Russian aggressive military acts. But after 1972 the Chinese began to send to the border sufficient

---

26. Harrison E. Salisbury, "Marco Polo Would Recognize Mao's Sinkiang," *New York Times Magazine,* November 23, 1969; *New York Times,* March 3, July 5, and August 16, 1970; *Far Eastern Economic Review* (January 16, 1971), pp. 46–67; *New York Times,* August 5, 1973, and January 3, 1974; Tania Jacques, " 'Sharqiy Turkestan' or 'Sinkiang'?" *Radio Liberty Research,* March 7, 1975.

reinforcements—men and weapons—to make a major Russian ground offensive very costly. Still later, in 1976 and after, continuation of the Soviet buildup in sophisticated weapons, communications, and nuclear missiles combined with increasing Chinese military backwardness (the product of neglect during the Cultural Revolution) produced an even greater imbalance in favor of the Soviet Union. The Chinese buildup, which by 1975 was thought to have evened the balance sufficiently to prevent Soviet military actions in or threats against China, only betrayed Peking's military weakness. This resulted in a flurry of Chinese military window-shopping missions to Europe, Peking's extreme diplomatic tilt toward the United States and Japan, near military alliance with Washington, and prominence given to such military components of the post-Maoist modernization drive as nuclear missiles.

It is difficult to accurately describe the size and quality of opposing forces: authoritative estimations depend not only on unavailable data about the actual number of men along the border, their specific location, their weapons, and their logistic backup, but also on such qualitative estimates as the strategy and tactics of the two sides, their morale and training, and specific assumptions about war initiation and goals.[27] Much of the effort to estimate the qualitative factors turns out to be unnecessary, however, because neither side intends to launch a major land offensive against the other (either to overthrow the other's government or to seize large parts of its territory) and because the nuclear retaliatory capability of both sides is so high.

Moscow was alarmed at Chinese behavior at Damansky and after, which it attributed to Cultural Revolution excesses and to Mao Tsetung's perfidy. Soviet leaders therefore resolved to garrison their (and the Mongolians') border with China heavily enough to make a repetition of the March 1969 events very costly to Peking and to use the threat of more widespread military action to force the Chinese to settle the border issue on its merits as the Soviet leaders understood them. Hence, the Russians increased the number of divisions in the border regions from fifteen understrength formations to over forty at higher levels of readiness; provided them with the most advanced equipment, including nuclear missiles and tactical warheads; filled out the border troop divisions; en-

27. This section is based on Robinson, *Sino-Soviet Border Situation*, pp. 8–31, which in turn was based on a variety of published sources, mostly International Institute for Strategic Studies, *The Military Balance, 1969–70 to 1977–78*, and IISS, *Strategic Survey*, 1969 to 1977.

gaged in constant patrolling of land and water; undertook augmented civil defense measures in cities within Chinese nuclear range (which included more and more of the Soviet Union with each passing year); and initiated a massive construction program to lay the necessary logistical base for a large, permanent border force.

Considered by the Russians a set of defensive measures, the program nonetheless could be, and was, construed by the Chinese as threatening. Because Peking was innately suspicious of Moscow for ideological reasons and because it had to judge the Soviet military machine by its capabilities and perceived tactics (which are often offensive), the Chinese were forced to increase the size, change the disposition, and upgrade the equipment of their own formations. The immediate cost was high: the Cultural Revolution had to be curtailed; the People's Liberation Army had to divide itself between politico-industrial administration and training and defense duties; support of such allies as Pakistan in 1971 and North Vietnam until 1974 had to take second place to opposing the Soviet threat; compromises had to be made with the United States over the Taiwan issue to alleviate the possibility of a two-front conflict; and China's policy toward every issue and nation had to be governed on the basis of their relation to the Sino-Soviet conflict. The Chinese did match the Soviet increase in manpower, if not in modernity of equipment (although they were unable to send significant additional ground divisions to the border regions until 1972, four years after the Russian buildup began). Peking also increased its defense budget; mobilized large numbers of urban youths to serve in the Production and Construction Corps in the northern and western provinces; strengthened the militia program; and began a crash civil defense effort, including the well-known tunnel networks in major cities. Finally, Peking made a number of administrative changes in provincial boundaries, one of which was the division of Inner Mongolia among its neighbors, allegedly for defense purposes. By 1974 these changes had gone some distance to redressing, if only temporarily, the 1969 imbalance of forces.

Equally important, the Chinese continued to develop their nuclear and missile program but changed its direction: more effort was made to counter the Soviet menace by concentrating on short- and medium-(3,000-mile) range missiles, forgoing the development of intercontinental-range missiles expected by the Americans, and deploying them in diverse, semi-hardened locations capable of reaching most large Soviet cities, even—after 1976—Moscow. Moreover, the Chinese continued producing and testing nuclear weapons and, through increased production capacity and the use of older jet bombers, developed a significant air-delivery capability by the mid-1970s. China dispersed these aircraft and weapons around the full complement of about two hundred Chinese bases reasonably near the Soviet border, thereby ensuring that a Soviet preemptive strike could not destroy Chinese retaliatory ability without risking obliteration of a sizable number of Soviet cities.

It is difficult to describe and evaluate the details of Soviet and Chinese dispositions. Not only are particulars closely held by both sides for obvious reasons, but force composition varies with the circumstances postulated, measurement of forces and their locations by outside authorities varies from year to year, and manpower figures signify increasingly less as sophisticated weaponry is deployed. It is usually stated that the Soviet Union had by 1975 built its ground forces up to a level of forty-five divisions, including two in Mongolia, with others in the Trans-Baikal Military District available for quick reinforcement. This remained relatively stable through 1980 (forty-three divisions, including three in Mongolia). Only about one-third of these were in the highest category of readiness. But because of the heavy investment in logistics, construction, and pre-positioning of equipment that had taken place since 1969, many more divisions could be brought in without too much effort.

Much the same could be said of the Chinese. By 1975 they had about fifty Main Force divisions in the Shenyang and Peking Military Regions, fifteen in the Lanchow Military Region, and perhaps eight in Sinkiang. By 1976 these had increased to about sixty-seven Main Force divisions in the first two regions, and they remained relatively stable thereafter. As in the Soviet case, not all of them carried out border duties. On the other hand, in an emergency additional formations could quickly be sent from other areas of the country.

Each state also maintained a certain percentage of its forces for possible duty in areas not associated with the Sino-Soviet border problem: the Soviet Union in Eastern and Western Europe and in the Middle East; China in South and Southeast Asia, the Fukien Strait, and Korea. Both also maintained large numbers of men for internal duties; this was particularly important for China in the post-Mao era, when there could be disorder; also for the past decade the PLA had been centrally involved in politics and administration. Moreover, there was the problem of how to evaluate the real strength, in any major test with the Soviet Union, of China's Local Forces (some of whom were border defense troops) and

Production and Construction Corps. Evaluations of the forces available to both the Soviet Union and China could thus vary widely.

Geographic circumstances determined much of the specific location of Russian and Chinese formations and forced Moscow and Peking to adopt differing strategies. Because so much of the Soviet population in Siberia and the Far East is concentrated along the Trans-Siberian Railway and because this vital transportation artery often runs, because of weather and terrain, quite close to the Chinese border, Moscow had to deploy many of its forces and station much of its equipment close to the boundary, even south of the railway. Since the Chinese could not know the exact nature of Soviet intentions, they had to see this location as a threat to Chinese territory to the immediate south—Sinkiang, Kansu, Inner Mongolia, and Heilungkiang. Since the Russians had nowhere to retreat in a northerly direction except onto tundra and ice (or, in the case of the Primorskaya, into the sea), Moscow had to adopt a strategy of preventing incursion by any Chinese force and to reject out of hand any Chinese suggestion for mutual withdrawal from the border to any but short distances. This was especially the case near such cities as Khabarovsk, which was right on the border, across the river from land claimed by China, and Vladivostok.

The Chinese dared not move their main force too close to the border since this would have risked destruction or entrapment in the wastes of Sinkiang, Kansu, and Inner Mongolia. Moreover, most of the Chinese population live quite a bit to the south. Those who do live near the Soviet border are minority peoples whose cousins are Soviet citizens and who, in the case of the Sinkiang Kazakhs, have shown a propensity to try to reunite themselves with their relatives.

Chinese strategy and force locations followed from these facts: the main army force had to be held back from the border to defend important cities (such as Peking) and facilities (such as the Lop Nor and Shuang Ch'eng-tze nuclear and missile sites) to the south; the minority peoples had to be watched, a job for the influx of Han settlers, who at the same time, by spreading themselves out through agricultural colonization, acted as a paramilitary barrier to advancing Soviet forces; and in case of invasion, the army and the people (mostly peasants on communes) would have to coalesce to present the Russians with a combination of conventional defense and guerrilla war tactics—"people's war." As the colonization effort proceeded and as the military grew stronger, regular army formations would advance even closer to the Soviet border until at some point—depending on the thickness of the logistical supply network, the density of troops and population, and the type of weaponry supplied— the main Chinese forces could be located as close to the border as the Soviet formations were. Meanwhile, aggressive patrolling and surveillance by border divisions, local forces, and Production and Construction Corps cadres would presumably forestall or warn of Soviet attack.

Central to the strategies of both the Soviet Union and China, and modifying the above conclusions to some extent, was their possession of sizable numbers of nuclear weapons. Since the beginning of the Sino-Soviet dispute, Moscow has had enough nuclear weapons to punish China severely for any territorial transgression. This constituted only a background factor until the 1969 clashes, however, and even then their use would hardly have been practical except in the most severe circumstances, scarcely imaginable despite talk in the summer of 1969 of preemptive strikes against Chinese nuclear production and test facilities, rocket and nuclear storage sites, and air bases. But once the Soviet Union began to deploy its increasingly strong ground forces in the border region, the entire Chinese position—stategic and tactical—was threatened, because tactical nuclear weapons were integral to Soviet (not Chinese) motorized and armored divisions and because Soviet (but not Chinese) formations were trained and equipped to fight from the outset on a nuclearized battlefield.

For a while before 1972 a Soviet preemptive attack could have destroyed nearly all Chinese nuclear and missile facilities, air bases, sea bases, and army camps, and then have occupied significant portions of the Chinese land mass, including the capital region. Hundreds of millions would have been killed, of course, including millions in neighboring countries. It was this wider effect, together with the resultant weakened Soviet strategic position in relation to the United States and the strong possibility of an alliance of all other major states against the Soviet Union, that made such a situation unlikely.[28] Nonetheless, the Chinese

28. The Soviet strategic position as compared to that of the United States would obviously decline since the Soviet Union would have expended a certain portion of its deployed missile strength, whereas that of the United States would be intact. Moreover, the Soviet system was probably deficient in accuracy, actual and advertised megatonnage of warheads would differ, misfires would occur, and so on. This would surely result in increased Soviet reluctance to invite a strategic confrontation with the United States until such deficiencies were remedied. A Soviet nuclear attack on China of the scale noted would also probably precipitate an anti-Soviet alliance of all the other major states, which would fear that the Soviet Union might use such

leaders apparently found it plausible and adjusted their military and diplomatic posture accordingly. To judge from their statements and acts, the Chinese continued to take the Soviet threat seriously even after the Soviet Far Eastern buildup eased in 1976, for they increasingly realized their own weakness.

Peking also had to face other, more realistic contingencies. Perhaps the most serious was the possibility of attempted Soviet interference in the politics of the post-Mao succession struggle, supporting militarily one or another faction to help establish a pro-Soviet government, or occupying such critical border regions as Sinkiang or parts of Heilungkiang.[29] While the Soviet Union probably reacted to this with incredulity and was quick to disclaim any offensive intentions, the Chinese, combining an evaluation of actual Soviet military capabilities with heavy criticism of Soviet ideological policies (which informed the Chinese of Soviet military intentions), could only plan for the worst. It was thus the nuclear potential of a very strong Soviet military force adjacent to the Chinese border that drove the Chinese to reinforce their own border defenses heavily; to devote increasing portions of their domestic production to conventional hardware and nonintercontinental-range ballistic missiles; to look to NATO for sales of military hardware; to encourage NATO to increase its readiness; and to interrupt the revolutionary activities of the Red Guard and transfer its members to Production and Construction Corps units next to the boundary. The Soviet threat was one of

---

weapons against each of them separately and realize that the Russians were now willing to use the ultimate means of destruction in support of their overall policy goals. It would be a classic case of the unification of several strong, relatively unaggressive states against a stronger, more aggressive nation and therefore an attempt to reestablish a stable global balance of power.

29. While the factual basis is slim, it is nonetheless true that all deposed Chinese politicians since 1959 have been accused by the victorious side of advocating compromise with the Soviet Union. This is true of P'eng Teh-huai (the former minister of defense), Lo Jui-ch'ing (a former army chief of staff), Yang Ch'eng-wu (another former army chief of staff), Lin Piao (Mao's erstwhile successor), and the so-called Gang of Four (Mao's closest supporters in the early 1970s). Where there is allegedly smoke, there may be fire. Furthermore, at certain times from 1969 to 1976, during the politics of Maoist succession, it sometimes seemed that military factions might well set up local strong points opposed to the central government, which could have led to open fighting among political-military factions. Finally, since 1971, the Soviet Union has had the military potential to occupy at least parts of Sinkiang, Inner Mongolia, or Heilungkiang.

the major catalysts in the post-Mao drive to modernize the economy at any cost.

By 1975 the Chinese had to some extent redressed the imbalance. A few infantry divisions had been converted to armored formations, demonstrating that Peking had the productive capacity for such changes. And in the next three years, Peking added over a million men to the PLA, which provided the flexibility needed for a conventional response to Soviet attack. Those forces, when equipped eventually with modern arms, will be able to make the Soviet Union pause before attempting to invade or punish. Moreover, by the mid-1970s, China had sufficient nuclear retaliatory potential to deter all but the largest Soviet preemptive attacks and to threaten major cities in European Russia, including Moscow. China had thus advanced from the minimal deterrence posture of the 1960s to a strategy based on increasingly hardened and dispersed missiles aimed at the Soviet, if not yet the American, homeland. With or without prolongation of the border conflict, this trend will continue.

Despite these improvements, however, by 1978 the Soviet Union had managed once again to weigh the balance in its favor. Its border force had become a well-oiled machine of increasingly high mechanical quality, and the maneuvers staged for the spring tour by Leonid Brezhnev that year alarmed Peking anew. A new factor emerged in 1977 and became prominent in 1978 with the Vietnamese-Cambodian war. Beginning for different reasons, it quickly took on Sino-Soviet dimensions as Moscow and Peking supported the opposing Southeast Asian combatants. That was bad for Peking: (1) it could not afford to go to war in Southeast Asia, to say nothing of against the Soviet Union directly, at the very beginning of its modernization drive; (2) on the other hand, it could not sit by and watch the Vietnamese upset the balance in Southeast Asia by absorbing Cambodia; (3) it now had to face the prospect of immobilizing, at great distance from the Sino-Soviet border, a large portion of its own forces deployed in central, south, and southwest China; and (4) in 1978 it faced the unpalatable prospect of a two-front conflict—Sino-Soviet and Sino-Vietnamese—as a result of the new Soviet-Vietnam alliance. This last development—seen as defensive and justifiable by the Russians—added a tragic dynamic to the Sino-Soviet border problem. Each power misperceived the policy and the tactics of the other, causing a spiral of events that could well have ended in war. In early 1979 China took military action against Vietnam in response to the latter's Soviet-assisted conquest of Laos and Cambodia. The thirty-day punitive action was costly in casualties and material losses to both China and Vietnam. Nor did it solve Peking's dilemma about the Moscow-Hanoi alliance, since the Soviet Union, through mere verbal threats and arms supplies to Hanoi, was able to short-circuit the Chinese offensive. Peking learned that no military success in Asia was possible as long as Soviet armed forces stood on the Sino-Soviet border ready to quell any Chinese advance elsewhere around China's periphery. China was "contained" in Asia by the Soviet Union, and its rapid diplomatic movement toward the United States was a direct outcome. By 1980, an all-but-official military alliance between Peking and Washington was nearly in place, a move spurred to completion by the Soviet invasion of Afghanistan in late 1979.

The tremendous disparity in overall strength favoring the Soviet Union was evident if one compared numbers of nuclear-capable delivery vehicles and, therefore, minimal quantities of nuclear warheads. While the Soviet Union had to hold a large proportion of these in reserve for the deterrent relationship with the United States and for waging war against America and its allies in Europe and elsewhere, the residual available for potential use against China was still enormous and represented (assuming that each vehicle was capable of delivering at least one nuclear warhead) a destructive potential of horrendous proportions. By 1980 China had about 500 nuclear delivery vehicles (not counting MIG-19s, MIG-21s, and F-9s, all of which presumably had to be used for interceptor, reconnaissance, and tactical support functions); the Soviet Union had over 6,000 vehicles (again not counting its large supply of jet fighter aircraft, many of which were nuclear capable). Even if only 20 percent of the Soviet force were earmarked for the Chinese theater, about 1,200 vehicles would still be available. And this presumed only one nuclear warhead per delivery whereas an increasing percentage of medium-range Soviet missiles were being equipped with MIRVs. The Soviet Union also had a strong and dispersed air defense system that could probably have intercepted and destroyed a large percentage of, if not all, Chinese IL-28s and TU-16s. Finally, each Soviet ground unit had a nuclear capacity, either in the form of ground-to-ground missiles or small-unit tactical nuclear weapons. When the 1970 International Institute for Strategic Studies figure of 3,500 such warheads is used, expanded proportionate to the number of additional Soviet divisions in 1980 (twelve), and assuming that such weapons were available for use against China roughly in proportion to the percentage of the Soviet army deployed against China, another 970 warheads could be added. This ignores the absolute superiority the Soviet Union enjoyed in conventional firepower, artillery, armor, and battlefield mobility. Thus in 1980 the overall military balance was heavily weighted in favor of the Soviet Union.

This imbalance in numbers of nuclear weapons, delivery capability, and modernity of equipment was likely to continue for about five years since basically it was the product of the differences in degree of industrialization in the two countries. However, China's own nuclear deterrent, together with its large, trained, and increasingly modern ground force, its mass of paramilitary units in the border regions, and its active militia made any large Soviet attack unlikely. China's possession of a more than minimal nuclear deterrent therefore partly neutralized the Soviet advantage in numbers of delivery vehicles and modernity of conventional equipment in any reasonable (less than all-out attack) near-term situation.

The more time China had to increase its own nuclear supply and modernize its military, the closer to actual equality the two military machines would come. Even before the achievement of long-run military stability, however, approximate equality could exist between the Soviet Union and China in the border military situation. Reaching that point would restore Chinese interest in settling the issue. The three necessary conditions would be rough equality in force capability; mutual realization that further competition in military preparedness would be excessively costly and not even marginally effective; and a stable balance of power in Asia as a whole, including as elements the policies and instrumentalities of the United States and Japan.

Analysis of Soviet Behavior

If the above represents the generalities of the Sino-Soviet border conflicts in 1969 and beyond, what about the particulars of Soviet behavior? The foreign policy of any state stems from its general concerns and interests, on the one hand, and its specific operational objectives (greatly dependent on time and policy issues), on the other. Moscow felt it had no choice but to respond strongly, directly, and militarily to perceived Chinese threats at specific border locations and to the long-term challenge presented by China's ever-increasing power and unfriendly attitude. In other words, the Russians genuinely believed their actions were defensive and prophylactic and that not to react would have been to show weakness under provocation. Moreover, with its increasing problems at home,[30] the Soviet leadership could not domestically admit weakness and need not have admitted it internationally. After all, the USSR was rapidly growing in most of the physical measures of national power, particularly military. Thus Soviet use of the military instrument (more Soviet-initiated incidents and the border buildup) served three ends: to force the Chinese back to the negotiating table, to keep them there (even if no progress took place) as a means of defusing border tension, and to set the stage for eventual agreement on that and other divisive issues.

Although there is no direct evidence, it seems likely that a second Russian motivation was to keep the talks going as a counter to the effort by China and the United States to improve their own relations. Such an improvement, if it resulted in an anti-Soviet Sino-American entente, would be a diplomatic disaster for the Soviet Union. One way to forestall such an eventuality would be to maintain contact with the Chinese, as far as possible, in attempting to resolve outstanding issues.[31] The talks thus had taken on a different character by 1972, when it became apparent that progress on the merits of the question was impossible. Thereafter, the Russians probably felt increasingly inhibited from using military force against the Chinese, from carrying the border buildup beyond the bounds that *they* regarded as defensive, and from making major probes or tests of China's military reactions, to avoid driving Peking even more quickly toward Washington.

The border buildup policy thus impaled Soviet policymakers on the horns of a dilemma. On the one hand, they had to defend their home-

30. These include the division between the modern military-oriented sector of the economy and the increasingly less modern agricultural and consumer sectors; the burden on the rest of the economy of the military sector's demands; technological backwardness in the nonmilitary sectors of the economy and unwillingness to adopt the necessary measures to solve the chronic agricultural problem; unreceptiveness of the younger (post–World War II) generations to the ideological beliefs of the older revolutionaries; growing separation between party and people and unrepresentativeness of the party; local nationalism and religion in the areas of the Soviet Union not part of Great Russia, as beliefs competed with Marxism-Leninism; and the policy rigidities usually associated with presuccession periods.

31. The same reasoning seemed to motivate the Russians to remain in contact through negotiations with the United States, principally in SALT II but also in the MBFR talks, the Helsinki human rights talks, and in less critical but symbolic areas such as cultural exchange. In a three-sided game, all participants must constantly fear a deal at their expense made by the other two, and the Soviet Union was not immune to this fear. Moscow also wished to stay in close contact with Washington because the ongoing series of negotiations, especially SALT II, prevented the United States from adopting strong military measures to counter the Soviet buildup.

land and encourage the Chinese to negotiate a settlement. Together with the occasional use of minimal force, the border buildup did deter the Chinese from perpetrating another Damansky Island incident and did keep them at the negotiating table. On the other hand, the Russians wanted to discourage the Chinese from modernizing their own military forces and from forming an anti-Soviet entente with the United States. The buildup and the use of force against the Chinese, however, drove the Chinese straight in that direction. The Soviet role in the Vietnamese invasion of Cambodia, in assisting Hanoi during the Chinese "counterattack," and in the USSR's own invasion of Afghanistan only accelerated the pace of Sino-American alliance-building. As the Kremlin solved its short-term security problem, therefore, it created a much greater long-term threat. The cure turned out to be worse than the disease.

There is no overt indication of disagreement among members of the Soviet Politburo about the border question. It may be that there have been internal differences over the timing and the magnitude of specific military actions, but available evidence points to almost complete unanimity on policy toward China. Indeed, it seems likely that Brezhnev has used the China issue to increase the degree of agreement in the Kremlin and throughout the country on issues not directly related to China. It is too much to say that Moscow became dependent on the "China threat" as a principal means of carrying out its general domestic program of political suppression and heavy industrial development. But it seems reasonable to suppose that the China factor did contribute heavily to the decision to build up Soviet military forces to very high levels, did influence many other aspects of Soviet foreign policy, and was used as one excuse to continue biasing the economy against a consumer orientation.

At times there may have been disagreement in the Politburo over what general or specific policies to adopt toward China. Several observers have claimed the existence of factions that take consistently different positions on a range of issues, including China.[32] For instance, the "Neo-Stalinists" were said to be in favor of improving relations with China, but the "Russian Nationalists" allegedly professed great fear and hatred of Peking. The "Conservative Authoritarians" (presumably led by Brezhnev) were thought to favor a compromise agreement with China

32. These observers include Wolfgang Leonhardt, "The Domestic Politics of the New Soviet Foreign Policy," *Foreign Affairs* (October 1973), pp. 59–74; Roy A. Medvedev, *On Soviet Democracy* (Norton, 1975); and Alexander Yanov, *The Russian New Right* (University of California, Institute of International Studies, 1978).

as were the "Limited Modernizers," but neither supposedly wished to go as far toward China ideologically as did the Neo-Stalinists. If there were divisions in the leadership along these lines, and if Soviet Politburo policy was the product of a balance among them (with the Brezhnev group having its way because of its centrist position), it follows that Moscow's China policy (among other Soviet foreign policy orientations) could change with the end of the Brezhnev era.

Soviet Communications with China

Investigation of how the Russians communicated with the Chinese about the border issue other than through use of force reveals additional facets of Soviet behavior in force-related situations.[33] Soviet verbal behavior toward the Chinese varies with the kind of communicator, the style and tone of the communication, the forum, and the communication's content. Three propositions emerge from such an investigation. First, there is a hierarchy among Soviet communicators, according to the seriousness of the situation, moving from the most serious to the least serious situation:

1. Named Politburo member
2. Victor Louis (the Soviet "journalist")
3. "I. Aleksandrov" (pseudonym for a variety of party and government officials)
4. Ambassador or negotiator
5. Tass
6. Lower-level official
7. Scholar

Second, certain communicators appear only *during* a crisis or military incident (for instance, Victor Louis), others only just before or to ward off a crisis (top officials, "I. Aleksandrov"), some just *after* a crisis or incident (Tass), and some only in noncrisis situations (low-level officials, scholars). Third, the threat content varies according to the degree of seriousness of the situation and parallels that of the level of the communicator. This is not the case, however, for the *style* and *tone* of the

33. Investigation based on a reading of about a thousand articles in the Soviet press, periodicals, and radio broadcast translations between 1969 and 1975, which formed the Soviet data base for Robinson, "The Sino-Soviet Border Dispute" and *The Sino-Soviet Border Situation.*

reportage where the communications most indicative of trouble (Victor Louis interviews and "I. Aleksandrov" editorials) are sometimes the least ideological in tone, but the "scholarly" articles are often the most propagandistic. The Russians deliberately used these differences to warn the Chinese of the growing danger of Peking's pursuing a given course of action, to support the Soviet campaign to solve the border question by negotiation, and to accompany—and afterward justify—the use of force against the Chinese. Moreover, although direct evidence is lacking, subsequent Chinese behavior indicates that Peking understood the import of this hierarchy of communications and acted accordingly. This is not to say that Peking always behaved as Moscow desired it to; in the long run, the Chinese became more stridently anti-Soviet than ever. But for communications about the border incidents of which we have knowledge, it appears that the Chinese were more cautious the more the threat content—implied or expressed—increased.

Finally, public Soviet communications during border incident periods were nonexistent. This is not surprising, since the duration of each period was short, usually no more than a few days. Most often, there was no announcement of any sort after an incident, a practice usually paralleled by the Chinese. When one side did choose to make a public issue of an incident, as for instance the March–September 1969 clashes, the 1974 helicopter incident, or the 1978 "escaped criminal" affair, the purpose was to forward some related but nonmilitary policy goal—negotiations, a better agreement, or propaganda and patriotism on the Soviet side; and the necessity for defense and economic construction, anti-Sovietism, or justification for the negotiating position on the Chinese side. The communications pattern thus tended to be: (1) escalation of the seriousness of the communicated threat on the Soviet side, often paralleled by increasingly strident propaganda and self-justification on the Chinese side; (2) occurrence of a planned military option against the Chinese, when no public communications were exchanged; and (3) the phase after the incident, when the propaganda content of communications peaked even though announcement of the actual incident was not necessarily made.

Chinese Behavior

It is clear that the Soviet Union overreacted to the March 2, 1969, incident, overgarrisoned its side of the Sino-Soviet border, frightened the

Chinese into thinking a major attack was coming, and contributed to its own long-term insecurity by controlling the problem in the interim. But the Russians cannot be blamed entirely for their predicament. China's anti-Russian attitudes, its overly anti-Soviet policy of two decades, its Damansky Island military initiative, and its post-1968 attempt to construct a world anti-Soviet alliance all contributed to frightening the Russians into overreaction. But it is still unclear why the Chinese ambushed the Russians on March 2, 1969—why they acted in cold blood.[34] And it is still unknown whether there were acute divisions in the Chinese leadership over whether to carry out the Damansky Island operation and over how, in general, to respond to the Soviet military initiatives of March 15, 1969, and afterward. It seems clear that, while post-1949 Chinese Communist political history does provide several examples of policy differences over how to deal with the Soviet Union, after 1969 the Chinese leadership was more nearly unified than ever before on this question. Although the Chinese themselves charged Lin Piao with advocating rapprochement with the Russians during the 1969–71 period, no strong factual evidence has been advanced to support that charge.[35] In fact, both Maoist and post-Maoist Chinese leaders seem to have been convinced of the need to deal with the Soviet Union both directly through China's military buildup and changed military dispositions and indirectly through China's opening to the United States, Japan, Western Europe, and other states perceived to be anti-Soviet.

It also seems likely that there was little or no argument among Chinese leaders over general policy toward Russia on both military and other issues. The Chinese often seemed as emotional about the Russians as the Russians were about them, an attitude not produced just by the post-1960 decade of Sino-Soviet relations but thoroughly ingrained in the Chinese psyche by centuries of dealing with China's northern neighbors. To be sure, in so thoroughly opposing the Russians on all fronts, the Chinese merely carried out what they perceived to be the objective interests of the Chinese state: standing as a bulwark against the spread into Asia of ever-expanding Soviet military, political, and economic power. But this also accentuated deep-seated emotional and racial attitudes toward the Rus-

34. For speculation on why the Chinese initiated the military activity at Damansky, see Robinson, "The Sino-Soviet Border Dispute," pp. 1190 ff.

35. These charges are detailed in internal Chinese documents published in Michael Y. Kau, *The Lin Piao Affair: Power, Politics and Military Coup* (Sharpe, 1975).

sians. It seems likely that by early 1969 the Chinese had concluded that the time had come to draw a line against further Soviet expansion or threat of expansion directly on their border and indirectly in other regions of Asia. They seem to have reasoned that, if they could throw the Russians off balance, perhaps the Russians could be discouraged from proceeding with the military buildup they had begun in 1966. Peking seems not to have expected or realized that carrying out the Damansky Island operation would prompt Moscow to respond in ways difficult for the Chinese to handle. So whereas Peking's purpose was at first prophylactic, from March 15 the Chinese at best were able to hold their own defensively and at worst found themselves pushed around by the Russians at any time or place Moscow desired.

On the other hand, the Chinese understood all along Soviet motivation in using force against them. Their conclusions about Soviet ideology and political purposes were precisely those described above for the Soviet Union. While it is not known what the Chinese were able to do to prepare for the anticipated Soviet blows, they could and did conclude that the blows were coming and that they themselves could do nothing short of delaying as long as possible and, in the end, giving way to the Russians.

After March 15 Peking dared not respond to the Russians tit for tat, lest Moscow escalate the level of violence. And at no time thereafter were the Chinese sure that the Russians would not escalate even further, in response to Chinese retaliation, to levels that they could not handle. Still, the Chinese apparently did not believe the Russians would move to such a high level of violence that the security of the Chinese state or the leadership's existence would be imperiled. Hence, they concluded that they were under no acute pressure to give way to Moscow, except provisionally, over the border issue. In this they seem to have gauged the Russians correctly. So while taking an occasional beating from the Russians, Peking calculated that its very existence was not at stake, that it would not have to compromise at the negotiating table, and that there was still time to move against the Russians in several ways.

Of course, the Chinese public had to be assured that the situation was under control and that the leadership knew how to deal with it. That is one reason Peking put so much propaganda effort into the anti-Soviet aspects of the Lin Piao campaign after 1971 and linked most departures from domestic and foreign policies to the need to stand up to the Russians. A threat similar to that of the Soviet Union has toppled many a government, but in the Chinese case it was carefully turned to account, first by Mao and later by his successors. Both found the policy of daring the Soviet Union a workable strategy in a bad situation.

The Chinese also used the Soviet threat, first, to reconstitute their international political position, which had been severely degraded during the Cultural Revolution, and second, to begin the long process of restructuring world politics around Peking's division of the globe into first, second, and third worlds. By the late 1970s, those two processes had been so successful that, in contrast to 1969, China had managed politically, if not always militarily, to contain Soviet expansion in Northeast and East Asia, although surely not in South and Southeast Asia; loosened Moscow's grip on such former allies as India; made a friend out of its principal former enemy, Japan; convinced many in the third world that their interests lay with Peking, not Moscow; fully restored relations with the United States; and even caused many to think about the desirability of establishing a worldwide coalition against the Kremlin led by China and the United States.[36] So whereas the Russians were successful in coercing the Chinese in every particular instance of military operations along the border, the cost was exceedingly high in terms of deleterious changes in the long-term balance of power in Asia and throughout the world. Finally, although the Chinese policy of anti-Sovietism was based on interests besides those arising from the military clashes, the Chinese probably would not have gone so far or so fast along the roads just indicated had it not been for the USSR's use of force.

The Role of the United States

No third parties were directly involved in any of the border incidents between the Soviet Union and China. However, in a broad sense, Chinese and Soviet policy and actions toward each other after early 1969 were taken with one eye on the United States. Indeed, since 1950 China has been a major factor in Soviet-American relations and hence in the configuration of world politics. To decisionmakers in Washington, Moscow,

36. See Edward Luttwak, "Against the China Card," *Commentary,* vol. 66 (October 1978), pp. 37–44; letters from readers and Luttwak's response, *Commentary,* vol. 67 (January 1979), pp. 4–8; Seyom Brown, "An End to Grand Strategy," *Foreign Policy,* no. 32 (Fall 1978), pp. 37–39; Chalmers Johnson, "The New Thrust in China's Foreign Policy," *Foreign Affairs,* vol. 57 (Fall 1978), pp. 125–37; and Lucian W. Pye, "Dilemmas for America in China's Modernization," *International Security,* vol. 4 (Summer 1979), pp. 3–19.

and Peking the basis of post–World War II international relations has been the triangular interaction of the United States, China, and the Soviet Union.[37] This generality is clearly illustrated by the American reaction to the Sino-Soviet border incidents and related changes in the shape of the international system after 1969. The Damansky Island incidents formed the dividing line between the cold war and the era of multipolar international political maneuver in which we now live.

American reaction to the incidents and to subsequent Russian use of force is usefully expressed by juxtaposing short- and long-term policy interests. In the short run, American statesmen feared that the incidents would lead to Sino-Soviet war, to a change in the East-West balance of power, or to the possible reduction of China, by Soviet nuclear attack, to a minor political actor. Perhaps until the end of 1971 it was not clear in Washington whether the Soviet Union would carry its campaign against China to the point of initiating a Sino-Soviet war. Washington was quick to realize that American interests lay in preserving a strong and united China as a bulwark against Soviet expansion in Asia and globally, even though China would still be strongly Communist and basically anti-American as well. Desire to maintain the balance of power overcame fundamental ideological differences with Peking.

Moscow was therefore publicly and privately warned that the United States would view any use of force against China with extreme disfavor, and after 1971 initiatives were taken to help redress the military balance of power between Moscow and Peking through material, at first strictly nonmilitary, support of the Chinese regime. This is not to suggest that at that early stage the United States would have rendered actual military support to Peking if the Soviet Union had attacked China. American involvement in Vietnam precluded that possibility, just as did domestic opposition to too close a relationship with Peking under any circumstance. Nonetheless, such possibilities were at least discussed in Washington, and the groundwork was thereby laid for the reconstitution of ties with Peking. The Damansky Island incidents had much to do with the Kissinger trip to Peking in mid-1971, the Nixon visit and the Shanghai communiqué in 1972, and détente between Peking and Washington in the years that followed.

In the long term, the two initial incidents, coupled with Soviet coercion of the Chinese after 1969, led to a reorientation in world politics. Equally

37. See the author's "Detente and the Sino-Soviet-U.S. Triangle," in Della W. Sheldon, ed., *Dimensions of Detente* (Praeger, 1978), pp. 50–83.

important, Soviet willingness to use force also contributed to the increasingly negative American reappraisal of Soviet-American détente that pushed the superpowers apart in the mid-1970s. Washington policymakers were at first willing to grant that the large buildup of Soviet conventional and nuclear forces was motivated by Moscow's perception of the Chinese threat. Later when the magnitude of the Soviet buildup on the Western as well as the Eastern frontier became apparent, American appraisal became much less charitable. At first it was thought that the Eastern border buildup against the Chinese would divert Soviet attention from Europe and perhaps lead to Soviet willingness to compromise on such issues as strategic arms limitation and mutual and balanced force reductions. But when it became clear that the Chinese threat was fueling an even greater acceleration of Soviet force augmentation in Europe as well as globally, American sympathy for the Soviet plight declined precipitously. As the Soviet buildup continued, the feeling grew in Washington that the United States and China had a common interest in containing the spread of Soviet influence everywhere. Soviet-Cuban intervention in southern Africa and the Horn of Africa after 1974 reinforced this feeling. Vietnam's invasion of Cambodia was the last straw for China, as was the Soviet invasion of Afghanistan for the United States. The Sino-American exchange of defense ministers in January and May 1980 followed naturally.

Soviet military actions against China, including both the initiation of border incidents and the military buildup along the Sino-Soviet border, changed American policy toward both Communist states. It is true that the United States did very little to directly support China. To the end of 1978, no American military equipment had gone to China, and policymakers in Washington had not seriously considered the demonstrative use of U.S. military power on behalf of the Chinese. Still, the possibility of obtaining American military support and the reality of growing Sino-American political and economic ties increased China's confidence and its resistance to the Soviet Union.[38] These changes in American policy were read in Moscow as the beginning of a Sino-American entente designed to

38. The linkage between better Sino-American ties and boldness of Chinese actions against the Soviet Union or its allies is graphically demonstrated by the quick Chinese decision to normalize relations with Washington in mid-December 1978 in response to the Soviet-Vietnamese treaty of alliance in November, and by the Chinese invasion of northern Vietnam in February 1979 following the Soviet-assisted Vietnamese invasion of Cambodia in January and immediately after Teng Hsiao-p'ing's visit to Washington.

contain the Soviet Union, despite clear American statements to Moscow that such was not Washington's intent.[39] The Russians thus confused a policy of renewed containment—this time a joint Chinese-American-European policy—with an attempt to prevent the Soviet Union from achieving its minimal goal of forcing world acceptance of its superpower status. The Damansky incidents therefore strained Soviet relations with Washington; contributed, more than anything else, to the continuing deterioration of Soviet relations with Peking; and provided the catalyst for Peking-Washington détente.

By 1980, the results were already apparent. The American-Chinese-European-Japanese anti-Soviet entente that Moscow feared most was rapidly coming into being. Washington and Peking were engaged in joint military planning. Japan, frightened by the Soviet buildup, was building a viable defense structure, and Europe was starting to think in terms of linkages between its Soviet policy and that of China. There was danger as well as opportunity in this rapid reconfiguration of the global balance of power. Although Moscow might eventually be contained by the new entente, it could also react violently by attempting to break up the coalition before the new configuration solidified.[40]

Conclusions

I have already argued that the USSR forced China to conform to its wishes on the border question, in the sense that China perpetrated no further military provocation similar to the first Damansky incident. Moreover, China was constrained to enter into negotiations with the Soviet Union, even though it had no intention, before restoring relative military equality, of coming to any final agreement on the border question or on any other issue. I have also concluded that China would not have found itself in this position had it not been for the Soviet willingness to use military force against it. But the long-term outcome displeased Moscow in three ways: (1) China became even more anti-Soviet than

39. The authoritative Soviet statement is contained in the note from Soviet Premier Brezhnev to President Carter of December 22, 1978 (*CDSP*, vol. 30, no. 51, January 17, 1979, pp. 2–3); the American verbal assurance is best conveyed by the President's normalization speech of December 15 and the accompanying background briefing (*New York Times*, December 16, 1978).

40. See Miles Kahler, "Rumors of War: The 1914 Analogy," *Foreign Affairs*, vol. 58 (Winter 1979–80), pp. 374–96.

before; (2) the United States and China moved first to détente and then toward rapprochement in the face of the mutually perceived Soviet threat; and (3) as a result the pattern of world politics changed in a way that did not favor the Soviet Union. Moreover, American attitudes and policies toward it were significantly affected when Washington saw how ready the Soviet Union was to use force to attain its goals. This readiness was demonstrated not merely by the Sino-Soviet border incidents, but also by its invasion of Czechoslovakia in 1968; its threat to intervene in the Middle East in 1973; its machinations in Africa, Southeast Asia, and South Asia in the middle and late 1970s; its enormous strategic and conventional military buildup throughout the 1960s and 1970s; and the Afghanistan invasion in 1979–80. If not the principal cause of Sino-American détente, then, American perception of this Soviet propensity to turn to the military, of which the Chinese case was an illustration, was nevertheless a major contributor.

Of central importance to the outcome of the border clashes was the general political-strategic atmosphere surrounding Soviet use of force against the Chinese and the effect of that atmosphere on the political-military situation between Moscow and Peking. The Soviet Union would not have moved so quickly and with such confidence against China had the Kremlin believed that the United States would intervene on the side of the Chinese. But it knew with certainty that the United States would not. Not only were Peking and Washington not on speaking terms in 1969–71, but it was a long time after the initial breakthrough in mid-1971 before China and the United States began to solve their outstanding differences. Of equal significance was American preoccupation with Vietnam; at no time between 1969 and 1974 was direct American military support of China likely, given the disturbed state of domestic American politics, the increasing desire to withdraw from Southeast Asia and perhaps from the Pacific as a whole, and the need to shift American attention from Asia to the Middle East and Europe. The Russians knew this and took advantage of it.

Then, too, in the post-1969 period, the Soviet-American strategic nuclear balance was moving toward equality. Even if the United States had wished to aid China by threatening strategic nuclear reprisal against the Russians for pushing the Chinese around, this would have been disastrous since the Soviet Union now had the power to destroy American society. There would be no repetition in the 1970s of the overt nuclear threat elements of coercive diplomacy as practiced during the Cuban missile crisis except where vital American interests might be directly threatened. Moscow realized that, from the strategic nuclear point of view, its concerted buildup after 1962 had successfully isolated its battle-field with China. Concomitantly, the Kremlin counted on the general atmosphere of détente, however ephemeral, and on American desire to preserve at least minimal Soviet-American ties. It would have been un-thinkable for the United States suddenly to declare détente at an end merely because of a few military incidents between Communist countries halfway around the globe from the North American continent.

As the Russians had succeeded in neutralizing, through détente, direct American influence on Sino-Soviet military outcomes, much the same was true of Soviet and Chinese links with other Asian states. Moscow had taken care since the early 1960s to repair or strengthen its relations with each of the eight states surrounding China except South Korea. The most obvious examples, aside from North Vietnam, were India and Japan. On the subcontinent, Moscow replaced Washington as the security guarantor of South Asian international politics. The Tashkent agreement of 1965, the alliance with India in early 1971, and the Bangladesh conflict later that year all demonstrated that Moscow had the ability to influence events decisively in that region. If the relationship with Japan was less felicitous because of the traditional Japanese attitude toward the Soviet Union and Moscow's intransigence over the northern islands issue, the Kremlin was still able to influence Tokyo significantly by enticing the Japanese to par-ticipate in Siberian economic development and gain access to its natural resources. Japan therefore thought it prudent to walk a tightrope between China and Moscow (though continuing to take its general policy orienta-tion from the United States).[41] Only with the large Soviet Far Eastern maritime buildup did Japan feel it was necessary to jump off that tightrope —in China's direction—in 1978 and after.

China, of course, was greatly to blame for its own isolation, for during the Cultural Revolution it had deliberately cut off all contact with every country except Albania. In 1969 Peking faced Soviet threats and guns absolutely alone. The contrast a decade later was stark. China had emerged from its self-imposed isolation, and India and Japan had moved away from Moscow's attempted embrace. The Vietnam War was long over and the United States had regained some freedom of action in world

41. See Robert Scalapino, ed., *The Foreign Policy of Modern Japan* (University of California Press, 1977); and Donald C. Hellmann, ed., *China and Japan: A New Balance of Power* (Heath, 1976).

politics. Soviet-American détente had suffered a series of blows and the United States at least was beginning to reduce the military imbalance strategically and in Europe. So Moscow could no longer deal with China entirely as she wished. In the last two publicized border incidents (the intrusion of the Soviet helicopter in 1974 and the military incursion of Soviet forces in mid-1978) Moscow found it necessary to apologize and even to court Peking's favor to gain the release of the imprisoned helicopter crewmen.

In 1971 Moscow pointed out to Peking that the latter's support of its erstwhile South Asian ally, Pakistan, against a Soviet-backed India was useless. As the Kremlin put it, the Soviet Union "could not be responsible" for what might happen along the Sinkiang-Soviet Central Asian border were the Chinese to send troops against India in response to cries for help from Rawalpindi. By contrast, in 1978 China could threaten to and then actually go to war against Vietnam on its southern flank to protect the remnants of its Cambodian ally, even while continuing to face the Soviet threat from the north. While the contrast between 1971 and 1978 is not perfect and while the linkage between the Southeast Asian and the Sino-Soviet situations was still fraught with danger, China in the late 1970s and early 1980s could afford to behave more aggressively, whereas in 1971, at the height of its troubles with Moscow, it dared not speak or move boldly.

Whatever the balance between short-term benefits and long-term costs to Moscow of its military actions against China, it is clear that emplacing a very strong Soviet force in Siberia and the Soviet Far East has altered the entire balance of power in Asia. Moreover, at the end of the 1970s, it seemed exceedingly unlikely that the Russians would agree to draw that force down to levels approximating those of the mid-1960s. The most important outcome of the change was the mortgaging of Chinese military and foreign policy to the deterrence of Soviet threats and defense against Russian invasion.

Other aspects of the balance of power in Northeast Asia were also affected by the Soviet force buildup, including its naval buildup, for the mere presence of these forces close to Korea and Japan altered the military equation. Japan viewed the Soviet Union as its natural enemy and explicitly justified its rearmanent effort in anti-Soviet terms. On the Korean peninsula, the Soviet naval buildup changed the overall military balance between North and South, although the separate efforts of China and the United States were directed, respectively, to lessening the degree of Soviet influence in Pyongyang and to stabilizing the local military balance.[42]

In the Taiwan Strait there was and probably would be no military threat from the Chinese mainland against the Republic of China so long as the Sino-Soviet border situation remained tense. In Southeast Asia, the Soviet Union had become a major, if indirect, military power because of its close security ties with Hanoi and its ability to supply military equipment and advisers to the Vietnamese Communists. Finally, in South Asia, even though India had moved into a position of more even balance between the United States, China, and Russia, Soviet military influence remained important, and Soviet involvement in helping to sustain in power a group of pro-Soviet sympathizers in Afghanistan upset the delicate balance on the subcontinent as a whole.[43]

In sum, whereas the Soviet Union was unable to convert its commanding military presence in Northeast Asia into a decisive political and economic influence in the rest of Asia, the Soviet military instrument shaped the Asian balance of power, political and military, if not economic. As in other areas of the world, Moscow found that military power was its most

42. On the one hand, significant augmentation of the Soviet Far Eastern fleet based in Vladivostok, together with a much-strengthened, shore-based naval air arm, materially increased the Russian threat to the American ability to supply the Korean and American military in the South. On the other hand, American naval strength deployed west of Pearl Harbor declined significantly after the end of the Vietnam War, accentuating the Soviet buildup. Were the Soviet Union to interpose its fleet between Japan and Korea or give significant intelligence assistance to the North Korean navy and air force, some American authorities doubt whether, in the critical first days and weeks of a renewed Korean conflict, American ships could reach South Korea in the requisite numbers.

43. The South Asian political balance traditionally rested on a standoff between India and its supporters on the one hand and Pakistan and its friends on the other. Until the mid-1960s, the United States played the role of balancer and hence security guarantor. Since then, the Soviet Union has played that role, principally as a means of excluding American influence from the subcontinent, and secondarily to counteract Chinese pressure on India. After 1971, however, Pakistan was weakened by the Soviet- and Indian-backed Bangladesh struggle for independence, a conflict in which neither China nor the United States was able to support Pakistan. Attention centered on the remnants of Pakistan in the west, since Bangladesh had become an Indian client, and the question was whether Pakistan could find external support sufficiently strong to withstand combined Indian-Soviet political pressure. In this situation the overthrow of the Daoud government in Kabul by leftist forces became critically important, for Soviet influence was then to be found on both sides of an increasingly weak Pakistan. The problem was exacerbated by the Soviet overthrow of two successive Communist, but nationalist, governments in Kabul and by the late-1979 invasion.

efficient device, and sometimes its only one, for serving its foreign policy goals and applying its overall power from a distance.

American security interests changed accordingly. The defense of Japan against Soviet air and naval threats needed much greater attention. The United States had to consider more carefully its access to South Korea in case the North rekindled the Korean War. In East and Southeast Asia, Soviet naval forces were much in evidence and it appeared only to be a matter of time before the Russians had a naval base on the Vietnamese coast. American security interests in the Philippines, access to Indonesian oil and Southeast Asian natural resources, rights of passage through the Strait of Molucca, and American naval operations in the Indian Ocean would all be threatened directly by such a base.

On the other hand, American economic interests were probably not affected by the Soviet force in Northeast Asia. On the contrary, the free market economies of Japan, South Korea, Taiwan, Hong Kong, Singapore, and Malaysia, and to a lesser extent Indonesia and Thailand, flourished despite the Soviet military presence. Indeed, so long as China acted as a bulwark to Soviet influence in Asia, all of these economies not centrally planned continued to show continued rapid rates of growth and enrichment of their peoples. They have not had to devote an unreasonably high portion of their social and economic product to countering Soviet military threats.

Attitudes toward the United States in Asia and elsewhere were generally unrelated to the Sino-Soviet border conflicts. If anything, world public opinion as well as American public opinion has favored the American opening of relations with China for its own sake, even though some perceived, correctly, that the entire process, from the Shanghai communiqué in 1972 to normalization in 1979 was, among other things, Washington's diplomatic response to the emerging Russian threat against China. While differences remained in the United States as expressed in competing policies and declarations of the executive and congressional branches about the status and defense of Taiwan after normalization, the American body politic seemed united behind the policy of improving relations with Peking.

This seemingly felicitous situation could change suddenly should the Soviet Union conclude that it was in its interest to bring the conflict with China to a head. While that probability appears low, some consideration would have to be given to Soviet fears that China, the United States, Japan, Western Europe, and their respective allies were ganging up on Moscow to form a worldwide anti-Soviet coalition. Nothing could be worse from the Soviet Union's point of view. If the Russians concluded that such a trend was inexorable, they might move to forestall it directly by attacking China or indirectly by a military move elsewhere—an extreme measure designed to break apart such a nearly unbeatable combination before it solidified.[44] But Moscow would be more likely to conclude that Peking needed to be taught that the United States is an unreliable ally, unwilling to come to its assistance (or, for that matter, to that of more closely allied partners) when needed. A series of much more serious and bloody border incidents or the mauling of one or two Chinese divisions in Sinkiang might thus be attractive, if also exceedingly dangerous and provocative. The United States might then be asked by Peking to greatly increase its material support of China, including transfer of much military equipment and military technology. The United States could, it is true, help the Chinese resist the Russians through direct American military action against the Soviet Union, but the probability of that is near zero, in view of the risk of World War III and the destruction of the United States. The United States would be able to maximize its leverage in Sino-Soviet conflict situations by helping to convince Moscow—by American actions as well as words—of American support of China before conflict breaks out. Washington would lose most of its leverage and be faced with unpalatable choices, however, if fighting were to begin. American strategy, therefore, must be based largely on deterrence rather than a war-fighting capacity.

Suppose the Russians had not used military force at Damansky in 1969 and elsewhere along the border thereafter? Would the USSR have been farther ahead or farther behind, and what of American security interests? It is, of course, impossible to rewrite history, but two things can be said. First, the Russians carefully controlled their use of force against the Chinese on all occasions. They had, and for the most part still have, the Chinese at their mercy.[45] But their actions were much less forcible than their

44. Some examples of forestalling such action, aside from direct attack on China, might be enmeshing China in dislocating conflict in Southeast Asia that it could not win; demands that Western Europe demilitarize to a significant extent or face military consequences; or greatly stepped-up Soviet support for radical groups and states in the Middle East and North Africa. While at this writing each of these possibilities seems extreme, they might not be, under the postulated circumstance of entente between America, Europe, Japan, and China.

45. The Soviet strategic military advantage over China may be declining. First, China is likely to continue to gain disposable military power, including nuclear weaponry. Second, to the extent that the Russians continue to dominate the Chinese militarily, Peking will lean more and more to the American side of the new Soviet-

capabilities allowed; instead they were tailored to broader Soviet diplomatic goals in China. It was impossible for Moscow to eschew using military force: that would have shown weakness and forbearance, impossible for any ruling group in Moscow, Communist or not. The Russians believe that state borders must be defended at all costs and that most of their actions against the Chinese were for no other reason. If they had reacted to the Chinese with minimal force, however, it would probably have been better for them in the long run, since the Chinese would not have been so thoroughly frightened and would not have aimed every policy act at stopping the perceived Soviet threat.[46] Minimal Soviet use of force would have been worse for the United States, since the opening with China probably would have been slower and would not have come so far. Moreover, the imbalance of military power in Europe would probably have tilted in Moscow's favor even more and the threat of Soviet invasion would have been made even more believable had Moscow opted for minimal augmentation of its forces in Northeast Asia.[47]

Could the Russians have attained their policy objectives—settlement of the border issue in particular and improvement of Sino-Soviet relations in general—had they not used force? The answer can never be known, of course, but it seems likely that they perceive force as necessary to short-term goal attainment. Moscow felt it had no other choice, given the seriousness with which it regarded the short- and long-term Chinese threat, a conclusion strongly supported by the emotional Russian attitude toward the Chinese. Moreover, it is important to realize that the Chinese were

---

American cold war. Third, even though the Soviet Union may be moving even farther ahead of China in all aspects of modern weaponry, Peking can argue that the growth of its own nuclear forces makes increasing percentages of Soviet territory, population, and industry vulnerable to Chinese missiles.

46. What if the Soviet Union had decided to use much greater force against China? In that case, Soviet security interests would have been threatened to an extreme degree. Not only would the Chinese have declared a holy Maoist "people's war" against the Russian invaders, but the United States would in all probability have done all it could to aid the Chinese. That option for the Soviet Union, however, was never seriously considered and remains unlikely.

47. My argument here is contentious, I realize. It depends on the assumption that the Russians would have continued to augment their nuclear and conventional forces at approximately the same rate as they have in the last decade even if they had not had to face a "Chinese threat." It is true that the Soviet Union might not have built up its forces against Europe and the United States to fully replace those diverted to the Chinese front. On the other hand, the equipment and forces now on the Chinese front would probably have been produced and trained even without the perceived threat from Peking.

(and are) impervious to other forms of Soviet influence—economic aid or punishment, offers of compromise on other issues, personal appeals, cultural ties, and so forth. If these had ever been effective policy instruments, they had long since become useless. Force was all that was left to the Russians and force was what they understood and knew how to use best. So they went ahead and used it.

The tragedy for Moscow was, and continues to be, that its use of force did not attain its *longer-term* goals. Not only did the Chinese not give an inch on the border issue, but they redirected their entire military effort and foreign policy to resisting the Soviet Union. The upshot of a decade's effort was a terrible defeat for Moscow: by 1980, the USSR faced a rapidly strengthening and modernizing China in league with the United States, both of whose leaders seemed united on the necessity of opposing Moscow in most territorial and policy areas where its influence was felt or threatened. Perhaps the Chinese will one day decide that it is better to settle their differences with the Russians, but in 1980 there was no sign of that. The Soviet Union has itself to blame for this state of affairs. Its fault was overreaction to the Chinese, an error typical of its whole foreign policy style, to be sure, but one that could only have led to an impasse between the two Communist giants.

CHAPTER EIGHT

The Korean and Vietnam Wars

WILLIAM ZIMMERMAN

AT THE OUTSET of the 1970s a Soviet scholar was asked to deliver a paper on Lenin's significance for Latin America. He dutifully began his paper by noting that from Lenin's *Complete Works* he had ascertained that Lenin not only had never been to Latin America but had had virtually nothing to say about it. Nevertheless, he contended Lenin's ideas and his contribution to the course of revolution were relevant to an understanding of Latin America. He then proceeded to comment at great length on this.

My assignment bears a superficial resemblance to the task confronted by the Soviet scholar. This chapter deals with the Soviet use of armed forces for political purposes in the Korean and Vietnam wars. In a narrow sense, Soviet armed forces played virtually no role in either war. I was therefore tempted to dismiss the topic as uninteresting and to pass on to other, more potentially fruitful areas of inquiry. For a number of reasons, however, I resisted this temptation.

First, Soviet personnel did play a role, though a modest one, in both wars. Second, the political purposes of the Soviet Union were served by its having provided its allies with considerable amounts of weapons and some military personnel. Third, the possibility that the involvement of Soviet armed forces would be far greater than it actually was had to be taken into consideration by the states more centrally involved in the fighting. Finally, it is important to determine why the Soviet role was as limited as it was and what this implies about Soviet goals, priorities, political skill, and propensity for taking risks.

The Korean and Vietnam wars were central events in the post–World War II period. In each war the United States committed hundreds of thousands of troops to deal with military threats thought to emanate

314

wholly or in part from the Soviet Union. (John Kennedy's 1961 meeting with Nikita Khrushchev in Vienna appears to have been an immediate precursor to Kennedy's decision to send 18,000 advisers and support troops to Vietnam, "to make," as Kennedy told James Reston, "our power credible" to the USSR.)[1] Although direct Soviet participation was minimal, it is necessary to reconsider both the role Soviet armed forces actually did play in these two wars and the implications of Soviet behavior to arrive at an understanding of Soviet foreign policy.

In this chapter I describe the events leading up to and during the two wars and discuss their outcomes. The examination of the Soviet role in the Korean War focuses on two issues. (1) Did the Soviet Union start the Korean War and, if so, what were its motives? Were the North Korean troops merely an extension of the Soviet armed forces serving the political purposes of the Soviet Union? (2) The North Koreans failed in their attempt to unify Korea and were driven back by South Korean and United Nations (almost entirely American) troops to the Yalu and Tumen rivers, the rivers that divide the Democratic People's Republic of Korea (North Korea) from the People's Republic of China (PRC) and the Soviet Union. From Allen Whiting's work one can be reasonably certain why China crossed the Yalu.[2] But why did the Soviet Union fail to cross the Tumen? What would have prompted it to use force directly and on a large scale?

Next, I assess the Soviet role in the Vietnam War. Again, the focus is on a few incidents. (1) In the summer of 1964, ostensibly in reaction to attacks on American ships by North Vietnamese patrol boats in the Gulf of Tonkin, the United States bombed North Vietnam. Why did the Soviet Union respond in such a limited way to an attack on a socialist country and what does this imply? (2) A second incident, prompting a more overt Soviet response, occurred several months later. In February 1965 the United States launched a major air attack on North Vietnam. The attack took place immediately after a Vietcong attack on Pleiku in South Vietnam, rather than in response, for instance, to an attack on American military shipping in the South China Sea. Why did Moscow react as it did and what did that indicate about Soviet foreign policy? (3) After Pleiku, the American escalation continued for three years, until 1968, when on March 31 President Lyndon B. Johnson first restricted the bomb-

1. As reported in David Halberstam, *The Best and the Brightest* (Fawcett, 1973), p. 97.
2. Allen S. Whiting, *China Crosses the Yalu: The Decision to Enter the Korean War* (Stanford University Press, 1960).

ing of North Vietnam and then in the fall completely halted it. What role did the USSR play in advancing or impeding the various ill-fated efforts to stop the fighting? In the process of escalation and subsequent de-escalation did the Soviet Union compete with the United States in risk-taking? How and to what extent did the Soviet Union use its military might to offset the American escalation? (4) The role of the Soviet Union in the North Vietnamese offensive in the spring of 1972 and its response to the bombing of Hanoi and the mining of Haiphong harbor by the United States, which followed the offensive, are assessed, as are the implications and underlying politics of the May 1972 visit to the USSR by President Richard M. Nixon, a trip that produced manifest anxiety in Hanoi.

A Synopsis of the Conflicts

The Korean War began on June 25, 1950, when the North Koreans crossed the 38th parallel, which until then had been the demarcation line between the Democratic People's Republic of Korea (North Korea) and the Republic of Korea (South Korea). The Communist takeover in North Korea was similar to that in Eastern Europe. The Soviet Union was bent on creating a state, in the Yalta formula, democratic and friendly to the Soviet Union. As General Terentyi F. Shtykov, the Soviet representative to the Joint American Soviet Commission on Korea, put it in 1946, "The Soviet Union has a keen interest in Korea being a true democracy and an independent country friendly to the Soviet Union, so that in the future it will not become a base for an attack on the Soviet Union."[3] The USSR used many of the same techniques in consolidating its preeminent position in North Korea as it had in Eastern Europe. Joint stock companies for oil and shipping were created and Soviet advisers were attached to "the Cabinet, the National Planning Council and the Ministry of Defense."[4] Many of the leaders in post–World War II regimes in Eastern Europe had been Soviet citizens (Marshal Konstantin Rokossovsky was a member of the Polish Central Committee as late as 1956); so, too, in North Korea "Soviet-Koreans"—Soviet citizens of Korean extraction who had lived in

---

3. *New York Times,* March 21, 1946, as cited in Robert R. Simmons, *The Strained Alliance: Peking, Pyongyang, Moscow and the Politics of the Korean Civil War* (Free Press, 1975), p. 21. For an excellent critical review of Simmons' book, which is an important source in this chapter, see William Stueck, "The Soviet Union and the Origins of the Korean War," *World Politics,* vol. 28 (July 1976), pp. 622–35.
4. Whiting, *China Crosses the Yalu,* p. 42.

the USSR before 1945—occupied important positions in the North Korean government and in the Korean Labor party when the independent Democratic People's Republic of Korea (DPRK) was established in 1948. (Again, as in many Eastern European states, several groupings made up the Korean Labor party: the Soviet-Koreans; Koreans who had been in Yenan with the Chinese Communist party; the "Kapsan" group, which had conducted guerrilla activities against the Japanese; and a "domestic" faction that had remained in Korea during World War II and consequently had close ties with Communists in South Korea.)

The timing of the North Korean attack on South Korea seemed to be related to the drawing of lines between the two blocs that followed the Communist takeovers in Europe and Asia and the burgeoning of the cold war. Specifically, major American spokesmen had demarcated an American defense perimeter that excluded Korea. In 1949 General Douglas MacArthur had implicitly placed South Korea outside the perimeter by defining the U.S. line of defense as extending through the chain of islands near the coast of Asia from the Philippines through the Ryukyu archipelago, Japan, and the Aleutian Islands. In 1950 Secretary of State Dean Acheson spoke of the " 'defense perimeter' of the United States in the Pacific" as "including the Aleutians, Japan, the Ryukyus, and the Philippines. . . . So far as the military security of the other areas of the Pacific is concerned, it must be clear that no person can guarantee those areas against military attack."[5]

Because of the nature of Soviet-North Korean relations and the global emergence of tight bipolarity, the beginning of the Korean War was viewed as a Soviet ploy in the cold war. Western specialists were naturally skeptical of vague Communist assertions that the war was "unleashed by the imperialists" and of the specific North Korean version of the beginning of the war: "Early on the morning of June 25 so-called national defense troops of the puppet government of South Korea initiated a sudden offensive onto the territory of North Korea all along the line of the 38th parallel [and] . . . invaded the territory of North Korea to a depth of one or two kilometers north of the 38th parallel in the region west of Haiju and the Kunchon and Chorwon regions."[6] (One observation from a Communist source they found notable, however: "The advantages which an

5. Ibid., p. 39.
6. Declaration of Ministry of Internal Affairs of People's Democratic Republic of Korea, as reported in *Pravda,* June 26, 1950 (in *Current Digest of the Soviet Press* [*CDSP*], vol. 2, no. 22, July 15, 1950, p. 12).

aggressor wins during a sudden attack are well known to everyone.")[7]
Adam Ulam stated the consensus of Western commentary when he declared: "Everything . . . would point to the conclusion that the Korean
affair was undertaken at Soviet initiative. That the North Koreans would
have attacked on their own is inconceivable."[8]

At any rate, what happened next is beyond dispute. In the weeks after
June 25, the North Koreans advanced rapidly to the south and nearly succeeded in occupying all Korea. The advance was finally halted in midsummer by the combined efforts of the South Koreans, the United States,
and a small contingent of U.S. allies operating under the aegis of the
United Nations. (The legitimizing umbrella of the United Nations was
made possible by the Soviet Union's boycott of the Security Council meetings in protest over the failure of the United Nations to recognize the credentials of the Chinese Communists as the ruler of China.) In these efforts
the American role was obviously paramount. By mid-August 1950 an
"observer" was asking in *Izvestiya,* "Who does not see now that the civil
war in Korea would have ended long ago had it not been for American
intervention?"[9]

Events moved rapidly. In September MacArthur undertook a major
and daring amphibious action at Inchon, which allowed the American and
South Korean armies to extricate themselves from the Pusan perimeter
and to launch a counteroffensive, creating, according to *Pravda,* a "situation [which] is very serious."[10] By October the South Koreans had crossed
the 38th parallel, taking little notice of Chinese Communist threats to intervene.[11] Now the United States aspired to unify Korea on *its* terms. The
American ambassador to the UN, Warren Austin, declared: "The opportunities for new acts of aggression should be removed. . . . The aggressor's
force should not be permitted to have refuge behind an imaginary line. . . .
The artificial barrier which has divided North and South Korea has no
basis for existence either in law or reason."[12]

7. *Literaturnaya Gazeta,* August 31, 1950 (in *CDSP,* vol. 2, no. 35, October 14,
1950, p. 13).

8. Adam B. Ulam, *Expansion and Coexistence: Soviet Foreign Policy, 1917–73,*
2d ed. (Praeger, 1974), p. 518.

9. *Izvestiya,* August 20, 1950 (in *CDSP,* vol. 2, no. 34, October 7, 1950, p. 22).

10. Sergei Borzenko, "Battle for Seoul," *Pravda,* September 23, 1950 (in *CDSP,*
vol. 2, no. 37, October 28, 1950, p. 13).

11. Whiting, *China Crosses the Yalu,* p. 111.

12. Ibid. As early as August 17, Austin had declared: "The United Nations must
see that the people of Korea attain complete individual and political freedom. . . .
Shall only a part of this country be assured this freedom? I think not." Ibid., p. 78;
Whiting's italics deleted.

By mid-October, however, the Chinese "volunteers" had crossed the Yalu, and from October 26 to November 7, they fought South Korean and American forces along a broad front extending west to the coast. By November 27 the Chinese army was heavily engaged in North Korea. Greatly overextended, the American troops retreated rapidly to positions somewhat south of the 38th parallel. Once again the battlefront stabilized; a near stalemate existed militarily. From late January 1951 to July 1953 the Americans and South Koreans did achieve modest gains at the expense of the Chinese and North Koreans: notably, they recrossed the 38th parallel across much of the peninsula. Meanwhile, MacArthur was relieved of command by President Harry S. Truman in 1951, Dwight D. Eisenhower was elected president in 1952, and Stalin died in March 1953. Finally, in July 1953, an armistice was agreed to which resulted in boundaries that essentially restored the prewar condition.

The Vietnam conflict was much longer and more fluid than the Korean War. It might reasonably be called this century's Thirty Years' War. The Vietnamese, under Ho Chi Minh, had waged a guerrilla war against the Japanese in the last months of World War II. Immediately after the war the Vietnamese continued their fight for an independent Communist Vietnam against the French, whose possession Indochina had been before World War II.

The emergence of communism as a powerful force in Vietnam bore little resemblance to the standard pattern of Soviet-dominated takeovers as typified by Eastern Europe and exemplified by the formation of the Democratic People's Republic of Korea. Instead, in 1945–47 Soviet policy in Indochina was based almost exclusively on Stalin's aspirations for the French Communist party (PCF). (The PCF, it will be recalled, was part of the early post–World War II French governmental coalition.) The PCF initially supported the French government's fight against the Vietminh. In 1947 Maurice Thorez, as vice-minister of France, "countersigned the order for military action against the communist-led Republic of Vietnam." Verbal Soviet and PCF support for the Vietminh came only after the PCF had been ousted from the French coalition government and after the Truman Doctrine and the Marshall Plan had been announced in March and June 1947.[13]

The Communist seizure of power in China greatly facilitated Ho Chi Minh's fight against the French since Chinese Communist control of the border between China and Vietnam ensured Vietminh access to weapons

13. Donald S. Zagoria, *Vietnam Triangle: Moscow, Peking, Hanoi* (Pegasus, 1967), pp. 37, 38.

and other military equipment. Gradually, the Vietminh prevailed in the fighting, its greatest military victory over the French being the capture of Dienbienphu in 1954.

The withdrawal of the French from Indochina was consummated by the 1954 Geneva conference. Once again, the Vietnamese had reasons to feel that other Communists had strange notions of proletarian internationalism. The Soviet Union urged a cease-fire on the Vietminh largely because its major concern was with Europe, particularly with having the French defeat the proposed European Defense Community. As summarized in the *Pentagon Papers*: "Soviet interests dictated the sacrifice of the Vietminh goals if necessary to prevent German remilitarization."[14] The People's Republic of China similarly allowed concern about its own security to take precedence over Vietminh interests. Peking was anxious to ensure the security of China's southern borders and to delay an American military buildup in Indochina. For Peking, in Marek Thee's words, the "main emphasis was on the prohibition of foreign bases, withdrawal of foreign forces and neutralization of Indochina."[15]

The 1954 Geneva conference resulted in another country artificially separated by a cease-fire line, in this instance the 17th parallel. The Geneva documentation emphasized the provisional nature of the cease-fire and envisaged that a general election would be held in 1956, to be followed by reunification. The "reality of partition," however, was clear.[16]

There then followed a brief period in which Hanoi concentrated on the internal economic development of the north rather than on accelerating reunification. By 1960, however, the National Front for the Liberation of South Vietnam had been created. In the next year or so, "the rate of infiltration from North to South Vietnam increased sharply."[17] In response partially to this, partially to more general fears of Communist—Chinese and Soviet—commitment to wars of national liberation, the United States began to play a far more active role in South Vietnam. Specifically, President John F. Kennedy approved a Program for Action for South Vietnam, which contemplated "a set of detailed instructions . . . for operations in the military, economic and psychological fields," including "covert actions

14. *The Pentagon Papers: The Defense Department History of United States Decisionmaking on Vietnam*, Senator Gravel ed. (Beacon Press, 1971), vol. 1, p. 168.

15. Marek Thee, "The Indochina Wars: Great Power Involvement—Escalation and Disengagement," *Journal of Peace Research*, vol. 13, no. 2 (1976), p. 123.

16. Ibid.

17. Geoffrey Jukes, *The Soviet Union in Asia* (Sydney: Angus and Robertson, 1973), p. 218.

in the field of intelligence, unconventional warfare, and political psychological activities." Throughout the next three years, the position of the South Vietnamese regime continued to deteriorate. American decision-makers contemplated more drastic actions to curb the infiltration from North Vietnam and to bring pressure on Hanoi. In August 1964 the Tonkin Gulf incidents occurred. The United States mounted reprisal air strikes against Hanoi; the Tonkin Gulf resolution was passed by Congress. In October 1964 Khrushchev was removed as head of the party and state in the Soviet Union. In November President Lyndon B. Johnson defeated Barry Goldwater. One of Johnson's central campaign themes was that the United States was "not going north and drop bombs at this stage of the game, and we were not going south and even out and let the Communists take over either."[18]

But, in fact, the United States was going north. After declining to retaliate for the Vietcong attack on Bienhoa just before the U.S. elections, Johnson in February 1965 ordered the bombing of North Vietnam, ostensibly in response to a Vietcong attack on the American base at Pleiku. American officials were spoiling for an opportunity to enlarge the U.S. role in the war, and Pleiku offered such an opportunity. Townsend Hoopes reports that McGeorge Bundy had noted cynically that " 'Pleikus are streetcars,' i.e., if one waits watchfully, they come along."[19]

The attack on the north, which occurred while Soviet Premier Aleksei Kosygin was in Hanoi, constituted a new phase in the war. As the *Pentagon Papers* make clear, "By contrast with the earlier Tonkin strikes in August 1964, which had been presented as a one-time demonstration that North Vietnam would not attack U.S. forces with impunity, the February 1965 attacks were explicitly linked with the 'larger pattern of aggression' by North Vietnam, and were a reprisal against North Vietnam for an offense committed by the Vietcong in South Vietnam."[20]

The war intensified in the three years after February 1965. The North Vietnamese and the Vietcong, on the one hand, and the United States and the South Vietnamese, on the other, engaged in a competition of will and commitment. A crucial stage came in early 1968 when, in the aftermath of the Vietcong's Tet offensive, General William Westmoreland requested that the American military contingent of 510,000 men in South Vietnam be augmented by an additional 206,000 troops during 1968.

18. *New York Times*, September 29, 1964.
19. Townsend Hoopes, *The Limits of Intervention* (McKay, 1969), p. 30.
20. *Pentagon Papers*, vol. 3, p. 271. Italics in original deleted.

What followed was a thoroughgoing reassessment of the American military position against the backdrop of domestic political crisis, highlighted by Senator Eugene McCarthy's success in the March 12, 1968, New Hampshire primary and Senator Robert Kennedy's announcement on March 16 that he would seek the Democratic presidential nomination. On March 22 President Johnson relieved General Westmoreland of command and made him army chief of staff. On March 25 and 26, the Senior Advisory Group on Vietnam—a distinguished group whose members included Dean Acheson, Omar Bradley, McGeorge Bundy, Douglas Dillon, Arthur Goldberg, Henry Cabot Lodge, Matthew Ridgway, Maxwell Taylor, and Cyrus Vance—met for a stocktaking. As Cyrus Vance, then deputy secretary of defense, remarked, the group was "weighing not only what was happening in Vietnam, but the social and political effects in the United States, the impact on the U.S. economy, the attitude of other nations. The divisiveness in the country was growing with such acuteness that it was threatening to tear the United States apart."[21]

The reassessment culminated on March 31, when President Johnson announced that there would be a two-stage halt of the bombing of North Vietnam—first at the 20th parallel and later a complete halt—and that he would not "seek," and would not "accept, the nomination of my Party for another term as President."[22] Four days later the North Vietnamese government declared its "readiness to appoint its representatives to contact the United States representative with a view to determining with the American side the unconditional cessation of United States bombing raids and all other acts of war against the Democratic Republic of Vietnam so that talks may start."[23]

The "talking while fighting" dragged on until 1972. In the first half of the year, the United States undertook two bold diplomatic moves. President Nixon visited first the People's Republic of China and then the Soviet Union. Hard on the heels of the Nixon visit to China, the military front in South Vietnam changed dramatically. On March 31, precisely four years after Johnson's 1968 bombing-cessation speech, the North Vietnamese army crossed the demilitarized zone en masse. The United States resumed the bombing above the 20th parallel, expanding its attacks on North Vietnam to include the bombing of Hanoi and the mining of Haiphong harbor, actions that did not preclude Nixon's visit to the Soviet Union in May

21. Hoopes, *Limits of Intervention*, pp. 215–16.
22. *New York Times*, April 1, 1968.
23. *Pentagon Papers*, vol. 4, pp. 602–03.

1972. The presidential visits to China and the Soviet Union were an integral part of the U.S. disengagement from Vietnam and "produced almost immediate results."[24] Unsure now of the support of its backers—the Soviet Union and China—North Vietnam quickly came to an agreement with the United States, and in January 1973 the Paris Agreements on Ending the War and Restoring Peace in Vietnam were signed. (In the Paris negotiations, it should be stressed, neither the Soviet Union nor China participated directly. The North Vietnamese had evidently had enough fraternal aid in such matters at Geneva in 1954.) The essentials of the 1954 Geneva agreement—reunification through a general election —were reaffirmed, and provisions were made for the United States to withdraw its remaining troops and for the release of American prisoners of war.

The prewar condition, however, was not restored. "All parties became quite resigned to a military solution. . . . Hanoi rejected all proposals for a continuous cease-fire line, as adopted in the 1954 Geneva agreement. . . . Instead it demanded categorically, and was granted, the 'leopard spot' solution, a cease-fire in place, which favored the guerilla forces."[25] Two years later, after a brief hiatus during which it appeared that the Republic of Vietnam might solidify its position vis-à-vis the Vietcong (by February 1974 the Vietcong had lost some 15 percent of the territory it controlled at the time of the signing of the peace agreement), the thirty-year quest came to a rapid end. In early 1975 the North Vietnamese increased their "revolutionary violence" to put pressure on the South Vietnamese government. What followed was "totally unplanned and unexpected": within fifty-five days the Republic of Vietnam and its armed forces disintegrated and surrendered unconditionally. Vietnam was unified.

Soviet Armed Forces and the Korean War

In the first months of the Korean War, a majority of the American public thought the United States had entered World War III.[26] It is difficult to imagine that public opinion polls in the Soviet Union in 1950—had they existed—would have shown that a majority of the Soviet people thought

24. Thee, "The Indochina Wars," p. 125.
25. Ibid., p. 126.
26. Kenneth N. Waltz, "Electoral Punishment and Foreign Policy Crises," in James N. Rosenau, ed., *Domestic Sources of Foreign Policy* (Free Press, 1967), p. 229.

the Soviet Union was in World War III. A central thrust of Soviet foreign policy in those months was to ensure that the Soviet Union not be involved, at least overtly, in any direct fighting and certainly not in Korea. The main theme of the Soviet media was the Stockholm Peace Appeal, a campaign to obtain the signatures of millions of people opposed to the atomic bomb.

This attitude flies in the face of the two usual explanations of the origin of the Korean War: that Korea was a "testing ground" and that the North Koreans were attempting to "tie down U.S. military strength in Asia so as to reduce resistance to Communist aggression elsewhere."[27] Hindsight, however, makes a simpler, Korean-centered explanation seem the most likely. The North Koreans attacked for a combination of reasons. They gave some credence to the possibility that the South Koreans might attack, hence the attractiveness of a preemptive "do unto others before they do unto you." The unification of Korea could be accomplished solely by Koreans; the North Koreans appear to have convinced themselves and Stalin that Communist guerrillas in the South would rise in response to a call from the North. This expectation probably enhanced the sense that a North Korean attack upon South Korea would be successful and that the unification could be accomplished quickly. Furthermore, since the affair was to be exclusively a Korean action and since the Americans had excluded Korea from their defense perimeter, there was virtually no risk of American involvement. In short, a North Korean invasion would extend Communist domain through a war in which Soviet armed forces played no direct role and the Soviet Union took no risk.

This is, of course, merely a plausible reconstruction of events, but there is some evidence to bear out the particular proposition above. Syngman Rhee was on record as having said, "We shall respond to the cries of our brothers in distress" in the North. Nikita Khrushchev stated that Kim Il-Sung had assured Stalin that "an internal uprising [would occur] after the first shots were fired and Syngman Rhee was overthrown."[28] Kim may well have believed this. After the North Korean attack had failed, Pak Hon-yong, a leading figure among the Korean Communists who had spent World War II in Korea, was charged, in an indictment brought against him by the North Korean Labor party, with having circulated "a false report that in South Korea, the South Korean Labor Party had an

27. Whiting, *China Crosses the Yalu,* p. 41. Whiting reports both these explanations as unsubstantiated by events.

28. Simmons, *Strained Alliance,* p. 115.

underground organization of 500,000 members who were ready to take action in concert with the North."[29] Certainly Kim made an appeal to South Koreans once the war had begun, urging them "to render active assistance to the People's Army, to expand the national struggle, to destroy the enemy, to disrupt his communications, and restore the people's committees."[30] Indeed, the North Korean statements of June 10 and June 21, 1950, can be construed as calls to South Korean "patriots" to prepare for an incipient uprising. The interview by Kim Tu Bong, president of the Presidium of the DPRK Supreme People's Assembly, on June 23 is particularly open to such a construction: "As everyone knows," Kim Tu Bong observed,

all the democratic political parties and social organizations of the Southern Half of the Fatherland and all the Korean people . . . have taken *every possible* step and have exerted their utmost to unify the Fatherland peacefully . . . [There then follows a long list of various unsuccessful proposals.]

More recently on the basis of the aspiration of all of the democratic political parties and social organizations of the Southern half of the Fatherland and all the Korean people, the Presidium of the Supreme Korean People's Assembly has gone to the extent of directly proposing to the South Korean National Assembly a plan for expediting the peaceful unification of the Fatherland.

However, the Syngman Rhee country-selling traitor gang . . . *wants a division of the Fatherland and an internecine civil war instead of the peaceful unification of the Fatherland.* . . .

Leading traitors of the Syngman Rhee gang have openly talked about the northern expedition on many occasions. . . . The country-selling traitors may launch their adventurous northern expedition which they are talking about. However, the northern expedition will not be an easy one. . . .

The people of the northern half will launch their struggle vigorously in opposition to the Syngman Rhee traitor gang in order to defend the democratic rights and freedoms and traits of democratic reform which they have won and the people of the Southern Half of the Republic will also rise in unison in the struggle to oppose the Syngman Rhee traitor gang in order *to defend the democratic system established in the northern half and to extend it to the southern half.*[31]

If this Korean line of argument can be sustained, it probably also stands to reason that Khrushchev (certainly not one to shrink from blam-

29. "The North Korean Labor Party's Internal Factions," published anonymously in the Japanese publication *Jiyu* and reproduced in Simmons, *Strained Alliance,* p. 109.

30. As reported in *Pravda,* June 27, 1950 (in *CDSP,* vol. 2, no. 22, July 15, 1950, p. 14).

31. As reported in U.S. Foreign Broadcast Information Service (FBIS), *Daily Report,* Supplement Korea, no. 124 (June 27, 1950), p. PPP11; emphasis added.

ing Stalin for misdeeds) is believable when he testifies "that the war wasn't Stalin's idea, but Kim Il-Sung's. Kim was the initiator." (Khrushchev quickly adds, "Stalin didn't try to dissuade him. . . . I don't condemn Stalin for encouraging Kim. On the contrary I would have made the same decision if I had been in his place.") [32]

Whoever originated the idea, Stalin seems to be the one who took steps to further increase the prospects that the Korean attack would succeed, to further minimize the risk to the USSR, and to reduce the likelihood that a Soviet finger would be found on the trigger. Well before the attack, the Soviet Union had been the sole provider of equipment and training for the North Korean army, except for those Korean troops which had been part of the Chinese Communist forces in 1949–50. In April–May 1950 the Soviet Union made large deliveries of tanks, trucks, and heavy artillery to North Korea, presumably in anticipation of the attack.

At the same time, the number of Soviet advisers was greatly reduced. Khrushchev stated it was "absolutely incomprehensible to me why [Stalin] did it, but when Kim Il Sung was preparing for his march, Stalin called back all our advisers who were with the North Korean divisions and regiments, as well as all the advisers who were serving as consultants and helping to build up the army." Robert R. Simmons reports data that bear out Khrushchev's description of the events. "In 1948, there were 150 advisers in each North Korean army division (approximately one per company); in 1949 the number was reduced to 20 per division; by the spring of 1950 there were only between 3 and 8 per division." [33] He also reports the testimony of an alleged Russian defector who had been in North Korea before the outbreak of the Korean War that the "Soviet Union's military adviser group numbered only 40 before June 25." [34]

At the outbreak of the war, therefore, there were almost no Soviet forces in Korea, even in the form of advisers—with the probable exception of some Soviet pilots. (Khrushchev states that Soviet "air force planes were being used to shield Pyongyang and were therefore stationed in

32. Nikita S. Khrushchev, *Khrushchev Remembers* (Little, Brown, 1971), p. 370.

33. Simmons, *Strained Alliance*, p. 120, drawing from *North Korea: A Case Study in the Techniques of Takeover* (Washington, D.C.: Government Printing Office, 1961), p. 114.

34. Simmons, *Strained Alliance*, p. 120, citing Kyril Kalinov, "How Russia Built the North Korean People's Army," *The Reporter* (September 26, 1950), pp. 4–8. Robert F. Futrell, *The United States Air Force in Korea, 1950–1953* (Duell, Sloan and Pearce, 1961), p. 92, reports that U.S. Air Force intelligence thought it likely that Soviet instructor pilots participated in the initial phase of the war in Korea.

North Korea.")[35] This may have meant some Soviet loss of control over North Korea; one of the strong points in Simmons' sometimes flawed book is the case he makes that the North Koreans jumped the gun by attacking in late June rather than late July or early August. The near absence of its forces certainly reduced the Soviet Union's risk in the short run, and the sizable amount of military aid seemed adequate to achieve the political purpose of Korean unification. At the same time, however, going to such lengths to avoid being implicated in the North Korean attack may have reduced the effectiveness of the Soviet armed forces as a deterrent to U.S. intervention without affecting Western perception of who was responsible for the war. (One of the most intriguing comments issuing from North Korea in the summer of 1950 was an article accusing Rhee of having attacked North Korea when he knew full well that "in the final analysis the U.S.A. would be blamed for the situation.")[36] It is ironic that the Soviet Union, by being relatively inconspicuous militarily and by seeming to signal that it would not intervene in Korea, may have made American leaders less fearful that American intervention would prompt a direct Soviet response. Those in the U.S. government charged with monitoring the Soviet press and radio, for instance, were probably not troubled by the threats implicit in a July 2 *Pravda* editorial stressing the need for even more signatures to the Stockholm Peace Appeal in light of American actions in Korea and in Moscow radio's announcement that the event of greatest significance in the week of June 25–July 2, 1950, was the collection of signatures in the Soviet Union for the Stockholm Peace Appeal.[37]

35. Generally, Stalin's penchant for control was as strong in the Korean case as elsewhere. Gasoline supplies, for instance, were reportedly kept down to one-month levels with reserves kept in the USSR, according to Whiting, *China Crosses the Yalu,* p. 43. This may have affected North Korea's chances of success, at least after the initial blitzkreig had failed, inasmuch as it left the DPRK short of bullets and other matériel.

36. At least this is what *Izvestiya* reported the North Korean newspaper *Mindchu Choson* as having said. *Izvestiya,* August 1, 1950 (in *CDSP,* vol. 2, no. 31, September 16, 1950, p. 15).

37. The *Pravda* editorial (which was monitored by FBIS, *Daily Report,* no. 128, July 3, 1950, p. AA16) read: "The Soviet people brand with indignation the open act of aggression committed by the American Government against Korea. All the peoples of the USSR, says the resolution of the plenary session of the Soviet Committee of Peace, have always warmly supported and are still supporting the efforts of the organized front of Peace Partisans aimed at the furthering of the cause of peace and against the incendiaries of a new war." The same issue of the *Daily Report* (pp. AA23–24) includes a Soviet Home Service report that "the most important

The American intervention prevented the attack by the North Korean army, using Soviet arms, from being successful and in a matter of months changed the military situation. As a result, the Soviet Union seemed about to witness the collapse of a socialist state—to be replaced by a pro-American, unified Republic of Korea on its border. It was torn between writing off a bad venture, encouraging the Chinese to intervene, substantially augmenting its overt contribution to the war effort, and reacting to pressure from its ostensibly docile client state, the Democratic People's Republic of Korea.

The Soviet Union Fails to Cross the Tumen

The initial Soviet efforts to regain a modicum of control over the deteriorating situation came in July 1950 and were diplomatic in nature. Stalin responded favorably to Jawaharlal Nehru's mid-July proposal to negotiate an end to the war. The Soviet media in fact went so far as to publish a quotation from the *Washington Post* characterizing the North Korean action as aggression in order to highlight the USSR's enthusiasm for a settlement. The *Washington Post, Izvestiya* observed, "admits that *'Stalin would use his influence to end the aggression in South Korea.'* "[38]

Soviet diplomatic moves at this juncture must at best be classified as temporizing. U.S. leaders felt that a minimum condition for a negotiated settlement was a restoration of the prewar status quo, as the Soviet press acknowledged: "The real aspirations of the U.S.A. [are] . . . to create 'realistic conditions' for settlement of the Korean question. These 'realistic conditions' . . . consist of Truman's impending messages to Congress, in which he will request special allocations of dollars and manpower to make it possible for him 'to carry out his mission to the end.' "[39]

---

event which has had great influence on the international situation during the last week is the collection of signatures for the Stockholm Peace Appeal which has started in the Soviet Union. This campaign for the collection of signatures in the Soviet Union links the ranks of the supporters of peace still more closely and is yet another telling blow against the warmongers' plans and their anti-Soviet propaganda. They no longer limit themselves to preparations for aggression. They have committed direct acts of aggression. And in this connection I want to continue with the second international event. I have in mind the events in Korea."

38. Article signed "Reviewer," *Pravda,* July 23, 1950 (in *CDSP,* vol. 2, no. 30, September 9, 1950, p. 6); emphasis added.

39. "Reviewer," *Pravda,* July 23, 1950. The internal quotations are purportedly from an Agence France Presse correspondent.

In fact, the prevailing mood in July 1950 in Washington (though not, for instance, in London) favored an advance beyond the 38th parallel. George Kennan was, by his account, a member of the minority: "I made it clear as early as July 1950, in the internal discussions of our government, that I was opposed to any advance behind the 38th parallel." In August Kennan stated his belief that a change in the military situation favoring the United States, especially the crossing of the 38th parallel, would produce a Russian response:

When the tide of battle begins to change, the Kremlin will not wait for us to reach the 38th parallel before taking action. When we begin to have military successes, that will be the time to watch out. Anything may then happen—entry of Soviet forces, entry of Chinese Communist forces, new [pressures for a] UN settlement, or all three together. The Russians will not be inclined to sit by if our forces or United Nations forces . . . of any sort push the North Koreans beyond the 38th parallel again. . . . They may . . . reoccupy North Korea, or they might introduce other forces which would be nominally Chinese Communist forces . . . (goodness knows who would be really controlling them). . . . Obviously they are not going to leave the field free for us to sweep up the peninsula and place ourselves forty or fifty miles from Vladivostok.[40]

Kennan was, after a fashion, correct. According to Khrushchev, there was an initial temptation to write off North Korea: "At first, Stalin and [Chou En-lai] seemed to conclude it was fruitless for China to intervene."[41] By late August the Soviet Union and the People's Republic of China had agreed that the Chinese would use their troops in Korea if the North Korean position deteriorated further. (Chinese intervention was conditional on U.S. troops crossing the 38th parallel; this act prompted the famous midnight session between Chou and M. K. Panikkar, India's ambassador to the PRC, on October 2.)[42] Once again, however, as at the outset of the war, Soviet ground forces did not cross the Tumen, even as volunteers—not when South Korean forces crossed the 38th parallel on October 1, nor when American troops crossed the parallel on October 7, nor when the South Koreans approached the Yalu and the far north corner of North Korea, nor when the Americans advanced to the Yalu did Soviet troops "reoccupy North Korea." The forces that were introduced were not "nominally" Chinese Communist forces, they were Chinese Communist forces. No Soviet official disturbed Panikkar's sleep in October 1950.

40. George F. Kennan, *Memoirs: 1950–1963* (Little, Brown, 1972), pp. 23–24.
41. Khrushchev, *Khrushchev Remembers*, p. 371. Khrushchev did not witness the encounter between Stalin and Chou; rather, the Politburo seems to have been briefed.
42. Whiting, *China Crosses the Yalu*, pp. 108–09.

At this point, though, Soviet armed forces demonstrably did play a role. They served in Manchuria to back up Chinese troops and to deter American reprisals against China. The Soviet Union armed the Chinese troops, and Soviet air and antiaircraft forces were directly, if limitedly, involved in the fighting. It appears, moreover, that Chinese participation was conditioned on such Soviet commitments. It was not simply that "Mao yielded to Soviet pressure";[43] rather, it seems that the Soviet Union took several steps that reduced the risk for the Chinese and that these steps were in some way related to the February 14, 1950, Sino-Soviet treaty of alliance. The instruments of ratification for that treaty were exchanged September 30, 1950;[44] it seems a reasonable assumption that by that date Chinese and Soviet leaders had a fairly explicit understanding of what each country would do in various eventualities. Whiting speculates that the treaty "offered a firm guarantee of all out Russian support should the U.S. attack mainland China in response to PRC intervention in Korea."[45]

At any rate, the Soviet Union did more in the fall of 1950 than merely provide armaments to go along with Chinese manpower. In fact, Moscow initially provided rather meager amounts of weaponry to the Chinese "volunteers," which has led to speculation that Soviet aid to the Chinese was deliberately inadequate.[46] Whiting's construction of the chronology makes such speculation seem as if the Vietnam War and the Sino-Soviet split of the 1960s and 1970s were imposed on the Korean War of the early 1950s: the combination of the timing of an agreement, the probable conditions of Chinese involvement, and the necessity for training People's Liberation Army units to handle Soviet weapons probably explains the Soviet Union's failure to equip the Chinese in any way similar to what it had done for the North Koreans before June 1950.

A reasonably good picture of the extent to which Soviet personnel were involved in the direct conduct of the war has emerged.[47] If the role

43. Vladimir Petrov, "The Soviets and World Communism," in O. B. Borisov and B. T. Koloskov, *Soviet-Chinese Relations, 1945–70* (Indiana University Press, 1975), p. 28.
44. Simmons, *Strained Alliance*, p. 158.
45. Whiting, *China Crosses the Yalu*, p. 90.
46. Simmons, *Strained Alliance*, p. 181.
47. It should be stressed that "Soviet personnel"and "Korean troops" are not completely exclusive categories. "Soviet Russian" and "DPRK Korean" are physically distinguishable but Soviet Koreans in the sense of, first, an ethnic Korean citizen of the Soviet Union and, second, a former Soviet citizen of Korean extraction who had become a Korean citizen are not.

of Soviet advisers is ignored, the first clear-cut direct encounter occurred October 8—a day after American troops had crossed the 38th parallel—when two U.S. F-80s strafed a Soviet airfield eighteen miles southwest of Vladivostok and sixty miles north of the Soviet-Korean border.[48] The first occasion on which Soviet-built MIG-15s were used took place three weeks later when a sizable number of them crossed the Yalu from Manchuria. The MIG-15 was an infinitely better plane than anything the United States had in Korea until the F86-F Sabre Jet was introduced in 1952; the crack pilots who flew MIGs evidenced a "skill in maneuver [which] argued against their being Chinese in terms of the known capabilities of PLA pilots."[49]

During the remaining years of the war, several more incidents involved planes with Soviet pilots. In 1952, Futrell notes, "there was no longer any doubt that some of the . . . pilots were Russians. On July 4 a Sabre pilot pulled in close to a stricken MIG and observed that the enemy had a ruddy complexion and bushy eyebrows of light red." In November 1952 "unmarked but obviously Russian MIG-15s swarmed down from Vladivostok. A flight of three Panther jets engaged several MIGs . . . and shot one of them down. At General [Mark] Clark's recommendation, the Joint Chiefs of Staff agreed to make no public disclosure of the Navy's clash with the Russians."[50]

According to American intelligence estimates, which were accepted by the State Department's Office of Chinese Affairs, there were fifteen Soviet divisions in Manchuria in the fall of 1950 and "about 40,000 Soviet artillery troops 'attired in Chinese Communist uniforms' in the Yangshui Mountain area near Fengcheng."[51] Soviet writers tell us that "crack" Soviet "air divisions" were sent to the Chinese northeastern provinces; these "provided dependable air cover against enemy air attacks for the industrial centers in North Eastern China."[52] According to M. S.

48. The Soviet version of this incident is contained in the protest of the Soviet government that appeared in *Pravda,* October 10, 1950, and in the *New York Times* on the same day. The United States acknowledged later that the incident had taken place as a result of "navigation error and poor judgment" and informed the United Nations that the "commander of the Air Force group concerned [has] been relieved and appropriate steps have been taken with a view toward disciplinary action against the two pilots involved." *New York Times,* October 20, 1950.

49. Whiting, *China Crosses the Yalu,* p. 135.

50. Futrell, *United States Air Force in Korea,* pp. 477, 567.

51. U.S. Department of State, *Foreign Relations of the United States, 1950,* vol. 7: *Korea* (GPO, 1976), p. 1025.

52. Borisov and Koloskov, *Soviet-Chinese Relations,* p. 71.

Kapitsa, a Soviet diplomat with long experience in Chinese affairs, these Soviet planes "downed dozens of American planes."[53] And Futrell reports that while "in Mukden a 'Supreme Joint Headquarters' of Chinese and North Korean forces apparently served policy-making and administrative functions for the Communist air forces . . . an 'Allied Joint Headquarters' at Antung exercised day-by-day control of Red air activities over North Korea. The Antung center appeared to be managed by Chinese Communist officers, but an intelligence informant reported that it was actually run by Russian advisers who were present in the control room at all times."[54] In short, the Soviet air force was used to increase the cost to Americans, in lives and planes, of violating the Chinese sanctuary, and it probably supervised the air war over North Korea; and Chinese volunteers, acting (as a Soviet scholar recently described it) out of "both internationalist and nationalist considerations,"[55] ensured that the DPRK would continue to exist. Finally, Kapitsa maintains that the Soviet Union was committed to a bail-out operation in Korea if things got too bad: "In case of a worsening of the situation the USSR was prepared to send five divisions to render aid to the DPRK in rebuffing the aggression."[56]

In the fall of 1950 the Soviet Union made more explicit its threat to use force to deter further expansion of the war by the United States and the United Nations. "There were hot heads [in the United States] who recommended transferring the war onto the territory of the PRC," Kapitsa writes. "The USA could not but reckon on the presence of the mighty Sino-Soviet alliance."[57] He quite properly points to President Harry S. Truman's *Memoirs* as evidence that Truman was deterred: Truman believed that the United States must expect a Soviet response if it attacked China.

Thus the Soviet Union, by its actions, direct and threatened, helped set limits on the Korean conflict. Apparently it was committed to using its troops if necessary to avert certain outcomes. It was anxious to keep the United States out of northeastern China. Had American troops gone across the Yalu to China, Soviet troops would have crossed the Tumen in force. Stalin was evidently willing to sacrifice some Russian lives to

53. Mikhail S. Kapitsa, *KNR: dva desiatiletiia-dve politiki* (Moscow: Politizdat, 1969), p. 36.
54. Futrell, *United States Air Force in Korea,* p. 370.
55. Personal conversation.
56. Kapitsa, *KNR,* pp. 36–37.
57. Ibid., pp. 38–39.

reduce the danger that North Korea would collapse. After the front in Korea had been stabilized, the Soviet Union reintroduced enough military personnel into North Korea to affect the waging and the outcome of the war at very little risk to itself since the United States was no longer disposed to seek total victory in Korea. By September 1951, according to U.S. intelligence estimates, 20,000 to 25,000 Soviet troops were in North Korea, including roughly 5,000 ground air troops, a 5,000-man artillery division, 2,000 military advisers, and 1,500 engineers.[58] The effect was to reinforce the American disposition to settle for the restoration of the prewar status quo. Since the United States was deterred by its clash with the Chinese when American forces had approached the Yalu, there was almost no risk to Soviet security in implanting troops in North Korea *after* the front had stabilized. Moscow also seems to have understood the distinction between crossing a border to fight the United States to prevent the United States from unifying Korea and placing Soviet troops in North Korea to increase the cost and risk to the United States of an attempt to unify Korea. The former risk—the risk the Chinese took —Moscow *might* not have been willing to take, Kapitsa notwithstanding, had the Chinese intervention failed to prevent the UN forces from unifying Korea, even if it meant the collapse of a socialist country and a pro-American Korea on the Soviet border. The latter risk—analogous to placing American troops in Berlin as hostages—Moscow was willing to, and did, take. Ultimately, therefore, Soviet troops did cross the Tumen but only after the Chinese had crossed the Yalu, when the prospects that the war might again come close to the Soviet border had become remote.

Patron-Client Bargaining and Soviet Support for North Korea

Although the Soviet Union rendered a modicum of aid to the People's Republic of China and to the DPRK, there is much in the open record to suggest that it was determined to avoid entanglement in the conflict if at all possible and that the North Koreans mounted a vigorous campaign in the fall of 1950 to persuade the Soviet Union to increase its support of them. On October 19, while the North Koreans were fleeing north and after the Chinese had begun to cross the Yalu, Kim Il-Sung made a rather striking broadcast. He began by saying, "The Korean people [are] . . . receiving absolute support from the Soviet Union, the People's Republic

58. Simmons, *Strained Alliance,* p. 202.

of China and all democracies and progressives of the world." What is striking are the two examples given of such absolute support:

One of the examples for the world wide support to the Korean people is the medical mission from Hungary. Another support comes from the Chinese people; we, the Korean people will never forget the warm support of the Chinese people delivered by the People's Delegation on the occasion of the second anniversary of our Republic. Premier Chou En-lai also declared that China cannot remain indifferent at the invasion of the Democratic People's Republic of Korea.[59]

Doubtless some listeners wondered whether Kim had intentionally omitted a Soviet example.

If so, it might have been partly a result of the chilly letter he had received from Stalin a week before in response to a fawning cable sent by Kim. (In mid-October 1950 North Korean leaders were unlikely to have stood on ceremony.) The cable from Kim had stated in part:

The Korean people are ardently grateful for the U.S.S.R.'s constant, friendly support of our people in the struggle for the unification and independence of our motherland.

Thanks to the disinterested aid shown us by the U.S.S.R. in accord with the agreement on economic and cultural cooperation concluded in March, 1950, between the two countries, the Korean people have achieved huge success in the development of our Republic.

The U.S.S.R.'s foreign policy, which invariably fights for democracy, freedom and the independence of large and small nations, is strengthening in our people the belief in a triumphant conclusion to the sacred war of liberation against the American interventionists and their lackey—the treacherous Syngman Rhee clique.

We know that in this war the support and sympathy of the peace-loving nations of the whole world, headed by the great U.S.S.R., are on the side of the Korean people.[60]

Stalin's response was terse at best and probably rude. It was addressed to Mister (gospodin)—not Comrade—Kim Il-Sung. After thanking Kim for the "kind sentiments and good wishes" he had conveyed, Stalin stated: "I wish the Korean people, heroically defending the independence of their country, a successful conclusion to their struggle of many years' duration for the creation of a united, independent and democratic Korea."[61] Utterances such as these have generated, over the years, cynicism about the Soviet commitment to proletarian internationalism.

59. FBIS, *Daily Report,* no. 205 (October 20, 1950), pp. BB1, BBB1.
60. *Pravda,* October 12, 1950 (in *CDSP,* vol. 2, no. 38, November 4, 1950, pp. 21, 55).
61. Ibid., p. 55.

There were further pointed remarks from the Soviet side. On October 31, 1950, broadcasting from Khabarovsk *in Korean,* Soviet radio took the occasion to describe to its listeners what was happening in Vietnam. At a time when North Koreans desperately needed Soviet aid, one can readily imagine how discomforting it was for the North Koreans, their backs against the Yalu, to hear the conclusion of the Soviet broadcast:

The Vietnam People's Army has made the imperialist American and French rulers angry. *The imperialist American Government has announced that they are going to send planes, tanks, cannons, and other equipment from Korea to the Vietnam French forces.* They are going to set up a second brutal action in Vietnam and they are disturbed by the Vietnam people's victory. The People's Army victory has struck a blow against the imperialist American and French colonialists.

All of the democratic nations support and sympathize with the Vietnam people's forces.[62]

Remarks such as these must have made the North Koreans rather nervous about the steadfastness of Soviet support. On the anniversary of the Russian revolution, the North Korean leaders were probably trying to reassure themselves as much as their supporters. In a commentary bravely titled "The Victory of the Great Socialist Revolution of Russia Is a Victory in the Campaign for the Liberation of Small Nations," they noted that "the Korean people were liberated from the colonial yoke of the Japan bandits through the precious blood shed by the brave officers and men of the Soviet Armed Forces. Today the American imperialists are making every effort to deprive us of the happiness gained at the cost of the blood of the Soviet people." Consequently, the North Koreans asked, *"How could the great Soviet people . . . and peace loving peoples of the world sit back and do nothing about the brutal atrocities of the American imperialists, who are bent on aggression in Korea?"*[63]

The Soviet Union, it turned out, was going to do something (and the PRC much more). The degree of commitment and of risk would be carefully controlled; certainly Soviet leaders were not going to be pressured either by the North Koreans into extensive and risky support of North Korea or by anyone into diversionary actions elsewhere that might

62. FBIS, *Daily Report,* no. 215 (November 3, 1950), p. CC5; emphasis added. According to a defector, Vice Minister of Defense Kim Il "had complained about Soviet unwillingness to supply more planes, which had rendered North Korea defenseless against American bombing." Joungwon A. Kim, *Divided Korea: The Politics of Development, 1945–1972* (Harvard University Press, 1975), p. 178.

63. FBIS, *Daily Report,* Supplement Korea, no. 220 (November 6, 1950), p. PPP14; emphasis added.

prompt a vigorous response from the United States.[64] By its unwillingness
to risk its own forces in June 1950, the Soviet Union had contributed to
the failure of the North Korean effort to unify Korea—a failure that had
threatened the existence of the North Korean regime. Still, there was
little point in compounding the blunder, which at least entailed no risk
for the Soviet Union, by putting Soviet troops on the line in the fall of
1950 at very great risk. Far better to take a chance on the survival of
the DPRK—after all, the Americans were already on the Soviet borders
in Iran and Turkey—and to use Soviet armed force in more efficacious
and less risky ways as a deterrent in China and ultimately as a deterrent
in North Korea well removed from the battle.

Soviet Armed Forces and the Vietnam War

The relevant events preceding the Soviet responses to U.S. reprisals
against North Vietnam for the Tonkin Gulf incidents (August 1964)
and the Vietcong's attack on Pleiku (February 1965) date back to
1960–61. In those years Sino-Soviet doctrinal differences about national
liberation wars became manifest, first at the 1960 meeting of the eighty-
one Communist parties and then in Nikita Khrushchev's famous January 1961 *Kommunist* article. Khrushchev's position was that Soviet
nuclear might was sufficient to deter the "export of counter-revolution"
and that revolution in individual countries could therefore proceed apace
without interference from the outside. Fearful of the risks of escalation,
Khrushchev put forth a plausible and attractive rationalization for a
policy that did not involve large amounts of military aid, much less large
deployments of Soviet troops abroad, to foreign Communists engaged in
waging national liberation wars—namely, the Vietnamese.

At the same time, however, the Soviet Union had become modestly
involved in Indochina, specifically in Laos, where Soviet transport aircraft flew almost 200 missions in the last half of December 1960.[65] This
spilled over into South Vietnam: "In the spring of 1961, Soviet transports began airlifting military supplies to Tchepong, a town twenty miles

---

64. The Chinese may have wondered why Moscow did not undertake such a
move. For instance, a November 21, 1950, broadcast from Peking quoted Omar
Bradley as having said the United States was "left without an adequate margin of
military strength with which to face the enemy at any other specific point." FBIS,
Daily Report, no. 228 (November 22, 1950), p. AAA1.

65. Zagoria, *Vietnam Triangle,* p. 42.

from the Vietnam border in eastern Laos believed to be a major base of operations for the Vietcong."[66]

Where the Soviet Union did not play a significant role in 1960–63 was in providing military assistance to North Vietnam. Rosser states that the North Vietnamese specifically asked the Soviet Union for increased military assistance and that this produced a worsening of Soviet-Vietnamese relations.[67] The occasion for the Soviet evaluation of the request, his argument runs, was December 1962, when General Pavel Batov, chief of staff of the Warsaw Pact countries, visited North Vietnam. During a January 1963 visit, party secretary Yuri V. Andropov delivered the rejection of the request. The timing of the North Vietnamese request was presumably not propitious: in the aftermath of the October 1962 Cuban missile crisis and the Sino-Indian border clash, there was little disposition in Moscow to encourage adventurism.

In any event, Soviet-Vietnamese relations worsened in 1963–64, and Vietnamese ties with the People's Republic of China improved. The North Vietnamese were consequently not counting on Soviet support should the United States decide to escalate its role in Vietnam to one involving overt operations, bombings in particular, against North Vietnam. In February 1964 it seemed likely that the United States would decide to undertake such measures. The Vietnamese assessment of Soviet policy seems to have been well founded, even though Moscow's response to the increasing evidence of a propensity in Washington to escalate the war conveyed a willingness to assist North Vietnam if the United States should attack: on February 25, 1964, in a statement by Tass, the Soviet Union promised to render the Vietnamese national liberation struggle the "necessary assistance and support" and declared that "the Soviet people cannot remain indifferent to escalatory events in Vietnam."[68] But the Vietnamese media conveyed the distinct impression that the Soviet Union was proffering such "necessary assistance" *if* the United States attacked, not as a deterrent to such an attack; that the North Vietnamese were much less confident of Soviet nuclear strength as a deterrent to the United States than were Soviet leaders; and that Soviet assistance came with too many strings—Moscow, in particular, appears to have insisted that Vietnam side with the USSR against the People's Republic of China. In a

66. Richard Rosser, "The Soviets and Vietnam: A Tragic Miscalculation?" *South Atlantic Quarterly,* vol. 72 (Summer 1973), p. 392.

67. Ibid., p. 393.

68. *Pravda,* February 26, 1964.

June 1964 article in *Hoc Tap* Vice-Premier Pham Hung insisted that "to insure the defense capability of the socialist camp it is imperative to strengthen the defense capability of all socialist countries and not just one country" and criticized potential donors for employing aid "as means of compelling others to abandon their independent political stand."[69]

The record indicates that the North Vietnamese knew whereof they spoke. In 1964 the importance the USSR attached to Southeast Asia, never high, seemed to dwindle still further. Soviet deliveries of all kinds to North Vietnam decreased substantially—this in a year when *Hoc Tap* was affirming that "support for the international revolutionary movement by the countries in which socialism has achieved victory should cover all fields"[70]—from 51 million rubles in 1963 to 42.5 million rubles in 1964, the difference being largely accounted for by an 8-million-ruble "reduction in deliveries in machinery and equipment (from 30.6 to 22.3 million)."[71] And in June 1964 Khrushchev was prepared to have the USSR resign as cochairman of the permanent body of the International Control Commission for Laos and evidently to extricate the USSR from Indochina.[72]

Despite these intimations, the Soviet Union did continue to accord Vietnam limited support. As Khrushchev said in July 1964, "we have more than once warned" the United States not to act as a "world gendarme" and "we support the people of South Vietnam" who "have every right to engage in [any] armed struggle . . . a sacred struggle for their freedom and independence."[73]

It is against this background that the Soviet reaction to U.S. actions against North Vietnam after the Tonkin Gulf incidents can be best understood: consonant with recent practice, the reaction was modest, vague, and verbal. A Tass statement of August 6 declared that "authoritative Soviet circles resolutely condemn the aggressive actions of the U.S.A.," characterized the incident as one that might result in "dangerous intensi-

69. As reported in *New York Times,* June 6, 1964.

70. Ibid.

71. Jukes, *Soviet Union in Asia,* p. 218.

72. Zagoria, *Vietnam Triangle,* p. 43. Zagoria also reports that *Pravda* on July 7, 1964, warned that should the Soviet Union's call for an international conference on Laos be received negatively by other states this "would place the Soviet government in a position in which it will feel compelled to review the question in general of whether the Soviet Union can carry out its functions as co-chairman."

73. *Pravda,* July 9, 1964 (in *CDSP,* vol. 16, no. 28, August 5, 1964, p. 4).

fication of the already tense situation," and asserted that "such actions, or further imprudent steps or provocations in this area can cause events capable of turning the incidents which have taken place into a widespread military conflict with all the dangerous consequences ensuing therefrom."[74] Two days later, on August 8, Khrushchev characterized the American actions as "aggressive" and "piratical." The operative paragraphs, however, contained little specific commitment. " 'Madmen' and 'semi-madmen' and other people, normal and abnormal" were warned. "The peoples," Khrushchev declared, ". . . are fighting and will continue to fight for their independence":

Should the imperialists thrust a war upon the socialist countries, the people of the Soviet Union will carry out their sacred duty. . . . The Soviet Union today has enormous military strength at its disposal and by relying on it we are able to labor and create in peace.

Directing all its forces into communist construction, the Soviet Union is following the behests of the great Lenin and is pursuing the sole correct path.[75]

Peking Review, rarely one to miss a trick, noted dryly that "neither the Tass statement nor that of Khrushchev referred to giving support to the just struggle of the D.R.V. against U.S. aggression."[76]

Two months after Tonkin, Nikita Khrushchev was a pensioner. His longtime associates, Leonid Brezhnev and Aleksei Kosygin, were first secretary (later general secretary) of the Communist Party of the Soviet Union (CPSU) and chairman of the Council of Ministers, respectively. The assertion that Khrushchev's ouster produced a change in Soviet behavior cannot be explicitly substantiated. Khrushchev might well have reacted to events—specifically, to the obvious indications in Washington after the election that the United States was moving toward a major escalation in Vietnam—as his successors did. Substantial documentation exists to suggest that in the months before and after Khrushchev's ouster

74. *Pravda,* August 6, 1964 (in *CDSP,* vol. 16, no. 32, September 2, 1964, p. 26).

75. *Pravda,* August 9, 1964 (in *CDSP,* vol. 16, no. 33, September 9, 1964, pp. 11, 12). The careful reader will have noted that the last two paragraphs in the text are probably best read as a reaffirmation of the previous Soviet position and a skillful rebuttal to critics: that the USSR's deterrent capacity was adequate, and there would be no increase in military aid to North Vietnam; and that the Soviet Union was directing "all its forces into communist construction"—"the sole correct path."

76. *Peking Review,* no. 33 (1964), p. 27. The *New York Times,* which has been known to miss a trick, headlined its report of Khrushchev's speech, "Khrushchev would go to war for Hanoi."

Soviet audiences were being prepared for a major reconciliation between the United States and the Soviet Union.[77] Much of the motivation, moreover, that apparently prompted a change in Soviet policy toward North Vietnam was characteristic of Khrushchev's policy as well: confidence that a political solution would ultimately produce a Communist victory in South Vietnam, interest in extricating the United States from Vietnam so that the USSR and the United States could address other problems, and a desire to maintain some presence in the Democratic Republic of Vietnam (DRV) as a counter to China.[78] At the same time, the new leaders probably perceived themselves as being under greater pressure than Khrushchev to demonstrate that the Soviet Union still supported revolutionary causes globally; and they were probably less fearful than Khrushchev that a modest American-Soviet confrontation in Vietnam would escalate.

What is clear is that there was a shift in Soviet signals toward the end of 1964. Tass on November 27 used the same phrases it had used in February—"cannot remain indifferent" and "render necessary assistance"—but it differed in that it expressed concern about "the fate of a fraternal socialist country."[79] Kosygin informed the Supreme Soviet in December that the USSR "will not remain indifferent" and declared it "is prepared to give . . . the necessary assistance, if the aggressors dare raise a hand against" the DRV,[80] a commitment conveyed that month by Brezhnev and Aleksandr Shelepin as well. Finally, on December 30, Andrei Gromyko affirmed Soviet arms assistance if "the aggressors dare to infringe upon [the DRV's] independence and sovereignty" and invoked "the principles of proletarian internationalism."[81]

Evidence of the new Soviet leadership's intention to follow through with assistance came in February as Kosygin headed a Soviet delegation to Hanoi whose main mission, presumably, was to concretize increased Soviet economic and military assistance. Plans by the United States to

77. In particular AN SSSR, *Dvizhushchie sily vneshnei politiki SShA* (Moscow: Nauka, 1965).

78. The new leaders differed from Khrushchev in that they were willing to attempt to repair relations with China.

79. *Pravda,* November 28, 1964. *Pentagon Papers,* vol. 3, p. 266, indicates that there was "a reported Soviet pledge in November to increase economic and military aid to North Vietnam."

80. *Pravda,* December 10, 1964 (in *CDSP,* vol. 16, no. 49, December 30, 1964, p. 12).

81. *Pravda,* January 5, 1965 (in *CDSP,* vol. 17, no. 1, January 27, 1965, p. 22).

undertake reprisals against North Vietnam were delayed in deference to Kosygin's visit for three reasons. First, it was feared that the reprisals "could be interpreted," the chairman of the Joint Chiefs of Staff wrote, "as a reaction to [the] visit, thereby impairing and complicating U.S.-Soviet relations." Second, American leaders had "the hope, if not expectation, that Kosygin would from the U.S. point of view, weigh in constructively in the Vietnam struggle." Third, "the Soviet Union [was] the only alternative source of economic and military support to Hanoi" other than China.[82] However, on February 7, the day after Kosygin's arrival in Hanoi, the Vietcong, in what was probably a deliberate provocation, attacked the U.S. barracks at Pleiku and a helicopter base at nearby Camp Holloway. The Americans, who were itching for an opportunity to launch Operation Flaming Dart, proceeded to bomb the southern regions of the DRV during Kosygin's visit.

The overt Soviet reaction, while restrained, was considerably more specific than it had been at any time in 1964. Kosygin, in a speech in Hanoi on February 9, continued to use such phrases as "necessary assistance" and to assert that "peace is an ally of socialism." He explained that during his trip "ways will be outlined for the future expansion of cooperation along economic, political, cultural, *and other lines*."[83] The Soviet government in *Pravda* made explicit the operative definition of "other" on February 9: "In the face of the above mentioned actions by the U.S.A., the Soviet Union, together with its allies and friends, will be forced to take further measures to guard the security and strengthen *the defense capacity* of the Democratic Republic of Vietnam. Let no one have any doubts that the Soviet Union will do this, that the Soviet people will fulfill their internationalist duty with respect to a fraternal socialist country."[84]

In mid-1964, the Soviet Union was on the verge of extricating itself from Southeast Asia. Soviet military advisers were playing a decreasing role in Indochina generally and in Vietnam especially. Soviet military personnel in Vietnam (although I have no explicit figures from open sources) must have numbered well under a thousand. Weapons transfers were being reduced, and the Soviet effort to deter the United States relied on noncredible hortatory remarks and the Soviet nuclear arsenal.

According to the Chinese (and they are apparently correct), the Soviet

82. *Pentagon Papers*, vol. 3, pp. 301, 302.
83. *Pravda*, February 9, 1965 (in *CDSP*, vol. 17, no. 6, March 3, 1965, pp. 5, 6).
84. Ibid., p. 7.

leaders set out in January–February 1965 to use their military aid to get some control over events in Vietnam. They "have ulterior motives in giving a certain amount of aid—they are trying to hoodwink the people at home and abroad, to keep the situation in Vietnam under their control, to gain a say on the Vietnam question and to strike a bargain with U.S. imperialism on it."[85]

The bargain evidently entailed a negotiated settlement that would (as Kosygin is supposed to have told the Chinese when he passed through Peking on his visit to North Vietnam, in February 1965) help the United States "find a way out of Vietnam"[86] and at the same time reactivate the Sino-Soviet alliance. Instead, Pleiku produced a situation in which the USSR found itself using its armed forces for political purposes—on a far more modest and less risky scale than the United States, to be sure— paralleling one of the U.S. reasons for intervention in Vietnam. The USSR, that is, felt it had to demonstrate the credibility of its commitment —that it was a "strong" and *"reliable"* friend of small socialist states.[87] In this instance, the small socialist state may have manipulated the Soviet Union so that Soviet military power served the political purposes of the smaller state as much as those of the Soviet Union. Bipolarity among socialist states may have created a straddle point at which small (socialist) states could encourage the great (socialist) powers to compete in providing war matériel, some personnel, and enhanced deterrent capabilities.

After February 1965 the bombing of North Vietnam became a central feature of the general effort by the Americans to stop "the Communist aggression" rather than a response to particular incidents. The American escalation—U.S. troops in South Vietnam and increased air strikes— continued until March 1968. The war itself dragged on for the United States until January 1973, although the United States gradually disengaged itself after President Johnson's March 31, 1968, speech. The Soviet contribution to the North Vietnamese war effort by and large paralleled that of the United States to South Vietnam but on a much smaller scale, involving far less risk-taking than U.S. actions but representing roughly two-thirds of the total foreign assistance to North Vietnam.

Focusing on Soviet media utterances makes it readily apparent that

85. *Peking Review,* no. 46 (1965), p. 16.
86. Ibid., p. 15.
87. *Pravda,* February 9, 1965 (in *CDSP,* vol. 17, no. 6, March 3, 1965, p. 7); emphasis added.

Moscow was intent on convincing external and domestic audiences that the Soviet Union would match the United States step for step, though Soviet leaders preferred to climb shorter steps. In 1964 Moscow's themes had been that "it would not remain indifferent" and that it would take "necessary measures" (unspecified). In 1965–67 it stated that it was taking *"practical* measures . . . to strengthen the security and build up the defense capability" of the DRV or, in Brezhnev's words, to provide "real support."[88] Such phrases were generally coupled with declarations that the USSR would compete with the United States by matching U.S. escalation. "The Soviet Union is prepared to give the Democratic Republic of Vietnam whatever assistance it needs. . . . We have not been and will not be found wanting in this regard."[89] "The Soviet Union has given and will continue to give fraternal Vietnam its full political support and the necessary economic and military aid" (Dmitri S. Polyansky).[90] "The Soviet Union has given, is giving, and will continue to give the Vietnamese people all-round support and aid" (Supreme Soviet).[91] "The U.S. ruling circles must realize that new steps to expand the war will inevitably call forth correspondingly more efforts by the Vietnamese people and the countries friendly to them. . . . The Soviet Union has given and will give all-round aid" (Nikolai Podgorny).[92]

There was some indication, moreover, that there was a kind of competition in risk-taking going on among the Soviet elite, which relates to differences in opinion about whether the U.S. actions in Vietnam were part of an overall confrontation between the forces of imperialism and revolution or a relatively separable phenomenon. For those like Shelepin and Marshal Rodion Malinovsky, both of whom characterized the United States as "worse than Hitler," the war in Vietnam was not an isolated event but evidence that the United States confronted Soviet interests in revolution in every corner of the globe. However, the core political leadership—Brezhnev, Kosygin, Podgorny—spoke as though they regarded Vietnam as a more or less isolated event. One evidence of this difference

88. E. Primakov, *Pravda,* March 15, 1965 (in *CDSP,* vol. 16, no. 11, April 7, 1965, p. 23), and Brezhnev's speech in Warsaw, *Pravda,* April 9, 1965 (in *CDSP,* vol. 17, no. 14, April 28, 1965, p. 11).

89. *Pravda,* April 9, 1965 (in *CDSP,* vol. 17, no. 14, April 28, 1965, p. 11).

90. *Pravda,* November 7, 1965 (in *CDSP,* vol. 17, no. 44, November 24, 1965, p. 7).

91. *Pravda,* December 10, 1965 (in *CDSP,* vol. 17, no. 51, January 12, 1966, p. 7).

92. *Pravda,* March 10, 1967 (in *CDSP,* vol. 19, no. 10, March 29, 1967, p. 4).

in view showed up in late 1966 when *Izvestiya* censored a speech by Shelepin in such a way as to bring his position more in line with the prevailing Soviet stance. The speech as published by *Red Star* (the army newspaper) describes the worsening international situation in 1966 as a consequence of a general confrontation of imperialist and revolutionary forces:

As a result of the intensification of the aggressive schemes of the imperialists, a serious aggravation of the world situation has taken place. *World reaction, headed by the main force of war and aggression—American imperialism— now here, now there kindles the hotbeds of conflict. The imperialists in a number of regions are striving to restore by force the colonial order, to stifle the national liberation movement of the people.* The U.S.A. has been waging for several years now a plundering, colonial war against the peoples of Vietnam.[93]

Izvestiya, on the other hand, by omitting the italicized words in the above text, seemed to suggest that the primary reason for the aggravated international situation was the war in Vietnam. Whether Vietnam was a relatively separable problem or a clash of the forces of imperialism and revolution led to some differences in policy formulation by Soviet leaders about the magnitude of future commitments to the Democratic Republic of Vietnam. Shelepin declared in August 1965 that the Soviet Union would provide "necessary and ever-increasing assistance"[94] to the DRV at a time when others in the leadership were merely pledging the support deemed necessary.

It certainly was the case that *non-Soviet* Communist elite groups were willing to let the Soviet Union take greater risks. The Chinese responded to Soviet criticism about difficulties in shipping aid across China by pointing out that "besides ground and air communications there are sea routes to link various countries in the world."[95] The Cubans similarly had the indelicacy to use the occasion of the CPSU's Twenty-third Congress in 1966 to advise the Soviet leadership:

Considering the situation that has arisen in connection with the war in Vietnam, it is necessary to establish a military force capable of stopping the bombings of the Democratic Republic of Vietnam, that is, capable of putting the American planes that bomb Vietnamese territory out of action. For victory over imperialism in Vietnam, it is of decisive importance, using all available means and taking the necessary risk, to halt the criminal aggression, which is what the bombing of the Democratic Republic of Vietnam constitutes. It is

93. *Krasnaya Zvezda* and *Izvestiya,* December 10, 1966; emphasis added.
94. *Pravda,* August 18, 1965 (in *CDSP,* vol. 17, no. 33, September 8, 1965, p. 8).
95. *Peking Review,* no. 19 (1965), p. 26. In fact, the USSR after 1967 used the sea as the major means of conveying its aid to Vietnam.

Table 8-1. *Soviet and Chinese Military Aid to the Democratic Republic of Vietnam*
Millions of U.S. dollars

Year	USSR	China
1965	210	60
1966	360	95
1967	505	145
1968	209	100
1969	120	105
1970	75	90
1971	100	75
Total	1,660	670

Source: International Institute for Strategic Studies, *Strategic Survey, 1972* (London: IISS, 1972), p. 50.

necessary to make the utmost effort and to render decisive assistance in order to turn the territory of the Democratic Republic of Vietnam into a "graveyard of American aircraft."[96]

While in general the speech of the Cuban delegate, Armando Hart Davalos, was enthusiastically received by the Soviet Congress audience, his advice on risk-taking and rendering sufficient antiaircraft aid to deter U.S. B-52s received no applause. (No B-52s were shot down until December 1972.)

The Vietnamese, however, did receive other forms of military aid, including antiaircraft missiles, batteries, and planes, as the Soviet leadership made plausible its argument that fidelity to proletarian internationalism (that is, countering the Chinese challenge) consisted in providing concrete assistance, in which the USSR naturally had a comparative advantage, not ideological fervor. Table 8-1 summarizes the estimates of the International Institute for Strategic Studies (IISS) of Soviet and Chinese military aid to Vietnam from 1965 to 1971. The Soviet figures were apparently derived from the official exchange rate, which at that time was one ruble to $1.11; in other IISS calculations, Soviet defense expenditures are estimated at 0.40–0.50 ruble to one dollar, implying that the figures should be doubled. (The usual estimate of U.S. expenditures for the Vietnam War is about $112 billion.)

96. *Pravda*, April 2, 1966 (in *CDSP*, vol. 18, no. 15, May 4, 1966, p. 19). The author happened to be in the Soviet Union during the Twenty-third Congress. I well remember a conversation with a senior specialist in the Institute of World Economics and International Relations during which I was asked whether I had read what that "lunatic Cuban" had said at the Twenty-third Congress.

As early as April 5, 1965, U.S. intelligence found evidence of the first SA-2 SAM site under construction. According to the *Pentagon Papers,* "the SAM's were only the most dramatic form of considerably increased quantities of modern military equipment beginning to be furnished to the DRV by the Soviet Union."[97] MIG-17s were sighted in June 1965.[98] In April 1966 the first announced use of MIG-21s occurred in the war,[99] and in May Soviet "Shyster" missiles with a range of 750 miles—Saigon and Hanoi are roughly 700 miles apart—were reported as having been seen by neutral observers in the Hanoi area.[100] By summer 1966 the Soviet Union was publicizing its role in training Vietnamese pilots to fly the MIG-21s.[101] By fall American intelligence was estimating the presence of 130 SAM sites in North Vietnam[102] and disagreeing about whether there were 5,000 or 7,000 antiaircraft batteries in North Vietnam. "One highly placed [U.S.] source" described the Vietnamese defense as "the most advanced that American pilots have ever faced. Indications are the system will be further elaborated and strengthened."[103]

Soviet military personnel were also made available. In March 1965 Brezhnev even floated the possibility of Soviet volunteers going to Vietnam: "Our central agencies are receiving many declarations from Soviet people expressing readiness to take part in the Vietnamese people's struggle for freedom and independence."[104] In April 1965 a carefully phrased Soviet-North Vietnamese declaration was issued which declared: "The Soviet government, if need be and if the DRV government so requests, will give its consent to the departure for Vietnam of Soviet citizens who, guided by a sense of proletarian internationalism, have expressed the desire to fight for the just cause of the Vietnamese people."[105] (The Chinese in March 1965 charged that "the Soviet leaders proposed that

97. *Pentagon Papers,* vol. 3, p. 365.

98. *New York Times,* June 25, 1965. I do not know whether these were built by the Russians or the Chinese.

99. Ibid., April 25, 1966. "Air Force officials" were reported as not knowing "to whom the MIG 21s belonged although they presumed the fighters were North Vietnamese Air Force planes."

100. Ibid., May 20, 1966, reporting an article appearing in *Aviation Week and Space Technology.*

101. *Pravda,* August 28, 1966 (in *CDSP,* vol. 18, no. 35, September 21, 1966, p. 20). See also *New York Times,* August 29 and 30, 1966.

102. *New York Times,* October 4, 1966.

103. Ibid., September 28, 1966.

104. *Pravda,* March 24, 1965 (in *CDSP,* vol. 17, no. 12, April 14, 1965, p. 16).

105. *Pravda,* April 18, 1965 (in *CDSP,* vol. 16, no. 16, May 12, 1965, p. 13).

China permit transit of 4,000 army personnel to Vietnam without first obtaining her [Vietnam's] consent" and that China should let the Soviet Union "occupy and use one or two airfields in Southwestern China and station a Soviet armed force of 500 men there."[106]

Exactly how many Soviet military and civilian advisers were in Vietnam is impossible to determine. *Za rubezhom* in December 1968 reported that about 3,000 experts were helping "in various fields of the national economy and the defense of Vietnam";[107] but estimates for 1968–72 by the International Institute of Strategic Studies in *Military Balance* use the figure 1,000 (versus 21,000 in Egypt according to Heikal) as the number of Soviet military personnel in Vietnam.[108] Whatever the number, they played an important part in managing SAM sites, especially, it seems, in 1965–66. (Presumably, North Vietnamese cadres later played a larger part.) Max Frankel reported in August 1965 that "from radio interceptions, ground espionage, aerial reconnaissance and deductions from other known facts, most, if not all, the missiles are believed to be under Soviet management."[109]

Initially, Soviet sources, as part of a tacit agreement between Moscow and Washington, gave no indication that Soviet citizens were playing an active role, but in October 1966 *Krasnaya Zvezda,* the Soviet army newspaper, described the putative advisory role Soviet missile specialists were playing under fire. American military intelligence sources, however, asserted that "Soviet advisers were helping the North Vietnamese to coordinate the radio network that ties the antiaircraft system together under a central command."[110] Whatever their exact role, it is difficult not to conclude that Soviet military personnel were in North Vietnam and actively involved in ground-to-air combat against the United States in the three years from February 1965 until the bombing halt in 1968.

The central purpose of the Soviet involvement in the escalation seems to have been straightforward: to deter the United States from actions that would threaten the DRV's existence and to prevent the United States from attacking Hanoi and Haiphong. The latter limited goal the USSR could achieve with 1,000–3,000 Soviet personnel. There can be no doubt

106. Hannes Adomeit, "Soviet Risk-Taking and Crisis Behavior: From Confrontation to Coexistence?" *Adelphi Papers,* no. 101 (London: International Institute for Strategic Studies, 1973), p. 12.

107. As reported in *New York Times,* December 15, 1968.

108. Mohamed Heikal, *The Road to Ramadan* (Ballantine, 1975), pp. 177–78.

109. *New York Times,* August 27, 1965.

110. Ibid., October 4, 1966.

that the USSR had some success in deterring U.S. actions. The *Pentagon Papers,* for instance, are replete with evidence that concern about the possible Soviet response to U.S. escalatory steps affected American calculations and resulted in options being precluded and forces being deployed in less than optimal ways.[111]

The deterrent role of the Soviet armed forces was created in several ways. Obviously, American cost estimates were influenced. More subtly, by making public in the Soviet media such actions as the presence of Soviet technicians at missile sites, Moscow made its commitment manifest by yielding the initiative and leaving the choices to U.S. leaders, who could easily imagine the possible consequences of killing dozens or hundreds of Soviet citizens. (A similar hostage role was played, evidently deliberately, by the Soviet merchant marine in Haiphong harbor.)

The biggest political gain the Soviet Union derived from its assistance to the DRV stemmed from the DRV leaders' open expressions of gratitude, which were quite appropriate since Soviet (and Chinese) aid more than offset the damage done to the DRV by the United States. This praise blunted the effectiveness of Chinese attacks on the USSR for "revisionism" and "collusion" with the United States, and allowed Moscow to claim correctly that a socialist country which really was advancing the revolution appreciated the assistance being rendered by the fraternal Soviet Union.

The Soviet Union made gains such as these at low risk and low cost. A large number of possible actions were never undertaken and, I suspect, never seriously entertained; there was no apparent disposition, for instance, to open a second front despite, or because of, Chinese pressure. A few highly visible low-cost actions were taken to show displeasure with American policy in Vietnam. (One such incident was the canceling of a Soviet-American track meet. The USSR ultimately reimbursed the Americans for revenue losses suffered.) Much of Soviet-American relations during the Vietnam War could be described as business as usual.

In war it is not necessarily true that what goes up must come down. In Vietnam, though, the level of the war did decrease after President Johnson halted the bombing north of the 20th parallel in March 1968. "Fighting while talking" was the pattern for four years. In 1972, however, Nixon's visits to China in February and to Moscow in May set in motion events that brought about an end to the war. As Adam Ulam remarks, "The

---

111. *Pentagon Papers,* especially vol. 4. As an example, the Seventh Fleet stayed offshore out of respect for the Styx missile (which had sunk the Israeli ship *Eilat*) although it is generally asserted that the Styx was not used in the war.

Chinese trip . . . accomplished what was undoubtedly in Washington leaders' minds its main objectives: an invitation to Moscow with its sequels, a prospect of a compromise settlement in Vietnam, and a number of important agreements between the United States and the USSR."[112]

North Vietnamese leaders were made uneasy by these events. Once again, as in 1954, the possibility loomed that the great powers might act in concert and undermine Vietnamese interests. The DRV's response was to launch a major attack directly across the anachronistically labeled demilitarized zone, which in turn prompted heavy U.S. bombing of North Vietnam. This time the United States bombed Hanoi and bombed and mined Haiphong. With a great deal at stake, the issue again was what role the Soviet armed forces would and did play.

It is doubtful, first of all, that Moscow encouraged the DRV to launch its attack across the boundary separating North and South Vietnam. Certainly there is no evidence for this of which I am aware. But several things are clear. The weapons, particularly the tanks, used by the North Vietnamese were primarily Soviet in origin. Moscow's overt response to American protests about its role in arming the North Vietnamese was scornful: V. Kudriavtsev, writing in *Izvestiya,* observed:

> The U.S.A. complains that the Vietnamese patriots are now "using heavy military equipment in battle," "blames" the Soviet Union for this, and uses this to "justify" the bombing of Hanoi and Haiphong. It is understandable that the American warriors would like it if their B-52 heavy bombers were opposed only by Vietnamese with rifles in their hands. It is even easier to fight against unarmed old men, women and children. [The Vietnamese Provisional Revolutionary Government], naturally and rightfully, sees to it that its fighting men, who are defending freedom, are well and effectively armed.[113]

Moreover, the North Vietnamese were equipped with much more modern weapons than they had been in 1965–68 and had enormous stockpiles of SA-2 missiles. "According to U.S. sources, 1,600 of the latter were fired against U.S. aircraft between April and July." "During the spring of 1972, two new missiles began to appear in the North and with the National Liberation Front in South Vietnam. These were the Sagger wire guided anti-tank missiles, and the shoulder-fired SA-7 Strela surface-to-air missile . . . which appears to have been highly effective against helicopters."[114]

112. Ulam, *Expansion and Coexistence,* p. 767.
113. *Izvestiya,* April 29, 1972 (excerpted in *CDSP,* vol. 24, no. 16, May 17, 1972, p. 6).
114. Stockholm International Peace Research Institute, *World Armaments and Disarmament* (SIPRI Yearbook 1973) (Stockholm: Almqvist and Wiksell, 1973), pp. 301, 302.

Finally, in this vein, the Soviet leadership was sufficiently concerned about North Vietnam's anxiety about the forthcoming Nixon visit to Moscow to dispatch a delegation headed by CPSU Secretary Konstantin Katushev, "in accordance with an agreement reached earlier," to discuss "the further development and strengthening of Soviet-Vietnamese relations as well as certain questions of mutual interest."[115]

At the same time Soviet leaders were not so concerned about events in Vietnam or the attitudes of the North Vietnamese leaders as to let the bombing of Hanoi or the bombing and mining of Haiphong harbor—or for that matter the damage to some Soviet merchant ships and the injuries to members of their crews—stand in the way of Nixon's visit to the USSR. The immediate Soviet response was almost entirely verbal. Moscow did resupply North Vietnam, with the result that in December 1972, when the last U.S. bombing spasm occurred, the North Vietnamese succeeded in downing B-52s for the first time in the war. Moreover, the American blockade and mining produced "the first Soviet naval reaction in the long history of U.S. operation in Southeast Asia." Submarines and six surface warships including a Sverdlov-class cruiser sailed "at a relatively slow transit speed" from Vladivostok to a place "some 300 miles from the principal operations of U.S. carriers." While Soviet intelligence-collection ships, which previously had often been present at U.S. naval activities off Vietnam, sailed among the American ships, the Soviet "reaction force remained at a distance of 300 miles until it departed in late June 1972."[116] In general, however, Soviet behavior reflected priorities in which minor wars on the periphery of Asia were peripheral as well to the strategy of those in Moscow calling the shots. To Soviet Politburo member Pyotr Shelest (who may have shared with East Germany's Walter Ulbricht a preference for rapprochement with China rather than improved East-West relations, and whose position as first secretary of the Ukraine probably disposed him to emphasize the development of coal rather than natural gas and oil) the idea of having Richard Nixon come to Moscow (and Kiev) immediately after the mining and blockade of Haiphong and the bombing of Hanoi may have been abhorrent; it probably was.[117] (Shelest

115. *Izvestiya,* May 1, 1972 (in *CDSP,* vol. 24, no. 17, May 24, 1972, p. 1).

116. Bradford Dismukes, "Soviet Employment of Naval Power for Political Purposes, 1962–75," in Michael MccGwire and John McDonnell, eds., *Soviet Naval Influence: Domestic and Foreign Dimensions* (Praeger, 1977), pp. 501–02.

117. My assessment of Shelest's reaction benefits from Grey Hodnett, "Ukrainian Politics and the Purge of Shelest," paper delivered at the annual meeting of the Midwest Slavic Conference, Ann Arbor, Michigan, May 5–7, 1977.

was removed from his post as first secretary of the Ukraine on May 25, the day before Nixon arrived in Kiev.) To Brezhnev and Kosygin, however, progress in the SALT negotiations and the prospect of explicit recognition that the Soviet Union's strategic forces had achieved parity with those of the United States, the prospect of a burgeoning trade with the United States, including American investment in the development of natural gas and oil deposits in Siberia, and the fear that the Nixon visit to Peking in February 1972 might lead to an adverse shift in the global distribution of power were far too important for them to show squeamishness about American behavior in Vietnam.

Conclusions

Superficially, the Korean and Vietnam wars have much in common. The actors were similar: the fighting involved the United States and a vigorously anti-Communist client state, on the one hand, and on the other, a Communist state bent on forcibly unifying the country. Though these wars are often portrayed as major episodes in the Soviet-American cold war, no direct confrontation of any scale between the United States and the Soviet Union took place. The locations were similar: each war took place on the periphery of Asia in countries bordering on China. Each war was limited. No nuclear weapons were used. Sanctuaries relevant to the delivery of military supplies were generally observed. No efforts were made to interfere with the shipment of weapons and material before their arrival in the country for which they were destined. Diversionary moves were not initiated elsewhere as a means of inhibiting the involvement of one or another state. Each war was terminated through a long process of talking while fighting. The Korean truce negotiations dragged on for two years; in Vietnam (where everything took longer) the negotiations lasted more than four years.

On the whole, however, the differences were more significant. The outcomes of the two wars were certainly different. The Korean War ended with the essential restoration of the status quo ante and seemed to establish the proposition that "export of revolution" across state boundaries would be countered by U.S. military action. The Vietnam War ended in the unification of the country under Communist leadership. In the process the point most clearly established seems to have been that a small state fighting a total war has considerable advantage over a superpower engaged in a war for limited goals. Other differences in the context and conduct of the war helped make more likely the particular, and different, outcomes. Far fewer viewed the United States' actions in Vietnam as legitimate than did its actions in Korea; the Rhee government in Korea was more capable of governing than the South Vietnamese governments; the jungles of Vietnam provided a physical environment conducive to guerrilla warfare; and the Vietcong was a much more effective force than the South Korean Communist guerrillas. Another difference between the style and conduct of the two wars arose from the simple fact that the Vietnam War took place (largely) after the Korean War, in which both the United States and the PRC had learned some lessons. The United States was much more mindful of Chinese signals and concern than it had been during the Korean War.[118] Also, it is worth remembering that the Soviet Union neither borders on Vietnam nor played a significant part in the founding of North Vietnam (whereas in North Korea the Soviet Union's role was crucial). Finally, in the Korean War the relation between the United States, China, and the USSR had been almost entirely a bipolar one between the United States and "the Sino-Soviet bloc," whereas the Vietnam War was fought against the backdrop of the Sino-Soviet split, which produced, to use the title of Donald Zagoria's book, a Vietnam Triangle.

One area where the similarities outweighed the differences, however, is the focus of this study: Soviet use of armed force as a political instrument. In Korea and Vietnam the Soviet Union provided the socialist state with weapons in support of that state's efforts to unify its two-state nation by force. One failed, the other succeeded. In both wars the Soviet leadership was disposed to let others do the fighting. The actual use of Soviet troops —as opposed to Soviet weapons—was quite restricted. In each instance only a few thousand Soviet troops were involved and they were employed primarily to deter and defend a socialist state against American bombing. (In the last months of the Korean War the number of Soviet troops in Korea may have reached 20,000.) In both Korea and Vietnam, the Soviet use of armed forces was largely, to use a phrase that gained some currency in the initial phase of U.S. involvement in Vietnam, "covert and deniable." Even when Soviet accounts described Soviet involvement in Vietnam, Soviet leaders could always maintain that their missile specialists were not actually involved in the fighting but were merely training the Vietnamese. What stands out in boldest relief is that, even when an effort was being

118. Allen S. Whiting, *The Chinese Calculus of Deterrence* (University of Michigan Press, 1975).

made to extend Communist power by force, the actions of the Soviet Union were quite limited and entailed low risk.

In this chapter I have concentrated on what actually happened. An awareness of the general Soviet propensity for low-risk undertakings is, however, probably heightened by reflecting on a number of instances in which advocated alternative courses of action were not pursued. At the outset of the Korean War, for instance, no Soviet troops were used, and Stalin had actually reduced their number in Korea before the war began. Khrushchev argued that with "one Soviet tank corps, or two at the most,"[119] the North Koreans would have gone all the way to Pusan before the United States could have responded. Khrushchev's policy might have worked. Stalin, to his credit, presumably understood the risk to the USSR of such a Soviet commitment; if the United States intervened and actually fought one or two Soviet tank corps, the prospects for escalation would be great indeed. In this instance the old refrain "Emu vidnee"—"It's clearer to him [Stalin]"—seems appropriate. Similarly, in the fall of 1950, the North Koreans apparently pressed the Soviet Union for greater aid than they actually received. Again, more aid would have helped North Korea attain its goals but at a risk to the Soviet Union that Stalin evidently considered unacceptable. There is nothing to suggest that the USSR under Stalin was ever disposed to provoke incidents elsewhere in an effort to weaken the U.S. capacity to act effectively in Korea, even though there is an occasional hint that the Chinese hoped for such moves.

In Vietnam, Khrushchev—his bluster about Stalin's behavior in Korea notwithstanding—pursued a policy of minimum commitment in 1963–64. As in Korea, the Soviet Union was reluctant to respond favorably to requests from a small ally for greater support in the conduct of the war. Instead the Soviet leadership under Khrushchev proposed to provide the requested support only on conditions that, in effect, required the North Vietnamese to divorce themselves from China. Although some shift in Soviet policy was detected after the October 1964 ouster of Khrushchev, only after the direct bombing of North Vietnam while Premier Kosygin was in Hanoi did Moscow furnish more support and reduce its conditions for that support. Throughout the years 1965–72 the USSR increased its support of North Vietnam as the United States increased its outlay for the war effort. The Soviet contribution, however, though of substantial assistance to the DRV, was minuscule compared with American expenditure on the war. Soviet assistance to Vietnam also fell short of that sought or

119. Khrushchev, *Khrushchev Remembers*, p. 370.

advocated by those, inside and outside the Soviet Union, who demanded a direct confrontation with the United States and a willingness to take risks. In Vietnam, as in Korea, the Soviet Union was not disposed to provoke incidents elsewhere to "tie down" American imperialism. No effort was made to interfere with American delivery of materials or men or to interdict the U.S. Navy's actions even during the bombing of Hanoi and the mining of Haiphong. These incidents did not even delay Nixon's visit to the Soviet Union, a course one presumes that Shelest and others advocated. Regardless of the many differences between Stalin, Khrushchev, and Brezhnev, all three in their decisions rejected the blandishments of those prone to greater Soviet risk-taking and greater willingness to use Soviet forces for political purposes. Brezhnev and Kosygin in 1972, moreover, made it as obvious as Khrushchev had in 1964 that improved relations with the United States were considerably more important than developments in Vietnam.

Despite the many similarities in the Soviet use of armed force in Korea and Vietnam, it is true that in one instance a Communist state, North Vietnam, succeeded in unifying the country, and in the other, a Communist state, North Korea, failed in the effort. Moreover, Soviet–North Korean relations more nearly approximated our image of modal Soviet-satellite relations than did Soviet–North Vietnamese relations. In drawing up a balance sheet on the effectiveness of the Soviet use of its armed forces as a political instrument, should it be concluded that the Soviet Union was more effective in Vietnam than in Korea? The foregoing summary of the differences between the two wars suggests the need for caution. The situations were radically different, and it does not necessarily follow that the divergent results indicate greater Soviet effectiveness in the Vietnam War than in the Korean War. Moreover, the part played by the USSR in both wars was sufficiently modest to raise doubt about whether the outcome of the wars is a reasonable indicator of the effectiveness of the Soviet use of force.

It might be better to evaluate effectiveness as the enhancement of state interests as some function of that state's resources expended. Viewed this way, the extremely modest role of Soviet armed forces in the two wars may be evidence of the effectiveness of the Soviet use of force for political purposes. If a state can get other states to do its fighting for it, after all, in a certain sense it is being almost optimally effective.

In Korea, for instance, there was a possibility that by merely providing weapons and limited air support the Soviet Union had done enough for the

North Koreans to unify Korea. Placing Soviet troops in Manchuria as a deterrent to American attack in exchange for having Chinese troops prevent the United States from unifying Korea represents an impressively effective use of Soviet armed force. Introducing Soviet troops into North Korea after the Americans had been driven back to the 38th parallel was also an effective political use of the troops—as hostages. Although these troops never engaged American forces, their presence ensured the continuation of socialism in North Korea by increasing the likelihood that the United States would not make a second attempt to go north.

In Vietnam, the USSR's use of force was also highly effective in some respects. The Soviet Union, and the People's Republic of China, substantially affected the conduct of the war because of American perception of what help would be given to North Vietnam if the United States took certain courses of action. It is difficult not to regard the Soviet provision of North Vietnam with weapons and "advisers" as having served its purpose. The Soviet Union's limited contribution to the North Vietnamese war effort did affect the outcome of the war. With almost no cost in Soviet lives, an expenditure by the USSR of at most one-thirtieth the annual amount of U.S. outlays in Vietnam went a long way toward offsetting the U.S. contribution. What several of the above examples suggest, in short, is the relevance to Soviet foreign policy of some old verities about the use of armed force for political purposes: its use is more likely to be effective in denying an opponent something than in coercing him to do something specific; and force is most effectively applied when it is not actually used.

A wider perspective on the effectiveness of Soviet actions in Korea and Vietnam produces additional insights. The reaction of the other actors in the Korean War forces a correction in the assessment of the Soviet use of armed forces as a political instrument. The Soviet effort to appear uninvolved, at the very beginning of the war, increased the likelihood that the United States would intervene and hence that the North Korean adventure would fail. The Soviet Union, nevertheless, did not succeed in persuading non-Communist leaders that it was not responsible for the North Korean invasion. As a result, the North Korean action made it possible for the U.S. administration to persuade Congress that an enormous increase in American military spending was necessary to counter the Soviet threat, and this greatly expanded the global military capabilities of the United States. And it appears that, if the Chinese had failed to stop the United States in North Korea in the fall of 1950, the Soviet Union might have acquiesced in the reunification of Korea rather than cross the Tumen to engage American forces. Certainly, despite North Korean pressure, the USSR set limits on the aid it would provide. The Soviet reluctance to engage in risk-taking and the modesty of the commitment forced the North Koreans to rely much more on their own devices. In an important sense, therefore, the Korean War and the Soviet use of force therein has to be seen as an important stimulus not only to the rearming of the United States but also to the emergence of a nonsatellite North Korea with a deliberately self-reliant ideology.

In Vietnam, the reaction of the other actors in the conflict affects but does not diminish one's view of the effectiveness with which the Soviet Union used its armed forces for political purposes. Soviet behavior had a significant effect on U.S. foreign policy. It may reasonably be speculated that, as Soviet support of Vietnam increased after 1965, the willingness of the United States to play the China card also increased. North Vietnam, in turn, had cause to appreciate both the importance and the fragility of Soviet support for its cause. Nevertheless, the results of the Vietnam War—the unification of Vietnam and the strengthened ties of socialist Vietnam with the Soviet Union—probably have reassured the Soviet elite about the wisdom of its course in Vietnam. The low-risk policy of a measured response to American acts was doubtless considered a success, which probably reinforced the Soviet Union's belief that it could engage profitably in other low-risk efforts on the periphery of Europe while continuing to attach primacy to the superpower relationship.

CHAPTER NINE

Crises on the Korean Peninsula

DONALD S. ZAGORIA *and* JANET D. ZAGORIA

AN ANALYSIS of Soviet behavior during the *Pueblo* crisis in 1968, the EC-121 crisis in 1969, and the poplar tree incident in 1976 shows clearly that Soviet support for North Korean initiatives has been cautious and declining. In the *Pueblo* crisis Soviet ships and planes trailed and harassed U.S. ships and Moscow gave strong public support to the North Korean position, but it was only after the threat of war had passed that the USSR brought its naval deployment up to task force size. In the EC-121 crisis the Soviet Union made a token military response, gave lukewarm political support to Pyongyang, and actively joined the United States in looking for survivors from the plane. After the poplar tree killings the Russians did virtually nothing to help Pyongyang. Indeed, they may have urged Kim Il-Sung to send a conciliatory message to the United States.

Soviet caution in these three incidents seems to have been guided by a number of factors. First, the Soviet Union has been unwilling to risk confrontation with the United States over North Korean interests, which were mainly, during the period under discussion, to oust the United States from South Korea and reunify Korea by force. Here the Soviet attitude is directly analogous to its lack of support for Chinese provocations during the Taiwan Strait crisis of 1958. In both situations, Moscow was simply not prepared to risk a military confrontation with the United States for local Communist goals.

Three other considerations have entered Soviet calculations about Korea: the unpredictability of North Korean leader Kim Il-Sung, North Korea's proximity to the Soviet Union, and Soviet fear of China. Kim has

357

never inspired great trust in Moscow. Relations between Moscow and Pyongyang during the 1960s and 1970s varied between cool and luke-warm. Moscow is clearly wary of becoming involved in a military situation in which Kim controls the degree of risk. Soviet caution is evident in all three incidents discussed here. In the case of the EC-121 crisis, Moscow went so far as to warn Pyongyang publicly about taking independent mili-tary initiatives against the United States that could involve the Russians.

Geographically, North Korea is situated uncomfortably close to the Soviet Union and, in particular, to Vladivostok and other points in the Soviet Far East where Russia's Pacific forces are based. This means that a U.S. military threat to North Korea automatically becomes a threat to the Soviet Union and to its military position in the Far East. North Korean initiatives have forced the Soviet Union to protect itself against the possi-bility of U.S. retaliatory action, as well as to avoid provoking the United States to such action. In the *Pueblo* and EC-121 incidents, therefore, as long as U.S. military action seemed possible, the Soviet Union kept a lim-ited military force in the area; but the moment the United States gave signs of dropping its military options by removing the larger part of its crisis deployment, Soviet forces withdrew.

The third constraint on Soviet policy in Korea is China. Ever since the Chinese Communists intervened in the Korean War in 1950 and saved the North Korean regime from defeat, Pyongyang has—with the exception of a period during the Cultural Revolution in China—tilted toward Peking. The tilt has increased since the end of the Cultural Revolution in the late 1960s, although North Korean–Chinese relations have cooled somewhat since China normalized relations with the United Nations in 1979. Mos-cow has feared that a Korea unified by the North Korean Communists would move into the Chinese orbit and greatly complicate Soviet strategic problems in Northeast Asia.

Détente with the United States seems to have been another constraint in this period. Tension was just beginning to relax at the time of the *Pueblo* incident, and the USSR certainly did not want a military crisis with the United States over the incident to reverse this. By the time the North Koreans shot down the EC-121, Soviet-U.S. talks on limiting offensive and defensive missiles (ABMs) were planned. When the poplar tree kill-ings took place, the Soviet Union was involved in discussions and agree-ments with the United States and other Western countries on a whole range of issues, including strategic arms limitation (SALT), European security and cooperation (Helsinki), and technological and other aid to the Soviet Union. Moscow was reluctant to endanger these discussions for

Pyongyang's interests, which are marginal to its own. During the poplar tree crisis, its public support for the North Korean case was cool.

The *Pueblo* Crisis

On January 23, 1968, North Korean patrol boats and submarine chasers suddenly surrounded the U.S. Navy electronic surveillance ship *Pueblo* outside the twelve-mile limit off the North Korean port of Wonsan. Claiming that the ship was in North Korea's territorial waters, the patrol boats opened fire on the *Pueblo,* injuring the ship's captain, Commander Lloyd M. Bucher, and several crew members, one critically. An armed North Korean party then boarded the ship, which was taken under guard to Wonsan.

The Johnson administration responded to the North Korean seizure with intense diplomatic activity and a show of military force in the Sea of Japan that was the largest naval buildup since the Cuban missile crisis in 1962. On the day the attack occurred, the United States sent an emergency call to North Korea through the Soviet Union asking Pyongyang to release the ship. Meeting with North Korean representatives next day at armistice talks in Panmunjom, U.S. representative Rear Admiral John V. Smith again demanded the return of the *Pueblo* and its crew but was rebuffed.

Washington twice requested—on January 24 and 26—Soviet mediation with Pyongyang to bring about the ship's release; both times Moscow brusquely rejected these requests. The United States then brought a complaint against North Korea before the United Nations, asking that the Security Council act "with greatest urgency" to obtain the release of the ship and its crew. The United States indirectly warned that the UN Charter reserved the right to member states to defend themselves against unilateral military action.

Meanwhile, the United States ordered Task Force 77—comprising twenty-five ships—to enter the Sea of Japan. By January 24 a task group consisting of the attack carrier *Enterprise* and five destroyers was on station southeast of Korea. A second task group (the attack carrier *Ranger* and three destroyers) arrived in the area on January 31, and a third consisting of the antisubmarine carrier *Yorktown* and six destroyers arrived on February 2. The arrival of the carriers *Kearsage* and *Coral Sea,* the frigate *Truxton,* the intelligence ship *Banner* (the *Pueblo*'s sister ship), and four more destroyers soon after completed Task Force 77. It was specifically instructed by General Earle Wheeler, chairman of the Joint Chiefs of Staff, not to attempt to free the *Pueblo* or approach it too closely.[1]

The Fifth Air Force established advance headquarters at Osan Air Base in Korea, two fighter-bomber squadrons were deployed from the United States to South Korea, and additional Strategic Air Command bombers were sent to the western Pacific. The U.S. Eighth Army in South Korea and South Korean military forces were put on alert, and land-based tactical air units in South Korea were reinforced. Finally, President Johnson called up nearly 15,000 air force and navy reserve personnel.

The Soviet Union countered this buildup with a naval buildup of its own. A Soviet intelligence ship and a destroyer were on patrol in the Tsushima Strait when the crisis began, and they were spotted in the vicinity of U.S. ships on January 24.[2] As Task Force 77 moved into the Sea of Japan, the USSR began interposing ships between the North Korean coast and the U.S. fleet—close to the U.S. ships. The Soviet ships included *Kotlin-* and *Kashin*-class destroyers (one equipped with surface-to-surface missiles), tankers, submarines, a single AGI (intelligence-gathering ship), and the trawler *Gidrolog,* which had electronic devices to intercept communications. On January 26 the *Gidrolog* was shadowing the U.S. attack carrier *Enterprise,* which was in the middle of the task force.[3] Soviet ships shadowed and harassed incoming U.S. units, bringing about a dozen incidents by mid-February. In an incident on February 1, the Soviet merchant ship *Kapitan Vislobokov* collided with the U.S. destroyer *Rowan* after failing to yield the right of way.

Soviet media began reporting on the *Pueblo*'s capture immediately, and the Soviet international service carried news of developments as they occurred. An editorial in the *Red Star* on January 28 spoke of the Soviet Union's reinforcing its "peaceful policy" with its "defensive might."[4] But Moscow withheld official comment on the episode for more than a week after it took place. Until the end of January, therefore, the situation was somewhat uncertain, with intentions on both the Soviet and the American sides not entirely clear.

1. Robert R. Simmons, "Case Studies: The *Pueblo,* EC-121, and Mayaguez Incidents," in Barry M. Blechman and Stephen S. Kaplan, *The Use of the Armed Forces as a Political Instrument,* prepared for U.S. Department of Defense, Advanced Research Projects Agency (unpublished report, Brookings Institution, 1976), p. 7.

2. *Japan Times,* January 25, 1968.

3. *New York Times,* January 27, 1968.

4. U.S. Foreign Broadcast Information Service (FBIS), *Trends,* January 31, 1968.

The situation began to change on January 31, when North Korea hinted to the United States that it should request closed meetings at Panmunjom. The United States immediately responded, and U.S.–North Korean meetings began on February 2.

Two days later the Soviet Union issued its most authoritative comment on the *Pueblo* affair, when *Pravda* ran an article signed "Observer," indicating that it directly reflected the opinion of the Politburo. Called "The Policy of Adventure and Provocation Is Doomed to Failure," the article recalled Communist support of North Korea during the Korean War: "The DPRK with the support of the countries of the socialist community with all peace-loving forces, demonstrated its courage and fortitude so convincingly a decade and a half ago in its fight against the American interventionists." The article concluded with a warning against U.S. military moves and a demand for withdrawal of the U.S. naval force from the Sea of Japan:

Is it not clear that endeavors to win something from a sovereign socialist state—the DPRK—with the aid of threats and pressure have no chance of success?

It is of particular importance now that the United States take no rash steps which could complicate the situation still further.

The United States must proceed . . . on the basis of respect for the sovereignty and territorial integrity of the DPRK and its national dignity . . . [meaning] first of all a complete cessation of the campaign of blackmail and threats in relation to the DPRK.[5]

This was Moscow's most belligerent statement since the crisis had begun. Coming when it did, it seemed to suggest that if the United States would withdraw the *Enterprise* and most of the rest of its forces from the Sea of Japan, the Panmunjom talks might get moving and the *Pueblo* crew might be released. At the same time, a Hungarian delegate to the UN who was in close touch with the North Koreans hinted to the United States that it should send the *Enterprise* away from Korea, suggesting that such a move would bear fruit at Panmunjom. Probably to back up these suggestions, on February 5 and 6 the Soviet Union reinforced its naval contingent in the Sea of Japan with more ships—six cruisers and destroyers, three of which were equipped with surface-to-surface missiles—bringing to sixteen the number of Soviet ships in the area.

On February 6 Washington sent the *Enterprise* south through the Tsushima Strait away from Korea. Although land-based tactical air units

5. FBIS, *Trends,* February 14, 1968.

were retained in the area and in late February U.S. F-106s were deployed in Korea, the withdrawal of the *Enterprise* signaled Washington's abandonment of military options and its willingness to rely on the Panmunjom negotiations to free the *Pueblo* and its crew. Following this event, on February 8, *Red Star* ran an article mentioning—for the first time since the crisis had begun—the Soviet-North Korean defense treaty of 1961, implying that if North Korea was attacked the Soviet Union might come to its defense.[6]

Meanwhile, Radio Pyongyang repeatedly broadcast charges that confessions made by *Pueblo* crew members indicated that the ship was 7.6 miles from North Korea's Yo Island when it was seized, that is, inside the twelve-mile limit claimed by North Korea. The confessions purportedly said further that the ship had made four other incursions into North Korean territorial waters before it was captured.

U.S.–North Korean negotiation efforts continued steadily for a time at Panmunjom; by March 4, the two sides had met ten times. The talks then resumed periodically throughout 1968, with both sides putting forward different formulas under which the *Pueblo* crew might be released.[7] Finally, on December 22, the United States announced that an agreement had been reached at a private meeting of the Korean Military Armistice Commission. The same day, U.S. negotiator Major General Gilbert H. Woodward signed a North Korean document stating that the ship had violated North Korean territorial waters and was spying when seized. The document contained a U.S. apology (drafted by North Korea) for the intrusion and a promise by the United States that it would send no more intelligence ships into North Korean waters. But the United States repudiated the apology before the document was signed with the full and prior knowledge of the North Koreans. On December 23 the *Pueblo*'s surviving crew members were returned to U.S. authorities at the demilitarized zone (DMZ), along with the body of the crew member who had died. The *Pueblo* itself was never returned.

A North Korean Initiative

The capture of the *Pueblo* appears to have been a North Korean venture initiated without consultation with or the prior knowledge of either the Russians or the Chinese. Several things point to this conclusion.

6. Ibid.
7. For an account of the terms desired by both sides, see Simmons, "Case Studies," p. 7.

There is no evidence of collusion by either Communist power.[8] Indications are that North Korean relations with both of them were not close in 1968. Destalinization, differences over the Cuban missile crisis, the Soviet Union's pursuit of détente with the West, and North Korea's support of China in the Sino-Soviet dispute had combined during the late 1950s and the 1960s to produce substantial tension between Moscow and Pyongyang. Under these conditions North Korea had carried out a purge of pro-Soviet elements in its leadership. The Soviet Union had sharply curtailed its own and Eastern Europe's economic aid and had completely cut off military aid, actions that directly affected North Korea's ability to carry out its seven-year plan (1961–1967). In October 1966 the Pyongyang government was forced to extend its economic plan for three years. In late 1964 the North Korean paper *Nodong Sinmun* virulently criticized the Soviet Union, charging that it was economically exploiting North Korea under the pretext of rendering economic aid.[9]

Relations between the two countries began to improve only after Nikita Khrushchev's ouster in 1964, but the improvement was slow. In February 1965 Premier Aleksei Kosygin went to Pyongyang for an official state visit. On that occasion, he assured North Korea that the Soviet Union was prepared to furnish all moral and material assistance within its means, saying it was the "sacred duty" of all socialist countries and Communists to combat imperialism and to support the struggle for national liberation.[10] Kosygin also evidently agreed in principle to a resumption of Soviet military assistance and an increase in economic aid.

In May a Soviet–North Korean agreement that the Soviet Union give military assistance to strengthen North Korea's "defense potential" was signed in Moscow. Moscow promised to supply jet fuel, spare parts, antiaircraft missiles, and a limited number of MIG-21s, and Soviet military

---

8. A Czechoslovak defector, General Jan Sejna, formerly with his country's defense ministry, did contend in the July 1969 issue of *Reader's Digest* that the Soviet Union collaborated in the *Pueblo* attack. He based his conclusion on remarks made in 1967 by Soviet Defense Minister Grechko at a drinking party to the effect that the United States showed great arrogance in deploying its reconnaissance ships along Communist coasts and the Soviet Union would have to teach it a lesson; and an account given to Czechoslovak officials by a Soviet general after the event saying that "we have humiliated the United States." (*Washington Post,* January 22, 1969). This evidence is too thin and self-serving to warrant serious attention, particularly without supporting evidence.

9. Byung Chul Koh, "The *Pueblo* Incident in Perspective," *Asian Survey,* vol. 9 (April 1969), p. 267.

10. Byung Chul Koh, *The Foreign Policy of North Korea* (Praeger, 1969), p. 85.

academies were to resume training North Korean military personnel.[11] In June a major new economic agreement was signed.

In early 1966, when a North Korean delegation attended the Twenty-third Congress of the Communist Party of the Soviet Union (CPSU), party leader Leonid Brezhnev reaffirmed Soviet support for the Korean people in their struggle for the unification of Korea. The same year, Soviet party organs carried an increasing number of articles friendly to North Korea.

By May 1967, when Deputy Premier Vladimir Novikov paid a good-will visit to Pyongyang, he was able to express satisfaction at growing Soviet–North Korean relations "not only in the economic sphere but also in the realms of party, social, cultural and other activities."[12] Moscow had begun to resupply Pyongyang with limited kinds of military equipment. From 1967 through 1968 it reportedly furnished 250 of North Korea's 500 military airplanes and between 1965 and 1968 supplied eight of its ten missile bases.[13] North Korea was also said to have acquired 500 air defense missiles, and its air force was estimated to include 21 MIG-21s, 350 MIG-17s, and 80 IL-28s.[14]

Still, the process of warming up Soviet–North Korean relations was just getting under way at the time the North Koreans seized the *Pueblo.* This did not prevent Kim Il-Sung's making an important programmatic speech on October 5, 1966, expressing his unhappiness with the Russians. He elaborated on the theme of North Korean independence, railed against "modern revisionism," and criticized the USSR for "compromising with U.S. imperialism" and for attempting to dictate war policy to North Vietnam. Most significantly of all, Kim's speech expressed apprehension that "the U.S. imperialists, while refraining insofar as possible from worsening their relations with big countries, concentrate their aggression mainly on Vietnam and try to swallow up such divided or small countries as Cuba, Korea, and East Germany, one by one." He clearly feared a standoff between the United States, the Soviet Union, and China that would work against the goals of smaller Communist states such as North Korea.[15]

11. Chin O. Chung, *Pyongyang Between Peking and Moscow: North Korea's Involvement in the Sino-Soviet Dispute, 1958–1975* (University of Alabama Press, 1978), pp. 112 ff.

12. Koh, *Foreign Policy of North Korea,* p. 99.

13. *New York Times,* August 22 and 23, 1968.

14. *New York Times,* February 1, 1968.

15. For this analysis, see Sheldon W. Simon, "The *Pueblo* Incident and the South Korean Revolution in North Korea's Foreign Policy: A Propaganda Analysis."

Implicit in Kim's remarks, too, was his dissatisfaction with the level and quality of Soviet arms sent to North Korea. Moscow consistently held back, for example, its most advanced fighter planes, long-range bombers, and other weapon systems that could be used for offensive purposes against the South.

North Korean–Chinese relations were, as one analyst put it, merely "formal" at the time of the *Pueblo* incident.[16] Although Pyongyang still owed Peking a debt of gratitude for Chinese help during the Korean War and had sided with China in the Sino-Soviet dispute, it had stubbornly resisted Chinese control. Kim Il-Sung had never praised Mao Tse-tung's thought. Nor was Chinese required as a foreign language in North Korea.[17] North Korea's independence and the improvement in its relations with the Soviet Union may have spurred China to make territorial demands on the North Korean border. For in July 1965 North Korean embassy officials in India revealed that China was claiming a hundred square miles near Mount Paektu as "compensation" for its aid during the Korean War.[18] By early 1968 there were reports that the border had been sealed.

But it was the Cultural Revolution that put the greatest strain on relations with North Korea. Kim Il-Sung denounced it. The Chinese Red Guard responded with posters accusing "fat" Kim of sabotaging the Vietnam struggle, slandering China, and causing famine in his own country; they even reported that he had been arrested by the army for following a revisionist line. A month later, veterans of the Chinese People's Volunteers, who had fought in Korea during the war, verbally attacked Kim. North Korea responded by threatening China with "consequences" if it persisted in its attacks.[19]

Moreover, Kim's policy statement of October 1966 was directed as much at China as it was at the Soviet Union. Attacking "left opportunism" generally, Kim also criticized China specifically for obstructing unity over Vietnam—by its rejection of a Soviet plan to transport Soviet arms to Vietnam through Chinese territory—and for attempting to dictate its own policies on North Vietnam. Far from being close, then, North Korean–Chinese relations were deteriorating at the time of the

16. Roy U. T. Kim, "Sino-North Korean Relations," *Asian Survey* (August 1968), p. 722.

17. See Koh, "The *Pueblo* Incident in Perspective," p. 267.

18. Chung, *Pyongyang Between Peking and Moscow,* p. 120.

19. Robert R. Simmons, "China's Cautious Relations with North Korea and Indochina," *Asian Survey,* vol. 11 (July 1971), p. 633.

Pueblo incident, and it is unlikely that the two would have colluded in a military operation.

Finally, the *Pueblo* attack was part of a larger pattern of North Korean aggression. The North Korean campaign was touched off by an August 12, 1966, editorial in the party paper *Nodong Sinmun* stressing independence.[20] Then, speaking in October to the North Korean Labor (Communist) party, Kim announced his abandonment of the policy of trying to unify Korea by peaceful means and the adoption of a new, militant policy toward the South. He said reunification could be accomplished only by armed force.

In the months that followed, North Korean statements employed harsher and harsher rhetoric, and there were repeated warnings that war could break out at any time. The North Koreans insisted that the withdrawal of U.S. troops from South Korea was a precondition for Seoul's "liberation." By the beginning of 1968 the North Korean attitude toward the United States was seen by U.S. observers in South Korea as more belligerent than at any time since 1953.

At the same time the number of armed incidents along the DMZ rose.[21] North Korea also seized South Korean fishing boats in increasing numbers, accusing South Korea of sending warships in disguise. Pyongyang asserted on January 6, 1968, that such "reckless aggression" would result in "one hundred-fold retaliation" by North Korea.[22]

These incidents were accompanied by a substantial increase in the North Korean defense budget in 1967. A new purge of North Korean leaders completed in mid-December of that year put professional military men in control of the country; army generals were appointed to the North Korean defense, construction, education, interior, and food procurement ministries, and an estimated hundred people regarded as moderates were weeded out of official positions. Jack Anderson contends further, citing "top U.S. Army officers," that North Korean army training was shifted from defensive to offensive tactics, important military installations were placed underground, families were told to stock emergency supplies for war, and Kim Il-Sung issued a proclamation permitting forced removal of "hostile" elements in the population to mountain camps where they

20. Joseph C. Kun, "North Korea: Between Moscow and Peking," *China Quarterly*, no. 31 (July–September 1967), pp. 55–56.

21. In 1966 there had been 50 such incidents; in 1967 the UN Command reported 543; in 1968 there were more than 750, making that year the bloodiest since the end of the Korean War.

22. Simmons, "Case Studies," p. 3.

could be kept under surveillance.[23] We cannot be sure of this, but throughout 1968 the North did step up its campaign to infiltrate guerrillas, saboteurs, and agents into South Korea, and its propaganda reported a rising revolutionary tide in the South comparable to that said to be developing at the time in South Vietnam. All this suggests that North Korea was preparing a decisive military confrontation with the South.

This impression is strengthened by the North Korean attempt to assassinate South Korean President Park Chung Hee on January 21, 1968, two days before the seizure of the *Pueblo*. A group of twenty-one North Korean agents penetrated to within a thousand yards of the presidential residence on the outskirts of Seoul before they were stopped by South Korean police, who battled them in the streets. The next day, the lone survivor of the North Korean squad—a twenty-six-year-old lieutenant—said at a news conference held by the Seoul regime that the sole mission of the group, which had undergone intensive two-year training, was to kill President Park. He added that it was his understanding North Korea would soon launch a major offensive aimed at unifying the peninsula by 1970.[24]

The timing of these events in 1968 indicates that the North Korean move was linked to what was happening in Vietnam. The attack against the *Pueblo* and the attempted assassination of President Park took place in the week before the Communists' Tet offensive in South Vietnam. Relations between North Korea and North Vietnam were close throughout the Vietnam War, and it is likely that Pyongyang knew of Hanoi's plans for the Tet offensive. In moving when they did, the North Koreans may have wished to signal to Russia and China that they too meant to press forward against a non-Communist South. They undoubtedly hoped to take advantage of the American plight in Vietnam. Their attack would force the United States to face the dilemma of backing down—with all of the consequences that might ensue—or of responding militarily and thus becoming embroiled in two Asian land wars at once. That Pyongyang had its eye on the Vietnamese situation is clear. After the *Pueblo* attack it ran a statement by Le Van Ha, head of the South Vietnamese National Liberation Front (Vietcong) mission in Hanoi, saying that the North Korean action represented "powerful support for the South Vietnamese people."[25]

23. *Washington Post,* February 18, 1968.
24. Koh, "The *Pueblo* Incident in Perspective," p. 272.
25. North Korean Press Agency, February 6, 1968.

One can only speculate about how much the North Koreans hoped to gain by their move. They must have figured that if the United States went to war, the Soviet Union and China would have to come to their defense under their respective treaties. In this case, the two Communist superpowers might be encouraged to patch up their quarrel. Pyongyang might have been able to exploit the newfound unity for an all-out offensive to get the United States out of South Korea and reunify the peninsula. The seizure of the *Pueblo* came on the eve of a preparatory meeting for a world Communist party conference, scheduled for February 26. Pyongyang may have thought to force the conference to take up the question with the aim of obtaining a reaffirmation of the Russian and Chinese defense commitments and perhaps increased military, political, and economic aid.

Undoubtedly, North Korea's determination to move decisively in 1968 was strengthened by the sight of South Korea flourishing economically and appearing to stabilize politically. Seoul's first five-year plan (1962–66) had been highly successful. Per capita income and foreign investment had both increased dramatically.[26] And Seoul's political climate was improving. In May 1967 President Park was reelected to a second term, and the following November the country's six-month impasse over the fraudulent June 1967 elections ended when the major opposition party stopped boycotting the National Assembly. These developments dimmed prospects for an imminent breakup of the South Korean political setup and must have heightened Kim's desire to move quickly before the situation could solidify. The *Pueblo* attack might also drive a wedge between South Korea and the United States by raising doubts in Seoul about the strength and trustworthiness of its major ally. It would thus give Pyongyang more leverage in the South. Soon after the *Pueblo* was taken, reports circulated at the United Nations that the North might be willing to swap the ship's crew for North Koreans held prisoner by South Korea.[27] Or North Korea may have hoped by its combined actions against Park and the *Pueblo* to force Seoul to bring back the thousands of military troops it had in South Vietnam and thus give up the political and economic benefits it gained from this policy.

Domestic purposes, too, would be served by the attacks. They would justify to a population doubtless demoralized by the North's sorry eco-

26. Joungwon A. Kim, "The Long March," *New York Times Magazine,* February 25, 1968.
27. *New York Times,* January 29, 1968.

nomic performance a continued austerity program and would demonstrate to any waverers in the North Korean leadership the need to rally around Kim. War preparation and the danger of an attack became prominent propaganda themes in Pyongyang's domestic media after the *Pueblo* was captured.[28]

The *Pueblo* incident occurred when the peace movement in the United States, urging a retreat of American power from the Asian mainland, was reaching its peak. By seizing the *Pueblo* Pyongyang might have hoped to bring home to the United States how costly its support of South Korea was and perhaps gain a reduction, if not a withdrawal, of this support. Pyongyang may have sought, in particular, to deter future U.S. reconnaissance efforts along the North Korean coast that could impede its campaign against the South. In any case, North Korea would be certain to humiliate the United States in the eyes of the world.

Pyongyang might have hoped for a few peripheral gains. At this time U.S.-Japanese relations were strained, mostly because of the U.S. involvement in Vietnam. Japan was worried about being drawn into the conflict, and the United States was pressing Tokyo to give stronger support to its policy in Vietnam. The *Pueblo* was based in Sasebo at the time of its capture; an attack on it might raise once again for Japan the question of whether it should provide such U.S. ships with port facilities.[29]

Perhaps, too, the North Korean attack was motivated, as one writer has contended, partly by the fact that Kim was approaching the age of sixty, when Koreans traditionally finish the first phase of life. Kim had made clear that his "life goal" was to reunify the peninsula.[30] The year 1968 was the anniversary of the legendary founding of the Korean nation and of the Silla Unification, when the country was brought under a single central political rule.[31] It would have been a perfect time for Kim to realize his goal.

U.S. Reaction: Surprise and Caution

The move surprised the United States for several reasons. Intelligence ships had operated successfully before without being apprehended. The

28. Simon, "*Pueblo* Incident," pp. 5–6.

29. For a discussion of North Korean fear of Japan and Chinese efforts to play on that fear, see Robert R. Simmons, "China's Cautious Relations with North Korea and Indochina," *Asian Survey,* vol. 11 (July 1971), pp. 633–34.

30. Joungwon A. Kim, "North Korea's New Offensive," *Foreign Affairs,* vol. 48 (October 1969), pp. 176–77.

31. Ibid., p. 166.

Pueblo had been stationed off the North Korean coast for two weeks and had been working in the Wonsan area for some days before it was attacked. Also, North Korea's aggressive statements over the years had lost much of their impact because of their virulence and frequency. U.S. observers in Korea apparently did not detect any change in Pyongyang's statements indicating that it was about to make a move against the United States. As it happened, in the U.S. government there was no experienced person monitoring the North Korean navy on a day-to-day basis.[32]

The attack began at about 11:30 p.m. (EST) on January 22. At the time, it was not known either how close the *Pueblo* had been to the North Korean coast or whether the North Korean action was part of a larger Communist military operation that had Russian or Chinese backing.

The administration proceeded almost immediately to consider a series of military options. These eventually narrowed down to four: (1) an attempt to storm Wonsan harbor and retrieve the ship; (2) aerial bombardment and sinking of the *Pueblo* at Wonsan to deny the Communists access to the intelligence-gathering equipment on board; (3) retaliation against North Korea or the Soviet Union by seizing or destroying a Communist ship, raiding Wonsan or Pyongyang, or knocking out a large military installation; and (4) blockading North Korea.[33]

The first, and probably most appropriate, response proved to be impossible. It was quickly determined that conventionally equipped forces could not reach the ship before dark.[34] Air force units on alert in South Korea had only nuclear weapons, which would have meant immediately escalating the conflict, possibly encouraging Soviet or Chinese intervention. Conventionally equipped aircraft were sent from Okinawa, but by the time they reached South Korea, darkness had begun to fall, so they were not sent on. South Korean aircraft under United Nations command were not asked to assist. In any case, they did not have the delivery capabilities necessary for the rapid response required to free the *Pueblo*.

The other courses were rejected as being too risky, unacceptable, or ineffective. A bombardment of Wonsan or retaliatory action against the Communists might elicit countermeasures by Pyongyang and its allies; the administration was anxious to avoid any action that would justify further Communist aggression. After the Tet offensive began in South

32. Trevor Armbrister, *A Matter of Accountability* (Coward-McCann, 1970), p. 145.
33. Ibid., p. 261, and Simmons, "Case Studies," p. 6.
34. The *Enterprise* was en route to the Gulf of Tonkin when it was ordered to the Wonsan area; of the 59 fighter aircraft aboard the carrier, only 35 were operational.

Vietnam, Washington was even more wary of doing anything to encourage the opening of a second front in Asia. Air strikes in the Gulf of Tonkin had led to a large-scale U.S. involvement in Vietnam and public disapproval, and the administration was reluctant to undertake new strikes. North Korea's trade was mainly overland with the USSR and China; a blockade would therefore have little effect. Other suggestions that were offered—for example, luring the *Gidrolog,* then shadowing the *Enterprise,* into South Korean waters and encouraging the South Koreans to seize her—were given short shrift.[35]

Moreover, none of these courses would have brought about the return of the *Pueblo* crew, a consideration that weighed heavily with the administration. Early signals by the Soviet Union and its Eastern European allies encouraged U.S. optimism about prospects for gaining the crew's release through diplomatic means, and the North Koreans themselves soon opened up the possibility that talks could bring about a resolution of the situation. President Johnson, with an election coming up and with plans at the time to run for a second term, was eager to take a moderate course that might bring about the crew's release. And Congress, the press, and the American public were all on the side of caution. Opinion in other countries—those of Western Europe and Japan—was also for caution.

These considerations, all of which were probably reinforced by the Soviet military buildup, combined to promote a U.S. response that was highly visible but restrained. When Task Force 77 sailed into the Sea of Japan, it went under the code name "Formation Star," designed to avoid giving the impression that it was going to war.[36] The air force and navy reservists were neither ordered overseas nor sent to bases for eventual deployment; that is, they were never positioned to go to war. Even when the Soviet merchant ship collided with one of the U.S. destroyers, the United States did not respond. Instead, administration officials excused the ship, although under international practice it should have given way to the U.S. warship.

Very early, in fact, the Johnson administration showed a predisposition for diplomatic action to effect the crew's release. It immediately asked Ambassador Llewellyn Thompson in Moscow to solicit Soviet

35. According to Armbrister, Walt Rostow, President Johnson's assistant for national security affairs, was very keen on this idea because he felt it had the virtue of "symmetry," but Secretary of State Dean Rusk rejected it out of hand, observing that its only symmetry lay in its equal outrageousness. *A Matter of Accountability,* p. 261.

36. Ibid., p. 266.

mediation. When this request was rejected, Washington made another bid for Soviet help. Even after the second request was rejected, it maintained contact with the Soviet Union on the issue. From the beginning of the crisis it was evident to Washington that Soviet influence in Pyongyang was limited and that Moscow could not afford to appear to be talking too openly with U.S. officials, particularly after Kim's October 1966 statement charging the Soviet Union with collusion with the West. For this reason apparently, spokesmen for the administration were careful not to interpret the Soviet rejections of its requests for help as being Moscow's last word. This suggests that in the contacts between U.S. and Communist representatives Washington was given some assurance that the Soviet Union might help behind the scenes, to ease tension.

On January 25, after the initial U.S. requests to Moscow had been turned down, Clark Clifford—President Johnson's nominee for secretary of defense—told the Senate Armed Services Committee he believed Johnson would make every diplomatic effort to rescue the *Pueblo* crew.[37] The following day, the President spoke on national television of finding a "proper and peaceful solution." He said he was confident that the American people would exhibit in this crisis, as they had in others, "determination and sanity."[38]

On January 27 a State Department spokesman said that the Soviet attitude on the crisis was negative but not hopeless and that the possibility of Soviet intervention had not been ruled out, adding, "The Russians do not agree with our explanation of the incident, but they are not moving to heat up the situation."[39] Washington was leaving room for Moscow to come around.

When the North Koreans suggested on January 31 that the United States ask for closed talks, it quickly did. The talks went on for many sessions even though they were not proving fruitful, and U.S. representatives wondered why Pyongyang was continuing them.[40] The United States also quickly picked up the hints North Korea gave about how the *Pueblo* crew's release might be brought about.[41]

37. *New York Times,* January 26, 1968.
38. *New York Times,* January 27, 1968.
39. *New York Times,* January 28, 1968.
40. *New York Times,* February 11, 1968.
41. The North Koreans put up photographs at Panmunjom showing two U.S. helicopter pilots shot down in 1963 who had been released after they signed a letter of apology and the United States acknowledged that they had been spying. See also Wayne S. Kiyosaki, *North Korea's Foreign Relations: The Politics of Accommodation, 1945–1975* (Praeger, 1976), p. 82.

As early as February 1, therefore, it was clear to all, including the Soviet Union, that the administration was giving up its military options. The removal of the *Enterprise* from the Wonsan area demonstrated the administration's decision to rely on diplomacy. Johnson maintained this course even though during the 1968 presidential campaign Republican candidate Richard Nixon tried to exploit the government's lack of action. The administration may even have turned Nixon's criticism to its own advantage. By playing on Communist fear that Nixon, if elected, would be sure to take a tough stand on the matter, perhaps including retaliatory military action, it may have encouraged the release of the *Pueblo* crew before 1969.

Soviet Policy: Mixed Signals and Low Risk

At the time of the *Pueblo* incident, the Soviet Union was engaged in developing a dialogue with the United States on various questions of mutual concern—notably, Vietnam, the Middle East, and arms limitation. Talks had been held between Premier Kosygin and President Johnson at Glassboro, New Jersey, in June 1967. Plans were being developed for a nuclear nonproliferation treaty. These steps undoubtedly raised the hopes of Soviet leaders that they might be able to divert some of their limited resources into nonmilitary areas and move forward with economic development.

Meanwhile, Soviet influence in Eastern Europe was threatened by the rise of anti-Soviet forces in Czechoslovakia. On January 5, 1968, these forces put Alexander Dubček into power in Prague. Moscow must have feared the contagious effect this might have elsewhere in Eastern Europe.

In 1968 the Sino-Soviet dispute was in full swing. Moscow was preoccupied with mustering forces inside the Communist bloc against the Chinese. Largely for this reason, it was trying to reestablish influence over Pyongyang, going so far as to begin resupplying North Korea militarily. Moscow was doing this at some cost to itself, since its scarce resources were already being siphoned off by Hanoi, just then mounting the Tet offensive against South Vietnam. Moreover, knowing it was Kim Il-Sung's declared intention to reunify Korea by force, Moscow must have been concerned about how its weapons would be used.

When the *Pueblo* crisis developed, then, the Kremlin must have been of two minds. This is indicated by Soviet behavior, which showed two noticeably different sides, one hard-line and belligerent, the other conciliatory. On the one side, Moscow must have been pleased for several reasons. First, to judge from the Soviet media's handling of the crisis, it must have gained satisfaction from seeing its major adversary put on the spot. On January 25, for example, *Pravda* crowed, picking up a North Korean phrase, that the Pentagon had been caught "redhanded."[42] The Russians also abruptly turned down the first two American efforts to obtain their mediation. When Ambassador Thompson approached the Soviet foreign ministry to ask for Soviet intervention, his message was not even accepted. Kosygin, traveling in India at the time, confirmed that the United States would have to deal directly with North Korea.[43] Little sympathy was shown publicly for the plight of the United States.

Second, Moscow may have felt that the capture of the *Pueblo* would teach the United States a useful lesson: not to encroach with its sophisticated intelligence-gathering equipment onto the territory of the Soviet Union and its allies.

Third, the Russians may have welcomed an opportunity to put North Korea in their debt by supporting it. Unlike Peking, Moscow reported the incident promptly on January 24. At that time, Tass noted that an American intelligence warship had been apprehended in North Korean territorial waters and repeated the North Korean charge that this "provocation by the American armed forces" was the most serious since the armistice of 1953. The article added that the U.S. press was seeking to distract public attention from "U.S. aggressive actions against the DPRK."[44] At the United Nations, where in the absence of North Korean representation the Soviet Union was guardian of North Korean interests, the Soviet delegate consistently upheld North Korea's position that the *Pueblo* had violated its territorial waters. Kosygin said the same thing.[45] Clearly the USSR's public statements backing North Korea's case were meant to serve a political purpose.

The timing and scope of the Soviet military buildup suggest the same thing. Certainly, the Soviet Union must have feared that the United States would take retaliatory action after the *Pueblo* attack. Since the United States was on the defensive in Vietnam, it might try to recoup its losses with a move against Communist targets in North Korea and perhaps a Soviet vessel. The administration did in fact consider such a move.

42. FBIS, *Daily Report,* January 26, 1968.
43. *New York Times,* January 28, 1968.
44. FBIS, *Daily Report,* January 26, 1968.
45. *New York Times,* January 28, 1968.

On the other side, therefore, after their first comments on the *Pueblo* incident, the Russians took pains to downplay the situation. Kosygin said that the *Pueblo* affair was merely a case of one country's ship straying into the territorial waters of another, suggesting that it could have been an accident.[46] Asked on the same occasion about a possible Soviet role in mediation, Kosygin did not reject the possibility but hinted broadly to reporters that Moscow might act as mediator.[47] On January 28 a report from Seoul said that the Soviet Union had quietly indicated its willingness to play a peacemaking role; Kosygin was reported to have said so directly in talks with Indian Prime Minister Indira Gandhi.[48] Reporters following Kosygin gained the clear impression that the Soviet Union was attempting to defuse the crisis.[49]

Moscow may have passed along to the United States soon after the *Pueblo*'s capture a report on the crew, assuring Washington that the men were being properly treated.[50] All the while, Soviet and Eastern European representatives maintained contact with U.S. representatives. In these ways, Moscow tried to encourage the United States to rely on diplomatic action to obtain the release of the *Pueblo* and its crew.

But Moscow could not afford to seem to conciliate the United States publicly. This may have been the reason it turned down the initial U.S. requests for help, since these had been made public. The day after it was reported that the Soviet Union might play a peacemaking role, this was denied by Soviet representatives in the group traveling with Kosygin. Similarly, on January 30 Moscow denied the accuracy of a newspaper report alleging that Kosygin had said the *Pueblo* crew might be traded for captured North Korean agents.[51]

Soviet moderation seems to have gone further than indirect hints. Indications are that the Soviet Union expended some of its limited credit with

46. *Washington Post,* January 27, 1968. While Kosygin's remark may have been a trial balloon, there is no evidence that the line being taken privately by Soviet representatives in Moscow and elsewhere was different. Other Russians were saying that the affair should not be blown up: at the United Nations Soviet Ambassador Platon D. Morozov referred to the incident as a North Korean "domestic matter." FBIS, *Trends,* January 31, 1968.

47. *Washington Post,* January 27, 1968.

48. *New York Times,* January 29, 1968.

49. *New York Times,* January 28, 1968.

50. *The Times* (London), January 31, 1968. Presidential spokesman George Christian said the White House had received reports but declined to give the source. He did say, however, that no word had come from the International Red Cross.

51. *New York Times,* January 31, 1968.

North Korea by pressing it to enter talks with the United States. Very possibly, Moscow signaled Pyongyang that it would receive no support if the United States were provoked to a major military confrontation. And Moscow may have pressed Pyongyang to enter talks at Panmunjom to get U.S. forces out of the Sea of Japan.

By early February, the United States had evidently chosen to pursue diplomatic, rather than military, action to free the *Pueblo* crew. Probably both to strengthen the American commitment to diplomacy and to pick up points in Pyongyang, the Soviet Union then issued its *Pravda* warning and reinforced its naval contingent in the Sea of Japan. By then, such moves must have seemed safe to Moscow. Just to be sure, however, it demanded that the *Enterprise* be moved out of the area. *Pravda,* for its part, used a tone that the *New York Times* found imploring rather than denunciatory.[52] Only after the *Enterprise* was safely out of the Sea of Japan did the Soviet Union mention its defense treaty with North Korea.[53] As in the Taiwan Strait crisis, the Soviet Union's most belligerent moves came after the real danger of large-scale conflict had passed.

The purposes of the Soviet naval buildup were three: to gather information on U.S. intentions in the Sea of Japan; to deter the United States from any of a variety of military moves it might have been tempted to make against North Korean or Soviet targets in an effort to rescue the *Pueblo* crew or to retaliate for the attack on it; and to maintain credibility with North Korea and other Soviet allies who might regard inaction as a sign of Soviet weakness.

This interpretation of the Soviet military response is supported by other evidence. First, the incident was not immediately reported on the domestic news service. On January 24 it was reported on the international service; a day later it was reported domestically, then international service reports only were resumed. This suggests that the Soviet population was not being readied for war.

Then, the two Soviet ships on patrol in the Tsushima Strait shadowed U.S. vessels as they entered the Sea of Japan; they did nothing more. When Soviet planes arrived, they flew around the U.S. ships in what seems clearly an exercise in reconnaissance and harassment. Rear Admiral Epes of the *Enterprise* said that the Soviet planes were Badgers, some equipped for reconnaissance only and others armed with air-to-surface missiles. At first they simply flew down to take a look at the U.S.

52. *New York Times,* February 5, 1968.
53. FBIS, *Trends,* February 14, 1968.

ships, and after being intercepted, they turned back. But then they started going through the U.S. formation (evidently south) toward the Tsushima Strait, one day conducting thirty "raids" at all altitudes, a few as low as thirty-five or forty feet above deck.[54] Epes apparently did not take the raids seriously. This seems to have been the first case of Soviet harassment of U.S. ships, clearly a controlled one that operated at a relatively low level.

In addition to the raids, the *Pueblo*'s sister ship *Banner* one evening saw the nuclear-powered frigate *Truxton* bearing down at full speed. The *Banner* passed a message to a nearby carrier that there was a Soviet intelligence ship in the middle of the task force. The carrier responded: "Hey, *Truxton,* knock it off, that's our buddy."[55] The carrier evidently had been trailed by the Soviet ship for some time and was confident it was merely carrying out a reconnaissance assignment.

Armbrister suggests that the Soviet Union, which had long considered the Sea of Japan its special preserve, was simply protecting its interests.[56] Probably it was also ensuring that it would have warning if the United States should decide to make any aggressive move while attempting, through harassment, to deter such a move.

The February 1 incident between the *Kapitan Vislobokov* and the *Rowan* occurred well south of Wonsan. It is not clear whether it was an independent action by the Soviet captain or a slap by Moscow. Soviet merchant captains are notorious for their violation of agreements made between their country and other countries, so the captain could have acted on his own. He may, however, have been acting on instructions. After the incident, the Soviet Union made an official protest but gave it no publicity. This suggests that if the incident was designed by Moscow it was meant simply to warn the United States that Moscow was not happy with the U.S. military presence in the area. U.S. officials clearly did not feel the action was intended as a provocation. They knew that the Soviet Union was worried by the presence of the U.S. task force in the area, as evidenced by Washington's quick response to the suggestion that the *Enterprise* be moved, as it was on February 6.

One Soviet specialist has suggested that Moscow encouraged North Korea to return the *Pueblo* crew.[57] Max Frankel, writing in April, seemed

54. Armbrister, *A Matter of Accountability,* p. 266.
55. Ibid.
56. Ibid.
57. Jane P. Shapiro, "Soviet Policy Towards North Korea and Korean Unification," *Pacific Affairs,* vol. 48 (Fall 1975), p. 349.

confident that Moscow was trying to help arrange the release of the ship.[58] The matter was probably taken up during the February visit to Pyongyang of CPSU Secretary Boris N. Ponomarev and in the course of other Soviet–North Korean contacts in 1968; and it may have been in the initial period from January 23 to February 1 as well.

The Ponomarev delegation visited North Korea on February 9 and 10. Although there was no public indication of the substance of the talks, it seems plausible that the Soviet Union insisted on an explanation of the incident and at the same time assessed North Korean military needs in light of the new development. The visit apparently did lead to an increase in certain kinds of Soviet military aid to North Korea, as well as a speeded-up delivery of previous commitments. According to one report, by mid-August North Korea had underground hangars in several of its fifteen airfields, and its MIG-21 fleet had been doubled to sixty.[59] The Soviet Union had also more than doubled—from fourteen to thirty-five —North Korea's surface-to-air missile (SAM) sites since January and had supplied other equipment.[60] But neither then nor later did it supply North Korea with MIG-23s or with more advanced SAMs of the kind it later delivered to Egypt. In other words, while the USSR was ready to support the North Koreans, it was prepared to do so only if it could be done relatively cheaply and with minimum risk to Soviet interests.

If the Soviet response to the crisis was cautious, the Chinese response was even more so. China did not report the incident until January 26, three days after it had occurred, and then gave merely a brief factual account. At the time, China was caught up in its dispute with the Soviet Union and concerned about the Soviet military buildup on the border, which threatened China's security. On its southern flank it was committed to supporting Hanoi, as North Vietnam launched its offensive against the South. Internally, China was going through a major upheaval as the Cultural Revolution reached new heights of fervor under the Red Guard. It could not have welcomed a North Korean–U.S. confrontation that might threaten its industrial areas in the northeast. The Chinese may even have suspected that the seizure was a Soviet–North Korean venture. They therefore confined themselves to playing on North Korean fear of Japan.[61] This form of Chinese support could not have been well received by a Pyongyang bent on pursuing its campaign against South Korea.

58. *New York Times,* April 17, 1968.
59. *New York Times,* August 15, 1968.
60. *New York Times,* April 20, 1969.
61. Simmons, "China's Cautious Relations with North Korea and Indochina," pp. 633–34.

North Korea was, in fact, unhappy with both the Soviet and the Chinese response to the crisis. On January 27 the Pyongyang regime issued a statement saying it hoped "all socialist countries will pay deep attention to the affair" and express "active support and solidarity to the Korean people in their just struggle."[62] The admonition must have been directed particularly to the Chinese, and the Chinese seem to have understood it so. For on January 28 they responded with a statement—the only other one Peking made about the *Pueblo* affair—saying that North Korea was "entirely right" in its "decisive measure of self-defense" and that the Chinese government and people "firmly support the just stand" of the North Koreans in countering "U.S. imperialism's flagrant provocation." They added: "Should U.S. imperialism dare to embark on a new adventure, it is bound to taste the bitter fruit of its own making and receive even more punishment."[63] This was hardly the "active" support North Korea had asked for; China was merely a bystander. The Soviet Union's response was so much stronger, it must have expected to gain some credit in Pyongyang.

The Soviet Union may also have welcomed the prospect of obtaining valuable intelligence information from the *Pueblo*. Although all reports from the *Pueblo* crew indicate that at the time of the capture the North Koreans were quite uninterested in the ship's intelligence-gathering equipment,[64] the Russians must have expected to profit handsomely from it. Armbrister says that, according to U.S. intelligence reports, within a couple of days dozens of Soviet technicians had flown to Wonsan and boarded the ship.[65] A Czechoslovak defector has said that briefings given the Czechoslovaks after the *Pueblo*'s capture indicated that the Russians were getting valuable information from the ship.[66] Moreover, the ship was never returned. From an intelligence standpoint the Russians could have been gratified by the North Korean action.

However, Moscow also had reason to be worried by it, and the other side of Soviet behavior in the crisis reflects this. The Russians may have wanted to see the United States embarrassed, but they must have been worried that if the United States were humiliated in both South Vietnam *and* Korea it might react aggressively, setting off a major conflagration

62. Ibid.
63. Ibid.
64. See Lloyd M. Bucher with Mark Rascovitch, *Bucher: My Story* (Doubleday, 1970); Armbrister, *A Matter of Accountability*; and Ed Brandt, *The Last Voyage of USS Pueblo* (Norton, 1969).
65. Armbrister, *A Matter of Accountability*, p. 258.
66. *Washington Post*, January 22, 1969.

that would activate the Soviet–North Korean defense treaty and threaten to embroil the USSR in war. This would explain why Russians were heard saying off the record at the United Nations that while they felt North Korea had taught the United States a lesson it deserved it would be a mistake to try to humiliate a great power, particularly when it was on the defensive in Vietnam.[67]

The Russians must also have suspected North Korea of deliberately creating the crisis to force Moscow into granting it increased military aid. Moscow would have resented this pressure both because its aid to North Vietnam was already draining its resources and because it feared encouraging North Korea to attack South Korea, dragging the USSR into a war against its will. Far from wanting a war or even heightened tension in Asia in early 1968, Moscow appears to have sought a reduction of tension. It was then engaged in negotiations with the United States on an antiballistic missile treaty and with the Japanese on plans to develop Siberia. Tension in Korea could only harm both sets of negotiations. Also, the Soviet Union probably has not wanted to see Korea unified by the North Koreans, much less by the intransigent Kim Il-Sung. A Korea reunified under Kim could become linked to China; this would be a nightmare to Moscow, politically and strategically. Finally, Moscow was engaged in its own extensive naval electronic intelligence operations, which were equally vulnerable to seizure. North Korea's action in effect violated the tacit Soviet-American understanding on these activities. Moscow must have feared for the safety of its own reconnaissance ships.

These conflicting considerations did not leave the Soviet Union with too many options. It could not afford to permit the United States to threaten either Soviet or North Korean security. Nor could it allow U.S. ships to move freely into the Sea of Japan. It also could not permit Pyongyang to slide into the Chinese camp. It thus had to make some military response and a public show of support for Pyongyang. At the same time, Moscow did not want, by its own military or political behavior, to provoke the United States to retaliatory action. Nor did it want to encourage the North Koreans to follow their initiative with other aggressive moves. It therefore made a conservative military response while trying to persuade the United States privately that diplomatic action was likely to bring results. Possibly Moscow could have reacted more forcefully to the U.S. military buildup without provoking the United States to take retaliatory action. It could, for example, have sent in a matching number of ships. It

67. *Christian Science Monitor,* February 2, 1968.

could have marshaled more impressive air power. It could have hampered the movement of Task Force 77 ships. It chose to lean toward caution.

Similarly, on the political front the Soviet Union was conciliatory. It also refrained from supporting Pyongyang's more extravagant claims. During the first week or two after the *Pueblo* seizure North Korea contended that the guerrilla movement in the South was growing in strength and breadth. The Soviet media ignored these claims, and after the immediate crisis was over, they were virtually silent about the *Pueblo* affair.[68]

In September 1968, when Politburo member D. S. Polyansky visited North Korea for the twentieth anniversary of the founding of the state, he noted that North Korea had contractual relations with the Soviet Union for "the joint defense of socialist gains, and the enemies should not forget this."[69] The "joint defense" was almost certainly a reflection of Soviet insistence that the North Koreans not undertake unilateral action against the United States.

Soviet leaders may have, on this and other occasions, sought to persuade Pyongyang to release the *Pueblo* crew by Christmas. Being more sophisticated than the North Koreans in their understanding of Americans, they may have realized the favorable effect the crew's release at that season could have. They would also have been more sensitive to the threat posed by President-elect Nixon, who was to enter office in January. Moscow must have been relieved when the *Pueblo* crew passed across the "Bridge of No Return" at Panmunjom on December 23.

In its traditional year-end roundup of important events in 1968, *Pravda* on December 29 did not even mention the *Pueblo*.[70] Clearly the Soviet Union meant to put this episode behind it as quickly as possible.

Soviet policy in the *Pueblo* case, then, was ambivalent. Caught between its fear of a confrontation with the United States and its desire to maintain credibility in Pyongyang and the Communist camp, Moscow made both conciliatory and belligerent moves. These moves were geared in part to its American audience, and indications are that that audience was responsive. Washington quickly abandoned its military options, partly because it was already involved in Vietnam. But the Soviet Union's military buildup, moderate though it was, probably contributed to U.S. caution, while conciliatory Soviet statements encouraged the Johnson administration to believe that the release of the *Pueblo* crew might be brought about

68. Simon, "*Pueblo* Incident," p. 10.
69. Tass, September 4, 1968; cited by Simon, "*Pueblo* Incident," p. 10.
70. Simon, "*Pueblo* Incident," p. 11.

by means short of war. The United States was already sensitive to the Soviet Union's fears about North Korean security and, even more, about its own. Soviet behavior in the *Pueblo* crisis—its public statements in behalf of North Korea and the nature and timing of its military buildup—probably clarified American understanding. In sum, Soviet objectives for its relations with the United States were well served.

Soviet belligerent statements and moves were also aimed at North Korea. There Moscow seems to have had less success. It did what it thought necessary, during the first week or two after the crisis developed, to preserve credibility in Pyongyang, going further than Peking in its support. Despite this, Moscow seems to have gained little ground in the North Korean capital.

Moreover, if the Soviet Union did in fact—during the Ponomarev and Polyansky visits—warn Pyongyang against taking future initiatives against the United States, it failed to gain its objective. For within a short time the North Koreans had attacked another U.S. target: the EC-121.

Whether the Soviet Union anticipated such a North Korean move or not, in retrospect the *Pueblo* incident represents a landmark in the Soviet attitude toward North Korea: the point at which Moscow began to conclude that it could gain few concessions to Soviet interests from the North Koreans and abandoned efforts to conciliate them.

The Shooting Down of the EC-121

On April 15, 1969, less than four months after the *Pueblo* crew had been released, North Korean aircraft shot down an unarmed U.S. Navy EC-121 with thirty-one men aboard while the reconnaissance plane was off the North Korean coast.

The Nixon administration knew only that the plane had been missing for a couple of hours when a North Korean news agency report was monitored which said that the plane had been brought down by North Korean forces. The same day, North Korea proposed a meeting of the Korean Military Armistice Commission without specifying what it wished to discuss. A meeting was arranged for April 18.

The administration meanwhile ordered into the Sea of Japan Task Force 71, which was officially put at twenty-nine vessels but unofficially at close to forty;[71] with four aircraft carriers (*Enterprise, Ticonderoga, Ranger,* and *Hornet*), carrying 256 war planes, it had more firepower than the U.S. Sixth Fleet[72] and was a substantially larger force than that sent after the *Pueblo* incident. Two other carriers, the *Kitty Hawk* and the *Bon Homme Richard,* were ordered from Hong Kong to the Sea of Japan, and the battleship *New Jersey,* en route home from Vietnam, was diverted to the area. Other U.S. forces were put on alert. Further U.S. reconnaissance flights were temporarily suspended, however.

At the same time, the United States requested Soviet, Japanese, and South Korean help in looking for survivors of the EC-121 crash. The day the plane was shot down, Secretary of State Rogers met in Washington with Soviet Ambassador Dobrynin to ask for Soviet aid. The Soviet Union responded favorably and promptly to the American request. On April 16 two Soviet destroyer-type ships in the Sea of Japan began to assist in the search and rescue effort. With U.S. aircraft from bases in Guam, the Philippines, Okinawa, and Japan, the Soviet ships spent three days helping to look for survivors. At one point, guided by a U.S. Navy patrol plane to some debris, one of the Soviet destroyers picked up the debris and described it by radio to a low-flying U.S. Hercules C-130. The Soviet ship invited the plane to photograph the wreckage of the EC-121. It then radioed a message to the departing U.S. plane, which said: "Soviet Destroyer, Red Banner Pacific Fleet, sends condolences in connection with the loss of your aircraft."[73] Two days later, the Soviet ship gave the debris to a U.S. destroyer. On April 18, the United States publicly thanked the Soviet Union for its help. Two bodies but no survivors had been found. Also on April 18, the United States and North Korea met at Panmunjom, as arranged. At that meeting, the U.S. negotiator, Air Force Major General James P. Knapp, read a statement protesting the North Korean action in shooting down the EC-121 and demanding that the North Koreans take measures to prevent such incidents in the future.[74] In response, the North Koreans only demanded repeatedly to know to what unit the aircraft belonged.

The same day, President Nixon said at a nationally televised press conference that the United States was resuming its reconnaissance flights and that they would be protected. He contended that the EC-121 had

71. *New York Times,* April 20, 1969.
72. Simmons, "Case Studies," p. 18.
73. *New York Times,* April 20, 1969.
74. *New York Times,* April 18, 1969.

been ninety miles off the North Korean coast when shot down and that at no time had it been closer than forty miles. He also spoke of the Soviet role in the incident, describing it as first

one of being of assistance to the United States in recovering the debris and looking for survivors. And we are most grateful to the Soviet Union for helping us in this respect. Our intelligence—and of course no one can be sure here— indicates that the Soviet Union was not aware that this attack was to be made. North Korea is not a nation that is predictable in terms of its actions. It is perhaps more than any other nation in the Communist bloc completely out of control of either the Soviet Union, or for that matter, Communist China. . . . It was completely a surprise attack in every sense of the word and, therefore, did not give us the opportunity for protective actions that I would have taken had it been threatened.[75]

On April 20 Task Force 71 entered the Sea of Japan reinforced by jet fighters dispatched from Osan Air Base in South Korea. As the U.S. ships came in, three Soviet intelligence ships and three Soviet destroyers appeared. These carried out surveillance activities only. The Soviet Union may also have put a standby force to sea; if so, it remained close to Vladivostok, out of contact with U.S. forces. On the evening of April 21 the Soviet Union complained orally to American officials in Washington and Moscow about the U.S. naval presence. The United States responded by explaining that the reinstituted reconnaissance flights needed protection, emphasizing that it was North Korea (not the Soviet Union) that had brought down the EC-121.[76] On April 22 Washington publicized the Soviet protests.

On April 26 the United States announced that it was withdrawing Task Force 71 south of Korea to the Yellow Sea. A government spokesman said that North Korea had been sent a message that retaliation might follow future shootings.[77] The *New Jersey* returned to the United States at this time. Shortly thereafter, Task Force 71 was reduced to eight ships.

North Korean Action

As with the seizure of the *Pueblo,* the shooting down of the EC-121 seems to have been on North Korean initiative alone. In April 1969 the

75. *New York Times,* April 19, 1969.
76. *New York Times,* April 27, 1969.
77. *New York Times,* April 26, 1969. No indication was given of how the message was sent.

North was still actively pursuing its militant policy of attempting to undermine the Seoul regime by force.

The attempted assassination of President Park and the attack on the *Pueblo* had increased tension between South Korea and the United States. After these events, Seoul undoubtedly wanted to take retaliatory military action.The Park regime must have felt a stop should be put to the North's continuing probes once and for all. Certainly, Washington seems to have feared a South Korean move in this direction, for it avoided calling in South Korean aircraft under the UN Command.

When the United States protested to the United Nations about the *Pueblo* seizure, the South Koreans entered a protest of their own, condemning the attempted assassination of President Park. After the United States agreed to enter into private talks with North Korea, the South Korean government radio said U.S. policy had aroused "burning indignation and resentment on the part of the ROK people."[78] Seoul wanted some expression of U.S. concern about its own situation in the face of North Korean attacks. The major Seoul newspaper warned against U.S. "connivance" at the *Pueblo* affair.[79] Soon after, anti-American demonstrations erupted in Seoul and along the DMZ for the first time since the Korean War, and the South Korean National Assembly unanimously passed a resolution strongly critical of the United States.[80]

Meeting with U.S. Ambassador William J. Porter and Commander of UN Forces General. Charles Bonesteel, South Korean Premier Chung Il Kwon demanded that the problem of infiltration from North Korea to the South take precedence over the *Pueblo* case, that South Korea be included in all negotiations, and that the United States increase its aid to Seoul beyond the amount projected by President Johnson.[81] Seoul also wanted an improvement of the 1953 mutual defense treaty to provide for "immediate and automatic" U.S. response to a common U.S.–South Korean danger,[82] and the reassignment of South Korean forces from the UN Command to purely South Korean control. The United States resisted these demands then and during a February 11

78. Seoul Domestic Service, February 5, 1968; cited in Simon, "*Pueblo* Incident," p. 13.

79. *Dong A-Ilbo*, February 11, 1968; cited in Simmons, "Case Studies," p. 13.

80. Koh, "The *Pueblo* Incident in Perspective," p. 290.

81. Simmons, "Case Studies," p. 13.

82. Soon Sung Cho, "North and South Korea: Stepped Up Aggression and the Search for a New Security," *Asian Survey*, vol. 9 (January 1969), pp. 30–31.

visit by President Johnson's special envoy, Deputy Secretary of Defense Cyrus R. Vance, to Seoul.

Yet U.S. aid to South Korea was increased. A few weeks after the *Pueblo* incident, President Johnson reaffirmed the U.S. commitment to defend South Korea against Communist aggression and asked Congress for $100 million in emergency military aid for Seoul. Later, he promised aid to South Korea's new Homeland Defense Corps. Within a few weeks, nearly 200 U.S. jets were flown to South Korean airfields from Japan, Okinawa, Guam, and Hawaii, and specialists and spare parts were sent to two U.S. Army divisions in South Korea. South Korea also received a destroyer, air-defense missiles, radios, anti-infiltration devices, and ammunition.[83]

Meanwhile, the Park regime announced that it was going to build up the South Korean militia to 2.5 million men. By March 14, more than 1.6 million reservists were organized and the remainder were scheduled to be mustered by the end of the month. In addition, the South Korean armed forces were brought to their full strength of 623,000 men by delaying discharges.[84]

All this must have been worrying to North Korea, which seems to have concluded it had to act quickly if it expected ever to take the South. In August 1968 the South Korean CIA announced the discovery of a large Communist underground, whose members were said to have made repeated journeys to the North and to have met with North Korean leaders, including Kim Il-Sung. Later in the year, on November 3, a party of at least sixty North Korean commandos landed on the east coast of South Korea near Ulchin in what the Seoul government thought to be part of an effort to establish bases for permanent guerrilla operations in the South. According to accounts by the captives, they had been ordered to recruit South Koreans for subversion, terrorism, and sabotage. The North Korean commandos held at least one village before they were cleaned out by South Korean military, policy, and security forces.[85] The following month, South Korean President Park warned at a national security meeting in Seoul that North Korea had begun a new type of irregular war.

These North Korean actions were combined with three armed clashes initiated by Pyongyang in the DMZ in October and with the replacement,

83. *New York Times,* December 23, 1968.
84. Koh, *Foreign Policy of North Korea,* p. 154.
85. *Washington Post,* April 14, 1969.

in December, of Defense Minister Kim Ch'ang-bong by General Ch'oe Hyon, widely regarded as Pyongyang's top guerrilla warfare strategist.[86] The militants evidently were gaining strength in the North Korean capital. One Western analyst asserts that the U.S. failure to retaliate in the *Pueblo* incident had strengthened the militant policy of the "hawks" in the North Korean leadership.[87]

In mid-March 1969 the United States began an operation called "Focus Retina," the airlift of 1,200 U.S. combat troops from North Carolina to South Korea to participate with South Korean soldiers in maneuvers against a "surprise attack from a third country," clearly North Korea. This move especially appears to have heightened North Korean fear and anger; for on April 16, the day after the EC-121 was shot down, a Pyongyang broadcast spoke of "Focus Retina" as being "very provocative."[88] From the North Korean capital it probably seemed that, with the Vietnam War beginning to wind down, the United States was turning its attention to Korea and that time was not in Pyongyang's favor.

Meanwhile, North Korea's relations with the two Communist superpowers had not improved since the time of the *Pueblo*'s seizure; if anything, they were even cooler. After the Ponomarev visit to Pyongyang in February 1968, the Soviet Union had doubled North Korea's SAM sites, reaffirmed the Soviet defense commitment, and increased economic assistance to the North. It was on its way to becoming North Korea's largest trading partner. North Korea had promptly and unqualifiedly endorsed the Soviet invasion of Czechoslovakia, as was consistent with Pyongyang's opposition to liberal pressure in the Communist bloc. But North Korea had failed to get from the Soviet Union the kind of support it had undoubtedly sought after the *Pueblo* incident. Probably to show his unhappiness, Kim Il-Sung refused to give in to the request reportedly made by Ponomarev that North Korea send a representative to the April Budapest conference, which was to prepare for the international conference of Communist parties scheduled for Moscow later in the year.[89]

Thus the *Pueblo* incident seems to have left both sides frustrated with one another. The Soviet Union must have been warier than ever of its North Korean ally. The *Pueblo*'s seizure had humiliated the United States and caused some strain in U.S.–South Korean and U.S.-Japanese

---

86. Koh, "The *Pueblo* Incident in Perspective," p. 280.
87. Simmons, "Case Studies," p. 17.
88. BBC Overseas Service, April 17, 1969.
89. *New York Times*, February 23, 1968.

relations.[90] It had given Moscow a certain edge over Peking with Pyong-yang, and it may have netted the Soviet Union useful intelligence infor-mation. But it had complicated the Soviet Union's tenuous political relations with both the United States and Japan.[91] It had led to greater aid to South Korea and justified Johnson's calling up the reserve at home, a move he had long wished to make. It had brought a large U.S. military force into the Sea of Japan, within reach of vital Soviet territory and installations in the Far East. Most important, the seizure of the *Pueblo* demonstrated that North Korea was ready to take, without Soviet knowl-edge, unilateral actions that could involve the USSR in a military con-frontation with the United States. The Russians had not been happy when China, a major ally, had gotten them into such a predicament. They must have been doubly unhappy to have a minor ally, North Korea, threaten to take them to war. Moreover, Moscow must have been irri-tated that Pyongyang had resisted attempts to nudge it away from Peking.

Meanwhile, North Korean relations with China had not yet improved beyond the "formal" stage of early 1968. China could not have liked the fact that Moscow rendered comparatively greater support to Pyongyang in the crisis and was supplying North Korea militarily. This was not a situation in which China could feel friendly toward North Korea, since China's own relations with the Soviet Union were deteriorating at the time. The Chinese Communist party newspaper had condemned the Soviet invasion of Czechoslovakia in August 1968, calling it a "shame-less act."[92] Although Czechoslovakia's "revisionist" policies were not to China's liking, Peking clearly feared that the Soviet action might pro-vide a precedent for similar action against its own territory—something particularly to be feared after the "Brezhnev doctrine" of November justi-fying Soviet intervention in socialist countries and in light of Soviet activi-ties in Sinkiang and along China's western border.

In March 1969 armed Sino-Soviet incidents developed on the Ussuri River dividing China and the Soviet Union. The EC-121 may have been monitoring these incidents before it was shot down.[93] China was deeply involved in its dispute with the USSR and would not have wanted a con-

90. See *The Times* (London), January 31, 1968.

91. The Russians were trying to arrange a visit by Politburo members M. A. Suslov and B. N. Ponomarev to Japan. Their efforts had to be pushed into the back-ground when the *Pueblo* crisis developed. See *Japan Times,* January 27, 1968.

92. *Renmin Ribao,* August 23, 1968; cited by *Economist* (London), August 31, 1968.

93. *Japan Times,* April 16, 1969.

flict with the United States on the Korean peninsula. China was, in any case, still preoccupied with internal problems. Liu Shao-chi had been expelled from the Communist party in November 1968, culminating a campaign waged by the radical Red Guard against "revisionists." The Chinese Communist party was preparing to meet for the first time since 1958 to adopt a new party constitution and elect a presidium, central committee, and politburo. This congress began on April 1, 1969. North Korea had not sent a representative.

On April 23, after the EC-121 was shot down, Pyongyang issued a statement contending that the United States was seeking to provoke a new war. "The entire Korean people and the people's army," the statement said, "must sharpen their revolutionary vigilance and be fully prepared to return retaliation for retaliation and all-out war for all-out war."[94] U.S. analysts thought at the time that the statement was aimed at the Soviet Union and China as much as at the United States. Again, frustrated by the lack of support it was getting from its two Communist allies, particularly after the successful *Pueblo* attack, Pyongyang appears to have acted alone.

April 15 was Kim Il-Sung's fifty-seventh birthday. Shooting down the EC-121 on that day could have been a way of commemorating the event. David Willis of the *Christian Science Monitor* speculated at the time Kim may not have known of the attack before it occurred: as of April 19, Kim had not said a single word about it, there were few statements in the North Korean press and radio about it, and the North Koreans' opening statement at Panmunjom did not even refer to it. Noting that this was in strange contrast to North Korean reports after the *Pueblo* crisis, Willis suggested that the attack on the U.S. plane may have been on the initiative of Defense Minister Ch'oe Hyon as a birthday gift to Kim.[95] Americans at Panmunjom supported this notion. They thought that the North Koreans seemed confused about their instructions and speculated that someone in Pyongyang may have made a mistake in calling for the meeting. They too wondered if Ch'oe had acted on his own initiative against the wishes of other North Korean leaders.[96]

If Ch'oe did act independently, he may have had more than one domestic purpose in mind. First, taking place when it did, the incident could have bolstered his standing with Kim, by contributing to the cult of personality

94. *New York Times,* April 24, 1969.
95. *Christian Science Monitor,* April 19, 1969.
96. Ibid., and *New York Times,* April 19, 1969.

Kim had built around himself. Then, on April 17, Ch'oe commended the 896th army unit for bringing the plane down "with one shot."[97] He may have been trying to shore up morale in the North Korean army by hinting to North Korean soldiers and their foreign enemies alike that Pyongyang had units capable of successfully firing surface-to-air missiles, then being supplied by the Soviet Union.

On April 18 an editorial in *Nodong Sinmun* called for heightened North Korean vigilance and maintenance of a constant state of mobilization and stressed the importance of stepping up military and political training. It spoke of President Nixon as the "new boss of the U.S. imperialists, ranting that a third world war will break out not in Europe but in Asia." These comments may well have reflected the fear, of some North Korean leaders at least, that after years of austerity and militancy the North Korean population was beginning to slacken its efforts and let down its guard. In view of U.S. restraint in the *Pueblo* crisis, shooting down an unarmed U.S. plane may have been judged an easy way to boost North Korean military preparedness.

U.S. Response: Military Force and Political Sensitivity

The attack on the EC-121, like the seizure of the *Pueblo*, took the United States by surprise despite a warning.[98] The Defense Department explained this by saying such flights had been flown in the Sea of Japan for more than twenty years with few incidents and that in the first three months of 1969 there had been 190 similar flights in the area that had not been attacked.[99] Although the United States was confident that neither the Russians nor the Chinese were involved, Nixon's advisers urged caution. The military men were aware of the risks of military action, which could have precipitated war at a time when the United States was still engaged in Vietnam. The civilians also favored restraint. Defense Secretary Melvin R. Laird, for example, was described as "not enthusiastic" about air strikes.[100] Secretary of State Rogers said the next day: "The weak can be rash; the powerful must be more restrained," and spoke of acting "responsibly" in the crisis.[101] Aside from a few hard-liners, most of Congress

97. *New York Times,* April 16, 1969.
98. Just before the attack, the plane was alerted to possible danger and ordered to abort its mission and move further south. It is not clear why it failed to do so.
99. *New York Times,* April 17, 1969.
100. Simmons, "Case Studies," p. 19.
101. *New York Times,* April 17, 1969.

called for caution. Public opinion also supported a restrained response, although this time there was no question of retrieving hostages.

After considering a series of military options, therefore, the administration quickly turned to a policy combining a dramatic show of military force with a low-key political stance that was conciliatory, especially toward the Soviet Union.[102] On the one hand, the administration ordered Task Force 71—with its 40 vessels and 256 warplanes—into the Sea of Japan. It denounced the North Korean attack, warning Pyongyang not to attempt to repeat it because U.S. military power represented by the task force would be prepared for a quick response.[103] And on April 18 President Nixon announced that the United States was resuming its reconnaissance flights, this time with fighter escorts.

On the other hand, at his April 18 press conference, President Nixon publicly acknowledged Soviet assistance in the search and rescue operation and absolved the Soviet Union from any responsibility for the attack. The United States did not raise the issue at the United Nations for fear such a move might force the Russians to publicly support North Korea, as they had in the case of the *Pueblo*. Washington also made a point of specifying that Task Force 71 was aimed at warning North Korea, not the Soviet Union, against interfering with future reconnaissance flights.

In other words, the administration did everything it could to separate the Soviet Union from the attack while making a show of military strength designed mainly for political effect in Pyongyang. Washington's position

102. The administration originally considered (1) a limited air strike on the North Korean bases that had sent up the planes responsible for shooting down the EC-121; (2) a blockade of the North Korean coast; (3) an air strike on all North Korean air bases; and (4) an attempt to lure a North Korean ship or plane outside of its territorial waters in order to destroy it (*New York Times*, April 17, 1969, cited by Simmons, "Case Studies," p. 19). The Nixon administration was constrained from the use of these options by many of the same factors that held the Johnson administration back in the *Pueblo* crisis. For one thing, there were not enough U.S. planes on "strip alert" to carry out a retaliatory action quickly (Simmons, "Case Studies," p. 16). And although North Korean targets were actually selected for a retaliatory U.S. move and a speech was prepared for President Nixon to give on the occasion of a U.S. attack, it was determined that U.S. military forces were not ready.

U.S. leaders did not think the Soviet Union had endorsed North Korea's attack, but they did fear that use of military force on any large scale might risk a Soviet, Chinese, or North Korean counterattack, touching off a major armed conflict in the area. North Koreans had no American hostages this time, but there were unconfirmed reports that two North Korean destroyers were speeding to the scene of the EC-121's crash, raising fear that they might pick up survivors and hold them.

103. *New York Times*, April 18, 1969.

was made possible by the Soviet Union's initial conciliatory response to the attack.

Soviet Disenchantment with North Korea

At the time of the attack the Soviet Union was pursuing détente and discussing with the United States a range of issues that would affect Soviet planning for years to come. In May 1968 the two countries had ratified a consular convention. Two months later they had, with Britain and fifty-nine nonnuclear nations, signed the nuclear nonproliferation treaty and agreed to open talks "in the nearest future" on limiting and reducing offensive and defensive missiles. Relations between Moscow and Washington appeared to be on the upswing as the end of the Vietnam War came in sight.

Moscow had just carried out its invasion of Czechoslovakia. Militarily, it was trying to stabilize the situation there, and politically, it was still marshaling Communist bloc support for its action. It also was preparing for the world conference of Communist parties to be held in Moscow in June 1969.

Moscow was more and more on the defensive against Peking. Chinese criticism of the Soviet invasion of Czechoslovakia had hampered Soviet efforts to make that move palatable to other Communist countries, and China's continuing attacks—both verbal and actual—on the eastern border were a constant irritant. In October 1968 it was reported that the Soviet Union had established missile bases in Outer Mongolia on the Chinese border.[104] The same month the Soviet Union sent journalist Victor Louis to Taiwan, the first time in nineteen years a Soviet citizen had visited the island. Going even further, Moscow received a member of Chiang Kai-shek's Chinese Nationalist party. Then in March 1969, after the first skirmishes along the Ussuri River, Moscow bitterly attacked China in *Kommunist,* contending that China was attempting nuclear blackmail of its Asian neighbors.[105] The Kremlin followed this up with an April 11 proposal for the renewal of Sino-Soviet border talks; Western analysts thought this overture was designed mainly to show up the Chinese.[106]

In this situation, the Soviet Union could hardly have welcomed another North Korean attack on the United States. Besides going against

104. Sunday *Times* (London), October 6, 1968.
105. Sheldon W. Simon, "Some Aspects of China's Asian Policy in the Cultural Revolution and Its Aftermath," *Pacific Affairs* (Spring 1971), p. 22.
106. For example, see the Swiss paper *Neue Zurcher Zeitung,* April 14, 1969.

Moscow's probable warnings to Pyongyang after the *Pueblo* incident, such a move must have contributed to Russian reservations about a Korea unified under Kim Il-Sung.

One can only guess about the Russians' reaction to Nixon's acknowledgment of their help in the search for survivors.[107] They probably did not want attention called to their help; in their own press they did not report it. But they must have been gratified when Nixon absolved the Soviet Union of any responsibility for the attack, since this suggested that the Soviet-U.S. dialogue could continue undisturbed. And it is likely they were relieved that the United States did not raise the issue at the United Nations, where they would have been forced by North Korea's continued absence to present its case.

When the EC-121 incident occurred, the Soviet press picked up the April 15 KCNA report of it. Next day, the purportedly unofficial Radio Peace and Progress broadcast in English to Asia gave some support to Pyongyang's contention that the plane had intruded into North Korean airspace; and an April 17 Radio Moscow broadcast in Korean did the same. But the Soviet Union's strongest support of North Korea did not come until April 18, when an *Izvestiya* article said that the Pentagon had "prepared loopholes in advance in the event of various kinds of accusations and declared that the crew of the aircraft had instructions to keep 60 miles from the limits of DPRK airspace." The article added that since the *Pueblo* episode "this sort of declaration is not taken seriously even in Congress." However, there was no support for North Korea's contention that its self-defense had been "legitimate."[108]

Moscow protested Task Force 71's entry into the Sea of Japan only mildly and orally; it was thought in Washington that its protests on April 21 were pro forma and made mainly to express Soviet solidarity with North Korea.[109] Perhaps to help the Soviet Union as well as to avert any stronger Soviet response, Washington publicized the protests.

It is not clear to what degree the Russians feared for their own security at the time. U.S. behavior in the *Pueblo* case and President Nixon's assurance that Task Force 71 was directed against North Korea only should have allayed their fear. This is probably why they assembled such a small

107. The Soviet eagerness to help may have been spurred by the hope that they would get intelligence information from the debris. The EC-121 had, after all, carried six tons of electronic equipment. However, there is no indication that the Russians found anything worthwhile or kept what they did find.

108. FBIS, *Daily Report,* April 16 and 23, 1969.

109. *New York Times,* April 23, 1969.

naval force in the Sea of Japan. At the same time, they could not be sure what the newly elected, "hard-line" U.S. president might do, particularly since the U.S. buildup was so large.

In any case, Moscow could not permit the North Koreans to take risks that might involve the Soviet Union. On May 14, just a few weeks after the EC-121 was shot down, the Russians sent a delegation headed by Soviet President Nikolai V. Podgorny to Pyongyang for a few days.[110] There seems little doubt that Podgorny expressed Soviet disapproval of the new North Korean action to Kim Il-Sung. Repeating Polyansky's September 1968 remarks, Podgorny spoke of the need for *"collective* action" to repel U.S. warships and planes and noted that North Korea had contractual relations with the Soviet Union for the *"joint* defense of socialist gains and the enemies should not forget this."[111]

In sharp contrast to the line then coming from Pyongyang, Podgorny stressed the need for, and the tactical utility of, a relaxation of tension in the Far East. In a line pointedly omitted from the North Korean version of Podgorny's speech, the Soviet leader said: "Experience shows that periods of relaxation of tension in international relations and the implementing of the principles of peaceful coexistence in the final analysis have always been more beneficial for socialism and the national liberation movement than for imperialism."[112]

Finally, all of Podgorny's speeches in North Korea emphasized the need for "peaceful" reunification of Korea. They mentioned the Soviet-Korean mutual defense treaty only as the basis of friendship between the two countries, not in the context of the U.S. "imperialist" threat, as North Korean media usually spoke of the treaty.

One purpose of Podgorny's visit to North Korea after the shooting down of the EC-121 was thus to express Moscow's displeasure at North Korea's unilateral actions and to try to convince the North Koreans that they could achieve their goals better through peaceful than through violent means.[113] Podgorny may have spoken even more bluntly to the North Koreans in private. For after the EC-121 incident the number of cases of North Korean subversions and violence across the demilitarized zone fell sharply, from 761 in 1968 to 134 in 1969.[114]

110. FBIS, *Survey,* May 22, 1969.
111. Ibid.; emphasis added.
112. Ibid.
113. *New York Times,* May 15, 1969.
114. Simmons, "Case Studies," p. 25.

The Russians also sought to gain North Korean support against China. After his visit to North Korea, Podgorny visited Outer Mongolia, apparently as part of a concerted Soviet effort to consolidate relations with Asian allies after the border clashes with the Chinese the previous year. To get North Korean support against Peking, Podgorny evidently felt he must make some gesture to Pyongyang, and he signed a joint communiqué with Kim Il-Sung that was harder on "U.S. imperialism" than Soviet propaganda usually was.[115] Beyond this limited gesture he did not go.

The Chinese were quick to sense the situation and profit from it. Peking's reaction to the EC-121 incident was to try to make points about Soviet-American collusion. The Chinese were slowly beginning to follow a more pragmatic foreign policy after the excesses of the Cultural Revolution had worsened relations with Pyongyang and other states. Although Peking responded to the incident with praise for North Korea,[116] most of its comment was criticism of the Soviet response. It particularly censured Soviet willingness to assist the United States in the search for survivors and debris and asserted that a U.S. official had said: "Russian willingness to render assistance has been astonishing. From the way they are doing things at present they look like allies instead of opponents in the cold war."[117] The Chinese press agency NCNA called the assistance "servile compliance" and "a new ugly performance of U.S.-Soviet collusion."[118]

On the whole, then, the Soviet Union wanted to preserve its relationship with the United States while offering Pyongyang aid and support as an incentive to move away from Peking (though it was clearly giving up hope of bringing the North Koreans around).

Under these circumstances, Moscow decided to help the United States look for survivors. Its support of North Korean arguments was equivocal. Despite the large U.S. military buildup, the Soviet Union made only a token military response, and this was designed to gather information on U.S. intentions. Three of the six Soviet ships were intelligence vessels; the other three—destroyers—may only have been intended to ensure their security. The Soviet military response also was meant both to remind the United States that Moscow viewed with disfavor such a large buildup close

115. FBIS, *Survey*, May 22, 1969.
116. Simmons, "China's Cautious Relations with North Korea and Indochina," p. 634.
117. BBC Monitoring Service, *Summary of World Broadcasts*, FE/3055/A2/1 (April 23, 1969); cited by Simmons, "Case Studies," p. 22.
118. Cited by *New York Times*, April 24, 1969.

to Soviet territory and to reassure the United States that the Soviet Union had nothing to do with initiating the incident. Finally, the small size of the Soviet naval presence was a warning to Kim Il-Sung that Moscow was not going to encourage him in such provocative action, particularly at a time when it was engaged in fruitful negotiations with the United States and armed conflict with China.

As in the *Pueblo* case, the Soviet Union appears to have succeeded in its objectives with the United States. Its naval presence probably reinforced the U.S. decision not to take retaliatory military action, while its aid to the United States helped reassure Washington that Moscow had not helped precipitate the EC-121 incident. Task Force 71 was moved out of the Sea of Japan quickly. Soviet objectives in Pyongyang were less well realized. North Korean subversion slackened, but the North did not shift ground against Peking. Nor was a new anti-U.S. attack precluded.

The Poplar Tree Incident

Seven years after the North Koreans shot down the EC-121, North Korean soldiers axed and clubbed to death two U.S. Army officers on duty at the DMZ.

The episode began on July 28, 1976, when the UN Command in Korea (manned mainly by Americans) advised the Korean People's Army (KPA) and the Military Armistice Commission that UN personnel would be in the Joint Security Area (JSA) during August for construction, beautification, and routine maintenance.[119] Not long after, UN forces surveyed a poplar tree that had long been a problem for UN guards because it obstructed the view from one observation post to another. It was decided that the tree would be cut down.

On August 6 a UN work crew attempted to do this, but it was warned off by a KPA guard. The crew then withdrew, reporting the situation to JSA commander Lieutenant Colonel Victor S. Vierra, who noted that any further work on the tree might require special precautions. It was also determined that the tree could be merely trimmed, not cut down.

Accordingly, on the morning of August 18 Vierra sent a reinforced work detail of fifteen men to trim the tree. The detail was headed by Captain Arthur G. Bonifas and included one other U.S. officer and South

119. This kind of activity had been carried on for years in the JSA without serious incident.

Korean Army Captain Kim. Vierra also made arrangements for monitoring the operation and for quick reaction in case of trouble.

The group entered the Joint Security Area in a truck and drove to the deserted poplar. Within a minute, two North Korean army officers and nine guards arrived in a similar truck. Captain Kim told the KPA the work detail meant to trim, not fell, the tree. The head of the KPA group, later identified as Lieutenant Pak Chul, a seven- to eight-year JSA veteran, replied that this was "good." The North Koreans then proceeded to comment on the tree trimming, while other North Korean guards gathered at the scene. When the work was nearly done, Pak told Captain Bonifas to stop, warning him there might be trouble if he did not. Captain Bonifas directed that the work continue. Lieutenant Pak sent a runner, apparently for more North Korean guards. Soon after, a second North Korean army truck arrived with eight to ten guards, and other guards moved to the scene, bringing the total of North Koreans to nearly thirty. Pak again directed that the work stop, saying, "The branches that are cut will be of no use, just as you will be after you die." Captain Bonifas told his men to continue working. Meanwhile, JSA commander Vierra, monitoring the situation in the rear, called the UN command post closest to the scene and told the men there to tell Bonifas to stop work. As this order was given, however, Pak attacked Captain Bonifas with his feet. Several North Korean guards then jumped on Bonifas and beat him, and the remaining guards attacked the UN security force, first with fists and feet and then with clubs and metal pipes from the back of their truck and the axes being used to trim the tree. Within minutes, two U.S. Army officers—Bonifas and First Lieutenant Mark T. Barrett—were dead, and nine other men in the UN force were wounded. (The North Koreans later claimed casualties of their own.)

General Richard G. Stilwell, commander of UN and U.S. forces in Korea, learned of the events almost as they occurred; he returned to Korea from Japan, where he was touring Japanese self-defense forces, the same evening. The U.S. Joint Chiefs of Staff, the White House, and Secretary of State Henry Kissinger were all advised immediately. Shortly thereafter, President Gerald Ford was informed in Kansas City, where he was attending the Republican National Convention. He expressed strong indignation over the murders. Within a day, the administration was considering a range of possible alternative responses to the North Korean action. These included doing nothing; staging a show of force by U.S. units in Korea; deploying forces from other Pacific units to Korea; deploying a squadron of fighters from the United States to Korea; sending an aircraft carrier to Korean waters; increasing the combat readiness of U.S. forces; and carrying out a retaliatory action. The administration decided to make a show of force.

The same day, the State Department demanded that North Korea accept responsibility for the killings, provide assurances that such incidents would not occur in the future, and punish the men responsible. Secretary of State Kissinger met with both the Japanese and Chinese representatives in Washington and was in touch almost immediately with the Soviet ambassador. Kissinger apparently obtained Japanese consent to the deployment of Japan-based U.S. forces. He probably assured the Chinese and Russian ambassadors that any military actions the United States undertook would be aimed solely at North Korea. He may also have urged the Chinese and Russians to put pressure on North Korean leader Kim Il-Sung to meet the U.S. demands. He reportedly emerged confident from his talks with Chinese Ambassador Huang Chen that China would not give material support to Pyongyang.[120]

By August 19 a squadron of F-4 phantom fighter planes had arrived in South Korea from Okinawa; the alert status of U.S. forces in Korea had been raised to defense condition 3 and flights from Guam to Korea were made by B-52s; an F-111 squadron was on its way from Idaho, supported by KC-135 refueling aircraft; and Task Group 77.4, comprising the aircraft carrier *Midway* and four frigates, was sent from Japan to the area. Most of these forces were in place by early morning, August 21. Then, at General Stilwell's suggestion and with Washington's approval but with little notice to North Korea, U.S. and South Korean troops carried out Operation Paul Bunyan: cutting down the poplar tree.

Within the hour, North Korea's senior representative to the Military Armistice Commission, Major General Han Ju-kyong, requested a private meeting with the U.S. representative to the Military Armistice Commission at Panmunjom, Rear Admiral Mark P. Frudden, to convey a message from his supreme commander, Kim Il-Sung. This meeting took place at noon the same day, when General Han passed along the following statement for delivery to General Stilwell:

It is a good thing that no big incident occurred at Pan Mun Jom for a long period. However, it is regretful that an incident occurred in the Joint Security

---

120. Richard G. Head, Frisco W. Short, and Robert C. McFarlane, *Crisis Resolution: Presidential Decision-making in the* Mayaguez *and Korean Confrontations* (Westview Press, 1978), p. 243.

Area, Pan Mun Jom this time. An effort must be made so that such incidents may not recur in the future. For this purpose both sides should make efforts. We urge your side to prevent the provocation. Our side will never provoke first, but take self-defensive measures only when provocation occurs. This is our consistent stand.[121]

General Han added that the cutting down of the tree that morning had been a serious provocation and that measures should be taken on the United Nations side to avoid such provocations in the future. The message he transmitted was the first personal message from Kim to the UN commander in the twenty-three-year history of the Korean armistice. After a brief delay, the State Department, revealing that the message had been sent, called it a "positive step." For several days, however, B-52 bombers continued to fly daily "practice bombing missions" over South Korea and flew three at a time between South Korea and their bases in Guam. On September 6, after nearly two weeks of meetings, the UN Command and North Korea concluded an agreement in Panmunjom on new security arrangements for the truce area.[122] The same day, the *Midway* left the Sea of Japan. On September 7 U.S. forces in Korea were returned to normal alert status. The rest of Task Group 77.4 left the Sea of Japan on October 12. No Russian military buildup during the entire period is reported.

The 1976 Setting

These events took place in a political climate quite different from that which prevailed during the *Pueblo* and EC-121 crises. First, earlier North Korean provocations had been counterproductive. The EC-121 crisis had led, among other things, to an affirmation of Japanese support for the U.S. position[123] and increased U.S. military aid to Seoul.[124]

121. *New York Times,* August 23, 1976.

122. The new arrangements were based on a formula proposed by the United States in 1970.

123. In contrast to its reluctant support for the United States in the *Pueblo* case, Japan gave the United States relatively strong support over the EC-121; *New York Times,* April 17 and 18, 1969. The Russians, then interested in dampening any Japanese militarism, could not have been happy with this outcome.

124. After the EC-121 was shot down, the United States agreed to send the F-4 fighters it had promised after the *Pueblo* incident; these were scheduled for delivery in August 1969. In addition, 20 F-4 jets were added to the 128 U.S. planes already in South Korea. Two more F-4 squadrons were also sent to replace the Air National Guard F-100 squadrons mobilized after the *Pueblo* attack. Simmons, "Case Studies," p. 22.

Second, by 1976 Soviet–North Korean relations were extremely strained. In March 1970, scientific cooperation between the two countries had broken down. Later that year, at the Fifth Party Congress in Pyongyang, North Korea attacked "revisionism" for "yielding to U.S. imperialism," clearly an attack on the Soviet Union for pursuing détente.

The Russians had never acknowledged Kim's pretensions to being a "creative" thinker. They did not quote him or use his name in connection with North Korean accomplishments, a practice in marked contrast with that of North Korean media, which had built up a Kim cult surpassing the cults of both Stalin and Mao. For an egomaniac like Kim, this must have rankled. He responded by ranking visiting Soviet delegations lower than Chinese.[125]

The Russians took a bold step in September 1971, when, for the first time since the division of Korea at the end of World War II, a Soviet citizen, Igor A. Neto, entered South Korea. North Korea immediately protested the action, warning Moscow not to engage in contacts of any kind with the Republic of Korea. But after the Neto visit, the Soviet Union issued passports to several South Korean businessmen, a few scientists, and a dramatist. In August 1973 North Korea boycotted the Universaid (World University Games) in Moscow because the Russians were allowing a South Korean team to participate. In September 1975 the Soviet Union also granted entry visas to South Korean sportsmen.

By 1975 the signs of discord were unmistakable. The most dramatic was Kim's failure to visit Moscow during his first trip outside Korea in ten years, which took him to China, Eastern Europe, and North Africa. The only close ally he visited was Bulgaria, and the North Korean–Bulgarian communiqué suggests that substantial differences existed between the two countries.[126]

After this episode Russian and North Korean relations continued to cool, with the media of both countries consistently playing down anniversary occasions that in the past had been used to stress friendly relations between the two. In August 1975, on the thirtieth anniversary of the

125. See Byung Chul Koh, "North Korea: A Breakthrough in the Quest for Unity," *Asian Survey*, vol. 13 (January 1973), p. 88.
126. FBIS, *Trends*, June 11, 1975. Whether the Russians snubbed Kim or Kim snubbed Moscow is not clear. It was probably the former, however. A high-ranking Soviet official said in the summer of 1975 that Moscow had asked Kim to defer his planned visit to Russia until later in the year because Soviet officials were then "too busy" to see him. Another Soviet official described Kim as a "hot potato" that Moscow thought China should handle first.

Soviet liberation of North Korea, Pyongyang disparaged the value of Soviet aid to North Korea since 1945. No high-level Soviet delegation went to North Korea for that occasion.[127] A month later, the twenty-seventh anniversary of the nation's founding was not attended by a Soviet delegation, nor was the thirtieth anniversary of the founding of the Korean Workers (Communist) party. Only three Communist states—Rumania, Cuba, and Hungary—sent delegations to commemorate the latter occasion and Kim snubbed the closest Soviet ally, Hungary.[128] Pyongyang treated the fifty-eighth anniversary of the Russian revolution coolly.[129]

Meanwhile, after reaching a high in the early 1970s, trade between the two countries stagnated. The Soviet Union did little to help North Korea out of its economic difficulties resulting from heavy defense expenditures, but instead attempted to use trade as a political weapon to gain Pyongyang's support in the Sino-Soviet dispute.[130] After completing the program of military assistance to North Korea it had begun before the *Pueblo* incident, the Soviet Union did not undertake any major new military commitments.[131]

By contrast, Chinese–North Korean relations improved from April 1969 on. Unlike the Russians, the Chinese acknowledged Kim Il-Sung's greatness as a leader, quoting him generously. At the October 1969 celebrations in Peking, for example, the North Korean delegation was met at the airport by Premier Chou En-lai although North Korea had belatedly decided to attend; moreover, after the opening day North Korea appeared first on official lists of visiting delegations.[132]

In 1970 the North Korean ambassador to China reappeared after an absence of two years, after which Chou visited Pyongyang, his first trip abroad after the end of the Cultural Revolution. Other high-level Chinese

127. Ibid., August 20, 1975, p. 21.

128. Ibid., October 16, 1976, p. 16; also ibid., September 10, 1975, p. 20.

129. Ibid., November 12, 1975, p. 11.

130. The Soviet Union did not, for example, help North Korea to meet its international debts, nor did it reschedule the $700 million debt that was outstanding to itself.

131. By 1971 North Korea had 900 airplanes, of which 500 were MIG fighter-bombers. It also had thirty missile bases, twenty more than in early 1968. (*New York Times,* April 16, 1969.) But whereas in 1972, 80 percent of North Korean military assistance came from the Soviet Union and the rest from China, from early 1975, half came from Russia and half from China. For a fuller discussion of the deterioration in Soviet-North Korean relations, see Donald S. Zagoria, "Korea's Future: Moscow's Perspective," *Asian Survey,* November 1977.

132. Simmons, "China's Cautious Relations with North Korea and Indochina," p. 634.

visits followed. Subsequently, the Chinese dropped the claim to North Korean territory that they had advanced during the Cultural Revolution.

In July 1971 China attended, for the first time since 1966, a meeting of the Korean Military Armistice Commission. Soon after, Mao sent a message to North Korea's Kim on the tenth anniversary of the Chinese-Korean friendship treaty assuring North Korea of joint military aid.

China was even partially successful in selling its own policy of détente to North Korea. After the visit of President Nixon to China had been planned but before he went, Li Teh-sheng, an alternate member of the Chinese politburo and director of the People's Liberation Army general political department, visited North Korea. Possibly he told the North Koreans about the prospective visit, explaining the trip as a sign of U.S. weakness and arguing that it would help China offset the growing threat from Japan feared by both Peking and Pyongyang.[133] The North Koreans probably did not like the move, but they swallowed it. After a month, Kim commented on the planned visit, saying that Nixon was going to Peking with a "white flag."[134]

In April 1975 Kim visited Peking for the first time in fourteen years and met with the ailing and rarely seen Mao. In the communiqué that resulted from this visit, the Chinese, unlike the Russians, backed Kim's claim that North Korea was the "sole and legal sovereign state of the Korean nation," but they indicated that they would support only "peaceful reunification," not any plans Kim might have for forcibly taking over South Korea. When Kim spoke of intervening in South Korea, Vice Premier Teng Hsiao-p'ing asserted several times that reunification must be by peaceful means. Other Chinese statements stressed North Korean military strength rather than joint Chinese–North Korean military action.

Peking was preoccupied during this entire period with its struggle with the Soviet Union and, as the Chinese dialogue with Washington developed, with maintaining that link as a possible counter to Soviet power. Although Chinese–North Korean relations were improving, the Chinese remained cautious about North Korean interests, and Pyongyang must have been well aware of this.

Since neither Moscow nor Peking was willing to give much support to North Korea's efforts to get the United States out of South Korea and take over the South, Kim evidently decided to try direct pressure on both

133. Byung Chul Koh, "The Korean Worker's Party and Detente," *Journal of International Affairs,* vol. 28, no. 2 (1974), p. 177.

134. Ibid., p. 179.

Washington and Seoul. In 1972, for example, he told an American journalist—one of three allowed into North Korea that year—that "Washington should improve relations not only with big countries but with small countries as well."[135] The following April North Korea appealed to the U.S. Congress for withdrawal of the 40,000 U.S. troops then stationed in South Korea. In March 1974 Pyongyang proposed a bilateral peace agreement with the United States to supersede the 1953 Korean armistice agreement. Meanwhile, it tried to win over the American public by running ads in the *New York Times* and other papers with statements and pictures of a benevolent-looking Kim Il-Sung.

These efforts, however, drew little American response. In mid-1975 President Ford decided to make a show of force in Asia by rescuing the commercial container ship *Mayaguez* from the Khmer (Communist) forces that had just taken over Cambodia. Administration officials made it clear that one of the aims of the operation was to deter North Korean adventurism. Soon after, Secretary of State Kissinger reaffirmed the U.S. defense commitment to South Korea.

Evidently not completely discouraged, North Korea asked Japanese Premier Miki to help arrange talks between Pyongyang and Washington regarding an agreement to replace the existing Korean armistice accord. President Ford responded in his Pacific doctrine, announced in Honolulu in December, explicitly rejecting North Korean overtures for a separate agreement with the United States that would exclude South Korea. In the intervening period, on June 30, 1975, North Korean guards in the DMZ had surrounded, knocked unconscious, and seriously injured a U.S. army major during a Military Armistice Commission meeting. The incident involved Pak Chul, then a sergeant, of the KPA.

North Korea had little more success with South Korea. A dialogue developed between the two governments in April 1971 when, after overtures by Seoul, North Korean Foreign Minister Ho Dam unveiled an "eight-point program" for reunification that made certain concessions to the South.[136] On August 21 *Nodong Shinmun* called for unification of Korea by peaceful means "without interference of outside forces."[137] Also in August, North and South Korean Red Cross representatives held their

135. Koh, "North Korea," p. 90.
136. Koh, "The Korean Worker's Party and Detente," p. 182.
137. The North Koreans proposed confederation of North and South, with the political systems remaining intact; or, as a second alternative, carrying on "economic and cultural intercourse and mutual visits of personages" while laying aside political issues.

first meeting to discuss contacts between members of families and relatives separated by the Korean War.

A year later Kim Il-Sung indicated to visiting *Washington Post* correspondent Selig S. Harrison that he was willing to meet with South Korean President Park.[138] The next month, it was announced that high-level officials of the two governments had met and agreed on the principle of reunification, without outside interference, which was to set up a joint coordinating committee to solve various North-South problems and "not to slander or defame each other." The same day, a telephone hot line was opened between Pyongyang and Seoul. This June 1972 meeting was the high point of North Korean–South Korean contacts.

Almost immediately, the two sides gave differing interpretations of their joint statement. In October North Korea virulently attacked South Korea's ruling elite.[139] Soon after, in March 1973, North-South talks broke down. In August 1974 President Park's wife died of wounds received in an assassination attempt probably initiated by Pyongyang.

By late 1974–early 1975 North Korea was showing a new militancy, born in part no doubt of its continuing economic problems. In 1972 Pyongyang had had to cut its defense spending sharply. It also had difficulty paying its foreign debts; in October 1975 it managed to have its debts rescheduled only by agreeing to prepay the interest on them.

There was one area in which North Korea did have some success in this period: wooing the third world and other countries in an attempt to isolate and undermine the Park regime. In 1972 North Korea established diplomatic relations with six countries and received visits from representatives of others. The following year relations were established with nearly a dozen more third world countries and with several European countries as well. Pyongyang also gained admission to various international bodies, including the World Health Organization and the United Nations Conference on Trade and Development. It obtained status as a permanent observer at the United Nations. And it won a victory in the UN when the General Assembly passed two rival Korean resolutions: a U.S.-backed resolution calling for both Koreas to continue the North-South dialogue; and a pro–North Korean resolution advocating dissolution of the UN Command, negotiation of a peace treaty between the United States and North Korea, and the withdrawal of all foreign forces from Korea.

In mid-1975 Kim traveled to North Africa and Europe. In August

138. Koh, "North Korea," p. 90.
139. Ibid., p. 86.

North Korea gained admission to the conference of nonaligned countries in Lima. The next month, the UN Security Council refused for the second time to consider South Korea's application for admission. By this time, the North had diplomatic relations with nearly ninety countries, forty-four more than in 1972.[140]

It was against the backdrop of all these developments that the poplar tree murders took place. The year 1976 began with a rise in the number of incidents near the DMZ, and tension built as summer approached.

In February Soviet Communist party leader Leonid Brezhnev made a lengthy report on the world situation to the Twenty-fifth CPSU Congress in which he did not refer to the Korean question and included only one reference to Pyongyang in a ceremonial list of "fraternal Socialist states."[141] Three months later, in May, North Korea signed a joint communiqué with a visiting Pakistani delegation condemning aggression in all its forms, including efforts to achieve "hegemony," the code word long used by Peking to condemn Soviet expansion.[142] The same month, Pyongyang defaulted on debts of $130 million to Western countries.

In July the Chinese leadership—still under the sway of radical elements, possibly strengthened by the prospect of Mao's death—sent the North Koreans a message. In it the Chinese warmly stressed the "great unity of our two people cemented with bloodshed in their protracted fight against common enemies." They went on:

The Chinese people firmly support the Korean people in their just struggle for the independent and peaceful reunification of their fatherland and resolutely condemn all schemes aimed at creating "two Koreas." We are sure that the heroic Korean people will remove interference by any outside forces and accomplish the great cause of opposing U.S. imperialist aggression and realizing the independent and peaceful reunification of their fatherland.[143]

China also charged, in a *People's Daily* editorial the same day, July 10, that the United States had:

shipped into South Korea big quantities of modern weapons, and repeatedly staged military exercises to aggravate tension on the Korean peninsula. The U.S. must dissolve the "U.N. Command" and withdraw all of its troops from

140. Chong Sik Lee, "New Paths for North Korea," *Problems of Communism*, vol. 26 (March–April 1977), pp. 56–57.

141. Press release, Leonid Brezhnev on the World Situation, USSR Mission to the UN, February 25, 1976.

142. FBIS, *Trends* (June 3, 1976), p. 23.

143. New China News Agency (NCNA) broadcast in English, July 10, 1976. The message of congratulation and support was sent in the name of Chairman Mao Tsetung and Premier Hua Kuo-feng on the fifteenth anniversary of the Chinese-Korean Treaty of Friendship, Cooperation, and Mutual Assistance.

South Korea in accordance with the resolution of the 30th session of the U.N. General Assembly.

This was certainly grist for North Korea's mill, supporting its case that the United States was engaged in preparing for war in South Korea. The statements, as well as the warming ties with China, must have encouraged some in the North to think that there was still hope for decisive action to oust the United States from South Korea and reunify the peninsula.

Within a month, North Korea issued a strongly worded government statement attacking the United States and South Korea, accompanied by a memorandum purporting to document that the United States was about to make war on North Korea. It said the United States had *completed* war preparations and was entering into a "phase of directly triggering war" from a "phase of directly preparing for war." It also demanded that the United States withdraw all its military equipment from South Korea, give up its "two Koreas" policy, disband the UN Command, withdraw all foreign troops under the UN flag (that is, U.S. forces in South Korea), and replace the armistice agreement with a peace agreement. Then, the statement said, Korea could be reunified through a national congress.[144]

Thus, the July message from Peking—like Soviet military aid in the case of the *Pueblo* incident—may have emboldened Pyongyang to make a new, aggressive move against the United States. Or perhaps more accurately, North Korea was ready to use almost any sign of support from Russia or China as a pretext for taking new action.

Besides expressing North Korean frustration at its unsuccessful efforts to make a breakthrough—either by military action against South Korea and the United States or by direct negotiations with them—the poplar tree incident may have been staged to advance North Korean interests in two forums: at the nonaligned conference in Sri Lanka, which began on August 16, and at the United Nations. Kim had planned to attend the Colombo conference, but at the last minute he evidently changed his mind. According to Belgrade radio on August 15, he wired Yugoslav President Tito that he would not attend because of a "deteriorating situation on the Korean border,"[145] but North Korean Premier Pak Song Chul and Foreign Minister Ho Dam did go. On August 17 Pak Song Chul made a fiery speech against the United States repeating many of the

144. Head, Short, and McFarlane, *Crisis Resolution,* p. 208.
145. Ibid., p. 212.

demands that had been made in the government's August statement, but also adding that any attack on a nonaligned member should be considered an attack on all, requiring severance of political and economic relations with the aggressor. He proposed a resolution to condemn "imperialist maneuvers to provoke a war in Korea."[146] The next day Ho Dam charged at a press conference that the United States was preparing to "throw its aggressive forces into an all-out attack against North Korea."[147] That was the day the poplar tree incident occurred. It may have been timed to gain nonaligned support for the North Korean resolution.

At the UN General Assembly, pro–North Korean allies had entered, just before the poplar tree incident, a strong resolution calling for withdrawal from Korea of all foreign forces under the UN flag, withdrawal of "new types of military equipment" from South Korea, and an end to acts aggravating tension and increasing the danger of war. It too called for unconditional dissolution of the UN Command and replacement of the armistice agreement with a peace agreement. Pyongyang may have hoped that passage of the resolution would be facilitated by an incident in the DMZ.

That the poplar tree incident was premeditated seems clear because there was a noticeable pause between the time the North Korean guards appeared and the attack itself. That it was in line with the policies of at least some North Korean leaders also seems likely because of the sharp increase in incidents initiated by North Koreans along the DMZ in early 1976 and the provocative North Korean statements on the eve of the incident.

Soviet Reaction

The Russians did not immediately report the killings. Although they were in touch almost immediately with U.S. officials in Moscow and Washington, they first reported the incident on August 20 in a broadcast that spoke of "heightened tensions" and "provocative actions" by the U.S. forces in Korea.[148] *Pravda* reports on August 21 and 22 noted that the clash had taken place and that there was a U.S. military buildup in South Korea; no mention was made of the KPA forces being placed on alert. On

146. *Washington Post,* August 18, 1976.
147. *Far Eastern Economic Review,* September 3, 1976.
148. Head, Short, and McFarlane, *Crisis Resolution,* p. 288.

August 23 a broadcast from Moscow in English reported that Kim Il-Sung had sent a message to the United States; Moscow inaccurately, but significantly, claimed that the message expressed "regret" that the "provocation" initiated by the United States had led to the deaths of two American officers.[149] Finally, on August 29, an *Izvestiya* editorial lightly rapped the United States for using "threats and sabre-rattling" methods that were inconsistent with détente.[150] This mild rhetorical support seems to have been the extent of Soviet aid to North Korea in the incident.

There are no indications of any Soviet military buildup either while the United States was carrying out its show of force during the tree-cutting or afterward. Possibly the Russians were not worried about the U.S. military action. Perhaps they had learned from the previous two incidents that the United States was unlikely to take retaliatory military action against either North Korean or Soviet targets. Undoubtedly Secretary of State Kissinger assured the Russians, during his talks with the Soviet ambassador on August 18, that any U.S. military action would have a limited purpose and be of short duration. The mention of the U.S. buildup reflects some Soviet uneasiness about the reappearance of the U.S. military forces in the area.

Perhaps the Russians were also being extremely careful not to provoke President Ford. After the *Mayaguez* operation, they may have feared that Ford would look for another opportunity to reaffirm U.S. military strength, this time on the Korean peninsula. They would have understood that the presidential campaign was an appropriate time for such a show of strength and avoided giving him an opening for such action.[151]

It is more likely, however, that Soviet relations with North Korea were by this time so attenuated that Moscow simply did not feel it worthwhile to give more than the blandest sort of support to the North Korean position. At the time of the murders North Korea was actively in the process of warming up relations with China. With little to gain, the Soviet Union decided to do next to nothing.

In any case, it could have done little, since its influence over North Korea at the time was limited. It could have put pressure on Kim to produce his grudging apology, and Soviet specialist Zbigniew Brzezinski argued that the Russians preferred Ford because he was a known quantity,

149. FBIS, *Trends,* August 25, 1976.

150. Head, Short, and McFarlane, *Crisis Resolution,* p. 288.

151. Indications are that Ford's response to the poplar tree incident may, in fact, have helped him in the campaign. Ibid., p. 279.

and they did not want to see him embarrassed; so they urged Kim Il-Sung to comply.[152] This is quite possible.

However, no one felt they had much influence in Pyongyang in August 1976. Attention was directed to what the Chinese could do for the United States in the situation. They probably played the largest part in bringing about the Kim message, as press reports indicated.[153]

China was even quieter than the USSR about the poplar tree incident, reporting the killings but toning down the North Koreans' inflammatory remarks about them and refraining from any comment of its own for two weeks although it was present at talks in Panmunjom.[154] The Chinese also had an interest in seeing that President Ford, with whose administration they were beginning a dialogue, was not humiliated. They may have used their improved relationship with Kim to tell him to cool down. Reports to this effect were not disputed in Washington.[155] Perhaps Ambassador Huang Chen indicated something along these lines to Secretary of State Kissinger.

Both the Soviet Union and China probably encouraged North Korea to accept the new arrangements in the DMZ instituted in September. The Soviet Union may have joined China in urging North Korea to abandon its hostile activities along the border. At Military Armistice Commission meetings the North Koreans were businesslike and uncharacteristically subdued.

Whether or not the Soviet Union did push the North Koreans in these ways, Moscow certainly tilted toward the United States. Far from aiding Pyongyang, it helped make good the American case; this seems to have been understood in Washington. By the same token, North Korean restraint after the incident indicates that the Soviet message that the Russians would not support North Korean attacks on U.S. personnel or targets finally got through to Pyongyang. Soviet objectives were well served on both counts.

Conclusions

The poplar tree incident did nothing to advance North Korea's cause in marshaling third world and international support, getting the United

152. *Far Eastern Economic Review,* September 3, 1976.
153. See, for example, *Korea Herald,* August 28, 1976.
154. *Washington Post,* August 31, 1976.
155. *Far Eastern Economic Review,* September 3, 1976.

States out of South Korea, reunifying the peninsula under Northern control, or shoring up Soviet and Chinese support. On the contrary, at Colombo, although the North Korean resolution passed on August 20, it did so over the strong objections of fifteen members of the conference and after one of the sharpest public disagreements in the nonaligned movement's fifteen-year history. Since then, North Korean prestige and influence in the movement has shown a steady deterioration, and South Korea's relations with the third world have shown a correspondingly steady improvement.

The same counterproductive results of North Korea's militance have been evident at the United Nations. The pro–North Korean resolution that had been entered in 1976 was withdrawn by its sponsors before revulsion over the killings could bring about its defeat. And the North Koreans have not bothered to introduce a resolution at the United Nations since. They proved to be their own worst enemies. The third world countries blamed North Korea, not the Americans, for the poplar tree incident.

In testing the U.S. resolve in such a barbarous manner at such a juncture in American politics,[156] Pyongyang—deliberately or inadvertently—brought about a show of American force that compelled it to put its own military forces on a wartime footing. The incident also helped strengthen the support of many Americans, including congressmen, for the defense commitment to South Korea. President Jimmy Carter met substantial congressional resistance to his planned withdrawal of combat troops from South Korea—much of the resistance because of a general perception in the United States that Kim Il-Sung is reckless, unpredictable, and bloodthirsty.

The incident also helped to bolster foreign support, especially in Europe, for the U.S. position in South Korea. The Swedish moderate newspaper *Swenski Dagbladet* said after the incident, for example: "If the most recent crisis . . . shows anything it is that the U.S. presence is still indispensable as a guarantee against an armed North Korean attack against the border to the South."[157] Kim's grudging apology was also a political loss. It neither erased the stain of the killings in the eyes of foreign countries nor increased his prestige with his own people.

---

156. It is not really possible to determine whether the incident was actually ordered in Pyongyang, perhaps by reckless elements in the North Korean leadership, or whether it was an initiative by local military forces. But the extremely tense atmosphere at the DMZ was consistent with Pyongyang's unyielding policy at the time.

157. Quoted in Head, Short, and McFarlane, *Crisis Resolution,* p. 279.

In addition, whatever hopes Pyongyang may have retained for dealing with the Seoul regime were dashed. South Korean President Park responded to the incident by pledging to retaliate in case of another North Korean provocation, "minor or major." He said angrily, "There is a limit to our patience. A stick is needed for a mad dog."[158] Although there was some South Korean irritation with the United States over its vacillating response to Kim's message, this was generally offset by the show of U.S. force at a time when South Korean policies were under critical scrutiny in the United States.

Finally, in provoking the United States again and in such a way, North Korea may have used up much of the support it could expect from the Soviet Union and China. The North Korean leadership has maneuvered, with considerable success, between the Soviet Union and China since their dispute began. It is strategically placed in Asia, and neither Communist superpower wants to see it replaced by a non-Communist regime. But both Soviet and Chinese support for the North Korean position has been decreasing. This is particularly evident in the case of the Soviet Union. From a cautious military show of force and strong political support for North Korea in January 1968, it moved to markedly weaker support, both militarily and politically in April 1969, when it also actively helped the United States. In August 1976 there was no Soviet military reaction at all, and Moscow gave only the mildest kind of verbal backing to the North Korean case. Moscow's support for North Korean initiatives had become practically nil. This undoubtedly contributed to the poor Soviet–North Korean relationship evident in 1980.

158. *Japan Times,* August 21, 1976.

CHAPTER TEN

The Arab-Israeli Wars
of 1967 and 1973

PAUL JABBER *and* ROMAN KOLKOWICZ

BECAUSE OF THE high priority Moscow gave the normalization and stabilization of relations with the industrialized West during the late 1960s and early 1970s, it was careful not to give the United States any provocation in the Middle East. Moscow preferred protracted, low-level, controlled instability in the Middle East to radical and violent rearrangement of the regional political and military balance. The latter, however, was at the heart of the policy objectives of Arab clients in the area. Thus a frustrating, dissonant, and counterproductive relationship ensued between patron and clients. Moreover, neither the primary Soviet security objectives in the Middle East (in our view, long-term access to naval and air facilities) nor those of the clients (superior offensive weapons systems) were granted by either side. In short, while Moscow was impelled by ideological, political, and security motivations to penetrate the Middle East, its behavior there was constrained by superpower balancing and deterring relations with the United States.

In the aftermath of Nikita Khrushchev's ouster from power in 1964, a fundamental realignment occurred in Soviet priorities and tactics. Instead of following a single Stalinist, either-or policy of confrontation with the West or Khrushchev's provocative and discredited policy based on camouflaged weakness and lacking internal consistency or clear purpose, the Brezhnev-Kosygin regime set a new course. This policy was trifurcated: to *hold and stabilize* relations with the industrialized West; to *contain* China; and to *explore and expand* in the areas south of Russia. Soviet policy toward the West became stabilizing across the board (détente, deterrence, arms control, cultural and scientific exchanges, technological transfers, trade, and so forth) ; policy toward China was one of containing ideological hostility, military pressure, and political challenges; policies in the Middle East and the third world were exploratory and expansionary and included massive arms transfers, technical assistance, anti-imperialistic agitation, and support of radical and revolutionary movements.

While eagerly seeking to expand its presence and influence among the "progressive" Arab countries, the Soviet Union continued to give stabilizing relations with the industrialized West a higher priority than destabilizing and quasi-revolutionary activities in the Middle East. On the whole, it may be proper to characterize Soviet interests and constraints in the Middle East during the 1967–73 period as reflecting a long-range investment of resources—a policy of nonprovocative and gradual penetration into societies that are receptive because of partial ideological congruence, dependence on Soviet arms and credits, or sheer desperation resulting from looming defeat in war. Soviet policy was challenged to maneuver between the fear of superpower confrontation and the ideological, political, economic, and strategic lures set by the porousness and instability of the Middle East.

The Middle East and the Mediterranean basin assumed significant security interests for the Soviet Union from the mid-sixties on as a result of several developments: the movement of Soviet strategic doctrine and policy away from the rigid finite-deterrence, quasi-massive-retaliation position supported by the Khrushchev regime toward concepts of limited, conventional wars as a probable, even desirable, Soviet policy variant;[1] a huge military and merchant naval building program that changed Russia from a minor naval actor into a global naval power and aroused its interest in certain naval facilities and a presence in the Mediterranean region;[2] and a shift in Soviet strategic policies so that the navy's role changed from one that was largely defensive and supportive to a forward-deployed, deterrence-related anticarrier and anti-Polaris mission.[3]

1. See Thomas Wolfe, "Russia's Forces Go Mobile," *Interplay*, March 1968; Thomas Wolfe, *Soviet Power and Europe: 1945–1970* (Johns Hopkins Press, 1970); "Military Power and Soviet Policy," P-5388 (Santa Monica, Calif.: Rand Corp., 1975).

2. Michael MccGwire, "The Evolution of Soviet Naval Policy: 1960–1974," in Michael MccGwire, Kenneth Booth, and John McDonnell, eds., *Soviet Naval Policy: Objectives and Constraints* (Praeger, 1975).

3. Bradford Dismukes, "The Soviet Naval General Purpose Forces: Roles and Missions in Wartime," in MccGwire and others, *Soviet Naval Policy*; and Harlan Ullman, "The Counter-Polaris Task," ibid., pp. 585–97.

All of these developments motivated the Soviet military and political leadership to provide for reliable naval support facilities outside the Black Sea bottleneck and closer to the Sixth Fleet sea-lanes.[4] Moreover, with renewed interest both in building influence in "progressive" and other states of the Mediterranean and in maintaining freedom of maritime passage, high mobility, and effective forces for on-shore intervention, the Soviet Union began showing its flag, visiting ports, and generally maintaining a high profile.[5] Finally, the heightened strategic value of certain countries along the eastern seacoast of Africa and the Red Sea clearly led the Soviet Union to rely on its navy in those areas too.[6]

After Albania terminated the USSR's use of a naval base at Vlone in 1961, the Russians were eager to obtain naval facilities and air bases elsewhere in the littoral region as a replacement. The need for this became even more urgent after the United States announced in 1963 that Polaris submarines would regularly patrol the Mediterranean.[7] The Soviet Union concentrated its efforts on Egypt and embarked on some intensive and expensive wooing of Gamal Abdel Nasser and subsequently of Anwar Sadat. Top Politburo members as well as ranking military leaders visited Cairo regularly.[8] The minister of defense and commander in chief of the Soviet navy, Admiral of the Fleet Sergei I. Gorshkov, made at least four visits to Egypt between 1961 and 1966 trying to persuade the Egyptians to provide his country with naval support facilities.[9] But it was not until the fiasco of the six-day war that the Egyptians, urgently needing Soviet arms aid, provided extensive naval and air support facilities. The USSR thus obtained virtual control over seven air bases in Egypt (Jianaklis, El Mansura, Inchas, Cairo West, Beni Suef, Aswan, and Mersa Matruh), as well as preferential treatment at four harbors in the Mediterranean (Port Said, Alexandria, Mersa Matruh, and Sollum) and one (Berenice) in the Red Sea. These privileges were terminated after March 1976, when Egypt

4. Robert G. Weinland, "Land Support for Naval Forces: Egypt and the Soviet Escadra 1962–1976," *Survival* (London), vol. 20 (March–April 1978).

5. See Michael MccGwire and John McDonnell, eds., *Soviet Naval Influence: Domestic and Foreign Dimensions* (Praeger, 1977), pt. 7.

6. George Dragnich, "The Soviet Union's Quest for Access to Naval Facilities in Egypt Prior to the June War of 1967," Oles Smolansky, "Soviet Policy in the Persian Gulf," and Michael MccGwire, "Foreign-Port Visits by Soviet Naval Units," all in MccGwire and others, *Soviet Naval Policy.*

7. Dragnich, "The Soviet Union's Quest"; Mohamed Heikal, *The Road to Ramadan* (Collins, 1975), p. 40.

8. Dragnich, "The Soviet Union's Quest."

9. Ibid.

abrogated its Treaty of Friendship and Cooperation with the Soviet Union. Since then Moscow has been searching, with mixed results, for alternative naval and air facilities in the region, particularly in Syria, Algeria, Libya, Somalia, Yemen, and Ethiopia. It seems to have concluded, however, that it cannot rely on the volatile regimes and leaders in this region for long-range air and naval facilities and has restructured the size, time on station, scope, and mission of its Mediterranean squadron and the air support units in the region accordingly.[10]

Soviet political interests in the Middle East from 1967 to 1973 appear to have been closely related to the emerging Brezhnev-Kosygin policy realignment. Specifically, the policy of the Soviet Union was to support progressive regimes and movements in the region, link them under Soviet aegis in anti-imperialist, anti-Western entities, make them dependent on the USSR, and finally shape and influence their domestic and foreign policies to conform with its own.

Soviet political and strategic objectives were to (1) maintain a suitable level of tension in the area, forcing the Arab regimes to remain dependent on Soviet military assistance; (2) obtain concessions from Arab clients that served Soviet strategic and national security interests (air and naval support facilities); and (3) obtain and increase Soviet influence in internal affairs of the client state to enhance socialist and Communist values, structures, and political-economic reforms. Above all, the Soviet Union sought to avoid situations in which it would lose control over events while being forced to maintain or even increase its presence and commitment. Faits accomplis by its clients, blackmail, and catalytic developments were to be avoided at any cost; excessive Arab offensive strategic strength was thus to be avoided as well as excessive Arab vulnerability to Israeli offensive superiority. Either one of these contingencies could provoke violent confrontation ("wars of annihilation") between the local protagonists, with superpower involvement inevitable. Since the Soviet Union clearly preferred a protracted stalemate in the area—a state of "no war, no peace"—it used its influence to shape the regional military balance and its clients' national capabilities and strategies to conform with these primary objectives.

Soviet military aid was designed to accomplish the following:

1. To develop strong *defense* postures in Egypt and Syria to make Israeli aggression costly (in lives and material), while allowing the USSR

10. Weinland, "Land Support," p. 79.

to be a highly visible supporter and protector of Arab national security, but without providing its clients with the superior offensive strategic capabilities that might provoke a superpower confrontation by raising the danger of "wars of annihilation" against Israel.

2. To develop credible deterrence capabilities, further reducing Israeli incentives for attacks against Arab states. The Egyptians and Syrians were provided with weapons that enabled them to limit Israeli penetration of their airspace but did not give them offensive superiority.

3. To use defense and deterrence policies, combined with economic and diplomatic pressure on the West, as a strategy of compellence against Israel.[11]

Soviet policy preferences in the Arab-Israeli arena may be summarily described as based on a policy of deterrence that would reduce incentives for unilateral full-scale aggression and of compellence that would enable the Soviet Union and its clients to wrest concessions from Israel without going to war. This strategy therefore shaped the military and political activities of the Kremlin, whose aim was to retain Arab-Israeli qualitative arms balances but not necessarily quantitative parities.

Soviet policy toward the Middle East has changed with the departure of each party leader. Stalin's indifference to the third world was followed by Khrushchev's exuberance and activism and then by the calculating expansionism of the Brezhnev regime. Soviet policy is affected not only by changes of regime but also by the apparently conflicting interests of the ruling hierarchs in the coalition that has been governing Russia since Khrushchev's ouster. The evidence suggests that this is not a harmonious coalition and that important disagreements about priorities and policies have taken place inside the Kremlin.[12] The Politburo contains

11. Thomas Schelling, in an effort to avoid using *compulsion* (the usual noun formation for the verb *to compel*), coined the word *compellence* because the adjective form of *compulsion* is *compulsive,* which "has come to carry quite a different meaning." See Thomas C. Schelling, *Arms and Influence* (Yale University Press, 1966), pp. 69–71. [Editor's note]

12. Evidence of sharp leadership disagreements includes the succession crises of recent decades, the antiparty conflict of 1957, the military disaffection and ensuing "strategic debates" of the 1950s, 1960s, and 1970s, and the remarkable behavior of the Politburo in the Czechoslovak crisis of 1968. Heikal also made caustic observations about Politburo behavior on the occasion of his 1970 visit with Nasser in Russia: "The Soviets decided that the sending of their own crews to man the SAM-3 sites in Egypt was such a critical step that it should be put before the whole Politburo. Its members were summoned from everywhere in the country and one by one they began arriving in their big black cars with the curtains drawn. For the first time in

among its eighteen members the leaders of the major Soviet bureaucracies. With its consensus mode of operation, the group has tended to avoid radical policy innovations and their attendant risks. Instead it has coalesced around minimal cost-risk-threat policies. The main axis of disagreement on the Middle East among the institutional representatives in the Politburo has run between those who prefer a vigorous, massive, and direct involvement and those who advocate prudence, moderation, and economy. The former may be characterized as interventionists, the latter as "détentists." The interventionists are less concerned about superpower détente and the possible effect on it of a more vigorous Soviet political-military policy in the Middle East than the détentists, who worry about the dangers of superpower confrontation and the damage to Soviet-American relations that might be provoked by Soviet behavior in the Middle East.

The scanty evidence available on these internal Soviet bureaucratic politics suggests that the interventionists make up much of the military establishment, the hard-line orthodox party sectors, and the defense-related industries and that the détentists include the large nonmilitary industrial-managerial bureaucracies of the government, the bulk of the party membership and of the Central Committee apparat, and the foreign policy establishment, including the most important "think tanks" and research institutes.

The détentist position on the Middle East has centered on the primacy of political solutions rather than military ones, on avoiding provocation of the other superpower, and on maintaining a reasonable balance of political and military relations in the region. This was expressed candidly by a ranking apparatchik of the Central Committee in a speech given in Cairo at the height of the 1969–70 "war of attrition":

We are working for a political settlement, and a political settlement does not mean just words from one side only, but both means and prescribes the existence of a certain balance of power. . . . A political settlement is not surrender,

---

peace twelve Soviet marshals were brought in to share the deliberations of the Politburo." He also quotes Nasser, whose briefing of the Politburo was interrupted by some kind of message that began circulating among his hosts. The message turned out to be of secondary importance, and Nasser observed, " 'Did you see what happened?' 'Over that bit of paper, you mean?' I asked. 'Yes,' said Nasser, 'It is too bureaucratic. If a telegram to General Siad in Somalia needs the signature of all those three [Brezhnev, Kosygin, Podgorny] then we are in trouble.' " Heikal, *Road to Ramadan,* pp. 83–90.

although some people see in it the devil itself, and claim that a popular war is the only hope. But where? In Sinai?

We have to face reality: Sinai is not Vietnam. A popular war in relation to Sinai is absurd. Furthermore, launching a popular war from the West Bank may not be absurd, but it is difficult because of the terrain there. . . . Therefore you need to have an optimistic outlook and patience.[13]

The interventionist viewpoint was less sanguine. The military lectured that "words and wishes are not enough. Practical steps are necessary, along with active participation in the struggle of other nations for freedom and independence."[14] Moreover, "it will be a grave mistake to place all hopes and attention on political settlement and to forget military needs." Although "the UAR made great efforts to achieve political settlement. . . . Tel Aviv's stubborn position renders the increase of the UAR's military might absolutely necessary."[15]

Actual Soviet policy in the Middle East in the past two decades indicates a compromise between these two extreme positions. It followed a middle-of-the-road, low-committal, nonconfrontational approach drawing heavily on Soviet economic resources. Yet, in failing to provide Moscow with effective political leverage, such a policy satisfied no one. The hard-line party traditionalists (for example, Mikhail Suslov, Aleksandr Shelepin, Pyotr Shelest) found it difficult to accept Sadat, Assad, or Qaddafi, who hardly fit the Leninist revolutionary leader mold. The pragmatists in the governmental-managerial bureaucracies were critical of the expenditures of scarce resources in the bottomless quagmire of Egypt and Syria and of the corrupt and inefficient Arab bureaucracies managing these resources. The Soviet military, while coveting Arab naval and air bases, were openly contemptuous of the Arab allies and found them poorly trained and disciplined and utterly unreliable. Soviet diplomats and governmental leaders considered their Arab counterparts unpredictable and disloyal.

The pull of the Middle East on Soviet interests and imagination has been powerful enough to overcome internal dissonance and shape Soviet policies in a long-range, expansionist direction, thus defining the operational modus vivendi among the interventionists and détentists. The

13. Speech by Rotislav Ulyanovsky, deputy head of the International Department of the CPSU Central Committee, delivered in April 1970 at Al Ahram, Cairo, cited in Yaacov Ro'i, *From Encroachment to Involvement: A Documentary Study of Soviet Policy in the Middle East, 1945–1973* (Halsted, 1974), p. 106.

14. *Krasnaya Zvezda,* March 14, 1970.

15. Colonel Ponomarev, *Krasnaya Zvezda,* February 28, 1969.

Soviet Union has declared the region to be of vital interest and has made it so through repeated and escalating commitments to and support of the several regimes among the "progressive" countries.

The Six-Day War

After the 1956 Suez crisis and ensuing Sinai war, the simmering Arab-Israeli conflict was relatively dormant for a decade. A United Nations Emergency Force, charged with policing the Sinai borders and ensuring freedom of Israeli navigation through the Strait of Tiran and the Gulf of Aqaba, separated the forces of Israel and Egypt, the two main contenders. But this was a fragile truce. In 1964 a flare-up of the long-standing dispute over access to the Jordan River caused by Israel's completion of its national water carrier project—designed to channel some of the Jordan's flow into the arid Negev Desert in the south—ruptured the relative calm of the preceding years. Shortly thereafter, a number of new underground Palestinian groups began small terrorist operations across Israel's eastern borders. Heavy Israeli retaliation and increasing Syrian support for the Palestinian *fedayeen* produced repeated frontier skirmishes. Rising tension reached a climax on April 7, 1967, with an aerial and artillery battle between Syria and Israel over Lake Tiberias and the Golan Heights. This escalation was accompanied by weekly exchanges of verbal threats and accusations by Damascus and Tel Aviv.

In February 1966 an internal coup in the Syrian ruling Baath party brought to power in Damascus a left-wing faction with strong Marxist leanings. The new leaders immediately declared not only their total commitment to Arab rights in Palestine, but also their strong conviction that a "revolutionary people's war" was requisite in the Arab confrontation with Israel. From mid-1966 on, though *fedayeen* raids were mainly across the Jordanian-Israeli border, Israeli leaders increasingly pointed accusing fingers at Damascus. On February 5, 1967, Israel sent a warning to Syria through diplomatic channels that a large retaliatory raid would be forthcoming if Syrian support for the guerrillas did not cease.[16] Statements of similar import attributed to Prime Minister Levi Eshkol and Chief of Staff Itzhak Rabin appeared in the press in the first half of

---

16. *A Select Chronology and Background Documents Relating to the Middle East*, prepared for the Senate Committee on Foreign Relations, 91 Cong., 1 sess. (Government Printing Office, 1969), p. 22.

May.[17] The *Jerusalem Post* reported that planning was under way for "a military expedition intended to take the wind out of the Syrian sails once and for all."[18] On May 12 a United Press dispatch, featured in the *New York Times* and other major newspapers, reported that "a highly placed Israeli source [believed at the time to be Premier Eshkol] said here today that if Syria continued the campaign of sabotage in Israel it would immediately provoke military action aimed at overthrowing the Syrian regime."[19] For their part, Syrian leaders regularly denounced Israeli threats as a manifestation of the "imperialist-Zionist-reactionary conspiracy" against the Arab left, yet defiantly vowed continued support for the Palestinian "commandos, sons of the occupied territories, who have a natural right to return to and liberate their homes."[20] Strong support for Damascus came from the Soviet Union, which, though unhappy with the destabilizing effect of commando activities, appeared determined to protect the precarious hold of the new Marxist leadership.

Indeed, for the Soviet Union, the 1966 coup was a welcome development. Moscow was irritated by its failure to make ideological inroads into the Arab world, despite large amounts of military, economic, and technical assistance to several Arab countries since 1955 and the emergence of a number of friendly anti-Western regimes—including Egypt, Syria, Iraq, Algeria, and North Yemen. A region politically inflamed with postcolonial nationalist fervor and socioculturally suffused with Islamic values and a generally conservative religious outlook, the Arab Middle East had proved singularly impervious to Marxist dogma—at least to the Soviet version. Communist parties had been systematically curbed and often outlawed in most Arab states. Only in Iraq, during the later years of Qasim's rule, had an Arab Communist force been close to obtaining power, and it had been swiftly and bloodily crushed by its nationalist opponents at the first opportunity.

After Khrushchev's fall in 1964, a reappraisal of the socialist potential of third world regimes, prompted partly by Soviet failures in the Middle East, produced a more tight-fisted and conservative attitude toward the

17. For a good factual account of this period, see Shiloah Center for Middle Eastern and African Studies, Tel Aviv University, *Middle East Record,* vol. 3 (1967), particularly pp. 159–81.

18. *Jerusalem Post,* May 14, 1967.

19. *New York Times,* May 13, 1967.

20. Speech by Nureddin al-Attassi, Syrian head of state, excerpted in Institute for Palestine Studies, *International Documents on Palestine, 1967* (Beirut: IPS, 1970), pp. 501–02.

Afro-Asian world. A year later, through no particular Soviet effort, a government was installed in Damascus that was willing to admit Communists into the cabinet, employed a Marxist lexicon, and looked to the Kremlin for political support. For all their caution, "the Soviet leaders must have felt a certain eagerness at this renewed opportunity, after a break of six years, for the enlargement of Soviet influence in the heart of the Arab world."[21]

Russian support began immediately. By early May 1966 *Izvestiya* was accusing Israel of border provocations and of conducting a campaign against Syria reflective of Western imperialism's displeasure with the "progressive changes" in Syria. As tension along the Syrian-Israeli border rose, Soviet media began to warn of Israeli troop concentrations facing Syrian lines. In his detailed analysis of the buildup of the 1967 war, Walter Laqueur points out that such news regularly made headlines in the Soviet press throughout the year preceding the crisis and that an item about the planned overthrow of the Syrian government by Israel had been featured in *Pravda* at least once a month from October 1966 on.[22] At an official level, the Soviet government repeatedly sent Israel diplomatic notes warning against intervention. The strongest was delivered on April 21, 1967, after the major clash on April 7; it spoke of "dangerous playing with fire on the part of Israel in an area near to the borders of the Soviet Union," warned that "a policy of aggression against its neighbors is bound to result in serious consequences" for Israel, and counseled the Israeli leaders to shun a course of action that could "endanger the vital interests of their people and the fate of their State."[23] Economic and military aid to Syria was also forthcoming. An arms supply agreement believed to be worth $200 million and to have included MIG-21 aircraft and SA-2 missiles was reportedly signed in the summer of 1966.[24]

21. David Morison, "The USSR and the Middle East War of 1967," in W. Raymond Duncan, ed., *Soviet Policy in Developing Countries* (London: Blaisdell, 1970), p. 212.

22. Walter Laqueur, *The Road to Jerusalem: The Origins of the Arab-Israeli Conflict, 1967* (Macmillan, 1968), pp. 73–74.

23. Avigdor Dagan, *Moscow and Jerusalem: Twenty Years of Relations between Israel and the Soviet Union* (London: Abelard-Schuman, 1970), pp. 202–03. This is a semiofficial account by a senior Israeli diplomat of Soviet-Israeli relations up to the 1967 crisis.

24. Stockholm International Peace Research Institute, *The Arms Trade with the Third World* (Stockholm: Almqvist and Wicksell, 1971), p. 548; International Institute for Strategic Studies, *The Military Balance: 1967–1968* (London: IISS, 1968), p. 53.

So by May 1967 the Soviet Union had taken on the role of major protector of the Syrian regime, in a relationship that appeared based not only on traditional Soviet support for progressive Arab nationalist governments but also on a novel ideological kinship. Soviet solicitude was further manifested by Moscow's vigorous promotion of a progressive front among Egypt, Syria, North Yemen, and Algeria. Aleksei Kosygin had urged a closing of the ranks during his visit to Cairo in May 1966, and a mutual defense pact between Syria and Egypt had been concluded in November.

The Slide to War

The 1967 crisis began on May 15, after major Egyptian troop movements were reported in Sinai and a state of emergency was declared by Cairo. The Egyptians said this was necessary to deter an expected Israeli attack against Syria. Later President Nasser would explain his actions as having been prompted by warnings of impending Israeli aggression conveyed to him by Syria and the Soviet Union:

We all know how the Middle East crisis started in the first half of May. The enemy had a plan to invade Syria; this was frankly admitted in all the statements of enemy politicians and military commanders, and there was ample evidence of premeditation to that effect.

Syrian sources were quite definite on this point, and we ourselves had reliable information confirming it—our friends in the Soviet Union even warned the parliamentary delegation that visited Moscow at the beginning of last month that there was a plot against Syria.[25]

These moves were followed by Secretary General U Thant's hurried withdrawal of the UN Emergency Force (UNEF) on May 18, Syrian and Israeli mobilization, and Egypt's closure on May 22 of the Strait of Tiran to Israeli shipping and all other vessels carrying strategic cargoes to Israel. The Egyptian blockade of the Gulf of Aqaba immediately became the center of the gathering storm. Earlier, Israel had defined this act as a casus belli. Amid rising tension, intensive Israeli-American consultations were held in which Israel sought to enlist U.S. aid in restoring the status quo ante on the basis of an American commitment to freedom of Israeli navigation through the straits made by the Eisenhower administration at the time of the 1957 Israeli withdrawal from Sinai. Deeply engaged in the Vietnam conflict and fearful for its interests in the Arab world, the United

25. Resignation speech by Egyptian President Nasser, in *International Documents on Palestine, 1967,* pp. 596–97.

States was reluctant to act alone; however, President Lyndon B. Johnson's efforts to arrange a multinational flotilla to challenge the Egyptian blockade came to nothing. Finally, at the end of May, King Hussein of Jordan flew to Cairo and, putting aside his long political quarrel with Nasser, signed a mutual defense treaty with Egypt that placed Jordan's army under overall Egyptian command in case of war. On June 5, after forming a broad coalition government, Israel opened hostilities with a successful surprise air attack that decimated the air forces of Egypt, Syria, and Jordan and determined the course of the war from its outset. Six days later, when military activities came to an end, the Israelis had decisively defeated their three Arab opponents and gained control of the Sinai peninsula, the Gaza Strip, the West Bank of the Jordan, and Syria's Golan Heights.

Soviet Behavior

Soviet objectives in the 1967 crisis could be described in the following terms: to avoid a military confrontation with the United States, since no vital Soviet interests were at stake and there was a marked American preponderance of power in the area; to maintain a posture of determined political support for the Arabs designed to safeguard cordial Soviet-Arab relations and exert a deterrent effect on Israel and its patron, the United States; and to prevent the strongly pro-Soviet, internally shaky Marxist regime in Syria from losing power—a likely development if there was a large Israeli punitive thrust across the border.

STAGE 1 (APRIL 7–MAY 22). Although Soviet sources had for over a year periodically warned of Israel's aggressive intentions toward Syria, the April 7 fighting over Lake Tiberias probably brought about a major review of the Middle East situation in Moscow. The official Soviet reaction to this incident took fully two weeks to materialize. Only on April 21 was the Israeli ambassador in Moscow, Katriel Katz, given the stiffly worded note mentioned earlier. Scarcely four days later, however, a second statement was handed to Katz; this time Israel was formally accused of massing troops on the Syrian borders with hostile intent:

The Soviet Government is in possession of information about Israeli troop concentrations on the Israeli-Arab borders at the present time. These concentrations are assuming a dangerous character, coinciding as they do with the hostile campaign in Israel against Syria. . . . In this context it is impossible not to draw attention to the bellicose statements by Israeli military personalities against Arab countries.[26]

26. Dagan, *Moscow and Jerusalem,* pp. 203–04.

The April 7 battle—the largest Arab-Israeli clash since 1956—had gone badly for the Syrians, who had lost six MIG-21s but failed to down a single Israeli aircraft. The vehemence of the Israeli response to the initial Syrian artillery shelling must have been read in Moscow as indicating Tel Aviv's serious intention to cause the downfall of the Damascus government by humiliating it militarily. Because of Syria's demonstrated weakness, it was imperative to ward off further Israeli action. This could be done in only one of two ways: through a threat of direct Soviet intervention, which would have lacked credibility if based on the meager Soviet military presence in the area or would have prompted a U.S. response had it conjured up the possibility of Soviet resort to home-based forces; or by involving Syria's only effective political ally in the Arab world—Egypt. In similar situations in the past, Nasser had ordered a show of force in Sinai (February 1960) or mobilized his military (August 1963) to dissuade Israel from threatened retaliation against Syria for border incidents. With a seven-month-old mutual defense treaty between Egypt and Syria in effect, another dissuasive intervention by Nasser could be expected if a sufficient case could be made for an impending Israeli move. Thus the Soviet operational objective in this phase was to induce the United Arab Republic (UAR) government to make a show of force designed to ward off a large Israeli raid against Syria. There is no evidence that the Soviet Union undertook any military action during this phase to affect the Middle East situation, nor did it threaten to do so.

Soviet diplomacy was primarily directed at two targets: Israel and Egypt. The Soviet communications of April 21 and 25 warning Israel not to engage in retaliation were accompanied by increased press coverage of the situation, emphasizing the alleged Israeli troop concentrations and blaming Israel exclusively for the increased tension. The advisability of restraint was urged on Israel's permanent UN representative, Gideon Rafael, who was visiting Moscow, in meetings with both Deputy Foreign Minister Vladimir Semyonov and the head of the Middle East department, Alexander Shchiborin. Semyonov cautioned that "local conflicts could easily get out of control [and] therefore the Soviet Union could not remain indifferent should they occur near its frontiers. Those who invited a conflict close to the Soviet borders might pay a very high price."[27] Subsequent Soviet-Israeli contacts in Moscow and Tel Aviv throughout this phase were in the same vein.

The most crucial Soviet moves in this period were directed at Egypt, however. Information regarding a likely Israeli strike against Syria before

27. Ibid., pp. 205–06.

the end of May and the actual massing of eleven Israeli brigades in the north was "officially" relayed to a parliamentary delegation headed by National Assembly speaker Anwar el-Sadat, which visited the USSR from April 27 to May 14.[28] Between May 8 and 12 similar news was conveyed to Nasser in Cairo by the Soviet ambassador and by Syrian intelligence sources.[29] Apparently Nasser asked Moscow for its opinion of the validity of these estimates and received confirmation. On the other hand, contradictory evidence was provided by the Egyptian army chief of staff, General Mohammed Fawzi, who was dispatched to Syria on May 14. Despite Fawzi's report that no Israeli troop concentrations were in evidence, on the same day Egyptian armed forces were mobilized and the ostentatious movement of troops into Sinai began.

Whether Nasser believed Syria to be actually threatened or whether he chose to act as if he did because a confrontation with Israel suited his own political needs of the moment is not clear. In any case, his actions, which were followed two days later by the withdrawal of the UNEF, accomplished the Soviet purpose admirably. Overnight, attention shifted from the Syrian-Israeli border to Sinai.

Egypt's actions elicited immediate unofficial approval from Moscow. The Soviet media commented positively on the Egyptian troop movements and continued to assail Israel's "active preparations for military adventures."[30] No negative commentaries on the termination of the UNEF mission are apparent. On May 12 Soviet Ambassador Chuvakhin turned down an invitation from the Israeli Foreign Ministry to visit the northern areas and ascertain for himself that there were no special troop concentrations.[31] On May 19, the day Israel ordered heavy mobilization of reserves, Israeli Foreign Minister Abba Eban's request to Chuvakhin for Soviet cooperation in organizing "a reciprocal deescalation of troops in the South" was met with the by now standard response that the crisis was of Israel's own making and Arab actions were legitimately in self-defense.[32] On May 22 Israeli Ambassador Katz was told by Shchiborin at the Foreign Ministry in Moscow that "we cannot be responsible for what is

28. According to Sadat, the Soviet Union "informed me officially that Israel had massed eleven brigades along the Syrian border and had communicated this information to Jamal 'Abd an-Nasir." From Sadat's serialized memoirs on Egyptian relations with the USSR, *As-Siyasah* (Kuwait), November 19, 1976.

29. Nasser's resignation speech; Laqueur, *Road to Jerusalem*, pp. 71–72.

30. *Pravda,* May 19, 1967.

31. Michael Brecher, *Decisions in Israel's Foreign Policy* (Yale University Press, 1975), p. 362.

32. Ibid., p. 372; Dagan, *Moscow and Jerusalem,* pp. 211–13.

happening in the atmosphere which was poisoned by your leaders' statements."[33] Throughout this phase, Soviet diplomatic behavior was strongly supportive of the Arab position and careful not to weaken the deterrent value of Nasser's moves by words or deeds that might allay Israel's anxiety. On May 22, however, the Soviet Union was suddenly faced with a radically altered situation. Egypt blockaded the Tiran Straits, and a full-blown crisis quickly ensued.

STAGE 2 (MAY 23–JUNE 4). From the available record it is impossible to determine whether Moscow was consulted or even informed about the decision to close the Gulf of Aqaba to Israeli navigation and Israel-bound strategic cargoes before it was announced by Nasser in his May 22 speech. In any case, subsequent Soviet behavior suggests growing wariness of the dangers of entanglement in the looming military confrontation. Moscow understood clearly that an Israeli military response to Nasser's challenge was likely: on May 19 Eban had told Chuvakhin that Israel would go to war if its freedom of navigation was interfered with.[34] Soviet conduct was extremely cautious during this phase. All efforts seemed directed toward preventing war while seeking a diplomatic solution that would preserve the political gains of the Arab clients and, if war broke out, toward avoiding military involvement unless the United States became directly engaged.

Nevertheless, the single most important military action undertaken by the Soviet Union in the 1967 crisis occurred during this phase. On May 22, the day the Gulf of Aqaba was closed, Moscow notified the Turkish government that under the terms of the Montreux Convention ten Soviet warships would pass through the Dardanelles from the Black Sea into the Mediterranean beginning on May 30. On this date, a tanker and a submarine supply ship went through; they were followed on June 3 by three frigates and two auxiliary vessels, on June 4 by a destroyer, and on June 5 by two additional warships, of which one was a minesweeper.[35] This reinforcement of the Mediterranean eskadra brought its total strength up to some thirty ships, the largest deployment in the Mediterranean since a permanent naval presence was established there in 1964.

Throughout the crisis and war, however, most Soviet units remained well removed from the immediate vicinity of the conflict. The major area

---

33. Dagan, *Moscow and Jerusalem*, p. 212.
34. Ibid.
35. *New York Times*, June 1, 1967; Jonathan Trumbull Howe, *Multicrisis: Sea Power and Global Politics in the Missile Age* (MIT Press, 1971), pp. 77–79.

of concentration was the offshore anchorage some 100 miles to the northwest of Crete, that is, some 500 miles away from the shores of Sinai and
behind a screen of U.S. Sixth Fleet units south of Crete. A small number
of Soviet units—although warships replaced the usual intelligence
ships—intensified their watch of Sixth Fleet ships, and others conducted
exercises in the Ionian Sea between Sicily and Greece.[36] Thus, by its
deployment and quality of reinforcement, the Soviet Union clearly signaled that it did not wish to challenge the U.S. Navy or be seen as trying
to directly affect the course of events in the Arab-Israeli area with its
fleet. "I am quite sure," U.S. Rear Admiral J. C. Wylie said, "that they
were even less anxious than the United States to have any of their forces
involved."[37]

The naval balance of forces in the Mediterranean in May and June
1967 certainly did not favor aggressive Soviet behavior. Although the
ships brought in from the Black Sea in the week preceding the war practically doubled the number of surface combatants in the eskadra, the
Sixth Fleet remained vastly superior in firepower and in its ability to project tactical air support. Facing the eskadra's single cruiser of the old
Kirov class, eight or nine destroyer-type ships, and two or three submarines were the Sixth Fleet's two aircraft carriers, the *Saratoga* and the
America, two cruisers, ten destroyers, several submarines, and an antisubmarine force that entered the Mediterranean from the North Atlantic
on June 2. The American carriers had about 200 F-4 and A-4 fighter
bombers and attack aircraft; these were unmatched on the Soviet side.
While no Russian amphibious forces of ships were deployed in the Mediterranean during this period, the United States had a marine battalion
landing team, with some 2,000 men, permanently detached to the Sixth
Fleet for action onshore. In addition, three destroyers and one command
ship patrolled the Red Sea throughout the crisis, with no Soviet counterparts.

The eskadra also had to contend with a substantial British naval presence in the region. Toward late May one British carrier, the *Hermes,* six
frigates, and a squadron of minesweepers assembled in the Gulf of Aden
for possible participation in a challenge to Egypt's blockade of the Tiran
Strait; and in the Mediterranean, a task group comprising the carrier
Victorious and four escort frigates hovered near Malta. One indicator of

36. Rear Admiral J. C. Wylie, Jr., Deputy Commander in Chief, U.S. Naval
Forces Europe, interviewed by Howe, *Multicrisis,* p. 76.
37. Ibid., p. 79.

the Soviet Union's concern about the British force in the Mediterranean, and perhaps of uncertainty about its potential role in a showdown, is that one destroyer and two minesweepers of the eskadra were assigned to tail it. Although the Soviet Black Sea fleet had more modern, missile-carrying, heavy ships available, Moscow chose not to bring them into the Mediterranean.[38]

If the Soviet intent was nonaggressive, were the naval reinforcements meant to be a deterrent to Israel and the United States? With an Israeli military response to the Egyptian blockade expected from one day to the next, was Moscow signaling that it would play an active protective role in case of war? Was the Soviet purpose to impress on the West the probability of a confrontation at sea if an attempt was made by the United States and Britain to lift the blockade by force? If such deterrent effects were indeed sought, the Soviet Union went about this in an indirect, low-key way, as evidenced by several facts.

First, fully one-half of the ten-ship Soviet complement sent to the Mediterranean consisted of auxiliary vessels; the largest fighting unit was a destroyer, which did not reach the area until June 4; and no amphibious capabilities were introduced, although an increase in the number of submarines added significantly to combat capabilities.

Second, no attempt was made to project a Soviet presence, however symbolic, into the conflict zone. While British and U.S. units—including aircraft carriers—converged on the Red Sea from the south and the U.S. carrier *Intrepid* traversed the Suez Canal southward on May 31, all Soviet units remained in the Mediterranean well to the west of the Israeli coast.

Third, the beefing up of the eskadra took place at a time when routine placements of Soviet units, following the pattern of previous Soviet rotations, were expected; and Western newspapers pointed out that the reinforcements merely raised the Soviet forces to the normal level for summer exercises. An overt deterrent posture required increasing the political visibility of these forces and some clear signaling that such naval movements were extraordinary, yet the Soviet media generally ignored them and avoided any references to or speculation about a Soviet balancing role while daily excoriating the presence of the Sixth Fleet in the region and Western "gunboat diplomacy."[39]

38. *New York Times,* June 1–8, 1967, especially dispatches by Neil Sheehan; Anthony R. Wells, "The 1967 June War: Soviet Naval Diplomacy and the Sixth Fleet—A Reappraisal," (Arlington, Va.: Center for Naval Analyses, 1977).

39. Howe, *Multicrisis,* pp. 76–77. A typical item is the column by Victor Mayevsky, "An Alliance of Colonialists?" in *Pravda,* June 4, 1967 (translated in *Current Digest of the Soviet Press* [*CDSP*], June 21, 1967, p. 26).

Not surprisingly, the deterrent effect of the naval reinforcements—and, indeed, of the entire Soviet naval presence—on the decisions of the presumptive target countries appears to have been minimal. Washington's efforts to assemble the multinational task force did not slacken because of Soviet actions. Their eventual failure was due to Pentagon opposition fueled by concern about the military implications of *Egyptian* resistance and congressional reluctance to become involved in other conflicts while an intense war was being waged in Vietnam. Moreover, other Western nations were not enthusiastic about the project, and American diplomats in the Middle East warned vigorously against the consequences for U.S.-Arab relations of a U.S.-Egyptian clash in the straits.[40]

Israeli decisionmakers similarly discounted any military danger from the Russians; by June 2 Foreign Minister Eban, perhaps the most cautious among them, "was convinced that the Russians would not intervene militarily, particularly if the war was of short duration."[41] Michael Brecher, in an exhaustive study of Israel's behavior during the 1967 crisis, asserts that Prime Minister "Eshkol and his colleagues did not attribute significance to Soviet hostility."[42] Israel's preoccupation in the days preceding the war was with guaranteeing a helpful political stand by the United States and the West generally, both to secure dependable sources of arms resupply in case of need and "to retain the fruits of victory" confidently predicted by its military leaders.[43] If such a supportive stand could be obtained, the West's superiority in the regional naval balance was expected to preclude any Soviet military action.

Indirect targets of the Soviet reinforcements undoubtedly were Moscow's chief Arab clients—Syria and Egypt. The expanded naval presence was tangible proof of sympathy for the Arab stand and added credibility to daily Soviet statements of "resolute support" in the crisis. At the same time, however, it was necessary to restrain Cairo and Damascus from further provocative actions, or even a military offensive encouraged by the bellicose mood whipped up in the Arab world by political rhetoric and Nasser's dramatic moves. These contradictory requirements probably best explain the low profile maintained by the Soviet naval contingent. The passage of ten additional ships through the Turkish straits, plus the coverage of Soviet fleet movements in the Western and Arab press, would

40. See the authoritative account in William B. Quandt, *Decade of Decisions: American Diplomacy Toward the Arab-Israeli Conflict, 1967–1976* (University of California Press, 1977), chap. 2; and Brecher, *Decisions,* pp. 412–17.

41. Brecher, *Decisions,* pp. 419, 421.

42. Ibid., p. 395.

43. Foreign Minister Abba Eban, ibid., p. 379.

accomplish the first objective; the unobtrusiveness of the naval presence and Soviet silence about its role helped achieve the second and kept the Americans and the Israelis guessing. The limits of the Soviet role must have been clear to the Egyptians. During his news conference with the world press on May 28, Nasser was questioned about whether the Soviet Union would be asked to intervene if the Sixth Fleet were to aid Israel directly. He responded:

If American military intervention of this kind takes place, naturally we shall regard it as a hostile act directed against the whole Arab nation. However, we shall not ask any of the friendly countries to intervene; we shall leave it to these countries to make their own decisions.[44]

In a May 29 speech Nasser again indicated that he was not counting on active Soviet help. After reporting that his war minister, Shams Badran —who had been sent to Moscow for consultation several days earlier, apparently at Soviet request[45]—had returned with a letter from Kosygin "in which he says that the Soviet Union supports us in this conflict, and will allow no country to interfere until the situation returns to what it was before 1956," he declared: "As I said yesterday, we have not asked the Soviet Union or any other country to intervene, because we do not want a confrontation that might lead to a world war."[46]

The official Soviet position—avoiding the outbreak of war while publicly supporting the Arabs—was expressed in a government statement issued on May 23 that blamed Israel for the onset of the crisis, defended the Egyptian actions as a legitimate honoring of joint defense commitments, and promised strong Soviet support against aggression aimed at the Arab states. The operative clauses stopped short of a military threat, however, and stressed instead the need to maintain peace in the region:

let no one have any doubts about the fact that should anyone try to unleash aggression in the Near East, he would be met not only with the united strength of Arab countries but also with strong opposition to aggression from the Soviet Union and all peace-loving states. . . .

The Soviet Government keeps a close watch on the developments in the Near East. It proceeds from the fact that the maintenance of peace and security in the area directly adjacent to the Soviet borders meets the vital interests of the Soviet peoples.

With due account taken of the situation, the Soviet Union is doing and will

44. *International Documents on Palestine*, p. 559.
45. Anwar el-Sadat, *In Search of Identity: An Autobiography* (Harper and Row, 1977), p. 173.
46. *International Documents on Palestine*, p. 565.

continue to do everything in its power to prevent a violation of peace and security in the Near East and safeguard the legitimate rights of the peoples.[47]

This statement appeared several hours after Nasser's announcement of the Aqaba blockade. Though approving the removal of the UNEF, it ignored the closing of the straits. Soviet disapproval of the blockade is shown by the lack of supportive statements on this issue by either official sources or the media throughout the prewar crisis. In fact, while commentators and editorialists continued to echo the "official line" of the May 23 statement and spoke of strong Soviet support for the Arab stance, the Soviet leadership took several steps in the week following the blockade to restrain the Arabs and reassure Israel.

The two most important demarches in connection with Egypt were an urgent message from the Kremlin conveyed orally to Nasser by the Soviet ambassador in the early hours of May 27 urging Egypt not to fire the first shot,[48] and consultations held with War Minister Badran in Moscow.[49] Both Badran and Syrian President Nureddin al-Attassi and Foreign Minister Ibrahim Makhous, who visited the Soviet capital on a hastily arranged visit on May 29–30, found the Kremlin unwilling to promise military support in case of war.[50]

At the same time, Kosygin sent a personal note to Prime Minister Eshkol urging a peaceful resolution of the crisis; the note was written in moderate, unaccusing language quite unlike previous and subsequent communications to Israel. "We want you to use all means to avoid the outbreak of an armed conflict which would have serious consequences for international peace and security," the note said. "We turn to you in order to avoid creating in the world another center of war, which would bring suffering without end . . . it is necessary to find ways to settle the conflict by unwarlike means."[51]

These Soviet contacts paralleled similar efforts made by the United States to dissuade both Israel and Egypt from striking first.[52] Bilateral Soviet-American exchanges also showed Moscow's objective to be the

47. Ibid., p. 12; *CDSP* (June 14, 1967), p. 2.
48. Mohamed Heikal, *The Cairo Documents* (Doubleday, 1973), p. 244.
49. Ibid., p. 242; Sadat, *In Search of Identity*, p. 173.
50. For the official Syrian statement on the visit and cables from Attassi to Brezhnev and Kosygin, see U.S. Foreign Broadcast Information Service (FBIS), *Daily Report,* May 31, 1967.
51. Dagan, *Moscow and Jerusalem*, pp. 216–17.
52. Lyndon Baines Johnson, *The Vantage Point: Perspectives of the Presidency, 1963–1969* (Holt, Rinehart and Winston, 1971), p. 291; Quandt, *Decade of Decisions,* pp. 42–43, 49.

avoidance of an Arab-Israeli military showdown. On the other hand, for deterrent purposes, Moscow continued to hold out the prospect of active opposition if Israel took the initiative. On May 27 the Kremlin advised President Johnson that it had information of an Israeli plan to attack and threatened to intervene. In Johnson's words, "The Soviets stated that if Israel starts military action, the Soviet Union will extend help to the attacked state." What the exact nature of Soviet "help" would be is unclear, but the President used the warning to good effect. His strong urging that Israel "must not take preemptive military action" is said to have tipped the balance in the Israeli cabinet against going to war in a close vote on May 28.[53]

STAGE 3 (JUNE 5–11). The outbreak of war on June 5 appears to have caught the Soviet Union by surprise. When by the end of May there had been no Israeli military response to the closing of the straits, it may have believed that Israel lacked the will to fight. Its assessment of the Arab-Israeli balance may have misled it into expecting that the massive, united Arab show of force would be a sufficient deterrent to Israeli initiative, and its contacts in Syria and Egypt confirmed that the Arabs would not attack first. Indeed, during the last week before the war, the Soviet Union behaved as if the crisis had peaked. Brezhnev, Kosygin, and Defense Minister Grechko left Moscow for a ceremonial visit to the Soviet fleet in Murmansk and Archangel that lasted several days, and Podgorny spent much of this period on a state visit to Afghanistan. Just before hostilities began, the only Soviet cruiser in the Mediterranean and ten other ships of the fleet were sighted lying at anchor one hundred miles north of Crete.[54]

The beginning of hostilities galvanized the Soviet leadership into action. Within a few hours, Premier Kosygin had activated the hot line for the first time in a crisis to convey to the United States Soviet concern about the fighting and the need for superpower cooperation to bring about a cease-fire.[55] This, plus the inactivity of the Mediterranean Squadron during the first day of the war, clearly indicated to Washington Moscow's desire to stay out of the fighting. Indeed, the six-day war phase was characterized by repeated communications between the two countries, through the hot line and diplomatic channels and by the behavior of their naval forces in the area, to assure each other that their intent was

53. Brecher, *Decisions*, pp. 339–340; Quandt, *Decade of Decisions*, pp. 54–55.
54. Wylie interview, in Howe, *Multicrisis*, p. 117; Wells, "1967 June War," p. 14.
55. Johnson, *Vantage Point*, pp. 298–301.

not aggressive. Once the early reports from the war zone had confirmed the destruction of the Arab air forces by the initial Israeli onslaught, the Soviet operational objective became one of minimizing Arab territorial losses while endeavoring to remain uninvolved in the hostilities and avoid a confrontation with the United States.

In keeping with its posture before the war, the USSR's main effort on behalf of its Arab clients was diplomatic, particularly in the United Nations. By the afternoon of June 6, despite reported Arab opposition, it had agreed to a Security Council resolution calling for a cease-fire in place and had dropped its demand for simultaneous Israeli withdrawal to the prewar lines. Caution and the absence of unusual military activity prevailed almost without exception. Only two cases have been recorded that suggest an effort to use military means to obtain specific policy objectives, and these contain ambiguities about either Soviet intentions or the purposefulness of the activity.

The first instance was the systematic harassment of the Sixth Fleet aircraft carrier *America* and its companion task force on the fourth day of the war, June 8. Two Soviet warships, one a destroyer and the other a patrol craft, repeatedly intruded into the *America* formation, at times on a collision course with U.S. units. The patrol boat "concentrated on the *America,* twisting in and out around the 77,000 ton carrier in dangerous maneuvers, attempting to force her to alter her course." The harassment continued for several hours, despite repeated demands by U.S. commanders that the Soviet ships withdraw.[56]

Since incidents of this type were fairly common (similar though less sustained interference had been engaged in by a Soviet destroyer with the same task group the day before), it is difficult to evaluate with confidence the significance of any one of them. In this particular case, the situation was further muddied by the fact that the task group was tracking a Soviet submarine that had been detected near the *America* on the previous afternoon. The obstructive maneuvers may have been intended to disrupt this pursuit, sparing the submarine the humiliation of a forced surfacing.[57]

An alternative explanation is that these actions were ordered by higher political authorities to make U.S. decisionmakers more aware of the Soviet presence in the Mediterranean at a time of increasing Soviet uneasiness about the course of events in the Arab-Israeli conflict. If this was the pur-

56. Neil Sheehan, "Russians Continue to Harass 6th Fleet," *New York Times,* June 9, 1967.
57. Ibid.

pose, all indications are that it did not affect Washington's perceptions or behavior. By June 7 the Egyptian defeat in Sinai was turning into a rout; deprived of air cover and faced with a collapsing communications network and a demoralized officer corps, Egyptian forces began to surrender en masse and largely ceased to defend against Israeli advances across the peninsula. On the eastern front, although Jordan had accepted the first cease-fire call on June 6, the fighting continued as Israel demanded that both Egypt and Syria also cease fire. Cease-fire calls on June 6 and 7 having gone unheeded, the United States and the Soviet Union on June 8 each submitted a draft of another cease-fire resolution that reflected for the first time the major differences between the superpowers. The American draft reaffirmed the terms of the previous resolutions and demanded compliance by the combatants. The Soviet version explicitly condemned Israel for aggression and demanded both a stop to the fighting and Israeli withdrawal behind the armistice lines.[58] Neither draft was voted on, but the debate emphasized the breakdown of unanimity and the increasing tension between Moscow and Washington. The Soviet reversal was almost certainly meant not as a legitimate change of position on the terms of a cease-fire but as a warning to the United States that, if Israel were not restrained, Moscow might give active support to the hard-line Arab position.

By the evening of June 8 both Jordan and the UAR had announced their willingness to accept a cease-fire, and on the following day Syria did so as well. While fighting subsided on the other fronts, Syrian-Israeli battles on the Golan Heights continued, however, as Israel launched a full-scale offensive on the morning of June 9 to capture the heights. By midmorning on June 10, most of the heights had fallen and the city of Quneitra was being abandoned by the Syrians. The road to Damascus appeared open, and Syrian leaders may have seriously feared an Israeli advance on the capital. Although it is not known whether Syria's government appealed to Moscow for direct military intervention, semiofficial Syrian bodies, such as the General Federation of Syrian Trade Unions, called on their counterparts in the Soviet Union and Eastern Europe—as well as Peking—"to urge your governments to extend immediate military aid," alleging that "hundreds of enemy planes are attacking Damascus and the other Syrian towns, destroying civilian homes and killing thousands of citizens."[59]

58. Texts in *International Documents on Palestine,* pp. 249–50.
59. Broadcast by Radio Damascus in Arabic, 11:46 GMT, June 10, 1967; FBIS, *Daily Report,* June 12, 1967.

This deteriorating situation in Syria brought about the only explicit Soviet threat of military intervention during the six-day conflict. It was conveyed in a hot-line message addressed by Premier Kosygin to President Johnson and received at 9:05 a.m. EST on June 10. According to the Johnson memoirs,

The Soviets accused Israel of ignoring all Security Council resolutions for a cease-fire. Kosygin said a "very crucial moment" had now arrived. He spoke of the possibility of "independent decision" by Moscow. He foresaw the risk of a "grave catastrophe" and stated that unless Israel unconditionally halted operations within the next few hours, the Soviet Union would take "necessary actions, including military."[60]

At the same time, the Israeli ambassador in Moscow was handed a note that charged Israel with ignoring Security Council resolutions and "proceeding in the direction of Damascus" after occupying Syrian territory. It warned that "should Israel not immediately stop its war activities, the Soviet Union, together with other peace-loving States, will apply sanctions, with all resulting consequences" and informed Israel that the USSR had decided to break off diplomatic relations forthwith.[61] On June 10 *Pravda* also carried the text of a statement on the situation in the Middle East issued the day before by a hastily called summit meeting in Moscow of the Communist party leaders of Bulgaria, Hungary, East Germany, Poland, Czechoslovakia, Yugoslavia, and the USSR. It accused Israel of "barbarically bombing cities in Syria" and pledged the states signing this statement to "do everything necessary to help the peoples of the Arab countries deal a resolute rebuff to the aggressor, protect their legal rights, extinguish the hotbed of war in the Near East and restore peace in this area" if Israel did not stop its aggression and withdraw behind the armistice lines.[62]

Two aspects of Soviet behavior on June 10 are worth noting here. Despite the urgency of the situation, only the secret communication directed to the United States spoke of possible military steps. The direct target of potential Soviet military action—Israel—was merely warned of unspecified "sanctions" to be applied multilaterally with the participation of "other peace-loving States," a formulation clearly not intended to conjure up the menace of an impending military move. Second, the Soviet Union refrained from any demonstration of force or low-key but deliberately detectable military preparations for intervention that might have

60. Johnson, *Vantage Point,* p. 302.
61. Text in Dagan, *Moscow and Jerusalem,* p. 236.
62. Text in *CDSP* (June 28, 1967), pp. 3–4.

enhanced the credibility of its threat. Only one report of a potentially related Soviet military action has appeared. On the morning of the Soviet warning, the chairman of the Joint Chiefs of Staff, General Earle Wheeler, is said to have commented that Soviet capabilities for intervention in the Middle East were minimal, although "they have alerted their paratroop divisions."[63] If this alert did take place, it would constitute a second known instance—in addition to the harassment of the *America*—of Soviet military activity related to the 1967 war. In any case, the Soviet moves do not appear to have worried American decisionmakers sufficiently to be mentioned in their accounts of these events.[64] Nevertheless, the teletyped warning alone apparently achieved the Soviet purpose: Washington immediately made strong recommendations to Israel to stop the advance into Syria.[65] By noon (Washington time) on June 10, an effective cease-fire had been achieved.

The Soviet Union's tepid show of support for its Arab clients as they went down to total defeat was received with dismay in Damascus and Cairo. Nonetheless, Nasser clearly understood Moscow's fear of precipitating a superpower clash and apparently made no attempt to urge the Russians to take a more active role.[66] Indeed, despite widespread anger and disenchantment with the Soviet Union—expressed in adverse media commentary and attacks by mobs on Soviet embassies and citizens in Cairo, Algiers, and other "friendly" capitals—after the war Nasser sought to involve Moscow in Egypt's security much more intimately, even re-

63. Michel Bar-Zohar, *Histoire secrète de la guerre d'Israel* (Paris: Fayard, 1968), p. 306. Wells, "1967 June War," p. 22, on the other hand, asserts that "as far as is known, the Soviets never placed any of their airborne forces on alert."

64. According to Quandt, *Decade of Decisions,* p. 63, Johnson's account of the Soviet-U.S. exchanges on October 10 has been judged "overly dramatic" by other participants. There is no mention in the President's account of any threatening activities by Moscow.

65. According to one authoritative Israeli account, "Secretary of State Dean Rusk got in touch with our foreign minister, Abba Eban, and our ambassador in Washington and asked them in near panic where we thought we were heading. He warned that our situation in the Security Council was getting worse, and he demanded that we obey the Council's ceasefire decision forthwith." Moshe Dayan, *Moshe Dayan: A Story of My Life* (Morrow, 1976), p. 377.

66. Nasser is reported to have told close associates just before he accepted the unconditional cease-fire on June 8 that the Russians "had been frozen into immobility by their fear of a confrontation with America" and that no military resupplies had been forthcoming in the course of the fighting because "they had been too scared of getting involved with the American Sixth Fleet." He added that a Soviet supply ship loaded with several thousand guns had turned back within sight of Alexandria for fear of Israeli bombings. Anthony Nutting, *Nasser* (Constable, 1972), p. 419.

questing in late June that the USSR take over the air defense of Egypt, both because his own smashed army could not fulfill this task and to effectively commit Moscow to an active military role in the regional conflict.[67]

For the most part, the Soviet eskadra—the only instrument available to the Russians for the regional projection of military power between June 5 and 10, 1967—behaved as if no Middle East war were under way. A few minor adjustments in routine procedures were made; for instance, Sixth Fleet carriers were closely trailed by several Soviet units instead of by just one, as was the usual practice.[68] At one point, on June 8, the only Soviet cruiser in the Mediterranean approached to within five miles of the *America*.[69] But these activities were negligible compared with the extensive American use of naval forces during the war.

On two separate occasions, the two U.S. carrier task groups approached the eastern shore of the Mediterranean from their holding stations south of Crete. The first was on the morning of June 6, when Moscow insisted on the imposition of a UN cease-fire calling for the retreat of all forces behind prewar lines. The U.S. task forces sailed some hundred miles eastward in the course of the day. By 6:30 p.m., as the Egyptian position in Sinai deteriorated further, the Soviet Union was ready to agree to an unconditional cease-fire, which was duly passed by the Security Council and announced by President Johnson in a televised statement at 8:00 p.m. One hour later, the Sixth Fleet was ordered to steam back to its earlier position south of Crete.[70]

The second instance was on June 10 immediately after receipt of Kosygin's threat of military intervention against Israel. At 9:30 a.m. the ships were ordered to sail at full speed toward the Syrian coast in a move explicitly designed, in Johnson's words, to convey to Moscow the "message . . . that the United States was prepared to resist Soviet intrusion in the Middle East." By 12:30 p.m. a Syrian-Israeli cease-fire was in effect, and the ships were ordered back half an hour later.[71]

Another flurry of activity involving the Sixth Fleet took place on June 8 in connection with Israel's attack on the U.S. intelligence ship *Liberty*,

67. Heikal, *Road to Ramadan*, pp. 46–48; Alvin Z. Rubinstein, *Red Star on the Nile: The Soviet-Egyptian Influence Relationship Since the June War* (Princeton University Press, 1977).

68. *New York Times*, June 8, 1967.

69. Ibid., June 9, 1967.

70. Howe, *Multicrisis*, p. 95.

71. Johnson, *Vantage Point*, p. 302.

which was some fifteen miles off Gaza. Two flights of fighter aircraft were scrambled from the carriers to provide cover for the stricken ship, and several combatants were dispatched to the area. The Soviet Union was informed of these actions over the hot line.[72]

What is perhaps most remarkable about these incidents from the perspective of this study is the lack of any recorded response by the Soviet navy. Furthermore, at no point during the six days of hostilities in the Middle East did Soviet ships engage in similar maneuvers or act in a manner that might be interpreted as a war-related "show of force" or "showing of the flag." Beyond the interference with the *America's* task force on June 8, Soviet naval behavior seems, in fact, to have been deliberately orchestrated to reassure the United States that the Mediterranean Squadron did not intend to take any part in the crisis.

The October War

In October 1973 the USSR had to face the major problem underlying its Middle East policy since the early 1960s, when it became a regional power with a permanent military presence, entrenched interests, and strong patron-client ties with local governments. Pared down to its fundamentals, this problem can be described as the necessity in a crisis for choosing between two desirable courses of action that could not be pursued simultaneously: on the one hand, maintaining a stable relationship with the United States and the West; on the other hand, supporting Arab clients in their dispute with Israel with the intensity required to maintain Soviet-Arab relations on an even keel. To this problem the Soviet Union had no easy solution, for its options in the region were constrained by three considerations. For the Arab states—Egypt and Syria in particular—active confrontation with Israel until the basic Palestine dispute was resolved was a national political and military priority. The Soviet Union's own presence and leverage in the Arab world rested heavily on its role as a major supplier of the sophisticated weapons required by the Arabs to sustain a credible anti-Israel posture. Yet continued assured access to Middle Eastern oil and the security of Israel were held by the West to be vital interests, which could not be threatened without evoking a forceful response.

72. Ibid., pp. 300–01.

It inescapably followed that Soviet Middle East policy, to be successful, had to maintain a fine balance between active and demonstrable
solidarity with the Arabs and avoidance of dangerous and counterproductive confrontations with the United States. This necessitated the imposition of limits both on the military capabilities the Soviet Union was willing
to put in Arab hands and on the political goals it could afford to be associated with.

Between the June 1967 and October 1973 wars, the nature of these
limits was clearly established, with significant resultant strains on Soviet-
Arab, and especially Soviet-Egyptian, relations. Thus, after the 1967
debacle, while moving quickly to rebuild the Egyptian and Syrian armies,
Moscow urged Nasser to seek a political solution to the Arab-Israeli
conflict.[73] Shortly before the Nixon administration came into office,
Moscow sent a diplomatic note to Washington "urging a more active
search" for a settlement.[74] In the first half of 1969 bilateral Soviet-
American discussions began; these were soon supplemented by four-power
talks in which the British and French participated. In these and subsequent contacts with Washington within the growing framework of détente
diplomacy, the Soviet Union hewed closely to the Arab position, demanding total Israeli withdrawal and satisfaction of Palestinian rights. Nevertheless, Moscow urged its Arab clients to accept both Israel's existence
behind the June 4, 1967, lines and peace treaties with Tel Aviv. Further
irredentist Arab claims did not enjoy Russian support.

This political posture was coupled with an arms supply policy aimed
at restoring sufficient Arab military power to deter Israeli "provocations"
and enable Egypt and Syria to negotiate a settlement from a position of
strength but not to initiate war. Long-range, offensive weapons systems
wanted by Cairo, such as the MIG-23 fighter-bomber, were withheld
before the 1973 war; shipments of weapons and training schedules were
subject to many delays; needed spare parts and consumables were released in limited quantities; and often weapons promised were not sent.

73. According to the Yugoslav newspaper Bo'rba, quoting "well-informed circles," Podgorny told Nasser during his visit to Cairo in late June 1967: "There is no
other way of liquidating the territorial gains of the aggressor except negotiations
and even some crucial concessions with respect to navigation and the recognition
of the fact of the existence of the Israeli state in the Middle East." Quoted in Rubinstein, Red Star on the Nile, p. 18.

74. Quandt, Decade of Decisions, p. 68.

"Arguments about arms supply . . . were the main theme of all four visits" Sadat made to Moscow after assuming power.[75]

Moscow capitalized heavily on its immediate response to Egyptian and Syrian military needs in the aftermath of the 1967 defeat to strengthen its military presence in the region, primarily the naval component. Access to Egyptian harbors for repairs, reprovisioning, and off-duty berthing permitted the establishment of a more balanced and much enlarged permanent fleet in the Mediterranean at a tolerable cost and substantially enhanced the political and prestige value of the eskadra. Scarcely a week after the 1967 hostilities ended, three cruisers, five destroyers, and two auxiliaries were added.[76] Some of these ships paid extended visits to Port Said and Alexandria in July–September and became "permanent" guests in October, ostensibly to deter Israeli air attacks on Egyptian harbors.[77] At the time of the Jordanian crisis of September 1970, the Soviet Union deployed twenty-three surface combatants and thirteen to fifteen submarines, more than double the force they had available during the six-day war. After this crisis the eskadra's normal composition was stabilized at ten to thirteen submarines, fourteen to twenty-two surface combatants, and twenty-three to twenty-six auxiliaries;[78] in other words, it leveled off at about the peak strength occasioned by the crisis. On the eve of the October war, there were seventeen surface combatants, which were steadily increased to twenty-six by October 24 and to a crisis high of thirty-four by October 31, following the U.S. nuclear alert. The firepower of the squadron was even more dramatically upgraded in the final stages of the war in direct response to American actions: the number of surface-to-surface missile launchers was more than doubled, from forty on October 24 to eighty-eight on October 31, and the number of surface-to-air missile launchers was increased from twenty-eight to forty-six.[79]

75. Heikal, *Road to Ramadan,* p. 67. Heikal's book and Sadat's autobiography, *In Search of Identity,* particularly chapter 8, contain sundry details on the difficulties in Soviet-Egyptian arms relations.

76. *New York Times,* June 19, 1967.

77. The continuous presence of Soviet units in Port Said and Alexandria lasted for eight and a half years, until their final expulsion in April 1976 following Sadat's breach with the Soviet Union. Bradford Dismukes, "Soviet Employment of Naval Power for Political Purposes, 1967–75," in MccGwire and McDonnell, *Soviet Naval Influence,* p. 485.

78. Robert G. Weinland, "Superpower Naval Diplomacy in the October 1973 Arab-Israeli War" (Center for Naval Analyses, 1978), pp. 43, 46, 47.

79. Ibid., pp. 46, 47.

The 1967–73 period thus witnessed a gradual but marked change in the naval balance. Whereas in 1967 the United States enjoyed absolute superiority, by 1973 the eskadra had acquired sufficient capability to counter the Sixth Fleet in regional crises.[80] The American advantage in tactical air support remained strong, but the Soviet Union gained some political ground with the deployment of helicopter carriers from 1968 on, either in the Mediterranean or in the Black Sea on short call, and the use of Egyptian airfields as home bases for naval intelligence aircraft that often overflew Western navies in the Mediterranean after 1967.

After the expulsion of Soviet troops from Egypt in July 1972 and Sadat's increasing public remonstrances, Moscow's concern over the possible waning of its influence in the area prompted a relaxation of restraints on arms supplies. In the year preceding the October war, SAM-6 missiles, the late-model Sukhoi-20 ground attack aircraft, and the modern T-62 tank were provided. A "strategic" offensive weapon with an assured capability of penetrating Israeli air defenses—the SCUD medium-range missile—was also made available for the first time.[81] Whether in the fall of 1973 Moscow was willing to support a military action to avoid further deterioration of its relations with the Arabs or whether it believed Sadat's war threats were mere posturing is not clear. What is clear, however, is that it continued to counsel Egypt against war, both publicly and privately,[82] and simultaneously beefed up the Arab armies, to hedge against the possibility of a politically ruinous Arab collapse like that of 1967 if war came. So long as the cease-fire was not breached, Moscow could follow the two-track policy of diplomatic peacemaking and military resupply with relative ease. Once hostilities began, however, a choice had to be made between hard-earned Arab friendship and stable relations with the United States.

Soviet Behavior

No attempt will be made here to describe in detail the course of the war or account for the multitude of military and political interactions of

---

80. Dismukes, "Soviet Employment of Naval Power," p. 502.

81. Jon D. Glassman, *Arms for the Arabs* (Johns Hopkins University Press, 1975), p. 113. The SCUDs were manned by Soviet crews but appear to have been under Egyptian operational control in the October war.

82. See Galia Golan, *Yom Kippur and After: The Soviet Union and the Middle East Crisis* (London: Cambridge University Press, 1977), pp. 37–71, for a good treatment of Soviet policy in 1972–73.

the major actors—Israel, Egypt, Syria, the United States, and the USSR
—that made up its history. The focus will be on Soviet behavior insofar
as it related to the use or contemplated use of Soviet military forces to
directly affect the course of events or to signal intentions and objectives.

Seen from this perspective, the crisis can be divided into four phases:

1. October 1–5, immediate prewar phase: dissociation from the Arab
war effort;

2. October 6–9, Arab offensive: search for an early cease-fire; assessment of the results of the Egyptian-Syrian offensive; decision to begin
resupplying weapons;

3. October 10–22, Israeli counterattack: massive resupply by air and
sea; renewed efforts to obtain a cease-fire; Kosygin's visit to Cairo; negotiation of the cease-fire with Henry Kissinger in Moscow;

4. October 23–26, cease-fire breakdown: warning to Israel; intervention threat to the United States; U.S. alert; third cease-fire holds.

OCTOBER 1–5. Between the time the Soviet Union was notified by
Sadat of an imminent military initiative[83] and the outbreak of fighting on
October 6, the Soviet Union took a number of steps designed to signal the
United States both that it was not an active partner in its clients' projected
campaign and that it wished to remain uninvolved in the crisis. On
October 4 and 5 it hastily and overtly evacuated its military advisers and
their dependents from Egypt and Syria, a move that angered the Arabs
because of the chance it might tip off the Israelis. Simultaneously, and for
the first time since October 1967, all units of the Mediterranean Squadron
in Port Said put out to sea; the *Nikolaev,* lead ship of the new *Kara*-class
guided-missile cruisers and the largest Soviet naval unit in the Mediterranean, returned to the Black Sea on October 5; and the squadron's general disposition in the Mediterranean remained unchanged, reflecting
peacetime conditions and behavior.[84]

To the Arabs, these measures conveyed the unmistakable message that
Moscow was washing its hands of the entire affair and that they could not
count on it to bail them out if their military offensive came to grief.
Through the ambassador in Cairo, Vladimir Vinogradov, Brezhnev had
informed Sadat, in response to the latter's message that a resumption of
fighting was imminent, that "the Soviet Union would give him the support

83. October 1, according to Heikal, *Road to Ramadan,* p. 24; October 3 in Sadat's
version, *In Search of Identity,* p. 246.

84. Weinland, "Superpower Naval Diplomacy," pp. 48–50; *The Times* (London), October 12, 1973.

of a friend."[85] However, the evacuation of Soviet personnel and the general Soviet attitude was read in Cairo as demonstrating, in Sadat's words, a "total lack of confidence in us and our fighting ability."[86] It made the Egyptians wonder if "it reflect[ed] some aspect of the global balance of power, and if so might it be that the Russians were not going to give us the help we were expecting?"[87]

While there is no reliable information on what transpired in the inner councils of the Kremlin during those first days in October, it is safe to assume that it was decided to safeguard détente even if it meant another Arab military defeat. The significance of the Soviet position in this prewar phase is that the Arabs were being left to their fate at a time when experts agreed that a war would lead to a quick and conclusive Israeli victory. What must have worried Soviet leaders at this point was the possibility that a quick Arab collapse accompanied by Israeli attacks in the interior, with Soviet units or personnel as planned or unwitting targets, might force Moscow to intervene in the fighting. Hence the alacrity with which Soviet personnel and naval units were withdrawn.

Was Soviet behavior also intended to alert the United States, in the hope that consequent U.S. and Israeli deterrent measures might dissuade Sadat from going ahead with his plans? This is an intriguing and not far-fetched possibility. Moscow did not know the exact date of the attack at the time the decision to evacuate was made, and it may have believed sufficient time was available to exert diplomatic pressure on Cairo. After all, Sadat had set other war deadlines in the past and later canceled them. The Soviet Union may not even have been averse to triggering an Israeli mobilization, such as the one the previous May when an Egyptian attack had appeared in the making. The Israelis had not preempted on that occasion, and political circumstances, as well as the reputed state of the Arab-Israeli military balance, were such that Moscow may have assigned a low probability to the contingency of Israeli preemption in October. If the Israelis mobilized again and Washington made strong representations in Cairo—perhaps Secretary Kissinger could advance his announced plan to launch a diplomatic initiative in November[88]—war might be averted. While this analysis must remain speculative, there can be little doubt that the Soviet Union regarded the approaching events with foreboding and

85. Heikal, *Road to Ramadan,* p. 34.
86. Sadat, *In Search of Identity,* p. 247.
87. Heikal, *Road to Ramadan,* p. 35.
88. Quandt, *Decade of Decisions,* p. 162.

worry about the potential effect of another Arab defeat on its interests in the Middle East.

OCTOBER 6–9. Fear of an immediate Arab collapse was proved unfounded in the first two days of the war, when Egyptian forces in the west rapidly overwhelmed the "Bar-Lev" line of Israeli defenses along the Suez Canal with few casualties and established beachheads several miles deep along the Sinai banks of the waterway. Meanwhile, Syria's two-pronged armored assault had succeeded in breaking through stubborn Israeli defensive lines (though sustaining heavy tank losses) and in regaining most of the southern half of the Golan area. In these efforts, the Arab armies appeared to have mastered the use of their sophisticated equipment, particularly antitank and antiaircraft missiles, of which they had large quantities, and the Israeli air force seemed largely neutralized. The strategic surprise achieved by the Arab offensive had given the attacking forces a few days to consolidate their gains before the Israeli war machine could mobilize fully and counterattack.

The two superpowers reacted to the outbreak of war with restraint and evident wariness. The crisis caught the United States in the thick of the Watergate crisis, which had practically paralyzed the government and diverted the President's attention almost exclusively to his own political survival. Although, in contrast with 1967, the country was no longer militarily involved in a foreign war, the Vietnam experience had created strong popular and congressional resistance to activism in foreign affairs, particularly in areas like the Middle East, where the possibility of military engagement was, in everyone's mind, always high. Further reinforcing the need for caution was the heightened American perception of a strong Soviet military presence in the area, especially its naval capabilities in the Mediterranean. Finally, American political objectives—resumption of a diplomatic dialogue and improved relations with the Arabs in order to move toward a political settlement—would be best served by a course of action that minimized negative repercussions on budding but tenuous U.S.-Egyptian relations but remained responsive to the demands of the special relation with Israel and faithful to standing commitments to Israeli security. From the early days of the war, American diplomacy—principally managed by Henry Kissinger—was aimed at ending the hostilities on terms that would promote, not hinder, postwar settlement efforts: an early cease-fire based neither on an Arab victory with Soviet arms nor on an Israeli success that would make peace negotiations politically and psychologically impossible again. At the same time, the crisis was held to be "crucial for U.S.-Soviet relations. If collaboration worked, détente would take on real meaning. . . . The worst outcome for the United States would be to appear crippled by the domestic crisis over Watergate."[89] Although President Nixon ordered one of the two carrier task groups of the Sixth Fleet—the *Independence* and its escorts—to steam from Athens harbor to a holding zone south of Crete on October 6 "as a visible sign of American power,"[90] beyond this precautionary move the Sixth Fleet carried on with business as usual. The second U.S. aircraft carrier, the *Franklin D. Roosevelt,* which was on a port visit in Barcelona, remained there until its scheduled departure on October 10.[91] No reinforcements of the fleet were carried out during this first phase.

The USSR had an urgent interest in an early cease-fire since it expected a crushing Israeli counterattack in short order. Barely six hours after the war began, Vinogradov in Cairo unsuccessfully sought Sadat's agreement to a cease-fire in place preserving early Arab territorial gains.[92] In bilateral diplomatic contacts with the United States, at the United Nations and between Kissinger and Ambassador Dobrynin in Washington, and in correspondence between Brezhnev and Nixon, the Soviet Union appeared "very conciliatory" and cooperative, and the Soviet media downplayed news of the war.[93] Soviet naval units continued to steam away from the zone of combat, and no additional ships entered the Mediterranean from the Black Sea.[94] In fact, the squadron's surface strength was decreased the day before the outbreak of war with the return of the cruiser *Nikolaev* and two other smaller units to the Black Sea, although the submarine component began to increase.

The ease with which the Bar-Lev line fell doomed the immediate Soviet operational objective, a quick cease-fire. The Egyptians have since stated that their war aims were not to regain territory, but "to bleed the enemy."[95]

89. Kissinger's sentiments, expressed at the first meeting of the Washington Special Action Group after the war began; ibid., pp. 172–73.

90. Quandt, *Decade of Decisions,* p. 171.

91. Weinland, "Superpower Naval Diplomacy," p. 32.

92. The Soviet Union repeated its request the evening of October 7 and, according to Sadat, practically every day thereafter. *In Search of Identity,* pp. 253–54.

93. Quandt, *Decade of Decisions,* pp. 173–75; Golan, *Yom Kippur,* p. 75.

94. "SovMedFlt was in a normal peacetime disposition during the first phase of the crisis (from the start of the war to October 12)." From a report on operations of the U.S. Sixth Fleet during the October war written by the fleet commander, Vice Admiral Daniel Murphy, and quoted at length in Elmo R. Zumwalt, Jr., *On Watch: A Memoir* (New York: Times Books, 1976), p. 437.

95. Heikal, *Road to Ramadan,* pp. 212, 220, quoting Sadat.

However, if Egypt had suffered losses as heavy as the Syrians' in their first two days on the Golan Heights, it might have been satisfied with its achievements of October 6–7. Sadat's determination to fight on, his persistent requests for arms, and the serious depletions of Syrian tanks and antiaircraft missiles in the vicious Golan fighting compelled the Soviet leadership on October 8 and 9 to make a number of crucial decisions based on a reassessment of the situation on the ground. These decisions were made when the Israelis were in the midst of successful counterattacks in the east that would, by October 10, push all Syrian troops back behind prewar lines. And an Israeli decision to begin strategic bombing of Syria resulted on October 9 in the accidental strike of the Soviet cultural center in the Syrian capital and caused several casualties.

Unable to seek a cease-fire resolution at the United Nations in opposition to Arab wishes and pleasantly surprised by its clients' military performance, the Soviet Union moved to provide Egypt and Syria with direct political and military support to enable them to pursue a more prolonged war effort. Several political measures were taken to boost Arab fighting capabilities: Iraq was encouraged to replace Syria's tank losses from its own stockpiles until Soviet replenishments could be sealifted and to send fighting units to the front;[96] Brezhnev, in private letters to a number of Arab leaders, urged similar active support for the front-line states while alluding to the "complexities" of the international situation, which presumably limited Moscow's ability to provide direct aid;[97] pressure on Sadat in behalf of a cease-fire was eased, though not lifted completely.[98] The major decision—to begin a vast resupply of the Arab armies by air and sea—was probably made on October 9.[99] Beginning on October 10, 12,500 tons of war material were delivered to Egypt, Syria, and Iraq by air during the course of the war, and 58,000 tons were sent by sea to Egypt and Syria.[100] Equipment provided included major weapons, such as tanks and fighter aircraft, and a whole range of consumables, including surface-to-air missiles (SAMs). The Syrians were desperate for this aid, having used up almost all their SAMs during the first few days of fighting.

96. Heikal, *Road to Ramadan*, p. 218.
97. Golan, *Yom Kippur*, p. 81.
98. See Heikal, *Road to Ramadan*, pp. 207–17, for an account of repeated Sadat-Vinogradov discussions about a cease-fire.
99. For an analysis, see Golan, *Yom Kippur*, pp. 85–86.
100. For details of the airlift and sealift from an authoritative source, see William B. Quandt, *Soviet Policy in the October 1973 War* (Santa Monica, Calif.: Rand Corp., 1976).

Also, all seven Soviet airborne divisions were placed in an increased state of readiness on October 8 for the remainder of the war.[101] It was not clear whether this was primarily connected with the contingency of a possible Soviet intervention or was a precautionary move taken once it appeared that an early cease-fire was not in the cards. Apparently U.S. decisionmakers were not alarmed by the move. It was not immediately reported by the media, and U.S. officials made no allusion to it. In his first extended press conference on the crisis, held on October 12, Secretary of State Kissinger—who had cautioned Moscow in a public address on October 8 that "détente cannot survive irresponsibility in any area, including the Middle East"—called Soviet behavior up to that point restrained and not irresponsible. "If you compare their conduct in this crisis to their conduct in 1967," he stated, "one has to say that Soviet behavior has been less provocative, less incendiary, and less geared to military threats than in the previous crisis."[102]

OCTOBER 10–22. During this phase, the military initiative shifted decisively in Israel's favor. On October 10 Prime Minister Golda Meir announced that the entire Golan had been retaken, and on October 11–13 the Israelis pressed their successful counterattack into Syrian territory beyond the 1967 cease-fire lines. After tank battles in which Iraqi, Moroccan, and Jordanian troops participated on the Arab side, the front stabilized along a line of ridges some twenty miles from Damascus; this line remained unchanged for the remainder of the war. The Israelis, though they failed to defeat the Syrian forces decisively, nevertheless occupied further territory and brought the outskirts of Damascus within reach of their long-range artillery.

On the Sinai front, the Egyptians, who had paused to consolidate their newly won positions on the eastern bank and successfully repulsed several badly coordinated Israeli armored attacks, launched a disastrous tank offensive on October 14, designed to take some pressure off the Syrian front and perhaps gain control of the strategic Mitla and Gidi passes. Without their missile antiaircraft defense umbrella, Egyptian armor fell victim to unchallenged Israeli air force attacks and to the superior range of Israeli tanks and better mobile marksmanship of Israeli crews. The Egyptian defeat in this major tank battle was probably decisive in allowing the Israelis on October 15–16 to cross the Suez Canal to the western bank and turning the tide of the war. An armored Israeli brigade, in de-

101. Golan, *Yom Kippur*, p. 86.
102. *Department of State Bulletin* (October 29, 1973), pp. 529, 535, 538.

stroying part of the Egyptian air defense system, created a defensive gap between the Second and Third armies deployed in Sinai that was quickly exploited by the Israelis, who poured in reinforcements and extended their salient sharply. By October 19 the Egyptian Third Army was in danger of encirclement and the road to Cairo was open (the Egyptians had committed most of the First Army's armored units, originally deployed between the canal and the capital, to the battle of October 14). On this day, President Sadat signaled his readiness to accept a cease-fire, which was adopted by the Security Council two days later.

Despite this turn for the worse in Arab military fortunes, Soviet behavior during this phase remained unchanged. It included efforts to secure a cease-fire, the resupply of the Arab combatants with weapons, and no significant or provocative show or use of military force beyond protection of the resupply effort. On the diplomatic front, the highlights of this period were Premier Kosygin's visit to Cairo on October 16–19 to obtain Egyptian acquiescence in a cease-fire proposal and the actual negotiation of an end to hostilities by Brezhnev, Gromyko, and Kissinger on October 20–21 in Moscow. In the early stages of the war, the Soviet Union had pressed for a cease-fire in place tied to a demand for total Israeli withdrawal from territories conquered in 1967; later, after Syrian reverses, it had privately informed the United States that it would support an immediate unconditional cease-fire.[103] By the time Kissinger flew to Moscow, Israeli advances west of the Suez Canal had forced the USSR and Egypt to accept a UN resolution that tied to the cease-fire a call for "immediate" negotiations between the parties to implement UN Resolution 242.

The airlift and sealift of military material continued throughout this phase and until October 23. The Syrian airlift, which totaled 3,750 tons, peaked on October 15 and remained fairly high until the 22d. Most of the weapons airlifted to Egypt—about 6,000 tons—arrived October 17–23. Altogether, 934 flights were made by AN-12 (10-ton loading capacity) and AN-22 (50-ton loading capacity) air transports. U.S. C-5 and C-141 planes carrying 22,395 tons of war supplies made 566 trips to Israel.[104]

The Soviet sealift reportedly included a total of twenty-five ships, which, after passing through the Bosporus between October 7 and 23, headed for either Latakia or Alexandria.[105] Some of these shipments,

103. Quandt, *Soviet Policy,* p. 20.
104. Ibid., pp. 21–26.
105. Ibid., p. 23.

particularly those of October 7–9 (on three ships), were probably carrying peacetime merchandise and military-related products from the Soviet Union. (In the months before the war and for most of 1973, an average of seven ships unloaded military equipment in Egyptian and Syrian ports every month.)[106] A peak in the sealift was not reached until the last days of the war; nine vessels passed through the Turkish straits between October 20 and 22 (five of them on the last date). Thus most of the equipment sent by sea was not used in the conflict.

The large resupply effort, the role it played in enabling Egypt and Syria to wage the war beyond the first week, the diverse military measures that Soviet forces were compelled to take to protect the operation, and the extensive, direct involvement of Soviet military personnel in the airlift and sealift make this episode significant. The operation was initiated and carried out during a crisis and had an important bearing on its course and outcome; it engaged large military contingents of three services not only in the logistical transportation effort but also in protecting it from hostile interference by opposing military forces; and it was a major and clearly intentional demonstration of Soviet commitments and purposes in the crisis.

From the outset, the Politburo was certainly aware that the airlift and sealift would assume the proportions of a full-scale military operation, which would place Soviet personnel in jeopardy. As the relevant decisions were being made in the Kremlin, the Israeli air force was bombing Damascus. In subsequent days, most Syrian airfields, including those used by Soviet transports, were repeatedly attacked and damaged. Syrian harbors were also bombed. Several Soviet aircraft were damaged or destroyed on the ground during the airlift, and a Soviet merchant ship, the *Ilya Mechnikov,* was sunk while lying at anchor in the port of Tartus on October 12.[107] This last incident occasioned the first of two Soviet warnings to Israel during the war. It stated that there must be "an immediate stop to the bombings of peaceful towns in Syria and Egypt and the strict observance by Israel of the norms of international law, including those regarding the freedom of navigation. The continuation of criminal acts by Israel will lead to grave consequences for Israel itself."[108] To keep sea-lanes open and provide protection for Soviet shipping, a number of units from the Mediterranean eskadra, including surface combat-

106. Ibid., p. 22.
107. Golan, *Yom Kippur,* p. 94.
108. Tass, October 12, 1973.

ants, converged on the area between the eastern tip of Cyprus and the Syrian coast and remained on patrol there until the U.S. alert of October 24.[109] To guard against Israeli air strikes, air-defense missile batteries, reportedly under exclusive Soviet operation and control, appeared at Latakia and Damascus.[110] Because of the damage to Syrian harbors, Soviet amphibious-lift ships were used to transport equipment, which was unloaded on the beaches. In addition to naval and air-defense personnel, Soviet tank crews participated in the supply operation, ferrying tanks from Latakia and Tartus to Damascus because of a shortage of Syrian personnel.[111]

By mounting this massive operation, the Soviet Union signaled that there were limits to its inactivity in the crisis. Not only did it reverse its previous dissociation from the Arab military gamble; its heavy commitment, whose dimensions were clear by October 13, indicated to Washington and Tel Aviv that Moscow would not tolerate a decisive Arab defeat. More specifically, the Soviet action was a warning to Israel not to march on Damascus—a live option on October 12–13 and apparently discussed by the Israeli leadership.[112] To the United States, the obvious message was that the USSR was now taking the Arab campaign under its wing and putting its prestige on the line in a way unprecedented in previous Arab-Israeli conflicts (except for the special case of the protracted war of attrition over the Suez Canal in the first half of 1970).[113]

At the same time, however, Moscow did not wish its position misunderstood by either its friends or its adversaries. When on the day the airlift began Dobrynin informed Kissinger of his government's willingness to press for an immediate unconditional cease-fire, Kissinger, according to one account, having failed to obtain Israeli agreement to halt hostilities before the Arab armies had been pushed back, had to

109. Weinland, "Superpower Naval Diplomacy," p. 52; Glassman, *Arms for the Arabs,* p. 134. The latter mentions that a *Kotlin*-class destroyer was positioned off Latakia harbor and provided antisubmarine protection for Soviet ships loaded with war supplies.

110. Glassman, *Arms for the Arabs,* p. 134.

111. Ibid.

112. Chaim Herzog, *The War of Atonement* (Little, Brown, 1975), pp. 136–37.

113. As Weinland aptly points out, "these two undertakings in support of the resupply of Syria—providing combatant protection at the terminus, and employing amphibious lift ships to insure that critical materials could be unloaded—represented significant departures from past Soviet practice. Prior to this, Soviet naval forces had rarely been employed for positive ends—to accomplish something. Most of their activity had been oriented toward the negative objectives of deterrence and defense—insuring that things don't occur." "Superpower Naval Diplomacy," pp. 54–55.

"persuade" Dobrynin "to delay his cease-fire call."[114] Also, assurances were said to have been conveyed by Brezhnev to Washington both directly and through West German Chancellor Willy Brandt, that "for him there is no question about the existence and viability of Israel" and that the Soviet Union did not wish to damage détente.[115] In other words, the air- and sealift did not mean Soviet support for unlimited Arab objectives or even for a continuation of the war, but rather a determination to see the fighting concluded under conditions that would not put the Arab clients at a political or psychological disadvantage.

Particularly striking is the way the resupply effort was downplayed to the Arabs. At no point during the war did Soviet media or official pronouncements explicitly mention the air- and sealift, even in statements designed to defend the Soviet record against biting Chinese and radical Arab criticism of Moscow's lukewarm attitude toward the Arab "liberation" effort. More important, there is some evidence that the early shipments fell far short of Egyptian and Syrian expectations or requests. Although the Syrians obviously were resupplied with ample quantities of SAM-6 missiles (which they had apparently run out of by October 8) during the first days of the airlift, President Boumedienne of Algeria claimed that early shipments consisted mostly of medical supplies and merchandise.[116] His talks in Moscow on October 14–15 with Brezhnev, Kosygin, Podgorny, Gromyko, and Grechko—which were triggered by Arab dissatisfaction with the Soviet assistance—were said by Tass to have been conducted in a "frank and friendly atmosphere," clearly indicating disagreements.[117] The tempo of the air- and sealift quickened after Boumediene's visit and reported arrangement of cash payment for the weapons.[118] However, Arab disenchantment was not allayed. Astonishingly, in major speeches both during and after the war, neither Sadat nor Assad so much as acknowledged the Soviet contribution to their military campaigns. When the resupply operation was at its peak during the second week of hostilities, Kosygin arrived in Cairo to persuade Sadat to stop the war. Thus, although forced by the heavy Syrian losses and the character of their relations with the Arabs to mount the airlift and sealift, the Russians were willing to pay a heavy price in the currency of

114. Marvin Kalb and Bernard Kalb, *Kissinger* (Boston, 1974), p. 476.
115. Golan, *Yom Kippur,* p. 93. See also *New York Times,* October 11, 1973.
116. Golan, *Yom Kippur,* p. 101.
117. Ibid., p. 100.
118. Sadat, *In Search of Identity,* p. 264.

forsaken propaganda and lost political value to ensure that it was not perceived by the Arab leaders as a green light for continuing the fighting.

While the Soviet signals appear to have been read accurately in Washington (and in the Arab capitals), the United States reacted by launching a similar air and sea resupply operation in behalf of Israel on October 13, after waiting two days in hopes that a cease-fire might materialize. Israel had asked for an airlift beginning in the early hours of the war, and domestic pressure on the Watergate-weakened administration was mounting. Besides, it was advisable to take precautionary measures in case the Russians were being duplicitous. The principal rationale behind the American airlift was to deny the Soviet Union the appearance of dictating the course of events with its weaponry. "The main considerations . . . were to convince Sadat that a prolonged war of attrition, fueled by Soviet arms, would not succeed, and to demonstrate to the Kremlin that the United States was capable of matching Soviet military deliveries to the Middle East. Above all, for the sake of the future American position globally and in the region, Soviet arms must not be allowed to dictate the outcome of the fighting."[119]

Unlike the U.S. airlift to Israel, the Soviet resupply effort encountered little difficulty in eliciting third-country cooperation for transit purposes. Soviet transport planes bound for Egypt and Syria were readily granted permission to traverse Yugoslav, Turkish, and Greek air space. The main routes were over Yugoslavia, where flights originating in Hungary would cross the border over Subotica, about 120 miles north of Belgrade, follow a line from Subotica to Belgrade to Dubrovnik to reach the Adriatric, then fly over the Strait of Otranto on their way to the Mediterranean. Planes carrying supplies from Bulgarian stores crossed the Yugoslav border over Nish, some 120 miles southeast of Belgrade, then flew due west to reach the Adriatic over Dubrovnik and join the Adriatic route southward. Overflights were made mostly by day, and Soviet planes were said to carry no markings. Pilots declared type of aircraft and registration number to the control tower at Belgrade, but no information on destination or type of cargo was given or requested. Turkey, a member of the North Atlantic Treaty Organization (NATO), did not allow Soviet military aircraft to overfly its territory, but permitted Aeroflot civilian transports to use its air space under existing commercial agreements. Greece, another NATO member, allowed Soviet overflights of the Cyclades Islands

119. Quandt, *Decade of Decisions,* p. 184.

but refused to allow the United States to use Greek bases in the military resupply of Israel.[120]

There were two other significant Soviet military measures during this intermediate phase: the alerting of three airborne divisions on October 11, and the gradual but continuing reinforcement of the naval squadron. Neither caused undue disquiet in Washington.

That seven Soviet airborne divisions had been placed in an increased state of readiness on October 8 became known in the United States on the night of October 10–11.[121] The further upgrading of the alert status for three of these divisions on October 11 may have been designed as a deterrent to an Israeli march on Damascus. If so, it is not known whether the Soviet intent was successfully communicated by this action or what role it played in Israeli decisionmaking. The United States did not perceive a substantial danger of Soviet intervention, nor did news of the alert become public until several days later.[122]

Also during this period occurred the first increase in the surface combat strength of the Soviet navy, when a cruiser and two destroyers were moved into the Mediterranean from the Black Sea on October 10. Between October 12 and 24 another destroyer and one escort ship apparently were added.[123] There were no indications of an increased alert status, even among the ships shadowing the U.S. task group nearest the war zone, in the area southeast of Crete.[124] As if to emphasize the atmosphere of normality, the cruiser and one of the destroyers that had entered the Mediterranean on October 10 headed west and began port visits to Italy.[125] Unlike the disruptive behavior of Soviet naval units during the 1967 war, that of the squadron in 1973 was "restrained and considerate," according to Admiral Worth H. Bagley, commander in chief of U.S. Naval Forces, Europe. "In fact, they weren't overtly aggressive. It looked as though they were taking some care not to cause an incident."[126] The

120. *Le Monde,* October 17, 1973, and April 26, 1974; *New York Times,* October 17, 1973; John C. Campbell, "Soviet Strategy in the Balkans," *Problems of Communism,* vol. 23 (July-August 1974), pp. 6–7.

121. Quandt, *Decade of Decisions,* p. 179.

122. According to the Kalbs, Kissinger chose not to inform the Israelis of the alert, which only became known to Israeli intelligence thirty-six hours later, on the afternoon of October 12. *Kissinger,* pp. 470–71, 472.

123. Weinland, "Superpower Naval Diplomacy," pp. 51, 47 (table 3).

124. From Vice Admiral Murphy's report, in Zumwalt, *On Watch,* p. 437.

125. Weinland, "Superpower Naval Diplomacy," p. 55.

126. Interview in *U.S. News and World Report* (December 24, 1973), pp. 27–28.

only abnormal activities of the eskadra during this phase were the positioning of some units near Syrian ports in the war zone to protect Soviet ships and the increase in the total number of surface combatant units from the " 'normal' strength" of seventeen on October 5 to twenty-six by October 24.[127]

OCTOBER 23–26. The cease-fire that went into effect the evening of October 22 in the battlefields did not last the night. By Tuesday morning, October 23, the Soviet embassy in Washington was in touch with Secretary Kissinger, accusing Israel of having "massively violated the cease-fire," and Moscow issued its second warning to Israel.[128] Which side was responsible for the resumption of fighting was not clear, but it soon became apparent that Israeli forces were taking advantage of the situation to complete their encirclement of the Egyptian Third Army. Although a second resolution calling for a halt to the renewed warfare was passed by the Security Council on October 23, late that day the Egyptian naval base at Adabiyah, on the Gulf of Suez, fell to an advancing Israeli armored column,[129] and on October 24 an attack was launched to occupy Suez City. Meanwhile, to the north, Israeli forces were on the outskirts of Ismailia, threatening the rear of the Second Army.[130]

It was in these circumstances that Egyptian President Sadat, who is said to have complained of Israeli violations almost hourly to both superpowers during this period, requested both Moscow and Washington to assume a direct role in enforcing the cease-fire. "You must," the identical messages are quoted as saying, "be in force on the ground to witness for yourselves Israeli violations of the cease-fire."[131] At the UN, Egyptian Foreign Minister M. H. Zayyat urged the Security Council "to call on the Soviet Union and the United States . . . each to send forces immediately from the forces stationed near the area to supervise the implementation of the cease-fire."[132]

Although the United States immediately came out with a public statement opposing the injection of superpower forces into the conflict area, Soviet Ambassador Anatoly Dobrynin informed Kissinger by telephone at 7:05 p.m. that the Soviet Union would support the Egyptian request at

127. Weinland, "Superpower Naval Diplomacy," p. 47 (table 3).
128. Kalb and Kalb, *Kissinger,* p. 486; Golan, *Yom Kippur,* pp. 118–19.
129. Herzog, *War of Atonement,* p. 248.
130. Ibid., p. 250.
131. Heikal, *Road to Ramadan,* p. 251.
132. Insight Team of the Sunday *Times, Insight on the Middle East War* (London: Angus, 1974), p. 204.

the UN. Shortly thereafter, in a second communication, he told the secretary of state that the Soviet delegation itself might introduce the resolution. About two hours later, the ambassador called again and told Kissinger he had "a very urgent" message from Brezhnev to Nixon. The stiffly worded four-paragraph text accused Israel of continued cease-fire violations that challenged its two architects, the Soviet Union and the United States. It stressed the need to "compel observance of the cease-fire without delay." To achieve this, Brezhnev wrote, "Let us together . . . urgently dispatch Soviet and American contingents to Egypt." Then he added: "I will say it straight, that if you find it impossible to act with us in this matter, we should be faced with the necessity urgently to consider the question of taking appropriate steps unilaterally. Israel cannot be allowed to get away with the violations." The threat was followed with a closing paragraph that sought to strike a conciliatory note: "I value our relationship."[133]

Believing that there was a "high probability" of some "unilateral Soviet move," the United States alerted most of its military forces shortly after midnight on October 25, upgrading the readiness of all units to no less than defense condition 3 status. Although no large Soviet intervention was feared, this response was reportedly to impress upon Moscow American unwillingness to accept any unilateral Soviet injection of military forces between the Middle East combatants.[134] At the same time a message from Nixon to Brezhnev stated that the United States would consider a deployment of Soviet troops to the Middle East in violation of the June 1973 agreement between the two superpowers on the prevention of nuclear war.[135]

Although the full text of the Brezhnev note has not been published, there can be little doubt from reading the available excerpts that the Kremlin did intend to convey to the United States a clear warning that, unless the Israeli onslaught on the west bank of the Suez Canal was stopped at once, the USSR would intervene directly. Nor is there any

133. Quandt, *Decade of Decisions*, p. 196; Kalb and Kalb, *Kissinger*, p. 490; *New York Times*, April 10, 1974.

134. "I would like to state on behalf of the President the United States position on this matter very clearly. The United States does not favor and will not approve the sending of a joint Soviet-United States force into the Middle East. . . . The United States is even more opposed to the unilateral introduction by any great power, especially by any nuclear power, of military forces into the Middle East in whatever guise those forces should be introduced." "Secretary Kissinger's News Conference of October 25," *Department of State Bulletin* (November 12, 1973), p. 587.

135. Quandt, *Decade of Decisions*, p. 197.

doubt that the Soviet move was successful in prodding the United States into action. From all reports, Washington exerted heavy influence on Israel on October 25 to make no further attempts at military advances, to move into defensive positions, and to cease firing. During the two following days, after the cease-fire had generally taken hold, similarly harsh pressure was used to force Israel to allow food, water, medicines, and other nonmilitary supplies to reach the Egyptian Third Army,[136] whose forcible surrender the Israelis now sought to annul any possible Arab claims to military victory and strengthen their hand in postwar diplomacy. Immediately after the Soviet "ultimatum" and the U.S. alert, a third UN cease-fire order did prove effective, Israeli advances did stop, the Third Army did not fall, Suez was not taken, and Cairo was not further threatened. By October 28 small Soviet and American contingents of unarmed observers had joined a peacekeeping force made up of troops from nonpermanent Security Council member-states,[137] the U.S. alert had been called off, and the 1973 war crisis was substantially over.

Whether the Israelis would have gone on to make further military gains if there had been no Soviet threat—that is, whether the Soviet move was superfluous—is another important but unanswerable question. In all likelihood, the United States would have acted to prevent an Egyptian debacle fatal to Kissinger's plans for an effective mediating role in the postwar search for a settlement. Moreover, the threat was issued at a time when the Israeli forward movement had run out of steam: the second cease-fire call had been heeded in many sectors of the front, UN teams were fanning out to supervise its implementation, Israel had already acceded to U.S. demands that the Third Army be provided with plasma and other humanitarian aid from Red Cross sources, and Israeli attacks on Suez and Ismailia had been repulsed with heavy losses. In his news conference of October 25 Secretary Kissinger stated that, until the previous evening (when the Soviet push for superpower intervention materialized), the U.S. government "had every reason to believe that the basic direction that had been established, and to which all parties had agreed [that is, the cease-fire resolution], would in fact be implemented."[138] On the other hand, in Cairo and Moscow there probably was great uncertainty about both Israeli intentions and U.S. willingness or ability to restrain its client. Any

136. Ibid., p. 198.
137. The Soviet Union sent seventy observers, the United States thirty-five.
138. *Department of State Bulletin* (November 13, 1973), p. 590.

further Israeli movements closer to Cairo—even if there were no attempts to penetrate or surround the city—could be politically and psychologically disastrous for the Egyptian leadership. Just as crippling, however, was the continuing apparent intention of Israel to capture the Third Army. By the afternoon of October 24, no medical or other urgently needed supplies had actually been allowed to reach the encircled forces, Israeli troops having turned back three convoys sent by the Egyptian Red Crescent and the International Red Cross.[139] In Tel Aviv, General Chaim Herzog—an authoritative, semiofficial commentator on military affairs during the war—stated on Israeli radio that the Third Army's only option was "surrender with honor."[140] In making his appeal for direct joint superpower intervention, President Sadat probably sincerely believed that only such drastic action could stave off the worst.

Soviet leaders may have concurred in this assessment. It is likely that Brezhnev and his colleagues had by this time become upset at Washington's failure to carry out the bargain negotiated with Kissinger in Moscow three days earlier—Arab acceptance of a cease-fire and agreement to postwar peace negotiations in exchange for Israeli compliance with and immediate implementation of the cease-fire.[141] Also, Soviet credibility and determination in relation not only to the Arabs but also to the other superpower were being severely tested. A forceful move was called for. In any case, the Soviet Union must have calculated that it had little to lose by sponsoring Sadat's request. The call was for "joint" superpower action; it had already gained the endorsement of a number of Security Council members; the sending of forces would be part of a United Nations operation to enforce a resolution introduced by both the United States and the Soviet Union and almost unanimously supported by the council's members (the People's Republic of China had abstained from voting). At best, the United States would consent, in which case the Soviet Union would have gained a legitimate direct military role on the ground in the area. At worst, raising the issue would convey to Washington the urgency of the need to pressure Tel Aviv. In either case, useful credit would be earned with Sadat and disgruntled Arab public opinion generally.

In both 1956 and 1967 Moscow had threatened to come to the aid of its Middle Eastern friends in the closing stages of the crises, but in neither

139. *Insight on the Middle East War*, pp. 204, 213.
140. Ibid., p. 204.
141. Quandt, *Decade of Decisions*, pp. 191–92.

case had the threat been backed up with perceptible, serious military preparations for such a contingency. On October 25–26, 1973, although the beefed-up Mediterranean Squadron and the airlift to resupply Arab forces showed some potential for quick intervention, the Soviet Union continued to refrain from provocative shows of force or low-profile but threatening military preparations that might have added significant military credibility to Brezhnev's conditional statement of intent. Even the Soviet military activities cited at the time as having contributed to the United States' decision to alert its forces—the naval buildup, the airlift stand-down, the alerting of airborne troops, communications intercepts, the arrival of nuclear materials in Egypt—were sufficiently ambiguous to cast serious doubts on their status either as deliberate signals of a will to intervene or as bona fide preparations for impending unilateral action. As Secretary of Defense James Schlesinger admitted in his news conference of October 26, the United States and the Soviet Union "were very far away from a confrontation." About the U.S. alert, he added: "If the question refers to a military confrontation, under the circumstances I think that we were taking the actions that were necessary to preclude the development of a military confrontation."[142]

Although a major Soviet naval buildup did occur in the Mediterranean at the end of the war, it took place *after* the U.S. alert was declared and appears to have been a response to both the American show of force and Washington's own buildup of the Sixth Fleet, which occurred on October 25, when a third U.S. aircraft carrier, the *John F. Kennedy,* and its accompanying task group, and a second helicopter carrier, the *Iwo Jima,* with an 1,800-man marine assault force on board, passed through the Strait of Gibraltar and headed east to join the other two carriers near Crete.[143] The increase in Soviet surface combat units from seventeen to

142. "Secretary of Defense Schlesinger's News Conference of October 26," *Department of State Bulletin* (November 19, 1973), p. 622. Schlesinger generally downplayed the probability of Soviet intervention, spoke of "mixed reactions and different assessments" among National Security Council members about Soviet behavior immediately before the alert decision, and referred to the need to counter the possible effects of Watergate on others' perception of the American will to act as an important component of the U.S. response. These were remarkably candid statements, considering he was speaking while the alert was in effect, and on the day that President Nixon had labeled the situation as "the most difficult crisis we have had since the Cuban confrontation of 1962," a crisis caused by the belief that "the Soviet Union was planning to send a very substantial force into the Mideast, a military force." Ibid., pp. 581, 583.

143. Weinland, "Superpower Naval Diplomacy," p. 39.

twenty-six between October 5 and 24, while significant, was not unusual in the circumstances. By October 31, however, the total of surface combatants had risen to thirty-four units, which included one cruiser.[144] Seven submarines also arrived from the North Sea Fleet. By October 31 the Mediterranean Squadron was at its highest combat level ever. Its total strength "had increased to 96 vessels, including 34 surface combatants and 23 submarines, possessing a first launch capability of 88 SSMs, 348 torpedoes, 46 SAMs."[145]

Similarly, the activities of the Soviet navy, which had heretofore maintained a semblance of peacetime normality, changed after the U.S. alert had been declared in response to the American concentration of its naval forces southeast of Crete on October 25. According to the report of the Sixth Fleet commander:

On 25 October a Soviet surface action group (SAG) composed of a Kynda [cruiser] and a Kashin [destroyer] joined the Soviet units monitoring TG 60.1 [the aircraft carrier *Independence* and its escorts]. As other U.S. forces joined in the holding area, each task group was covered by a separate Soviet SAG which included an SSM and SAM capability. On 26 October, the Soviets began large-scale anti-carrier warfare (ACW) [exercises] against TF 60 with SSG and SSGN [guided missile submarines, diesel and nuclear] participation; this activity was conducted continuously for the six days following 27 October. . . . Both fleets were obviously in a high readiness posture for whatever might come next, although it appeared that neither fleet knew exactly what to expect.[146]

Previously the three U.S. task groups had been scattered the length of the Mediterranean, with the *JFK* group stationed just west of Gibraltar, to provide logistic support for the airlift to Israel. Their concentration only a few hundred miles from the battle zone represented a change of posture to one preparatory for offensive action, a move designed to enhance the credibility of the U.S. alert.[147] The eskadra anticipated this action by maneuvering into a position from which it could most effectively engage the carriers—with their ability to direct nuclear attacks against the Soviet heartland—in the unlikely contingency of full-scale combat between the superpowers. More immediately, and also more to the point, its new posture was meant to create an effective deterrent to any attempted intervention ashore on the Egyptian-Israeli front by Sixth Fleet forces. To this end a full surface action group was assigned to cover the U.S. amphibious

144. Ibid., p. 47; Zumwalt, *On Watch*, pp. 439, 447.
145. From Admiral Murphy's report, in Zumwalt, *On Watch*, p. 447.
146. Ibid.
147. Weinland, "Superpower Naval Diplomacy," p. 38.

units. According to Admiral Bagley, the Russians "deployed their ships and submarines so that our forces were targeted for instant attack from multiple points."[148] In addition, several components of the eskadra, including ships earlier positioned off the Syrian coast, were relocated north of the Nile Delta and thus interposed between the Sixth Fleet and the battle zone.[149] Despite the proximity of the two navies, however, there were no reported attempts by Soviet ships to interfere with Sixth Fleet operations.

Although the presence of amphibious-lift ships among the units of the eskadra—augmented during the war from the normal one to three to a reported maximum of nine[150]—might be construed as evidence of Soviet plans to use the navy for intervention, Western intelligence knew that these vessels carried few troops and were actually loaded with supplies for Syria and Egypt, that they were being used to supplement merchant ships in sealift operations. On October 24–25 two of the troop carriers were reportedly awaiting clearance through the Dardanelles to return to the Black Sea, and two others had already departed.[151] Furthermore, these nine LSTs and LSMs together could have carried no more than 2,000 men.[152] Had the Soviet Union decided to initiate military intervention in the Middle East around October 25, available evidence indicates that instruments other than the Mediterranean Squadron would have been relied on. The squadron's role would have been to deter and, failing deterrence, to complicate, limit, and obstruct counterintervention by the Sixth Fleet.

A related and even more ambiguous development was the reported transit on October 22 through the Dardanelles en route to Alexandria of a Soviet freighter that appeared to be carrying nuclear materials. The vessel arrived in the Egyptian harbor on the 25th, and when it departed an unspecified number of days later, it was still carrying neutron-emitting materials on board. Although U.S. intelligence sources are said to have ascertained the presence on Egyptian soil of equipment related to the Soviet-supplied SCUD missiles and evidence that indicates the missiles were armed with nuclear warheads, U.S. officials after the war denied that there was concrete evidence of nuclear weapons of Soviet origin in Egypt. In any case, the report on the arrival of the nuclear shipment in Egyptian

148. *U.S. News and World Report,* December 24, 1973.
149. Weinland, "Superpower and Naval Diplomacy," p. 57.
150. Ibid., pp. 52–54.
151. Golan, *Yom Kippur,* p. 123; Glassman, *Arms for the Arabs,* pp. 162–63.
152. Weinland, "Superpower Naval Diplomacy," p. 54.

waters did not reach Kissinger and other top decisionmakers until the morning of October 25, several hours after the alert had been ordered.[153]

Speculation that the detected nuclear materials were indeed weapons and that they were probably meant for the missiles of the eskadra[154] rather than Egyptian forces must, given the paucity of verifiable information, remain at the level of conjecture. The presence of the suspicious shipment in Alexandria is not in dispute, however. Regardless of the actual destination of the material, the Soviet Union did send a freighter into Alexandria with a nuclear load in the tense and delicate circumstances of October 25. Three days earlier, Egypt had deliberately fired two SCUDs at the Israeli forces in the Deversoir area west of the Suez Canal only moments before the first cease-fire was to have gone into effect. The actual firing had been conducted by Soviet crews, who were manning all the SCUD batteries.[155] Sadat says he ordered the firing because he "wanted Israel to learn that such a weapon was indeed in our hands and that we could use it at a later stage of the war."[156] On October 16 Sadat had warned Israel in his major speech of the war that surface-to-surface missiles would be used against Israel if Egypt were subjected to strategic bombing. "Our . . . trans-Sinai . . . rockets are now in their bases ready to be launched at the first signal to the deepest depth of Israel. . . . The Israelis should remember what I once said and still say: an eye for an eye, a tooth for a tooth and depth for depth."[157] In the rather desperate circumstances the Egyptian leadership faced on October 24–25, Sadat's warning might have been stretched to include an Israeli march on Cairo or further advances west of the canal. It is probably safe to say that a Soviet motive in allowing the nuclear shipment to Alexandria was to warn that continued Israeli progress on the west bank of the canal might precipitate a nuclearization of the

153. Kalb and Kalb, *Kissinger*, p. 493; Glassman, *Arms for the Arabs*, p. 163; *Washington Post*, November 21 and 22, 1973; *Aviation Week* and *Space Technology*, November 5, 1973. For U.S. official assessment, see Kissinger's news conference of November 21, 1973. Quandt, who at the time was in the Middle East section of the National Security Council and attended Washington Special Action Group (WSAG) meetings, categorically states that "it is virtually certain that the Soviets did not turn over the control of nuclear warheads for SCUD missiles to the Egyptians," and "there is no reliable information that nuclear weapons of any sort have ever been introduced into Egypt by the Soviets." *Soviet Policy*, p. 31.

154. Weinland, "Superpower Naval Diplomacy," p. 58.

155. Golan, *Yom Kippur*, p. 87. Though the Soviet Union allowed the SCUDs to be fired at Israeli troops in the front, it did not agree to Sadat's request that the missiles be used against the landing of American supplies in the Sinai.

156. Sadat, *In Search of Identity*, p. 265.

157. BBC Monitoring Service, *Summary of World Broadcasts*, ME/4426/A/16.

Arab-Israeli conflict. This might have been expected to put more pressure on Washington to dissuade the Israelis from further action.

The developments U.S. spokesmen at the time of the alert most directly linked with the heightened threat of Soviet military intervention were the increase in the readiness status of a number of Soviet airborne divisions on October 23, and the presumably related pause in the airlift to Syria and Egypt.[158] U.S. intelligence first noted that Soviet airborne divisions had been alerted on October 11 (apparently three days after the alert had gone into effect). On October 23 it became known that the alert status had been further increased.[159] At the same time, a diminution in airlift flights to Egypt and Syria was noticed on October 23, and all flights ceased on October 24. Late that afternoon, the Brezhnev note was delivered. The enhanced readiness status of the airborne forces does not seem to have unduly worried U.S. decisionmakers while the airlift was in full swing, but the stand-down suggested that transport aircraft were being freed for the eventuality of intervention.[160] There were also reports on intercepted communications suggesting the movement of Soviet troops by air, the establishment of an airborne command post in southern Russia, and the spotting of a flight of some ten Antonov-22s heading toward Cairo.[161]

Yet all of these indicators were vague. The petering out of the airlift occurred in conjunction with the cease-fire and may have reflected a Soviet judgment that no further arms supplies were necessary. The sealift was interrupted at the same time. Five ships went through the Bosporus on October 22, but only one on the 23d, and none on the 24th, for the first

---

158. "Secretary of Defense Schlesinger's News Conference of October 26," p. 617.

159. Quandt, *Decade of Decisions*, p. 197.

160. "Secretary of Defense Schlesinger's News Conference of October 26."

161. Ibid.; Kalb and Kalb, *Kissinger*, p. 488; Glassman, *Arms for the Arabs*, p. 161. There is an important discrepancy between the defense secretary's statement that the airlift decreased on the 22d, and ceased completely on the 23d, and Quandt's study, which shows that some 550 tons were delivered to Syria, Egypt, and Iraq on the 23d, with no deliveries on the 24th; *Soviet Policy*, pp. 25–26. If Schlesinger was correct and there were no Antonov flights on the 23d, the spotting of ten or twelve transports heading for Egypt on the 24th could have given rise to the fear that they carried the advance party of a Soviet intervention force. If Quandt's figures are correct and the airlift continued through the 23d, prima facie the flights on the 24th were part of the continuing supply effort. The planes, upon landing in Egypt on the 25th, were reportedly found to be carrying arms, not troops (Glassman, *Arms for the Arabs*, p. 161), and Schlesinger himself stated that WSAG members considered "the probability of Soviet forces being en route . . . to be quite low."

time since October 14.[162] Preparedness measures detected in the Soviet
Union for the transfer of troop contingents to the Middle East do not
necessarily point to unilateral intervention. They are easily explained by
Moscow's attempt to persuade the Americans of the merits of sending a
joint peacekeeping force on short notice and its logistic preparations for
U.S. acceptance.

Thus the possibility that the Soviet Union was contemplating the unilateral injection of ground forces into Egypt if it became absolutely necessary to salvage Cairo's position cannot be ruled out. But the more reasonable inference from the scanty available evidence is that Soviet diplomatic
moves and military signals were orchestrated on October 23–25 mainly
to increase pressure on Washington to restrain the Israelis. From Moscow's perspective the Soviet objective must have appeared fairly limited
and noncontroversial: to secure full implementation of a cease-fire that
was already partially effective, that had been negotiated and cosponsored
by the United States, and that had occurred when Washington's protégé
had a clear military advantage. For Brezhnev and his colleagues, the
chance that they would have to act upon the threat contained in his note
of October 24 must have seemed slight.

Conclusions

How influential was the Soviet Union in shaping Egyptian and Israeli
policies and behavior in the two crises and how closely did these conform
to Soviet preferences? In 1967 the USSR played important roles in both
the crisis of May 15 to June 5 and the subsequent six-day war. It was a
"loser" as a result of its Arab clients' defeat, but it was also a major
beneficiary of the outcome. Soviet actions were crucial in sparking the
conflict in mid-May, and Soviet intervention on the last day of the war
raised for a few hours the possibility of a superpower military confrontation. Yet of all the major participants in these events, on balance, Moscow's behavior was the most restrained, conservative, and cautious. While
the local parties undertook armed hostilities that engaged all their military
forces and the United States maneuvered sizable naval task forces near the
combat area, threatened to break a blockade in disputed waters, and
suffered an attack on one of its ships in which heavy casualties were in-
flicted, the USSR restricted itself largely to diplomatic demarches, politi-

162. Quandt, *Soviet Policy*, p. 23.

cal contacts, and the signaling of intentions through policy statements and the media. The use of military instruments to influence events was resorted to sparingly, and when it was invoked, the circumstances were such that either the Soviet Union's intent was (purposely) unclear or its commitment and determination were doubted. In fact, it may be said that of all the means available to the Soviet Union to influence the course of events in the Middle East, military power was the one least used.

The primary Soviet objective was to *deflect* Israeli aggressive intentions from Syria alone onto the more powerful Syrian-Egyptian joint military capabilities. To achieve this, Moscow wanted the Egyptians to confront Israel with a more threatening posture without giving Israel sufficient provocation to launch a preemptive strike and unleash war. The Russians miscalculated their control over Egyptian behavior and passions, however, and started a momentum toward war that could not be stopped.

The Soviet Union tried to influence Israeli choices and policies by both threats and assurances. It wanted the Israelis to be sufficiently impressed by a united Arab front supported by Moscow and by a sense of near-abandonment by the United States, to enable the Arabs to win a symbolic victory while directing Israeli aggression away from the vulnerable Syrian regime.

The outcome of this was in the short run highly undesirable for the Soviet Union. Its own clients and the Israelis went beyond their assigned roles, and a reversal of roles took place: the Israelis emerged victorious and the Arabs suffered a humiliating defeat. But in the longer run this defeat turned out to be a victory of sorts for the Russians since it enabled them to become the badly needed protector of Egypt and Syria as never before.

In 1973 preferences and behavior were again asymmetrical: the Soviet Union preferred the Egyptians to pursue a political solution rather than war to attain their territorial and security objectives. It provided the Egyptian armed forces with large quantities of weapons, including up-to-date sophisticated systems, to increase the credibility to Israel of their deterrence and compellence, though making sure that these did not significantly alter the regional balance of power or provide its clients with a capability for launching a "war of annihilation." Soviet expectations were therefore sanguine: Egypt and its allies were to be made strong enough to deter a preventive Israeli attack, but not strong enough to start a war. Toward Israel, the USSR seems to have assumed in the early 1970s an attitude similar to that of 1967, trying to persuade Israel of the futility of obtaining a political settlement through military force, thus compelling an accommodation to Arab demands without war.

When Egypt and Syria initiated hostilities on October 6, however, the Soviet Union, as in 1967, followed a course of action that appears to have been primarily designed to minimize the chances of a confrontation with the United States. While Moscow resupplied its clients with weapons and publicly supported Arab political objectives, its general behavior was restrained and cautious. From the first it acted to bring about an early halt to the fighting, and it was cooperative at the United Nations and in bilateral efforts with Washington. Its use of military means for demonstrative political purposes or deterrence was limited. Even at the declaratory level, where its practice has often been to compensate for inaction with verbal bombast, Moscow "tempered its domestic propaganda so as not to implicate the U.S. too seriously and presented the war effort as a pan-Arab (and totally local) struggle; it even moderated its official statements and warnings to Israel."[163] Only when, in the final stages of the war, Egypt seemed likely to suffer a crippling military and political defeat did the Soviet Union show willingness to raise the stakes by threatening unilateral intervention. However, as in 1967 and in the Suez crisis of 1956, the Soviet move was made in circumstances that suggested a low probability that the threat would have to be carried out, and it was accompanied by signs of military readiness that were vague and inconclusive.

The Soviet Union did not shun the use of military power to influence events because such use was superfluous, costly, politically inappropriate, or operationally impractical. The remarkable restraint exhibited both in 1967 and in 1973 when the tide of events was clearly moving against its interests and overwhelming its clients and protégés was mainly the product not of Soviet self-denial but of Western deterrence. The USSR was deterred by a regional military balance that favored the United States, by its conviction that the United States was seriously committed to the defense of regional interests, and by its fear of the harmful consequences of a military confrontation in the Middle East for a host of developing East-West political and economic relationships.

The Kremlin did not appreciate the risks for Soviet regional interests entailed in keeping such a relatively low military profile while clients were defeated. Nor did the Arabs hide their disappointment or mute their reprobation. A steep decline in influence was averted after the June war by massive and immediate weapons resupply and stepped-up economic

163. Golan, *Yom Kippur*, p. 126.

assistance, and Arab-Western relations were at such a low that Cairo and Damascus had no practical alternative to reliance on Moscow. Besides, the virtually complete destruction of Egypt's and Syria's military machines dictated quick rearmament as a preeminent national objective, and the Arabs possessed neither the money nor the political leverage to obtain non-Soviet equipment; hence the paradox, in the three years that followed the six-day war, of maximum Soviet expansion of actual presence and political as well as ideological influence in the Arab world on the heels of the worst defeat suffered by Soviet arms.

In October 1973 the Soviet Union paid a heavy political price for its lukewarm support of its Arab friends. Again, the actual degree of military involvement or noninvolvement of Moscow in the war bore no perceptible relation to its political fortunes in the region during ensuing years. It is conceivable that a much more substantial Soviet interventionist role, either to protect Damascus in the first week of the war or to salvage the Egyptian position in the third week, would have produced a different result, one more favorable to the Soviet position. On the other hand, any imaginable Soviet military intervention would have been basically defensive and would not have changed the military outcome of the war; the Arabs would still have had to turn to the United States to obtain a political settlement with Israel that yielded the requisite territorial withdrawals.

In any case, the limited Soviet military involvement in 1973, though surpassing that of 1967, gained Moscow little credit with its Arab friends. Despite the wartime airlift and sealift and Moscow's apparent willingness to risk a confrontation with the United States to forestall the loss of Egypt's Third Army, the leaders of Egypt and Syria discounted and pointedly ignored the role of Soviet aid in official pronouncements made during and after the war, and Egypt moved rapidly after the cease-fire to mend its relations with Washington and orient its diplomacy exclusively toward the United States. The decline of Soviet influence continued apace over the next three years, culminating in 1976 with Egypt's denunciation of the 1971 Treaty of Friendship and Cooperation and Syrian intervention in the Lebanese civil war against Moscow's express opposition. In Arab-Israeli conflict diplomacy, the Soviet Union found itself relegated to the sidelines, an impotent witness to a resurgence of American influence in Arab states.

In all likelihood, the Soviet Union has learned two critical lessons from the 1967 and 1973 events, which may importantly affect its future conduct. First, neither large-scale military assistance nor a substantial regional military presence ensured much influence on the behavior of clients on issues important to them or much control over the course of events in crisis situations. Second, retaining influence over client states, even where relationships are of long standing and acquired at high cost in economic and military aid, may require a commitment to military intervention on the clients' behalf when necessary, even at the risk of nuclear confrontation.

To the extent that these lessons have been absorbed by Soviet decision-makers, future Soviet behavior in the Middle East should reflect greater caution in the building stages of international crises (as contrasted with behavior during crises), more selectivity in the choice of clients and causes with which Moscow could become militarily associated, and increased readiness to commit military power in furtherance of preferred outcomes while supporting chosen friends.

In short, the USSR will act in ways that are both more restrained and more dangerous than in the past. With the changing balance of military strength between the superpowers, in the Middle East as well as globally, the Soviet leadership will no doubt feel in a future confrontation that it commands the requisite capabilities for more assertive behavior than in 1967 and 1973. What the ensuing clash of wills will bring forth if the conflict is joined cannot be foreseen. Clearly, however, the choices for the two superpowers will be even harder, and the risks more terrible, than in any previous Middle Eastern crisis.

CHAPTER ELEVEN

Air Support in the Arab East

ALVIN Z. RUBINSTEIN

DEVELOPMENTS in the Middle East often take on a dynamic of their own and sweep superpowers along on a course they had neither anticipated nor desired. From 1955 to the early 1970s Arab needs and Soviet interests and capabilities led from Soviet arms transfers and verbal support in crises to deployments in defense of vulnerable clients. Soviet involvement in the Arab East began in the early post-Stalin period as part of a foreign policy shift from a continental-based strategy to a global one. Entrée into the Middle East followed easily upon Moscow's willingness to sell arms. Initially motivated by a desire to undermine the Western-sponsored Baghdad Pact and the network of bases available to the U.S. Sixth Fleet and Strategic Air Command for use against the Soviet Union, arms transfers paved the way for the establishment of a presence and expanded ties. Eventually, though, Moscow's clients sought much more than this.

Moscow was shocked by the Arab collapse in the 1967 June war. So rapid was the Israeli advance that there was nothing the Soviet Union could do to prevent the outcome, even had it been inclined—which it was not—to intervene militarily on the Arab side. On the diplomatic front the USSR mounted a major campaign in the United Nations on behalf of the Arabs, promised "all necessary material assistance," and broke off relations with Israel. Militarily, it limited itself to closely watching the Sixth Fleet aircraft carriers. The Kremlin acted quickly once the fighting was over, however. On June 12, 1967, two days after the UN cease-fire had gone into effect, the Soviet government sent a squadron of TU-16 bombers to Egypt to show the flag and bolster Egyptian morale; and a massive airlift of military equipment began, including the delivery of "200 crated fighters" within several weeks.[1] By October, it had sent an additional 100 MIG-21s, 50 MIG-19s, 50 to 60 SU-7s, and 20 IL-28s; and by the end of 1967, 80 percent of the aircraft, tanks, and artillery that Egypt had lost in June had been replaced.[2]

In the Soviet leadership there were undoubtedly differences over what course to follow, though the evidence of the intraparty debate on foreign policy is meager. One indication was the dismissal of Nikolai G. Yegory-chev, first secretary of the Moscow City Committee of the Communist Party of the Soviet Union (CPSU), a week after the CPSU Central Com-mittee Plenum of June 21. Since November 1962 Yegorychev had held this post, to which he had been promoted, presumably by Nikita Khru-shchev, shortly after the Cuban missile crisis. Yegorychev led a party dele-gation to Egypt (April 11–24, 1967) after Foreign Minister Andrei A. Gromyko's sudden visit in late March and perhaps was implicated in Gamal Abdel Nasser's decision to precipitate the crisis with Israel in May, supposedly to forestall a preemptive Israeli attack against Syria. Yegory-chev may have been critical of the Politburo's handling of the June war, thus placing him at odds with the Brezhnev faction and exacerbating a rivalry born of disagreements over how to implement economic reforms and how to treat the liberal intelligentsia.[3]

Whatever the divisions in the Politburo, Soviet leaders decided to reprovision the Arabs. This entailed a major commitment of military advisers to ensure the effective use of the modern weapons provided and to create a system of defense against further attacks. In early November 1967 Marshal Matvei V. Zakharov, chief of the Soviet general staff, who had personally supervised the strengthening of Egypt's defenses, reported to Nasser that "Egypt can now stand up to anything Israel can deliver."[4] Soviet advisers began to train the Egyptian and Syrian armed forces at all levels. The military vulnerability and dependence of Egypt and Syria made the Soviet presence and position seem secure. Both states needed

1. Lawrence L. Whetten, *The Canal War: Four Power Conflict in the Middle East* (MIT Press, 1974), p. 398.

2. International Institute for Strategic Studies, *Strategic Survey, 1967* (London: IISS, 1968), p. 37.

3. Christian Duevel, "The Political Code of N. G. Yegorychev," Radio Liberty Research Paper, no. 17 (1967), and Duevel, "Soviet Party Press Attacks Left Opposition," Radio Liberty Dispatch (August 25, 1967). John R. Thomas argues that Yegorychev "apparently advocated direct involvement" in the June war; see "Soviet Foreign Policy and the Military," *Survey*, vol. 17 (Summer 1971), pp. 147–53.

4. Mohamed Heikal, *The Road to Ramadan* (London: Collins, 1975), pp. 51–52.

Soviet arms, expertise, and tactical guidance to redress Israeli superiority. Soon other Arab states—Sudan, Iraq, and the People's Democratic Republic of Yemen (PDRY)—overcame their hesitation to place heavy reliance on Soviet military assistance and followed suit.

Moscow quickly realized strategic dividends by obtaining sought-after naval facilities in Egypt. To allay U.S. uneasiness as its military buildup of Egypt unfolded, it regularly proclaimed the defensive nature of its assistance, whose stated aim was to secure justice for the Arabs and a return of their territories. The Soviet naval presence not only deterred Israeli attacks on Egyptian ports but also warned Washington that it no longer had an unlimited range of options for intervention in the region.

There were other reasons for the massive infusion of arms and the Soviet military buildup in the Mediterranean and the Indian Ocean. First, it was essential for the Soviet Union's future in the area to maintain in power regimes that pursued policies congenial to its interests. Whatever their past differences with Nasser, Soviet leaders perceived that a set of convergent goals now bound Egypt and Syria to the USSR, and vice versa. The strategic stakes made the cost of arms and advice seem moderate, the risk tolerable. Coming to the aid of "progressive" regimes in the Middle East could also have a ripple effect of long-range significance.

Second, having embarked on a policy of acquiring influence in the Arab world, Moscow pressed its diplomacy on a broad front. The Arab-Israeli conflict was by no means the only promising pond to fish in, though it was the largest; the prospects were bright elsewhere in the Middle East. In the Persian Gulf, the Red Sea–Horn of Africa littoral, and North Africa, Moscow saw situations that could weaken its global adversary and improve its own position. Third, Moscow purveyed arms to restore its tarnished credibility as a superpower patron, with an eye to impressing fence-sitters and prospective suppliants as well as its heavily dependent clients.

Soon, however, the Kremlin received Arab requests not only for armaments, military advisers, and supportive naval deployments, but also for combat support on the battlefield. Egypt at the end of 1969 was desperate for assistance against deep-penetration raids by Israeli aircraft; at the same time, Sudan sought support for its counterinsurgency effort against the Anyanya rebellion; and in 1974 Iraq called on Moscow for help in suppressing the Kurds. To each of these requests the Kremlin responded affirmatively by providing combat air support. These Soviet military actions and related diplomacy are the subjects of this examination.

The Air Defense of Egypt

As early as 1955 Egypt was the focal point of Moscow's strategy for exercising influence in the Arab world. Differences cropping up from time to time between Moscow and Cairo were never permitted to jeopardize the Soviet leadership's courtship of Nasser.

To Egypt's crushing defeat in June 1967 the Soviet Union's response was immediate, generous, and far-reaching: it undertook to restore Egypt's military capability and assist in the struggle against "the aggression," as Israel's victory was called. Some 2,000 Soviet advisers, including about 800 attached to the air force, arrived to help in the retraining. They counseled extensive reforms in the Egyptian military, especially in the air force, the bastion of social privilege, and Nasser did introduce many reforms; the Kremlin was less successful in persuading him to undertake meaningful economic and social reforms.

Egypt's military recovery was rapid, leading to differences over how to deal with Israel. Basically, Moscow wanted to keep the Arab-Israeli front quiet, but Nasser was otherwise inclined. In the first year after the June debacle, he had accepted the possibility of a political solution; lacking military capability, he had no option other than to talk about a political solution. Also he hoped the United States would, as in 1957, force Israel to surrender captured Arab territory; and he believed world public opinion would see the justness of the Arab cause.[5] However, with the failure of political means to effect a solution, his desire for an alternative to stalemate led him to consider the military option. So in the fall of 1968 he began a series of minor military engagements in the Suez Canal area. Artillery barrages and air attacks along the canal paralleled intensified diplomatic activity at the United Nations.

Also impelling Nasser's military activity were domestic restiveness and growing criticism of his leadership in the Arab world. From early March to late June 1969, Egyptian activity along the canal increased as Nasser launched the "war of attrition"—his interim answer to unacceptable stalemate. Soviet leaders, confronted with a serious situation in the Far East, where clashes with the Chinese along the Ussuri River threatened to explode into war, sought to contain the Suez brushfire. They tried to dis-

5. Alvin Z. Rubinstein, *Red Star on the Nile: The Soviet-Egyptian Influence Relationship Since the June War* (Princeton University Press, 1977), p. 63.

suade Nasser from his collision course with Israel, but failed, despite his total military dependence on the Soviet Union.

By summer the war of attrition had escalated to a major conflict. Slowly but steadily Nasser's military option turned sour. From early September, when Israeli forces landed along the Egyptian coast south of Suez and ranged over a thirty-mile strip destroying missile batteries and manned outposts, to late December, when Israeli planes began to fly virtually unchallenged over Egypt's now exposed heartland, Nasser's predicament deepened. The Soviet-Egyptian joint communiqué, issued in Moscow on December 12, 1969, suggested that Vice-President Anwar Sadat's mission to obtain additional Soviet arms had been successful, that the Soviet leadership had promised to send increased quantities of weapons and advisers. However, between December 12, 1969, and January 22, 1970— the day Nasser flew in secret to Moscow to urge an expanded military involvement—Egypt's plight and Nasser's own situation worsened. Israeli planes dominated the skies over Egypt, and Soviet combat troops were needed to save Nasser's regime. The Soviet response set in motion a chain of momentous developments.

The Kremlin Acts to Save a Client

Soviet leaders knew of Egypt's dire situation in the fall of 1969 from their subordinates on the scene, so Nasser's appeal in January 1970 came as no surprise and found the Politburo favorably disposed and ready to act. First, Nasser's political survival, which was in jeopardy, had to be assured. Moscow was not about to abandon the man who had brought the Soviet Union into the mainstream of the Arab world; he was a known factor with whom it could work, and his policies were for the most part congenial to Soviet long-term interests. Second, Nasser agreed to Soviet conditions and provided unrestricted use of sections of six major airfields from which Soviet planes could reconnoiter the eastern Mediterranean and the Red Sea to the Horn of Africa; unhindered access to the Egyptian ports of Alexandria, Port Said, and Sollum; and freedom to deploy Soviet ground air defense personnel and combat pilots. This enormously improved not only the Soviet military position in Egypt, but also its strategic position in the eastern Mediterranean. Third, the defense of Nasser was linked to Soviet credibility in the Arab world. To permit a U.S.-supported client to defeat Moscow's most important one would mean, in effect, acknowledging by default U.S. preeminence in the area and running the risk of the USSR finding itself without any role there at all. Finally, those who had favored the "forward policy" in the Arab world—notably Leonid Brezhnev and his closest associates—could not shy away from the consequences of that policy without laying themselves open to attack on their original decision from opponents in the Politburo and the Central Committee. A careful reading of Soviet writings at the time suggests that the decision to commit forces if needed was made sometime in the late summer or early fall of 1969; left open, pending political-military developments in Egypt, were the timing and type of forces required.[6]

In contrast to June 1967, when Nikolai Podgorny's request for exclusive control over the areas quartering Soviet advisers was rebuffed by Nasser,[7] the Soviet Union in 1970 was given a blank check for the deployment and defense of its personnel. The general arrangements for the Soviet troops were settled before Nasser returned to Cairo:

we were told the number of SAM-3 batteries they were going to give us and the positions in which they would be placed, and the number of men who would come with them. Eighty Soviet aircraft were going to be sent, preceded by four high-altitude supersonic reconnaissance planes—X500s the Russians called them, though the West now knows them as MIG-25s. About 1800 Egyptians were to come to the Soviet Union for six months' training [to learn to operate the SAM-3s].[8]

According to Mohamed Heikal, the editor of the semiofficial newspaper *Al Ahram,* who was a close confidant of Nasser's and had accompanied him to Moscow, the Russians made their decision at the meeting attended by the members of the Politburo and all twelve Soviet marshals.[9] However, the precision with which they laid out their plan of action hardly suggests the spur-of-the-moment decision that Heikal reports. Rather, it supports the view that Soviet leaders had anticipated the contingency of a massive intervention to save Nasser, prepared accordingly, and were ready with their reply when Nasser made his request. Brezhnev asked that the results of their discussions be kept secret as long as possible.

Soviet operational objectives called, first, for bringing an end to Israeli deep-penetration raids over Cairo, Port Said, and other cities; second, for pushing the fighting back to the canal area; and third, for restoring an approximate balance of power between the Egyptians and the Israelis. The Soviet plan involved the assumption of responsibility for Egypt's air de-

6. Ibid., p. 105.
7. Heikal, *Road to Ramadan,* p. 48.
8. Ibid., p. 88.
9. Ibid., pp. 87–88.

fense. For the first time, Soviet combat troops in significant numbers were to be sent to fight in a non-Communist third world country. Soviet capabilities and confidence had reached the point where Moscow was willing to go beyond the supply of weapons and advisers to support its clients and pursue political-military objectives in the third world.

Soviet missile crews, estimated at about 1,500 air defense personnel, arrived in early March and began installing SAM-3 sites around Cairo and Alexandria and in the Nile Valley.[10] In addition to SAM-3s, a missile designed specifically to counter low-flying aircraft and effective up to fifteen miles, "the first Soviet-piloted MIG-21J interceptors (a more advanced version of the MIG-21) and accompanying ground support crews began arriving" soon afterward at Egyptian air bases.[11] Soviet aircraft operated out of six airfields (El Mansura, Inchas, Cairo West, Jianaklis, Beni Suef, and Aswan; by 1971–72 small numbers of IL-38 patrol craft and AN-12 electronic surveillance planes were also operating from an airfield at Mersa Matruh). Supplementing these formidable defensive measures were thickened SAM-2 sites (SAM-2s are partially effective at high altitudes but quite ineffective below 2,000 feet) and large numbers of radar-controlled ZSU-23-4 four-barreled 23 mm antiaircraft guns designed for use against low-flying aircraft. By the end of March, about 4,000 Soviet military personnel were manning missile sites alone; by the end of June, the number had risen to some 8,000; and by the end of 1970, it was up to almost 15,000.[12] If the estimated 3,000 to 4,000 Soviet instructors and advisers attached to the Egyptian armed forces and the 150 to 200 Soviet pilots flying MIG-21Js are included, Soviet armed forces in Egypt at the end of 1970 numbered about 20,000. The first Soviet-manned SAM-3 sites became operational on March 15, 1970, leading Israel's Minister of Defense Moshe Dayan to observe several days later that where SAM-3s were stationed and successfully operated "things would become difficult for us."[13] At the beginning of April Soviet soldiers dressed in Egyptian army fatigues with no insignia or marks of rank were observed in various parts of Egypt.[14] Moscow was no longer keeping its commitment secret. The growing number of SAM sites and the reports that Soviet pilots

10. Roger F. Pajak, "Soviet Arms and Egypt," *Survival,* vol. 17 (July-August 1975), p. 167.

11. Ibid.

12. International Institute for Strategic Studies, *Strategic Survey, 1970* (London: IISS, 1971), p. 47.

13. BBC Monitoring Service, *Summary of World Broadcasts,* ME/3336/A/8, March 23, 1970.

14. *New York Times,* April 2, 1970.

were flying in defense of Cairo and Alexandria prompted Dayan to announce the end of Israeli deep-penetration raids on April 6. The first confirmation of the use of Soviet pilots came on April 17, "when Israeli pilots overhearing exchanges in Russian in a MIG-21J formation, returned to base rather than challenge the adversary."[15] After April 18 Israeli pilots did not venture beyond the Suez Canal region, to avoid encountering Russian-speaking pilots who scrambled into attack formation to meet every potential approach to the Nile Valley by Israeli aircraft.[16] The presence of Soviet combat forces made the Egyptian heartland and, with it, Nasser's position once again secure.

In May and June Soviet-manned SAM units buttressed the Suez Canal air defenses. Not only did the introduction of the new SAM-3 installations and the improved SAM-2 models make Israeli attacks more costly, but the Soviet-piloted MIG-21Js, "which, during their first weeks in Egypt, had restricted their patrols to the Nile Valley, extended their operations forward to areas on the flanks of the Canal front."[17] Having denied Israeli aircraft access to central and upper Egypt, Moscow then moved its forces forward to the fiercely waged struggle in the canal area. Despite heavy Israeli bombing and mounting Egyptian casualties, the Russians and Egyptians continually pushed the network of SAM sites closer and closer to the canal.

The Soviet-Egyptian success in reestablishing the SAM defenses was achieved by setting up the SAM sites often overnight with minimum consideration for reducing vulnerability and making fine adjustments for accuracy. By this technique, Israeli raiders were frequently surprised by new SAM installations. Moreover, new weapons were introduced, such as the SAM-3 and improved models of the SAM-2. The new SAM-2s possessed better computer fire control and a capability of launching salvos of six rockets in an integrated time sequence. This technique of so-called ripple firing was, of course, extremely expensive, but it did compensate for accuracy losses because of speedy installation, and it also better assured the imposition of high Israeli losses, which was the goal of the Soviet campaign.[18]

The nearer Soviet crews and pilots drew to the incendiary canal area, the more ominous became the potential for a Soviet-Israeli crisis. In early July, this took on new meaning when Israeli Chief of Staff Major-General

15. J. C. Hurewitz, "Weapons Acquisition: Israel and Egypt," in Frank B. Horton III, Anthony C. Rogerson, and Edward L. Warner III, eds., *Comparative Defense Policy* (Johns Hopkins University Press, 1974), p. 489.
16. *New York Times,* April 29, 1970.
17. Jon D. Glassman, *Arms for the Arabs: The Soviet Union and War in the Middle East* (Johns Hopkins University Press, 1975), p. 78.
18. Ibid., p. 79.

Haim Bar-Lev announced that three Israeli planes had been shot down by SAM-2 missile batteries, whose crews included Soviet personnel.[19] Israeli air losses continued to rise.

However, on Secretary of State William Rogers' initiative and because of Nasser's readiness for a respite to strengthen his military-political situation and give U.S. diplomacy a chance, a cease-fire was put into effect on the evening of August 7, 1970. At that time, there were an estimated fifteen to twenty SAM sites within the fifty-kilometer zone on either side of the canal into which no further military installations were supposed to be introduced; two months later, "between 40 and 50 missile batteries—about one-third of them SAM-3s—had been set up by the Egyptian army within the 50 km stand-still zone. Of these, 30 to 40 were within 30 kms of the Canal, and the closest battery was about 12 kms from the waterway. Taking reserves into account, some 500 to 600 missiles were newly emplaced within the stand-still zone."[20] The Soviet-Egyptian violation of the cease-fire "was apparently a calculated move to definitively eliminate Israel's air supremacy over the canal," the Russians probably reasoning that this "would best guarantee the maintenance of the cease-fire and, by increasing the insecurity of Israel's hold on the east bank of the Canal, would provide incentive for an Israeli pullback."[21] Also, the Soviet air defense system in the Nile Valley made Cairo, Alexandria, and Aswan among the best protected centers in the world.

Throughout the crisis of January to July 1970, Soviet leaders always spoke in broad terms, stressing the defensive nature of their military involvement. A few days after Nasser's secret visit to Moscow, *Pravda* addressed itself to the "inflamed" situation in the Middle East. Those in the West who expected that the Arabs would find "themselves all alone" and easy prey of the Israelis were given notice of the reaffirmation of the strong ties between the Soviet Union and Egypt and the even greater significance "at the present time" of the "many-faceted Arab-Soviet cooperation."[22] The article noted Egypt's increasing "combat potential" and the USSR's resolve not to abandon Egypt. On January 31 Premier Aleksei Kosygin sent a letter to President Richard Nixon warning of the dangerous situation developing in the Middle East and demanding an end to Israeli

19. *New York Times,* July 7, 1970.
20. *Middle East Record, Volume Five: 1969–1970* (Jerusalem: Keter, 1977), p. 16.
21. Glassman, *Arms for the Arabs,* p. 81.
22. *Pravda,* January 27, 1970.

air attacks. In the letter, which was the first known direct message sent by Kosygin to Nixon since the President had taken office a year earlier, the Soviet leader was quite direct:

We would like to tell you in all frankness that if Israel continues its adventurism, to bomb the territory of the U.A.R. and other Arab states, the Soviet Union will be forced to see to it that the Arab states have the means at their disposal with the help of which due rebuff to the arrogant aggressor can be made.[23]

On February 2 he communicated with British Prime Minister Harold Wilson and French President Georges Pompidou as well. Unsatisfactory replies led Tass to report on February 12 that Kosygin had told the Western powers: "The Soviet Union is fully resolved to help foil imperialist ventures and there should be no doubt about that."[24] Four days later, Tass announced that the Soviet Union would provide the Arab states with "the necessary support" to uphold their security and their just interests.[25] The SAM-3 crews and Soviet-piloted aircraft were dispatched with background music of anti-Zionist denunciations in the Soviet media.

Moscow's combat intervention was undoubtedly made easier by the attitude of many officials in Washington that "Israel has brought on the Soviet response by a reckless bombing campaign and irresponsible rhetoric aimed at the Nasser regime's existence."[26] Moreover, when Washington did not object to the dispatch of Soviet arms and personnel, apparently because "the United States received advance assurance that the introduction of Soviet fighting personnel into Egypt . . . was essential for the defense of a hard-pressed protégé," Moscow may have felt assured that no confrontation would ensue.[27]

On April 14 Brezhnev optimistically observed that the progressive Arab regimes had not only stood their ground but strengthened their position and that at the same time Israel's international isolation was growing. A peaceful solution, he said, was possible provided Israel withdrew from occupied Arab territories; the Arabs would never accept the occupation of their lands, and the USSR was ready to give "all the necessary assis-

---

23. *Arab Report and Record* (March 1–15, 1970), p. 167.
24. *Soviet News,* February 7, 1970.
25. *Pravda,* February 17, 1970 (translated in *Current Digest of the Soviet Press* [*CDSP*], vol. 22, no. 7, March 17, 1970, p. 10).
26. William B. Quandt, *Decade of Decisions: American Policy Toward the Arab-Israeli Conflict, 1967–1976* (University of California Press, 1977), p. 95.
27. See J. C. Hurewitz, "Superpower Rivalry and the Arab-Israel Dispute: Involvement or Commitment?" in M. Confino and S. Shamir, eds., *The U.S.S.R. and the Middle East* (Wiley, 1973), p. 160; and Glassman, *Arms for the Arabs,* p. 85.

tance" to help achieve a settlement.[28] By late April Soviet policy had achieved the end of Israeli deep-penetration raids and the security of the Nile Valley, a critical tactical objective. However, what Soviet statements never dealt with was how far the USSR was prepared to go to alter the situation: was it only to effect a return to the status quo before the war of attrition, or was Moscow willing to help Egypt cross the canal?

Israeli reports about the expanding combat role of Soviet pilots prompted Premier Kosygin to hold a press conference at which he confirmed the Soviet military involvement, justifying it as being in conformance with Egyptian wishes and in opposition to what he termed U.S.-supported Israeli aggression.[29] Two weeks later, in an apparent effort to persuade the United States not to provide Israel with additional aircraft, he divulged his reply to a message sent him on May 7 by the heads of state of Iran, Turkey, and Pakistan. In his answer Kosygin emphasized the Soviet Union's interest in a political settlement in the Middle East in compliance with all the provisions of UN Security Council Resolution 242 of November 22, 1967, saying Moscow's "extensive aid" was designed to help the Arab states "successfully defend their legitimate national rights."[30] While heavy fighting continued, so did uncertainty about Soviet intentions, particularly as the battle shifted toward the canal. On the whole, Moscow's statements sought to convey the "defensive" character of its involvement, both to reassure the United States about its objectives and to keep Washington's resupply of Israel to a minimum.

On the battlefield Soviet air defense forces were crucial: they created new political facts that motivated the Rogers initiative of June 1970 and Nasser's acceptance on July 22 of a cease-fire effective on August 7. The cease-fire ended the dangerously escalating Soviet-Israeli confrontations. From June 30, when Soviet-manned SAMs downed two Israeli F-4s over the canal, to July 30, when the Israelis ambushed scrambling Soviet planes as they climbed to intercept the approaching F-4s and downed four MIG-21Js, the two engaged in an increasingly serious series of feints and countermoves.[31] Having accepted responsibility for the defense of Egypt and considering its prestige on the line, Moscow was not prepared to settle for a situation "that risked a compromise or defeat of Soviet arms by

28. *New York Times,* April 15, 1970.
29. *Pravda,* May 5, 1970.
30. *New York Times,* May 21 and 22, 1970.
31. Lawrence Whetten analyzes this affair in illuminating detail in *Canal War,* pp. 117–28.

Israel."[32] When Moscow observed that Israel would not shy away from confrontation with the USSR if its security was at stake, it decided to expand the air defense belt along the canal, even though this required violation of the August 7 cease-fire. To induce greater prudence in the Israelis and to convey to Washington its determination to defend Egypt, Moscow decided to construct "a virtually impregnable air defense wall,"[33] comparable to that of the most heavily defended areas in the Soviet Union.

After the cease-fire of August 7, 1970, and until June 1972, the Soviet Union continued to expand Egypt's military capability. The improvement in Egypt's Soviet-operated air defense system was immediately evident:

> By the end of October [1970], some 500–600 surface-to-air missile launchers covered the western approaches to the Canal, about 200 of them being within 19 miles of that line. Moreover, the forward sites in the system, carefully spaced 7½ miles apart along the Canal itself in order to give overlapping coverage, also covered an area extending 12 miles into Israel-occupied territory.[34]

To the thickened interlocking network of SAM-2s and SAM-3s, the Soviet Union introduced some SAM-4s (medium-altitude air defense weapons designed to provide combat troops with umbrella protection against air strikes) and, in 1971, SAM-6s (the tracked version of the SAM-3, especially useful against low-flying aircraft).[35] In 1970–72 it also expanded Egypt's air force, increasing the number of Cairo's MIG-21C/Ds "from about 150 in July 1970 to 220 two years later, and of SU-7s from 105 to 120":

> On the other hand, the operation of the MIG-21Js [about 150 of them] was never handed over to Egyptian pilots or ground crews. Moreover in 1971, a token number, perhaps as many as a half-dozen, of the new but still not fully tested MIG-23s were deployed in Egypt for reconnaissance experiments, and a squadron or possibly two of SU-11 fighter-bombers wholly for display. Only Soviet personnel were allowed to handle the two classes of aircraft. . . .

> The helicopter fleet, nearly trebled in size from 70 in 1970 to 180 in 1972, included an additional 20 MI-6 Hooks, each capable of lifting a fully armed paratroop company. Finally, the number of T-54/55 tanks had been enlarged from 950 in 1970 to 1,500 two years later, of the T-34s from 250 to 400, and of armored personnel carriers from 900 to 2,000.[36]

This sustained military buildup was hardly disturbed by the political quarrels that increasingly troubled the Soviet-Egyptian relationship in

32. Ibid., p. 127.
33. Ibid., pp. 127–28.
34. IISS, *Strategic Survey, 1970,* p. 48.
35. Hurewitz, "Weapons Acquisition," p. 491.
36. Ibid., pp. 490–91; Glassman, *Arms for the Arabs,* pp. 105–06.

the period from Nasser's death on September 28, 1970, to the expulsion of Soviet missile crews and combat pilots in July 1972. And when the Russians left, the SAM system, which had been manned by between 12,000 and 15,000 Soviet military personnel, was kept intact. With the aid of 100 or so Soviet technicians who remained and the additional advisers who may have returned when relations improved in early 1973, the air defense system was maintained and its lethal effectiveness was demonstrated in October 1973.[37]

Nasser's Strategy

Nasser's secret visit to Moscow in January 1970 was born of desperation. A greatly expanded Soviet commitment, including the use of Soviet armed forces, was needed to restore his domestic equilibrium and international prestige. Such a commitment accorded with his strategy of enmeshing the Soviet Union in the military defense of Egypt, not only to strengthen Egypt's defense capability but also to heighten tension between the superpowers and force the internationalization of the Arab-Israeli conflict.

Though military matters took precedence, Nasser did not overlook political and diplomatic opportunities to strengthen Egypt's position in relation to Israel. His main target was the United States, which he hoped to induce to withhold the twenty-five Phantoms and one hundred Skyhawks it planned to send to Israel. On February 2, 1970, at an international conference of parliamentarians in Cairo, Nasser charged that the United States bore the greatest responsibility for the violence in the Middle East because of its support of the "aggression" against Egypt and aid to Israel.[38] As long as U.S. arms poured into Israel, he implied, the Arabs would seek arms from the USSR. A week later, in an interview with two American journalists, Nasser said that, if the United States sold more aircraft to Israel, he would do everything he could to get Soviet help, including SAM-3s.[39] The theme that U.S. support for Israel was

37. In the summer of 1973 the Egyptian air defense system consisted of "130 SAM sites, each of 6 SA-2, SA-3 and some SA-6 launchers; 20mm, 23mm, 37mm, 57mm, 85mm and 100mm AA guns; all integrated, through a warning and command network, with 9 Air Force squadrons of MIG-21MF interceptors." International Institute for Strategic Studies, *The Military Balance, 1973–1974* (London: IISS, 1974), p. 32.

38. BBC Monitoring Service, *Summary of World Broadcasts,* ME/3296/A/3, February 4, 1970.

39. Ibid., ME/3302/A/1–4, February 11, 1970.

pushing Cairo to turn to the Soviet Union for military aid was repeated by Nasser in an interview given James Reston on February 14. Nasser used the Western press to convey reasonableness and to justify his reliance on the Soviet Union.

The Egyptian (and presumably Soviet) strategy of dissuading President Nixon from fulfilling Israeli requests for more aircraft, even while Egypt was accepting the influx of Soviet arms and military personnel, was effective. Though Nixon was disposed to supply the F-4s and A-4s, "the rest of the bureaucracy was generally opposed . . . arguing that Israeli military superiority was still unquestioned and that Soviet arms shipments were a response to Israel's reckless campaign of deep-penetration bombing using the Phantoms."[40] Moreover, Nixon's deferral of a decision in February, March, and April was shaped by several other factors: his "displeasure at the way in which the American Jewish community had treated French President Pompidou during his visit in late February"; Washington's resumption of talks with the Soviet Union against the promising backdrop of political concessions Soviet Ambassador Anatoly Dobrynin said Moscow had obtained from Nasser in return for new arms shipments; and the fear that further aid to Israel might adversely affect the already weak position of Jordan's King Hussein.[41] The disposition to accept Soviet assurances of the "defensive" character of its deployment of SAMs was no doubt reinforced in the frequent talks of Donald Bergus, head of the small, unofficial U.S. mission in Cairo, with Nasser; though formal diplomatic relations with the United States had been broken during the June war, Nasser maintained close contact through Bergus.

With military relief at hand, Nasser's political dilemma was clearly expressed by his de facto spokesman, Mohamed Heikal: "The parties to the local struggle cannot impose peace and the parties to the international struggle cannot declare war. Therefore, the Middle East crisis has entered a strange state—a vacuum in which it is lost between war and peace."[42] Encouraged by Rogers' announcement on March 23 that the United States had decided not to sell Israel the additional Phantoms and Skyhawks, Nasser agreed to meet with Assistant Secretary of State for Near Eastern and South Asian Affairs Joseph Sisco. The talks (April 10 to 14) with the first high-ranking American official to visit Cairo since the

40. Quandt, *Decade of Decisions,* p. 97.
41. Ibid.
42. BBC Monitoring Service, *Summary of World Broadcasts,* ME/3336/A/3, March 23, 1970.

June war, and Nasser's uneasiness over Egypt's heavy losses and military dependence on the Soviet Union, prompted him, in a major speech on May 1, to call for a new American initiative. It was delayed, however, by Nixon's preoccupation with Vietnam, specifically, the U.S. invasion of Cambodia on April 30 and the consequent domestic backlash. But on June 19, on receiving Rogers' proposal for a three-month cease-fire and a resumption of talks under Dr. Gunnar Jarring, the UN secretary general's special representative, Nasser hurriedly arranged a trip to Moscow (June 29–July 20), where talks led to decisions of far-reaching importance and resulted in Nasser's acceptance on July 22 of Rogers' proposals.[43] The cease-fire effective on the evening of August 7 was predicated on assumptions of continued Soviet protection against Israeli military power and increased American political pressure on Israel for extensive concessions.

In the interim, Egypt was to be systematically built up and prepared for the eventuality of another round of fighting. Nasser had used his Soviet connection for the defense and promotion of Egypt's interests. On his death in September 1970, he bequeathed his successors a Soviet legacy that was to serve Egypt well in the following years.

American and Israeli Reactions

The failure of an intensive American initiative in the fall of 1969, the essentials of which were publicly set forth by Secretary of State Rogers on December 9, 1969, meant that the war of attrition would continue until the situation on the battlefield made the combatants more receptive to diplomacy. Moscow did not accept Nixon's attempt to link patron pressure on its warring clients in the Middle East with improvement in U.S.-Soviet relations and progress toward a SALT agreement. The Nixon administration's absorption with SALT, the war in Vietnam, West German Chancellor Willy Brandt's *Ostpolitik,* and probings for an opening to China led Washington to adopt a watch-and-wait attitude toward the fighting in Egypt. The President reacted mildly to Kosygin's warning letter of January 31 and only a bit more forcefully in his State of the World message a few weeks later. Although he urged restraint on the Russians, he accepted their assurance of the defensive nature of the Soviet arms and troops dispatched to Egypt; and he shelved Israel's request for

43. Rubinstein, *Red Star on the Nile,* pp. 118–21.

additional aircraft, content for the moment to let battlefield developments form political initiatives.

The Israelis, intent on forcing Nasser to comply with the 1967 cease-fire agreement, sought to sustain their devastating air war. The "disappointment and concern" expressed by Foreign Minister Abba Eban the day after Rogers announced (on March 23, 1970) that President Nixon had decided to hold Israel's request for additional aircraft in abeyance turned to mounting uneasiness as the scale of direct Soviet military involvement became clearer. On March 20 Dayan described the expansion of SAM sites as "the first stage of the Sovietization of the Egyptian war machine"; on April 14 he held the manning of missile sites by Soviet personnel to be "a very grave matter" and warned the Russians that if need be "we shall bomb you"; and on April 29 the Israeli government formally charged that "for the first time Soviet pilots are flying operational missions from military installations under their control in Egypt." The Israeli contention that Soviet armed forces were changing the military balance was no longer dismissed by Washington, and President Nixon became more receptive to Israeli requests for aircraft replacements; hence toward the end of April the White House took over from the State Department responsibility for the day-to-day supervision of American policy toward the crisis.

Though Vietnam and Cambodia still absorbed most of the President's attention, he could no longer ignore the regional and global implications of the deepening Soviet participation in the Egyptian-Israeli war. Washington was encouraged by Nasser's speech of May 1, calling on Nixon to understand the Arab position and urge Israel to comply with the principles of Resolution 242, and making clear that a decisive moment in Arab-American relations had been reached—"either we will be estranged forever or there will be a new serious and definite start . . . the situation is delicate and . . . the consequences are extremely dangerous." However, without tangible evidence of Soviet restraint or indeed of some definitive statement from Moscow on where it intended to draw the line of involvement, Nixon decided to resume the supply of military equipment promised to Israel in the December 1968 arms agreement. Eban was so informed on May 21 and was asked only that the Israeli government withhold publicity and show "a degree of flexibility on terms of a settlement. This was forthcoming on May 26, when Prime Minister Golda Meir formally announced that Israel continued to accept UN Resolution 242 as the basis for a settlement and would agree to something akin to the Rhodes formula for talks."[44] Ignoring a Soviet overture in early June for a joint approach, Nixon authorized the Rogers proposal, which was presented to Cairo and Jerusalem on June 19. Although the Israeli cabinet rejected the proposal, Ambassador Itzhak Rabin in Washington "objected to the tone of the message to Nixon and did not communicate it to the White House."[45] For more than a month Washington and Jerusalem negotiated their differences, agreeing finally on July 25 after Prime Minister Meir had received various assurances from President Nixon. In overriding the strong opposition in her coalition government, Meir decided that the risks of a rejection were greater than those of acceptance, a judgment expressed in Dayan's comment that "Israel is not so strong that she can afford to lose allies."[46] The Israeli government publicly accepted the American plan on July 31.

In seeking the "expulsion" of Soviet forces from Egypt, the White House saw the Soviet military entrenchment in Egypt as part of a more general Soviet challenge to U.S. world influence and as a Middle East complement to Soviet arms aid to Hanoi. On July 1 President Nixon said: "You cannot separate what happens in Vietnam from the Mideast or from Europe or any place else."

That is why, as the Soviet Union moves in to support the UAR, it makes it necessary for the United States to evaluate what the Soviet Union does, and once the balance of power is upset, we will do what is necessary to maintain Israel's strength vis-à-vis its neighbors, not because we want Israel to be in a position to wage war—that is not it—but because that is what will deter its neighbors from attacking it.[47]

Nixon's determination to end the fighting and avoid a confrontation with the Soviet Union required the exercise of pressure on Israel. Inevitably, the asymmetry in American-Israeli priorities created difficulties between Washington and Jerusalem.

Outcomes

Soviet leaders had cause for satisfaction after the implementation of the cease-fire agreement of August 7, 1970. First, owing to the Soviet mili-

44. Later, on July 4, President Nixon also quietly "authorized the shipment of electronic-counter-measure (ECM) equipment to be used against the SAMs in the canal zone." Quandt, *Decade of Decisions,* pp. 99–101.

45. Michael Brecher, *Decisions in Israel's Foreign Policy* (Yale University Press, 1975), p. 491. Chapter 8 gives a detailed account of the Israeli reaction to the Rogers proposals.

46. *New York Times,* July 29, 1970.

47. *New York Times,* July 2, 1970.

tary involvement, Egypt had blunted and then reversed the Israeli offensive and reestablished an approximate military balance of power along the Suez Canal axis. Egypt's continued viability as a credible belligerent and Nasser's political survival, two prime Soviet objectives, had been realized and enhanced Soviet prestige among the courted progressive Arab states. Second, in his dependence on the Soviet Union, Nasser had granted military privileges that capped a decade of Soviet diplomatic effort and well served Soviet strategic objectives in the eastern Mediterranean and Red Sea areas. The Soviet navy gained access to Egyptian ports without having to secure permission for each visit and extensive repair and supply depots to facilitate the forward deployment of the Soviet Mediterranean fleet; the range of Soviet air reconnaissance was also greatly extended by the use of the Egyptian airfields under Soviet control. The Soviet military presence, enormously expanded from the level before the war of attrition, seemed solidly entrenched, based as it was on Nasser's complete reliance on Soviet equipment, expertise, and protection, and an impressive Soviet performance. Third, Moscow thought it had a dependent client capable of resisting but not defeating Israel and subject to Soviet restraint; for despite its massive aid, Moscow sought only to protect Nasser from collapse, not to regain Egyptian lands. Fourth, Nasser's acceptance of the cease-fire suited the Soviet objectives of avoiding a confrontation with the United States and returning the conflict to the conference table, where the USSR would play a leading role in the negotiations for a political settlement. To sweeten Nasser's return to the diplomatic process, Moscow promised to extend and widen the air defense system, which, within a few months, would effectively neutralize Israeli air supremacy over the canal and protect Egypt in the event of a resumption of hostilities. Finally, as Brezhnev emphasized in a speech on August 28, 1970, it was Soviet military power that had given added impetus to political initiatives and had forced Israel to the conference table, though "with clenched teeth."

That the intervention could be mounted so expeditiously was due to the USSR's greatly expanded capability for projecting power abroad and its sense of confidence deriving from a nuclear arsenal matching that of the United States. In an era of nuclear stalemate, a superpower commanding powerful conventional forces can engage in low-cost, low-risk, far-ranging, intensive rivalry in the third world. The Soviet Union's response to Egypt's legitimate request for assistance was limited, focused on air defense, and cautiously escalatory, thereby limiting and complicating the reactions open to U.S. policymakers.

Israel and the United States could not ignore the Soviet use of armed forces. A tough, self-confident Israel was made to face up to the limits of its power, the extent of its dependence on the United States, and the impossibility of defeating an Egypt protected by the Soviet Union—or even of intimidating Nasser into making concessions. The United States could not remain a passive bystander once the Soviet Union became directly involved in the fighting: committed to the existence of Israel as a state, though not to its post-1967 boundaries, suspicious of Soviet intentions and policies, and eager to shore up Western-oriented Arab regimes and prevent the radicalization of Arab politics, it could not maintain a situation of Israeli superiority without doing severe harm to its extensive economic and strategic interests in the Arab world.

After Nasser's death Moscow expanded its military and economic ties with Egypt, expecting continuity to prevail with his successors. However, some of Anwar Sadat's moves disturbed Moscow: his tentative retreat from Nasser's policy of nationalization; his downgrading of socialism; and in early February 1971—as a surprise foreign policy initiative—an offer to reopen the Suez Canal coupled with an underlying combativeness. Moscow's uneasiness was soon compounded by the domestic crisis in Egypt. In early May, charging a plot to unseat him, Sadat purged most of the Nasserist elite with whom Moscow had begun to feel comfortable. In an attempt to preserve the privileged Soviet position in Egypt and prevent Sadat from looking to the United States, Moscow induced him to seal Egypt's relationship with the USSR in a treaty of friendship and cooperation. Sadat agreed, seeing in the treaty, signed on May 27, 1971, Soviet recognition of his legitimacy and reaffirmation of promises of weapons and support in the event of another war.

In the following year, though, Sadat became convinced, first, that Moscow's reluctance to provide "offensive" weapons concealed a basic opposition to Egypt's resort to the military for regaining occupied Arab territory, and second, that Moscow was content with the existing situation of "no war, no peace," because it allowed the Soviet Union to pursue détente with the United States. These conclusions led to the expulsion of Soviet military personnel in July 1972 and a period of Soviet-Egyptian tension. Five months later, his exploration for a Western alternative having proved unrewarding, Sadat again turned to Moscow, which, eager to keep a military foothold, responded by reopening the arms tap, making possible the fourth Arab-Israeli war in October 1973.

By the summer of 1973, three years after Moscow had saved the Egyptians from certain defeat, the Soviet position in Egypt had slipped considerably, but still retained a number of advantages. In the economic sphere, the Soviet Union played an important role in the industrial sector. In the military sphere, though forced to relinquish its unlimited use of Egyptian airfields, it was permitted the continued use of ports and anchorages, though on less preferential terms than before. It retained these concessions on an increasingly constricted basis after the October war until April 1976, one month after Sadat unilaterally abrogated the 1971 treaty and ended the once significant Soviet military presence.[48]

The Soviet-Egyptian estrangement (only partially eased by Sadat's conciliatory moves from December 1972 on) contrasted with the Soviet-American détente. The superpower differences of 1970 had faded in the glow from SALT I, the Nixon-Brezhnev exchange of visits, and mushrooming economic, cultural, and scientific agreements. For the time, Moscow was content to keep its relations with Egypt in a minor key. Despite the strain, there were advantages. The forced removal of Soviet troops from Egypt engendered improvement in Soviet-American relations by easing Washington's concern about the Soviet challenge in the Middle East. Also, believing that Washington would not pressure Israel into making concessions that could occasion a major reorientation in Egyptian foreign policy, Moscow expected the Egyptians to maintain a Soviet connection. The American relationship was of great importance to Moscow, which looked forward then to the extensive credit and trade concessions recommended to the Congress by President Nixon—at least until the October war, which reversed Washington's sanguine outlook about the future of the U.S.-Soviet détente.

In retrospect, it seems clear that had Moscow not used its forces to support Egypt in 1970, the improvement in U.S.-Soviet relations that sprouted briefly in 1972 would not have withered after October 1973: 1970 was an essential precursor to 1973. Without the Soviet intervention to save Nasser and reverse the Arab-Israeli military imbalance, the Arab-Israeli conflict would have remained locked in the situation of "no war, no peace." One concomitant of this might have been a Soviet policy of

48. A recent analysis suggests that, since it had no comparable naval facilities elsewhere in the Mediterranean, losing the Egyptian shore-based facilities led the Soviet Union to reduce the number of surface combatants deployed in the Mediterranean and, possibly, to increase the number of submarines deployed. See Robert G. Weinland, "Land Support for Naval Forces: Egypt and the Soviet Escadra, 1962–1976," *Survival*, vol. 20 (March-April 1978), pp. 78–79.

greater restraint in arms transfers to Egypt and Syria. If so, Sadat would not have had a feasible military option in October 1973, no superpower confrontation would have occurred, and détente might have developed more fully. This would have entailed tacit Soviet recognition of the limits of its possibilities in the Arab East and acceptance of a lesser presence. But no vital Soviet security interest would have been jeopardized; indeed, the infusion of American capital and technology into the USSR that might have resulted from a less imperial Kremlin policy in the Arab East would probably have resulted in a significant boost to its economy and overall position in Europe. But this would have meant curtailment of the ambitious "forward policy" started by Khrushchev and continued by Brezhnev.

On the other hand, had Moscow backed an Egyptian crossing of the canal in 1970, the result might have been a Soviet-American confrontation. Assuming it would have stopped short of a nuclear showdown, a Soviet challenge of such magnitude might have greatly enhanced Moscow's standing in the Arab world. However, it would also have precluded a SALT agreement, détente in Europe, and economic concessions; it might also have pushed the United States closer to the People's Republic of China. In such an environment, U.S.-Soviet relations would have been worse than they actually became after the October war.

Soviet Relations with Sudan and the Anyanya Insurgency

When Sudan joined the other Arab states in June 1967 in breaking ties with the United States, the USSR's interest in improving their modest relationship was whetted. For its part, Sudan hoped to acquire modern weapons to offset traditional reliance on Britain, with whom it had broken diplomatic relations the previous year over the Rhodesian issue. A Sudanese military mission went to Moscow in late July 1967, and an arms agreement was announced on August 6.[49] At the end of September a Soviet military delegation visited Khartoum to discuss the details, which reportedly included the establishment of Sudan's first air academy.

Implementation of the agreement languished, however, because Moscow was already heavily committed in Vietnam, Egypt, and Syria and, the Sudanese need for arms not being critical, Moscow could afford to dole out small, irregular packages of weapons in an attempt to gain better treatment for the Sudanese Communist Party (SCP). The arrest of

49. *Middle East Record, Volume Three: 1967* (Jerusalem: Keter, 1971), p. 56.

Moawiya Ibrahim, the secretary of the SCP, in late October 1967 brought a strong denunciation in *Pravda*. Labeling the actions against Ibrahim and other Communists "of a clearly provocative nature," *Pravda* blamed "rightist forces" and wrote that "instead of struggling against the accomplices of imperialism and aggression, the Sudanese reaction plans to concentrate all its fire on the Communist patriots"; it noted that this would "weaken the possibility of Sudan making a positive contribution to the Arab cause against Israel."[50] The implication was that Soviet arms could be put to better use than support for such a regime.

Despite a number of delays, by mid-September 1968 Sudanese officials said that "a new agreement on the reinforcement of the Sudanese Air Force has been concluded." By the end of the year, a trickle of Soviet arms had arrived, and Soviet advisers "were selecting officers for training in the USSR."[51] Arab sources placed the value of the Soviet-Sudanese arms agreement at well above the frequently mentioned $100 million price tag. But continued Soviet annoyance with the treatment of local Communists kept the arms deliveries minimal, a succession of Sudanese military missions to Moscow notwithstanding. Indeed, on the eve of the May 25, 1969, coup in Sudan, there was a mission in Moscow, seeking, as had its predecessors, a speedup in the Soviet supply process.

The nine army officers led by Colonel (later Major-General and then President) Gaafar Mohammed al-Nimeiry, a thirty-nine-year-old graduate of the military academy at Omdurman, who seized power on May 25, 1969, immediately made known their leftist orientation, denouncing imperialism, calling for close ties with the Soviet Union, and recognizing East Germany on May 28, thus becoming the second "progressive" and anti-imperialist Arab country to do so within a month (Iraq had taken the step on April 30). Though banning all political parties, Nimeiry did place Communists in the cabinet and courted the goodwill of leftists to counterbalance the might of "conservative, traditionalist, religious, and pro-Western forces" and gain the support of the trade unions, students, and intelligentsia.[52] In so doing he reinforced Moscow's belief in the progressive character of the regime. Four members of the Revolutionary Command Council (RCC) were Communists or leftists: Major Hashim Mu-

50. *Pravda,* October 30, 1967.

51. *Middle East Record, Volume Four: 1968* (Jerusalem: Keter, 1973), p. 56.

52. Haim Shaked, Esther Souery, and Gabriel Warburg, "The Communist Party in the Sudan, 1946–1971," in Confino and Shamir, *The U.S.S.R. and the Middle East,* p. 353.

hammad al-Ata, Major Faruq Uthman Hamdallah, Lieutenant Colonel Babikr an-Nur Uthman (these three were to be leading actors in the Communist-supported abortive coup of July 1971), and Prime Minister Abubakr Awadallah, the only civilian on the RCC. At least eight of the twenty-one cabinet members were leftists or Communists.

The new leadership took steps to end corruption, solve the problems of agriculture and the rebellion in the south, and strengthen the armed forces by obtaining modern arms and improving military training and institutes. From the very beginning, it looked to the Soviet Union for arms and assistance in upgrading the Sudanese armed forces. Nimeiry needed Soviet pilots and advisers, in particular, to assist in counterinsurgency operations in the south. Not only had Sudan been without a great power patron since the break with Britain in 1966 and with the United States after the June war, but it faced disintegration because of the growing challenge from the insurrectionists, who were encouraged by the aid they were receiving from Uganda, Zaire, and Ethiopia, traditional enemy of Sudan and staunch ally of the United States.

An Opportunity Seized

The Soviet leadership was quick to recognize the new military government of Sudan. In the Soviet press, unadorned reporting of Prime Minister Awadallah's affirmation of peaceful coexistence and opposition to colonialism and neocolonialism gave way, within one week, to praise for the new government's strengthening of "the front against Israeli aggression and imperialist prying in the Middle East."[53] The initial actions of the ruling RCC were unquestionably congenial to Soviet interests: diplomatic recognition of the German Democratic Republic; identification with Nasser and "progressive" Arab and African states; sharp criticism of "Western imperialism and Zionist intrigues"; and overtures for closer ties with the Soviet bloc.

Soviet leaders were aware of Sudan's difficulties: a civil war in the south against the Anyanyas—the military arm of the amorphous coalition of black Christian tribes and clans of the Southern Sudan—who had started insurgency operations in 1963;[54] a troubled economy; and powerful social and economic groups whose outlook was antithetical to Nimeiry's reformist bent. But as the largest country in Africa and a stra-

---

53. *Pravda,* May 28, June 1 and 2, 1969.
54. Robert O. Collins, *The Southern Sudan in Historical Perspective* (Tel Aviv: Shiloah Center for Middle Eastern and African Studies, 1975).

tegic land mass between Arab and Black Africa bordering on eight countries and the Red Sea, the Sudan was a tempting political target. Soviet planners may well have argued that securing a foothold there would help forge an anti-Western Arab coalition and would open up new opportunities for the Soviet Union, such as the use of Sudanese ports to facilitate the forward deployment of the Soviet navy, which had started calling at Aden and Hodeida the previous year, and a greater ability to move easily in Central Africa in the future.

Nimeiry's foreign policy orientation was commendable. Moreover, he seemed genuinely committed to a political solution of the "southern question." Whereas his predecessors had sought to suppress the Anyanya movement by increasingly bloody and costly military campaigns, Nimeiry impressed Soviet observers with his willingness to grant the southerners, who were ethnically Africans, not Arabs, substantial autonomy and to bring them into the central government.[55] His promise of regional autonomy assumed immediate credibility with his appointment of "a prominent southerner (the Communist lawyer, Joseph Garang) to the newly created Ministry of Southern Affairs in June 1969";[56] and his conciliatory position toward the Anyanyas suggested that Sudanese requests for accelerated and expanded arms assistance were intended to strengthen the regime against "reactionary" enemies and were not likely to enmesh the Soviet Union in an unending civil war. By late June the Soviet government's positive attitude toward Nimeiry was reflected in the statement Sudanese Communist Party Secretary-General Mohammed Abdul Khalek Mahgoub made at the Moscow Conference of Communist and Workers Parties, calling for support of the "Sudanese revolution."

Nimeiry's anti-Western, pro-Nasser, Soviet-bloc-oriented position was essentially what motivated a favorable Kremlin reaction to requests for arms and military advisers. Nimeiry's antifeudal, anticonservative, generally progressive domestic line no doubt also helped, as did minor events like the creation in Moscow in late August of the USSR-Sudan Friendship Society.[57] Throughout the summer the Soviet press continued its commendatory coverage of events in Sudan.

55. *Izvestiya,* June 12, 1969; *Pravda,* June 28 and July 18, 1969. See also Malumud Ata Alla, *Arab Struggle for Economic Independence* (Moscow: Progress Publishers, 1974), pp. 142–43, 148–49.

56. Peter K. Bechtold, *Politics in the Sudan* (Praeger, 1976), p. 263. See also Eric Rouleau, "Sudan: A Putsch With a Popular Front," *Le Monde Weekly Selection* (September 10, 1969), p. 4.

57. *Izvestiya,* August 29, 1969.

By late 1969 Soviet arms and advisers began to arrive in appreciable numbers. During the buildup and modernization of the Sudanese armed forces in the next eighteen months, the Russians divorced their interest in military advantages from their political disappointment with Nimeiry's changing attitude toward Sudanese Communists and his inability to find a solution to the southern problem. Regarding Nimeiry's foreign policy orientation and reliance on Soviet military support as the basis for future intimacy, they accepted the disquieting aspects of his domestic policy. The 1968 arms agreement had brought a few Soviet military instructors by midsummer and some arms by early 1969. After the May 1969 coup Moscow had stepped up its flow of arms because it saw the Nimeiry regime as a target of opportunity; because it expected arms and economic aid to establish a solid long-term relationship; and because it could not afford to ignore Nimeiry's disclosures of plots—allegedly with Ethiopian, U.S., West German, and Israeli backing—to topple his regime.

In anticipation of a visit by Nimeiry in early November 1969, *Pravda* devoted a lengthy article to the situation in Sudan and revealed the problems faced by Soviet decisionmakers.[58] It praised the "progressive" regime for conducting "an active anti-imperialist foreign policy" and taking important steps to strengthen relations with the Soviet Union. Acknowledging that the internal problems confronting the Sudanese government were "very complex," the *Pravda* article criticized "reactionary circles" who have turned "to stirring up anti-communism and downgrading the policy of the Sudanese Communist Party in hopes of attracting nationalist elements," and who, realizing that open attacks "on socialist goals" would fail, try to pass themselves off as supporters of "socialism without communism." *Pravda*'s admonishment of Nimeiry was moderate. Whatever disappointment Moscow felt over the SCP's diminished status in the cabinet, it continued to praise the regime's general domestic and foreign policies. The prospect of closer state-to-state relations was enough to warrant the expanded military commitments, especially since most of the arms were destined for use in the south, where there was minimal danger to Soviet advisers.

Monetary estimates of Soviet military assistance during the 1969 period vary; figures of $65 million and $150 million have been mentioned, demonstrating a combination of difficulty in assigning dollar values to Soviet equipment and uncertainty about certain magnitudes

58. *Pravda,* November 5, 1969 (in *CDSP,* vol. 21, no. 45, December 3, 1969, pp. 23–24).

involved.[59] The equipment provided included tanks, armored personnel carriers, surface-to-air missiles (SAMs), and several types of aircraft— jet fighters, transports, and helicopters. The aircraft and helicopters included sixteen MIG-21 short-range, supersonic fighters; six AN-12 heavy cargo planes, with a 44,000-pound payload, capable of transporting about one hundred troops; five AN-24 twin-turboprop transports, capable of carrying about fifty troops; ten MI-8 helicopters and three MI-4 utility helicopters, each capable of carrying a small number of troops; and one battery of SAM-2s. Most of the aircraft were delivered from mid-July 1970 on, when the fighting in the south once again intensified. Presumably, they were useful for counterinsurgency actions.

If behavior is an indication of intent, the diverse aircraft signaled Soviet support for the Nimeiry government's military operations against the Anyanyas and apparent decision to press for a victory in the field. Given the nature of the enemy, the commitment required of Moscow would have remained modest compared to that made to Egypt if Nimeiry had continued the counterinsurgency campaign for several years; the fighting was at a low level and posed little danger to the Soviet pilots who accompanied the above mentioned aircraft and who apparently flew combat missions; the battlefield was far from the public eye and operations could be carried out with impunity against a poorly armed foe. But political developments in Khartoum in July 1971 dramatically altered Nimeiry's approach to the rebellion. As a result, the Russians had little, if anything, to do with the nonmilitary solution that Nimeiry finally fashioned.

There is little information on the role Soviet military personnel played in actual operations against the southern insurgents from 1970 to July 1971. Neither the Sudanese nor the Russians write about it, and Western accounts, even those from the field, rely heavily on rumor and inference. I piece things together as follows.

Despite the government's efforts at reform, which went slowly, the

59. The lower estimate is cited in U.S. Department of State, Bureau of Public Affairs, *Communist States and Developing Countries: Aid and Trade in 1971* (Government Printing Office, 1972), p. 18; the higher estimate in *The Almanac of World Military Power,* 2d ed. (Bowker, 1972), p. 260.

The figures on Soviet force levels and equipment in the Sudan during the 1969–71 period have been culled from various sources: International Institute for Strategic Studies, *The Military Balance* and *Strategic Survey*; Arms Control and Disarmament Agency, *World Military Expenditures and Arms Transfers*; Stockholm International Peace Research Institute publications on disarmament and arms transfers; *Arab Report and Record*; and the references noted above.

fighting in the south never completely stopped. By early 1970 it had erupted again with considerable intensity and it continued intermittently throughout the year. The government used about two-thirds of its army of 28,000 to 35,000 men (expanded between 1969 and 1971) in the south, where the terrain, unlike that in the north around Khartoum, is overgrown and marshy. Poor roads made operations and the deployment of armor difficult, and the Sudanese army depended on Soviet aircraft for bombing villages, flushing guerrillas, and moving troops quickly to places where guerrilla units had been sighted. Though about 525 Sudanese officers were being trained in Soviet bloc countries,[60] relatively few, if any, had finished flight training or were able to fly the MIG-21s or the helicopters. Since the logistics of supplying Sudanese troops in the south and the tactics of dealing with the insurgents placed a premium on air support, presumably some of the 500 Soviet military advisers flew both supply and combat missions, although possibly only as copilots with Sudanese officers. Given the isolated areas in which the insurgents operated and the absence of trained Western observers, detection was virtually impossible, and the Russians could freely have flown missions to track the Anyanyas. It is also conceivable that some of the pilots were Egyptians: after the June war, Egypt had helped Sudan establish an air academy, partly to train Egyptian cadets out of range of Israeli aircraft. Certainly, relations between Nimeiry and Nasser were close.

As in Iraq in 1974–75, the Russians were prompted to help a progressive regime suppress an insurgent movement as a way of ensuring the survival of a leadership deemed congenial to Soviet strategic and political interests. Throughout 1970 and early 1971, Moscow, to judge from Soviet press coverage, continued to view Nimeiry as progressive, beset by domestic intrigues of right-wing sects and groups, and bogged down in a rebellion fomented by imperialist forces. Although Moscow was disappointed that he had turned on pro-Moscow Communists, his anti-imperialist foreign policy and extensive nationalization of foreign enterprises tilted the balance in favor of accelerated deliveries of weapons and such air support as was needed. Moreover, the new challenge to Nimeiry from traditionalist, anti-Communist Muslim sects, notably the Mahdists, strengthened Moscow's determination to support his regime.

On March 25 and 26, 1970, Nimeiry suppressed the Ansar (Mahdist) insurrection on Aba Island, setting off a widespread crackdown on the

---

60. Central Intelligence Agency, *Communist Aid to the Less Developed Countries of the Free World, 1976*, ER 77-10296 (CIA, 1977), p. 6.

Mahdists that included the killing of their leader. According to one report, as yet unconfirmed by other sources, MIG aircraft flown by Egyptian or possibly Soviet pilots strafed the island in support of government troops.[61] Two weeks later, in a move apparently designed to convince other religious groups that the crushing of the Mahdists was not motivated by Communist tendencies in his government, Nimeiry deported the secretary-general of the pro-Moscow wing of the SCP. Mahgoub's deportation (he returned in late July and was placed under house arrest) improved, to some degree, the position of the rival Communist faction of Ahmad Sulayman and Moawiya Ibrahim, who were willing to dissolve the party in order to remain in the government, which they thought they could influence from within.[62] In May, to reassure his leftist adherents, Nimeiry nationalized all banks and major trading corporations, "Sudanized" many foreign enterprises, and signed a new agreement with Moscow, adding Soviet experts to various ministries. The factional infighting between Nimeiry and the Communists came to a head in November 1970, not long after the departure from Sudan of a Soviet delegation led by Politburo member Dmitri Polyansky. Three leftist members of the RCC were purged: Major Faruq Uthman Hamdallah, Lieutenant Colonel Babikr an-Nur Uthman, and Major Hashim Muhammad al-Ata. None of these actions interfered with the continued supply of Soviet aircraft for use against the Anyanyas.

In February 1971 Nimeiry saw "no room for the Communists in the Sudanese revolution."[63] Moscow (and Sadat) tried to mediate, but without success, as Nimeiry attacked the Communist strongholds in the trade unions and youth organizations. Nonetheless, Moscow maintained close relations with the Nimeiry government, receiving, for example, an RCC delegation at the Twenty-fourth Congress of the CPSU (March 30 to April 8, 1971).

On July 19, 1971, Major Hashim al-Ata, who had been removed from the RCC in November 1970, in turn deposed Nimeiry, imprisoning him

61. *Middle East Record, Volume Five,* p. 1095.

62. The split between Mahgoub and his associates was caused by the latter's belief that the SCP be dissolved as the price of playing a leading role in Nimeiry's Sudanese Socialist Union. Mahgoub believed the party should retain its independent existence and moved to form alliances with the banned anti-Nimeiry religious Umma party and coalition National Front party. The role of the Communists in the Sudan is treated in considerable detail in the first scholarly treatment of the subject in the English language: Gabriel A. Warburg, *Islam, Nationalism and Communism in a Traditional Society: The Case of Sudan* (London: Frank Cass, 1978).

63. Shaked and others, "Communist Party in the Sudan," p. 359.

and his supporters. However, the failure to execute the old leaders "proved to be a fatal tactical mistake of the new revolutionaries since, on July 22, a successful 'counter-counter-coup' " brought Nimeiry back to power.[64] Unlike the unsuccessful putschists, Nimeiry took a bloody revenge, executing the officers as well as leading Communists, including Mahgoub and Joseph Garang. His relations with Moscow deteriorated sharply because, though there was no evidence that it had engineered the coup, the Soviet Union, in a departure from its characteristic treatment of coups in progressive states, had come out immediately in support of al-Ata's government and tried to pressure Sadat into following suit, thereby heightening Nimeiry's suspicion of its complicity. Nimeiry ignored Soviet appeals to spare those sentenced to death in connection with the events of July 19 to 22. Although relations between Moscow and Khartoum recovered, they never again approached the closeness of the previous two years.

The coup and worsening domestic tension prompted Nimeiry to make essential concessions to the southerners. A settlement was finally reached in Addis Ababa on February 27, 1972, between the Sudanese government and the Anyanya leaders, without any Soviet influence. It came about through Nimeiry's decision to shelve Pan-Arab ambitions, offer the southern Sudanese a substantial measure of autonomy, include them in the political leadership of the ruling one-party Sudanese Socialist Union, and concentrate on internal development. Changed attitudes in neighboring nations, particularly Ethiopia, further improved the chance for a settlement.

Support from abroad was crucial in sustaining the Anyanya revolt. Uganda and Ethiopia, and Zaire to a much lesser degree, took in refugees and provided funds and staging grounds that made sustained rebel resistance possible, though victory proved elusive. Their assistance derived from identification with the blacks and antipathy to Arabization; it predated Nimeiry's coup and Soviet involvement.

All three countries were anti-Soviet, anti-Communist, and basically pro-Western (though Uganda's Milton Obote, a leading member of the nonaligned grouping, was a frequent critic). Their behavior was not

64. Ibid. Warburg, *Islam, Nationalism and Communism,* believes that the coup was motivated by Hashim al-Ata's desire to bring about a settlement of the southern problem. The coup failed for a number of reasons: the interventionary role of Egyptian troops stationed at the Egyptian Military College in Gabal Awlia and the Egyptian air base in Wadi-Seidna, outside Khartoum; the role of Egypt, Libya, and British intelligence; the lack of leaders; and the failure of al-Ata to execute Nimeiry and his aides.

shaped by cold war pressure; superpower rivalry took a back seat to local animosities. Moreover, the Soviet factor was too negligible to have any noticeable effect on their foreign policy position, whose sharp changes were consequences of domestic shifts of power and perception.

In Uganda, Obote had started by 1969 to lessen his support of the Anyanyas and his close ties with Israel and to improve relations with Nimeiry and the Arab countries. But he was deposed in January 1971 and his successor, Idi Amin Dada, reversed this line, at one point accusing the Sudanese of abetting incursions into the country by pro-Obote groups. However, after the 1972 agreement ending the Sudanese civil war was signed in Addis Ababa, Amin became friendlier with Nimeiry, broke with Israel, and turned to Libya for subsidies. In Ethiopia, Emperor Haile Selassie played a major role in mediating an end to the conflict. Pleased by Nimeiry's anti-Communist tack after the July 1971 event, he improved relations with Sudan, thereby weakening the Anyanyas' military option and persuading them to settle. He welcomed Nimeiry's reconciliation with the southern Sudanese, his turn toward Central Africa and away from Arab world affairs—specifically, his downplaying of the cause of Muslim secessionists in the Ethiopian province of Eritrea—and his attempt to normalize relations with the United States. With these changes in the diplomatic environment, Zaire lost interest in the Anyanyas: President Mobutu's interest had stemmed only from animosity toward a Sudanese leadership, no longer in power, that had supported the rebel Simbas against him in the mid-1960s.

A Good Hand Squandered

Nimeiry had been pleased with Soviet air support in the counter-insurgency war in the south. However, the alacrity with which Moscow backed Hashim al-Ata's coup was its undoing. Whether through over-confidence, poor advice, ignorance of the local scene, or underestimation of Arab reaction, Moscow blundered. In its eagerness to see the SCP in a position of power, Moscow undermined a strong position. It intensified Nimeiry's domestic anticommunism and suspicion of the Soviet Union (despite the resumption of a relationship of sorts within a couple of months) and turned him toward the West and closer relations with the People's Republic of China, the former being far more important than the latter since Peking was unable to provide much assistance. Finally, it resulted in a diminished Soviet military presence. The setback in Sudan, unlike that in Egypt, was not due to Sudanese dissatisfaction with the level, quality, or performance of Soviet military advisers; it was due to faulty Soviet political judgment in backing a Communist dark horse that did not know how to finish the race.

The timely support that Nimeiry received from Egypt and Libya was crucial.[65] Both Sadat and Qaddafi acted to forestall a seizure of power by a Communist-inspired clique, irrespective of their assessments of what the Soviet Union was or was not doing. Quite simply, they opposed any Communist or Communist-oriented group coming to power in an Arab country on their borders.

Though regional developments can affect relations between superpowers, Sudan was peripheral to the U.S.-Soviet strategic relationship, so its change toward the Soviet Union had no notable effect. Moreover, the Soviet position in Sudan was still in the formative stages; it was more a case of an unrealized potential than an actual loss. Once the dust had settled, relations returned to a semblance of normalcy, but with a sharply reduced flow of Soviet arms and advisers and an end to the use of Soviet pilots in the south; this reflected Nimeiry's suspicion and his diminished need after the 1972 Addis Ababa agreement rather than Soviet second thoughts about the wisdom of trying to retain a foothold in the area.

Since then the situation has drastically changed. The political solution Nimeiry fashioned for the southern problem has so far held up. After July 1971, realizing that the future of his regime depended on his solving internal problems, Nimeiry widened his political base. He suppressed the Communists, downgraded relations with the Soviet Union, and negotiated an end to the civil war. In 1977–78 he effected a reconciliation with the Mahdist leadership. Reversing his nationalization policy, he encouraged foreign investment, especially from conservative Saudi Arabia and Ku-

---

65. Nimeiry's Defense Minister Khalid Hassan Abbas, who was in Yugoslavia at the time of the attempted coup, flew to Cairo. There, according to the story reconstructed by a Swiss journalist from the writings of a well-informed Lebanese journalist, Fuad Matar, Abbas conferred with Egyptian leaders and went on to Tripoli. "From there he called on the Sudanese by Libyan radio to rise against the coup. The countercoup took place on July 23, executed by tanks that appear to have come from the officers' academy established by the Egyptians at Jebel al-Awliya near Khartoum. Some sources affirmed that the tanks were driven by Egyptian officers. Another story was that a part of the Sudanese brigade stationed on the Suez Canal was flown to Khartoum. These troops seem in fact to have been moved, but it was tanks, not infantry, which liquidated the coup of al-Ata." Arnold Hottinger, "The Great Powers and the Middle East," in William E. Griffith, ed., *The World and Great-Power Triangles* (MIT Press, 1975), p. 135.

wait. Relations with the United States improved, though there was a temporary setback when the Palestinians who had murdered the American ambassador in Khartoum in March 1973 were turned over to the Egyptians and eventually freed. Overall, Nimeiry's tilt has been toward the West and away from the Soviet bloc. In May 1977 he expelled the remaining ninety Soviet military advisers and looked to France and to a lesser extent the United States for arms.

Although Moscow did not use its armed forces to assist al-Ata's coup, there is continuing speculation about whether the Soviet advisers tried indirectly through their relationship with junior officers at the military bases outside Khartoum to interfere with the rescue of Nimeiry or the reinforcement of his supporters in Khartoum by encouraging the Sudanese to obey the orders of the al-Ata government only.[66] But even if the Soviet advisers had persuaded the Sudanese troops to stay in the barracks, the outcome in Khartoum would have been the same, because the main forces used to bring Nimeiry back to power were the Egyptian troops based in the area and the Sudanese flown in from the Suez Canal front.

A direct use of Soviet armed forces to affect the political outcome was just not feasible. It would have alienated most of the Arab world. Even had the Russians contemplated it, they had only five hundred advisers in the country, and these were largely isolated in a few military installations. There was no way they could have mounted a major intervention on their own so far from home bases. Had Moscow stayed out of the Sudan altogether neither its credibility nor its position with Egypt, Syria, or Iraq would have suffered greatly; nor would it have been tempted into suddenly deserting a progressive leadership in the interests of advancing the cause of a Communist-backed one, the net effect of which was to exacerbate Sudanese—and Arab—suspicion of Soviet ambitions and possible duplicity. The prospective gains from pursuing a forward policy in the Sudan were not important to the advancement of Soviet interests in the region, at least in the short term, whereas the setback complicated, though far from precluded, Moscow's policy of meddling in the Horn of Africa.

Suppressing the Kurds in Iraq

On July 17, 1968, the Baath returned to power in Iraq. Unlike its predecessor, this regime sought to maintain, indeed to improve, relations

66. Bechtold, *Politics in the Sudan*, p. 270.

with the Soviet Union. Beset by internal troubles, determined to find a solution to the Kurdish problem, committed to an anti-Western policy and a more ambitious course in the Persian Gulf, the Baathists experimented with different ways of tolerating Iraqi Communists within a Baathist government, as part of their strategy of courting Moscow and exploiting divisions in the Kurdish movement, a part of which was Communist. For economic and strategic reasons, Moscow, too, was eager to strengthen the Soviet-Iraqi relationship and in the process downgraded the importance of the Iraqi Communist party and the Kurdish issue in its decisions.

Underlying a substantial Soviet economic commitment was Moscow's emerging strategic interest in the Persian Gulf. Initially, Moscow had seen the area as one of incipient threat. However, the once considerable Soviet concern over its "southern tier" had eased with Iraq's withdrawal from the Baghdad Pact in 1959 and the shah of Iran's pledge to the USSR on September 15, 1962, that the Iranian government "will not grant any foreign nation the right of possessing any kind of rocket bases on Iranian soil."[67]

Differences with Iraq over what should be the basis for a settlement of the Arab-Israeli conflict never caused serious tension or interfered with the improvement of Soviet-Iraqi relations. In the late 1960s and early 1970s the political climate turned even more favorable. The British withdrawal from the gulf, the emergence of independent ministates in an area of residual Iraqi-Iranian-Saudi Arabian tension, and the growth of the Soviet navy all stimulated Soviet interest in the strategic potential of manipulating the regional rivalries, quite apart from the prospects in the eastern Mediterranean that, in any event, derived essentially from the Arab-Israeli conflict. By the early 1970s the defensive aims that had shaped the early postwar Soviet policy of undermining the Western position in the Arab East had metamorphosed into a far-ranging policy of projecting Soviet influence for the promotion of regional and global objectives.

On April 9, 1972, during a visit to Baghdad, Soviet Premier Aleksei Kosygin and Iraqi President Ahmed Hassan al-Bakr signed a fifteen-year treaty of friendship and cooperation. The treaty signified the continual improvement in Soviet-Iraqi relations since the Baath had come to power in 1968. Moscow saw in the treaty the institutionalization of its expanding military, economic, and political presence in Iraq and the basis for a

67. Rouhollah K. Ramazani, *Iran's Foreign Policy, 1941–1972* (University Press of Virginia, 1975), pp. 315–16.

further consolidation of its overall position. Believing as it does in the positive role of treaties in advancing and cementing existing relationships between governments,[68] the Soviet leadership no doubt was highly pleased with this newest addition to its treaty network, others of the same model having been concluded the previous year with Egypt in May and India in August. The firm link to Iraq gave Moscow regular access to the Iraqi port of Umm Qasr and additional leverage in dealing with Iran; it also alerted the Arab states of the Persian Gulf to the Soviet quest for influence in the region.

The treaty brought Moscow problems as well. The Iraqis became signatories at least in part to enlist Soviet support in bringing the Kurds under control and the Communists into the Baathist fold. The Kurds are an unassimilated, fiercely nationalistic, non-Arab minority, constituting about one-quarter of the country's population and inhabiting the northeastern provinces, among them the oil-rich Mosul region.[69] After the failure of a major uprising in 1944, many Kurds, including the important tribal leader, Mullah Mustafa al-Barzani, fled to the Soviet Union. Permitted by Brigadier Abdul Karim Kassem to return in 1958 after the overthrow of the pro-Western monarchy, they pressed for fundamental autonomy. Though Kassem hoped to use the Kurdish demands to offset the pro-Nasser Iraqi nationalists who favored a merger with the United Arab Republic (the federation of Syria and Egypt that lasted from February 1958 to September 1961), he was unable to control the intense desire for autonomy that motivated Barzani's adherents. Fighting broke out in late 1961 and went on for almost nine years.

A provisional agreement of March 1970 that ended the Kurdish rebellion broke down in late 1971, and sporadic fighting started once again. In November 1971 the Baath published its Charter of National Action, which held out the promise of freedom for political groups and, specifically, of an alliance between the Baath and the Kurdish Democratic party (KDP). By giving Moscow a stake in the stability of the Baath regime, the Iraqi leadership expected the USSR to use its influence with the Kurds and the Iraqi Communist party (ICP) to help arrange a settlement. Moreover, the Baath knew that the Kurdish ability to wage war depended on military assistance from Iran, whose relations with the USSR were

68. Jan F. Triska and Robert M. Slusser, *The Theory, Law, and Policy of Soviet Treaties* (Stanford University Press, 1962), p. 282.
69. Oles M. Smolansky, *The Soviet Union and the Arab East Under Khrushchev* (Bucknell University Press, 1974), p. 187.

improving, so it hoped that a show of Soviet force on its behalf would keep Iran on the sidelines.

The treaty of friendship and cooperation signed by the Soviet Union and Iraq on April 9, 1972, was a landmark in their relationship: it denoted Moscow's full support for the Baathist regime and also Baghdad's readiness to rely on Soviet military and economic assistance and, perhaps more important, to use the Soviet connection to settle the Kurdish question. The treaty's significance was soon evident in the stepped-up pace of Soviet arms transfers (particularly tanks and aircraft) and trade, and the stream of Soviet technicians and advisers, all of which was extremely important to the Baathist government. Thus, for example, when Iraq nationalized the Iraqi Petroleum Company the new treaty relationship with Moscow made it feel more secure about any possible Western reaction.

After the October war, Baghdad resumed diplomatic relations with Iran, which cut back its assistance to the Kurds. This Iraqi diplomatic campaign was a prelude to concentrating on ending the Kurdish challenge by force if necessary and on terms less lenient than those set forth in the agreement of March 11, 1970.

As Soviet relations with the Baath improved and as the ICP drew closer to the Baath, agreeing on July 17, 1973 (after some pressure from Moscow), to join the National Progressive Front organized and led by the Baath, Moscow's impatience with the deterioration in relations between General Barzani's KDP and the ICP grew. The Soviet leadership tried unsuccessfully to mediate.[70] Barzani's purge of Kurdish Communists, reluctance to join the front, and acceptance of aid from pro-Western sources angered Moscow. His uncompromising position may have been the final straw that led Moscow to write off the KDP and accept the inevitability of a military solution to the Kurdish problem. Moscow had no choice, given its desire to consolidate state-to-state relations with Iraq, but to comply with the Baath's requests for military assistance.

Saddam Hussein Takriti, vice-president of the RRC and deputy secretary-general of the Baath, visited the USSR on February 24–25, 1974, undoubtedly to ensure Soviet support in the likely event that the Kurds rejected the government's offer of autonomy. On the fourth anniversary of the 1970 agreement, the government announced a watered-down plan for Kurdish self-rule, which, as Baghdad expected, Barzani termed inade-

70. Jean Riollet, "Moscow Worries About Political Stability in Iraq," *Radio Liberty Dispatch*, January 23, 1974.

quate. Heavy fighting began anew. To add to the complexities of the situation, a few weeks earlier there had been border clashes between Iraqi and Iranian troops that reversed the short-lived improvement in relations and threatened to complicate the Kurdish campaign, as well as to trigger hostilities between the two long-term regional rivals.

Calculations in Baghdad and Moscow

Though long a partisan of the Kurds, Moscow could not remain indifferent to the government's needs without risking its evolving special relation with the Iraqi Baathists. It knew that a Kurdish revolt threatened the stability of a regime whose predecessors had fallen because of this intractable issue and might undermine all that the Soviet-Iraqi relationship had brought Moscow: close ties with an important country in the Persian Gulf area; access to the port of Umm Qasr, whose significance for Moscow was political rather than military (not only is the port poorly equipped to repair modern vessels, but its location at the closed end of the gulf limits its value in times of crisis); participation of the ICP in the government; expanded economic ties and an important role in the exploitation of Iraq's rich oil fields; a lucrative market for Soviet arms, with payment in oil; and an opportunity to improve relations with both Iraq and Iran, thereby creating a more favorable strategic environment for the advancement of Soviet objectives in the region as a whole. The demands of Moscow were not excessive, the rewards could be significant—strategically, politically, and economically—and the risks of involvement were less than those of noninvolvement.

Baghdad exploited Moscow's dilemma, knowing the Kremlin preferred a political solution but would in the interests of better relations with the Baath reluctantly go along with a military solution rather than allow the Kurds and their "imperialist" supporters (Iran and covert U.S. assistance) to threaten the Soviet position in the country. By increasing its arms purchases from the Soviet Union and thereby its dependence, the Baath further assured itself of expanded Soviet involvement.

By supporting the Baath, Moscow hoped to prevent a war between Iraq and Iran; it also expected that Baghdad's need to draw on Soviet support would help increase Soviet influence on the Baathists and, at the same time, impress upon the Kurds the futility of fighting and the need to compromise. The seriousness with which the Kremlin viewed the situation may be deduced from the visit to Baghdad in late March 1974 of Defense

Minister Andrei Grechko and Minister of the Interior Nikolai Shche-lokov, one to talk about military requirements, the other presumably to share intelligence information on the Kurds and on internal security. Throughout the spring and early summer, the Soviet media counseled the Kurdish leadership not to isolate itself from "progressive forces in the country and abroad" and to consider that "a bad peace was better than a good quarrel." Reports of Barzani's quest for arms in the West and the determination with which the Baath pushed its military preparations, even while it left open the offer of a settlement to Barzani, meant that Moscow could not equivocate on Baghdad's requests for assistance.

Though detailed information of Iraq's purchases and military buildup is difficult to obtain, it is known that Soviet arms shipments, heavy throughout 1972 and 1973, increased in 1974. Iraqi tanks lost in the October war were replaced with newer models, and the Soviet Union also supplied "the *Frog* surface-to-surface missile in 1974, a reflection of the growing Iranian threat as well as the escalating post-October war rearm-ament among the combatant states."[71] In late May Soviet ships unloaded SAMs in Umm Qasr, possibly to protect Iraqi troops against Iranian air strikes.[72] Moreover, as the Iraqi army prepared a major offensive, Soviet air power played an important part. The Kurds claimed that Soviet pilots were assuming operational responsibilities at the Kirkuk air base, "the starting point for Iraqi Air Force bombing raids on Kurdish villages."[73] The accusation was plausible. Soviet TU-22 supersonic bombers had appeared in Iraq as far back as October 1973.[74] A year later, Western intelligence sources reported MIG-23 fighter-bombers being used against the Kurds.[75] British journalists wrote of TU-16 reconnaissance flights over Pesh Merga (as Kurdish rebels called themselves) lines,[76] yet Iraq was not known to have any pilots trained to fly the advanced MIGs or

71. Paul Kinsinger, "Arms Purchases in the Persian Gulf: The Military Dimen-sion," in *The Persian Gulf, 1975: The Continuing Debate on Arms Sales,* Hearings before the Special Subcommittee on Investigations of the House Committee on International Relations, 94 Cong. 1 sess. (GPO, 1976), p. 242. See also Roger F. Pajak, "Soviet Military Aid to Iraq and Syria," *Strategic Review,* vol. 4 (Winter 1976), pp. 53–54.

72. *Middle East Intelligence Survey,* vol. 2 (June 15, 1974), p. 48.

73. Arnold Hottinger, "A New Kurdish Insurrection," *Swiss Review of World Affairs,* vol. 24 (June 1974), p. 13.

74. *New York Times,* October 3, 1973.

75. *International Herald Tribune,* October 7, 1974.

76. *Observer Review* (London), November 3, 1974.

Tupolevs. The Russians could have calculated that willingness to use their personnel in support of the Iraqi offensive would appear as a commitment to the Iraqi regime and would give the shah pause for reassessment of direct Iranian involvement on behalf of the Kurds. The risks to Moscow were minimal, given the very limited commitment of pilots and planes and their minor role in the fighting.

Compared to the attention devoted to the Egyptian-Syrian-Israeli sector of the Middle East, the Soviet press's treatment of developments in Iraq was modest. But the message was clear; the right wing of the KDP, urged on by imperialist forces, was to blame for the resumption of military operations by isolating itself from progressive forces in the country and abroad. The nearest thing to a definitive Soviet statement was the assessment made by Lev Tolkunov, editor in chief of *Izvestiya,* in one of a series of articles that he wrote on the Middle East in late July and early August 1974.[77] He commended the Iraqi leadership for taking the road of progressive socioeconomic transformation, expressed concern over the separatist Kurdish movement that was being incited by external forces, and emphasized the 1972 treaty that served the common interests of the two countries.

At about that time the Iraqi offensive against the Kurds had advanced farther than any had before, squeezing the Kurds into a narrowing strip along the Iranian border. However, the Iraqis could not achieve victory because Iranian protective artillery barrages and supplies of antitank missiles and ammunition stiffened Kurdish resistance. With the weather worsening and the Iranians apparently willing to escalate their involvement, the Baath feared another indecisive campaign and pressed Moscow for additional assistance. In late September, in closely spaced visits, Iraq's foreign minister and its chief of staff each went to Moscow to discuss ways of "strengthening cooperation and friendship." A month later, First Secretary of the ICP, Aziz Muhammad, a Kurd elected to his post in 1964 and strongly identified with Moscow and ICP participation in the National Progressive Front, met with Politburo member Boris N. Ponomarev. The report in *Pravda* indicated that Aziz Muhammad emphasized the importance of the ICP-Baath cooperation and the front's progressive line in pressing socioeconomic reforms and a solution to the Kurdish problem,[78] and presumably backed Baghdad's request for additional arms. He may

77. *CDSP,* vol. 26, no. 30 (August 21, 1974), p. 7.
78. *CDSP,* vol. 26, no. 44 (November 27, 1974), p. 19.

also have alerted Soviet leaders that the ICP's prospects would be endangered if the Baath position was weakened as a result of failure against the Kurds.

The constant Iraqi pressure led Moscow to send Army Chief of Staff and Deputy Minister Viktor Kulikov to Baghdad on November 27 to assess the situation firsthand. The trip followed on the heels of a state visit to the Soviet Union by the shah (November 18 to 23), during which the Iraqi-Iranian situation had been discussed. Less than two months later, Beirut newspapers reported that Iraq and the Soviet Union had concluded their largest arms agreement to date.[79] What decided the issue for Moscow is not known: the breakdown in December of secret Iraqi-Iranian talks in Istanbul, the downing of two Soviet aircraft by Iranian missiles supplied by the United States,[80] the growing strain on the capability of the Baath, which was forced to call up reserve officers in their mid-thirties to continue the campaign, or the indications that covert U.S. support was sustaining the Kurdish revolt.[81] However, on January 13, 1975, a few days before the arms agreement was reported to have been signed, an article in *Pravda* accused the CIA, in cooperation with Israel, of having stirred up the Kurdish revolt, strongly implying that Moscow was disturbed by the American attempt to undermine a Soviet client through regional proxies.[82] Whatever the considerations that weighed most heavily with Moscow, the buildup of Iraqi armed forces proceeded quickly and included, among other things, improved artillery of all calibers, SCUD missiles, MIGs, and additional Soviet advisers.[83] Soviet shipments resulted in a noticeable increase in Iraqi military capability by late spring[84] and, combined with the

79. *Washington Post,* January 21, 1975.

80. *Arab Report and Record* (December 16–31, 1974), p. 576.

81. The covert American role was originally exposed in a leak to the press of a secret report prepared by the House Select Committee on Intelligence, which was chaired by Representative Otis Pike. See the *Village Voice,* Special Supplement, February 16, 1976. See also William Safire, *New York Times,* December 19, 1977.

82. *CDSP,* vol. 27, no. 2 (February 5, 1975), p. 17.

83. *Washington Post,* February 1, 1975. Jim Hoagland also reported that "at least one Soviet Colonel is known to have been killed in combat with the Iraqis against the Kurds, according to sources in touch with Kurdish intelligence."

84. The new Soviet arms enabled the Iraqi army to expand from two to three armored divisions, to add an infantry division, and to strengthen antiaircraft defense greatly. The air force increased by about 10 percent. This assessment is based on a comparison of the data given in International Institute for Strategic Studies, *The Military Balance, 1974–1975* (London: IISS, 1974), pp. 33–34, and IISS, *The Military Balance, 1975–1976* (IISS, 1975), pp. 34, 90.

sorties by Soviet-piloted MIG-23 aircraft, played a crucial role in the settlement reached between Saddam Hussein and the shah on March 5, 1975. Apparently, the expanded Soviet involvement had made the shah uneasy about the consequences of a protracted conflict and amenable to a settlement in which the Kurds were the dispensable pawns.

The View from Tehran

The Iraqi-Iranian settlement, which took place at a meeting of the Organization of Petroleum Exporting Countries in Algiers, transformed the political environment and doomed the Kurdish revolt. Although the Kurds were not specifically mentioned in the communiqué issued by Saddam Hussein and the shah on March 6, 1975, the reference to the restoration of "security and mutual confidence along their joint borders" and the maintenance by both sides of "strict and effective control over their joint borders in order to put a final end to all subversive infiltration from either side" meant that the Kurds could no longer obtain Iranian arms or sanctuary.[85] The shah made peace, abandoning the Kurds, because he obtained desired border adjustments (especially of the Shatt al-Arab River) and an end to anti-Iranian activity on Iraqi territory and because he was concerned about the growing Soviet involvement.[86] During his visit to the USSR in November 1974, he had heard Soviet President Nikolai Podgorny declare, "We must say outright that the tension existing in relations between Iran and Iraq is not in the interests of peace," and call for a settlement by the parties themselves. To this the shah had replied: "I would only observe that if in its relations with us Iraq will adopt the same position which you, our great neighbor, observe in your relations with us, and will refrain from following with such addiction the legacy of British imperialism, there will be no problem between us in this matter."[87] In the fighting in late 1974 and early 1975, Iran had provided a

85. The agreement also reestablished the border along "the Thalweg line in the middle of the deepest shipping channel in the Shatt al-Arab estuary" (where it had been before 1936) and settled the border through a disputed oil field. *Arab Report and Record* (March 1–15, 1975), p. 163. For details of the Iraqis' final offensive against the Kurds, see *The Economist* (March 15, 1975), p. 58.

86. Under a British-sponsored treaty in 1937, the Iraqi border with Iran was set along the eastern bank of the Shatt al-Arab, giving Iraq virtual control over the river and access to Iran's largest oil refinery at Abadan.

87. Quoted in *USSR and Third World*, vol. 4 (July and August 1974), pp. 466–67.

much-needed boost to the Kurds and stymied the Baath offensive. But this had resulted in stepped-up Soviet arms deliveries and involvement that were especially worrying because the delivery of SCUD missiles and MIG-23s—both handled by Soviet crews—seemed to the shah more a potential threat to Iran than an element in the campaign against the Kurds.[88] This heightened the shah's uneasiness, so that when the Baath agreed to settle the Iraqi-Iranian dispute on terms favorable to Iran, he seized the opportunity.

Outcomes

Moscow was pleased by the Iraqi-Iranian agreement. A month earlier it had noted with concern the seriousness of the border clashes and, reminding the shah of Podgorny's comment the previous November, had urged a peaceful settlement.[89] The Baath had solidified its internal position as a result of timely Soviet support, and prospects for Soviet-Iraqi relations seemed bright. Iraq would still require Soviet weapons, thus providing Moscow with needed hard currency though its leverage with a less dependent client was reduced. The far-reaching character of the agreement may have come as something of a surprise, but without doubt it was Moscow's willingness to back the Baath that had, in great measure, been responsible for its advantageous outcome. The elimination of territorial and political irritants from the Iraqi-Iranian relationship meant that Moscow, not having to take sides with one against the other in an armed conflict, could proceed with its policy of improving relations with both countries.

Though the superpowers have long-term interests in the Persian Gulf, their rivalry has so far only marginally affected the policies of the local actors. What was new for the area in the 1974–75 Kurdish affair, and what is of possible significance for the future, was the crucial role that the Soviet Union played in inducing the countries—each of which looked to a different superpower for backing—to settle their differences rather than risk an escalation that might lead them to seek intervention by superpower patrons. Escalation of the local conflict would certainly have intensified the superpowers' rivalry in the region, which, in turn, would have limited the local actors' independence of action and wrought major changes in the region's political-strategic character.

88. Kinsinger, "Arms Purchases," p. 244.
89. *Pravda,* February 2, 1975.

Since the incident, Soviet relations with Iraq have been far from close; indeed, since early 1978 they have deteriorated noticeably. Moscow's vital security interests are only minimally involved in the area, and its main political relationship is still with Iraq. It remains Iraq's principal arms supplier (for cash) and is likely to continue so for the foreseeable future. Nevertheless, the Baath has a policy of diversification and makes large arms purchases from France, much to Moscow's annoyance.[90]

Soviet naval vessels may call regularly at Umm Qasr but have to obtain permission for each port visit; and although Soviet aircraft en route to Aden (where arms were transshipped to Ethiopia) were permitted to refuel in Baghdad, this convenience was interrupted in the spring of 1978 because of policy differences over Eritrea—hardly a solid base for projecting power or influence in the gulf. In short, there is no Soviet military presence in Iraq that can be described as in a privileged position. If anything, the Baath has kept its political and military distance from Moscow and gone its own way in the Arab-Israeli conflict, Arab world affairs, and the Horn of Africa, where it supports the Eritrean separatists and the Somalis against the Soviet-backed Ethiopian regime. Moscow shows the flag with its port visits to convey its political interest in, and capability for, helping client states. Thus far, however, these visits have been mainly symbolic; they have not required the United States to do anything more than maintain its minor presence at the Jubair facility on Bahrain. Despite its important economic ties with Iraq, Moscow is less than pleased at seeing Iraq's enormous oil wealth being exchanged for Western technology and equipment. Iraqi Communists, though represented in the Baath government, are carefully circumscribed. Moscow must also be upset by the growing strain that developed when the Soviet embassy in Baghdad was forced to relocate because of Iraqi suspicion of Soviet electronic eavesdropping on official deliberations in government buildings and when twenty-one Iraqi Communists were executed for setting up party cells in the army.[91] None of this augurs well for future Soviet-Iraqi relations.

Had Moscow not helped the Baath, its position would probably have been much less favorable: a weakened Baath might have cracked down on the ICP, or worse still, it might have been deposed and replaced by a Western-oriented regime. If Iran had been allowed to turn the tide in favor of the Kurds, an American-supported client would have humbled a Soviet one, which would have been galling to Moscow. As matters turned

90. *Washington Post,* February 27, 1978.
91. *Washington Post,* June 8, 1978; *New York Times,* June 11, 1978.

out, Moscow was able to pursue a political, economic, and military relationship with Iraq and at the same time maintain an improving economic relationship with the shah. Of course, since the fall of the shah in January 1979 and the anti-Western revolution in Iran, Iran's relations with the Soviet Union, like those with the United States and Iraq, have been in turmoil.

Conclusion

When assessing the political utility of the Soviet use of armed forces, it is important not to impute to Soviet leaders yardsticks of success and failure that seem reasonable or compelling to us; for in diplomacy the success of a policy inheres not only in palpable increments but also in the value the party involved attributes to the overall consequences of its policy. Of the latter precious little is known. Given Moscow's far-ranging and increasingly determined pursuit of a number of simultaneous objectives in the Arab East—from undermining pro-Western governments and the position of the West to securing a presence for itself, promoting the noncapitalist path of development, and aspiring to the formerly British role of arbiter of regional conflicts—its use of military force was a logical extension of the foreign aid that initiated and sustained its developing relations with the courted Arab countries. In each of the cases examined, the Soviet Union expected that committing its armed forces to an objective that was important to the client would result in closer ties. And in the short run that is what happened. If relations later soured or failed to live up to Soviet expectations because of unanticipated and unforeseeable developments over which Moscow had no control, that is not reason enough to fault the policy the Soviet Union followed.

In all three cases examined, there appear to be a number of similarities in the Soviet use of armed forces as a political instrument. First, the USSR supported the legitimate government of a nation-state and acted in defense of national sovereignty and territorial integrity. Each of the three governments—Egypt, Sudan, and Iraq—faced, in varying degrees, a major crisis that threatened its stability and prospective tenure in office and saw in Soviet military support a means to surmount its difficulty. Second, the Soviet Union did not initiate the offers but acted in response to requests for military support and for the Soviet personnel needed for the effective use of Soviet armaments. Though Moscow did not offer

Soviet combat forces, it was not reluctant to supply them, presumably anticipating additional political advantage and the influence assumed to flow therefrom. Third, the Soviet government provided the arms and advisers on a government-to-government basis. The arrangements were made through regular diplomatic channels and touched on all aspects of the relationship, from the signing of the agreements through the scheduling of deliveries to the use of the assistance provided.

Fourth, notwithstanding their military character, the three recipient governments were deemed to be "progressive," an imprimatur bestowed primarily because of their policy of opposing "imperialism" (the United States) and not because of their internal reforms or platforms. Perhaps some weight was given to their professed commitment to "socialism," but pragmatism, not doctrine, shaped Soviet relationships with them. However, to bring ideological formulations into approximate concordance with Soviet support of certain regimes and with evolving political and socio-economic phenomena in the third world, Soviet analysts did devote considerable attention to detailed elaborations on the character of the "class struggle" in developing countries.

Fifth, the deployment of armed forces was necessary to maintain Moscow's credibility as a patron. If it was marginal in the Sudan and quite important in Iraq, it was essential in Egypt. Without it Moscow could not have hoped to fashion a special relationship or to receive military privileges. Refusal would have jeopardized—certainly in the case of Egypt and possibly of Iraq—the very existence of regimes favorably disposed toward the Soviet Union and would have discouraged prospective clients from turning to Moscow. Whether interpreted as a lack of capability, a reluctance to engage in protracted and costly rivalry with the United States, or a sign of political diffidence, refusal would undoubtedly have doomed Soviet ambitions in the Arab East and left the field to the United States. In the case of Egypt, Moscow demonstrated that it was prepared to go to hitherto uncharted lengths, including a crisis with its global adversary, to protect its client from defeat. Because of Soviet actions in 1970, the United States should not have been surprised by what Moscow did in October 1973 in the Middle East, and later in Angola and the Horn of Africa.

Sixth, Moscow was not lavish or indiscriminate in its largesse. Each time, the armed forces committed by Moscow were appropriate to the threat facing the client; they were prudently deployed to achieve limited military-political ends without unnecessarily alarming the United States or precipitating a superpower confrontation; overall, they were satisfactory to the client; and they were effective (in Egypt and Iraq) in signaling the adversaries of Moscow's client states to reconsider the implications of their behavior. In all three instances, Soviet actions avoided military overkill and showed a keen appreciation of the local situation and of the regional and global implications of the involvement.

Seventh, in all three cases, air defense and air power were the most effective types of military assistance rendered by the Soviet Union.

Finally, the USSR took care, generally speaking, to send, maintain, and use its armed forces in accordance with the client's wishes and without making the indigenous leaders fearful of domestic meddling. The task set was discreetly accomplished or facilitated, with minimum publicity and internal dislocation, and with no attempt to blackmail the client for concessions.

Comparative analysis also highlights the USSR's ability to respond flexibly and to graduate its assistance according to the needs and potentialities of different situations. First, in Egypt, where the Soviet Union showed a willingness to lend military support to a client enmeshed in a major interstate conflict, it made a major commitment of combat forces upward of 20,000 men, including pilots, missile and radar operators, and a full logistical complement. By contrast, in Sudan and Iraq, where the Soviet Union responded to insurgencies directed against its clients, the numbers were small, the equipment manned by Soviet troops was highly restricted, and the circumstances of their use were such that Soviet personnel were seldom in serious danger. The great disparity in force levels and combat participation make the Egyptian case qualitatively different.

Second, the inequalities in forces committed was in proportion to the political stakes involved. Egypt, the most important target of Soviet strategy in the Arab East, was being fiercely battered by Israeli air power. An immediate, large rescue operation was essential to secure the prime Arab client and to safeguard the strategic advantages already realized in Egypt. By contrast, the situations in Sudan and Iraq were less alarming. Neither regime was threatened by a pro-Western rival or apt to turn away from Moscow should assistance be denied, but each was being internally challenged by a fractious minority that was supported, however circuitously, by pro-Western forces intent on weakening an anti-Western Arab state. Moscow's response was to assist the soliciting government.

Third, only in the case of Egypt did the Soviet-American relationship significantly and unmistakably enter the picture. The Soviet government committed its armed forces not only to protect a beleaguered client, but also to signal the United States that it would not tolerate the defeat of its client at the hands of a U.S.-backed adversary. Undoubtedly this was intended to nudge the United States into taking steps to restrain Israel more than it had. In Iraq, on the other hand, the Baath was not threatened from without nor was a superpower clash of interests directly at issue, though behind the moves of the Soviet Union and the United States was a web of tangential geostrategic considerations. In Sudan there was no superpower competition of any consequence, and Soviet forces played a minimal role throughout.

Fourth, the regional context of each of the three cases was quite different. In Sudan and Iraq developments unfolded without relation to the Arab-Israeli conflict, though marginal Israeli connections could be adduced from aid given the Anyanyas through Uganda and Ethiopia and from the transshipment to the Kurdish rebels via Iran of Soviet arms captured in the June war. The crisis in Sudan stemmed from black African causes—racial, religious, and cultural. Events in Iraq bore on Iraqi-Iranian relations, on the stability of the Baath, and on incipient superpower rivalry in the Gulf. By contrast, the crisis in Egypt was a direct outgrowth of the Arab-Israeli conflict, which after the June war put the Soviet Union fully on the Arab side and brought it into open military rivalry with the United States in the Arab East. There may well be a long-term strategy underlying Moscow's behavior, but the specific responses of the Kremlin in these three cases were shaped by each crisis itself and not by any discernible linkage between them. Finally, whereas Moscow's decision to help Sudan and Iraq may have been made with some consideration of the brightening prospects of local Communists, that factor never entered into the Egyptian case.

It has been said of Middle Eastern politics that nothing fails like success. To paraphrase another epigram, the road to political disaffection is paved with good deeds. In pursuit of regional objectives and in support of progressive Arab governments, Moscow used its military power well, showing its understanding of the specific circumstances of each crisis and the realities of the Soviet-American relationship. The Soviet armed forces helped Egypt and Iraq to achieve their desired outcomes and to frustrate the bid of U.S. protégés for local advantage. In all three cases, they helped pave the way for further Soviet penetration. Yet for all that, they could not prevent abrupt political turnabouts. They could help courted countries but not secure Soviet influence. In third world settings, there is no safeguard against the unanticipated by-products of complex domestic and regional interplay, short of the colonial-style occupation that is counterproductive in today's international system. Changes of leadership and policy in developing countries can undo overnight the most elaborately planned Soviet presence.

In the Arab East, Soviet leaders relearned what they had first found out in Indonesia in 1965 and Ghana in 1966; namely, that they could help a third world country achieve certain objectives and themselves benefit in several ways from an expanded presence in the country and from changes in the configuration of power in the region, but that their ability to manipulate the country's internal or foreign policy was limited. Nor were Soviet leaders able to wield influence commensurate with the amount of aid rendered or the size of their armed forces in the country. The scope for initiative or leverage was proscribed because the Soviet leadership was unable to project power directly and fully into the political system of the target country.

Moscow has also learned that any policy depending for its success on the exercise of direct influence is bound to meet difficulty, frustration, and probably failure. There is a point beyond which Soviet influence cannot consolidate without occasioning a countervailing resistance from the United States, from the target itself, or from the region as a whole. A strong Soviet position in one country can adversely affect Soviet relations with that country's rival. Thus, when the Russians seemed to be entrenching themselves in Iraq, their relations with Iran cooled; and when relations with Iran showed improvement, Iraq grew suspicious. The area's internal rivalries restrict the Soviet Union's ability to develop lasting, close relationships.

The Soviet Union showed great skill in exercising influence over Middle Eastern protagonists in the Iraqi crisis. It used a limited display of military force to forestall a possible regional conflict without alienating either party—each of which it wanted to cultivate—while still facilitating the domestic objective of its Baathist client. This was an expression of superpower influence in its most sophisticated form. It demonstrated that Moscow knew how to restrain the behavior of a client state and the state's adversary through the deliberate and limited use of its armed forces. If there is a lesson to be learned from this experience it is that a superpower can *restrain* behavior more easily than it can *compel* action. But even the ability to restrain cannot be counted on, since the conditions of a given situation may limit the patron's ability to bring its power to bear in an effective way.

Strategic, military, and political considerations pertaining to Soviet national ambitions in the Arab East and global rivalry with the United States, as in the case of Egypt, may be a sufficiently accurate explanation of the Soviet decision to furnish armed forces. Nonetheless, Moscow's inclination to be slightly more solicitous and responsive to the wishes of Arab clients when their Communist parties are permitted to benefit from the "progressive" course of internal transformation, as in the case of Sudan and Iraq, should not be ruled out. Ideology may not be an imperative of Soviet foreign policy, but neither is it always irrelevant.

Moscow has learned to live with "failure," to accept the limits of its influence, and to recognize that constraints and disadvantages are concomitants of initiatives and benefits. The period of the early establishment of a presence and accumulation of privileged positions having passed, Moscow now finds that future gains are costly, difficult, uncertain, and limited. The more it becomes involved, the more it tries to exercise influence over beneficiaries and clients, the more it arouses nationalist resentment and resistance. Moscow knows this. Yet recent Soviet behavior indicates there is no wavering from the forward policy adopted in the mid-1950s. The leadership may have realized that influence-building in the Arab world is an untidy business, but it continues to give support and to do so on a substantial scale, convinced that it can benefit from the consequences of some Arab policies, a spin-off of the Arab-Israeli conflict, the pressure of Arab oil policy on the West, or the various subregional conflicts in the area. Moscow persists, apparently encouraged by what it perceives to be gradual improvements in its overall position. Whether rationalization or strategic wisdom, its willingness to stay the course and to place local setbacks in broader and longer-term perspective is indisputable, and it is also an unambiguous political statement.

If accurate, the foregoing has several implications for future U.S. foreign and defense policy and behavior. First, interest in the Middle East must be viewed as a permanent feature of Soviet foreign policy. Reflecting more than Moscow's understandable concern about the security of its southern flank, this interest encompasses the entire Arab world and constitutes an extension of the U.S.-Soviet adversary relationship in Europe and the Far East. For reasons that have proved compelling to a generation of Soviet leaders, the Arab East is conceived of as a vast strategic preserve in which the potential returns are believed to warrant a sustained, intensive pattern of interaction. Despite setbacks, disappointments, and irritations, Moscow considers the changes in the Middle East, whose evolution it has helped shape since its involvement in the mid-1950s, to have been generally propitious for the advancement of Soviet aims. However limited its present position in most parts of the Arab world and however little influence it wields in the formulation of policy in client states, the Soviet Union is committed to a policy marked by persistence of purpose and breadth of scope.

Second, the Soviet Union has demonstrated its ability to undertake military operations in the third world. What cannot be doubted any longer is its willingness to use its armed forces to support clients in the Arab East against external attack, against internal opposition that is aided from outside, and against pressure from a pro-Western regional rival. Since the June war, the USSR has poured an enormous amount of weaponry into the Middle East, not only to help its clients defend themselves, but also to enable them to pursue policy objectives detrimental to U.S. interests. Western analysts have devoted much attention to the impressive buildup of the Soviet navy, yet Soviet air power, air defense systems, armor, and artillery have overshadowed the naval dimension of Soviet military power and posed the major threat to Western interests in the Arab East. Any projection of Soviet force capabilities must recognize their balanced, multipurpose character. The Soviet Union possesses the military wherewithal to affect the outcome of any regional conflict in which it assists its clients.

Third, the Soviet Union's use of armed forces in pursuit of political objectives in the Arab world has been carefully managed. Though not reluctant to defend the security of a client state, Moscow has been sensitive to U.S. attitudes and interests. Each of the cases examined demonstrates Moscow's readiness to safeguard the domestic stability of a courted regime; that is, the Soviet Union has sought merely to preserve or consolidate the position of the government already in power. The remaining question is whether, and to what extent, the Soviet leadership is prepared to commit armed forces to help bring about major changes in regional alignments or to promote a client's objectives beyond the existing military or territorial situation.

Fourth, there is a very limited sample for evaluating the combat effectiveness of the Soviet forces that might be deployed in a Middle East conflict. Judging by their performance in Egypt in 1970—the only one of the three countries that engaged large numbers of Soviet troops in combat conditions—Soviet equipment and personnel acquitted themselves creditably. It is wise to expect that Soviet military forces will carry out effectively whatever tasks are assigned them in any future Middle East operation. An Arab client fully assisted by the Soviet Union would be a formidable adversary.

Fifth, the Soviet-American rivalry in the Arab world is a multifaceted struggle in which the military component is only one variable, though an important one. No single local battle or war is going to be decisive. Soviet power is not poised to swoop down on the area and incorporate large chunks of real estate into the Soviet imperial system. Like the United States, the Soviet Union covets influence, not territory. The superpowers are likely to find themselves engaged in an endless series of indeterminate miniconflicts of varying intensity, apt to spawn sudden upheavals and mercurial political shifts that may give one or the other superpower some temporary local advantages. But since their struggle in the Arab world is not always a zero-sum situation, as events in Iraq in 1974–75 clearly indicated, the United States need not always react to seeming Soviet advances or exaggerate Moscow's ability to bend a dependent client to its will. Dependency is not synonymous with helplessness. The Soviet (and American) experience in the third world has repeatedly shown that neither aid nor military privileges necessarily bring a superpower influence and advantage when these are most desired. A military presence that is not institutionalized and that can be peremptorily terminated will not ensure the political foothold without which no imperial policy is possible. In thinking about politics and alignments in the Arab East, one must remember that superpower behavior and ambition are confined by the uncertainty, the narrow range of feasible options, and the latent fickleness of local leaders that are the salient features of the regional landscape.

Sixth, the nuclear relationship between the superpowers operates on an entirely different plane from their rivalry in third world regions such as the Middle East. It imposes firm restraints and changes very slowly, since no technological breakthrough affecting the "essential equivalence" of their deterrent capabilty is likely. But it may be influenced by tension at the substrategic level. Thus the Soviet military involvement in Egypt in 1970 complicated efforts to limit nuclear delivery systems and reach agreement on a series of other issues. The reduction of tension in the Middle East in 1972 and up to the October war made SALT I and far-reaching economic and technical agreements possible; whereas the serious friction in the Middle East and black Africa since late 1973 have made the process of negotiating new agreements troublesome.

Finally, since there is no anticipating the periodic eruptions in the Arab world, U.S. policy must be capable of responding promptly and effectively to specific crisis situations. Soviet leverage came from a readiness to exploit concrete opportunities and not from any prepackaged design for expansion. It was exercised effectively from a position of growing military strength. Any successful policy toward a region so important to the stability and unity of the Western world requires a strong military capability, informed assessments, consensus on policy objectives, and a large amount of luck.

CHAPTER TWELVE

Naval Diplomacy
in West African Waters

DAVID K. HALL

IN FEBRUARY 1969 and again in December 1970, the Soviet Union deployed warships to West African waters—the first and second such appearances of Soviet naval power in this region of the world. The first was in response to Ghana's seizure of two Russian fishing trawlers in October 1968 in its territorial waters and subsequent refusal to release the ships and crew because of their suspected complicity in subversive activities designed to restore to power Ghana's former president, Kwame Nkrumah. After four months of unsuccessful diplomatic and economic pressure by the USSR to secure the trawlers' release, Moscow dispatched four naval vessels from the Mediterranean Sea into the Gulf of Guinea near Ghana. On March 3, with the Soviet ships in the area, the Ghanaians released the trawlers and most of the Russian seamen. On March 4, the Soviet naval contingent left the Gulf of Guinea for a port visit to Lagos, Nigeria, only to return again on March 11. On March 19, the last three Soviet seamen were released and the naval combatants returned to their Mediterranean fleet. This little-known incident exemplified both the expanding capability of the Soviet navy to project power into geographical areas far removed from the traditional sphere of Russian influence and an increasing willingness on the Soviet Union's part to employ coercive military threats, despite their accompanying risks, in defense of such state interests as Russian seamen and property.

I am grateful to my research assistant, Melinda Crane, for her diligent and indispensable aid, and to several U.S. officials familiar with West African affairs who have chosen to remain anonymous.

The second appearance of Soviet naval vessels in West African waters occurred in early December 1970, after Portugal had launched a small amphibious attack on Conakry, Guinea, from its African colony of Portuguese Guinea. The objectives of this seaborne attack by some 350 soldiers were to overthrow the government of President Sekou Touré and assassinate the leaders of the African Party for the Independence of Guinea and Cape Verde (PAIGC), a highly successful national liberation movement dedicated to ending Portugal's five centuries of colonial rule in Portuguese Guinea. Since 1960 Touré had permitted the PAIGC to openly operate its revolutionary schools and international information activities from the safety of Conakry and had allowed PAIGC guerrillas to use Guinea as a sanctuary from the colonial army in neighboring Portuguese Guinea.

In response to a personal appeal from President Touré for military defense against future Portuguese attacks, the Soviet Union dispatched a group of naval combatants to the waters of Portuguese Guinea to deter similar invasions. From this initial mission of the West Africa Patrol, as it came to be called in the United States, other Soviet missions in the region soon followed. Soviet combatants were used to deter and defend against internal unrest in Guinea, to cultivate political influence with other West African states, to expand the military facilities made available to the USSR in Guinea, and to watch the movement of North Atlantic Treaty Organization (NATO) ships in the Atlantic Ocean. Not only did the creation of the West Africa Patrol indicate an increased Soviet willingness to assume some military risks against a member of NATO (Portugal), but subsequent Soviet military activities in and near Guinea demonstrated how an initial military deployment could serve additional political and strategic objectives.

Ghana, 1968–1969

On October 10, 1968, two Russian fishing trawlers whose crews numbered fifty-two men were forcibly taken into custody by the Ghanaian navy just inside Ghana's twelve-mile territorial limit. While the seizure might have been expected to be resolved quickly by the two governments, the event instead became one of symbolic importance to both sides and precipitated a five-month dispute.

Soviet Behavior

Although several analysts of the trawler incident have ascribed the naval action taken by the USSR in early 1969 to the importance of protecting Russian seamen and property, this does not fully explain the Soviet response.[1] MccGwire has argued that "the Soviet Union has established a fairly consistent record of accepting the seizure of property and the expulsion, and even loss of personnel, in the interests of longer-term foreign policy objectives."[2] Moreover, the Soviet naval response to the trawler seizure did not result simply in the dispatch of ships to the vicinity of Ghana but included the first Russian port visits to any West African states —Guinea and Nigeria. The full scope of the Russian naval action can be satisfactorily explained only when viewed in several contexts. The Soviet Union's reaction to the trawler incident was conditioned by the economic importance of its fishing industry and maritime trade, the role of maritime activity in its foreign policy, the navy's growing capability and responsibility for protecting Soviet maritime interests, and, finally, a number of its political interests at stake in West Africa in late 1968 and early 1969.

"In order to use the sea the way she does," MccGwire has observed, "Russia has to rely on maritime stability and the freedom of the seas."[3] Certainly the prolonged incarceration of Russian fishing trawlers by a minor African nation could be perceived in Moscow as a challenge to the maritime law and order on which the nation's fishing industry and merchant marine depended. By the late 1960s the fishing industry played a major role in Soviet economic life. It had been greatly expanded in the 1950s to help offset the chronic inadequacies of Soviet agriculture. In the decade following 1957 the Soviet fishing fleet was doubled, making it the

1. This is the general interpretation of Soviet behavior in the excellent analysis of the event done by staff members of the Center for Naval Analyses in Arlington, Virginia. In particular, see James M. McConnell, "The Soviet Navy in the Indian Ocean," Professional Paper 77 (CNA, August 1971); Robert G. Weinland, "The Changing Mission Structure of the Soviet Navy," Professional Paper 80 (CNA, November 1971); and Bradford Dismukes, "Soviet Employment of Naval Power for Political Purposes, 1967–75," in Michael MccGwire and John McDonnell, eds., *Soviet Naval Influence: Domestic and Foreign Dimensions* (Praeger, 1977), pp. 485–86.

2. Michael MccGwire, "The Evolution of Soviet Naval Policy, 1960–74," in Michael MccGwire, Ken Booth, and John McDonnell, eds., *Soviet Naval Policy: Objectives and Constraints* (Praeger, 1975), p. 529.

3. Michael MccGwire, "The Navy and Soviet Oceans Policy," in MccGwire and McDonnell, *Soviet Naval Influence*, p. 145.

largest in the world. The metric tons of fish caught by the Soviet fleet quadrupled during the 1950s and 1960s. By the beginning of the 1970s about a third of the animal protein consumed in the USSR came from fish.[4]

Not only did the Ghanaians' lengthy impoundment of the two trawlers present a threat to an important sector of the Soviet economy; it also struck at a significant instrument of Russian foreign policy. The fishing industry was important to Soviet relations with the developing world; Moscow used gifts of fishing vessels, man-made ports, and navigational training as an effective form of foreign aid in a hungry world. Aid of this type helped expand Soviet international trade with third world countries and frequently gave the USSR access to port facilities in the nations aided. Since technical assistance was ordinarily required for the effective transfer of new fishing industry technology, initial gifts were often followed by Soviet administrators and technicians. Access to foreign ports and foreign waters had national security implications as well, for Soviet fishing fleets working strategic areas of the globe were likely to include trawlers specially fitted for intelligence work.[5]

The role of maritime activity as a "state interest" affecting military planning was formally acknowledged during the late 1960s, as the growing Soviet ability to project military power abroad led to the contemplation of new missions that both necessitated and rationalized increased defense expenditures. In 1967, the commander of the Soviet navy, Admiral Sergei G. Gorshkov, publicly stated that "with the growth of the economic power of the Soviet Union, its interests on the seas and oceans are expanding to an ever greater degree, and consequently new requirements are laid on the Navy to defend them from imperialist encroachments."[6] Two days after the Ghanaian seizure—although apparently without reference to it—another Soviet commentator observed that "the main task of Soviet ships in international waters . . . is to defend the work of the Soviet merchant marine, which today is subjected everywhere to direct provocations and attacks by aircraft and ships of some imperialist states."[7]

4. The material here is taken from Richard T. Ackley, "The Fishing Fleet," ibid., pp. 311–20.

5. See ibid., pp. 311–20; and MccGwire, "The Navy and Soviet Oceans Policy," p. 137.

6. Admiral S. G. Gorshkov, "The Development of Soviet Naval Art," *Morskoy Sbornik,* no. 2 (1967), p. 21.

7. Vladmir Davidov, Moscow Radio in Arabic to Algeria, October 12, 1968, quoted in McConnell, "The Soviet Navy in the Indian Ocean," p. 5.

The Soviet navy establishment may well have become sensitized to the new challenges it faced in the "prawn war," which occurred during July 1968 in the Gulf of Carpentaria between the Soviet ship *Van Gogh* and Australian fishermen. The *Van Gogh*'s electronic suction gear, capable of harvesting entire prawn beds, was accused of endangering the livelihood of hundreds of Australian fishermen and resulted in partially successful efforts to block Soviet fishing in Australian waters. While the Soviet navy could not be expected to choose Australia as the first target against which to defend the sanctity of Soviet property rights and the freedom of the seas, Moscow was increasingly prepared to exert its power against less imposing antagonists.[8]

The USSR's response to the trawler incident was conditioned not only by general concern about economic, foreign policy, and military matters, but also by the recent history of its involvement in Africa. Soviet policy toward Africa during the 1950s and early 1960s had been predicated on Nikita Khrushchev's optimism about African socialist development and an African foreign policy favoring the USSR in its competition with the Western powers. Ghana's Kwame Nkrumah, Guinea's Sekou Touré, and Mali's Modibo Keita proved to have policy positions quite compatible with Soviet preferences on a number of major international issues dividing the East and West, such as Algeria, the Congo, nuclear disarmament, reorganization of the UN, and the role of national liberation movements. As a result, these more radical West African leaders were given special attention and support during the Khrushchev years.[9]

Soviet trade credits were extended to Ghana, Guinea, and Mali; this helped bridge the economic gap left by the discontinuation of preferential treatment by Western Europe. Russian and Eastern European technicians helped provide economic planning, management of state enterprises, and military training. Hundreds of West Africans were sent to the USSR for technical, military, and ideological training. A modest number of jet fighters, military transports, tanks, and patrol boats were transferred by Moscow to provide the rudiments of a modern armed force. In successive years, Touré, Nkrumah, and Keita were honored with the Lenin Peace Prize.[10]

If the Khrushchev years were marked by the optimistic search for

8. Ackley, "Fishing Fleet," p. 319.
9. The best general introduction to these events is Robert Legvold, *Soviet Policy in West Africa* (Harvard University Press, 1970).
10. Ibid.

"African Cubas," the post-Khrushchev era was one of pragmatic adjustment to the internal weaknesses of radical clients and a broadening definition of Soviet interests in sub-Saharan Africa. The ethnic kaleidoscope of black Africa proved poor material for the national mobilization requisite to rapid socialist development. Nkrumah and Touré emerged as erratic and repressive leaders. Falling Russian expectations might have helped cushion somewhat the psychological blow of Nkrumah's overthrow in February 1966—a coup that came about despite the efforts of numerous Soviet security advisers and a Soviet-trained presidential guard. "Within a week of the coup d'etat," writes Legvold,

the new regime had sent all 620 Soviet technicians and teachers packing. Their ouster removed nearly the entire staff of Ghana's medical school (25), one third of all the qualified secondary educators in mathematics and science (125), 54 advisers attached to the Ministry of Defense, 200 workers at the Tamale airbase, 47 geologists, the staff of four state farms, 27 technicians completing atomic-research facilities and technicians aiding with a variety of other projects such as a fish-processing complex, a concrete panel factory, and so on.[11]

There soon followed a series of other Ghanaian acts that added insult to the Russian injury. In March 1967 Ghana charged the Soviet Union with smuggling arms into the country on the freighter *Ristna*. Ghanaian medical students returning from the USSR were denied licenses on the grounds that their training was inadequate. On August 23, 1968, a Soviet plane carrying passengers from Conakry, Guinea, to Moscow intruded into Ghanaian airspace and was forced to land. Relations were further strained by Ghana's sharp criticism of the USSR's invasion of Czechoslovakia. The seizure of the Soviet trawlers on October 12 was the latest in a series of acts that infuriated Soviet officials.[12]

In the aftermath of the Nkrumah coup, Soviet theoreticians were quick to note that many of the personal weaknesses that had brought down their Ghanaian client were not fully shared by Mali's Keita. (The absence of similar observations regarding Touré reflected the perpetually troubled state of Guinean politics.) *Pravda's* West African correspondent emphasized that Mali's leaders had centralized power against reactionary elements, seized the initiative in economic development, and seen the

11. Ibid., p. 263.
12. Ibid., pp. 307–11; W. Scott Thompson, "Ghana's Foreign Policy Under Military Rule," *Africa Report* (May-June 1969), p. 8; *Christian Science Monitor*, August 28, 1968.

importance of eliminating inefficient state enterprises.[13] In fact, as Legvold says, "in the circumstances it is hard to imagine what more any African regime could have done to satisfy Soviet expectations." [14]

It was therefore a cruel blow to the USSR when Keita's reign was cut short by a military coup on November 19, 1968—a month after Ghana's seizure of the Soviet trawlers. The chief African commentator for *Izvestiya* sadly observed that military coups "have become almost commonplace phenomena in Africa" and that these events "redound to the interests of the former metropolitan country, i.e., to the interests of neocolonialism."[15]

Events in Mali both heightened the symbolic importance of the remaining "radical" leader in West Africa—Guinea's Sekou Touré—and shifted Soviet policy in Africa further toward a pragmatic course that stressed the inherent importance of each nation rather than the ideological purity of regime policy. While Soviet relations with Guinea had been tumultuous since that state's independence in 1958, Touré remained the only West African leader unshakably committed to revolutionary socialism and a frequent supporter of Soviet positions. As a sign of the two governments' common interests, Guinea had been chosen by the USSR for the first joint meeting of Eastern European and African trade union leaders, to be held in Conakry in March 1969. Yet the fragility of Touré's continued rule was apparent to Moscow. In a January 24, 1969, broadcast to Africa, Radio Moscow likened the current situation in Guinea to that in pre-coup Ghana and Mali: in each instance, it argued, too much attention was given to politics at the expense of economic development and too much power was concentrated in the hands of one man.[16]

The USSR's increasingly pragmatic and opportunistic approach to West African affairs was most clearly demonstrated in its reaction to the Nigerian civil war being waged at the time of the trawler incident. When Great Britain and other Western powers refused in 1967 to provide the Nigerian central government with modern weapons for its fight against the secessionist Ibo tribe, Moscow seized the chance for influence by agreeing to sell and service some two dozen MIG-17 fighters and other

13. Legvold, *Soviet Policy,* pp. 291–92.
14. Ibid., p. 297.
15. V. Kudryavtsev, "African Horizons," *Izvestiya,* December 21, 1968, p. 4 (translated in *Current Digest of the Soviet Press* [*CDSP*], vol. 20, no. 5, February 21, 1968, p. 18).
16. BBC Monitoring Service, *Summary of World Broadcasts,* pt. 1: *USSR* (January 27, 1969), p. A5–1.

military equipment. It followed this sale with its usual long-term trade agreements, student exchange programs, and cultural tours.[17]

The importance of the trawlers to the Kremlin—or some bureaucratic element thereof—because of their possible use in covert intelligence operations must be a matter for speculation. During the months following Nkrumah's overthrow, Moscow had officially dissociated itself from his radio appeals from Guinea, where he was in exile, for a Ghanaian revolt against the military.[18] Moscow denied "slanderous allegations" that it was providing arms to Nkrumah's followers in Guinea. But events officially testified to by former Nkrumah guards during the investigation of the trawler incident cast serious doubt on Soviet denials. Several Ghanaians who had followed Nkrumah to Guinea claimed that they had received military training there with a variety of Soviet, Eastern European, Cuban, and Egyptian arms sent for the former leader's use. One guard described studying maps of Ghana's military facilities with Cuban advisers in the presence of the Cuban ambassador to Guinea. Another reported being told that arms and ammunition would be taken by boat to a coastal area in Ghana close to Nkrumah's home district, and it was near this district that the Soviet trawlers were detained.[19]

Additional testimony offered in January 1969 suggested that the Soviet boats had been engaged in more than fishing. Some of Nkrumah's former associates claimed that the trawlers were two of three such vessels permanently based at Conakry. A Ghanaian sergeant identified one of the Russian crewmen as a Soviet army major who in Nkrumah's days had lectured in Ghana on security problems. Another "sailor" was identified as a security instructor by his former Ghanaian driver. The captain of one of the vessels had lived in Ghana for a year, officially working as an oceanographer. While in most instances the Russian seamen flatly denied these identifications, the various strands of evidence suggested that the Ghanaian government had stumbled onto the initial phase of a covert Soviet operation designed to smuggle arms and exiles into Nkrumah's home province. If this was true, the longer the Russians were held and interrogated, the greater the risk that sensitive information damaging to Soviet interests in West Africa would be unearthed.

The fundamental Soviet objective during the incident was quite appar-

17. *New York Times,* March 9, 1969.

18. For official USSR policy toward Nkrumah's successors, see Legvold, *Soviet Policy,* pp. 267–68.

19. *West Africa,* February 8, 1969, p. 162, and February 15, 1969, p. 192.

ent—the immediate release of the trawlers and seamen detained by Ghana's navy on October 10. No evidence exists to suggest disagreement about this objective in the Soviet government, but there was some controversy about the best means of pursuing it.

Although there is every reason to believe that the Soviet embassy in Ghana conveyed a release request to the Ghanaian government immediately after the impoundment of the trawlers in Takoradi harbor, public knowledge of the Soviet demand did not exist until October 17, when, in the words of Tass, the Soviet embassy in Ghana "gave a press conference . . . at which it stated an emphatic protest against the detention of two Soviet trawlers" and "demanded that the Ghanaian authorities release the trawlers forthwith."[20] At the press conference, a Soviet spokesman explained that the trawlers' engines had been damaged and that they had been driven into Ghanaian waters by the wind and currents. Since they had not been fishing, he said, they had violated no international convention. Then the spokesman bitterly complained that the Ghanaian authorities had detained the men for six days without official explanation and, in violation of international law, had not permitted Soviet embassy officers to meet with the crew.[21]

During the following weeks, a war of words erupted between the Soviet embassy and the Ghanaian government, with statements occasionally added by the Soviet media for good measure. The Russian protest of October 17 gained the embassy a single visit with the arrested seamen, but no progress was made toward their actual release.[22] Radio Moscow claimed on October 21 that the incident was causing "friction" between the two countries.[23] On November 15 the Soviet embassy issued another public statement criticizing the Ghanaians' intensive investigation, accusing officials of "acts of violence" against the crew and ships and stating that it expected the vessels and men to be freed "in the near future."[24] In early December the Soviet ambassador in Ghana again protested the ill-

---

20. The argument for Soviet subversion is made by Thompson, "Ghana's Foreign Policy," p. 10. Other writings related to this topic are *West Africa*, December 28, 1968, p. 1551, and March 29, 1969, p. 367; *Africa Contemporary Record, 1968–69*, p. 493; Don Carl Steffen, "Little Ghana Takes On the Russians," *Life* (February 21, 1969), pp. 20–25.

21. U.S. Foreign Broadcast Information Service (FBIS), *Daily Report* (October 18, 1968), p. A11.

22. *West Africa* (October 26, 1968), p. 1270.

23. *Africa Research Bulletin* (October 1–31, 1968), p. 1222.

24. *Africa Research Bulletin* (November 1–30, 1968), p. 1250.

treatment of the crews and damage to the boats.[25] As Soviet frustration at the stubborn Ghanaians mounted, the first and only comment on the affair from a major Soviet leader was heard. In Moscow President Nikolai Podgorny referred on February 9 to "possible consequences" if the trawlers were not soon released.[26]

Almost immediately after the trawler dispute had gained public attention on October 17, the Soviet Union began a gradual escalation of coercive threats against Ghana. The first steps were economic and were taken on October 21, when Radio Moscow observed that the Ghanaians did not realize "the consequences of disrespect to Soviet sovereignty." If mutual relations were damaged, this could affect "technical cooperation." The Soviet commentator noted that the USSR had just agreed to assist in the construction of a cement factory and a canned fish factory in Ghana— two of the many Soviet aid projects that Moscow had suspended at the time of Nkrumah's fall.[27] More direct Soviet economic pressure was applied in late January, when the USSR discontinued its deliveries of fish and oil. The cancellation of Soviet petroleum shipments left Ghana's sole refinery with extremely low stocks. It was on this matter of actual economic coercion that the only known instance of division in the Soviet bureaucracy came to light, when the trade section of the Soviet embassy in Accra opposed such politically motivated manipulation of trade.[28]

Events in early February precipitated Moscow's move toward military pressure. First, in response to formal testimony given on February 3 by Nkrumah's former security guards about Soviet, Eastern European, and Cuban operations in Guinea, Ghanaian officials decided to fly their Russian prisoners to Accra for an appearance before the board of inquiry. The Russians had given Ghana little information during prior interrogations at Takoradi, and the decision to remove all fifty-two of the prisoners to Accra surely suggested to Moscow an increased effort to compel testimony. Second, Ghana's response to Soviet economic coercion in January quickly established the limited effectiveness of such pressure, at least in the short run. Several major American oil companies that had recently signed offshore prospecting agreements with Accra now consented to supply 72,000 tons of crude oil to the Tema oil refinery if the Ghanaian government would repay a portion of its defaulted 1.5-million-pound debt to them.

25. *West Africa* (December 7, 1968), pp. 1455–56.
26. Quoted in Dismukes, "Soviet Employment of Naval Power," p. 485.
27. *Africa Research Bulletin* (October 1–31, 1968), p. 1222.
28. Thompson, "Ghana's Foreign Policy," p. 11.

On February 16, a week after Soviet President Podgorny's warning of "possible consequences," Tass announced that the Soviet "missile ships *Boyki* and *Neulovimyi,* a submarine and a tanker, under the command of Captain V. Platonov, are paying a courtesy visit to Conakry from 14th to 20th February."[29] On February 20, the Soviet naval group left Conakry and slowly proceeded eastward around the West African bulge into the Gulf of Guinea. The contingent's itinerary was not announced. On February 26, with the Soviet ships approaching Ghanaian waters, the legal process in Accra seemed to accelerate. The captains of the Soviet trawlers were allowed to plead guilty to "navigating an unlicensed motor fishing vessel within Ghana's territorial waters" and pay a modest $150 fine.

Moscow apparently concluded that its pressure campaign had succeeded and on February 27 broadcast that "the Soviet trawlers and their crew reported to have violated Ghana's territorial waters have been released."[30] But this conclusion was premature. Radio Accra subsequently announced that "the two Captains and one member of the crew were . . . remaining behind to assist the Amissah Commission, which is investigating charges of subversion." Throughout the last days of February and the first three days of March, the Soviet naval contingent remained in the Gulf of Guinea. Finally, on March 3, the two trawlers and forty-nine crewmen were allowed to leave Ghana—but without their captains and one first mate.[31]

While Accra's decision to detain the three Soviet sailors for further interrogation cannot have pleased Moscow, other factors weighed against an escalation of military pressure. The Soviet Union was clearly worried that its military presence in the area would be publicly linked with the trawler incident and that it would be accused of blatant coercion of a small African state. This concern was evident in Radio Moscow's complaint on February 27 that the British Broadcasting Company had been airing "fabrications produced by its correspondent in Accra to cast a shadow on Soviet policy in Africa and to question Soviet loyalty to the principle of noninterference in the affairs of African states."[32]

Soviet caution was understandable. Throughout the previous year, the

29. BBC Monitoring Service, *Summary of World Broadcasts,* pt. 1: *USSR* (February 18, 1969), pp. A4–5.

30. FBIS, *Daily Report* (February 28, 1969), p. A16.

31. *Africa Research Bulletin* (March 1–31, 1969), p. 1364; Elmo R. Zumwalt, Jr., *On Watch: A Memoir* (New York: Times Books, 1976), p. 332; Dismukes, "Soviet Employment of Naval Power," p. 485.

32. FBIS, *Daily Report* (February 28, 1969), p. A16.

USSR had exploited the *Pueblo* incident, speaking of "the disgraceful spy mission of this American spy" and the "blackmail" and "war hysteria" that the United States had futilely generated in an effort to gain the ship's release.[33] And as recently as January 15 Radio Moscow had criticized the port visits of the U.S. frigate *Dahlgren* to West Africa as "only the first stage in naval penetration in the area" in support of "neo-colonialism and reaction."[34] Any evidence now in February of Russian gunboat diplomacy might illuminate a hypocritical gap between Soviet words and deeds.

Of equal importance, the Soviet invasion of Czechoslovakia in August 1968 had already tarnished the USSR's image in Africa. Even such socialist states as Tanzania expressed "profound shock" at an action perceived as "betrayal of all the principles of self-determination and national sovereignty." Comparable denunciations were heard from the Congo Democratic Republic, Ethiopia, Ghana, Kenya, Senegal, Sudan, Tunisia, Uganda, and Zambia.[35] Therefore, despite the only partial success of Soviet efforts to free the trawlers and their crews, on March 4 Tass hastily announced in Moscow:

The Soviet missile ships *Boiki* and *Neulovimyi,* a submarine and tanker, will arrive in the Nigerian port Lagos on an official visit on March 5, in accordance with an agreement reached by the Governments of the Soviet Union and Nigeria. The Soviet naval squadron . . . will stay there till March 10.[36]

The Soviet ships quietly steamed away from Ghanaian waters.

On March 11 the Soviet naval contingent left Lagos to take up station once again in the Gulf of Guinea.[37] Then on March 19 a spokesman for the Ghanaian government announced that the Russian captains and first mate held since October were now free to leave the country. Moscow did not publicly react to this final release—perhaps because of the announcement three weeks before indicating that it had already taken place. On March 26 the Soviet naval group returned to the Mediterranean, without the movements of the ships ever having been linked to events in Ghana by the world press or by Soviet spokesmen.

33. FBIS, *Daily Report* (December 26, 1968), p. A1.

34. BCC Monitoring Service, *Summary of World Broadcasts,* pt. 1: *USSR* (January 21, 1969), p. A5–1.

35. A selection of these hostile African reactions can be found in *Africa Contemporary Record, 1968–69,* pp. 611–18.

36. FBIS, *Daily Report: Soviet Union* (March 5, 1969), p. A36.

37. Dismukes, "Soviet Employment of Naval Power," p. 485.

While it is clear that the primary purpose of the task force had been to increase the pressure on Ghana, it is unlikely that the mission would have been undertaken if other Soviet relationships and interests in West Africa had not permitted the disguise of the ships' principal purpose from the press and other African states. And it is also apparent that the port visits to Guinea and Nigeria were something more than window dressing. The five-day stay in Conakry came at a time of threat to the USSR's unpredictable client, Touré: On January 14, the Guinean president spoke of a plot to overthrow him similar to that recently executed in Mali. In February Touré began a purge of his military and cabinet that would ultimately lead to death sentences for twelve opponents of his regime and the arrest of more than a thousand persons. The six-day port visit to Lagos was also wholly consistent with the USSR's intensifying campaign to cement relations with Nigeria and exploit the Western stand on the Biafran war. Quite possibly the Russian hierarchy could not have been persuaded that the first such deployment of Soviet combatants to West Africa was wise—particularly after Czechoslovakia—without the existence of these other Soviet interests in Guinea and Nigeria.

Ghanaian Behavior

Ghana's foreign policy during the trawler incident was the responsibility of eight military officers of the National Liberation Council (NLC) who had ruled the country since the exile of Nkrumah. The primary influence was the NLC deputy chairman and minister of external affairs, Policy Inspector-General John W. Harlley. Harlley's career in intelligence work and his experiences under Nkrumah had made him unusually sensitive to internal subversion and deeply suspicious of communism in general and the Soviet Union in particular.[38] Several 1968 events illustrate Harlley's leading role in foreign relations and the NLC's concern about Communist subversion. In September Harlley described an illegal railway strike as a "gigantic conspiracy to topple the military regime in Ghana" and as part of a plot "hatched from outside Ghana."[39] In November the NLC ordered the arrest of the commander in chief of Ghana's armed forces, Air Marshal M. A. Otu, for alleged complicity in a plot to return Nkrumah to power. At the time of Otu's arrest, Harlley announced that

38. Thompson, "Ghana's Foreign Policy," p. 9.
39. *Africa Contemporary Record, 1968–69,* p. 492.

the coup had been timed for around Christmas and that the two Russian trawlers taken into custody in October were believed to have been "on a reconnaissance mission" connected with the Otu coup.[40]

The other major influences on Ghanaian foreign policy at the time were the professional diplomats and economists of the foreign ministry who had been rehabilitated by the NLC after Nkrumah's fall. Generally, these career officers were far more mindful than the security-minded NLC of the benefits of international nonalignment and economic exploitation of East-West rivalry. To these foreign ministry personnel a number of difficult and technical problems had been delegated by the NLC, among them the necessary negotiations for new foreign aid and the rescheduling of foreign debt made essential by the crushing $800 million in borrowing Nkrumah had left behind.[41]

The enigma of the trawler affair is the absence of any *direct* evidence that Ghanaian officials knew of the furtive military pressure applied by the Soviet Union during the last part of February. Nonetheless, the few analysts who have studied the affair understandably conclude that "Ghanaian officials were almost certainly aware of the presence of the Soviet ships during the crucial period of the negotiations."[42]

With Tass announcing the arrival of four Soviet ships in Conakry and their scheduled departure date of February 20, and with a similar announcement of the Nigerian port visit, it is difficult to imagine that officials in Accra were unaware of the ships' presence in the Gulf of Guinea. At the same time, it is evident that the Soviet vessels were always deployed in an unprovocative manner—apparently a considerable distance from the Ghanaian coastline. None of the international press filing stories from Accra during this time ever referred to the presence of Soviet ships in the area; any sightings of the Russian naval contingent or public reference to it in Accra would certainly have been reported by some enterprising writer.

The NLC's lack of public reaction suggests that the ships' presence in the region was perceived for what it was—a discrete signal of Moscow's strong feelings about the injury being done to its prestige, personnel, and property. Yet presumably Ghanaian officials did not feel threatened by the appearance of the ships. If they had, a simple expedient would have been the kind of international publicity that the Soviet Union was trying

40. *West Africa* (December 28, 1968), p. 1551.
41. Thompson, "Ghana's Foreign Policy," pp. 8, 9.
42. Dismukes, "Soviet Employment of Naval Power," p. 486.

hard to avoid. That the NLC was well aware of this propaganda weapon at its disposal was implied in a statement made by Radio Accra when the forty-nine crewmen were released on March 3:

The Government . . . reiterated its desire to maintain friendly relations with the Soviet Union on the basis of equality, mutual respect for each other's sovereignty and territorial integrity, and non-interference in each other's internal affairs. It reminded the Soviet Union that, as a great and powerful state, it bore a special responsibility in ensuring that its attitude toward Ghana-Soviet relations was guided by these principles.[43]

In general, there is no evidence that the NLC perceived any major risk to its security in refusing to release the Soviet trawlers, even when word arrived of Soviet combatants in the Gulf of Guinea. It did perceive compliance with the Soviet demands without first establishing the actual extent of Russian complicity with possible attempts at subversion as a greater threat to Ghana's national security and the regime's survival. This prompted the obstinate refusal to be intimidated by increasing Soviet pressure. The paramount importance of internal security was emphasized by the arrest of Air Marshal Otu in November for possible plotting with Nkrumah supporters. Evidence offered to the board of inquiry on Communist support for Nkrumah in Guinea strengthened the NLC's determination to conduct a comprehensive investigation before releasing the crews.

Certainly there were valid grounds for the NLC's suspicions of the trawlers. They had first been spotted by a Ghanaian air force plane off the coast of Nkrumah's home province, and the pilot had observed six dugouts off-loading cargo from one of the trawlers. When a Ghanaian patrol boat arrived to apprehend the two Russian ships while they were still in Ghana's territorial waters, the trawlers headed for open sea. Only after the patrol boat had fired six cannon shots did the trawlers halt. Not only had their cargo been jettisoned during the brief escape attempt, but several of their logs were burned during the course of the chase.[44] Subsequent interrogation of some of the Ghanaians trading with the trawlers on October 10 established that this was the third time the Soviet seamen had visited the area. On October 2 the Russians had hailed three Ghanaian fishermen about fifteen miles offshore and arranged for a trade of fish for local fruit and animals, which was carried out on October 4. A similar exchange had occurred on October 10, the day the trawlers were im-

43. *Africa Research Bulletin* (March 21, 1969), p. 2.
44. Steffen, "Little Ghana Takes On the Russians," p. 22.

pounded. The NLC's theory was that the Russians had wished to develop contacts with local fishermen so that arms and exiles brought from Guinea could be smuggled ashore.[45]

Ghanaian investigators, however, failed to uncover much additional evidence in four months of effort. Police searches of villages in Nkrumah's district uncovered no smuggled arms. Despite obvious inconsistencies between actual events and the Russians' story about engine trouble, this explanation was clung to throughout numerous interrogations. Some of the urgency of the situation evaporated when information gathered by the inquiry board absolved Air Marshal Otu of any complicity in subversion or any knowledge of the Russians' activities. As Radio Accra reported on March 3 when the Russian crews were released, the decision had been made only when the NLC was "fully satisfied that the country's security was in no way compromised by this step."[46]

As fears for Ghana's internal security waned, international economic affairs—always important to foreign ministry professionals—assumed greater significance. Ghana's precarious economy made it vital to avoid any unnecessary rupture in trade and aid relations with the USSR. Ghana's per capita GNP grew only 1 percent in 1968, after no growth at all in 1966 and 1967. The economy was passing through a difficult phase of deflation made necessary by Nkrumah's undisciplined public spending. Although Ghana's trade with the Communist states had fallen since 1966, it still constituted 12 percent of the country's exports and imports in 1967. Moreover, in 1964–68 Ghana had enjoyed important trade surpluses with the Soviet Union, and in 1968 it was actually unable to meet Soviet demand for its principal export, cocoa. The trade surpluses had helped finance large oil imports from the USSR, and though petroleum could be obtained from Western oil companes, it had to be paid for in hard currency made scarce by Ghana's chronic trade deficit with the industrial democracies.[47]

Other factors complicated the economic picture. Because of its own financial problems, Great Britain had failed to provide the level of economic aid that might have been expected in response to its former colony's swing back to the West. And there was clear evidence that the Ghanaian public was not interested in the one-sided economic dependency likely to result from the complete severance of trade relations with the

45. *Christian Science Monitor,* March 21, 1969.
46. *Africa Research Bulletin* (March 1–31, 1969), p. 1364.
47. *Africa Contemporary Record, 1968–69,* pp. 496–502.

Soviet bloc countries. In December 1967, for instance, the NLC had agreed to permit Abbott Laboratories of Chicago to assume control of the country's unprofitable state pharmaceutical company, but the domestic storm aroused by the terms of the agreement compelled Abbott to withdraw from the contract.[48] In late February 1969 the Associated Press filed a story from Ghana stating that "to many proud young men, the sin of Mr. Nkrumah's relations with the Soviet Union, Communist China and other Communist bloc lands is matched by the Council's [NLC's] dependence on the West."[49] Such politicoeconomic factors pointed toward resolution of the trawler affair unless definitive evidence of Russian subversion could be established by the Ghanaian military regime.

The Question of Influence

Admiral Zumwalt has written that "Ghana brought her humiliation on herself by her refusal to engage in pre-gunboat diplomacy," implying that the release of the Russian trawlers and crew in March 1969 was the result of intimidation by the Soviet navy.[50] A careful reading of the available evidence, however, makes this proposition questionable, although sufficient data to settle the matter conclusively do not currently exist. Although Ghana eventually released the trawlers, this was done only after a five-month detention that was as humiliating to the Soviet Union as was any later intimidation to the Ghanaians. The NLC did not treat its Russian captives with traditional respect. When the Soviet crewmen initially refused to disembark from their boats in Takoradi harbor, one Soviet seaman was bayoneted and another knocked unconscious. During their first week in Ghana, the seamen were denied the right to see the Soviet ambassador. After finally being permitted to visit the crew in mid-October, the staff of the Soviet embassy was not allowed another visit until January 8.[51]

Although the Soviet trawlers were released while the Soviet task force was in West African waters, this was only after the NLC's failure to confirm any subversive actions by the Soviet trawlers and after it had demonstrated decisively its willingness to deal firmly with those suspected of such action. The professional diplomats in the Ghanaian foreign ministry

48. Thompson, "Ghana's Foreign Policy," pp. 10, 11.
49. *New York Times,* February 23, 1969.
50. Zumwalt, *On Watch,* p. 332.
51. *West Africa* (March 1, 1969), p. 254; *Christian Science Monitor,* March 21, 1969.

had felt from the outset that there was insufficient data to substantiate any accusations of clandestine activities.[52]

Perhaps the most telling evidence against Soviet coercion is the move the NLC was making toward release of the ships and crew before the Soviet naval combatants left Conakry on February 20 for Ghanaian waters a thousand miles away. In Lagos, Nigeria, on February 18, the chairman of the NLC and Ghana's formal head of state, Lieutenant General Joseph A. Ankrah, said that "it won't be long" before his government released the fifty-two Soviet fishermen and the two trawlers seized four months earlier.[53] At the very most, awareness of the Soviet naval group later in the week might have speeded up a decisionmaking process obviously well on its way. At worst, the latent threat of Soviet military action might have aroused new resistance in the NLC to the trawlers' release. Although the crews were formally fined on February 27 and their pending release announced in Accra on February 29, they were not permitted to leave the country until March 3. And even then the NLC decided to hold the three senior officers until March 19, as if to demonstrate its refusal to be intimidated by the Russians.

Moscow's own behavior suggests that it appreciated how little influence the naval task force had on Accra. No official linkage was drawn between naval movements and the trawler episode. The Soviet navy left Ghanaian waters for Nigeria on March 3 without gaining the release of the most senior Russian seamen.

Although a small deployment of combatants to West Africa was an unprecedented Russian act, the long-established political, economic, and military relationship with Guinea and the growing ties with Nigeria provided the USSR with a situation in which it was free to operate without attracting unwanted attention. The naval deployment itself represented a natural extension of Soviet worldwide operations: Moscow had steadily moved its port visits westward along the Mediterranean littoral between 1964 and 1968, reaching as far as Morocco in October 1968.[54]

This furtive gunboat diplomacy may have been encouraged by the complete absence of official comment on the matter by either the American or the British government during the four months of bickering leading up to the actual arrival of the Soviet ships. Certainly a deployment at this time could be viewed as taking maximum advantage of the transition

52. Thompson, "Ghana's Foreign Policy," p. 10.

53. *New York Times,* February 20, 1969.

54. Michael MccGwire, "Foreign-Port Visits by Soviet Naval Units," in MccGwire and others, *Soviet Naval Policy,* pp. 387–418.

in U.S. presidential administrations and the preoccupation of the U.S. Navy with events in Southeast Asia. But unquestionably of greater importance, in light of the negligible risks entailed by the mission, was the availability of Soviet naval power as an employable complement to diplomatic and economic pressure. Considering the already forwardly deployed Soviet warships in the Mediterranean, it was probably only a matter of time before Russian combatants would make their first voyage into the waters of sub-Saharan Africa. Indeed, combined events in Ghana, Guinea, and Nigeria brought this about.[55]

The long-term impact of the trawler affair on Soviet relations with Ghana proved to be nil, however. The NLC's suspicion of the Soviet Union was of declining importance to Ghana's foreign policy, as political power was officially transferred to a newly elected civilian government in September 1969. The existing level of trade with the USSR was maintained. And any lingering anxiety about Communist support for Nkrumah's return was abruptly ended in early 1972 with Nkrumah's death. Furthermore, in early 1972 Ghana's military once again intervened to depose the civilians elected in 1969, primarily because of continuing economic stagnation and inflation. The new military government, while maintaining a nonaligned status, sought better relations with the Communists, restoring diplomatic relations with Cuba and China and expanding trade and aid relations with the Soviet bloc.[56]

Nor did the incident have any immediate effect on the interests of the United States. While the American trading position with Ghana had greatly improved in 1966–68, establishing the United States as Ghana's second largest trading partner, no support was sought from Washington during the trawler affair.[57] With negligible U.S. awareness of the event and the growing opposition to American interventionism, the lack of White House concern did nothing to harm the President's standing with Congress or the general public. Only the U.S. Navy seems to have shown some natural interest in this unprecedented Soviet operation off West Africa, with former Chief of Naval Operations Zumwalt later describing it as a signal "that the USSR was ready, willing and able to protect its interests in parts of the world hitherto inaccessible to it." But the ad hoc and defensive nature of the action, and the rapid return of the four Soviet ships to

55. For a lucid summary of the growth of Soviet naval operations worldwide, see Robert G. Weinland, "Soviet Naval Operations: 10 Years of Change," ibid., pp. 375–86.

56. *Africa Contemporary Record, 1974–75*, pp. B650–51.

57. *Africa Contemporary Record, 1969–70*, p. B485.

their Mediterranean fleet on March 26, mitigated any concern the U.S. Navy might have felt about the implications of the deployment.[58]

While no aspect of the trawlers affair was of major importance in itself, this first exercise of Soviet naval power for coercive effect in African waters was conducted with a sophistication and subtlety at odds with the popular stereotype of the heavy-handed Russian. Although the principal objective was to secure the release of Soviet men and property, the less urgent aims of bolstering a Soviet ally, Sekou Touré, and cultivating political influence in Nigeria were also pursued. These ancillary objectives were sought in a way that concealed the primary purpose of the mission.

What if the USSR had chosen not to employ naval power at all in February 1969 to signal its seriousness? Currently available evidence indicates that the outcome of the incident would have been precisely the same. Ghana's failure to find confirming evidence of Russian subversion and its desire to continue, if possible, normal economic relations with the Eastern bloc would have proved to be adequate incentives for eventual release of the Soviet boats. Obviously, the NLC had not tried to exploit the affair for domestic or international propaganda. Its overriding concern was the number of real and imagined plots it suspected against its continued political control.

A direct resort to military force by the Soviet Union in response to the trawler seizure would have, on the other hand, severely damaged Russian interests in Africa. The two destroyers and the submarine were physically unsuited for an actual rescue of the Russian seamen. Presumably, a larger naval force would have not only ensured the permanent loss of the crew, but also confirmed the opinion that the crew had been engaged in operations that Moscow desperately wanted to conceal. African solidarity in the face of such Russian aggression could have been expected, and the smoldering memories of Czechoslovakia would have been rekindled in African capitals. It is unlikely that a military confrontation would have significantly altered American involvement or perception of U.S. interests in West Africa, given the groundswell of public opposition to foreign interventions. But increased West African receptivity to security collaboration with the original colonial powers, Great Britain and France, would undoubtedly have followed any such demonstration of Soviet willingness to use force against a poorly armed African state.

58. Zumwalt, *On Watch*, pp. 331–32.

The Conakry Raid, November 1970

During the 1960s Guinea harbored not only Nkrumah and his exiled entourage but also the adherents of several other political causes. Of these groups, the most important was the African Party for the Independence of Guinea and Cape Verde (PAIGC), the national liberation movement dedicated to ending Portugal's five centuries of colonial rule in neighboring Guinea-Bissau, or as Lisbon preferred to call the territory, "Portuguese Guinea." PAIGC-organized strikes in the capital city of Bissau during 1958–59 had ended in the shooting deaths of some fifty dock workers by the Portuguese colonial police and had forced a drastic revision of the PAIGC's strategy toward rural guerrilla warfare.

With Sekou Touré's blessing, PAIGC leader Amilcar Cabral and his secretariat took refuge in Conakry, where they openly operated schools for revolutionary training and solicited worldwide support for their anticolonial cause. Supplies for the PAIGC's guerrillas in Guinea-Bissau had to be transported through Guinea-Conakry. The PAIGC's soldiers frequently sought sanctuary from the Portuguese army in neighboring Guinea-Conakry, and Portuguese military positions were often shelled from the safety of Touré's republic—apparently by Touré's soldiers as well as the PAIGC.[59] A second base for the PAIGC was located in Senegal to the north. In 1969 the Portuguese army of some 30,000 troops began an aggressive campaign to locate and liquidate guerrilla training camps, including those located inside the frontiers of Guinea-Conakry and Senegal. The consequence was an escalating series of Portuguese bombings and incursions of Guinea and Senegal and a number of formal protests against Portugal lodged with the UN Security Council by these two African states.[60]

A second source of conflict in the region was the widespread resentment of Sekou Touré's rule among tens of thousands of Guineans who had

59. A useful description of the war in Guinea-Bissau is Neil Bruce, *Portugal: The Last Empire* (Wiley, 1975), pp. 62–70.

60. There is extensive literature on the PAIGC. Three useful sources are *Report on Portuguese Guinea and the Liberation*, Hearing before the Subcommittee on Africa, House, 91 Cong. 2 sess. (Government Printing Office, 1970); Richard Gibson, *African Liberation Movements* (New York: Oxford University Press, 1972), pp. 245–63; and John Biggs-Davison, "The Current Situation in Portuguese Guinea," *African Affairs* (October 1971), pp. 385–94.

fled their native country for Senegal, the Ivory Coast, Gambia, France, and other nations. Many had emigrated because of the harsh socialist measures Touré had imposed after independence in 1958: state monopoly of wholesale trade, collective farming, monopolistic state enterprises, and the nationalization of foreign investment. But despite Guinea's abundant natural resources, Touré's socialist planning was slow to produce. With a shortage of trained manpower, the departure of French technicians, and no modern economic infrastructure, goods disappeared from the shelves of the state stores and soaring inflation imposed a particular hardship on urban dwellers in the money economy. During the first half of the 1960s, real economic growth barely kept pace with population expansion, and by the end of the decade, per capita growth was actually negative.[61]

To move Guinea toward socialism and prevent his system's shortcomings from bringing him down, Touré was forced to rely on authoritarian mass mobilization and indoctrination. Plots against him increased, and frequent purges of the government and military were needed to prevent consolidation of the opposition. Mali's coup in late 1968 was particularly unsettling to Guinea's president and resulted in several precautionary acts: the army leadership was changed in early 1969; a people's militia was organized to counterbalance the army's power; and political committees were installed in army barracks. By 1970 Touré had become obsessed with the thought that a domestic counterrevolution or foreign invasion might sweep away the classless order to which he had devoted his life.[62]

In the early morning of November 22, 1970, Touré's worst fears seemed realized when there was an amphibious raid on Conakry. At 2 a.m., 350 to 400 soldiers came ashore from six unmarked troopships that had slipped into Conakry harbor. In small squads, the invaders spread out to strategic points in the city: Touré's summer residence, the home of PAIGC leader Amilcar Cabral, the national radio station ("Voice of the Revolution"), the prison holding numerous Portuguese soldiers captured by the PAIGC, the city power station, and the airport. Several of the squads quickly proved inadequate to their tasks. Touré's summer home was destroyed but the president was not found. Cabral, it developed, was in Bulgaria. The invaders assigned to seize the airport and neutralize Guinea's air force instead chose to defect to Touré's forces. The Portu-

61. Claude Riviere, *Guinea: The Mobilization of a People* (Cornell University Press, 1977), pp. 102–20; Harold D. Nelson and others, *Area Handbook for Guinea*, 2d ed. (GPO, 1975), pp. 197–209.

62. Riviere, *Guinea*, pp. 121–40.

guese prisoners were liberated and the city power supply knocked out, but the transmitter for the radio station was never located. As members of Touré's people's militia and the PAIGC began to fight back, many of the invaders withdrew to their troopships with their released prisoners and wounded. By early morning of November 23, the insurgents had withdrawn from Conakry's streets and sailed away, leaving behind as many as three hundred Guineans dead and nearly a hundred of their own party taken prisoner.[63]

Interrogation of the captured raiders quickly indicated that the attack had been planned by General Antonio de Spinola, the military governor and commander in chief of Portuguese Guinea. The participants had included about 150 black Portuguese soldiers from Portuguese Guinea, a like number of Guinean exiles recruited throughout West Africa, and a small number of white Portuguese officers. General Spinola's "Bay of Pigs" had been motivated by his desire to strike a decisive blow in the decade-long struggle against the PAIGC. Touré's replacement by a regime unwilling to provide sanctuary and assistance to the rebels would have been a crushing blow to the liberation movement.[64]

The invaders' failure to capture or kill Touré and Amilcar Cabral vitiated Spinola's plan. A number of the attackers had been poorly briefed and others quickly surrendered out of fear or indifference to the Portuguese cause. Yet even then, the relative ease with which the Portuguese and exiles had landed in Conakry, liberated prisoners, and sailed away demonstrated the inadequacy of Guinea's national security forces. A better executed invasion might have achieved Spinola's objectives.[65]

Touré's reaction to the raid was an immediate request on November 22, delivered by Guinea's ambassador to the UN, for an emergency meeting of the Security Council and an "immediate intervention of airborne UN troops to assist the national army of the Republic of Guinea."[66] When the Security Council chose to dispatch a fact-finding commission to Conakry instead of peacekeeping forces, the Guinean government was gravely

63. *New York Times,* November 26, 1970.

64. *United Nations Security Council Official Records,* 1560th meeting, December 5, 1970, p. 13.

65. Any serious student of this event should refer to the UN's published investigation of the raid: "Report of the Security Council Special Mission to the Republic of Guinea Established Under Resolution 289 (1970)," *United Nations Security Council Official Records,* Twenty-fifth Year, Special Supplement no. 2 (1971). Another helpful article is Margarita Dobert, "Who Invaded Guinea?" *Africa Report* (March 1971), pp. 16–18.

66. *Keesing's Contemporary Archives* (December 26–31, 1970), p. 24354.

disappointed. Only a slightly more encouraging response awaited Touré's appeal on November 23 for "all brotherly African countries" to provide "concrete support" for his regime. While several African countries pledged to send military forces if they were needed, only Nigeria and Egypt in subsequent days actually sent token units. Moreover, when the African states took up the issue of a Pan-African military force for such emergencies at a meeting of the Organization of African Unity on December 7, the idea was defeated just as it had been on previous occasions.[67]

Perhaps it was his low expectation of Pan-African support or his realization that few African states had modern forces at their disposal that led Touré to announce on November 25 that "we are now making the same appeal to all countries outside the African continent" for military assistance.[68] Guinea's president indicated that he especially wished to receive airplanes, both fighters and bombers. It was a request presumably related to the fact that Portuguese jets had violated and bombed Guinean territory with increasing regularity during 1970 and that on the morning of the November 22 invasion several unidentified aircraft had flown over the city of Conakry.[69]

If Touré and his ministers had any lingering doubts about Guinea's long-term need for external military support, they were laid to rest when word reached Conakry on November 27 of a ground incursion by two hundred Portuguese or exiled soldiers at Kondura—the principal military base for the PAIGC on Guinea's northern frontier. The outbreak of this new violence while the UN investigative mission was still in Guinea was taken by the government as further evidence of the ineffectiveness of the international body.[70] On November 29, Conakry announced that "36 mercenaries were killed and 18 captured" and "two members of our popular forces were killed" in battles in the Kondura area.[71]

Apparently it was this second major incident that prompted Touré's private appeals to the American and Soviet embassies in Conakry for some symbolic show of military support for his regime. This request set

67. Zdenek Cervenka, "The Organization of African Unity in 1970," *Africa Contemporary Record, 1970–71,* p. A37–38.

68. *New York Times,* November 25, 1970.

69. *New York Times,* November 26, 1970; *Africa Research Bulletin* (November 1–30, 1970), p. 1935.

70. "Report of the Security Council Special Mission to the Republic of Guinea," pp. 202–03.

71. FBIS, *Africa Regional Report* (December 4, 1970), p. W3.

off a series of subsequent military, diplomatic, and economic actions by the USSR whose long-term ramifications could be only dimly foreseen at the time.

International Reaction

Because of the apparent importance of third-party reactions to the Conakry raid in determining the eventual nature of the Soviet response, it is useful to begin with a discussion of them. The most visible and immediate reaction came from other African states. Despite a history of strained relations between Touré's radical regime and the more moderate African states, the image of a white colonial government attacking a poor black Islamic state was enough to rally support for Guinea in every corner of the continent. Every African government not under white control rushed a message to Conakry denouncing neocolonialism, imperialism, and racism, and in several cases the message included an offer of financial or military help to repel the Portuguese.

In Nigeria students marched through Lagos taunting passing Europeans and protesting in front of the American embassy U.S. military assistance to Portugal provided under the North Atlantic Treaty Organization. In Equatorial Guinea Portuguese homes were sacked and burned and their occupants driven from the country.[72] At an emergency meeting of the Organization of African Unity (OAU) held December 9–11, forty-one foreign ministers unanimously agreed to condemn "those states, particularly the NATO powers, who sustain Portugal in her colonial aggression, by their continued assistance to her." The OAU voted to establish a special fund "to provide financial, military and technical assistance to Guinea," and it directed its Liberation Committee to "substantially increase financial and material assistance to PAIGC."[73]

At the UN, the Conakry raid tapped the reservoirs of hostility toward white influence in Africa. In December 1969 the UN had designated the year 1971 as "International Year for Action to Combat Racism and Racial Discrimination" and had that same month formally condemned Portugal for its bombing and shelling of Guinean and Senegalese territory. In March 1970 the United States had for the first time exercised its

72. *Keesing's Contemporary Archives* (December 26–31, 1970), p. 24354; *New York Times,* November 28, 1970.
73. *New York Times,* December 12, 1970.

Security Council veto on a resolution calling for Britain to apply force against the illegal Rhodesian regime.[74] In October 1970 the United States had refused to support a General Assembly resolution outlining a program of economic, political, and military action against the remaining colonial regimes in Africa.[75]

It was hardly surprising, therefore, that the five days of Security Council debate over the Conakry raid quickly became an unrelenting attack by the third world and socialist states on Portugal, NATO, and vestiges of white influence in Africa. Even such pro-Western states as Saudi Arabia, Ethiopia, and Liberia called for Portugal's expulsion from NATO and castigated U.S. opposition to proposed economic sanctions against Lisbon.[76] In contrast, the Soviet Union was praised by African states for "its dynamic role in the struggle for the emancipation of Africa."[77]

One potential non-African source of military assistance for Touré was Cuba. Castro had taken a personal interest in Amilcar Cabral and the Portuguese Guinea liberation movement since January 1966, when Cabral appeared at the Tricontinental Conference of African, Asian, and Latin American leaders in Havana. As a result of his well-received speech on "Theory as a Weapon" and his endorsement of the independent revolutionary course being pursued by Cuba, Cabral had emerged from the conference as one of the third world's revolutionary leaders. Castro soon dispatched a number of Cuban instructors to assist the PAIGC. By the late 1960s Cubans had assumed responsibility for several PAIGC training camps in Guinea and Senegal and were accompanying these guerrillas into Portuguese Guinea. In January 1971, less than two months after the Conakry raid, authorities in Bissau listed four Cuban soldiers killed in the fighting of 1970.[78] Meanwhile, Cuban advisers were also playing an important role in the training of Touré's local militia.[79]

While the available information is understandably sketchy, there seem

74. *Africa Contemporary Record, 1970–71*, p. A52.

75. *U.S. Department of State Bulletin,* vol. 63 (November 16, 1970), pp. 635–37.

76. The relevant dates here are meetings 1558 through 1563 of the United Nations Security Council, held November 22 through December 8, 1970. Transcripts of these meetings are found in *United Nations Security Council Official Records* (1970).

77. This phrase was used by the UN ambassador from Burundi on December 8, 1970. *United Nations Security Council Official Records,* 1563d meeting, p. 11.

78. *Keesing's Contemporary Archives* (November 13–20, 1971), p. 24940.

79. Nelson and others, *Area Handbook for Guinea,* p. 222.

to be sufficient data to argue that Castro responded to Touré's worldwide request for help by agreeing to significantly increase Cuba's direct support of the PAIGC guerrillas. In light of Guinea's refusal to abandon the PAIGC cause, this was a contribution of considerable importance to the solution of Touré's own security problem. On May 24, 1971, it was reported in Lisbon that thirty-four Cuban "technical advisers" had arrived in Senegal to take charge of armaments, communications, and engineering units for the PAIGC. Early in September 1971 General Spinola stated in Lisbon that each guerrilla operational unit was now led by Cuban officers, of whom there were several hundred among the 6,000 trained guerrillas based in Guinea and Senegal.[80] Among the socialist countries of the world, Cuba was clearly bearing the physical burden of the fighting.

Surprisingly, one of the external powers to whom Touré looked after the Conakry raid was the United States. There was a certain logic to this in view of his deliberate unpredictability in international affairs. One of the secrets of his independence had always been the maintenance of an uneasy equilibrium between the great powers—particularly the Soviet Union, China, and the United States. As a result, despite Touré's bombastic Marxist rhetoric, the small West African nation was blessed with $103 million in American aid during the years 1961–71.

Furthermore, during the 1960s Touré had cautiously opened his nation to the direct private investment needed to transform Guinea's abundant mineral reserves into exports and foreign exchange. Fifty percent of Guinea's export earnings in 1970 originated with the Olin Matheson-controlled consortium, which operated the nation's principal bauxite mine and refinery. An even larger and more promising enterprise began in 1966 with the formation of an American and European consortium to develop the world's richest bed of bauxite. With assistance from the U.S. government and the World Bank, the consortium raised $185 million in capital to build the new railroad, deep-water port, and mining towns required for the project. Construction was well under way in late 1970.[81] Because of the growing American participation in Guinea's economy, it was less surprising that in late November 1970 Touré privately requested a symbolic display of American military support to help deter future external attacks.

80. *Keesing's Contemporary Archives* (November 13–20, 1971), p. 24940.
81. For details on the status of this project at the end of 1970, see *Africa Contemporary Record, 1970–71*, p. B374.

The probability of a positive response from the Nixon administration to Touré's request was nonexistent, however. The White House had already chosen to move away from the Kennedy-Johnson inclination to apply pressure to Lisbon in behalf of African self-determination, and the White House's judgment on African affairs was never seriously contested inside the government. Working from the premise that no existing African liberation movement could succeed in changing the policy of any of the white African regimes, Richard Nixon and Henry Kissinger formally adopted in January 1970 a policy of increased "communication" with the whites. For Portugal, the operational results were several executive steps, such as resumed negotiations on the Azores and full Export-Import Bank facilities for the Portuguese colonies, which were surely seen in Lisbon as tacit support for its colonial policy.[82]

In view of the new trend in White House policy, it is hardly surprising that the United States failed to respond to Guinea's public and private pleas for military support. Privately, the Nixon administration sent a confidential message to Touré around December 1. On December 2 the Guinean president *publicly* thanked Nixon for his "message of sympathy and support on the occasion of the grave and criminal aggression by Portugal," probably as a goad to the Soviet Union and a signal to Portugal.[83]

Soon the public release of the damning UN investigation and four days of unrelenting Security Council condemnation forced the White House into public action. During the last day of debate on December 8, the American ambassador to the UN officially criticized the invasion as contrary to the UN Charter and read into the record the contents of Nixon's confidential message to Touré. Even then, the United States abstained from voting on the watered down Resolution 290 that endorsed the UN report, demanded compensation from Portugal, and threatened sanctions in the event of any future attack. Perhaps as a result of White House reaction to intelligence reports that the USSR was responding militarily to Touré's appeal, a State Department spokesman announced on December 11 that the U.S. government had decided to grant Guinea $4.7 million in food aid "to contribute to the reconstruction made necessary by the attempted invasion."[84]

82. For the Nixon administration's policy toward the Portuguese colonies, see John Marcum, "The Politics of Indifference: Portugal and Africa, A Case Study in American Foreign Policy," *Issue,* vol. 2 (Fall 1972), pp. 12–16.

83. Quoted in *Keesing's Contemporary Archives* (December 26–31, 1970), p. 24354.

84. Ibid.

Soviet Behavior

What general Soviet interests, then, were engaged by the Conakry raid? The principal interest appears to have been the maintenance and expansion of Russian political influence in Guinea-Conakry, Guinea-Bissau, and Africa generally. Although the mid-1960s had been rather bleak years for Soviet objectives in Africa—with the loss of clients in Ghana, Mali, and the Congo—these setbacks had accentuated the importance of Guinea-Conakry and Guinea-Bissau to continued Soviet influence in West Africa. The PAIGC had emerged as Africa's most successful liberation movement, with Amilcar Cabral and his followers credibly claiming dominance in half of Guinea-Bissau's countryside. Furthermore, throughout the sixties, external support for the PAIGC had gradually gained an international respectability comparable to that achieved by the National Liberation Front in South Vietnam. In 1965 the UN General Assembly had appealed to all states to render moral and material support to the people of the Portuguese colony and requested that UN members sever all diplomatic, commercial, and military relations with Portugal. Such liberal governments as Sweden and Canada and several American church organizations were directly aiding the PAIGC by 1970.

Not only had material assistance to the PAIGC received official international sanction since 1965, but the liberation struggle in Guinea-Bissau also presented the Soviet Union with an unparalleled opportunity for expanded influence at the direct expense of NATO. Because of Portugal's membership in NATO, its active part in the North Atlantic trading community, and its receipt of U.S. economic and military aid, the diplomatic, commercial, and strategic costs of compelling an end to Lisbon's colonial wars fell squarely on the United States, Great Britain, France, and West Germany.

The opportunity to affiliate itself with one of the few successful and respected national liberation movements had not escaped the USSR's attention. Because of Khrushchev's early hope for revolution in Africa and the USSR's growing competition with China, Moscow had begun low-cost assistance to the PAIGC as early as 1960. Surplus rifles and ammunition shipped to Guinea found their way into the hands of PAIGC guerrillas. A small number of PAIGC cadres received training in the Soviet Union as well as in China, Czechoslovakia, and Algeria beginning in 1960. This Russian material assistance grew steadily throughout the 1960s, and though insignificant on a global scale, it was crucial to the outcome in Guinea-Bissau, a poverty-stricken country of no more than 600,000 inhabitants. Aside from that given by Guinea, no military aid from the newly independent African states was forthcoming. At an OAU meeting in 1964, PAIGC officials openly complained of the lack of tangible support from their liberated brethren. As late as 1970, the budget for the OAU's Liberation Committee, which funneled assistance to black guerrilla movements, was only $2 million for the entire continent. Small wonder, then, that in July 1970, while in Havana, Amilcar Cabral complained to the Cuban press about the "insufficient" aid of the OAU and took the opportunity to praise the Soviet Union, "which gives us almost all the new material, the arms and ammunition, we use in our struggle."[85]

By the end of 1970 this assistance had reached truly substantial proportions, as if to compensate for the fact that Moscow was still unprepared to provide guerrilla instructors and cadres as Cuba did. The weaponry now included long-range mortars, artillery, antiaircraft guns, machine guns, mines, and bazookas. The PAIGC had available as much weaponry as its 6,000 to 7,000 men could use—despite the Portuguese army's capture of fifty tons of Soviet arms in 1969 and another fifty tons in 1970.[86]

Not only did the Soviet Union use the opportunity to assist the PAIGC at the modest cost of surplus weapons, but it also made full use of the struggle in its propaganda war with the West. Verbal attacks escalated beginning in early 1969, as Moscow sought to counter its setbacks in Ghana and Mali and moved to exploit the more conservative policies of the new American and British governments. In an English broadcast beamed to Africa on March 25, 1969, for instance, Radio Moscow attacked the actions of the United States and Britain throughout Africa, criticizing their trade with South Africa, their indifference to the Namibia problem, and their lack of support for Rhodesian sanctions. The broadcast described the "dirty war of the Portuguese colonialists in Africa" as a "joint business undertaking for the Americans and British, who are making fabulous profits from the exploitation of Africans in Angola, Mozambique, and Guinea-Bissau."[87]

On the eve of the Conakry raid, Soviet analysis had moved into a self-congratulatory phase; Moscow seemed convinced that the efforts of the PAIGC and its supporters were about to pay off. A *Pravda* commentator

85. Quoted in Gibson, *African Liberation Movements,* p. 260n.
86. *Keesing's Contemporary Archives,* August 22–29, 1970, p. 24147, and November 13–20, 1971, p. 24940; *Washington Post,* February 21 and April 4, 1971.
87. FBIS, *Daily Report: Soviet Union* (March 27, 1969), p. A40.

wrote on November 12, 1970, that "the Lisbon rulers have been confronted with major successes by the patriots of Guinea (Bissau), whose national-liberation movement is of great significance for the cause to completely eliminate Portuguese colonialism in Africa. . . . Despite NATO assistance and the colonial authorities' use of every neo-colonialist stratagem and effort, the 30,000-man Portuguese army has sustained heavier and heavier losses."[88]

Moscow's growing commitment to, and political exploitation of, the liberation movement in Guinea-Bissau put a new face on its long and stormy relationship with Sekou Touré. Although Moscow no longer saw Touré as the pro-Soviet revolutionary he was taken to be in the 1950s, the late 1960s had brought a gradual warming of relations between the two governments based on converging practical interests. One area of interest was a common commitment to the PAIGC's success. Moscow recognized that Guinea's support was indispensable, since nearly all the PAIGC's supplies from overseas passed through the port of Conakry. *Pravda*'s August 1969 commentary on Guinea-Bissau observed that

in the South and the East the country borders on the Republic of Guinea, and in the North on Senegal. The friendly support of these states is very important to this small people. Aid to the patriots comes through Guinea and Senegal, and the severely wounded are evacuated to these countries. Conferences and meetings of the insurgents are frequently held on these friends' soil, and support bases have been set up there.[89]

Another common interest was bauxite. The Soviet Union had begun to participate in the development of Guinea's vast reserves, despite Moscow's pique at Guinea's deviation from the "socialist path" through agreements with Western corporations. In September 1970 an agreement was signed that called for a joint Soviet-Guinean mining and smelting development sixty-five miles east of Conakry and Soviet rights to import at least 2 million tons of Guinean bauxite for thirty years.[90]

Finally, the Soviet Union's renewed interest in Guinea during 1969–70 appears to have been associated with a more general cyclical trend toward greater Soviet awareness of African affairs, a trend created by a sudden turn of events for the better after successive disappointments in the mid-

88. Pyotr Yevsyukov, "Worthy Response to Lisbon," *Pravda,* November 12, 1970 (in *CDSP,* vol. 22, no. 45, December 8, 1979, p. 20).

89. V. Korovikow, "With Guinea's Guerrillas," *Pravda,* August 3, 1969 (in *CDSP,* vol. 21, no. 31, August 27, 1969, p. 14).

90. For comments on this agreement, see *Africa Contemporary Record, 1969–70,* p. B492, and *1970–71,* p. B374.

sixties. A coup in Sudan in May 1969, a similar power change in Libya in September 1969, and another shift to the left in Somalia in October 1969 led the Soviet press to comment exuberantly on "how logical and promising this path is becoming for many developing countries, notably in Africa."[91]

These broad Soviet political interests in both the PAIGC and Touré's regime were intensified by the events of November 1970. The fragile status of both the PAIGC and Touré became evident when an undisciplined band of invaders was able to wreak havoc on Guinea's capital for twenty-four hours. At the same time, the raid heightened the USSR's opportunity to cultivate closer relationships with African states at the expense of Portugal's embarrassed NATO allies.

During the week following the Conakry invasion, the Soviet Union joined the chorus of African states in demanding the "immediate withdrawal of all Portuguese armed forces from Guinean territory." While this Soviet objective was stated as early as November 22 by the USSR's ambassador to the UN, Yakov Malik, the demand was subsequently repeated by Tass, *Pravda,* and *Izvestiya.*[92] Not until November 30 did the Soviet Union hint that it might assume direct responsibility for deterring future military attacks on Touré and the PAIGC, and that hint came in an authoritative foreign policy address by Communist Party Secretary Leonid Brezhnev commemorating the fiftieth anniversary of Communist rule in Armenia. Buoyed by continuing American withdrawal from Vietnam, Brezhnev argued:

The bloody crimes committed by the imperialists and their hirelings—whether it is the war against the people of Vietnam, the bandit attack on democratic Guinea or the campaigns of terror against liberation forces in other parts of the world—are leading to a situation in which the anti-imperialist solidarity of the masses of people the world over is growing ever stronger.

The Soviet party chief implied that a firm Russian response would be forthcoming in such situations:

Soviet foreign policy . . . takes an implacable stand against any encroachments by the imperialists on the freedom and independence of the peoples and is directed toward administering a vigorous and decisive rebuff to such encroachments. The Soviet Union extends comprehensive support—political, economic and other kinds of support—to countries and peoples against which imperialist

91. R. Ulyanovsky, "Decolonization: Results and Prospects," *Pravda,* November 12, 1970 (in *CDSP,* vol. 22, no. 45, December 8, 1970, p. 16).

92. Ambassador Malik's statement is in *United Nations Security Council Official Records,* 1558th meeting, November 22, 1970, p. 13.

aggression is directed. . . . Joint actions by the freedom-loving and anti-imperialist forces in rebuffing aggression are the best means for sobering the extreme hotheads and adventurists in the imperialist camp, for preventing the unleashing of new "local" wars and their development into a war threat to all mankind. Life convincingly proves this.[93]

Brezhnev's remarks appeared to be addressed specifically to recent events in Guinea.

The Soviet Union's desire to arrange a "joint" deterrence effort against further Portuguese military action was clear in a statement unanimously approved by the heads of state of the USSR, Rumania, Poland, Hungary, East Germany, Czechoslovakia, and Bulgaria at the December 2 meeting of the Warsaw Pact countries. Published in the December 4 issues of *Pravda* and *Izvestiya,* the statement took cognizance of Portugal's attempt to "overthrow the progressive regime in Guinea" and "to retard the liberation struggle of the peoples of Guinea (Bissau), Angola, Mozambique, South Africa, Zimbabwe and Namibia." The invasion, the Warsaw Pact leaders argued, proved the importance of redoubling efforts toward the ultimate objective: "The imperialist aggression against Guinea demonstrates once again the insistent necessity of the speediest possible and complete liquidation of the colonial and racist regimes." And "in the struggle for their liberation, the African peoples can continue to count on assistance from the socialist states."[94]

The central importance of the Brezhnev speech and Warsaw Pact declaration became clear at the UN on December 5 as the Security Council took up the issue of action in response to the recently completed UN investigation of the invasion. Ambassador Malik asked rhetorically, "What must be done? What measures must be taken?" and then proceeded to quote the Soviet party leader's demand for "combined action" to ward off "adventurist hotheads." Malik referred to the Warsaw Pact statement of December 2—which was subsequently circulated for all to read—and quoted the pledge of "assistance from the socialist States." He repeated the ultimate Soviet objective: "It is becoming more obvious than ever that, until there is no longer a single colonial regime or colonial bridge-head on the African continent and until all troops have been withdrawn and all colonial military bases dismantled, the peaceful and inde-

93. Leonid I. Brezhnev, "Fifty Years of Soviet Armenia," *Pravda* and *Izvestiya,* November 30, 1970 (in *CDSP,* vol. 22, no. 49, January 5, 1971, pp. 2, 3).

94. "Statement on Putting an End to Imperialist Provocation Against Independent Africa," *Pravda* and *Izvestiya,* December 4, 1970 (in *CDSP,* vol. 22, no. 49, January 5, 1971, p. 5).

pendent existence and the development of the African States will be in danger."[95]

If any doubt existed about the Soviet Union's stand, it should have been dispelled on December 8 with the passage of UN Security Council Resolution 290. With the United States, the United Kingdom, France, and Spain abstaining, the resolution was approved with the hearty support of the USSR, third world countries, and several usually pro-Western regimes. Of the many elements in the resolution, the following were the most important to Soviet interests: "The Security Council"

4. *Appeals* to all States to render moral and material assistance to the Republic of Guinea to strengthen and defend its independence and territorial integrity;

5. *Declares* that the presence of Portuguese colonialism on the African continent is a serious threat to the peace and security of independent African States;

6. *Urges* all States to refrain from providing the Government of Portugal with any military and material assistance enabling it to continue its repressive actions against the peoples of the Territories under its domination and against independent African States;

7. *Calls upon* the Government of Portugal to apply without further delay to the peoples of the Territories under its domination the principles of self-determination and independence in accordance with the relevant resolutions of the Security Council and General Assembly resolution 1514 (XV);

8. *Solemnly warns* the Government of Portugal that in the event of any repetition of armed attacks against independent African States, the Security Council shall immediately consider appropriate effective steps or measures in accordance with the relevant provisions of the United Nations Charter.[96]

With formal adoption of Resolution 290, the full text was transmitted by cablegram to the governments of Portugal and Guinea.

The debate during the December 5–8 sessions of the Security Council gave the Soviet Union ample opportunity to clarify the nature of its objectives in the struggle between Portugal and the PAIGC and its supporters. However, the extent to which the Soviet Union was willing to act alone in this matter was not carefully spelled out in the debates. Moscow had vigorously but unsuccessfully advocated collective action in the form of mandatory economic sanctions against Portugal by the Security Council. And as a future deterrent Malik had called for a formal commitment

95. Quoted from *United Nations Security Council Official Records,* 1560th meeting, December 5, 1970, pp. 13–15.

96. The text of Security Council Resolution 290 can be found in *UN Monthly Chronicle,* vol. 8 (January 1971), pp. 18–19.

to military "demonstrations, blockade, and other operations by air, sea or land forces of members of the United Nations" if economic sanctions "do not produce the proper results and if Portugal persists in its acts of aggression against African states."[97]

It was impossible to determine during the UN debates whether the Soviet Union was merely playing to a gallery of sympathetic African states, knowing full well that the NATO allies would veto any collective punishment of Portugal. Therefore, a more credible sign of Moscow's willingness to defend Touré and the PAIGC was actual military action undertaken the first week of December. Several events occurred during this period to set off a Soviet military response. Following the November 27–28 ground battle in northern Guinea, Touré made a private request for military support from the Soviet Union and the United States. While this in itself might have sufficed to precipitate Soviet action, the Russians may have feared that the American government would unexpectedly pre-empt the Soviet role of third world protector. Finally, by the beginning of December it was well known at the UN that the recently completed mission to Guinea was drafting a final report that would demonstrate Portuguese culpability in the attack. All of these factors laid the foundation for a low-risk Soviet military response that would simultaneously signal Portugal, Guinea, and the PAIGC.

During the last week of November, a Soviet destroyer was detached from the Mediterranean fleet and sent around the West African bulge. Stopping first at Dakar, Senegal, immediately north of Guinea-Bissau, it was joined by a Soviet oiler also sent to the area. When a second Soviet destroyer arrived, the three ships began cruising the waters off Senegal, Guinea-Bissau, and Guinea-Conakry. On December 24 the three ships entered Conakry harbor without publicity and berthed in a remote section of the port. On December 30 the three ships slipped out of Conakry harbor for the return voyage to the Mediterranean.[98]

In succeeding months several similar cruises off Portuguese Guinea were made by two Soviet destroyers and an oiler. These missions were apparently prompted by Touré's continuing fear of invasion and by specific requests to the Soviet embassy for a show of military support. The

97. *United Nations Security Council Official Records*, 1560th meeting, December 5, 1970, p. 15.
98. Unpublished manuscript by Charles C. Petersen of the Center for Naval Analyses; MccGwire, "Foreign-Port Visits," p. 403; Dismukes, "Soviet Employment of Naval Power," p. 505.

USSR's first naval patrol in December was followed by three similar missions between February and the end of July 1971. Each deployment started from the Soviet Mediterranean fleet and consisted of from one to three destroyers. The locus of naval activity was adjacent to Portuguese Guinea—the area through which any new seaborne invasion of Guinea-Conakry or Senegal could be expected to travel.[99]

The Soviet media were silent about these deployments, perhaps suggesting high-level effort to control the risks involved. The possibility of a confrontation with Portugal could not be ruled out, and although NATO forces would be unlikely to join, Portugal had a sizable navy. Soviet silence may also have indicated some ambivalence about identification with Touré's regime. Although the Guinean leader had gained enormous sympathy in both the East and West as a result of the raid, a good deal of this sentiment began to evaporate in January—at least in the West—as the African nation seethed with mass arrests, "show" trials, and public hangings. Finally, Touré was noted for his quixotic independence, and any suggestion from Moscow that the Guinean leader had become dependent on Soviet military power might quickly have produced the opposite effect.

During the months following the Conakry raid, other steps were taken by the USSR to enhance the ability of its clients to deter or resist attack. In January 1971, presumably in response to Touré's November 25 request for aerial defense, three additional MIG-17 fighters were dispatched to Guinea, bringing the number of Soviet-donated planes of this type to eleven. However, as another Russian risk-avoidance measure, Nigerian and Algerian pilots assumed command of these planes, and they immediately began harassment sorties over the Portuguese-controlled towns of Guinea-Bissau.[100] The flow of arms, particularly defensive arms for Touré's army, also increased with the arrival of three more coastal patrol ships, tanks, antiaircraft guns, and radar equipment. One can only speculate about whether the simultaneous arrival of additional Cuban cadres for the PAIGC represented the active coordination of Soviet-Cuban military policy.

99. Abram N. Shulsky and others, "Coercive Naval Diplomacy, 1967–1974," in Bradford Dismukes and James McConnell, eds., *Soviet Naval Diplomacy* (Pergamon, 1979), p. 130; Dismukes, "Soviet Employment of Naval Power," p. 488.

100. Al J. Venter, *Portugal's Guerrilla War* (Cape Town, South Africa: John Malherbe, 1973), pp. 29, 84.

As during their previous naval deployment to West Africa in February 1969, the Russians seized low-risk opportunities both to improve their relations with other governments and to advance the liberation cause. Port calls by Soviet destroyers to Dakar in December 1970, twice in 1971, and at least six times in 1972 seem to fit this pattern. Leopold Senghor, the president of Senegal, was a supporter of decolonization but had refused to permit the PAIGC to operate military bases or receive arms shipments in Senegal. As the Portuguese stepped up their punitive attacks on guerrilla sanctuaries in Senegal during 1969–70, Senghor tried to protect his countrymen by closing down PAIGC offices and using his army to curb the PAIGC border movements that prompted Portuguese attacks.[101] Thus the visit of Soviet destroyers beginning in 1970 may have been designed to strengthen Senghor's courage in the face of Portugal's increasingly aggressive strategy and threatening events in Conakry.

There is evidence, in fact, that Senghor's support for the PAIGC cause began to increase in 1971, although several competing explanations for this policy change exist. Portuguese intelligence saw it as Senghor's attempt to deflect attention from his nation's deteriorating economic situation. But the surprisingly strong reaction of Africa and the UN to the Conakry raid also encouraged such a shift. Soviet port visits are likely to have played only a minor role in Senghor's change of heart, given the existing security provided by substantial French military forces in the Dakar area and a standing French pledge to assist Senegal against civil disorder.[102]

Beginning in September 1971, Soviet naval activity in West Africa showed signs of expansion and reorientation. The operational focus of the USSR's West Africa Patrol was shifted away from Portuguese Guinea and relocated at Conakry harbor. A Soviet destroyer, tank landing ship, and oiler took up permanent stations in the area. Port calls at Conakry became frequent and long; Portuguese intelligence reported that Soviet naval officers were often seen in the Guinean capital.[103]

Moscow's expansion and relocation of naval activity at Conakry represented not only an immediate response to Touré's latest charge of impend-

101. *Washington Post,* May 16, 1971; *Africa Contemporary Record, 1970–71,* p. B437; Nelson and others, *Area Handbook for Guinea,* p. 324.

102. Venter, *Portugal's Guerrilla War,* p. 187; *Keesing's Contemporary Archives* (November 13–20, 1972), p. 24940.

103. Petersen manuscript; Dismukes and McConnell, *Soviet Naval Diplomacy; Daily Telegraph* (London), October 28, 1971.

ing invasion but also, more important, a growing appreciation of Guinea's long-term potential as a forward military facility. The establishment of a permanent Russian naval facility along the West African bulge would permit more efficient and broader sea and air surveillance of the deployment areas for U.S. submarines in the Central and South Atlantic and facilitate wartime interdiction of the vital sea-lanes running between North America and the Mediterranean, Europe, and the Middle East. A facility in West African waters would largely offset the otherwise necessary transit of the hostile Greenland-Iceland-United Kingdom gap by Russian ships and perhaps submarines to reach stations in the Atlantic.[104]

In late 1971, however, Touré rejected a Soviet request that the USSR be permitted to build a permanent naval facility on Tamara Island, just off the coast near Conakry. Various sources have reported attempts by the Soviet navy since then to gain Touré's support for this project. One instance of this was reported by the London *Daily Mail* in January 1976, prompting Tass to hotly deny that the Soviet Union was building such a submarine base.[105]

Also supporting the proposition of significant expansion of Soviet objectives in Guinea has been the use of the port of Conakry for activities of little relevance to Touré, the PAIGC, or even West Africa generally. Kelly, for instance, has reported seven separate visits by Soviet submarines to Guinea between 1969 and 1973—most frequently, presumably, for replenishment and crew rest.[106] Submarine tenders have been deployed to the Gulf of Guinea since 1972, in association with annual fleet exercises.[107] Conakry has served as a replenishment stop for Soviet ships in transit to the Caribbean, the South Atlantic, and the Indian Ocean. An augmented West Africa Patrol was employed in the Gulf of Guinea and off the Angolan coast during the Angolan civil war, apparently to deter interference with arms and troop deliveries to the port of Luanda.[108]

104. For the details of these arguments, see Robert G. Weinland, "The State and Future of the Soviet Navy in the North Atlantic," in MccGwire and McDonnell, *Soviet Naval Influence,* p. 417.

105. For references to the Tamara Island issue, see *NAVSCAN* (Washington, D.C.: Department of Navy, Naval Intelligence Support Center), September 1, 1974, p. 2; *Le Monde,* January 31, 1974; *Christian Science Monitor,* January 13, 1976; *Africa Contemporary Record, 1976–77,* p. B594.

106. Anne M. Kelly, "Port Visits and the Internationalist Mission of the Soviet Navy" in MccGwire and McDonnell, *Soviet Naval Influence,* p. 52.

107. Petersen manuscript.

108. Michael MccGwire, "Naval Power and Soviet Oceans Policy," in *Soviet Oceans Development* (GPO, 1976), p. 143n.

Finally, the Soviet Union has used Guinean airfields in the pursuit of its strategic and broader African objectives. Under the direction of Cuban engineers, Conakry airport was expanded and improved in 1972–73, and upon its completion in July 1973, the Soviet navy immediately began using the new airfield for long-range reconnaissance flights of the mid-Atlantic to pinpoint the positions of U.S. ships and submarines.[109] During the 1973 Middle Eastern war, Soviet reconnaissance aircraft operating from Conakry helped keep track of U.S. naval movements to the Mediterranean. Other flights have been flown in conjunction with fleet exercises of the Soviet navy and, again during the Angolan war, over shipping lanes between the Caribbean and western Africa. On several occasions, these flights were coordinated with similar operations flown over the western Atlantic from Cuba.[110] The Angolan war enlarged the role that air facilities in Guinea could play in support of Soviet political and military interests. Soviet military aid airlifted to Angola during the war was staged through Conakry, and MIG-15s based in Guinea for the training of the Guinean air force were used by Soviet pilots for surveillance of the troops of the Western-backed factions in Angola.[111]

Portugal's Response

What can be said of Portugal's reaction to the Conakry raid and subsequent events? Lisbon immediately reacted by denying any responsibility for the attempted coup. Statements to this effect were promptly issued by General Spinola in Bissau, by the Portuguese foreign minister in Brussels, and by the Portuguese ambassador at the United Nations.[112]

Lisbon had good reasons for attempting to dissociate itself from any responsibility for the Conakry raid, for this unsuccessful aggression endangered Portugal's vital political, economic, and military links to the other North Atlantic nations. Portugal's ability to field and supply a sophisticated colonial army of 140,000 soldiers rested squarely on a continuing tide of military imports and domestic economic growth made possible only by American and European trade and direct investment. Seventy percent of its trade was with North Atlantic markets, and direct investment from the United States, France, West Germany, and the

109. Petersen manuscript.
110. *New York Times,* December 6, 1973, and November 19, 1977.
111. Kelly, "Port Visits," p. 528; *New York Times,* January 19, 1976.
112. FBIS, *Daily Report* (November 23, 1970), p. X1.

United Kingdom had helped foster the relative prosperity of the 1960s. As the UN vote on Resolution 290 indicated, only these NATO allies stood between Portugal's colonial practices and ostracism by the international community.[113]

Events during and following the Security Council debates of December 4–8, 1970, indicated that any repetition of the Conakry raid would seriously impair Portugal's vital relations with the Western powers. At the UN, "the delegates of the United States and Britain made it clear that they did not care to defend Portugal against the charges made against her."[114] The American, British, and French ambassadors ultimately acknowledged the veracity of the Security Council's investigative report. Western diplomats saw the affair "as extremely damaging to member countries in NATO."[115] When the presence of the West Africa Patrol was reported in the United States in February 1972, State Department officials implied that American economic interests in Guinea were more important than U.S. support for Portugal's African policy. According to the *Washington Post,* "the State Department is anxious to avoid any complications that might lead Touré's socialist regime to seize American aluminum companies. They have a $150-million investment in Guinea's booming bauxite and aluminum industry." State Department officials expressed no disapproval of the fact that "the Soviet task force is there primarily to protect Touré's regime from another invasion from neighboring Portuguese Guinea."[116]

Such lack of allied political and military support deterred Portugal's military strategy as much as did the objective military power interposed by Moscow after December 1970. In the spring of 1971 Portuguese Foreign Minister Patricio scoffed at claims that NATO support enabled Lisbon to carry on its African wars: "It is not true. We are complaining to our NATO allies that they don't give us any support. They won't even give us political support in Africa."[117] A *Washington Post* correspondent touring Guinea-Bissau, Angola, and Mozambique during the weeks following

113. A useful compilation of information on the relative importance of African and North Atlantic ties to Portugal's well-being can be found in "Portuguese Africa," *Africa Institute Bulletin,* vol. 12, no. 6 (1974).

114. *New York Times,* December 2, 1970.

115. *Christian Science Monitor,* December 2, 1970; *New York Times,* December 9, 1970.

116. *Washington Post,* February 9, 1972.

117. Quoted in *Washington Post,* April 4, 1971.

the Conakry raid quoted Portuguese officers as saying: "We should go get the guerrillas. . . . But if we did what the Americans do in Cambodia and Laos, the whole world would scream at us—including the Americans."[118]

There can be little doubt that the possibility of a military clash with the Soviet navy was an additional reason for Lisbon's lack of direct military action to stop Touré's considerable support of the PAIGC. In taking this new factor into account, Lisbon would only have been echoing the U.S. Navy's concern at the time that Portugal, should it sponsor another attack, might wind up facing the USSR alone.[119] But it is essential to recognize that Portuguese fear of possible Soviet action could not be separated from simultaneous fear of pressure from all points of the globe—from NATO, from several African states, from the United Nations, and from other Communist states such as China and Cuba. One high-ranking Portuguese official described his government's problem in the spring of 1971: "We can't afford to internationalize these conflicts any more than they already are. It would be more dangerous for us in the long run. Most of our trouble now comes from outside involvement in Portuguese problems."[120]

Other factors reinforced Portugal's hesitancy to sponsor another invasion of Guinea-Conakry. A major consideration was Lisbon's belief that there was an alternative strategy to that of eliminating the leadership of Guinea and the PAIGC. While the invasion planned by General Spinola held out the immediate possibility of "final victory" in the guerrilla war, the battlefield situation in Portuguese Guinea was by no means as desperate as was claimed by Portugal's enemies. Under General Spinola's leadership, Portugal's military position in Guinea-Bissau had gradually improved after 1968. Control of the countryside had stalemated in a rough parity between the government and the guerrillas, with the Portuguese army free to move where it chose.

Meanwhile, through new expenditures for roads, agriculture, industry, and media services, Spinola seemed to be making headway in the long-term battle for the "hearts and minds" of the native population. This apparently optimistic military picture in 1970–72 permitted Lisbon to

118. Quoted by Jim Hoagland, "Lisbon Hitting Rebel Bases," *Washington Post,* May 16, 1971.
119. For evidence of this concern, see Zumwalt, *On Watch,* p. 332; Weinland, "Changing Mission Structure of the Soviet Navy," p. 14; and *Washington Post,* February 9, 1972.
120. Quoted in *Washington Post,* May 16, 1971.

take a less anxious view of Touré's support of the PAIGC guerrillas.[121] Only with the increasing sophistication of the Cuban-trained PAIGC and the USSR's introduction of hand-held surface-to-air missiles and heavy artillery did the military situation shift decisively against Portugal in late 1972. Portuguese casualties began to rise rapidly as the PAIGC made massed assaults on isolated outposts, bombarded previously secure towns, and neutralized Portuguese jets and helicopters with surface-to-air missiles.[122]

Other factors militated against a repetition of the Conakry raid. For one thing, 1971 and 1972 were years when moderate leaders in Africa spoke of a "dialogue" with the white regimes that would avert a bloody war, and Portugal was loath to take any action that would undercut this gesture. Then, too, the Guinean exiles had proved to be rather incompetent soldiers. And in Lisbon the first serious signs of an effective antiwar movement were beginning to appear. By spring 1971, the *Washington Post* could report from Portugal that "students have begun to hold mild protest rallies, labor unions are less forthright in their support for the wars, and the number of army deserters and draft evaders has reached the point of being publicly mentioned by defense officials as a national shame."[123] Sabotage of Portuguese military equipment and NATO installations began in the winter of 1970–71, and the terrorism had reached such proportions by November 1971 that Prime Minister Caetano declared a "state of subversion" and postponed several long-awaited political reforms.[124]

Thus, while it seems likely that the presence of Soviet naval power in Guinean waters from December 1970 on was of some influence in the caution Lisbon exercised after the Conakry raid, this is a deterrent influence that cannot be disentangled from other important forces all pointing in the same direction: the complete lack of allied support for any offensive activities beyond Portuguese Guinea, a stabilizing military situation in Guinea-Bissau, the growing support of other African and Communist

121. This battlefield picture, somewhat at variance with the politically motivated descriptions provided by PAIGC supporters, can be found in Bruce, *Portugal,* and Jim Hoagland, "Portugal's Wars in Africa," *Washington Post,* April 27, 1971.

122. The appearance of Soviet missiles is noted in the *Christian Science Monitor,* June 5 and November 15, 1973. For the increase in Portuguese casualties, see *Keesing's Contemporary Archives* (September 10–16, 1973), p. 26088.

123. *Washington Post,* May 2, 1971.

124. On war protest and sabotage in Portugal, see *Washington Post,* June 4, 1971, and *Christian Science Monitor,* March 31, 1971.

states for the PAIGC and Touré, the near adoption of formal sanctions against Portugal by the UN after the first raid, the growth of an antiwar movement in Portugal, and the military ineffectiveness of the Guinean exiles.

The Guinean Response

As described by Claude Riviere, an international authority on Guinean affairs:

Sekou Touré's constant preoccupation with a possible attack by the imperialists and his obsessive fear of a domestic counterrevolution . . . could hardly promote fraternal cooperation with other states. At every turn, their leaders risked being accused of helping imperialism, or tolerating neocolonialism, or trying to undermine Guinea internally, either by giving asylum to Guinean emigres or by plotting to wreak the Guinean revolution.[125]

Such fear of attack and continuous alienation of potential African allies gave the Soviet Union bargaining power that it could use in pursuing its interests in and beyond Guinea.

There is no evidence to suggest that the Russians attempted to exploit Touré's fears during the first nine months of occasional naval protection. But the financial costs of their support steadily increased as Guinea made repeated requests for aid and evidence accumulated that the threat to Guinea's president was as much internal as external. Touré himself told the nation on the first anniversary of the Conakry raid that among those arrested after the attack were "sixteen Ministers, five former Ministers, several provincial governors, a large number of high-ranking officials, and most high-ranking officers of the Guinean Army."[126] To provide Touré with continuous protection from external and internal attack and to reduce the burden of frequent operations in the region, Moscow proposed to relocate the West Africa Patrol at Conakry and requested access to support facilities there. Because of the added security this change provided against his foreign and domestic enemies, it is not surprising that Touré gave his consent.

Other privileges subsequently extended to the Soviet Union seem easily explained by Touré's dedication to African liberation and his fear of counterrevolution. Permission to expand Conakry airport in 1972 to facilitate Soviet use jibes with Touré's fear of Portuguese air attack on the

125. Riviere, *Guinea*, p. 123.
126. *Africa Contemporary Record, 1976–77*, p. B589; *Keesing's Contemporary Archives* (July 8–15, 1972), p. 25353.

capital. His entrustment of the control of Guinea's planes and naval ships to foreign advisers and his use of Cuban bodyguards seem compatible with his deep and perhaps justifiable suspicion of the military's loyalty. And in light of Touré's unswerving support for African liberation movements as well as his espousal of the struggle against Portuguese colonialism, it is difficult to believe that Guinea's behavior during the Angolan war demonstrated undue Soviet influence. After Touré's announcement that he had sent troops to fight beside the Popular Movement for the Liberation of Angola (MPLA), it is not surprising that he permitted Soviet use of his airport and seaport in the same cause.[127]

Counterbalancing Touré's natural receptivity to anti-Western and pro-socialist causes has always been his fierce dedication to national and personal autonomy and the particular economic needs of African peoples. This has influenced his leadership since 1958, when Guinea alone chose independence from France rather than membership in a Franco-African community. The result of Touré's militant nationalism has been constant wariness of overdepending on any single benefactor and a deliberate exploitation of great-power rivalries for the economic gain of Guinea. Tactically, this nationalist policy has operated in a complex web of economic and military relationships with numerous Communist and capitalist states, often with impulsive ruptures in Guinea's foreign relations to counter excessive dependency and foreign indifference. Guinean concessions to the great powers have therefore often come in pairs, such as matching U.S. exploitation of the Boké bauxite deposits with a comparable mining agreement with the Soviet Union. Diplomatic rupture has been an inevitable risk of doing business with Touré, one that even the Soviet Union has not managed to avoid despite its historically close relations. In 1961 the Russian ambassador was expelled because of his opposition to Touré's flirtation with the Kennedy administration and the apparently overzealous Soviet propagandizing of Guinean youth.[128]

Touré's sensitivity to national dependence has been reflected in his reaction to Soviet requests since November 1970. The most obvious is his consistent refusal to grant Moscow the right to construct and use a naval base on Tamara Island. One method Touré has adopted to offset this Soviet pressure has been receptivity to Chinese offers of naval assistance. In 1973 a Chinese advisory mission was accepted, and in 1973–74 China

127. On Guinean troops in Angola, see *Africa Contemporary Record, 1975–76,* p. A29.

128. On Touré's strategy of counterbalancing the great powers, see Riviere, *Guinea,* pp. 141–71.

gave Guinea four coastal attack ships. These transfers have served to remind Moscow that other sources of aid are available.[129]

The Soviet Union, to be sure, is aware of Touré's tenacious independence; the unpredictable cost of violating it may explain Moscow's general refusal to take any public credit for the accomplishments of the West Africa Patrol. For this reason, the liberation war in Guinea-Bissau was a useful facade for both Touré and the USSR, with each hiding less idealistic interests in the West Africa Patrol behind the veil of support for the PAIGC and threat of external invasion. It must surely be concern for Touré's sensitivity that has made Moscow react so petulantly to leaked newspaper accounts of the possibility of a Soviet naval base on Tamara Island.

The USSR's contributions to Touré's external and internal security have provided leverage transferable into some Russian gains. The use of Conakry harbor for replenishment of Soviet submarines, naval combatants, and merchant ships passing through the region or participating in fleet exercises appears to be a clear gain little related to Touré's interests, as was the use of Conakry airport for Soviet navy long-range reconnaissance flights over the mid-Atlantic. Such flights were surely of negligible service to Guinea's interests, too.

Even these Soviet gains have proved to be fragile, however. With the end of the war in Guinea-Bissau and a decline in the fighting in Angola, the relative influence in Guinea of Soviet military protection and Western economic power has gradually shifted to the advantage of the latter. A serious disagreement emerged between Moscow and Conakry in 1976 over the low Russian prices paid for purchases of Guinean bauxite. Touré's socialist economic strategy and the continuing West African drought cut deeply into agricultural output and resulted in violent hunger demonstrations in August 1977 which shook the very foundations of the Guinean government. As a consequence, Touré commenced a fundamental reorientation of his foreign and domestic policies which is still in progress. In a major signal to the West, Touré ended Soviet use of Guinea for long-range reconnaissance flights in September 1977 and Cuban use of Conakry airport for transporting troops to and from Africa, and reduced Soviet naval operations allowed out of Conakry harbor. Missions were dispatched to the Western powers in search of economic assistance, and new liberalized terms were extended to foreign capital investors. Guinea's highly uncertain future as a staging area for Soviet military

129. The Chinese transfer of attack ships is noted in John E. Moore, ed., *Jane's Fighting Ships, 1976–1977* (Franklin Watts, 1976), p. 218.

activities prompted Moscow to look for other facilities in Mali, Sierra
Leone, Benin, and Guinea-Bissau.[130]

The PAIGC Response

Although Soviet military power appeared to be most directly aimed at
deterring Portugal and exploiting Touré's internal vulnerability, the
PAIGC leadership was an important secondary target of Soviet military
action. Air and naval facilities at Bissau and on the Cape Verde Islands
three hundred miles west of Dakar were of potential strategic value comparable to, if not greater than, those in Guinea-Conakry. These bases may
have become more important to the USSR in the 1970s because of Touré's
refusal to allow it to use Tamara. And the respect that Amilcar Cabral
and the PAIGC commanded throughout Africa and other states of the
third world and increasingly in the West made defense of his movement
a sound investment in Soviet global influence.

As noted, Moscow provided a steady stream of increasingly sophisticated weaponry and equipment until Guinea-Bissau's official independence from Portugal on September 10, 1974. In fact, the leadership core
of the PAIGC was saved from extinction by the West Africa Patrol on
January 20, 1973, when Amilcar Cabral was assassinated in Conakry by
a faction of PAIGC dissidents and Portuguese collaborators, and many
of his senior lieutenants were herded onto three boats bound for Portuguese Guinea. Alerted by Guinean and Cuban authorities, the Soviet navy
was able to intercept the assassins after a chase at sea.[131] However, in accordance with the low profile tacitly agreed to for the West Africa Patrol,
credit for this rescue was publicly given to the "Guinean Navy" or "Conakry naval units" by official spokesmen.[132]

Although the USSR assisted into power PAIGC leaders who tended to
share some of its international causes—for example, the liberation of
southern Africa and support for the Palestine Liberation Organization—
the lure of continued Soviet support after independence apparently did
not alter the PAIGC's definition of its own interests. Despite much consternation in NATO that the USSR would be granted at least as much
military access to Bissau and the Cape Verde Islands as was received in

130. *Africa Contemporary Record, 1976–77*, pp. B598–600; *West Africa*, May 8,
1978, p. 873; *New York Times*, November 19, 1977.
131. Shulsky and others, "Coercive Naval Diplomacy, 1967–1974," p. 131.
132. *Africa Confidential*, June 23, 1978, pp. 4–5, November 3, 1978, pp. 3–5,
and March 28, 1979, pp. 1–2; *New York Times*, November 19, 1977.

Conakry, the PAIGC rigidly denied foreign military traffic any routine use of facilities in Guinea-Bissau or the right to establish military bases there. The new state of Guinea-Bissau was as much preoccupied with economic matters as it was with military security, owing in part to the ravages of the long war and ten years of uninterrupted drought on the Cape Verde archipelago. Leaders in Bissau recognized that their economic well-being depended on broadening their previously narrow circle of benefactors to include the wealthier industrial nations of the West. As a result of vigorous PAIGC solicitation, the United States, Sweden, the Netherlands, Denmark, West Germany, and France all made important trade or aid concessions to the new nation. There has been little evidence that the Soviet Union has been able to translate its extensive military support of the PAIGC during the early 1970s into direct influence over the foreign policy of Guinea-Bissau.[133]

Significance of Outcomes

The Portuguese Guinea war has special significance in that the actual deployment of Soviet naval combatants to the area for deterrence represented a level of military involvement in third world affairs that went beyond the Soviet Union's normal inclination to operate *through* client governments and movements. The attempt to constrain Portuguese military reaction—while at the same time arming the PAIGC, the Cubans, and the Guineans for military action against Portuguese Guinea—represented a quasi-offensive action and a potential for *direct* combat involvement out of character with the historic focus of the Soviet Union on its responsibilities in Europe and Asia.

Soviet actions in the vicinity of Guinea do not suggest, however, that Russian leaders had abandoned their traditionally cautious management of the risks associated with the use of military power. It is an exaggeration, for instance, to argue, as has Admiral Zumwalt, that after the Conakry raid "the Soviets did not hesitate, in a part of the seas quite remote from their sources of supply, to challenge a member of an alliance accustomed to maritime supremacy."[134] In reality, the USSR did hesitate for at least ten days before committing ships to the area—until international events had clarified the risks and gains of such a deployment. By the time the first

133. For foreign aid to Guinea-Bissau, see Tony Hodges, "Guinea-Bissau: Five Years of Independence," *Africa Report* (January-February 1979), pp. 7–9.
134. Zumwalt, *On Watch*, p. 332.

Soviet destroyers arrived in early December, a number of events had greatly reduced the dangers of this action: an overwhelming show of international support for Guinea had emerged; even NATO members like the United States had made sympathetic gestures to Touré; the UN was in the process of formally accusing and condemning Portugal; and the Guinean president had made both public and private requests for military support. To these risk-minimizing factors could be added considerations of longer standing, such as the restriction of NATO's operational zone to an area north of the Tropic of Cancer (that is, some eight hundred miles north of Portuguese Guinea); increasing constraints on the U.S. commitment of military power to third world conflicts; and formal UN General Assembly encouragement of direct support to liberation movements in Portuguese Africa after December 1965.

Even under such favorable circumstances, the West Africa Patrol during its first year hardly seemed the naval "challenge" suggested by Zumwalt. No Soviet announcement was made of the presence or purpose of the ships, which provided an opportunity for face-saving withdrawal if there had been an actual Portuguese reaction or a NATO counterdeployment. During its first phase, which lasted until September 1971, the USSR did not provide Touré and the PAIGC with a permanent military deterrent but deployed ships in the area temporarily, in response to specific requests. And when the patrol assumed a permanent character in September 1971, its relocation toward Conakry not only increased its capability for intervening in Guinea's internal affairs but also reduced the risk of an inadvertent clash at sea with Portuguese ships off Guinea-Bissau.

Another element of the USSR's cautious opportunism during the Portuguese Guinea war was its willingness to commit mobile naval power for deterrence purposes but its consistent refusal to commit ground forces, which Cuba had done. This pattern has been repeated in other African states. In response to requests for military support from friendly regimes, Touré airlifted soldiers to Sierra Leone in March 1971 and to Benin in January 1977. At least on the first occasion, when internal order was restored several weeks later, the Soviet Union dispatched a naval combatant to this country as a show of friendship and support for the shaky regime and quite possibly as a sign of approval for Guinea's peacekeeping action. Similar timing prevailed during the Angolan civil war.[135]

Finally, the composition and operation of the West Africa Patrol suggests that the USSR, though reluctant to use its own ground forces in third

135. *Africa Contemporary Record, 1976–77*, pp. A84–90.

world countries, is more prepared to do so in internal support of a threatened client regime than in transgressing an international boundary to remove a hostile regime. Only after the West Africa Patrol was relocated in Conakry in September 1971 was a tank landing ship added to the Soviet combatants. The presence of this vessel suggested a conditional willingness to intervene directly in Guinean politics, which was never evident in Soviet assistance directed against Portugal.

Soviet military actions in West Africa after the Conakry raid proved to be of marginal importance to American politics. Not only were Americans generally predisposed against any additional overseas commitments, but few U.S. politicians and citizens were even dimly aware of Soviet activities in the area. A news blackout on the topic was in force at the White House and the State Department, as Nixon administration officials struggled to maintain working relations with both Portugal and Guinea. Only when the Soviet navy made extensive use of Conakry airport for long-range reconnaissance missions during the 1973 Middle East war did the Pentagon leak word of the USSR's military use of Guinea.[136] Not until December 1975, when once again Moscow effectively used Guinea's air and sea facilities in support of its Angolan intervention, did significant discussion of Touré's military relationship with the Soviet Union appear in the press.[137]

The Conakry raid and its aftermath marked another occasion when the interests of black African states were vigorously defended by the Soviet bloc and opposed by the North Atlantic states. The lack of an overt response from the United States and its allies allowed the Soviet Union to adopt the appearance of effectively deterring a future attack, although my analysis suggests that many other, probably more important factors contributed to the absence of invasion. The Soviet Union gained access to Guinean facilities useful to its broad interests both in Africa and strategically. For its part, the United States helped this process by refusing to openly choose sides in the struggle, though most of the world had concluded Portugal was in error.

Conclusion

In general, the Soviet Union's use of military power in the two cases examined here was successful in attaining its objectives. Although favor-

136. The first major U.S. story appeared in the *New York Times,* December 6, 1973.

137. *New York Times,* December 10 and 14, 1975, and January 19, 1976.

able outcomes were largely the product of political and economic factors, Soviet military power did apparently have a reinforcing effect and was used without incurring any significant costs. Of even greater long-range importance, the missions gave the illusion of decisive military influence and thus established with such important observers as President Sekou Touré and the U.S. Navy the presumption of Soviet military potency and credibility. The USSR's success was principally a function of its own sophisticated tactics. The objectives for Soviet naval power were established at a modest level—the return of two Russian ships and the deterrence of an unlikely second Portuguese invasion. Also, these objectives were pursued in an area of the world where the United States had no vital interests at the time. The USSR's subtlety further reduced risk. Naval power was deployed only when the passage of time had helped clarify potential benefits and costs. In the trawlers incident, military signals were resorted to only after the use of diplomatic and economic instruments had failed. The mission to Portuguese Guinea was in highly attractive circumstances, which emerged following the attempted invasion. In neither case was naval power employed in a binding fashion. Instead, force potential was modest and inconspicuous, public information was tightly controlled and restricted, targets were permitted to draw their own inferences, and port visits were employed to obfuscate intent (Nigeria) or pursue collateral opportunities (Senegal, Sierra Leone).

The lessons Soviet leaders learned from these deployments are difficult to decipher because of the dearth of Soviet commentary. It seems plausible to conclude that the lack of Western reaction to the first Soviet deployment to the Gulf of Guinea in February and March 1969 emphasized for Moscow the limited stakes the NATO allies had in that region and the improbability that they would react militarily to a more daring mission against Portugal in December 1970. A wider range of Soviet conclusions probably resulted from the Guinean experience. Soviet behavior after the Conakry raid suggests a growing awareness that the survival of African clients—notably those committed to internal or external revolution—depended on a more substantial commitment of Soviet armed might than had been previously made in the third world. The loss of Nkrumah and Keita demonstrated this. It may not be coincidental that the year the West Africa Patrol began the USSR also undertook stabilizing actions in Sudan and Somalia. Also, the Guinean experience probably reinforced the importance of avoiding a highly visible military presence in new third world states likely to find dependency on a superpower irksome. Tactics that mitigated this presence included the use of Cuban troops in Guinea, severe restrictions on information, and the deployment of a Soviet tank landing ship. The projected location of a Soviet naval facility on isolated Tamara Island may have been motivated by concern for Guinean nationalism. Such Soviet solicitude has been rewarded by continued access to Conakry harbor since December 1971. Finally, Moscow may have concluded that external influence on other governments' decisions is likely to be greatest in instances where a brutal, histrionic, and revolutionary leader, like Touré, has little chance of receiving substantial support from the democratic, capitalist Western powers. Regimes like Guinea, Ethiopia, and Uganda, with unsavory international reputations, may well be more vulnerable to Soviet military inducements.

The Ghana and Guinea cases do not indicate that the Russian manipulation of military inducements and threats is, in itself, the source of considerable international influence. Only where the political and economic interests of the targets were compatible with those sought by Moscow was Soviet military power capable of bringing about any identifiable change in behavior. Both Touré and the PAIGC were more receptive to Soviet desires during the Portuguese Guinea war, when the interests of the three parties were convergent. The USSR's inability to obtain routine military access to Guinea-Bissau and Cape Verde since their independence is a sign of how little permanent influence Moscow purchased with its extensive war aid and of how quickly the compatibility of two actors' interests can evaporate. Evidence of successful Soviet coercion is not discernible in these cases. Ghana appeared fully prepared to withstand all Soviet external pressure, including a show of military force, until it had completed a thorough investigation of possible Russian subversion. And so numerous are the alternative domestic and international explanations for Portugal's decision not to reinvade Guinea that only access to Portuguese government files could clarify what weight, if any, was given the implied Russian threat in Lisbon. The general success of Soviet military inducement and coercion and their threat to the United States turns principally on the compatibility of Russian objectives with those of other governments.

CHAPTER THIRTEEN

Angola and the Horn of Africa

COLIN LEGUM

THE SOVIET UNION took advantage of two historic changes that occurred on the African continent in 1974 to extend its military presence and expand its influence along the southwest Atlantic coast and in the Red Sea area. The first change came as the result of a military coup against the Caetano regime in Lisbon in April 1974, which led to the end of almost five centuries of Portuguese colonialism. There was little conflict over the successor governments in four of Portugal's five African territories, but in Angola three rival liberation movements contested for power in the political vacuum left behind by the Portuguese. The second change came in the Horn of Africa (Ethiopia, Djibouti, Somalia) in September 1974, after Emperor Haile Selassie had finally been dethroned. A new military regime, the Dergue, took power and committed itself to a Marxist-Leninist revolution.

The USSR became militarily involved in Angola in 1975 and, at about the same time, proposed to the Dergue that it replace the United States as Ethiopia's main source of arms supplies. This proposal was finally accepted by the Dergue in April 1976 and formalized in an agreement signed in December. Another new dimension of Soviet strategy was the introduction of large numbers of Cuban combat troops to complement the role of Russian military instructors and to handle the more sophisticated weapons under actual battle conditions.

This study of foreign intervention in two African crisis areas focuses on Soviet military and political methods to elucidate Moscow's strategy and interests in the third world—the vital new factor in the contemporary world balance of power.

As the newest of the world's naval powers, the USSR naturally has an interest in acquiring adequate facilities around the major oceans to improve the ability of its naval and fishing fleets (as well as its civil airlines and military aircraft) to operate worldwide and to free them from the climatic constraints of their home ports. Furthermore, for their own defense the Russians must be able to neutralize strategic areas to prevent Western powers from bringing their forward positions close to the Soviet borders, as well as to deal with the possibility that nuclear missiles will be launched from U.S. submarines in the Mediterranean, the Red Sea, or the northern Indian Ocean. These areas are also of vital strategic Soviet interest because the USSR needs to cover its Far Eastern front in all seasons against the possibility of war with China or to go to the assistance of its allies in Southeast Asia. Yet this aim of acquiring naval facilities is never mentioned in Soviet political statements or in the media; on the contrary, that it plays any part in USSR policy is vehemently denied. This attitude is in marked contrast to the insistence by Soviet spokesmen and writers that the USSR needs access to facilities to enable its naval and merchant fleets to enjoy freedom of movement in the world's oceans—an argument strongly advanced, for example, by the creator of the modern Soviet navy, Admiral of the Fleet Sergei G. Gorshkov.[1] There can be no question that Soviet policies in the Horn of Africa were determined by the age-old interest in access to Red Sea ports.

The Soviet wish not to seem to be pursuing a typical superpower interest no doubt explains the covertness of the pursuit. How to avoid being seen by the third world as being no different from "the imperialists" is a major USSR concern. Gorshkov's speeches and writings stress the differences between the Soviet naval role in political crises and that of the "imperialist navies." This concern is also reflected in discussions among Russian strategic planners on such issues as the deployment of ground forces in third world conflict situations, where they may be regarded as indispensable to ensure the effectiveness of military aid supplied by the Warsaw Pact countries.[2] Since Moscow remains strongly opposed to using Russian or other "white" troops from Eastern Europe as combat troops in the third world, this missing element in Soviet strategy has been the subject of considerable debate and controversy in Russian military cir-

1. Sergei G. Gorshkov, "The Development of Soviet Naval Art," *Morskoy Sbornik*, no. 2 (1976); *Red Star* (Moscow), February 7, 1978, as summarized in *The Times* (London), February 8, 1978. See also Gorshkov, *The Sea Power of the State* (London: Pergamon Press, 1979).
2. See Col. V. M. Kulish in *Military Force and International Relations* (Moscow: Institute of World Economics and International Relations, 1971).

cles. When the need for such ground forces arose, first in Angola and later in Ethiopia, the Cubans supplied the "nonwhite," or third world, element required by Soviet strategy. Afghanistan marked a departure from this policy.

The question is whether the Cubans can always be expected to fill the breach when the fulfillment of Soviet strategic interests requires it, or whether they will respond only in situations where Moscow's and Havana's interests coincide. In other words, are the Cubans merely Russian henchmen or are they capable of playing an independent role in third world situations?[3] Their major role in the two conflicts described in this chapter gives no firm answer to this question but tends to oppose the view (as stated, for example, by the Chinese) that the Cubans are simply "Russian mercenaries." There is also the further question of the limits of Cuban manpower and resources.

As an ideological power, the USSR is also able to pursue its state interests by championing causes that attract allies to its side from among third world anti-imperialist "progressive" elements. For example, Soviet foreign policy assumes responsibility for contributing to the "solidarity of the progressive forces in the international working-class movement" and supporting "genuine progressive revolutionary movements and movements of national liberation." These commitments enable the USSR to decide when, and how far, it should involve itself in any particular conflict in the third world.

A more recent development in Soviet policy is its acceptance of an *overt* commitment to help promote and consolidate revolutionary regimes oriented toward Moscow. Such a policy not only intensifies Sino-Soviet rivalry, but also disturbs nationalists in the third world who, though anti-imperialist, are usually anti-revolutionary. Moscow did not try to defend its intervention in Angola on the ground that it was assisting to consolidate a revolutionary regime there (although it subsequently did just that); but this was one of the three reasons it gave to justify its intervention in Ethiopia. Perhaps the most significant aspect of the USSR's role in the Horn of Africa is that for the first time it openly sought to promote and consolidate a "progressive" revolution outside Eastern Europe.

The USSR loses no opportunity to try to diminish the influence of Western powers in the third world (especially in areas where it has stra-

3. See Zdenek Cervenka and Colin Legum, "Cuba: The New Communist Power in Africa," *Africa Contemporary Record (ACR), 1977–78,* and "Cuba in Africa in 1978," *ACR, 1978–79.*

tegic interests of its own); but its policies toward the third world show an even greater desire to undermine the position of the People's Republic of China than that of the West. In the case of Angola, evidence suggests that Sino-Soviet rivalry was a crucial determinant of Soviet policy.

Angola

The new regime in Lisbon, which seized power on April 25, 1974, led by General Antonio de Spinola, fixed November 11, 1975, as the date for independence in Angola, although the question of who was to rule remained in contention among three rival forces. Each had received external backing from different sources in the period of armed struggle (1958–74).[4]

The Rival Angolan Parties

The Union for the Total National Liberation of Angola (UNITA), led by Dr. Jonas Savimbi, had received the least foreign aid. Despite appeals to it, Peking had withheld aid until late in 1974, and its first consignment of arms sent from Dar es Salaam (Tanzania) never arrived. UNITA's power base was in the south, along the Namibian frontier, among the Ovimbundu people, who are by far the most populous group in the country.

The Front for the National Liberation of Angola (FNLA), led by Holden Roberto, was supported by the Bakongo people along Zaire's frontier. It received most of its support either directly from or through Zaire. For a time, at the beginning of the Kennedy administration, some American aid was secretly channeled to the FNLA; this did not last long, because of Portuguese pressure on its NATO ally. Nevertheless, the CIA maintained contact with Roberto.[5] The FNLA was very much a client of Zaire, whose President Mobutu saw it primarily as an ally and an instrument for his foreign policy. This relationship contributed importantly to the subsequent course of the power struggle and probably also to the level of foreign military intervention. In 1973 the Chinese began to supply arms

4. For an informed study of the Angolan liberation movement, see John Marcum, *The Angolan Revolution,* vols. 1 and 2 (MIT Press, 1969).
5. John Stockwell, *In Search of Enemies: A CIA Story* (Norton, 1978).

and to train FNLA forces in their base camps in Zaire. North Korea, which had a training program for Zaire, also helped train FNLA forces.

The Popular Movement for the Liberation of Angola (MPLA), led by a Marxist poet, Dr. Agostinho Neto, had received Chinese military aid from 1958 to 1974, as well as economic and political support from some Western sources, notably Sweden, and from "support groups" in Western Europe and North America. But its main support came from the USSR, Cuba, and Yugoslavia. Soviet relations with the MPLA were not always smooth, partly because of Neto's suspicious personality, and partly because of splits within its ranks. Neto's two staunchest allies were the clandestine Portuguese Communist party (with whose leaders he was in prison in Lisbon for a time) and the Cubans. The MPLA's support lay among the Mbundu people in central Angola, but especially among the urban working classes and the intelligentsia, many of them Afro-Portuguese (mesticos). The MPLA was the only Angolan movement with Marxists in its leadership.

A mission sent by the Liberation Committee of the Organization of African Unity (OAU) early in 1975 to determine the relative strengths of the three movements reported that UNITA enjoyed the greatest popular support, followed by the FNLA, with the MPLA having the least.[6] Despite its large popular following, UNITA was militarily the weakest because of its failure to attract external support. In mid-1975 it joined the FNLA in a reluctant alliance, which assumed an anti-Communist character because of Soviet-Cuban support of the MPLA. When they failed to get Western military support to match that given by the Communist nations to the MPLA, Savimbi and Roberto sought South Africa's help. This led to the South African-FNLA-UNITA-Zaire operation.

External Actors and Their Interests

Throughout the Angolan crisis (early 1974 to early 1976) the OAU's policy, with little significant opposition from its members, was to support the idea of a coalition government to be formed by all three parties at independence. The OAU insisted that none of the parties was entitled to separate recognition; and it called on all African and foreign powers not to interfere in the country's internal affairs. This remained OAU policy

6. Colin Legum and Tony Hodges, *After Angola: The War Over Southern Africa* (Holmes and Meier, 1976), pp. 28–29.

until after the South African army intervened openly on the side of UNITA and the FNLA in late 1975. However, this policy was still fully operative when the Russians and Cubans first became militarily involved in early 1975.

The OAU had two main objectives in Angola: to avert a civil war following the Portuguese withdrawal and to prevent foreign intervention. This explains its consensus on the importance of recognizing all three rival Angolan movements as being genuine nationalist forces and its insistence that all were equally entitled to share in the government at independence. However, the OAU's attempts to discourage foreign intervention failed—largely because one of its members, Zaire, had a state interest in the future of its neighbor. Not only were Zaire's armed forces used to support the FNLA in Angola, but President Mobutu also worked strenuously to persuade others in Africa and abroad (especially the United States and China) to arm the FNLA.

Mobutu's objective was to prevent the extension of Soviet influence on his borders because of his own experience of Russian intervention in Zaire's affairs during Patrice Lumumba's short-lived regime in 1960 and again during the rebellion against his rule in the mid-1960s. Mobutu sought to convince the Western powers and the anti-Communist states in Africa (including South Africa) that they all had a common interest in keeping the Soviet Union out of Africa—an argument that had appealed to the Chinese in 1973.

Mobutu had two other interests in the Angolan conflict: continued access to the Benguela railway, which normally carried the bulk of the mineral exports from Shaba (Katanga) province to the sea; and the possibility of getting direct or indirect control of the oil-rich Angolan province of Cabinda, which forms an enclave within Zaire and the Congo. Mobutu insisted that "Cabinda is not Angola; it is separated by Zaire."[7]

Zambia, another of Angola's neighbors, also played a significant role in the conflict. Although President Kenneth Kaunda supported the OAU stand of support for all three Angolan movements, he developed close relations with UNITA after the MPLA had involved the Russians and the Cubans directly in the conflict. Zambia insisted on "non-intervention by foreign powers in any shape or form in African affairs."[8] Kaunda's speeches contrasted China's "model relations" (with Africa) with those

7. Radio Kinshasa, May 20, 1975.
8. For the full text of the declaration, see Legum and Hodges, *After Angola,* pp. 33–34.

of the Soviet Union; and he warned against the danger of "the tiger and his cubs" (Russia and Cuba) stalking the continent.[9] Like Zaire, Zambia also had a major economic-strategic interest in the Benguela railway, over which a large part of its copper exports normally crossed to the sea.

Former President Idi Amin of Uganda, a close political ally of Mobutu, was chairman of the OAU in 1975. In this role he was able to exercise considerable influence over the organization's policies. He used his position to maintain the African consensus despite strong Soviet pressure on him.

South Africa decided on military intervention in Angola for two reasons. First, it did not wish to see the growth of Soviet influence in the continent, especially so close to its borders. Second, it was concerned about the security of Namibia (South-West Africa), the international territory it controls on the border of Angola. The South-West Africa People's Organization of Namibia (SWAPO) used Angola's territory to make guerrilla incursions into Namibia, even during the time of Portuguese rule. After the Portuguese withdrawal, SWAPO moved its main training camps into southern Angola and was able to get direct supplies of Russian weapons. Later it was also able to get Cuban miltiary training for its guerrilla forces.

U.S. policy toward the Angolan crisis seems to have been largely dictated by four major interests: to avoid any new major foreign involvement, reflecting the post-Vietnam mood of the country and especially of its legislators; to deny any significant political or military gains to the Russians in Africa, but principally through diplomatic means and within the understood ground rules governing détente; to support American friends in Africa, especially President Mobutu of Zaire; and to defend an important American economic interest in Angola—Gulf Oil in Cabinda.

U.S. actions did not conform with all these objectives, even before the extent of Cuba's military intervention became known. Clandestine aid to the FNLA was apparently resumed as early as July 1974, within months of the coup in Lisbon, in response to strong pressure from Mobutu. The CIA station in the area, based in Zaire, was actively engaged in covert action,[10] which the Ford administration sought to supplement by an emergency aid program also channeled through Zaire. The Congress did not allow this, however.

Soon after the Forty Committee, the top-level U.S. review board that approves covert operations abroad, voted about $300,000 for a program

9. Ibid., p. 34.
10. Stockwell, *In Search of Enemies,* pp. 66–67.

of covert political support for the FNLA in January 1975, an interagency National Security Council Task Force on Angola was set up by security council staff directive.[11] Although the task force strongly opposed military intervention in Angola, President Gerald Ford in mid-July sanctioned a CIA plan for a $14 million covert action program to buy arms for the FNLA and UNITA.[12] Also in July, Secretary of State Henry Kissinger requested Congress to vote a $79 million emergency aid program for Zaire. His proposal met with considerable opposition, especially from the Senate, which adopted an amendment introduced by Senator John Tunney in late December 1975 opposing further covert aid to Angola. One other significant U.S. action was a State Department instruction to Gulf Oil on December 19, 1975, to suspend royalty payments of $125 million to the MPLA-controlled Finance Ministry.

The immediate Soviet objective in Angola was clear-cut: to ensure the victory of the MPLA as the successor government to Portugal. With the collapse of Portuguese colonialism the Kremlin was in a strong position to ask, "Where were the friends of the Angolan people in all those long years while the Angolans fought their foreign oppressors?"[13]

The initial Soviet position on Angola was to favor the right of all three rival Angolan movements to participate in the transitional government. Their position changed early in 1975. Soviet writers later ascribed the shift to a new turn of events in Angola for which "the blame lies with the leaders of the secessionist alignments which unleashed an armed struggle with active support from outside."[14] The official Soviet line was that there could be no talk of a civil war in Angola; it was a "war of intervention" forced on the country by the "splittists" and their foreign allies.[15] Accordingly they described their policy as assistance for "Angola's legitimate government, based on the internationalist principle of supporting the nations' struggle for freedom and independence."[16]

11. Nathaniel Davies, "The Angola Decision of 1975: A Personal Memoir," *Foreign Affairs*, vol. 57, no. 1 (1978), pp. 110–11. Mr. Davies was assistant secretary of state for African affairs in 1975. The task force report was reprinted in *Village Voice*, February 16, 1976.

12. Ibid. See also Leslie H. Gelb, *New York Times*, September 25, 1975.

13. *Radio Peace and Progress* (Moscow), January 6, 1976. This is a Russian program broadcast to third world countries.

14. Statements by Professors F. Kozhevnikoy, N. Uzanakov, and I. Blischcaenko, in *Izvestiya*, January 10, 1976.

15. Thomas Kolesnichenko, Tass, February 3, 1976. All references to Tass are to the Soviet news agency's statements as broadcast by Radio Moscow on the dates given.

16. *Pravda*, January 3, 1978.

This position brought the USSR into open conflict with the declared policy of the OAU. Soviet policy also stirred other African reactions, principally from Zambia's President Kaunda, who warned that "assistance to liberation movements must not be an excuse for establishing hegemony in Africa. In this respect we should learn from the People's Republic of China."[17]

Sino-Soviet rivalry was a major feature of Moscow's approach to the Angolan conflict. Moscow put much of the blame for what had happened in Angola on the Chinese. A typical charge was that "the Maoists sent weapons, money and military instructors to Angola. They sent them not to the legal government recognized by many countries in Africa, Asia and other continents, but to those separatist elements which embarked on an armed struggle against the government. . . . Angolans are killed in their own land by Chinese arms."[18] Moscow repeatedly accused the Chinese of pursuing world hegemonistic ambitions.[19]

Cuban objectives in Angola essentially reflected Fidel Castro's view of his country's "tricontinental role," with Cuba as the vanguard of revolution in the third world. The extent to which this Cuban interest meshes with Soviet interests will be considered presently; but considerable evidence supports the view that the Cubans seek to pursue an independent role in the affairs of the third world, whatever their ties with Moscow or their dependence on Soviet economic and military support.[20] The popular view of the Cubans as "puppets of Moscow" or the Chinese view of them as "Russian mercenaries" is not borne out by available evidence. However, this does not contradict another view that the Cuban role in both Angola and Ethiopia helped carry out Soviet objectives, which could not have been achieved without the active combatant role of Cuban soldiers.

Cuba's explanation of its role in Angola was supplied by its foreign minister, Carlos Rafael Rodriguez:

Look, it's obvious that we have a close relationship with the Russians. But when we first sent troops to Angola we did not rely on a possible Soviet participation in the operation. We started it in a risky, almost improbable fashion, with a group of people packed in a ship and in those British Britannia aircraft of ours. Eventually, the operation was coordinated with the Russians, who were

17. Legum and Hodges, *After Angola,* p. 31.
18. Tass, November 17, 1975.
19. Radio Moscow in Arabic to Algeria, December 30, 1975.
20. Zdenek Cervenka, "Cuba and Africa," *ACR, 1976–77,* pp. 84–90. This view was also supported by Sir Herbert Marchant, British ambassador to Cuba from 1963 to 1965, in *The Times* (London), August 16, 1977.

beginning to send military supplies to help President Agostinho's MPLA government in Angola. But the thing started off as a purely Cuban operation.[21]

Fidel Castro claimed that Cuba's cooperation with Africa was the natural "result of our principles, our ideology, our convictions and our blood."[22] It is therefore not without significance that the Cuban exercise in Angola was given the code name Operation Carlotta, after a female slave who had led a black revolt in Cuba in 1843. The "blackness" of many Cubans was especially useful in this operation since they blended more easily into the African milieu. A conspicuous number of the first Cuban troops to arrive in Angola were black.

Cuba's modern connections with Africa go back to 1959, when Ernesto "Che" Guevara first established links with the Front for the National Liberation of Algeria in Cairo; but the closest ties were with the anti-Portuguese liberation movements, especially that between Guevara and Amilcar Cabral, the charismatic hero-martyr of Guinea-Bissau. Except for the Mozambicans, all the anti-Portuguese movements had close links with Cuba, where they went for military training and education.

The objective of the People's Republic of China in Angola was primarily to assist the liberation movements in the struggle against colonialism; this was in conformity with its international role in the third world. China began to support the MPLA in 1958 as the "progressive element" in the anti-Portuguese struggle and continued to supply it with arms until 1974 even though relations were strained—partly because of the gradual ascendancy of pro-Moscow elements in the MPLA but, more important, because of China's decision in 1973 to arm and train the FNLA. (China, as mentioned, had refused to supply weapons to UNITA until late 1974.)

China's involvement with the FNLA came about in response to an African initiative. When the struggle against the Portuguese in Angola slackened in 1973—mainly because of troubles within the MPLA, low morale in the FNLA, and lack of arms for UNITA—Tanzania's President Nyerere and Zaire's President Mobutu decided to ask China to train the FNLA. The Chinese agreed to send more than a hundred military instructors and supplies to the FNLA's camps in Zaire.

Unlike Russia, China responded positively to the OAU's initial policy declaration requesting all external forces to stay out of the Angolan power

---

21. Interview with Hugh O'Shaughnessy, *The Observer* (London), February 26, 1978.

22. Castro's speech to Congress of the Cuban Communist Party, Radio Havana, December 22, 1975.

struggle. Almost three weeks before Angola's independence—on October 27, 1977—China withdrew all its military instructors from the FNLA camps.[23] This move was badly received by the FNLA and Mobutu.

China saw the Angolan crisis almost exclusively in the context of its quarrel with the USSR. It blamed the Russians for "starting the war in Angola";[24] criticized them for having deliberately created a split among the liberation movements and for sending large quantities of arms to only one side; and accused them of "wantonly slandering and attacking the other two movements—and thus single-handedly provoking the civil war in Angola."[25]

The Peking view was that the Russians' actions in Angola "fully revealed their ferocious features as social imperialists." China also accused them of engaging in a "scramble for hegemony in Africa, the aim being to place strategically-important Angola, which is rich in natural resources, in their neocolonialist sphere of influence."[26]

The Course of Events

The Alvor Accord for independence signed by the Portuguese government with the FNLA, UNITA, and the MPLA on January 15, 1975, pledged the four signatories to cooperate in a transitional government until independence, which was set for November 11, 1975. The aim was to produce a smooth transfer of power, with Portugal acting as chairman over two interim bodies in which the three rival Angolan movements were equally represented. Security was to remain the responsibility of the Portuguese forces.

The Alvor Accord was implemented on January 31, 1975, but quickly broke down as the mistrustful leaders of the rival parties maneuvered for position.

Fighting broke out in the Angolan capital, Luanda, on February 13, 1975, in a clash between two wings of the MPLA—Neto's faction and the "Eastern Revolt" faction led by Daniel Chipenda. (The latter had received Moscow's support for a time during 1973.) When Neto's sup-

---

23. AZAP (Zaire government press agency, Kinshasa), October 27, 1975. For a farewell statement by Li Tung, leader of the Chinese military training unit, see Legum and Hodges, *After Angola*, p. 21.

24. PRC Foreign Minister Chiao Kuan-lua, in *The Times* (London), November 15, 1975.

25. Statement by Chiao Kuan-lua in Peking, November 15, 1975.

26. *Peking Review*, no. 391 (September 26, 1975).

porters succeeded in driving Chipenda out of the capital, he decided to join the FNLA. As Chipenda had been the only prominent Ovimbundu leader in the MPLA, his defection critically weakened the movement's ability to win control over southern Angola, the territory held by UNITA. In the next few weeks fighting broke out between the FNLA and the MPLA, which rapidly escalated in March and April. The fighting at this early stage did not involve UNITA. The initiative during much of this first period lay with the FNLA, and the MPLA found itself heavily on the defensive.

The military strength of the Angolan rival forces in the first half of 1975 was roughly the following. The MPLA had 6,000 men and the support of 3,500 to 6,000 former members of the Katangese gendarmerie. The FNLA had 15,000 men, assisted by regular Zaire soldiers in FNLA uniforms. They were also the best armed. Besides Zaire army weapons, they had received 450 tons of Chinese weapons in 1974.[27] UNITA had at most 1,000 men, with few sophisticated weapons.

UNITA's forces at Lobito came under MPLA attack for the first time in late May. In the first week of June, the MPLA and the FNLA were engaged in heavy fighting in the northern and eastern parts of the country, as well as in the capital and in the Cabinda enclave—the principal oil area. Except for Cabinda, where the FNLA was defeated, no side showed clear military superiority in the fighting in this early phase. However, the MPLA had strengthened its position in the capital sufficiently to turn its guns against UNITA in early June.

May and June brought the first clear evidence of external intervention in Angola: the FNLA was being openly assisted by Zaire army units, with clandestine support from the United States.[28] At the same time, the MPLA's rivals claimed that it was receiving Soviet military aid, which later evidence supported.

The OAU took a firm hand in attempting to reconcile the rivals. Under President Jomo Kenyatta's chairmanship, they signed the Nakuru agreement on June 21. But by July 9 fighting had started again and rapidly assumed the proportions of a civil war. It resulted in Angola being divided roughly into three arenas, each controlled by one of the rival forces.[29]

The first six months of 1975 proved crucial in the struggle for power.

27. Davies, "The Angola Decision," p. 116.
28. Stockwell, *In Search of Enemies.*
29. For a fuller account of the fighting in 1975, see Legum and Hodges, *After Angola,* pp. 13–17, 49 ff.

The FNLA started in the strongest position—with the largest armed forces and the strongest regional backer, Zaire. But it was unable to use its apparent superiority effectively, mainly because it lacked real popular support in its areas of operations, including the capital and Cabinda. UNITA, on the other hand, was unable to mobilize its substantial popular support effectively because it lacked military supplies and sufficient trained fighting cadres.

The MPLA was rapidly able to improve military organization and to increase its supply of weapons so that it could drive both its rivals from the capital, establish its control over the center of the country (running east from Luanda to the Zambian border), and confine the FNLA to the northwest corner of the country despite the latter's buildup to 17,000 troops, many of them Zairean soldiers.

By the beginning of August, the MPLA was strong enough to launch a second front offensive against UNITA's forces, compelling them to retreat from a string of southern cities—notably the three ports of Lobito, Mocamedes, and Benguela. By the end of the month the MPLA controlled twelve of the sixteen provincial capitals as well as Cabinda. During this period the Portuguese army had virtually given up trying to keep the opposing forces apart, confining themselves mainly to controlling arms being flown into Luanda.

UNITA's loss of the ports in the south and inadequate airfields made it difficult for it to bring in supplies, especially since Zambia, though strongly sympathetic to Savimbi, was then still complying with the OAU's guidelines and so would not allow arms for UNITA to pass across its territory. The route through South Africa and Namibia had not yet been opened up. Only the MPLA had been able to attract and absorb large additional supplies of arms between March and July. It had also acquired the strategic and psychological advantage of substantially controlling the capital.

The MPLA's growing military superiority forced UNITA to enter into an unwilling alliance with the FNLA in July—much against Savimbi's wishes, since he saw his own movement as a third force, capable of winning a major share of the power in a coalition government. Nor did he like the FNLA's policies, and he mistrusted those of Roberto's chief backer, President Mobutu. But in adversity he accepted the need to coordinate his military efforts with those of the FNLA.

Several international developments during the crucial first eight months of 1975 explain why the local balance of power changed so completely.

When the Forty Committee decided to provide $300,000 in support for the FNLA, it earmarked the money for political action, not for the purchase of arms.[30] Neither the Russians nor the Cubans seemed to be shipping arms directly into Angola at this time, apparently having ceased to do so after the military coup in Portugal in April 1974. They had provided the MPLA with arms estimated at $55 million during the period of the armed struggle (1958–74).[31]

Beginning March 25, a relay of thirty Russian cargo planes arrived in Brazzaville (Congo) with military equipment, which was later shipped either into Cabinda or to Luanda.[32] This was the beginning of the use of Brazzaville as a staging post for the buildup of Soviet material and Cuban forces. According to Kissinger, the USSR supplied $200 million worth of arms between April and June.[33]

In April 100 tons of arms were flown directly to MPLA-held airfields in central Angola from Dar es Salaam. A chartered Bristol Brittania, being flown to Serpa Pinto by a British crew, was forced to land at Luso because of bad weather. The Portuguese at first confiscated the arms but later released them to the MPLA. Sympathetic Portuguese soldiers also allowed two Yugoslav vessels to unload arms for the MPLA in Luanda. In May and June four Soviet ships unloaded arms, as did two ships from East Germany and one from Algeria.[34] In June a Cypriot-registered ship, *Sun Rise,* was prevented by Portuguese troops from unloading arms at Luanda. It went on to Pointe-Noire (Congo), where it discharged its cargo.

The Cubans appear to have made their decision to send military instructors to Angola in April 1975, after a visit by an MPLA envoy, P. Jorge, who was sent to Havana to report on the MPLA's difficult position in Luanda after the FNLA attacks of March. During this visit Castro seems to have decided on a change in Cuba's intervention, switching from supplying military advisers and instructors only to providing ground forces. Jorge's mission was to explain to Castro that the MPLA cadres did not have enough time to familiarize themselves with the sophisticated weapons supplied by the USSR and needed Cubans to man tanks and artillery in the actual military operations. Although the Cubans were in-

30. Davies, "The Angola Decision," pp. 109 ff.

31. Brig. W. F. K. Thompson, *Daily Telegraph* (London), April 11, 1975.

32. Ibid.

33. Henry A. Kissinger, "On World Affairs," *Encounter* (London: November 1978), pp. 9–25.

34. David Martin, *The Observer* (London), August 24, 1975.

troduced as "advisers" (according to Jorge[35]), they became involved in the fighting at Caxito as early as the end of May, when for the first time tanks were used by the MPLA forces. A Cuban spokesman later confirmed that a decision had been made in May or June to send 230 military advisers to establish training camps in territory held by the MPLA at Benguela, Cabinda, Henrique de Carvalho, and Salazaro.[36] This figure corresponds with information gathered by the CIA.[37]

By July heavy supplies of arms and an increasing number of foreign military instructors were reaching Angola; this coincided with the successful military initiatives launched on July 14 by the MPLA.[38]

About a hundred Chinese and thirty North Korean instructors were still training FNLA units in their camp at Kinkuzu inside Zaire. Another forty to fifty Cuban advisers arrived in Angola in early July, via Congo-Brazzaville, bringing the total number of Cubans to three hundred.[39] FNLA sources reported the arrival of fifty Cubans in Brazzaville on July 25 to assist in handling the Russian arms arriving there. UNITA's commanders first saw Cubans in operation at the fighting for the port of Lobito in mid-August 1975.[40]

Zaire sent a commando company and an armored-car squadron across the border and into active combat in mid-July.[41] President Ford decided on July 17 to act on a CIA action-plan, which provided for UNITA and the FNLA to acquire arms with funds channeled through Zaire.[42] Meanwhile, Holden Roberto had sent Daniel Chipenda to Namibia in July for talks with General Hendrik van den Bergh, chief of the South African Bureau of State Security (BOSS). Although U.S. intelligence reports suggested that South Africa had begun to support both the FNLA and UNITA in July,[43] the official report from South Africa claimed that its support had only begun in September.[44] What seems likely is that South

35. Radio Luanda, May 7, 1975. See also Jorge interview in *O'Seculo* (Lisbon), April 12, 1975.
36. *New York Times,* January 12, 1976.
37. Stockwell, *In Search of Enemies.*
38. Martin, in *The Observer,* August 24, 1975.
39. Davies, "The Angola Decision."
40. Personal report to the author by Dr. Jonas Savimbi in September 1975.
41. Martin, in *The Observer,* August 24, 1975.
42. Leslie H. Gelb, *New York Times,* September 25, 1975.
43. Davies, "The Angola Decision."
44. *Nature and Extent of the South African Defence Forces' (SADF) Involvement in the Angolan Conflict.* White paper published by the Government of South Africa (Pretoria: February 1977). Hereafter *SADF* report.

African support of the FNLA began in July but that its collaboration with UNITA did not begin until September.[45]

The crucial round in the power struggle started in mid-August 1975 and ended in a major MPLA political victory on November 11, the date of independence. This new phase saw a serious intensification of the civil war, less disguised foreign intervention, and the beginning of the breakup of the OAU's consensus on Angola. During this three-month period, according to official U.S. estimates,[46] twenty-seven shiploads of military equipment and thirty to forty supply missions were flown in by Soviet AN-22 military cargo planes. Most of this equipment was off-loaded in the Congo and transshipped from there to Angola before independence. The number of Soviet military advisers in Angola was estimated at 170 to 200.

In mid-August larger numbers of foreign troops began to participate in the fighting. Two additional Zaire paratroop companies were committed to action in Angola in support of the FNLA.[47] At the same time South African troops, which had moved from late June to early July into southern Angola to protect the Ruacana and Calueque pumping stations, occupied the Cunene Dam complex,[48] which supplies Namibia with electricity. One Cuban taken prisoner by the FNLA gave details of his unit's arrival from Brazzaville in August 1975, at least a month after leaving Cuba.[49] There can be no doubt that the first Cuban combat soldiers arrived in Brazzaville before the South Africans had sent their first small force across the border to defend the Ruacana installations in July 1975. From Brazzaville, they were quickly sent in batches to Cabinda and to other points in Angola.[50]

In September U.S. military aid began to reach the FNLA. Soviet 122-millimeter rockets were used for the first time in fighting north of Luanda. In the middle of the month two more Zaire battalions were sent across the border into Angola.

Three Cuban merchant ships left Cuba for Angola in early September.[51] A fortnight later the Congo's President Marien Ngouabi arrived in Havana and signed a bilateral agreement whose terms were unspecified;

45. Legum and Hodges, *After Angola.*
46. Thompson, in *Daily Telegraph,* April 11, 1975.
47. Davies, "The Angola Decision," p. 121.
48. *SADF* report.
49. AZAP, December 20, 1975.
50. Davies, "The Angola Decision," p. 121.
51. Ibid.

but a joint communiqué issued September 19, at the end of his mission, expressed Congolese-Cuban solidarity for Angola's "heroic combatants." A Cuban delegation arrived in the Congo in early October, coinciding with the arrival of the first Cuban troopship, the *Vietnam Heroica,* which carried several hundred armed units. Most of the troops were transported to Angola in a local coaster or overland to Cabinda. At least one of the Cuban ships disembarked troops directly at Porto Amboim, south of Luanda, where the Cubans had established another training camp. Some Cubans went to the training camp at Benguela; others appear to have linked up with MPLA units moving toward Nova Lisboa from Lobito, where they made their first contact with South African forces at Norton de Matos on October 6.[52] The Cuban combat troops that began to arrive after September are believed to have been largely tank troops drawn from the independent armored division of the Cuban armed forces, sometimes referred to as the Special Reserve of the Commander in Chief.[53]

Toward the end of the month South Africa was shipping material to the FNLA and UNITA and had established a training base for the FNLA in southeast Angola.[54] According to an official account, the South African Defence Force (SADF) sent an officer to Silva Porto on September 24, 1975, to help plan an operation to stop the MPLA march to Nova Lisboa. His assignment was to advise UNITA on the training and reorganization of its forces and to hold Nova Lisboa "at all costs." A team of eighteen instructors, with three antitank weapons and a few machine guns, joined the liaison officer. The MPLA march was halted on October 6. Meanwhile, according to the same report, it soon became obvious that "the struggle, with strong Cuban support, began to take on a conventional colour."[55]

For a short time in October it seemed as if the tide had begun to turn against the MPLA when South African forces, spearheading a UNITA-FNLA offensive, made rapid progress across south-central Angola to within seventy miles of Luanda.

Also in October, the U.S. State Department asked Congress to approve a $79 million military aid program for Zaire, which had remained stalled since early 1974, when President Mobutu had expelled the American ambassador. At the end of the month, Zaire sent another battalion to the

52. *SADF* report.
53. M. L. Vellinga, "The Military and Dynamics of the Cuban Revolutionary Process," *Comparative Politics,* vol. 8 (January 1976), p. 253.
54. Davies, "The Angola Decision," p. 121.
55. *SADF* report.

south. The number of Cuban ground troops was estimated to have increased to about 3,000.[56]

With the final outcome in the balance, reinforcements of men and matériel were rushed to both sides in the last days of October and the first weeks of November. From late October, aircraft of Soviet Military Transport Aviation were used in the airlift. American supplies were being flown in via Zaire by U.S. C-130 military transport aircraft. Dr. Neto later confirmed that the Russians had supplied him with MIG-21s, T-34 and T-54 tanks, APCs, antitank and SAM-7 missiles, rocket launchers, and AK-47 automatic rifles; he did not mention the 122-millimeter rocket launchers (the Stalin Organs).[57] (No Angolans could fly the MIGs, so the presumption is that they were flown by Cubans.) A mixed Zaire-FNLA force failed in an attempt to capture Cabinda. The Cuban airlift was increased to as many as five troop flights a week, and there was an increase in the sealift.[58] The big Cuban buildup started on November 7, when 650 commando troops were flown to Angola via Barbados, Guinea-Bissau, and Congo. The Cubans held up the South African-led UNITA-FNLA strike force on the outer perimeter of Luanda. According to South Africa's P. W. Botha (then defense minister, later prime minister), the strike force was prevented from attempting to capture the capital by American pressure. Further operations were temporarily stopped on November 11 "after mediation by go-betweens," according to the official South African report, which is silent about who the mediators were, though Prime Minister J. B. Vorster strongly hinted that the United States was involved.[59] At that time, the UNITA-FNLA South African forces held the general line north from Lobito to Santa Coimba, and from there east to Luso. The South African forces were officially said to consist of about three hundred adviser-instructors and personnel and a limited number of armored cars, mortars, and antitank weapons.

Two independent republics were proclaimed in Angola on November 11, 1975—the People's Republic of Angola by the MPLA in Luanda and the Social Democratic Republic of Angola by UNITA and the FNLA in Huambo. The MPLA government was at once recognized by a dozen African countries, the Soviet bloc, and Cuba; the republic at Huambo received no official recognition.

56. Davies, "The Angola Decision," p. 121.
57. Radio Luanda, January 31, 1976.
58. Davies, "The Angola Decision," p. 122.
59. *ACR, 1976–77,* p. 848.

Six days later, on November 17, the FNLA-UNITA-South African forces undertook a three-pronged attack against Luanda, but it was easily contained. By then, Cuban combat troops numbered an estimated 15,000. On November 27 a Cuban artillery regiment and a battalion of motorized and field troops landed on the Angolan coast after a sea crossing of twenty days in two cargo ships, each carrying 1,000 men plus armored vehicles, guns, and explosives. According to García Marquez' account, more troops and weapons were flown into Angola over the next few months in "up to a hundred flights."[60] He claims that the Cubans were flying "blind" without meteorological information and flying low to save fuel. The first air route they took necessitated refueling at Bridgetown, Barbados, but this was stopped because of U.S. representations to the Barbados authorities. An attempt to fly via Guyana also had to be abandoned when American oil companies refused to provide the necessary fuel. For a time, flights were routed through Cape Verde, but, according to Marquez, this had to be stopped to "avoid bringing harm to a defenceless country."

The first significant sign of any naval deployment appeared in late November when a Soviet *Alligator*-class amphibious landing ship (LST) was sent from Conakry (Guinea) to Pointe-Noire (Congo), where it stayed from December 1 to December 6 before patrolling outside Angolan waters. It carried a full complement of naval infantry as well as vehicles equipped with antitank and antiair missiles. The immediate reason for this deployment appears to have been the FNLA attack on the Cabinda enclave in mid-November, which also posed a threat to Russian merchant ships unloading arms for the MPLA less than twenty miles away at Pointe-Noire. In synchronization with the FNLA's strike, Zaire had moved three of its naval patrol boats into the area. The largest of these, a *Swift*-type patrol boat, carried 81-millimeter mortars and 40-millimeter grenade launchers, which can severely damage a merchant vessel. In early January 1976 the LST was joined in its operating area by a *Kotlin*-class guided missile destroyer (DDG) and an oil tanker. They had been diverted from routine operations in the eastern Mediterranean in December and had entered the Gulf of Guinea on their way south. The destroyer was followed out of the Mediterranean on January 4, 1976, by a *Kresta II*-class guided-missile cruiser; it too headed for Conakry—at above normal transit speed.[61]

60. *Processo* (Mexico City), January 1977.
61. Charles C. Petersen and William J. Durch, "Angolan Crisis Deployments," in Bradford Dismukes and James McConnell, eds., *Soviet Naval Diplomacy* (London: Pergamon, 1979), pp. 146–47.

These Soviet naval movements brought several warnings from Washington. On January 6 official sources registered "grave concern" at the Soviet naval activities.[62] The following day a White House spokesman announced that Soviet naval deployments to Angolan waters were "further evidence of a continuing Soviet involvement in an area where they have no legitimate interests." These protests were met by a Tass denial that any Soviet warships were in Angolan waters. In fact, the LST and the destroyer did immediately move further north. The former took up a surveillance position in the Gulf of Guinea, and the latter proceeded to Conakry, where it joined the cruiser.[63]

In January and February Soviet naval surveillance of U.S. warships was intensified, both at the outlets from the Mediterranean and in mid-Atlantic, where the *Vertikal,* an intelligence collector, joined the LST. It is also possible that a *Juliett*-class cruise-missile submarine was involved in the Atlantic surveillance operation. It put into Conakry in February. The USSR also deployed TU-95D naval reconnaissance aircraft over the Atlantic, operating from Conakry and Havana. After mid-February there were no significant Soviet naval operations in the area.[64]

Soviet naval deployment in the Angolan crisis was probably motivated by several considerations. First, there is little doubt that the LST was sent to Pointe-Noire in late November in response to a potential FNLA and Zaire land and naval threat to Russian vessels unloading supplies at the port, as well as to Cabinda, where the MPLA was being assisted by Cubans and reinforced with Russian arms. A naval response would have been appropriate to the kind of risks being run at that time by the Soviet Union. Subsequent use of Soviet naval units seems to have been in pursuit of three main purposes: political, intelligence gathering, and support for the air bridge, especially from Cuba.[65]

The USSR appears to have had several political-strategic objectives: to deter the small Zaire navy from interfering with the unloading of arms from Russian merchant ships at Pointe-Noire; to discourage South Africa from using its navy to block access to Angolan ports; and to signal opposition to any possible use the United States might make of its navy to impede

---

62. *Washington Post,* January 7, 1976.
63. Petersen and Durch, "Angolan Crisis Deployments," pp. 147–48.
64. Ibid., pp. 148–50.
65. Petersen and Durch have tentatively suggested that the LST and the DDG might have been needed to evacuate Soviet military personnel from Angola if the South African army's operations had succeeded. This does not appear to fit in with the logistical requirements of evacuation. Ibid., p. 146.

the air bridge or the sea bridge from Cuba to the Congo and Angola, or from the Soviet Union, via Conakry, to the Congo. A natural consequence of these aims would be to create a more general impression in Angola and elsewhere of the degree of Moscow's commitment to support the MPLA.

In early January 1976 the USSR made two Aeroflot IL-62s available to Cuba. These aircraft transported troops from Holquin to Luanda, stopping at either Bissau or, more probably, Conakry for refueling. The flights continued from January 7 to January 21, carrying troops at a rate of 200 a day. The flights were resumed in late February, but at a lower rate. Troops were also arriving at Pointe-Noire by ship.

South Africa's involvement increased substantially after Angolan independence. More battle groups were formed to bring their strength up to just under 2,000 (logistic element included) shortly before withdrawal on January 22, 1976. As a countermove to the Cuban buildup—and especially to the 122-millimeter rocket launchers—140-millimeter guns were introduced into the fighting: "this caused chaos among the Cuban ranks."[66] The FNLA-Zaire troops failed to achieve much military success despite South African support. But UNITA managed, with South African support, to continue the military struggle, which, despite a sharp increase in Cuban troops to 19,000 in 1976–77, was still continuing in 1980. According to South Africa's official account: "The allied FNLA/UNITA forces, supported by South African forces, could have conquered the whole of Angola, but Dr. Savimbi insisted that he was only interested in controlling his traditional area because he was determined to reach a settlement with the MPLA to the advantage of Angola."[67]

After South Africa's withdrawal, UNITA and the FNLA had to rely on an army of about 1,200 foreign mercenaries, paid for with CIA funds.[68] Meanwhile, however, opinion in the OAU had swung strongly toward the MPLA after it became known that both UNITA and the FNLA were collaborating with the South African army. In February 1976 the OAU member states divided equally on a proposal to recognize the MPLA regime; but before the end of the year the great majority of African states, as well as other states around the world, had decided to recognize the regime's legality.

66. *SADF* report.
67. Ibid.
68. Stockwell, *In Search of Enemies;* also Legum and Hodges, *After Angola,* p. 28; and *International Herald-Tribune* (Paris), February 3 and 12, 1976.

Soviet Behavior

Soviet actions in Angola in the crucial period from the coup in Lisbon (April 1974) to the territory's independence (November 1975) suggest not a carefully thought out strategy but rather a rapid response to changing conditions and to new challenges, developing from a low-level response (April 1974 to early 1975) through a medium-level response (March to June and July 1975) to a high-level response (July and August 1975 to early 1976).

There is no lack of evidence, however, to show that the Soviet Union was carrying out a long-term strategy (involving both Portugal and its African territories) to create opportunities that might be exploited as they occurred. But it would be wrong to describe such a policy as opportunistic: a more accurate description would be pragmatic and tactical.

The long-term planning of the Soviet Union's African strategy is shown by its consistent support of the national liberation movements on the continent. In the case of Angola, support for the anti-Portuguese movements had a double purpose, since Moscow was at the same time assisting Alvaro Cunhal's clandestine Communist party to overthrow the Salazar-Caetano regimes: by supporting the anti-Portuguese liberation struggles it could (and, as it turned out, did) contribute to the overthrow of the Portuguese political system.

Having begun to support the MPLA in 1958, Nikita Khrushchev publicly predicted its success in 1961.[69] Despite the vicissitudes of Moscow's relations with Neto, its support throughout went to one or the other of the factional leaders in the MPLA. Neto also enjoyed Cunhal's support and personal friendship. Cunhal is believed to have introduced Neto to Moscow on his first trip there in 1964.[70]

Angola's geopolitical position was undoubtedly an important Soviet consideration. A sympathetic regime there could be expected to assist in influencing developments across its borders in neighboring Zaire—a primary target of the Soviet Union's Africa policy, as is shown by its intervention there since the early 1960s. Angola's other two close neighbors, Zambia and Namibia, are also high on the list of Soviet policy priorities in Africa. A breakthrough in Angola could extend Soviet influence into Namibia, and so to the threshold of South Africa. South Africa and the

69. *Pravda,* June 16, 1961.
70. Michael Kaufman, *New York Times,* December 28, 1975.

Horn of Africa are, perhaps, the two most important target areas of Soviet "ocean politics."

In late 1973, after China had reestablished diplomatic ties with Zaire and had decided to train FNLA cadres, Soviet policy also showed more concern about the Chinese role in Angola. Sino-Soviet rivalry was undoubtedly a major element in Moscow's decisionmaking on Angola—perhaps even the most important element in it.[71] This is supported by a typical Soviet geopolitical view of China's role in Africa expressed by one of its senior China watchers:

The Chinese are determined to expand their influence throughout Africa. Their target area is southern Africa. They have established a strong hold in Tanzania on the Indian Ocean, and are closely involved with FRELIMO in the struggle in Mozambique. The railway line they are helping to build from Dar es Salaam to the copperbelt in Zambia is an aspect of their policy. Their clear aim is to help extend the railway from Zambia into the copper area (Shaba) of Zaire. Thus they will have succeeded in establishing a major strategic railway right across the narrow waistline of Africa, linking the Indian and Atlantic oceans.[72]

This background makes it easy to understand the vigorous reaction of the Soviet bureaucracy to the restoration by the Chinese of diplomatic links with Zaire and their decision to help the FNLA in 1973. It may also help explain their policy of increasing their military intervention in support of the MPLA early in 1975. The military situation in Luanda and northern Angola at that time strongly favored the combined Zaire and FNLA forces (that is, the forces backed by the Chinese as well as by the Americans). The Russians repeatedly alleged that China's role in Angola proved that it had again "done a deal with the most reactionary international elements."[73] Hence, if the FNLA and UNITA (the latter was regarded by the Russians as Maoist) were to succeed in defeating the MPLA, the result from the Soviet position would be a victory for the Chinese, as well as for the Americans. The Soviet Union sees the Chinese as an even greater threat to its interests in the third world than the Americans.

Soviet policy in Angola after the collapse of the Caetano regime continued to be linked with its policy in Portugal, where it was closely engaged in 1974 and early 1975 with the bid for power by Alvaro Cunhal's

71. Colin Legum, "The Soviet Union, China and the West in Southern Africa," *Foreign Affairs,* vol. 54, no. 4 (1976), pp. 745–62.
72. Statement to the author by a Soviet diplomatic observer at a seminar on the Indian Ocean held at Brussels University in 1970.
73. Tass, November 17, 1975.

Communist party and its allies. The Portuguese Communists had endorsed the Alvor Accord of January 1975. So had the Russians, who appear to have held that position until possibly March 1975, when the MPLA, under heavy pressure in Luanda, sent its urgent requests to the Soviet Union and Cuba for military aid.

For the Russians to have given such aid openly at that time would have been seen by the OAU as hostile to its demand that no foreign support be given to any one of the three rival Angolan movements. It would therefore have suited the purpose of the USSR (especially that part of its bureaucracy most directly concerned with maintaining good relations with Africa) for the Cubans to act as the channel of military support for the MPLA. (Cuba had never made a secret of its lack of regard for the OAU.)

Thus the initial Soviet reaction to developments in Angola was to adopt a low-risk policy after March 1975, when it began secretly to fly arms into Brazzaville for shipment to the MPLA. That decision may also have been influenced by evidence of covert American support. This factor was, in any case, decidely less important than the open support of the FNLA by China and Zaire—two of Moscow's bêtes noires. Nor can there be much doubt about the close coordination between Cuba and the Soviet Union in establishing a bridgehead for military supplies to the MPLA at Brazzaville, since Cubans are known to have handled the shipments of Soviet arms arriving there.[74]

It would be difficult to exaggerate the importance of the air and sea facilities available at Brazzaville to the success of the Soviet-Cuban operation in making the MPLA's victory possible. Before July 1975 two difficulties stood in the way of the Russians' and the Cubans' getting substantial military supplies directly into Angola, especially into Luanda, where they were most urgently needed. First, the Portuguese authorities in Luanda were still fairly successful in intercepting arms shipments. Second, the OAU was being extremely vigilant about transgressions of its policy on foreign intervention.

The People's Republic of the Congo was one of the few OAU members that did not go along with the consensus—partly because of its rivalry with Mobutu's policies arising from its interest in the future of Cabinda if that enclave (which abuts on the Congo's territory as well as Zaire's) were to secede from Angola.

Another important advantage of Brazzaville to the Soviet Union was

74. French military intelligence source.

that it made any visible military presence in Angola unnecessary; this could be left to the Cubans. Neto confirmed in a statement in January 1976 that, while substantial military supplies had been received from the USSR, none of its military advisers had come to Angola. He added: "Such advisers were only in Congo-Brazzaville, and from there they have tried to help MPLA."[75] The Soviet link with the MPLA in Luanda was Igor Ivanovich Uvarov, a Tass correspondent, who is also believed to be a leading member of Soviet military intelligence, GRU.[76]

The Russians moved into a third, high-risk phase in mid-July 1975, at about the same time that President Ford endorsed the Forty Committee's proposal to provide covert military aid for the FNLA-UNITA. At that time, there was also some evidence that Chinese arms were being used by the Zairean armed forces who were intervening in the fighting with the FNLA. The Soviet media gave prominence to a report by Leslie Gelb in the *New York Times* on September 25, 1975, suggesting that the United States and China were coordinating their covert military support for the anti-MPLA forces.

However, of greater concern to the Soviet Union in early August 1975 was the growing MPLA conviction that the South African army was about to play a major military role in Angola. This fear had been aroused by relatively small South African incursions into southern Angola to "protect" the hydroelectric project in the Cunene valley. These fears were soon justified by South Africa's open military intervention in late October. The MPLA had foreseen this new danger and had obviously succeeded in convincing the USSR and Cuba about the gravity of any major intervention by the South African army.

All the evidence leads to the conclusion that the decisions to greatly increase Soviet aid and to commit large numbers of Cuban combat troops had been made by August, primarily to check this new "imperialist" threat, which the MPLA, the Soviet Union, and Cuba naturally saw as collusion between the United States, South Africa, and China—a view put forward by, among others, V. G. Solodovnikov, director of the USSR Institute of African Studies.[77]

It is hard to believe that, if the Russians and the Cubans had not made their final decision to intervene massively in late July or early August, the South African military intervention would not have succeeded in tipping

75. Radio Luanda, January 29, 1976.
76. *Manchester Guardian*, November 20, 1975.
77. Tass, November 12, 1975.

the military balance against the MPLA. What is open to argument is whether the South Africans would have undertaken this commitment if they had been aware of the earlier substantial buildup of Cuban combat troops.

The Soviet-Cuban military buildup did not, however, end when the MPLA formed the government of independence in November 1975. This is understandable for a number of reasons. While the MPLA had won a substantial political victory, it was by no means militarily secure. A rival government had been established by the FNLA and UNITA, whose forces controlled well over half the country, and the South African military forces had not yet been withdrawn from Angola but stood ready to help consolidate the forces of the FNLA and UNITA in their traditional areas.

Thus, to ensure a total MPLA victory in Angola, the Russians and the Cubans probably perceived little choice other than to increase their level of military intervention. This they did after November 1975, when the numbers of Cuban troops rose from between 12,000 and 15,000 to about 19,000.

The only two constraints on Soviet decisionmaking were Cuba's own view of its commitments and the possible damage to the cause of détente. The Kremlin discounted the possibility of serious U.S. intervention in Angola.

Statements by the USSR throughout 1974–75 were designed to show that its policy was in full accord with UN decisions on support for anti-colonial liberation movements; that it had adopted a principled stand in opposing "imperialist conspiracies" (a concerted U.S.-China conspiracy); that it supported the legitimate and most popular Angolan party; and that it served no selfish interests. Even before South Africa's military intervention, the USSR's statements suggested that it was engaged in fighting "South African racism" but denied that there was a civil war in Angola and that the Soviet role was in any sense "interventionist," since the USSR was acting in response to, and in defense of, the "legitimate authority." A notable feature of these statements was the emphasis they put (especially in propaganda to third world countries) on the dangers of the Chinese wish for "world hegemony."

South Africa's open intervention in late October 1975 greatly strengthened the Soviet case. Moscow could then claim with even greater justification what it had been saying for months: that it and Cuba were preventing aggression by the South African "racist" regime in Pretoria. From then on, the Russians had much less difficulty in countering African objections to their role in Angola. After Angola's independence, their position was that they were supporting, as they claimed they were fully entitled to do, a sovereign African government.

The Russians consistently and firmly rejected the idea that their role in Angola could damage détente. This is exemplified by the views of Georgi Arbatov, a senior Soviet adviser on U.S. affairs to Leonid Brezhnev: "If Dr. Kissinger saw Angola as a major issue of East-West relations, even some sort of confrontation, I think he was absolutely wrong. It was a counterproductive way to deal in general with the African situation."[78]

There is little evidence that the Soviet Union at any time seriously expected the United States to intervene openly or actively in Angola, although clearly it knew that the United States was covertly supporting the anti-MPLA forces. Moscow appears to have distinguished between U.S. policies in support of the anti-Communist forces in Portugal and what was likely to happen in Angola. Its assessment of U.S. public and congressional opinion in the aftermath of Vietnam was justified in October 1975, when Congress opposed the State Department's proposal to renew military aid to Zaire, and especially in December, when the Tunney amendment forbidding all clandestine aid to Angola and Zaire was adopted by the Senate.

The clear conclusion is that the Soviet Union did not anticipate any serious American military intervention in Angola that could have brought the two superpowers into a military confrontation harmful to détente. Equally clearly, the strong congressional and public constraints on the U.S. administration's ability to intervene on any significant scale in Angola removed any possible Soviet hesitation about expanding its military intervention. After November 1975 Moscow also felt itself completely free to act because of the "legitimization" of its support for the new "sovereign" MPLA government in Luanda and because of the intervention by the South African army.

Soviet public statements show little concern about the damage to U.S.-Cuban relations after Castro had pointedly rejected Washington's demands that he withdraw his troops from Angola as a precondition to the resumption of normal diplomatic relations. Moscow may in fact have welcomed the postponement of normal relations between Washington and Havana, since this could open the way for Castro to end his complete dependence on the USSR.

78. *The Observer,* November 12, 1978.

Perceptions of Soviet Policy and Actions

Soviet policies polarized Africa's political leaders. In Angola two camps grew up—one strongly pro-Soviet, the other bitterly anti-Soviet. The MPLA behaved as a Soviet and Cuban ally throughout; its leaders invited Soviet and Cuban intervention and defended it against all critics. After independence, however, Neto showed his readiness to move into a less aligned position by seeking Western economic cooperation.

Savimbi and other UNITA leaders were initially not anti-Soviet; they remained willing, until July 1975, to enter into a coalition government with the MPLA. They finally turned for help to the major anti-Communist country in the region, South Africa, when they failed to find effective allies either in Africa or in the West. Holden Roberto, on the other hand, was always hostile to the Russians and remained their implacable foe, along with his close ally, President Mobutu.

Mobutu's deep fears about "the spread of Russian influence" were further strengthened by Soviet behavior in Angola. He reacted by making desperate efforts to persuade the Western powers to intervene in Angola and to encourage the emergence of an anti-Soviet front of African states. He succeeded in winning support for this idea from about a dozen African leaders—including those of Egypt, Sudan, Ivory Coast, Senegal, and Morocco. But although Mobutu maintained his close alliance with Idi Amin, the Ugandan leader's animosity toward the Soviet role in Angola was short-lived. He felt deeply humiliated by what he regarded as the Soviet Union's bullying to get him to do its bidding; but while he resisted it on this point, his reliance on Soviet military supplies was obviously a major factor in causing him to restore his diplomatic relations with Moscow.

Zambia's President Kenneth Kaunda reacted particularly strongly against the Soviet and Cuban actions in Angola, which he repeatedly denounced as a danger to the continent. While not publicly supporting U.S. military intervention, he expressed his understanding of the reasons for which the FNLA and UNITA leaders decided to seek American military aid.

South Africa's reaction to events in Angola was predictable since its regime has always felt threatened by any spread of Communist influence in Africa. What was not so predictable was its decision to commit itself to a military role in Angola.

Overall, African reactions were largely ambivalent. Most African leaders were strongly opposed to intervention by any of the foreign powers, but they tended to blame both superpowers for engaging in "big power politics." After South Africa's military intervention, the Soviet-Cuban role was more generally accepted. However, many African leaders have made a clear distinction between the role of the Russians and that of the Cubans.

Cuba's influence in Africa was undoubtedly increased by its role in Angola, a paradox that may be explained by admiration for a small third world country that took on such a massive commitment and carried it through so successfully. Positive feelings toward Cuba were undoubtedly a major factor in diminishing African hostility toward the Soviet Union.

Western European countries played a singularly low-key role in the Angolan affair, although they strongly criticized the Russians and the Cubans. France promised support for Zaire and possibly also gave covert aid to the FNLA. Sweden, while opposed to the Soviet intervention, supported the MPLA.

The Ford administration took a much graver view of the Soviet-Cuban intervention than did its NATO allies. In response to the escalation of the Soviet-Cuban military intervention in mid-1975, it began to support the idea of playing a more activist part.

American policy on Angola was made largely by Secretary of State Henry Kissinger, often against the advice of his own senior advisers in the State Department[79] and very much against the grain of the post-Vietnam mood of Congress. Kissinger believed that it was necessary to "stop this first major Soviet adventure in Africa in 15 years." His view of the Soviet Union's action was that it was engaged in

for the first time massively introducing military equipment and starting a cycle of upheavals similar to the impact of their first introduction of military equipment into the Middle East, into Egypt, in 1954, which led to over 20 years of constantly growing tension. At this point, we sought to stop this by assisting the Black forces that were resisting the takeover. When we did this, the Soviets escalated yet another level by introducing Cubans.

However, he was later to state:

There was no intention of sending American troops to Angola under any circumstances; there was no possibility of anybody introducing 500,000 troops into Angola. In fact, it was the Russians through the Cubans who were in our

79. Davies, "The Angola Decision."

position, that is to say, in the position we were in in Vietnam. We were backing the local population against foreign invaders, or at least against foreigners.[80]

Kissinger continued to believe that "it was relatively easy to stop the Cubans and Soviets in Angola."[81] He attributed what he saw as the U.S. failure to react effectively to Soviet intervention in Angola to the fact that the country had "lost the capacity to create incentives for responsible behavior [by the Soviet Union], and the capacity to create penalties for irresponsible behavior—both the result of the decline of executive authority. I think this was the reason why the Soviets made their attempts in Angola in 1975."[82]

American concern about the Soviet intervention and the risk of souring détente was communicated in private discussions with top Soviet leaders (including Brezhnev and Kosygin), through direct diplomatic exchanges, and by repeated public warnings from the President and the secretary of state. As late as November 24, 1975, Kissinger was still publicly warning Moscow that the United States could not "remain indifferent" to Soviet intervention.[83] However, the Russians had already decided that there was little risk of American action to back up that kind of threat. The behavior of Congress had clearly shown them the limitations on the administration's options.

Outcomes

The Russians achieved their immediate objectives in Angola, but their longer-term goals have not been secured and remain in some doubt. With the Cubans' indispensable assistance, they were able to help their local ally, the MPLA, establish itself as Angola's legal government against its Western-supported opponents, the FNLA and UNITA. Soviet and Cuban military support made it possible for the MPLA to fight back from what had appeared to be a losing position in March 1975 to achieve a commanding position only nine months later. Moreover, the close relations that had grown up between Neto and his Communist allies in those critical nine months played a crucial part in his decision to reverse his earlier dis-

80. Kissinger, "On World Affairs."
81. Ibid.
82. Ibid.
83. *New York Times,* November 25, 1975.

avowal of the MPLA as a Marxist-Leninist organization[84] and to establish the new Angola as a Marxist state. This fulfilled one of Moscow's longer-term political-strategic objectives. There is no evidence to suggest that Neto's decision was made because of Soviet pressure, but there is every reason to suppose that he was strongly encouraged to move in that direction, especially by the Cubans.

Nevertheless, Soviet military intervention was not completely effective. The addition of Soviet arms and Cuban troops, although essential to the MPLA's gaining political power, were yet not powerful enough to crush the MPLA's opponents who continued to threaten the MPLA regime.

The FNLA and, especially, UNITA remained in control of a sizable part of the country. They could expect immediate support from neighboring Zaire and South Africa, as well as from further afield, and they continued to present a military challenge to the MPLA and the Cuban ground troops. Thus at the time of independence there was an insecurely based regime, heavily dependent for its survival on Soviet and Cuban military aid, and faced with serious internal and external enemies.

Nevertheless, the immediate outcome of the conflict favored the Soviet Union in a number of ways.

First, the defeat of South Africa's military intervention was symbolically important. Although most of the serious fighting was done by the Cubans—who won praise in Africa for "driving out" the South Africans—it was understood that they could not have been successful without Soviet military backup. This praise was expressed by African leaders not previously well disposed toward the USSR—for example, Joshua Nkomo, the leader of the Zimbabwe African People's Union (ZAPU), and Sam Nujoma, the Namibian leader of SWAPO—as well as by some who had been actively hostile—notably, President Kaunda of Zambia. The effective commitment of Soviet military power attracted many Africans' interest in the potential value of the USSR as an effective ally in their fight against the minority white regimes in southern Africa.

84. Dr. Agostinho Neto had said in an interview with the Nigerian magazine *Afriscope* (Lagos, August 1975): "MPLA is not a Marxist-Leninist organization. Also, our leadership is not Marxist-Leninist. Some of us have read Marx and Lenin, but we don't consider ourselves Marxist-Leninists. We are a large organization with various shades of opinion and different types of groups united solely under the flag of liberation. As a heterogeneous organization, it contains both Marxist and other points of view. But it is true that many people in the world consider the MPLA as a movement linked with Moscow. Again, I say this is untrue. This image exists only in the imagination of outsiders."

Second, the active military presence of the Russians and the Cubans in southern Africa enabled them to intervene more directly in the conflicts on the continent. Their close ties with the MPLA regime (fortified by the signing of a Treaty of Friendship and Support on October 8, 1976) assured them of at least a chance of acquiring access to naval, air, and other facilities. They used their military units in Angola to begin large training programs for SWAPO, the Zimbabwe Independence People's Republican Army of Joshua Nkomo, and the African National Congress of South Africa.

Third, the Russians were able to extend their military reach into the south central Atlantic region. The Soviet navy's West Africa Patrol was no longer exclusively dependent on facilities at Conakry (always risky because of the unpredictability of Guinea's President Sekou Touré); it could expect to extend its operations as far south as Luanda and Lobito. The Soviet fishing fleet could also hope to get important facilities in the area, and Soviet air links (Aeroflot and military) were extended several thousand miles down the West African Atlantic coast. In these ways the USSR's military potential was strengthened.

Fourth, the reversal of the OAU's stand on recognizing only the MPLA and on military intervention in Angola meant that no permanent damage was done to Soviet relations with most African states. For this the Russians could thank South Africa's decision to intervene militarily, as well, of course, as the success of its own intervention.

Fifth, the outcome was damaging to two of Angola's neighbors, Zaire and South Africa, both of which were Soviet target areas. Moscow has sought the overthrow of Mobutu since 1963. South Africa saw its security position made more perilous (especially in Namibia) by the defeat of the anti-Communist front, which its army had unsuccessfully supported.

Sixth, the defeat of China's allies in the conflict (Zaire and the FNLA) was especially satisfactory to the Russians, who saw this as a serious setback to Peking's third world role in Africa. China's failure to produce effective military support for its allies strengthened the belief of some leaders in southern Africa that, so far as military support went, the USSR was likely to be a more effective strategic ally. Furthermore, the Chinese had very limited success in Africa with their high-pitched propaganda campaign aimed at exposing the Soviet Union as being engaged in "imperialist expansion."

Finally, the defeat of the pro-Western forces and the loss of political, economic, and military influence in an area that they had dominated for centuries represented a decided setback for the United States and the Western European powers. This reduction of Western influence in a part of the world hitherto dominated by a NATO power satisfied another Soviet objective. The ambiguities and, in the end, the ineffectiveness of the American response in Angola damaged U.S. interests without achieving any worthwhile results.

Some of the other outcomes were not so satisfactory for the Soviet Union. While, as has already been noted, a majority of African states and leaders ended by approving the Soviet-Cuban military intervention, this was to some extent offset by a number of African leaders' increased hostility toward the USSR because of what they felt to be clear evidence of "Soviet expansionism." A more active anti-Communist front began to develop in Africa, supported by such countries as Egypt, Morocco, Sudan, Ivory Coast, Senegal, Somalia, and Zaire.

American-Soviet relations were also damaged by the events in Angola, particularly because of American concern about the large deployment of Cuban combatants. The Angolan episode placed new strains on the process of détente and contributed to the tension produced by Soviet-Cuban intervention in the Horn of Africa soon afterward.

The Russians, having tested the responses of the United States to the phased increase of their military intervention in Angola, were apparently encouraged to believe that the mood of the U.S. Congress and the American people, reflecting the Vietnam experience, had considerably reduced the chances of the administration's being allowed to mount an effective military response to Soviet intervention in situations such as that in Angola. This evaluation of future American policy in the third world undoubtedly influenced the USSR's decisions in the Horn of Africa.

The U.S. position on Angola lacked credibility to Africans. The African leaders and forces that had looked to the United States for support felt betrayed. While this was especially true of the anti-MPLA forces in Angola and Zaire, it was also the case for Zambia and a number of other African states, including Ethiopia. South Africa particularly felt aggrieved at U.S. policy; its leaders publicly complained of having been let down. On the other hand, African leaders opposed to intervention by any of the major powers (notably, Nigeria) criticized U.S. policy for having contributed to the Soviet-Cuban intervention because of the covert (though well-publicized) CIA operations. The open debate in the United States made it certain that the administration could not engage in effective clandestine operations. Angola was seen by both the Russians and the

Africans as a watershed in American attitudes about U.S. military intervention in third world conflicts.

While Angola represented a breakthrough for USSR political and military strategy, important questions remain undecided about the long-term possibilities of consolidating these initial gains. More than four years after Angola's independence, the MPLA was still not successful in consolidating its power or in rescuing the country's economy from the dangerous state into which it had fallen when the Portuguese withdrew. Several major events since Angola's independence must be considered in evaluating the Soviet Union's chances of exploiting its initial advantage.

First, internal power struggles in the MPLA surfaced in 1977 when a powerful army and political faction, led by Alvo Nites, came close to overthrowing Neto's faction, which was saved largely by Cuban military intervention. Although this attempted coup was not, as was reported at the time, favored by the USSR, there is no reliable evidence to show what the attitude of the Nitists would have been toward the Russians and the Cubans if the coup had succeeded. A major grievance of the Nitists was the preponderance—as they saw it—of "whites" in the MPLA regime, that is, mesticos (Afro-Portuguese) and Portuguese Communists. It is not known whether the Nitists included the Soviet bloc and Cuban advisers in their grievances about "white domination." Many Angolans make a clear distinction between the "whiteness" of Russians, East Germans, and so on, and the "nonwhiteness" of Cubans—a distinction, incidentally, that is encouraged by the Cubans. However, after the Cuban role in crushing the Nitist coup, there is no reason to suppose that the surviving Nitists in the MPLA feel much affection for either the Cubans or the Russians.

Second, the continuing failure of the MPLA to overcome its internal tension was shown by the dismissal of Prime Minister Lopo do Nascimento and a number of other important ministers in 1978.

Third, in 1978 the Neto regime's policies toward Zaire and Namibia unexpectedly changed in a way potentially harmful to long-term Soviet objectives. As a result of OAU mediation (and with American encouragement), Neto and Mobutu agreed to end hostilities. If this reconciliation holds up (and it is in the interest of both local parties that it should), it could contribute importantly to stabilizing both the MPLA and the Mobutu regimes. This would reduce the opportunities for the USSR to use Angolan territory to work against Mobutu. The official Soviet line has been to welcome this reconciliation.

Fourth, Neto unexpectedly took a leading part (as a member of the African Frontline states) in supporting the efforts of the five Western members of the UN Security Council to find a peaceful settlement for Namibia. He was largely instrumental in influencing SWAPO's leader, Sam Nujoma, to drop his opposition to the Western proposals. The end of the guerrilla war against Namibia and Namibia's emergence as an independent state would remove the risk of an escalated conflict against the South African army by SWAPO forces using Angola as a base. An independent black state would act as a buffer between Angola and South Africa, cutting off South African and other support for UNITA, facilitating the task of pacifying southern Angola, and reducing the need for Cuban troops in the country.

The major short-term advantage of a peaceful settlement in Namibia would be the breathing space it would give the MPLA to consolidate its position—an obvious Soviet interest. Another possible advantage would be SWAPO's coming to power in Namibia; the USSR could then hope to develop good relations with such a regime. The disadvantage would be the loss of opportunities offered by an armed struggle to exploit the atmosphere of violence in the region to undermine the South African regime—a strategic Soviet interest. The Russians remained quiet about Neto's decision to cooperate in the Western initiative, but they continued to attack the Western moves as "imperialist maneuvers designed to help the South African racist regime."

Fifth, the MPLA regime has continued to show a keen interest in improving its relations with the West, mainly for economic reasons. Serious economic difficulties have produced strong popular feelings against the regime, further contributing to its instability. Economic recovery has been painfully slow. Since Angola's natural markets lie in the Western economy, it obviously needs to improve relations with Western Europe and North America. The MPLA has acknowledged this reality and has adopted policies to reflect it.

However, relations with the United States have been impeded by Washington's insistence that diplomatic relations could be resumed only after Cuban troops had left Angola. This demand was contemptuously rejected by Neto, who nevertheless received U.S. ambassadors in his capital and continued to express an interest in establishing normal ties with Washington. Jose Eduardo dos Santos, who succeeded Neto after his death in 1979, has acted similarly.

Although the Angolan authorities took a 51 percent interest in Gulf

Oil's operations in Cabinda, they have publicly expressed a desire that this U.S. multinational continue to exploit their oil. They have disavowed any intention of nationalizing the oil industry.

In some ways, therefore, Angola's Marxist regime has shown evidence of wishing to adopt pragmatic policies in pursuing its economic and foreign policy interests.

Finally, on the other hand, Angola's military links with the Soviet bloc and Cuba have been greatly strengthened since independence. In early 1980 there were more Cuban soldiers (possibly 19,000) in the country than at independence because of the threats to Angola's northern and southern borders and the continuing challenge from the MPLA's internal opposition. Angola relies for all its military supplies on Warsaw Pact countries and for much of its military training on Cuba. And East Germany has helped build up Angola's air force and a paratroop division.

The Horn of Africa

The five political entities that make up the Horn of Africa are Ethiopia; its dissident province, Eritrea; the Somali Republic (Somalia); the Djibouti Republic; and the Republic of Sudan.

The Principals and Their Allies

The Amhara-dominated Christian Kingdom of Ethiopia had for centuries been the dominant power in the region, except for a brief interregnum (1936–39) of Italian occupation. During World War II Haile Selassie's imperial regime became a Western ally; after the war it was almost entirely dependent on the United States for its arms. It also developed close links with Israel and maintained a suspicious hostility toward its Arab neighbors. Its closest African ally was Kenya. Ethiopia's relations with the West changed after Haile Selassie's dethronement in September 1974, when the successor military regime, the Provisional Military Administrative Committee (PMAC)—also known as the Dergue (an Amharic word for committee)—embarked on a Marxist-Leninist revolution. It ended its military ties with the United States and entered into a close alliance with the Soviet bloc and Cuba while still retaining its alliance with Kenya and, until February 1977, with Israel. Like the Haile Selassie regime, its relations with most of the Arab world (except Libya, South Yemen, and the Palestinian organizations) and Somalia were hostile. By 1978 the Dergue had also quarreled with China.[85]

At its independence in 1960, the Somali Republic flew a flag with a five-pointed star, each point representing a territory in the Horn inhabited mainly by Somalis to which the new republic laid claim. Two of the points —British Somaliland and Italian Somalia—had joined to form the new republic, leaving three points to be collected: the Ogaden province of Ethiopia, Djibouti, and the northeast province of Kenya. Although Somalia joined the Arab League, its closest political and military ally was the USSR from 1967 until the USSR began to replace the United States as Ethiopia's main source of arms in 1976. After finally severing its military ties with Moscow (as well as with Havana) in 1977, Somalia was forced to rely almost entirely on its fellow members in the Arab League— especially Saudi Arabia, Egypt, and Sudan—and on Iran. It also sought to win allies in the West, and it drew closer to China. Somalia has been an unwavering champion of Eritrean independence.

The tiny Djibouti Republic achieved its independence from France in 1976, but it retained a military link through an alliance that provided for the continued presence of 2,150 French troops. Its 220,000 inhabitants are divided between Afars, who have close ethnic links with clans in Ethiopia, and Issas, who are directly related to Somali clans. Djibouti has sought to maintain a careful neutrality between its two rival neighbors.

The Sudan has traditionally controlled the back door into the Horn, but it is also a Red Sea state. After severing its military ties with the USSR in 1972, it developed close ties with the Arab League, particularly with Egypt, with which it has a military defense alliance. Its relations with Libya have been troubled since the mid-1970s. Although Sudan attempted to maintain a neutral position in the conflict between Ethiopia and Somalia, its relations with the former have been uneasy for years because of its support for the Eritreans. With the rise of the Dergue, Sudan sought more military aid from Western countries, especially from the United States and Britain. It also relies on China for military supplies.

Eritrea is still formally a province of Ethiopia, but it has played an increasingly independent and disruptive role since 1962, when it launched an armed liberation struggle for at least a measure of independence from Ethiopia. Because the opposition originated in the Muslim parts of Eri-

85. For a more detailed account of these developments see Colin Legum and Bill Lee, *Conflict in the Horn of Africa* (New York: Africana, 1977); and *Continuing Conflict in the Horn of Africa* (Africana, 1979).

trea, it attracted sympathy and support from other Muslim countries, especially in the Arab world. Another reason for this Eritrean-Arab alliance was their shared interest in opposing Haile Selassie's pro-Israel stand. The Soviet bloc and Cuba gave some support to two of the three fronts making up the Eritrean liberation movement—the Eritrean Liberation Front (ELF) and the Eritrean Popular Liberation Front (EPLF). The third faction is the Eritrean Liberation Front-Popular Liberation Forces (ELF-PLF), which was the first to use the Muslim issue to appeal to the Arab world. Despite the Marxist tendencies of the leadership in the EPLF and the ELF, all three fronts are essentially nationalistic. Soviet and Cuban support for the Dergue produced serious tension with the Eritrean leaders. The Eritreans receive no support from the West or from black Africa. The EPLF is much the strongest of the three fronts. The ELF largely ceased to count as a military factor after mid-1978. The ELF-PLF has increasingly oriented itself toward Saudi Arabia but is itself internally divided.

Regional Forces

The pattern of regional alliances has been shaped by four factors: the Horn's strategic location at the nexus between black Africa and the Arab world and at the crossroads of a network of international sea routes; inter-Arab rivalries; the Arab-Israeli conflict; and the rival interests of the major world powers.

President Gamal Abdel Nasser of Egypt was the first to propose turning the Red Sea into an "Arab Sea"—an idea that has survived his time. Nasser's rationale for controlling the Red Sea was that it was essential to tightening the stranglehold on Israel. Saudi Arabia, which was suspicious of Nasser's designs, became attracted to the idea of creating an "Arab Sea" after the buildup of a Soviet naval presence in the Red Sea, particularly after the Russians had acquired naval facilities in Somali ports. This Saudi defense interest was shared by the shah's Iran. Israel and Ethiopia both saw the Arab design for the Red Sea as a threat, which was a major reason for their close military cooperation in the region.

The Arab world saw the secession of Eritrea, under Muslim leadership, as a major step toward asserting effective control over the Red Sea and at the same time weakening the historic power of Ethiopia's "Christian Kingdom" in the region.

Libya was drawn into the region's politics because of Colonel Qaddafi's enmity toward the Egyptian and Sudanese regimes; but though it took the side of the Dergue against Somalia, it continued to give its political support to the Eritreans.

The People's Democratic Republic of Yemen (PDRY, or South Yemen) took the side of "revolutionary Ethiopia" largely because of its close military and political ties with the USSR and Cuba; but it, too, continued to support the Eritreans.

Kenya, while sharing the suspicions of other regional powers about the nature of Soviet expansion in the area, nevertheless continued to give its strong backing to Ethiopia because of its overriding concern about the Pan-Somali threat to its territorial integrity.

These manifold and often contradictory interests produced two strangely assorted alliance systems in the developing conflicts in the Horn. Ranged alongside Ethiopia were Kenya, Libya, South Yemen, Israel, and the Palestinian organizations, as well as the Soviet bloc, Cuba, and Yugoslavia. Support for Somalia and Eritrea came from Saudi Arabia, Iraq, Syria, Iran, Sudan, and Egypt.

Global Factors

Aside from Ethiopia, the Red Sea area had traditionally been dominated by Britain, France, and Italy, mainly as competitors concerned with expanding or defending their colonial spheres of influence. Italy faded out after its defeat in World War II. Britain largely withdrew when it began in the 1960s to wind down as a military power east of Suez. Only France has maintained a residual military role in Djibouti as part of its defense network in the Indian Ocean.

The United States became the dominant Western military power in the Red Sea area in the 1950s, mainly through its defense agreements with Haile Selassie's Ethiopia, its alliance with Saudi Arabia, and its greater naval interest in the area. The main American interests have been two. In the words of a senior State Department official, Edward Mulcahy, the United States "needed a strong friend [Haile Selassie] who could be trusted."[86] Its other interest was in its communications relay center at Kagnew on the high plateau near Asmara in Eritrea—then still vital to its naval communications. U.S. economic and military aid to Ethiopia between 1949 and 1974 was in a sense "rent" for Kagnew. In 1973, after it became possible to "float" the communications center in navy ships, Kag-

86. Legum and Lee, *Conflict in the Horn of Africa,* p. 10.

new lost its value, and the Nixon administration decided to make a substantial reduction in its military commitments to Ethiopia. The U.S. arms agreement was ended in April 1977. The Israelis, however, continued to give some military support to Ethiopia until a year later, when an incautious public boast by Foreign Minister Moshe Dayan resulted in Colonel Mengistu's ending Ethiopia's relations with Israel.

After Somalia finally broke its military ties with the USSR in November 1977, the United States and other NATO members were under considerable pressure from Saudi Arabia, Egypt, and Sudan to help the Somalis make up for the loss of Soviet arms. None of the Western powers yielded to the pressure because they did not wish to become militarily involved in the local conflicts. By then, too, it was clear that Somalia had become an aggressor by sending regular army units across Ethiopia's borders. The Western position was that the conflict should be mediated through the Organization of African Unity and that the security of the area should be left to the regional powers. The United States also refused to allow Saudi Arabia and Iran to pass American-procured military supplies to a third party. This attitude could not be expected to convince the USSR that the NATO powers were not militarily involved; it argued that Saudi Arabia, Iran, and Egypt were simply acting as Western surrogates in buying arms for the Somalis. The United States was also constrained from helping to arm the Somalis by Kenya, a staunch pro-Western country, which feared that sooner or later the Somalis would repeat their Ogaden venture in its northeastern province.

In fact, neither the United States nor any other Western power played a significant military part in the conflicts in the Horn after the American cutoff of military aid to Ethiopia in 1977—much to the distress of its regional allies. Although Saudi Arabia, Egypt, Iran, and Sudan wished to see the Western powers arm the Somalis, the Israelis and the Kenyans argued that continuing to support Ethiopia militarily would keep the Dergue from becoming completely dependent on the Soviet Union.

China attempted to play a neutral role, refusing to supply either side with arms and maintaining its development projects in both Ethiopia and Somalia. However, after the Somalis' March 1978 defeat in the Ogaden and after Ethiopian denunciations of Peking in characteristic Moscow language, China expressed a readiness to provide spare parts for Somalia's Russian-supplied tanks and aircraft.

The Russian interest in the Red Sea is of long standing. Alexis and Peter the Great in the seventeenth century, and Paul I and Catherine the

Great in the mid-eighteenth century, all pursued the idea of establishing "blue sea ports" in the Mediterranean and the Red Sea.[87] However, not until the mid-1950s was this idea translated into practice, when Khrushchev accepted the strategy of Admiral Sergei Gorshkov that the USSR create "a modern navy capable of dealing with the latest innovations in the enemy camp . . . in any part of the globe."[88] The clearest public statement of the Soviet interest in the region was made by V. Sofinskiy, head of the Soviet Foreign Ministry Press Department, in a televised speech in Moscow on February 3, 1978: "The Horn of Africa is first and foremost of military, political and economic significance. The importance of the area lies in its location at the link-up of the two continents of Asia and Africa. There are a lot of good sea ports in the Persian Gulf and the Indian Ocean. Moreover, there are sealanes which link oil-producing countries with America and Europe."[89]

Although the Somalis had begun to receive a small amount of Soviet military aid in 1963, the Russians had to wait until 1972 to get effective access to naval facilities at Berbera. But the meager naval facilities that the Somalis could offer and their unreliability as a long-term ally never really satisfied the Russians.

In the meantime, with Haile Selassie on the throne, the Russians took a close interest in the development of the Eritrean liberation movement, to which they gave only cautious public support and minor military and economic aid. Military training was provided by the Cubans. But Moscow actively began to encourage and support the creation of Marxist cells in both the ELF and EPLF in 1968.[90]

The Soviet Union's patient wait for its opportunity in Ethiopia finally came in July 1976, when its military alliance with the Dergue began to take shape. However, the Russians hoped that, with the rise of a revolutionary state in Ethiopia to complement the Marxist-Leninist state in Somalia, they would be able to establish a foot in both camps. "With peace, everything will become possible," they promised both the Somalis and the Ethiopians.[91] What Moscow offered both sides was, in fact, a *Pax Sovietica* in the Horn, with the USSR as the sole supplier of arms to both Somalia

---

87. For an excellent exposition of the Russians' historic interest in the area, see Edward Wilson, *Russia and Black Africa Before World War II* (Africana, 1974).

88. *Pravda,* July 26, 1964.

89. Reported by New China News Agency, March 14, 1978.

90. *ACR, 1978–79,* p. B232.

91. This statement was repeated to the author by an aide to Somalia's President Siad Barre.

and Ethiopia and the guarantor of their redrawn borders within a federal system.

When this plan was angrily rejected by Somalis because it ignored basic Pan-Somali interests, the Russians were faced with a choice between Somalia and Ethiopia. Moscow seems to have had little difficulty choosing the latter, even though the revolutionary process in Ethiopia was, to say the least, hazardous and uncertain. However, at the end of 1977, when it could no longer be disguised that Somalia was using its Russian-trained army and equipment in the Ogaden, the USSR threw its full military weight behind the revolution in Ethiopia.

Weeks after Moscow conferred its official approval on Mengistu's revolutionary program in March 1977,[92] Fidel Castro hailed the Ethiopian revolution as "Africa's first genuine Marxist revolution." The Cubans had previously maintained cordial relations with the "Somali revolution"; but their only active role in the region was through their military training support for the Eritrean liberation movement and a relatively strong military training program in South Yemen. On March 14, 1977, Castro arrived in Addis Ababa with the express purpose of helping to promote a "progressive alliance" on the Red Sea, which was to include Djibouti, Eritrea, and South Yemen as well as Ethiopia and Somalia. He envisaged it as a bloc capable of opposing the Red Sea alliance between Sudan, Egypt, and Saudi Arabia. Having won Colonel Mengistu's approval for the plan, he made a secret trip to Aden, where he met with the Ethiopian and Somali leaders to urge on them the possibility of two "scientific socialist" regimes merging their revolutions. But Somalia's President Siad Barre reacted angrily to Castro's proposals. With the failure of this enterprise, Cuba followed the Russians in giving its full support to the Ethiopians.

The Cubans did not fully accept all the aspects of either the Dergue's or the Kremlin's policies. The major differences were over tactics to ensure the success of the Ethiopian revolution and over the approach to Eritrea. On the first of these issues, Castro insisted even more strongly than the Russians that Mengistu transform his military regime into a full revolutionary mass movement with a properly constituted Communist party. More serious, though, was Cuba's refusal to commit its combat troops to the battlefields of Eritrea after the 1978 defeat of the Somalis in the Ogaden. Having strongly supported the Eritrean liberation movement for many years, the Cubans insisted that the problem in Eritrea was

92. Radio Moscow, March 9, 1977.

political and should not be settled by force.[93] The absence of Cuban ground forces was acutely felt in Eritrea, where, despite the overwhelming superiority of Soviet-supplied armor and military aircraft, the resistance, though temporarily weakened, was not crushed.

The Course of Events

Ethiopia was wrenched out of its 2,000-year-old fuedal system and set on a new revolutionary course in March 1975—thirteen months after the beginning of the mutiny in the Ethiopian army and six months after Haile Selassie's dethronement. The committee of military officers, who had fought their way to the top of the leadership in the Dergue through a series of violent purges, abolished the monarchy, proclaimed a "Socialist Ethiopia" as a one-party state (but without creating the one party), abolished the feudal land system, nationalized all land including urban property, nationalized all industries, and curbed the medieval influence of the Orthodox Church. This lurch into revolution came at a time when virtually the whole country was engulfed in violent conflict; administration had collapsed; the Ethiopian army was divided in its political allegiances and stretched beyond its capacity; virtually all of its older army officers above the rank of captain had been liquidated or dismissed; military equipment was outdated, especially compared to the Soviet weapons in the hands of the Somalis, who stood as a threat along the Ogaden border.

Opposition to the military rulers was extremely diverse. Regional and nationalist forces in most of the thirteen provinces had rallied behind local leaders. Although their motives were complex and they were also in conflict with each other, all were agreed on demanding a fairer distribution of power in any postimperial constitution. The strongest of these nationalist forces were situated as follows:

—In Tigre in the north, where the traditionalists rallied behind Ras Seyyoum Mengesha and the young behind the Marxist-led Tigre People's Liberation Front (TPLF).

—In the Oromo (Galla) southern provinces of Bale and Sidamo, where the charismatic leader "General" Waagu Guta had long engaged in an armed conflict against the old emperor, with the back-door support of the Somali Republic.

—In Begemder, on the western border with Sudan, where the local

93. Statement by Cuba's vice-president, Carlos Rafael Rodriguez, *The Observer*, February 26, 1978.

leader, Bitwoded Adane, supported a modern nationalist and anti-Communist movement, the Ethiopian Democratic Union (EDU), which was joined by disaffected soldiers from the Ethiopian army. The movement received token military support from Sudan.

—In the Afar country, running alongside Eritrea, where the nomads on the Danakil plains took up arms under their prestigious sultan, Ali Mirreh. They were linked with the Afars in Djibouti and had financial and other support from Saudi Arabia and Somalia.

—In Gojjam and Wollega, two areas traditionally resistant to rule by Addis Ababa, where a number of dissident movements arose.

—In the Hararge province (Ogaden), where the West Somali Liberation Front (WSLF) led an insurrection movement closely supported by Somalia.

—In Eritrea, where the Dergue faced its most serious military threat.

—In Addis Ababa and other large towns, where violent opposition came from the political intelligentsia in the trade unions and teachers' and students' organizations, led by the Marxist Ethiopian People's Revolutionary Party (EPRP).

Faced with these multifarious internal challenges as well as the threat of a military attack by the Somali Republic and Arab support for all its opponents, the Dergue needed strong external allies if its own power was to be maintained and the country was to survive within its old borders. Not only were normal American supplies inadequate for the Dergue's purposes, but Congress had refused to increase the military aid program beyond a limit of $16 million. It included about a dozen F-5Es and the Maverick and Sidewinder missiles to go with them. Ethiopia was also allowed to purchase a squadron of secondhand F-5A Freedom Fighters from Iran with U.S. approval. During 1976 Washington still saw the limited supply of arms to Ethiopia as serving three purposes: a means of checking a further Soviet arms buildup in Somalia; a discouragement to the Dergue from looking to Moscow for substantial military aid; and support for pro-Western elements in the Dergue who were engaged in resisting the Communists. This aspect of U.S. policy was strongly encouraged by Israel and Kenya but discouraged by Saudi Arabia and Egypt.

As early as September 1974, the Dergue had turned down a tentative proposal from the USSR that it replace the United States as Ethiopia's source of arms supplies because the Dergue felt it could not count on a power that was still showing no sign of withholding its military aid from Ethiopia's principal enemy, Somalia.

Ethiopia's internal security problems continued to mount throughout

1976. These were further complicated by rivalries within the army and the Dergue—especially by a bitter struggle in the capital between the EPRP and *Me'ison* (an Amharic acronym for All Ethiopian Socialist Movement). The EPRP had emerged from its clandestine existence under the emperor's rule when the mutiny started but had soon quarreled with the Dergue because of its own simon-pure Marxist doctrine that there could be no shortcuts to revolutions; it argued strongly for the installation of a parliamentary system of government to facilitate the growth of a class struggle. When the Dergue turned down these ideas, the Marxists split, and *Me'ison,* led by Fida Tedla, rallied to Colonel Mengistu's side, arguing that a mass revolutionary party could be created in the ranks of the military regime. *Me'ison* was Moscow-oriented; it was largely instrumental in promoting the idea in the Dergue that the USSR be chosen as Ethiopia's "strategic ally." Throughout most of 1976 the Dergue and its *Me'ison* allies maintained what they called a "Red Terror" against the EPRP's "White Terror" of selective assassination and "kneecapping." Thousands died in the capital and the main towns, and many thousands of the intelligentsia were imprisoned.

A Soviet delegation visiting Ethiopia in March 1976 praised the Dergue's "correct progressive stand." Thereafter the Soviet media began to praise Ethiopia's national democratic revolution program, which was drafted by *Me'ison* and formally adopted by the Dergue in April 1976. In May the Dergue published its Nine-Point Peace Plan for Eritrea; it rejected independence for the province and proposed a federal solution instead. Moscow at once endorsed the plan for Eritrea as a policy deserving the support of all progressives. This endorsement marked the beginning of the USSR's rift with Somalia and Eritrea.

The Dergue issued a proclamation on the last day of 1976 restructuring its organization according to Marxist-Leninist principles. Its program, though notional rather than actual, pointed to the course the revolution was to take. Following a series of purges in the Dergue, Colonel Mengistu Haile Mariam emerged as the dominant leader on February 3, 1977. The Ethiopian press published pictures of Mengistu receiving the congratulations of the Soviet, Hungarian, and Chinese ambassadors in Addis Ababa. He also received a message of congratulation from Fidel Castro. Nevertheless, Ethiopia's sense of isolation was expressed by Mengistu on February 4, the day after his triumph, when he said in a broadcast: "In our region, Mother Ethiopia does not have any revolutionary friend, except the PDRY. The broad masses of Ethiopia should constantly ponder this fact." He followed this up by announcing that in the future Ethiopia would seek its military aid from the "socialist countries."

A few weeks later, on February 25, the Carter administration announced further reductions of its foreign aid to Ethiopia, as well as to Argentina and Uruguay, because of their consistent violation of human rights. The previously agreed upon military aid grants of $6 million were stopped, though not the $10 million in military sales credits.

As a result, Soviet approval of the Dergue's policies became more vocal. On March 9, 1977, Radio Moscow declared that "the present changes in Ethiopia have created the necessary prerequisites for a just settlement of the dispute in Eritrea." Fidel Castro hailed the "Ethiopian revolution" as Africa's "first genuine Marxist revolution." When Mengistu paid his first visit to Moscow in early April, he was toasted as a "genuine revolutionary leader." In the same month the Dergue expelled all American advisers from Ethiopia; the United States then cut off all military aid to Ethiopia. Soviet-Somali relations began to decline rapidly and visibly after Mengistu went to Moscow for official talks in May.

It soon became clear that a decision to ship Soviet arms had been made even before Mengistu's May visit—possibly in December 1976, when an influential Dergue delegation had first gone to Moscow to negotiate mutual agreements (these were apparently ratified by Mengistu during his May visit). The evidence for this came from French intelligence sources in Djibouti, which reported that *at the beginning of May* consignments of outdated Soviet T-34s and more modern T-54s as well as armored cars had arrived at the port and had been transshipped on the Djibouti-Addis Ababa railway line.[94] They had been shipped across the Gulf of Aden from South Yemen, where the Russians and the Cubans have teams of military advisers. Some of the tanks were unloaded at Diredawa, the main railhead in eastern Ethiopia, close to where the fighting had begun in the Ogaden. In subsequent weeks more arms shipments were reported to have arrived by the same route. Also, Western intelligence agencies reported that by July five planeloads of arms shipments a week were arriving at the Addis Ababa airport. Arab intelligence sources reported that the Soviet Union had agreed to supply Ethiopia with $385 million worth of matériel, as well as 48 MIGs of various types and up to 300 T-54 and T-55 tanks.[95]

94. *Le Monde* (Paris); quoted in Legum and Lee, *Conflict in the Horn of Africa*, p. 94.
95. Legum and Lee, *Conflict in the Horn of Africa*, p. 94.

However, the arms buildup did not show any significant increase over the next few months. One possible explanation for this is that handling and assembling the equipment after delivery was a problem. The only international airport, at Addis Ababa, was reported to be overstrained by the shipments that came in during July. In late September, knocked-down MIG-21s were flown by Soviet transport aircraft into Addis Ababa airport, where they were assembled with the help of Soviet and Cuban technicians. According to Western diplomatic sources in Addis Ababa, Eastern European pilots and flight crews were used to make test flights, but there is no supportive evidence to show whether they were also being used on the battlefronts. From September on, armored vehicles, amphibious aircraft, and other equipment were ferried across the Red Sea from Aden to Assab on the Eritrean coast. Some supplies also were brought by Soviet and other Eastern European naval vessels to Massawa, where they were easily observed by Israeli vessels, which were at that time still actively helping the Ethiopian side. The supplies sent by the Soviet bloc to these two ports seem to have been used mainly on the Eritrean front.

The first Cuban presence in Ethiopia was reported by the U.S. State Department on May 25, 1977.[96] A spokesman for the State Department said the apparent intention was that the Cubans help train Ethiopian forces in the use of Soviet military equipment. He added that this could be "a serious development," which might jeopardize U.S. efforts to normalize relations with Cuba.

Reacting to these Soviet and Cuban developments, President Barre said that Somalia would make "a historic decision" if the Soviet Union continued to arm Ethiopia. "We would not," he said, "be able to remain idle in the face of the danger of the Soviet Union's arming of Ethiopia."[97] He sent Defense Minister Mohammed Ali Samatar to Moscow on May 25— soon after Mengistu's visit—to seek assurance from the Soviet leaders that they were not planning to arm Ethiopia. In July there were reports that Soviet military personnel were leaving Somalia.[98]

In the end it was Moscow that made the first move to end its alliance with Somalia. The fighting in the Ogaden province had escalated rapidly in May, when between 3,000 and 6,000 troops of the West Somali Liberation Front (WSLF) captured one important town after the other. The

96. Ibid.
97. *Al Yaqsa* (Kuwait), June 27, 1977.
98. *Washington Post,* July 22, 1977.

Somali Republic was still insisting at the time that none of its own regular soldiers were involved in the fighting. It stated that the fighting was being done entirely by the Ogadeni Somalis, despite evidence of a considerable backup for the WSLF operations by Russian-type tanks and artillery.

Izvestiya on August 16 referred to the fighting in the Ogaden as an "armed invasion of Ethiopian territory" by "regular units of the Somali army." It added: "Even the plausible excuse of implementing the principle of self-determination did not justify such an act." President Barre flew to Moscow at the end of August in a last attempt to avoid a rupture with the Soviet Union, but although he got no satisfaction from his talks in Moscow, he took no immediate steps to end his treaty with the Russians. He explained to Arab diplomats in his capital that pushing the Russians out roughly would result only in their intensifying their support of the Ethiopians and, as had happened with Sadat, would encourage them to try to undermine his own regime.

By early September the Somalis were predicting a triumphant end to their campaign in the Ogaden. Plans were made to proclaim the liberation of "West Somalia" and its accession to the "rest of the Somali nation" before the end of that month. But the Somalis began to feel the strain of their long lines of communication and the weight of the Soviet armor brought in to sustain the rapidly expanded Ethiopian army, which was engaged in defending the last two strategic points in the Ogaden—Harar and Diredawa. By October the Somali campaign was stalled. With the arrival of more sophisticated Soviet weapons and technicians the initiative began to pass into the hands of the Ethiopians and their supporters. The critical month was October.

On October 15, Ethiopia's foreign minister, Colonel Felleke Girgis, flew to Cuba to report on the Somali "aggression against Ethiopia"—and no doubt to seek Cuban support urgently. A few days later, President Barre claimed that there were 15,000 Cuban troops fighting in the Ogaden, an allegation strongly denied by the Cuban Foreign Ministry, which insisted that "there is not a single Cuban combat unit there."[99] Western intelligence sources confirmed that there were no Cuban "combat units" but reported the presence of Cuban military instructors fighting with Ethiopians in Russian tanks and operating heavy artillery. They also reported the presence of Soviet military advisers and of several hundred

99. For the text of the full statement, see *ACR, 1977–78,* p. A108.

South Yemenis serving as drivers of military vehicles. The situation changed in November when U.S. reconnaissance satellites produced photographic evidence of a Cuban military presence.

The Soviet ambassador in Addis Ababa, Anatoly Ratanov, announced on October 19 that his country had "officially and formally" ended its arms supplies to Somalia. On November 13 Somalia abrogated the 1974 Treaty of Friendship and Cooperation with the USSR, ordered all Soviet experts and military technicians out of the country within seven days, and abolished the use of all air, sea, and land facilities in Somalia by the USSR. Relations with Cuba also were ended.

Somalia followed up its break with the Soviet Union and Cuba by addressing an urgent appeal for help to its fellow members in the Arab League as well as to the West and China.

According to official Somali sources, the United States had hinted at the possibility of military aid once the treaty with Moscow had been broken. The precise evidence for this claim is contradictory. Nevertheless, on July 26—two months after the Somali campaign had begun in the Ogaden—the United States, Britain, and France announced their preparedness, "in principle," to supply defensive weapons to help Somalia protect its "present territory." The fear at that time was that the Ethiopians might invade Somalia. A State Department spokesman said: "We think it desirable that Somalia does not have to depend on the Soviet Union." At the same time, the United States was in touch with its NATO allies, as well as with Egypt, Sudan, Saudi Arabia, Iran, and Pakistan, to arrange a consortium of nations willing to guarantee Somalia's security. However, Washington's position changed almost immediately. In early August a State Department official announced that President Jimmy Carter had changed his mind because of the "extreme nature" of Somali backing for the insurrection in the Ogaden, adding: "We have decided that providing arms at this time would add fuel to a fire we are more interested in putting out."[100] This reversal of policy, which was supported by Britain and France, was the result of two factors. First, the extent of the Somali army's actual involvement in the fighting in the Ogaden was not fully established until late July. Second, Kenya's pro-Western government strongly opposed the provision of any arms to Somalia since it feared for its own Somali-inhabited province.

The Somalis were understandably angry at this about-face, claiming

100. *Washington Post,* September 26, 1977.

that an unofficial U.S. envoy had carried specific assurances of U.S. aid if Mogadishu broke with Moscow.[101] America's friends in the region of much longer standing than the Somalis were no less upset. Saudi Arabia, Egypt, Sudan, and Iran all exerted considerable pressure on the United States and other NATO countries to facilitate the supply of weapons to the Somalis—if only through third parties. The United States refused to grant such permission to Saudi Arabia and Iran. Both President Sadat and President Nimeiry (Sudan) made personal representations to President Carter during their visits to Washington.

Although leading members of the Arab League had sought to persuade the United States to intervene in the Horn to replace the Soviet Union as Somalia's arms supplier, their own military role was fairly minimal. At their meeting in September 1977 the Arab League foreign ministers expressed deep concern about the situation in the Ogaden and urged all foreign powers to stay out; but it withheld support for Somalia's stand. Arms support of any significance did not begin until January 1978, after the Somalis' defeat in the Ogaden.

Fast Israeli naval units operated openly around Massawa and Assab, bringing special equipment for the Ethiopian army and serving the purposes of Israeli intelligence. About a dozen Israeli military instructors had helped in 1975–76 to train a new battalion of Ethiopian paratroopers, the *Nebalbal* (the Flame), which was especially active in fighting the urban guerrillas of the "White Terror." But the Israeli instructors had left before the end of 1976. Between twenty and thirty Israeli specialists arrived early in 1977 to assist in antiguerrilla training and counterinsurgency techniques; their presence was always vigorously denied by the Dergue but not by Israel.

The Libyans increased their presence in Addis Ababa during 1976–77 but played no military role. They reportedly pledged a total of £425 million of aid through bilateral economic and aid agreements, and they helped to guarantee Ethiopia's oil supplies.

The Organization of African Unity also failed to take a stand on the conflicts in the Horn, although it did attempt to play a mediatory role in August 1977, when a special committee was established to help produce a peaceful settlement. But its efforts petered out when Somalia walked out because of the committee's refusal to admit a delegation from the WSLF.

101. A full account of Dr. Kevin Cahill's message is given in *Newsweek,* September 26, 1977.

Just before the massive buildup of Soviet and Cuban military aid at the end of November 1977, the military picture looked like this:

—The eastern front (Ogaden) was stalemated, with the Somalis prevented from consolidating their hold on Harar and pinned down on the perimeter of Diredawa by perhaps 120,000 Ethiopian soldiers (most of whom had been hastily recruited), supported by Soviet tanks, artillery, and MIGs, with fewer than a hundred Cubans, several hundred South Yemeni driver-technicians, and a group of Warsaw Pact senior officers. The Cuban unit was under the command of General Arnaldo Ochoa, who had fought in Angola. On the periphery, the Ethiopian forces were pinned down to defensive operations in the main areas of Bale, Sidamo, and Arssi.

—On the northern front about 40,000 Eritrean liberation forces had further strengthened their position so that the Ethiopian forces were largely pinned down in the capital, Asmara, the two Red Sea ports of Massawa and Assab, and the second main city, Keren. The vital road from Assab to Asmara was cut. In the adjacent Tigre province, the TPLF was harassing the movement of troops and supplies across the mountain roads reinforcing the Ethiopian army in Eritrea.

—On the western front, the forces of the Ethiopian Democratic Union (EDU) in Begemder and Semien had begun to lose their earlier initiative.

The main point that emerges from this picture of the fighting is that, despite its huge advantage in manpower and despite having substantially more armament than had been provided by the United States, the Ethiopian army was unable to defeat its challengers by force of numbers.

Western intelligence estimated that there were 100 Soviet-bloc military advisers and 400 Cuban military instructors in Ethiopia when the big military buildup began in late November, although some Western and African diplomatic sources in Addis Ababa put the figure at about 1,000 Soviet-bloc and Cuban military personnel and 300 doctors and civilian technicians.

The Soviet-Cuban airlift and sealift got under way in early December. A navigational satellite, Kosmos 693, was sent up on November 24, followed by a reconnaissance satellite, Kosmos 964, on December 4 and a military satellite on December 8. Over the next few weeks U.S. "spy" satellites, naval scanners, and radar stations in Israel, Turkey, and Iran monitored extensive Russian air and naval movements. In the first stage of the airlift, U.S. intelligence monitored fifty transport flights believed to have originated from Georgievsk, near the Black Sea, and Tashkent. They flew to Aden, where they refueled before continuing to Addis Ababa. Soon afterward, the United States learned that flight clearances had been requested from a number of countries, including Pakistan, Afghanistan, and Iraq. The requests had given various destinations, including Maputo in Mozambique, Aden, and Tripoli. Washington at once protested, charging that the airspace of a number of countries was being used without permission.

Pakistan briefly detained three military transport planes, camouflaged as civilian aircraft, at Karachi after forcing them to land. Iraq officially protested its airspace being used for flights to Ethiopia via Aden. Its president, Saddam Hussein, said that after its protests to Moscow, Iraq got a formal undertaking that Soviet planes would go only to Aden, not to Ethiopia.[102] He added that because relations with both the USSR and South Yemen were "so good . . . it's not reasonable to expect that we could tell a friend what it could or could not do, once they got to the Yemen. We told the Soviets, however, that if their attitude towards the Eritrean conflict didn't change, we could not allow their transport aircraft to use our facilities."

The usual route taken by aircraft flying supplies to Ethiopia before December was from Black Sea bases, west across Bulgaria and Yugoslavia, then south over the Adriatic and Mediterranean to Tripoli, and from there across Sudan airspace (without permission) to Addis Ababa.[103] The pattern changed during December 1977 and early January 1978 when, at the height of the airlift operation, 225 Antonov-22s and Ilyushin-76s—about 15 percent of the Soviet military air transport fleet—simultaneously used widely different routes. Some took the regular route over Bulgaria and Yugoslavia to Tripoli; others flew from near the Caspian Sea over Iran and Iraq to Aden; others took off from Tashkent and flew across Afghanistan and Pakistan; and still others flew along the Persian Gulf from Georgievsk, across Iraq and Aden. For three weeks in early December, Antonovs were leaving Soviet airfields at Georgievsk at intervals of fifteen to twenty minutes. (There is some conflict about the number of flights at the height of the airlift; one State Department source put the figure at fifty, according to the *Washington Star,* January 17, 1978.)

A sizable sealift of arms was undertaken concurrently with the airlift.

102. Interview with André de Borchgrave, *Newsweek,* July 17, 1978, pp. 24–25.
103. *Air Force Magazine,* March 1978.

Turkish, Egyptian, and U.S. monitoring agencies recorded the passage of between thirty and fifty Russian and Bulgarian warships and freighters through the Bosporus and the Suez Canal. They unloaded their supplies at Massawa and Assab, where Israeli and other intelligence sources (including those of Eritrea) reported the arrival of T-54 and T-55 tanks, crated aircraft, 122-millimeter artillery, and undetermined missiles. Amphibious landing craft were used in this operation—mostly, probably, the two 1,000-ton *Polnocny*-class ships supplied to South Yemen in 1973— the first time the Soviet Union had provided these to any state except Nasser's Egypt, India, and the Warsaw Pact countries.[104] Two *Alligator*-class Soviet warships operated continuously off Massawa, and the EPLF claimed that missiles were fired from them at EPLF positions around the port.[105]

The intensified Soviet airlift and sealift ended suddenly in mid-January 1978. In addition to war matériel, the lift brought in a considerable number of Soviet-bloc and Cuban technicians to handle the equipment, as well as other military elements. U.S. intelligence reports estimated in mid-January 1978 that an additional 200 Soviet, Cuban, and East German military personnel had arrived in Ethiopia, bringing the total to 3,000.[106] However, the Ethiopians insisted that there were still only 450 Russians and Cubans in the whole country, none in a combat role.[107] At the height of the airlift Cuba's defense minister, Raul Castro, arrived secretly in Addis Ababa on a mission undoubtedly connected with the buildup of Cuban combat troops. U.S. intelligence agency reports spoke of the arrival of two Cuban battalions, each of 650 men.[108] Washington reported that Cuban forces were arriving by air from Aden at the rate of 200 a day from late November on.[109]

Reacting to the Soviet-Cuban operations, the Somali government began a frantic round of diplomacy among Arab League and NATO countries as well as China. The U.S. administration was reportedly surprised and shaken by the size of the Soviet operation.[110] The situation was handled directly by the President and a few top advisers, and an attempt was made to hamper the airlift by stimulating other nations to protest illegal Soviet

104. Desmond Wettern, *Daily Telegraph*, February 23, 1978.
105. Mike Wells, *The Guardian* (Manchester), January 20, 1978.
106. James Reston, *International Herald-Tribune*, February 7, 1978.
107. David Lamb, ibid.
108. *Newsweek*, January 23, 1978.
109. Ibid., March 5, 1978.
110. Don Oberdorfer, *Washington Post*, March 5, 1978.

use of airspace.[111] The United States warned the Soviet Union about the risk of expanding the Ogaden war across Somalia's international border.

NATO strategists were concerned about the implications of the demonstration of Soviet airlift capacity. "We used to console ourselves with the thought that the Soviets were not very good at this kind of thing," one NATO official commented. "Now they have shown first in the Middle East, then in Angola and now in Ethiopia that they can organize things very effectively when they want to. They are getting better all the time."[112] The West German defense minister, George Leber, said that Soviet transport capability had become "a new strategic element" in the East-West balance.[113]

In early February 1978 the Somalis claimed that 20,000 Cubans had arrived in Ethiopia; Western intelligence sources gave the much lower figure of 3,000 Cubans and 1,000 Russians.[114] However, thousands of Cubans were arriving by sea from Aden and were assembled in a military camp at Assab, which was established during February.[115] By February 24 U.S. intelligence had raised its estimates of Cuban arrivals to the much higher figure of between 10,000 and 11,000.[116] According to Zbigniew Brzezinski, they were organized into two infantry brigades and one mechanized brigade.[117] Somalia claimed that military personnel from other Warsaw Pact countries such as East Germany, Czechoslovakia, Poland, and Hungary were also involved in what it alleged was a plan for an Ethiopian army invasion of Somalia.[118] Moscow denied that there was any intention of attacking Somalia itself or that any Warsaw Pact soldiers were engaged in the fighting.[119] Their denial was directed especially to a Somali allegation that Marshal Dmitri Ustinov, the Soviet minister of defense, had arrived in Addis Ababa to oversee military strategy in Ethiopia.[120] What was more clearly established, though, was that two Soviet generals had arrived in Harar in the Ogaden—General Vasily Ivanovich Petrov, listed in July 1976 as first deputy commander in chief of Soviet

111. Ibid.
112. *The Guardian,* January 20, 1978.
113. Ibid.
114. David Lamb, *International Herald-Tribune,* February 7, 1978.
115. *The Guardian,* February 3, 1978.
116. *Daily Telegraph,* February 25, 1978.
117. *New York Times,* February 25, 1978.
118. *International Herald-Tribune,* January 21–22, 1978.
119. Tass, January 18, 1978.
120. *Daily Telegraph,* January 17, 1978.

ground forces,[121] and General Grigory Barisov, who had previously been in charge of Soviet military aid to Somalia.[122] Brzezinski claimed that Petrov was in "direct command" of military operations in the Harar region.[123] Somalia's minister of information, Abdul Kassam Salad Hassan, also claimed, while on a visit to Peking, that an unidentified East German general had been seen in Harar. According to him, the East Germans were in charge of communications, security, and intelligence in the Ogaden; the Bulgarians were in charge of food supplies; and the Hungarians and Czechoslovaks were involved in other operations.[12]

The NATO powers first began to show serious concern about Soviet military intervention in the Horn during the major airlift and sealift started at the end of November 1977. The U.S. ambassador made official representations to the USSR protesting the arms buildup.[125] In January 1978 the United States took the initiative in convening a conference in Washington of a number of NATO powers with special interests in the Red Sea area to discuss developments there. Those invited were Britain, France, West Germany, and Italy. Their conclusion was that no solution could be found by "force of arms," and they called for a negotiated settlement of the dispute.[126]

When the major counteroffensive in the Ogaden, with full Soviet and Cuban backing, started in the first week of February, concern grew in the West that the war would spill over into Somalia. Cyrus Vance warned on February 10, 1978, that if Somalia's border were crossed it "would present a new and different situation," and President Carter revealed on February 17 that he had warned Ethiopia that the United States would consider an invasion of Somalia "a very serious breach of peace, endangering even worldwide peace." A fortnight later, on March 2, he accused the Soviet Union of "overarming" the Ethiopians, which produced "a threat to peace in the Horn of Africa."[127]

President Carter moved late in February 1978 to limit the conflict by ensuring that the war did not spread into Somalian territory. As a first step he sent a delegation to warn Colonel Mengistu of the danger of Ethiopian

121. *International Herald-Tribune,* February 27, 1978.

122. *The Guardian,* February 11, 1978.

123. *International Herald-Tribune,* February 27, 1978.

124. *Daily Telegraph,* March 1, 1978.

125. Briefing by John Trattner, director of the Office of Press Relations, U.S. Department of State, January 30, 1979.

126. *International Herald-Tribune,* January 23, 1978.

127. Ibid., March 3, 1978.

troops crossing Somalia's border. Mengistu promised that this would not happen if two conditions were met: withdrawal of Somali troops from the Ogaden, and no American arms for Somalia.[128] But he ruled out a cease-fire "while Somali troops were still on Ethiopian soil."[129] At the same time, Carter approached the USSR and the OAU, asking them to cooperate on the basis of three principles governing U.S. policy in the Horn: Somali withdrawal from the Ogaden; removal of Cuban and Soviet troops from Ethiopia; and lessening of the tension between Somalia and Ethiopia by honoring international boundaries in Africa, even though these were sometimes arbitrarily drawn. While Moscow was ready to provide assurances that Ethiopian forces would not attack Somalia, it rejected the U.S. secretary of state's request that Russian and Cuban troops be withdrawn from the conflict, on the ground that they were entitled to assist the Ethiopians to repel aggression.[130]

Armed with Soviet and Ethiopian promises about Somalia's borders, the United States next asked President Barre to disengage from the Ogaden. On March 9 he announced that he was withdrawing Somalia's "regular forces" from the Ogaden. This was the first time it had even been admitted that the Somali army was fighting in the area. Barre's explanation for his decision was that he had received guarantees from the "big powers" that the Ethiopian forces would not cross Somalia's border and that other foreign forces would be withdrawn from the area. However, although the major powers had guaranteed that Somalia's borders would not be crossed if it withdrew its army, no assurances were obtained by the United States in its negotiations with the USSR about the withdrawal of Soviet and Cuban forces from Ethiopia. On the contrary, even before they had completed their immediate objective in the Ogaden, the Russians had turned their attention to the second major battlefield, Eritrea.

By February 1978, when Ethiopia's allies were beginning to build up their military presence in Eritrea, the EPLF and the ELF had a virtual stranglehold on the territory. Asmara was tightly surrounded; Massawa was cut off on the inland side, making it impossible for traffic to move out of the port; the road between the only other port, Assab, and Asmara had been cut; and Keren had been taken. The railway line from Djibouti to Addis Ababa was no longer usable. As in the Ogaden, despite its huge

128. *The Guardian,* February 20, 1978.
129. *International Herald-Tribune,* February 20, 1978.
130. Henry S. Bradsher, *Washington Star,* January 13, 1978; Graham Hovey, *New York Times,* February 11, 1978; *The Guardian,* February 1, 1978.

manpower superiority in Eritrea, the Ethiopian army was no match for the guerrillas. A senior Ethiopian government official at Asmara, Mengesha Gessesa, said when he defected early in 1978: "It is becoming clear that Eritrea will be a free country in a few months."[131]

The Russians built stockpiles of weapons, tanks, and artillery from ships unloaded in Massawa and Assab, and they flew quantities of arms to Asmara's airport, which was still open to traffic. Two MIG-21 squadrons (twenty-four planes) and one MIG-23 squadron (twelve planes) were located at Asmara. It is uncertain who was flying them; the EPLF claimed that they were piloted by South Yemenis. Mil-4 and Mil-8 helicopters, armed with antitank missiles and flown by Russian pilots, were used in Eritrea, as well as in the Ogaden.[132] (In December 1978 the EPLF shot down one of the helicopters, killing its Russian pilot.)[133] The EPLF reported that Russian crews were seen operating BM-21 multiple-rocket launchers at Massawa.[134] There were 3,000 Cubans in Asmara, but they stayed in the city and the airport. After the first Ogaden campaign was over in mid-March, General Vasily Petrov arrived in Asmara, presumably to direct the strategy as he had done in the Ogaden campaign. A Russian general (whose identity was never established) took charge of the Ethiopian air force base at Asmara. Eleven Russian officers of lieutenant-colonel rank commanded field units once the new campaign against the Eritreans developed momentum. Lower-ranking officers commanded smaller combat units, with between 50 and 250 officers deployed on each main front.[135]

An unsuccessful attempt was made in March to break out of Asmara and Massawa. After the main campaign in the Ogaden ended, about 120,000 Ethiopian forces were deployed against the Eritreans in an offensive that got under way in May. It achieved a number of initial successes, especially against the ELF on the Sudan border; the siege was broken at Massawa, Keren was retaken, and the road reopened from Assab to Asmara. Despite Ethiopian claims of victory, however, the main opposition force, the EPLF, still held out—and was continuing to do so almost a year later—even taking the initiative as late as April 1979. The only significant change was that the EPLF had been forced to return to its

131. Interview with Dan Connell, *ACR, 1978–79*, p. B223.
132. *The Guardian*, February 15, 1978.
133. Sudan News Agency (Khartoum), December 12, 1978.
134. Dan Connell, *Observer* Foreign News Service, February 10, 1978.
135. Ibid.; also *Le Monde*, February 4, 1978.

earlier phase of guerrilla tactics and was no longer able, or trying, to defend the towns.

The big difference between the campaigns in the Ogaden and Eritrea was that no foreign ground troops were engaged in fighting the Eritreans. The Cubans and the South Yemenis had both announced that their military units would not become involved in fighting the Eritreans, since they had supported them in the past. Nevertheless, the Cubans did not withdraw their troops from Asmara or Assab. Cuba officially declared that the problem of Eritrea was a political one, which should not be solved by military means.[136] Although the USSR also favored a political settlement of the Eritrean problem, it lent its support to the Ethiopian military effort to "crush the counter-revolution" in Eritrea while seeking to promote mediation between the two sides.[137]

Although the Russians ended their big airlift operation in mid-January 1978, a regular supply of arms continued to arrive by sea and air throughout the rest of 1978. U.S. intelligence reported that over 61,000 tons of military equipment had been unloaded in the first five months of 1978 from thirty-six freighters and fifty-nine transport planes.[138] NATO intelligence sources reported that Soviet and East German technicians were engaged in constructing airfields.[139] The Tigre People's Liberation Front said it could observe Cubans building a new strategic road and airfield in north Tigre.[140] The number of Cuban combat troops in Ethiopia was estimated at between 16,000 and 17,000. In August 1978 twice as many Soviet warships as usual were being regularly deployed in the Red Sea.

Soviet Behavior

Although apparently firmly allied by its Treaty of Friendship and Cooperation with the Somali Republic, the USSR showed early signs of having seen the possibilities opening up for it by developments in Ethiopia. Even before the Dergue dethroned Haile Selassie in September 1974 and steered the country in a revolutionary direction in 1975, Soviet diplomats in Addis Ababa told the Dergue that Russian arms were available to them if they chose to end their military ties with the United States.

136. This was stated by Cuba's vice-president, Carlos Rafael Rodriguez, in an interview with Hugh O'Shaughnessy, *The Observer,* February 26, 1978.
137. Dan Connell, *The Nation,* May 6, 1978.
138. *International Herald-Tribune,* June 18, 1978.
139. Ibid., July 6, 1978.
140. TPLF spokesman in interview with Colin Legum.

Soviet policy—with which Cuba was closely aligned except on the Eritrean question—moved through two distinct phases. The first phase opened in April 1976 when Moscow signaled its readiness to shift its support to the Addis Ababa regime by endorsing its program of "realistic documents," which, it said, were based on "the feasibility of the immediate tasks of the Ethiopian revolution, whose progress puzzles the uninitiated, maddens its enemies and is a source of satisfaction for the true friends of the new Ethiopia."[141] Moscow's attitude disturbed its Somali ally—especially when, two months later, it endorsed the Dergue's proposals for settling the Eritrean problem along federal lines. However, the Russians were still careful in their handling of the Somalis, possibly because they were not yet completely sure that the Dergue would suspend its arms arrangements with the United States. During this first phase the Russians, with Cuban support, began to sound out the Somalis about a *Pax Sovietica* in the Horn of Africa. Their argument was that, once the United States had been eliminated from the area as a military factor, it would become possible for them to help mediate border and other agreements between the Somalis, the Ethiopians, and the Eritreans,[142] since there would be no "imperialists" left in the area to divide Somalia and Ethiopia. The Somalis immediately rejected this idea, arguing that the Dergue, far from being Marxist, was fascist. The Russians nevertheless continued to press their arguments, while keeping up their side of the treaty obligations with the Somalis. The first phase ended in May 1977 after the United States' military assistance program in Ethiopia was terminated, and Colonel Mengistu signed a major multifaceted agreement with the USSR. Although the agreement did not specify military supplies, Soviet arms began to flow into Ethiopia from that time. Also in May Somalia's President Barre quarreled with Fidel Castro over his attempt at mediation along the lines proposed by the Soviet Union.

May 1977 was important because it was the month in which regulars of the Somali army began to cross into the Ogaden. Since the Soviet military advisers were still in Somalia at the time, it was impossible for them not to have known what was happening, yet relations with Mogadiscio were not broken until six months later, when Moscow gave as its official reason for the break: "Somalia had launched an armed aggression against Ethiopia, choosing as its target the Ogaden province. The Soviet Union had repeatedly emphasized that it had been, and always would be, on the

141. Radio Moscow, April 24, 1976.
142. Based on interviews of Somali officials by Colin Legum.

side of independent African states in the event of an attack. The Soviet Union's principled policy was expressed by the fact that despite its Treaty with Somalia, it came to the aid of the victim of aggression and did not support the Somali leaders' territorial expansion."[143]

The second phase of Soviet policy began in mid-1977 when—while still apparently hoping that the Somalis would in the end come round to accepting its *Pax Sovietica* plan—Moscow showed that, if faced with a choice between Somalia and Ethiopia, it would choose the latter. This was a bold policy in view of the kind of commitments the Soviet Union would have to make—first, to help Mengistu establish his ascendancy within the Dergue; second, to help his regime establish its control over a country engulfed by military insurrections; and finally, to consolidate the nascent Marxist-Leninist revolution.

Why did the Soviet Union decide to exchange its established foothold in Somalia for all the uncertainties of revolutionary Ethiopia? Ethiopia obviously offered far greater advantages to Soviet interests than Somalia. Not only did it have two ports (Massawa and Assab), which are far superior to Berbera and Mogadishu; but there was also the reasonable chance that a strong Ethiopia would someday dominate the important port of Djibouti. Another advantage of Ethiopia over Somalia was that it is potentially a rich country, holding a strategically important position in the African continent and in the Red Sea region. The Russians also probably took into account two other factors that militated against their continued alliance with the Somalis. They knew as well as anyone that Pan-Somalism is the dominant aspect of Somalia's foreign policy and that the army that they had helped to build would, at an opportune moment, attempt to wrest the Ogaden province away from Ethiopia. If the Russians remained in Somalia, they would inevitably be a party to the transgression of Ethiopia's border, which would seriously jeopardize their relations with the Organization of African Unity. The Russians' second concern was that they could never be sure when the Somalis would exercise their option of accepting Saudi Arabian support in exchange for expelling the Soviet presence from the Red Sea—an option that the Somalis have toyed with for some time. Seen in this perspective, the Soviet decision to shift its allegiance is not as surprising as it appeared at the time.

The Soviet Union stated that it was shifting its allegiance because (1) Ethiopia was a victim of Somali aggression, supported by the "imperialists" and their "proxies" in the area—the "reactionary Arab States" of

---

143. Vladimir Kudryavtsev, Radio Moscow, December 28, 1978.

Saudi Arabia, Egypt, and Sudan; (2) it had received an appeal for military support from a sovereign government, which was entitled to choose its allies; and (3) the Soviet Union had an "international duty to assist progressive revolutionary movements."[144] In the words of one Soviet authority on Africa, Vladimir Kudryavtsev: "The USSR supported Ethiopia because its people had started to implement their national and democratic Revolution, the struggle to liquidate feudalism and oppose foreign domination of the country."[145]

The Soviet Union chose to emphasize the first two aims rather than the third—that of supporting a revolution in Africa. This enabled it to score a number of political successes: it could align itself with the OAU principle of resisting forcible changes of borders; it could claim to be acting in conformity with the international right to assist a sovereign state faced with foreign aggression; and it could escape some of the responsibility for its contribution to making the "Somali aggression" possible in the first place by the Soviet role in training and arming the modern Somali army of 20,000 men.

The official reason given by the Soviet Union for its military intervention in the Ogaden fell away in March 1978 when the Somali army withdrew all its units to its own side of the border. Yet the level of Soviet and Cuban military support actually rose after the fighting had shifted to Eritrea and after the Somali withdrawal. Unlike Somalia, the Eritreans could not be accused of "aggression against Ethiopia's borders." The Russians justified their support of the Dergue against the Eritreans on the grounds that they were "secessionists" and that they had the support of "counter-revolutionary elements" abroad. They did not favor crushing the Eritreans by military force; like the Cubans, they saw Eritrea as a political problem. To judge both from their own statements and from independent information, the Russians and the Cubans appear to have done their best to dissuade Mengistu from mounting a major military offensive in Eritrea. They could point to the last sentence in Article 1 of the Soviet-Ethiopian Declaration on the Foundations of Friendly Relations and Cooperation, signed on May 6, 1977, in which "the two sides declare that inter-government relations must be based specifically on such principles as . . . non-interference in internal affairs and the settlement of disputed issues by peaceful means."

144. Radio Moscow, December 29, 1978.
145. Radio Moscow, in French, December 28, 1978, and in English, December 29, 1978.

Moscow saw its role not just as helping Ethiopia defend its borders against foreign aggression but as helping it by all means possible to safeguard and consolidate the revolution—an objective, according to both Moscow and Havana, that could be achieved only through a Marxist-Leninist proletariat party in Ethiopia. The Russians are known to have been concerned about Mengistu's refusal to convert his military regime into a mass popular organization, as he had apparently agreed to do as one of the conditions for Soviet support.[146] Although Mengistu continued to promise that he would create such a party, he showed great caution in establishing his proposed "Ethiopian Popular Organization of the Masses." The reason he gave for his caution was that previous efforts (when he was still supported by Me'ison) had proved "impractical."[147] He had therefore established a center to recruit "genuine communists" as a first step toward creating a proletariat party. The center to which he referred was a planning committee, whose members also included Marxist-Leninist advisers from the USSR, East Germany, and Cuba.[148] This is probably the first time that the Soviet bloc countries have actively helped to plan a local Communist movement to sustain a regime in a third world country.

At no time did the Russians show any real concern about the possibility that their role in the Horn might invite counteraction by the Western powers. They consistently accused the NATO powers (especially the United States) and China of military intervention through "third parties" —Saudi Arabia, Iran, Sudan, and Egypt. The aim of such an alliance, Moscow claimed, was to oppose countries "taking up a progressive path of development and to establish control over the Red Sea. The Soviet Union is against such a dangerous development of events."[149]

Toward the end of the campaign in the Ogaden, in mid-March 1978, the Soviet Union insisted that the Ethiopians had no intention of crossing Somalia's border and that all the prerequisites for peace had been established. What would help restore peace to the Horn was a pledge by other countries—"first of all by the United States and its NATO partners and also China"—that they would not interfere in the future. The Somalis

146. The source for this statement is Me'ison, whose leaders accused Mengistu of breaking his agreement with them.
147. Statement by Colonel Mengistu to Afro-Asian Writers; Radio Addis Ababa, March 12, 1979.
148. This information was communicated to Colin Legum from private sources in Addis Ababa.
149. Sergey Kulik, a Tass political writer, Radio Moscow, March 22, 1978.

had to withdraw their troops completely from Ethiopia and unconditionally give up their claims to parts of the territory of Ethiopia, Kenya, and Djibouti.

With a breathtaking display of cynicism, the Soviet media insisted that it was the NATO powers and China that "supplied weapons to the aggressor"—the Somali army. Furthermore, it was "the Western nations that encouraged Somalia to carry out an act of aggression against Ethiopia."[150] After Somalia had completed its withdrawal of troops to its side of the border, the Russians took a new tack. They said the United States was planning to supply Somalia with arms in order to establish itself firmly in Somalia, hoping to undermine relations of countries in the region with the USSR and to bar its access to the Red Sea.[151]

Perceptions of Soviet Policy and Actions

Only Kenya among the black African states declared itself an active ally of the Addis Ababa regime, but the great majority of OAU member states supported the Soviet-Cuban role insofar as it was held to be a response to a sovereign African state that had asked for help to repel a transgressor state, Somalia. The majority of African states were opposed to Eritrea's struggle for secession—an aim held to be incompatible with the preservation of the integrity of African states. OAU member states did not comment when the Russians justified their intervention as an effort to consolidate a Marxist-Leninist revolution in an African country.

Egypt and Sudan suspected that the USSR planned to use Ethiopia as a springboard from which to threaten them once the Communist regime was established in Ethiopia. President Sadat told the U.S. Congress in February 1977 that he envisioned the Russians and their Ethiopian allies as threatening Egypt's Red Sea trade route, as well as one of the sources of the Nile, Lake Tana: "Naturally, I am concerned at the Soviets controlling half my water." President Nimeiry of Sudan warned the OAU summit meeting in Gabon in July 1977, as he had before, against "the new socialist imperialism" of the Soviet Union, which was "threatening to turn the continent into a vast area of conflict." Saudi Arabia saw the Russians' objectives as being to promote Communist regimes in the region and to acquire bases in the Red Sea, both of which were inimical to Saudi Arabia's security. Iran, under the shah, expressed similar concern. These

150. Vladislav Chernuka, Radio Moscow, March 13, 1978.
151. Tass, March 16, 1978.

four countries took the lead in trying to achieve two aims: to help strengthen Somalia after its break with the Soviet Union and to persuade the Western nations to stand against expanding Soviet influence in the region, which, in the words of Nimeiry, was "a spreading cancer." The Arab League foreign ministers, meeting in Cairo on March 29, 1979, characterized Soviet-Cuban intervention in the Horn as "aggressive" and called for the immediate withdrawal of both countries' forces.

Until the end of 1977, the Western consensus was that the Soviet Union posed no serious threat in the Red Sea area. This view rested on two assumptions. The first was that a country known to be independent-minded and antagonistic to any form of foreign control, as Ethiopia was, was unlikely to allow itself to come under Soviet domination, even if its regime found it expedient to enter into temporary military agreements with the Soviet bloc. The second assumption was closely linked to the first: that even if the Soviet Union did succeed in temporarily establishing a position of influence in Ethiopia, it would in time be forced out, as had happened in Egypt and Sudan. It was therefore believed wise to avoid any military intervention in the Horn and not to adopt a hostile attitude toward any of the parties in the conflict.

Western perceptions about Soviet policy in the Horn, however, changed considerably as a result of the major airlift and sealift operations in late 1977 and early 1978. Cyrus Vance warned at his press conference on February 10, 1978, that the involvement of the Soviet Union and Cuba in the Horn was affecting the political atmosphere between those two countries and the United States—"a matter which we will obviously keep in mind as we proceed with the talks in the Indian Ocean because what is happening there is inconsistent with a limitation of forces in the area which is what we are seeking insofar as the Indian Ocean talks are concerned." The fourth round of Soviet-U.S. negotiations on the limitation and subsequent reduction of military activity in the Indian Ocean ended soon after Vance's statement. They had not been resumed at the time this was written, despite several efforts by the USSR to start them up again.

There was immediate concern that the conflict might expand across the border into Somalia, which, as Vance said, would "present a new and different situation" calling for possible intervention by the Western powers and their regional allies. Of greater concern was Soviet strategy in the Red Sea, the Indian Ocean, and the African continent.

Soviet policy in the Horn and in other parts of Africa was also seen by Western leaders as likely to jeopardize negotiations for a SALT II agreement. President Carter warned on March 2, 1978, that Soviet policies could sway American public opinion against approval of a new SALT accord. He explained: "It is Soviet actions in Africa, and not U.S. government policy, which has created a linkage between arms accords and developments in the Ethiopia-Somalia area." Only a day earlier, Carter's national security adviser, Zbigniew Brzezinski, had said that, while the administration was not itself "expressing any linkage" between Soviet actions in Africa and SALT, it was a matter of "realistic judgment" to conclude that "unwarranted intrusion of Soviet power into a purely local conflict would inevitably complicate the context not only of the negotiating process itself, but of any ratification process that would follow."

The clearest summation of the U.S. response to Soviet policy in the Horn was provided by Marshall D. Shulman, special adviser to the secretary of state on Soviet affairs.[152] He said that it should come as no surprise that the Russians had moved into an area where they felt they had an opportunity to expand their influence; this is characteristic of Soviet behavior. The Soviet Union was able to be on the side of legitimacy of the issue—the defense of territorial integrity—which is the side most African states were on. "The problem from our point of view arose from the fact that they did so with such obvious lack of restraint. The scale of the weapons they put into the area and the large number of Cuban soldiers they transported there exceeded any reasonable definition of restraint. . . . They were inclined not to appreciate what impact their actions would have. . . . As in the case of Angola they seriously miscalculated what the American reaction would be." The only reasonable U.S. response was to work in the diplomatic field. Shulman said he was skeptical about linkage. "Economic relations are not a feasible instrument because we don't have any trade agreements in force and we aren't able to put, say, limits on credits because these simply aren't being granted. . . . SALT is not a desirable instrument to use because the agreement, if and when we get it, would be in our own security interest. . . . What the Administration has been saying to the Russians is that lack of restraint in Africa would affect the general climate in this country, and that may have its effect in many ways."

Although the Western European nations were in close agreement with American perceptions of the USSR's role in the Horn, their leaders, with the exception of those in Britain, said little in public. The communiqué issued at the end of the NATO summit meeting in Washington on May 29–30, 1978, referred to the "repeated instances in which the Soviet Union

152. Interview with Bernard Gwertzman, *New York Times,* April 16, 1978.

and some of its allies have exploited situations of instability and regional conflict in the developing world." It warned that "disregard for the indivisibility of detente cannot but jeopardize the further improvement of East-West relations." But while the summit agreed on a long-term defense program, no specific proposals were advanced for responding to the immediate situation in the Horn.

Typically, China saw the Soviet intervention as part of Moscow's design for world hegemony. When the Russians failed to withdraw from Ethiopia after the Somalis had done so, the *Peking Review* declared on April 7, 1978: "One lesson that can be drawn from this is: Once the Soviet mercenary troops step on the soil of an African region or country, they will not quit easily. That is because the military intervention is not directed merely against one region or one country, but is closely connected with the social-imperialist bid for world domination, and its increasingly intense rivalry with the other superpower. The Soviet 'foreign legion,' to wit, the Cuban troops, is nothing but a tool of the Kremlin for world hegemony."

Outcomes

The USSR and Cuba have emerged as the main strategic allies of Ethiopia. They have replaced the Western powers, especially the United States, as the dominant military factor in Ethiopia and increased their ability to influence political developments in the Horn of Africa and the wider Red Sea area.

However, the Russians have not yet succeeded in their avowed aim of assisting the Ethiopian military regime to consolidate its Marxist-Leninist revolution. Nor have they succeeded in making Somalia part of their proclaimed design of creating a federation of Marxist-Leninist states in the Horn.

The principal, though by no means the only, obstacle delaying the consolidation of the Ethiopian revolution is the Eritrean resistance to Ethiopian and Soviet policies. Despite the considerable Soviet military support of the Ethiopian army in Eritrea, the secessionist forces still remain firmly lodged in the province. Unless the Eritrean liberation movement can either be defeated militarily or be persuaded or coerced into making a political settlement, the future of the Ethiopian revolution remains in doubt. Although the Somali army was defeated in the Ogaden, the forces of insurrection in the province remain active despite continuing Cuban ground support of the Ethiopian forces. Other centers of resistance, especially in the Oromo (Galla) areas in the south, have not yet been overcome. Opposition also still comes from a number of Marxist movements.

From being a state tied militarily to the USSR, Somalia has joined the regional alliance of anti-Soviet states, which includes Sudan, Saudi Arabia, and Egypt. Although deeply shaken by the defeat in the Ogaden, the Somali political system appears to have survived intact. Pro-Soviet elements in Somalia have apparently been unable to change the country's attitude toward the Soviet bloc to a friendlier one. Somalia has been left with a strong sense of grievance against the Western powers because of their refusal to replace the USSR as a source of military supplies.

The Red Sea regional powers—especially Saudi Arabia and Sudan—feel badly let down by the unwillingness of the Western powers to intervene actively in opposing the expansion of Soviet influence in the area. Their confidence in the likelihood of the Western powers intervening effectively if any of them should be subjected to Soviet pressure has been visibly affected. Their leaders complain about what they feel to be ambiguities in the policies of the Western powers as well as a lack of political will, especially on the part of the United States, to offer their military support in resisting any further expansion of Soviet influence and to enlarge their military presence in the Red Sea region. Because these Red Sea countries perceive Soviet strategy in their area as a serious threat to their own security, they are puzzled and concerned by the failure of their Western friends to see things their way. This has set up tension between the NATO powers and their natural allies in the region.

As in Angola, the Western powers have been left thrashing about to find means of deterring the USSR and Cuba from intervening militarily in the areas where the NATO powers are reluctant to become militarily involved themselves, even though they perceive the extension of Soviet influence in those areas as liable to upset the balance of power in strategically sensitive parts of the third world.

China has also failed to have any effective influence on developments in the Horn. Like the regional powers, the Chinese leaders blame the Western powers for not intervening actively against the USSR and Cuba. China lost its position in Ethiopia but somewhat improved its position in Somalia, though it is still reluctant to assume a significant military role in Somalia's support.

The final outcome of the conflicts in the Horn of Africa still remains in doubt. While the Soviet Union has gained an important advantage, it has not yet been able to demonstrate its ability to achieve its objectives. While the regional powers still look to the United States and other Western nations for the necessary support to thwart Soviet objectives, Western policy still appears to rely almost exclusively on local forces to accomplish this aim, though without active military intervention by the NATO countries or any substantial increase in arms to the region. This situation changed somewhat after the overthrow of the shah in Iran and, especially, after the USSR's military intervention in Afghanistan. The NATO powers began to give a greater importance to their naval forces in the Indian Ocean and the Persian Gulf; the United States negotiated for naval and air facilities at Mombasa with Kenya; attempts were made by the United States to secure naval and air facilities in Berbera and Mogadishu; and a higher priority was given by the United States to developing the British-controlled military base in Diego Garcia.

PART THREE

Conclusions

CHAPTER FOURTEEN

The Utility of Force

Now that the USSR has achieved strategic parity with the United States and its conventional military units are more capable than they were in the past, the use of Soviet armed forces as a foreign policy instrument is increasingly determined by decisionmaking in the Kremlin rather than by the USSR's ability to intervene militarily. Soviet leaders no doubt will be influenced by prior experiences bearing similarity to current issues. Foreign observers seeking clues to future Soviet behavior might also look to the historical record.

This chapter examines (1) the effectiveness of past Soviet uses of force; (2) the significance to operational outcomes of the type, size, deployment, and activities of Soviet armed forces; and (3) the effects of past strategic balances and specific U.S. military operations on the use of Soviet armed forces.

Standards for Assessment[1]

What is an effective act of coercive military diplomacy? This analysis focuses on the satisfaction of Soviet authorities' objectives by foreign actors and the Kremlin's achievement of specific situational outcomes. It does not consider the satisfaction of values held by Soviet leaders. Deciphering individuals' motives is extremely difficult in any instance and is virtually impossible to do with Soviet policymakers. What was on Leonid

---

1. Discussion in this section is drawn in part from Barry M. Blechman and Stephen S. Kaplan, *Force without War: U.S. Armed Forces as a Political Instrument* (Brookings Institution, 1978), pp. 59–74.

Brezhnev's mind after the clash between Chinese and Soviet soldiers on Damansky Island in early March 1969? Did Brezhnev want to ensure the security of his nation? Did he have a visceral desire for revenge or want to ensure Soviet prestige and dignity? Or did he feel that the integrity of his political position within the USSR or of his image in the minds of Soviet citizens and loved ones was at stake? It is impossible to know. Memoirs, biographies, accounts by journalists, and reports about the policymaking of Western leaders are hotly disputed; similar materials about Soviet leaders barely exist. And, at least at the public level, understanding of Soviet decisionmaking during foreign policy crises does not exist at all. Therefore it is questionable *whose* motivation should even be examined in specific cases.

Less contentious is the immediate behavior desired of foreign actors and the situational outcomes that were sought by the Soviet leadership. About these matters there is greater uniformity in the interpretation of verbal and written communications by Kremlin authorities, Soviet media statements, and Moscow's manipulation of military and other instruments of diplomacy. The identity of and lines of authority within the elite that directed Soviet actions after Ghana seized two Russian fishing trawlers in 1969 are difficult to determine; it is probably impossible to know what motivated individuals in their actions and whether their objectives were satisfied. More evident are the foreign behavior and outcomes sought most immediately in this incident by the Soviet leadership—the release by Ghanaian authorities of the seized trawlers and crews and the avoidance of damage to the USSR's image in sub-Saharan Africa. Similarly, following the initial Ussuri River fighting in 1969, Moscow tried to persuade Peking (1) to give up its belief in the utility of violence and its attempt to create a climate of uncertainty about the future of formerly Chinese territory that had been obtained by Russia in the nineteenth century, and (2) to enter into negotiations on at least this issue of dispute. Whatever the motivation and further objectives of Soviet policymakers were, the achievement of these immediate objectives was the focus of their attention and, presumably, necessary to the satisfaction of any additional goals they may have had.

Because desired outcomes may be achieved in the immediate sense but soon lost, this chapter assesses the achievement of outcomes both in the short term (defined arbitrarily as the period up to six months after the initial use of the Soviet military) and over a longer term (three years). Thus, durable positive outcomes may be distinguished from ephemeral ones. Of course, the persistence of favorable outcomes for several years may owe more to other factors and new developments than to an earlier use of armed forces. Whether positive outcomes have been sustained at all, however, is important to decisionmakers considering a new resort to force.

The achievement of operational goals and their retention does not necessarily imply that decisionmakers are satisfied with outcomes. Chosen goals may be the only ones that enough people can agree on or that seem feasible. Just as the use of armed forces is usually geared to some extent to customized goals, short-term objectives are formulated according to available means, perceptions of foreign attitudes, and acceptable risk.

To focus exclusively on the immediate behavior of actors and situational results desired would not take into account more general or strategic considerations of Soviet leaders during incidents—considerations more enduring and fundamental than operational objectives. For example, when the Kremlin decided to airlift Cuban soldiers and armaments to the Popular Movement for the Liberation of Angola (MPLA) during the Angolan civil war and to Ethiopa during its conflict on the Horn of Africa, Soviet leaders presumably were trying to do more than sway the outcome of the two conflicts. Other considerations might have been the USSR's global competition with the United States and China, the achievement of prestige with new regimes in Angola and Ethiopia, and thus, the ability to exert greater influence on developments in Africa and the Middle East. The Kremlin may have wanted to demonstrate the global reach of Soviet conventional forces and, more immediately, have had as a goal the acquisition of facilities for Soviet aircraft and warships. Despite the plausibility of these and other interests, strategic objectives, insofar as they involve motivation, are not as apparent as immediate operational objectives. So while this analysis explores outcomes important to presumed Soviet interests, these outcomes were not necessarily the ones of greatest concern to Moscow during particular incidents. For example, in responding to President Gamal Abdel Nasser's plea in late 1969 for air defense assistance, Moscow's principal operational objectives were to compel Israel to halt its deep penetration raids, to ensure Nasser's political position in Egypt, and to reinforce the USSR's relationship with Cairo (including, in this case, increased Soviet access to military bases in Egypt). Also at stake, but more difficult to identify as being influential in Kremlin decisionmaking, were the USSR's credibility and position in the Arab world and third world and the otherwise unchallenged military supremacy of a U.S. ally and American military technology over a Moscow ally equipped with Soviet arms.

Broad outcomes are examined in terms of a balance sheet that may include both calculated and unexpected gains and losses. An example of an unexpected loss would be the dissatisfaction of President Anwar Sadat with the demeanor and political activities of Soviet military men and diplomats in Egypt and with Moscow's attempt to use its expanded presence in Egypt to constrain Egyptian policy, and Sadat's openness to U.S. overtures toward friendly relations with Egypt and to U.S. aid to help reduce Egyptian dependence on the USSR. In short, broad outcomes are considered, but only in relation to presumed interests of the Soviet state and not as they relate to "known" goals of its leaders.

In addition to examining the short- and longer-term satisfaction of Soviet operational objectives and other important outcomes, this chapter also explores the utility of different ways in which Soviet armed forces were used. All of the case studies consider the political use of Soviet armed forces in situations of conflict or hostility between actors: in some instances fighting was continual and intense; in others, violence was sporadic or only a serious possibility. At the least, the political climate of the incidents included antagonism and tension. The essential role of Soviet armed forces in all but one of the incidents in which they were used was a coercive one. As a coercive instrument, Soviet military units were used to compel a foreign actor to do something or to stop doing something, or to deter a target against either taking an undesired action or stopping an activity that was appreciated. In many instances, a coercive use of force apparently was meant not only to deter behavior but also to compel an action. For example, Warsaw Pact maneuvers and exercises in late spring and early summer 1968 were intended to compel Prague to at least partially reverse its liberalization and to deter the Czechoslovaks from going further in this direction.

In some incidents the essential antagonism was between a foreign actor and the USSR itself and Soviet military power was orchestrated only on behalf of the Soviet Union. In other incidents the military were used to secure Soviet interests by coercing one foreign actor on behalf of another. Frequently when Soviet military power was used to support a foreign actor, that actor's conduct was probably more important to the USSR than the behavior of the target at which coercion was directed. Coercion was necessary for obtaining the honors sought from the actor the USSR was supporting. For example, although coercing Portugal in West Africa in 1970 may have had its own reward, the reinforcement of relations with Guinea was almost certainly Moscow's driving goal. In some instances the USSR did not enjoy at all its coercive role, such as when it had to sacrifice its relations with Somalia as a result of its support of Ethiopia in the 1977–78 conflict on the Horn of Africa.

Just as coercive military diplomacy may aim at deterrence or compulsion, armed forces, used as an instrument of support, also may assure that an ally continues to do something or not do something or induce a friend to do something or to stop doing something. Military force may be orchestrated to both assure and induce behavior at the same time, such as when Moscow sought to assure Sekou Touré's maintenance of good relations with the USSR and to induce the Guinean president to grant lodging for Soviet reconnaissance aircraft and warships.

Military force can be used to threaten an actor indirectly as well as directly—for example, by raising the stakes during a crisis, thereby leading a patron to discipline its client. The Soviet military measures and ultimatum that prompted the U.S. alert during the 1973 Middle East war also motivated the Nixon administration to pressure Israel to accept the previously agreed upon cease-fire.

Success and Failure

It is important to be clear about what is implied by the successful use of the military for political purposes. Success in using armed forces to reinforce desired behavior would imply that the actor was unsure about whether to continue performing the desired action and that Moscow's use of armed forces was recognized by the actor and did indeed persuade him not to change the behavior in question. If the desired behavior was going to be performed in any case, the use of force would be inconsequential, even if the actor did recognize and consider it. Failure would imply that the actor did not recognize the use of force or did but was not influenced by it. Thus, failure can be determined more easily than success: it is simply necessary to observe an actor not behaving in a desired way.

Success could imply that a use of the armed forces influenced the views of those around an individual leader, thereby causing him to behave in a desired way. Since few have ruled with absolute authority, the influence exerted on factions, individuals, and policy debates may have been Moscow's most frequently effective avenue to a satisfactory outcome. The con-

clusion that armed forces were used successfully when the objective was
to modify or change an actor's behavior also implies that the actor behaved desirably at least to some degree as a result of Moscow's use of the
military and that in the absence of this action the desired behavior would
not have been performed. However, despite the achievement and retention
of desired objectives in an incident and satisfaction with related developments, the relationship between the use of force and any outcome may be
tenuous or even nonexistent. Desired foreign behavior may occur in any
event.

The political use of the military may be accompanied by policy statements, diplomatic communications, the manipulation of economic assistance and arms transfers, and covert activities. These instruments may be
more or less important in achieving objectives than the use of the armed
forces. Such instruments may also either clarify and reinforce the meaning
of the military's activities or confuse and undermine them. The choices of
foreign decisionmakers whom Soviet policymakers are attempting to influence are also affected by their own domestic and foreign pressures and
constraints as well as by their perceptions, motivation, and degree of
commitment to a particular course or value. Although the Soviet Union
might clearly threaten a use of force, a foreign leader may perceive only a
weak Soviet commitment; domestic considerations may make a target act
against its own better judgment; or nothing at all may avail when an actor
identifies an objective with its own sense of destiny. The "confident use of
a strategy of coercive diplomacy" will include a consideration of all these
factors.[2]

The sum—clearly a complex one—of the variables influencing a target's decisions is a screen through which the armed forces used as a political instrument, as well as other Soviet policy instruments, must penetrate
to achieve a desired outcome. Different screens present varying degrees
of difficulty.

The Satisfaction of Operational Objectives

Soviet armed forces, when used as a political instrument, were an uncertain means for achieving specific objectives abroad. In the incidents
explored here in depth, positive outcomes and their retention for at least

2. Alexander L. George, David K. Hall, and William E. Simons, *The Limits of
Coercive Diplomacy: Laos, Cuba, Vietnam* (Little, Brown, 1971), p. 216.

a few years varied greatly with circumstances and with how Soviet military power was used. The realization of broader outcomes important to Soviet interests also was problematic.

China and Eastern Europe

The two most serious challenges to the USSR, which precipitated large Soviet political-military operations, were China's heightened hostility toward the Soviet Union in the late 1960s and periodic rebellions in Eastern Europe. The political character of Eastern Europe and relationships in Asia would probably be different if Soviet armed forces had been absent from these regions during the past several decades. Soviet military formations exercised almost continuous deterrence against major change opposed by the USSR. However, when general deterrence failed in Eastern Europe, Soviet military units were a virtual flop as a discrete political instrument aimed at compelling the reversal of unwanted developments or deterring other undesirable behavior. Moscow achieved its operational objectives against Peking, but only after many months of Soviet military activity and a threat to wage nuclear war against China—and at an enormous long-term cost.

The Soviet military buildup east of the Urals and in Mongolia during the several years before the clash on March 15, 1969, did not result in conciliatory Chinese behavior but rather in more blatant hostility toward Moscow. Although the border actions and further Soviet buildup after the violence on March 2, 1969, did not provoke new Chinese border provocations and may indeed have been an effective deterrent, it was only after the Kremlin threatened a nuclear strike against China that Peking felt compelled to enter negotiations with the USSR. Even then Peking did not accept Soviet positions in the negotiations, but used the talks as a hedge against preemptive Soviet military action and to buy time to build a favorable political environment in which to confront the USSR and increase its own military capabilities. Thus the USSR obtained relatively little after exerting maximum force short of war. By going so far to obtain a secure border in the short term, a dynamic dangerous to long-term Soviet security and global interests was set in motion.

As Thomas Robinson argues, the fear generated by this coercive diplomacy, which compelled an isolated China to enter into negotiations, also led Peking to mortgage its economic, foreign, and defense policy to create a greater military and global political base—an anti-Soviet global entente—that would make the USSR more wary of threatening China and increase Peking's ability to resist coercion. A decade after the Ussuri River clashes China was in political and economic alliance with the United States, Europe, and Japan against the USSR. Soviet attempts to intimidate China and the USSR's expanded air and naval presence in the Far East and Sea of Japan, which were related in part to the Sino-Soviet conflict, kindled serious Japanese anxiety about Soviet intentions and reinforced Tokyo's interest in closer relations with Peking and the acquisition of more capable defense forces. The United States and Europe became even more suspicious of the USSR when Moscow dramatically increased the capabilities of its conventional forces in the Far East at a time when Soviet forces in Europe were being reinforced. Improved Chinese relations with the United States and the European members of the North Atlantic Treaty Organization (NATO) and Japan caused considerable friction between the West and the USSR—the West welcoming a stronger China as a counterbalance to increased Soviet power and the USSR perceiving in this a global anti-Soviet entente.

In Eastern Europe military power was orchestrated to ensure subservience to the USSR and socialist orthodoxy. But the Poles stood up to Nikita Khrushchev and his cohorts in October 1956 and did not reform their leadership or hand power over to the Soviet-allied Natolinist faction. Movements by the Soviet army in and around Poland and of warships in the Baltic may have assured the loyalty and cohesiveness of the Natolinists, but this faction could not command the armed forces and remained an unpopular party minority. Nor is there a case for arguing that Moscow's show of force deterred a radical assertion of independence by Warsaw. Wladyslaw Gomulka himself was a stern Communist, opposed to liberalization and disposed strongly toward a firm alliance with the USSR. Having prevented Soviet military intervention with a unified following and a credible threat of violent and determined resistance, Gomulka assured further Soviet restraint by following *his* preferred course, which was acceptable to the USSR. What paid off was Khrushchev's gamble to back away militarily and give the Poles time to pursue their promised course. Moscow's political use of force was a failure, although the Poles could not ignore their environment and Soviet demands. But what Warsaw feared was military suppression—it was not impressed by mere demonstrations of force. Moreover, as Michel Tatu points out, Gomulka feared West Germany and the prospect of a united Germany at least as much as he did the USSR.

Nor did the deployment of Soviet units to Budapest during the first phase of the Hungarian crisis (October 23–31) or the buildup of forces and actions early in the second phase (beginning November 1) compel dissident workers and students to end their rebellious behavior and be content with promises of reform. Hence the new team led by Imre Nagy and János Kádár, who initially replaced Ernö Gerö, was unable to channel the rebellion. Had the dissidence been quelled early on, Nagy, like Kádár, probably would have been satisfied with mild reforms within a continued satellite framework. But Nagy turned away from Moscow completely after the insurrection and the USSR's new military moves. Kádár, who was more loyal to the USSR and more impressed by the Soviet army than Nagy, also was not emboldened by Moscow's behavior to try to rally Hungarians against the rebels and Nagy. Kádár merely took a back seat while Soviet authority and socialist orthodoxy were reimposed by force.

Soviet military demonstrations also did not induce effective bold behavior by Czechoslovak leaders loyal to the USSR in 1968, either before or after the August intervention by Warsaw Treaty Organization forces. Before the definitive action in August, Prague perceived the various movements and activities of Soviet and other Eastern European armed forces as theater. Alexander Dubček and his associates might have allowed the liberalization to proceed more rapidly in the absence of surrounding Soviet military power, but Moscow's political use of armed forces in the spring and early summer did not compel the reversal of developments distasteful to the Kremlin. The USSR's invasion and physical seizure of control, which the Czechoslovaks did not attempt to deter or resist violently, bought the Kremlin time, but more than seven months passed before Prague was compelled to accept Moscow's political diktat. This was brought about not by a show of force but by a verbal ultimatum delivered by Marshal Grechko.

The lessons of the political-military operations orchestrated against Poland, Hungary, and Czechoslovakia apply to the actions directed at East Germany, Rumania, and Yugoslavia. The East German riots in 1953 were not ended by shows of force or by bolstering the will of the East German authorities but by violent suppression, like that in Hungary. Nor was Tito coerced by Stalin's exertion of military pressure against Yugoslavia, or Nicolae Ceausescu by demonstrative actions ordered by Leonid Brezhnev's team. The danger of full-scale Soviet intervention caused both Tito and Ceausescu, like Gomulka and Dubček, to exercise self-restraint in their assertions of independent behavior; but this restraint appears to have been unrelated to the Kremlin's discrete uses of the military. Possibly, Soviet demonstrations of force caused other Eastern European leaders to fear suppression by and continue to respect Soviet military power; they might otherwise have inferred that the USSR was unwilling to resort to military means.

The restoration of loyalty and communist order in Poland, Hungary, and Czechoslovakia was not followed by the unraveling of the new regimes in those countries. In Poland, Gomulka remained a stalwart, conservative Marxist-Leninist. Decollectivization of agriculture, a less hostile relationship between church and state, and acceptance of economic assistance from the United States accompanied by a slow but sure tightening and then reversal of liberalization placed communism on a firmer footing, thereby giving the USSR a more stable and reliable ally. Still, Moscow had to consider that its failure in using the Soviet army to coerce the Poles and its willingness to gamble on Gomulka was taken as a sign of weakness in Eastern Europe and opened the way to the insurrection in Budapest.

Just as Gomulka had done with Poland, Kádár restored Hungary as a loyal Soviet ally and placed communism there on a stronger, national foundation. An important difference between the two leaders, however, was that Gomulka followed an increasingly conservative course and Kádár gradually introduced into Hungary the most liberal regime in Eastern Europe. The brutal suppression of insurgency in Hungary was probably a powerful deterrent to further eruptions of independence elsewhere in Eastern Europe in the short term. Such eruptions would have been plausible if both Poland and Hungary had successfully stood up to Moscow. Definitive Soviet action in Budapest gave credibility to the concurrent strengthening of the Soviet army elsewhere in Eastern Europe in November 1956.

The suppression in Hungary undermined the prospect of détente that had developed after Stalin's death. Yet if Moscow had been prepared in any event to enter into vigorous competition with the West over the then emerging third world and to provoke confrontation over Berlin and the future of West Germany, the cold war would probably have gained renewed vigor even if the events in Hungary had not occurred. The restoration of control in Hungary and of Soviet authority elsewhere in Eastern Europe was important to Khrushchev's diplomacy directed at the West and to the USSR's strategy for dealing with Peking's demands in the late 1950s and early 1960s. But Hungary was a dark stain on the image of the USSR in most of the world and undermined propaganda about principled Soviet behavior and the Kremlin's pretensions of moral leadership. The blow to the image of the USSR and its allies was greater still as a result of the 1968 intervention in Czechoslovakia. Earlier, many outside of the USSR believed the Kremlin had become more benevolent; and in the third world and even in the West, Moscow had capitalized on U.S. interventions in Southeast Asia and the Dominican Republic to build itself up and put the United States down. But the August intervention encouraged Eurocommunism and the further fragmentation of the Communist world. Once again Moscow reinforced the perspective that west of the Bug River the presence of the Soviet army was an imperial one, intended to control countries next to the USSR at least as much as to defend them and the USSR against Western aggression. Although dissidence in Eastern Europe was probably not responsible for the further buildup of Soviet military power there, Moscow nevertheless had greater reason to doubt the steadfastness of its allies in a European crisis. It was clear that despite the web of economic and social ties that the USSR had created in the preceding quarter of a century, its position in Eastern Europe remained exceedingly fragile.

The invasion of Czechoslovakia and the announcement of the Brezhnev doctrine also led to Albania's formal withdrawal from the Warsaw Treaty Organization and frightened China into reassessing its relations with the United States and adopting a firm antagonistic posture on the Sino-Soviet border. To the extent that the March 2, 1969, incident on Damansky Island was related to this stiffer attitude in Peking—aimed at showing Moscow that China was not a pushover—the intervention in Czechoslovakia may have caused a major rearrangement in global relations unfavorable to the USSR.

Still, not to intervene forcefully in Czechoslovakia would have meant accepting the possible disintegration of Soviet authority in Eastern Europe. Had Czechoslovakia been allowed to establish a new socialist democracy and distance its foreign policy from Soviet aegis, the repercussions might have included an even more serious situation in Poland in 1970, an emboldened Rumania, an even more liberal Hungary, and growing dissidence in East Germany. With no Soviet armed forces in Czechoslovakia, both the USSR and NATO would have perceived the Soviet security system in the west and Moscow's ability to intimidate Western nations as significantly weaker. The intervention into Czechoslovakia precluded these possibilities and led to the establishment in Prague of one of the tightest regimes in Eastern Europe. The establishment of Group Soviet Forces Czechoslovakia reinforced the USSR's military posture toward

NATO, which was not commensurately reinforced. Nor was détente very much delayed.

The Korean Peninsula and the Vietnam War

Moscow's cautious and subtle coercive diplomacy in response to conflict on the Korean peninsula and in the Vietnam War did not fail. Although largely the result of coincidence, U.S. behavior did conform to the objectives of Moscow's political-military diplomacy in these affairs. U.S. forces did not attack Manchuria after Chinese forces entered the Korean War or invade North Korea again in 1951; nor did U.S. forces direct violence at North Korea after the *Pueblo* was seized in 1968. Moreover, after the United States decided not to retaliate in 1968, the arrival of several Soviet warships around the U.S. *Enterprise* and its escorts in the Sea of Japan may even have played a role in compelling the task force's withdrawal. Finally, the 1972 presence of Soviet warships in the South China Sea was not followed by further U.S. bombing of Soviet merchantmen in the Haiphong harbor.

However, Stalin did not attempt to deter U.S. entry into the Korean War on the U.S.-led drive across the 38th parallel to the Yalu.[3] Nor did Moscow attempt to militarily deter the United States from beginning the air war against North Vietnam in 1965 or to compel U.S. withdrawal thereafter. The 1972 Soviet naval presence in Vietnam was not meant to compel the United States to stop its bombing against North Vietnam in response to Hanoi's Easter offensive; no Soviet military response accompanied the U.S. bombing attacks in December 1972. The limit to which the Kremlin went in using Soviet military men on behalf of Hanoi was to dispatch personnel whose technical skills quietly raised the cost of the war to the United States, as Soviet fighter pilots did during the Korean War. Soviet military men in North Vietnam, in the role of willing hostages, also constrained U.S. bombing decisions. The Johnson administration's decision not to invade North Vietnam or initiate strategic bombing of Hanoi and Haiphong resulted from U.S. concern about prospective Soviet and Chinese reactions.

The stance taken toward the United States by Moscow after North Korean airmen shot down a U.S. Navy EC-121 in 1969 also was not fol-

3. Had Chinese forces failed to rout U.S. ground units in North Korea in the fall of 1950, Stalin might even have accepted a Western reunified peninsula. After all, the United States had already obtained strong positions in Iran and Turkey, which also border the USSR.

lowed by retaliation against North Korea, and after a brief interval the large U.S. task force that had been deployed into the Sea of Japan was withdrawn. In this instance the Soviet stance was conciliatory and Soviet warships acted cooperatively to support the search and rescue effort. Rather than being used to deter a U.S. attack on North Korea or even to compel U.S. withdrawal from the Sea of Japan, Soviet military units were used instead to induce the Nixon administration to recall its armada. This the administration did, although Moscow's diplomacy, at most, probably only affirmed Washington's decision.

The Kremlin's restriction of its objectives and use of force to coerce the United States in these conflicts in Northeast and Southeast Asia, though accompanied by success in meeting narrow goals, seems to have been poorly received by the Communist nations threatened by the United States and whose allegiance Moscow wished to retain. However, Moscow wanted to avoid confrontation with the United States and, in the late 1960s and 1970s, to foster détente. The Kremlin's prudence, born out of concern to ensure paramount security and foreign policy interests, created dissatisfaction among Moscow's allies. Had it not been for their continuing dependence on the USSR for assistance, the Soviet Union's allies might have openly denounced Moscow.

It is unlikely that Peking was satisfied by the deployment of Soviet ground and air units in northern China in late 1950 after Pyongyang's aggression failed and U.S. troops approached the Manchurian border. If, as appears to be the case, Moscow pressed Peking to realize the utility of North Korea's invasion of the South and assured Mao Tse-tung and his colleagues that a quick victory could be obtained at little cost, it is likely that the Chinese expected the Soviet army and air units to accept the burden or at least fight alongside Chinese forces when things did not go according to plan and disaster loomed. At best, Peking may have viewed Soviet behavior with resignation, believing that Soviet-American fighting in Korea would escalate to include U.S. nuclear strikes against China. Kim Il-Sung wanted far greater support from the USSR, however. It was apparent to him that Stalin was not willing to wage war against U.S. forces on behalf of North Korea. After Moscow's military withdrawal from the North before June 1950 and then failure to avert the occupation of North Korea in the fall, Kim and his associates could not have been impressed by the Soviet deployment to North Korea of easily withdrawn aircraft or even of Soviet army units after the front had been stabilized and U.S. objectives sharply limited.

The Kremlin's delayed military response to the U.S. buildup after the *Pueblo* was seized also was not reassuring to Pyongyang, and Moscow's behavior in the EC-121 affair and after the murder of two U.S. officers in the demilitarized zone in 1976 seemed to leave Kim disgusted. Only North Vietnam may have expected little political-military support from the USSR and been relatively content with the military support it received. North Vietnamese doubts that the Kremlin would be ready to act coercively to derail the escalating air war against the North in 1965 may have owed much to their witness of Soviet support given to China during the 1958 offshore islands crisis and to Cuba during the missile crisis, when Peking and Havana were greatly disappointed.

The displeasure of the USSR's allies probably did not surprise Moscow. At best, Moscow could have hoped only to persuade its allies that Soviet military power was limited and that stronger action was futile, although Stalin also might have tried to rationalize Soviet caution with the argument that the USSR needed to be protected as the source of international communism.

Although Soviet deployments in China during the Korean War reinforced the credibility of the 1950 Sino-Soviet mutual defense treaty, the absence of strong coercive diplomacy on behalf of North Korea gave the West more than a hint of Soviet prudence and a greater sense of optimism and confidence in Western military capabilities. This more positive outlook than the one held in the beginning of the Korean War was also based on the absence of Soviet aggression toward Western Europe, despite Soviet hostility to both NATO rearmament and the movement toward the rearmament of West Germany. Soviet deployments in Manchuria during the Korean War possibly made the United States more circumspect in its thinking about China in the 1958 Quemoy crisis. Moscow's minimal support of North Korea in 1950 may have encouraged the Eisenhower administration to act more boldly in the Middle East in the late 1950s and the Johnson administration to attack North Vietnam in 1964. The limited Soviet support given to Hanoi may similarly have made U.S. policymakers more confident about Soviet restraint during the 1967 Middle East war.

Soviet caution in Southeast Asia was essential, though, to the improvement of U.S.-Soviet relations that was finally made possible when the air war against North Vietnam was ended in early 1968. Soviet military intervention on behalf of Hanoi might have unified American public opinion, galvanized NATO, and allowed the United States to escape the international stigma brought on by its unilateral military intervention in Southeast Asia. Moscow's restraint in reacting to the U.S. military buildup following the *Pueblo* seizure and Soviet cooperation after the EC-121 was shot down also allowed détente to go forward, as did Soviet reticence after the United States renewed air attacks on North Vietnam in 1972. The nuclear nonproliferation and SALT I treaties, agreements on Berlin and West Germany, the development of East-West trade, and Soviet economic relations with Japan all might have been delayed or precluded by a serious U.S.-Soviet confrontation. The complications of U.S.-Soviet and Soviet-Japanese relations, brought on by Soviet military activity and accompanying statements during the *Pueblo* affair—delayed and restricted as they were—reveal what might have happened if the Soviet show of force in these incidents had been larger and more pointed. A superpower confrontation in 1976, had the USSR reacted strongly to the U.S. deployments following the murders in Korea's demilitarized zone in July, might have severely threatened U.S.-Soviet relations.

Although North Korea and North Vietnam remained dependent on the USSR for military and economic aid, their recognition that Soviet support in the face of U.S. military power was fragile and that Moscow's global interests were preeminent weakened their trust in the USSR and belief in international communism as it was interpreted in Moscow. Soviet behavior seemed to endorse self-interested behavior and self-reliance. Whether a show of force in support of North Vietnam would have induced Hanoi to openly side with the USSR in the Sino-Soviet conflict during the period of U.S. military engagement in Southeast Asia is arguable. However, Soviet conciliation of the United States in the instance of the EC-121 clearly helped undermine relations between Moscow and Pyongyang and pressed the latter toward improved relations with Peking. What Moscow did appreciate was the absence of new provocation by North Korea against the United States, which might have threatened superpower accord. The attack on the EC-121 immediately followed the release of the *Pueblo* crew, despite Moscow's limited support—intended as a restraint—to Pyongyang in the *Pueblo* case. Moscow's distance from Pyongyang in the EC-121 affair made clear that allies who might get into trouble with the United States on their own account could not rely on the USSR for help.

The Third World

In the third world the USSR did not obtain very stable positions as a result of its coercive diplomacy on behalf of allies. Also, the ramifications of incidents to which the United States, China, and European NATO nations were attentive included serious debits to Soviet interests. Nevertheless, most of the outcomes related to Soviet operational objectives in the third world were positive in the short term and the gains were retained for several years. Soviet military units were most useful in coercing antagonists of Moscow's third world allies.

Moscow did not attempt to use its warships in the Mediterranean to deter an Israeli attack on Egypt and Syria in June 1967, although the squadron was probably meant to caution Washington against using the Sixth Fleet against the Arabs after hostilities ensued. In fact, the Sixth Fleet was not used militarily, and when paratroops in the USSR were alerted on the last day of the war, after Israeli units moved toward Damascus, the United States was motivated to pressure Israel against further movement in this direction. Although the United States had no intention of acting against the Arabs (at least when they were on the defensive) and Israel did not intend to assault the Syrian captial, coercive Soviet behavior did precede these favorable outcomes.

After the 1967 war, the deployment of Soviet warships to Egyptian harbors to deter new Israeli attacks seemed to be successful, and Moscow's deployment of missile crews and fighter aircraft to the Middle East in 1970 compelled Israel to end deep penetration raids on central and upper Egypt and, finally, attacks in the Suez Canal area. Israel was forced to face Soviet military resistance directly, and the United States again felt it necessary to pressure Israel by delaying new warplane sales and refusing to issue a declaration of caution to Moscow.

In the 1973 conflict, neither the United States nor Israel—after it had launched several attacks on Soviet merchant vessels and aircraft in Syria —interfered with Soviet airlifts and sealifts to Egypt and Syria; Israel did not move to seize Damascus; U.S. military forces played no role in the fighting; and, after Brezhnev coupled a threat of unilateral military intervention with demonstrative actions by Soviet airborne and aircraft units to threaten unilateral military intervention, the Nixon administration pressured Israel to recognize the cease-fire on the west bank of the Suez Canal, which Israel did.[4]

Coercion also did not fail in the other two essentially interstate third

4. It would be a mistake to view Israel's crossing of the Suez Canal and encirclement of the Egyptian Third Army as a failure in Soviet deterrence. The opportunity to carry out this brilliantly executed operation was not recognized until after Israeli troops were on the west bank.

world conflicts examined in the case studies (Guinea and Ethiopia) and in the one case of direct confrontation between the USSR and a third world nation (Ghana). Portugal did not attack Guinea again after Soviet naval vessels were deployed to West African waters. Although by themselves the global condemnation suffered by Portugal as a result of its attack on Conakry and Lisbon's fear of further isolation from the West might have deterred new violence against Guinea, it is also possible that Soviet gunboat diplomacy was a necessary condition for Portuguese restraint, particularly in the long term. Somalia was clearly disheartened by Moscow's political-military support of Ethiopia in the struggle over the Ogaden region, and Somali troops were forced to withdraw from Ethiopian territory. However, Mogadishu was not coerced by a threat of Soviet military action but was driven from the battlefield by Cuban and Ethiopian military men armed with Soviet equipment. And Ghana, after Soviet naval vessels had been deployed to the Gulf of Guinea in 1969, released the two Soviet trawlers and their crews that had been held in custody for five months. Although Accra probably would have released the vessels and crews in any case, Moscow's naval diplomacy probably influenced the timing of the release. Moreover, if Moscow had meant to deter the Ghanaians from harming the crew members to extract information, its effort did not end in failure.

Soviet leaders could take less satisfaction from the behavior of insurgent groups threatening Soviet friends, although no ally that Moscow supported was placed in more danger by domestic opponents after Soviet help was received; indeed, each ally found its position substantially improved. Also, in each incident involving an insurgency against a Soviet ally, antagonists suffered significantly and had to limit their objectives to avoid total defeat. Only the Kurds in Iraq were beaten decisively. The Soviet air support given to Gaafar Mohammed al-Nimeiry's government in Sudan did not compel the Anyanya rebels to end their struggle or compel Ethiopia, Uganda, or Zaire to stop helping the insurgents. Those outcomes were obtained two years later, after Moscow's relations with Nimeiry had weakened considerably and as a result of a political settlement that conceded many of the Anyanya demands. However, the decision to appease the rebels, made as it was in a climate of poor relations with the USSR, might indicate that continued Soviet military support had been essential to the containment of the secessionists.

More effective was the air support given to Iraq to help suppress the Kurdish rebellion. Iran did not increase its military support of the Kurds and finally withdrew it completely. The Kurds, who had already been forced to retreat, were thus forced to end their rebellion. That Iran reversed its position as it did seemed related not only to Baghdad's agreement to a favorable border adjustment and cessation of anti-Iranian activities in Iraq but also to Moscow's expanded—that is, military— presence in Iraq and Tehran's fear of additional Soviet deployments and clashes between Iranian and Soviet military men.

Angola was still a different story. With the aid of Soviet and Cuban military support, forces of the National Front for the Liberation of Angola (FNLA) and the National Union for the Total Independence of Angola (UNITA) were largely driven from the battlefield; moreover, neither Zaire, South Africa, nor the United States attempted to interfere with the Soviet airlift or sealift of Cubans and military matériel to southern Africa. It is important, however, that like the Anyanya insurgents and the Eritrean and Ogaden rebels, the FNLA and UNITA were not crushed completely or compelled to reach a political accommodation with the MPLA. Moscow's use of military means frustrated their objectives, but neither these groups nor their allies were intimidated enough to give up their cause. They remained a continuing threat requiring substantial governmental concessions in Sudan and the continued presence of a large Cuban garrison and commensurate Soviet military assistance in Angola and Ethiopia.

With the partial exception of the Arab side in the 1973 Middle East war, no Soviet ally involved in the third world cases examined occurring after the 1967 Middle East war was defeated by a Chinese or Western ally or an actor supported by a Western proxy. Nor was any regime receiving Soviet political-military support overturned. In the October war, although Syria lost some territory, Egypt at least achieved a political victory by crossing the Suez Canal and holding a position in Sinai.

But if antagonists of Soviet allies in the third world generally did what Moscow wanted them to do, the beneficiaries of Soviet military diplomacy did not often react so favorably. President Nasser, for example, was greatly disappointed by Moscow's support during the June war even if, having experienced Soviet behavior in the Suez and Lebanon crises, he was not terribly surprised. From Moscow's point of view, massive Soviet arms transfers and the show of force aimed at Israel after the 1967 war were critical to the USSR's retention of strong relations with Egypt and use of Egyptian bases; by providing air defense to Egypt in 1970 Moscow was able to reaffirm its relationship with Cairo, obtain further access to Egyptian military facilities in Egypt, and, in 1971, negotiate with Cairo a Treaty of Friendship and Cooperation. But these gains were not lasting. The creation of a powerful air defense, increasingly manned by Egyptians, and Israel's respect for the August 1970 cease-fire reduced Egypt's dependence on the USSR. At the same time, Cairo was angered by Moscow's refusal to deliver the armaments that the Egyptians believed were necessary to end the "no war-no peace" status quo with Israel. Exposure of the Ali Sabry plot and Soviet approval of the failed coup in Sudan made President Anwar Sadat positively suspicious of Moscow's intentions. Consequently, in 1972, Sadat terminated the large Soviet military presence in Egypt, took over the military equipment manned by Russian units and the facilities being developed for the Soviet navy, and denied Soviet naval aircraft the use of Egyptian airfields.

Soviet military diplomacy during the 1973 war did not prevent Syria from losing more territory and Egyptian forces from suffering a military disaster on the west bank. Sadat and President Hafiz al-Assad of Syria were not at all pleased by Soviet military diplomacy or the level of military matériel they received during the 1973 conflict. Moscow wanted to associate the USSR with the limited Arab gains made early in the conflict and to avoid blame for the success of Israel's counterattacks and further thrusts. But the USSR did not manage to secure an image of being a dependable patron supportive of the Arab cause. Rather, Soviet behavior was perceived in Egypt and in other Arab countries as calculated to limit Egyptian and Syrian military capabilities as a way to keep the Arabs dependent on the USSR; hence, Moscow was held responsible by the Arabs for their losses. Arms deliveries and Soviet threats on behalf of first Syria and then Egypt were not publicly acknowledged by Assad or Sadat during or after the war. In fact, Soviet relations with Egypt deteriorated after 1973 until finally, in early 1976, Sadat not only denied Soviet naval vessels the use of Egyptian facilities but also abrogated the 1971 Treaty of Friendship and Cooperation with the USSR. Cairo's disdain toward Moscow's help in clearing the Suez Canal, offered to supplement the work of U.S. and British teams, symbolized Egypt's declining interest in ties with the USSR.

India did not reject the USSR after its 1971 conflict with Pakistan, as Egypt did after 1973. Why did the Indians on the one hand and the Egyptians and the Syrians to a degree on the other react differently to Soviet military diplomacy on their behalf? Most important, perhaps, the Indians, unlike the Arabs, won a decisive military victory, leaving no need for a scapegoat. Second, the USSR appears either to have done everything New Delhi asked it to do to deter hostile behavior by China and the United States or else offered this assistance preemptively. Finally, India apparently did not consider itself or its victory dependent on the Soviet Union; its self-respect remained intact and it did not feel a strong need to assert itself in its relations with the USSR.

Syria suffered a major military failure between the June and October wars when it was forced to withdraw from Jordan in 1970. Moscow gave Damascus questionable military backing on that occasion—unlike its response to Egypt six months earlier and to India a year later—and conveyed to Damascus a prognosis of doom. This Soviet behavior, Syria's 1967 war experience, and the loss of further territory in 1973 convinced Damascus of the limited utility of a strong alliance with the USSR. Hence, despite Soviet replenishment of Syrian arsenals and diplomatic support given after the October war, Moscow ultimately found its relationship with President Assad rocky. Syria did not offer the USSR increased use of military facilities to compensate for the loss of those in Egypt; Assad refused to sign a treaty of friendship and cooperation with the USSR; and Damascus took positions far from the Soviet line on several important issues. Also, after the 1973 war, relations improved between Washington and Damascus.

In Sudan President Nimeiry was gratified by the USSR's counterinsurgency support in the early 1970s. But even before the USSR backed an ultimately unsuccessful coup in 1971, Nimeiry had followed a policy of socialism without communism and had grown increasingly wary in his relations with the USSR. When Moscow then overreached itself in Sudanese affairs in 1971, as was to occur soon in Egypt, Soviet relations with Sudan deteriorated precipitately.

The access to Guinean facilities that Soviet naval vessels and reconnaissance aircraft gained did appear directly related to Moscow's political-military support of Guinea. But in accepting Moscow's protection, President Touré, like Sadat and Nimeiry, became concerned about increased dependence on the USSR. Similarly, Prime Minister Sirimavo Bandaranaike of Sri Lanka, after gaining Soviet military support in 1971, reacted to the demonstration of Soviet and Indian military power in the Indo-Pakistani war by ending criticism of a U.S. naval presence in the Indian Ocean and welcoming port visits by the U.S. Navy and American military and economic assistance. In other words, the prime minister sought balance in Sri Lanka's relationships when its regime was fairly secure, since the country's fundamental interest lay in its freedom of action. In the case of Guinea, the Kremlin was not allowed to construct a naval facility on Tamara Island, and naval assistance was accepted from Peking.

Moscow appeared to obtain firmer relations with the MPLA in Angola and with President Mengistu's regime in Ethiopia. Moscow supported the MPLA and Ethiopian forces in their times of crisis, and both Angola and Ethiopia—formerly influenced by NATO members—maintained especially close relations with the USSR and Cuba. Both African regimes continued to be dependent, however, and may find this dependency less palatable if they become more secure. Before his death in 1979, President Agostinho Neto was already receptive to substantial economic exchange with the West and improved relations with Zaire and took a pragmatic view of the insurgency in Namibia. The Kremlin therefore had some reason to doubt the durability of cozy relations with at least Angola. But the USSR did obtain in these countries friendly, socialist-oriented regimes distrustful of the West, offering the USSR special entrée. Their identity with Soviet values is important. President Neto declared the MPLA a Marxist-Leninist organization, Addis Ababa accepted considerable tutelage from Soviet and Cuban advisers, and both regimes signed treaties of friendship and cooperation with the USSR. Moscow considers their sympathy to the cause of liberation in southern Africa another advantage. If, in the future, relations with Luanda and Addis Ababa sour over differences in policy, and military access previously obtained is lost—as has happened in other countries that have received substantial Soviet political-military and other support—these regimes might still be an asset to the Kremlin insofar as the West finds it difficult to deal with them.

A broad conclusion about the utility of Soviet political-military diplomacy as a way to reinforce relations with allies is that such support is appreciated and can help obtain access to military facilities and close political relations; but these gains are conditional. They depend on a continued identity of interests and harmony of strategies for the achievement of mutual objectives. When a third world leader perceives the USSR as being overbearing or unsupportive, the question "what have you done for me recently?" is more relevant to him than "what did you do for me in the past?" In this context a decline in dependence on the USSR for national or regime security has often led to a serious reversal in relations. Moscow thus has been able to preserve good relations most effectively (1) with governments especially insecure and isolated from other sources of support; (2) when it confined itself to helping a regime retain power rather than undermining it or redirecting its policies; and (3) when the demands made on the USSR were palatable. The status of the Soviet Union typically has not been that of imperial overlord but of guest worker. Still, nations, or at least regimes, sometimes find the support they receive to be necessary and can see no option other than dependency for long periods of time. "Put all your energy into remaining independent," Charles de Gaulle advised a young monarch a long time ago; but, at least for a while, national leaders often are willing to compromise their independence to retain the fruits of alliance.[5]

Increased independence of Soviet allies creates difficulties between them and the USSR that are well illustrated by longer-term developments in their relations. In the late 1970s President Sadat allied himself with the United States and the West and sought from the NATO bloc armaments, economic assistance, and foreign investments as well as support for his bold strategy for obtaining peace with Israel and, with it, the Arabs' lost territories. Unwilling to provide Egypt with the armaments Sadat considered necessary for bringing about a military victory and opposed to Sadat's independent stance in the Arab-Israeli conflict and conciliation of the United States, the USSR became thoroughly estranged from Egypt. President Nimeiry also drew closer to the West and China after obtaining a peaceful settlement of the Anyanya insurgency in 1972, which lessened his dependence on Soviet military support. As a part of this realignment Soviet advisers were expelled from Sudan in 1977. In close entente, Egypt and Sudan vigorously opposed the Kremlin's political-military support of Ethiopia in the conflict on the Horn of Africa.

Although President Assad of Syria did not reject the USSR and did allow Soviet warships increased access to Syrian facilities, Moscow remained unable to consolidate relations with Damascus.[6] Relations with the USSR suffered as a result of Syrian conflict with the Palestine Liberation Organization in Lebanon, and differences with Moscow also arose over Syrian openness to U.S. efforts to achieve an Arab-Israeli settlement. Evidence of President Assad's independence and flexibility included increased U.S. economic assistance to Syria, Syrian arms purchases in West-

5. The quotation is cited by André Malraux, *Felled Oaks: Conversation with de Gaulle* (Holt, Rinehart and Winston, 1972), p. 29.

6. Richard B. Remnek, "The Politics of Soviet Access to Naval Support Facilities in the Mediterranean," in Bradford Dismukes and James M. McConnell, eds., *Soviet Naval Diplomacy* (Pergamon, 1979), pp. 378, 381.

ern Europe, and decreasing numbers of Soviet arms transfers and military advisers in Syria. Closer accord between Moscow and Damascus after the 1978 Camp David summit conference pointed up President Assad's continued pursuit of a strategy different from the one followed by President Sadat, not a newfound identity with Soviet interests or objectives in the Middle East.

After the Kurdish insurgency was dealt with successfully, Soviet relations with the Baath party in Iraq also became unsteady. Baghdad adopted a stance independent from Moscow in the Arab-Israeli dispute, forced the Soviet embassy to move as a result of suspicions about eavesdropping, opposed Soviet support of Ethiopia directed against Eritrea, exchanged oil for Western technology, and circumscribed and executed local Communists. Such positions eventually led to the termination of Soviet aircraft refueling in Iraq and to expressions of anger about unauthorized overflights. Iraq also opposed the Soviet Union's activities in Afghanistan and South Yemen.

It is too soon to talk about long-term outcomes with reference to Angola and Ethiopa. President Touré did allow the USSR use of Guinean facilities for naval reconnaissance and for refueling transport aircraft en route from Cuba and the Soviet Union during the Angolan civil war; but relations weakened and the use by Soviet reconnaissance aircraft of facilities in Conakry was restricted when Touré sought economic assistance from the West and the USSR did not provide the desired volume of military assistance. President Touré may also have been irritated by Soviet intrusion into Guinean domestic affairs, as occurred in Egypt, Sudan, and perhaps Iraq. The regime in Guinea-Bissau, which gained independence in 1974, shared with the USSR a similar perspective on national liberation in Africa and appreciated the USSR's support. But the new government in Bissau did not allow the USSR to direct its decisionmaking; nor was Moscow given military bases or even routine access to local air or naval facilities. China, in fact, was a larger donor of aid than was the USSR. Bissau's ties with Moscow slipped considerably when, in the late 1970s, Soviet advisers became unpopular, dispute arose over Soviet fishing practices, and more Western aid was obtained.

On the other hand, Soviet relations with Ghana did not suffer long-term damage as a result of Moscow's coercive diplomacy in the 1968–69 trawlers incident. Neither Ghana nor the USSR ever publicized the Soviet naval presence in Ghanaian waters, and the coming to office of the Busia government less than a year later and the 1972 coup led by Colonel

Ignatius K. Acheampong may well have erased Accra's official memory of Moscow's gunboat diplomacy. Moreover, although relations with the USSR remained cool in the early 1970s, the new military government supported the cause of liberation movements in Africa and had difficult economic relations with the West. In 1975–76 Accra gave support to the MPLA in Angola, Soviet-Ghanaian economic relations were improved, and military attachés were exchanged for the first time in a decade.

Neither did Soviet relations with Iran suffer as a result of increased overflights of Iran in 1973 following large arms purchases by the shah from the United States or because of Moscow's coercion of Tehran to withdraw its support of the Kurds in 1974. After Iran and Iraq came to terms in early 1975 the shah was prepared to buy arms from the USSR as a partial counterbalance to his weapons purchases from the United States, which were endangered by anger in the United States about policies of the Organization of Petroleum Exporting Countries (OPEC).

What were the wider ramifications of Soviet efforts in the third world? Although U.S. policymakers awarded some legitimacy to Soviet actions intended to defend allies that supported international norms valued by the West, the larger the Soviet military effort the more damage was done to Soviet-American relations and the harder U.S. policymakers tried to follow policies harmful to Soviet interests.[7] The minimal Soviet military support given to Syria and Egypt during the June war and in its immediate aftermath provoked no serious U.S. countermeasures and did not hinder improved superpower relations. Soviet efforts on behalf of Guinea, Sudan, and Iraq as well as the bullying of Ghana attracted only the barest attention and no noticeable U.S. counteractions. Apparently the United States was willing to accept small doses of Soviet political-military diplomacy aimed at ensuring the territorial integrity of nations, preserving recognized regimes, and securing Soviet assets (Ghana). In addition, U.S. sympathy was evoked by Egypt's suffering of deep penetration raids by Israel in 1969–70, the encirclement of the Egyptian Third Army during the October war, and Ethiopia's disintegration in 1977.

7. I am indebted to the theoretical work on asymmetries of motivation and the protection of the status quo done by George, Hall, and Simons in *The Limits of Coercive Diplomacy* and by James M. McConnell, "The 'Rules of the Game': A Theory on the Practice of Superpower Naval Diplomacy," in Dismukes and McConnell, eds., *Soviet Naval Diplomacy,* pp. 240–80.

Nevertheless, the large Soviet deployment to Egypt and Cairo's greater dependence on the USSR in 1970 caused the United States to take a more balanced position between the Arabs and Israel—one that both Nasser and then Sadat sought as a way not only to satisfy Arab objectives in the confrontation with Israel but also to reduce long-term Egyptian dependence on the USSR. Soviet military support of the Arabs in the 1973 war reinforced this dynamic by leading the United States to further induce the Arabs with support while strengthening Sadat's view that reliance and dependence on the USSR was a mistaken strategy for regaining lost Egyptian territory, Gaza, and the West Bank. President Assad, too, was drawn closer to the United States. Moreover, the Soviet airlifts to Egypt and Syria, the Brezhnev ultimatum and related military activities in the USSR, and the consequent superpower confrontation in the Mediterranean during the 1973 war raised a serious question about détente in the United States for the first time, although U.S. support of Israel also led to serious discord within NATO and contributed to the Arab oil embargo, which was disastrous to Western economies.

Doubts of many in the United States and elsewhere in the West about Soviet intentions were reinforced by Soviet military support of the MPLA in Angola and of Ethiopia. Because of these interventions the United States spent more on defense, strengthened its relations with China, and became more cautious in negotiations with the USSR on strategic arms limitation and several other matters. European NATO nations slowly began to react similarly, and in Africa a number of nations entered into an overt, though informal, alliance against the Soviet presence on the continent. In addition, U.S. unwillingess to counter Soviet and Cuban activities in Angola contributed to French military intervention in conflicts in Chad, the western Sahara, Zaire, and elsewhere. These interventions may have led Soviet allies in Africa to think more critically about the utility of Soviet military intervention to their interests.

The other side to this Western and regional alarm in Africa, however, was the credibility and respect accorded Soviet military capabilities. Just as the image of the USSR had suffered when Moscow had offered the Arabs less than full support in 1967, doubts arose in the mid-1970s about American will and military capabilities because of U.S. restraint during the Angolan civil war and the conflict on the Horn of Africa. China appeared to be a completely unworthy patron. Hence, the climate was ripe for improved relations with the USSR, although not necessarily for Soviet influence. Leaders like Joshua Nkomo of the Zimbabwe African Peoples Union (ZAPU) and Sam Nujoma of the South West African People's Organization were given reason to rely more heavily on the USSR for support in their insurgencies in Rhodesia and Namibia. The apparent ability of the USSR to enable its allies to emerge triumphant may have led these revolutionary groups and perhaps others to discount the value of maintaining closer relations with the West. Also, although the USSR lost its military facilities in Somalia in 1977, President Siad Barre suggested in 1979 the possibility of a reconciliation with the Soviet Union.[8] Appearances of Soviet as well as U.S. naval vessels in response to the *Pueblo* seizure, the Indo-Pakistani war, the October war, and the civil war in Lebanon gave many the impression that the Soviet Union could render U.S. military power politically impotent. Uncontested Soviet military diplomacy in support of the MPLA, leading to the defeat of U.S. and Chinese clients (FNLA and UNITA), and of Ethiopia reinforced the impression of burgeoning Soviet military power and decreasing U.S. ability to affect the course of third world crises.

Moreover, although some African nations with close relations to the West disapproved of the Soviet interventions in Angola and Ethiopia, at least as many African capitals were not upset. Earlier the USSR had not been rebuffed when it had intimidated Ghana in 1969; the placid reaction was evidently made possible by the lack of publicity linking the deployment of Soviet warships to the release of the trawlers and their crews. Nor had the USSR offended African sensibilities by its naval support of Guinea and the PAIGC against Portgual, which had not been played up either. In the case of Angola, the considerable Soviet and Cuban effort mounted in 1975–76 was offset by the assistance, though limited, given to the UNITA and FNLA by South Africa, the United States, China, and even Zaire (perceived by many as a U.S. client and even stooge). Still others found Agostinho Neto's social values and attitudes toward economic development and national liberation in southern Africa congenial and were therefore willing to ignore foreign intervention on behalf of the MPLA. A large number of African and other third world nations were highly sympathetic to Soviet-Cuban support ensuring Ethiopian sovereignty and territorial integrity. In this, Moscow's claim of principled behavior was reinforced by its abandonment of Somalia, a long-time friend, and the USSR's consequent loss of access to Somali air and naval facilities.

8. U.S. Foreign Broadcast Information Service, *Sub-Sahara Africa* (January 23, 1979), p. B4.

The Tailoring of Soviet Political-Military Operations

Did the Kremlin use military power prudently or provocatively? Was Moscow sensitive to the ramifications of its use of force as a political instrument? Was the use of Soviet armed forces appropriate and well tailored to the USSR's operational objectives and larger interests? What difference did it make that some and not other types and sizes of armed forces units were chosen? And how significant to outcomes were particular military movements and activities? Standards used to obtain answers to these questions are the timing of Soviet military moves and consequent perceptions of target actors; the attention paid by Moscow to making coercive diplomacy appear legitimate as well as Moscow's subtlety when blatant coercion was likely to be counterproductive; and the extent to which forces of different size and character as well as varying activities were efficient and associated with favorable outcomes.

Deliberation and Prudence

Invariably Moscow used military power with great deliberation. In Eastern Europe shots were fired by Soviet troops only in East Germany in 1953 and in Hungary in November 1956, after an earlier intervention and withdrawal. Coercive (as opposed to suppressive) military behavior in Eastern Europe was not accompanied by any violent action; instead, warnings and threats were coupled with attempts at discussion and negotiation. Violence occurred periodically along the Sino-Soviet border, but Chinese territory was not seized and held, deep penetration raids were not made, and engagements were carefully limited. The threat to use nuclear weapons against China was preceded by six months of lesser coercion and attempts at more traditional diplomacy.

Particular circumspection was shown when the United States was an actor. Before hostilities broke out on the Korean peninsula in 1950 virtually all Soviet military men were withdrawn from North Korea; the later deployments of combat forces into Manchuria and North Korea were unannounced; and air operations were begun surreptitiously and only over Communist territory. U.S. naval operations were never interfered with. During the Vietnam War the supportive role played by Soviet military men was also minimal and deniable. Yet Soviet personnel were well placed in northern China and Vietnam during these two conflicts to provide practical support to Peking and Hanoi and to help deter U.S. air attacks.

Despite the presence of both U.S. and Soviet naval forces in the Sea of Japan after the *Pueblo* was seized, the timing of the major Soviet reinforcement precluded even the appearance of a superpower crisis; and while the harrassment of U.S. ships was unexpected, Washington recognized it as an expression of displeasure about the proximity to the USSR of a U.S. task force, not as a threat related to the issue at hand. Moscow's use of only intelligence-gathering vessels and several destroyers and its cooperative behavior following the shooting down of the EC-121 a year later clearly portrayed a desire to avoid superpower confrontation.

In the third world, where, in contrast to Europe and northern Asia, Soviet security was not directly at stake, Moscow used military power effectively and subtly, showing an ability to minimize damage to its interests abroad while applying its capabilities incisively. In general, Soviet leaders were adept at legitimating their use of force, timed their introduction of military means well, showed good sense in the types of forces called on, and did not gloat over successes. The Kremlin preferred a naval presence, covert tactical air assistance, logistical support, and the use of Cuban combat formations over the open deployment of Soviet military units in third world nations. Moscow knew that it was better to create new political facts rather than risk issuing ultimatums. In the Middle East, Africa, and southern Asia, Soviet armed forces were used neither recklessly nor clumsily, but with prudence and sensitivity.

When Soviet armed forces were used unilaterally in the third world, Moscow was aware of the risk of U.S. military intervention. The USSR's air defense of Egypt, naval support of Guinea, air support of Sudan and Iraq, the threat to Israel after it failed to observe the cease-fire during the October war, and aid to Ethiopia occurred either when the United States opposed the behavior of the target of Moscow's coercion or when Moscow's action could be justified by the principle of defending national sovereignty, which Washington was loath to oppose. The support given to Sudan and Iraq, moreover, was kept at a level easy to deny, and the U.S. political scene was carefully observed before and during Moscow's actions on behalf of Egypt in 1970, Angola in 1975–76, and Ethiopia in 1977–78. Presidents Richard M. Nixon, Gerald R. Ford, and Jimmy Carter were ill-disposed or unable to take military action in these instances on behalf of Israel, FNLA and UNITA forces, and Somalia.

Visits to Guinea before and to Nigeria after the passage of Soviet warships through Ghanaian waters in 1969 and the fact that this naval activity was not overtly linked to the trawlers' captivity was a classic performance of subtlety that illustrated the Kremlin's understanding of local sensibilities. Had the transit through the Gulf of Guinea been denounced by Accra as gunboat diplomacy, the Kremlin would have been discomforted; yet, as long as Conakry and Lagos were prepared to receive the ships, Moscow had a cover, albeit flimsy. Only warships were sent to West African waters after Conakry was assaulted in 1970; Nigerian and Algerian pilots, not Soviet airmen, flew Guinea's Soviet-supplied MIGs; and Cuban soldiers rather than Soviet army men bolstered Guinean ground security. Soviet military men were neither allowed to become hostages to the security of Sekou Touré's regime nor allowed to participate in direct violence against Portuguese Guinea. Moreover, by not announcing the role of the newly deployed warships, Moscow avoided agitating its client and lessened the risk of attracting a U.S. response that might have weakened the impact of the Soviet presence. Nor did the Soviet Union place the United States into a position of supporting Portugal. Although the Kremlin might have used such U.S. support of Lisbon to its own advantage, African leaders would not have received it well, which, in turn, could have hurt Soviet relations with them.

The Use of Nuclear Weapons

In the one instance when the USSR raised the specter of nuclear war, China quickly compromised its position and sought negotiations with Moscow. This unique instance of Soviet diplomacy—unlike the rocket rattling of the Khrushchev era—is supported by U.S. experience. Historically, when the United States has raised the prospect of nuclear attack in incidents, outcomes were invariably positive in the short term.[9] Like the U.S. threats against the USSR in earlier years, the practice of nuclear diplomacy by the Soviet Union might be particularly effective against actors over whom the Kremlin holds a position of massive nuclear superiority and when the issues are substantial enough to justify this level of threat. On the other hand, the longer-term outcome of Moscow's nuclear threat against China and the reinforcement of Soviet conventional forces in the Far East—implying Soviet preparedness for tactical nuclear war—drove Peking into a larger nuclear weapons program of its own and to im-

9. Blechman and Kaplan, *Force without War*, pp. 95–101. This, of course, is not to suggest that nuclear weapons should be used politically except in the gravest of circumstances and after the most careful consideration.

proved relations with the West. NATO and Japan also became seriously alarmed.

Almost certainly Moscow went beyond what was required to coerce Peking into toning down its border activities, both in the size of the Soviet conventional buildup and in the threat to use nuclear weapons. These moves were effective in the short term, but it is doubtful that so massive a response to China's behavior was necessary. A modest buildup and a few defeats of Chinese troops in border areas probably would have served to punish and deter the Chinese. The prospect of a major Chinese attack upon the USSR was extremely remote.

Major Ground Operations

The use of large conventional forces alone to compel Peking to enter negotiations and to show contrition did not achieve the desired results in the spring and early summer of 1969; nor were Eastern Europeans intimidated by the manipulation of large Soviet formations. Warsaw, Budapest, Prague, Bucharest, and Belgrade were each confronted with active multidivisional forces nearby; in every instance Moscow's threat was either faced boldly or ignored. That the Kremlin was seriously concerned and might finally order violent intervention was understood. Exercises by smaller forces would have sufficed to reinforce the message. Rather than coerce Eastern European nations, large Soviet deployments and maneuvers in Eastern Europe simply enflamed nationalist sentiments or galvanized citizens to follow their national leaders more closely.

Massive forces were necessary to the interventions in Hungary and Czechoslovakia and surely would have been against Poland if Khrushchev had not decided to gamble on Gomulka. No one knew in November 1956 that Soviet authority in Eastern Europe was not about to crumble and that the Hungarian army would not fight; or, in 1968, that Prague would assuredly choose nonviolent resistance. Although the violence used in Budapest was held against Moscow in international affairs, the restoration of authority and the absence of further outbreaks in the region may have convinced the Kremlin of the utility of that violence. It may have helped deter the threat of resistance by Czechoslovakia twelve years later. The USSR's deception and interventions in Hungary in November 1956 and in Czechoslovakia in August 1968 were well thought out in comparison to Soviet deployments in Poland and Hungary in October 1956 and in Czechoslovakia in July 1968. These latter actions illustrated Soviet indecisiveness and willingness to negotiate, not credible resolve. But if the Kremlin did secure a certain physical control of events in Czechoslovakia in August 1968, its desire to avoid violence and other harsh measures in the next six months demonstrated the limits of military power as a political instrument when it is apparent that an actor does not want to use force. The occupation of Czechoslovakia, like the U.S. interventions in Lebanon in 1958, in Southeast Asia in 1962, and in the Dominican Republic in 1965, bought time to achieve a solution, not the solution itself.

Projecting Power into the Third World

The Johnson administration felt real anxiety on June 10, 1967, after Soviet paratroopers had been alerted, implying the possible deployment of Soviet airborne units to the Middle East. Preparations for such a deployment six years later led the Nixon administration to declare a Defcon 3 alert and to press Israel to accept a cease-fire. Although Moscow had no desire to actually send forces to Egypt unilaterally during the conflict, the Kremlin's orchestration of airborne units and transport aircraft was particularly effective. No nonviolent naval activity could have implied such a degree of Soviet commitment to Egypt. Nor could tactical aircraft have been manipulated so subtly as to raise the prospect of such a commitment.

The earlier development of a large strategic transport capability must have pleased Moscow during the 1973 Middle East war. Although President Sadat wanted more military matériel than the USSR was willing to deliver, the Kremlin's ability to quickly replenish distant allies in the midst of conflict was impressive and boosted Soviet standing globally. A further development, however, was the U.S. airlift to Israel of an even larger volume of cargo. From this Moscow may have concluded that air transport of matériel should be used only to counterbalance a U.S. airlift or when the United States appears unwilling to use strategic transport aircraft to support an antagonist of a Soviet ally. The Soviet airlifts in support of the MPLA in 1975–1976 and of Ethiopia in 1977–78 proved the utility of rapidly transferring armaments abroad while at the same time deploying non-Soviet military personnel trained in Soviet weaponry and prepared to fight on behalf of a mutual ally. Using the Cubans was more prudent politically than using Soviet ground units and probably no less effective militarily.

Although Soviet planners were and probably remain concerned about the problem of overflight, the USSR was not prevented from carrying out supply efforts by the need to fly over numerous countries and to land for refueling. During the 1973 Middle East conflict U.S. C-5 and C-141 aircraft were unable to land in or fly over European countries. These planes had to fly over the Atlantic and the Mediterranean and refuel in the Azores and by tankers operating surreptitiously out of Spain. Soviet aircraft, however, were able to fly over Yugoslavia, Turkey, and perhaps Greece. Soviet aircraft en route from the USSR and Cuba during the Angolan conflict apparently stopped in Algeria, Guinea, and perhaps Somalia. Many African and Middle Eastern countries as well as Yugoslavia were overflown in this operation. The airlift to Ethiopia, which included a number of routes, included overflights of countries as widespread as Yugoslavia and Pakistan. Although permission was not obtained from many of the countries overflown, most of the countries ignored the flights. None, except Pakistan and Turkey, were prepared to seriously interfere with the airlift to Addis Ababa. Only Israel, during the 1973 war, ever threatened Soviet transport planes—by attacking aircraft on the ground in Syria. No nation has fired on a Soviet transport plane in the air for a violation of its sovereignty.

Airlifts during the October war, the Angolan civil war, and the conflict between Ethiopia and Somalia quickly provided Soviet allies with armaments, and tactical air support to Egypt, Sudan, and Iraq filled a critical military gap quickly and effectively. The Anyanya and the Kurds could not defend themselves from the Soviet aircraft, and their external supporters would not back them in this effort. In 1970, the United States did not become militarily involved in the Israeli-Soviet conflict in the Canal war, and, aside from skirmishing, Israel also was unwilling to militarily engage the USSR on a sustained basis. Israel was loath to regularly cause the deaths of Soviet military men, be it in air-to-air combat or attacks on ground-based air defense units.

Militarily effective and perceived as expressions of deep political commitment, Soviet actions in support of third world countries had the advantage of only being on or over the sovereign territory of an ally. Thus, like the air support given to North Korea and China during the Korean War and the air defense assistance to North Vietnam, these actions in the third world were prudent. Soviet fighter aircraft did not fly over Israel or Sinai; nor, apparently, did planes flown by Soviet pilots fly beyond Sudan and Iraq. By using tactical aircraft only to defend the sovereignty and territorial integrity of an ally, Moscow minimized the likelihood of expanding the conflict while providing valuable military support. Soviet military men also acted cautiously. For example, in the USSR's air defense of Egypt, Soviet units worked from the Egyptian heartland forward to the Suez Canal area, gradually filling out positions that had been sketchily established earlier.

Moscow could infer from its earliest experiences in gunboat diplomacy in West African waters that the use of small task groups to achieve limited objectives was practical and effective. Soviet operational objectives were satisfied, deployments of such task groups did not lead to a matching presence by U.S. naval units, and third world nations did not condemn the USSR for its actions. Outcomes related to the Angolan conflict further supported these inferences. Aside from just showing the Soviet flag after it became apparent that the United States would not intervene in any major way, Moscow probably meant to caution Zaire against interfering with the airlift or sealift being carried out in support of the MPLA. Zaire attempted no such action, and African nations did not find fault with the Soviet Union's naval activity. The result was that another third world nation was threatened with enough subtlety to avoid a charge of coercion. In addition, the concurrent deployment south of the West African patrol and of a cruiser from the Mediterranean to Guinean waters were of only secondary significance to the West. Détente did not falter because of this small naval activity.

Even if Soviet warships had not made their appearances Ghana would probably have soon released the captured Soviet trawlers and their crews, Portugal would have stopped attacking Guinea, and Zaire would not have interfered with the Soviet airlift or sealift in support of the MPLA. But no one can be sure that these outcomes would have resulted in the absence of the USSR's naval diplomacy. That being so, the association of small naval operations with satisfactory outcomes and the absence of negative ramifications allowed an interpretation of success.

During the 1967 and 1973 Middle East wars and in the intervening Jordanian crisis and Indo-Pakistani war, Moscow made full use of naval forces to express concern while maintaining flexibility. During the three Middle East conflicts Israeli officials did not perceive Soviet naval activities as provocative to Israeli forces, and U.S. policymakers viewed Soviet activities as cautious and restrained. (The dangerous face-off between U.S. and Soviet naval units in 1973 took place after hostilities had ceased.)

By responding in kind to large U.S. naval displays the USSR reinforced its global image as a superpower and reduced the political shadow cast by U.S. task forces. Such was the result of Soviet naval diplomacy during the *Pueblo* crisis, the Indo-Pakistani war, and the 1973 Middle East conflict.

Yet, because Soviet naval forces were unable to project power ashore and because both superpowers did not want to be the first to fire a shot at the other, a relationship between Soviet naval forces and the achievement of operational objectives in a crisis was not demonstrated. When Soviet allies fared poorly in a conflict (as in the 1967 Middle East war) or were seriously threatened by U.S. military power when they were doing well (Syria in the 1970 Jordanian crisis), a Soviet naval presence did not help them.

Being intent on avoiding conflict with the United States, Moscow wisely did not respond to U.S. naval operations during the wars in Korea and Vietnam. Large deployments of Soviet warships alongside American task forces launching carrier-based aircraft probably would have been exposed as bluffs rather than have compelled the termination of U.S. operations. However, the deployment of Soviet ships to the South China Sea, in response to U.S. operations in Vietnam in 1972, made sense as a caution to the United States against further attacks on Soviet merchantmen in Haiphong harbor.

Although New Delhi recognized the limits of Soviet backing during the Indo-Pakistani war, it also appreciated the support it did receive from Moscow. That the Kremlin ordered Soviet warships to follow British and U.S. carrier task groups into the Indian Ocean was gratifying to Indian leaders, despite expectations in both the USSR and India that the United States would not become militarily involved in that conflict. It is possible that the extra insurance provided by the Soviet navy allowed New Delhi to be more confident in completing its task in the former East Pakistan. During the *Pueblo* crisis and October war, however, the timing of Soviet actions and warship deployments earned little gratitude in Pyongyang, Cairo, or Damascus, which recognized that U.S. restraint had little to do with Soviet naval diplomacy.

Israel clearly did not restrain itself in 1973 because of the USSR's Fifth Eskadra, as it did not during the 1969–70 war of attrition or during the June war. Unable to project power ashore, the most the Soviet navy could do when its ally was on the defensive was to make itself a hostage in Egyptian ports, as it did after the *Eilat* was sunk in late 1967. Nor was Somalia coerced by the large Soviet flotilla marshaled in East African waters in 1977–78 although Mogadishu did not interfere with the Soviet supply effort to Ethiopia. This flotilla could have had a more serious effect only insofar as the USSR was prepared to mount some form of blockade against Somalia, which would have meant substantial risk to Soviet standing in the third world. While a small naval force may deter a nation politically isolated from the United States against engaging in violence, a large task group lacking ability to project power ashore may not be adequate to compel such a state to cease hostilities.

American Military Power and Soviet Use of Force

U.S. armed forces were more likely to be called on and were better able to deter and counter Soviet political-military operations when a well-recognized, important U.S. interest was being threatened—that is, when the United States had more at risk than the USSR in a particular incident; when Soviet forces were not already embroiled in combat activities and U.S. forces were; when Soviet leaders were not confident about the ability of their strategic forces to deter U.S. nuclear attack on the USSR; and when U.S. conventional forces were superior in the area of local disturbance or able to negate the support provided by Soviet military units.

No American president has ever perceived the United States militarily so strong or the USSR so weak that he reckoned war anything but a calamity for the West and acted incautiously when U.S.-Soviet conflict appeared plausible. American political leaders have always believed that avoiding Soviet violence against American allies was more important than causing death and destruction throughout the USSR. Thus U.S. strategic forces were never used to compel the USSR to withdraw from a position. In the words of McGeorge Bundy, former special assistant for national security affairs, "It was entirely clear" to President Kennedy that "a general nuclear exchange, even at the levels of 1961, would be so great a disaster as to be an unexampled failure of statesmanship."[10] President Kennedy's message to the USSR in the Cuban missile crisis was that a nuclear attack on the United States launched from Cuba would elicit a U.S. nuclear attack on the USSR, not that U.S. nuclear weapons would be used against the Soviet Union if the missiles were not withdrawn. First use of a nuclear weapon by the United States was threatened only as a response to a massive conventional offensive against U.S. allies in Europe and Japan.

American combat forces have never been deployed to an area where Soviet armed forces were using firepower. The Eisenhower administration kept its distance from Moscow's suppression of revolt in East Ger-

10. Speech by McGeorge Bundy, September 6, 1979, reprinted in *Survival*, vol. 21 (November–December, 1979), p. 269.

many in 1953 and in Hungary in 1956. President Lyndon B. Johnson acted no differently when Soviet troops marched into Czechoslovakia in 1968.

Serious American military action might have been threatened or even taken in response to Soviet intervention in Hungary and Czechoslovakia if President Eisenhower or President Johnson had believed that the United States was so powerful that it could have restricted hostilities to Eastern Europe and triumphed quickly. Not only was the latter out of the question, but by 1956 the USSR could devastate Europe and the United States with nuclear weapons, despite the even greater strategic capabilities of the United States. By 1968 the Soviet strategic arsenal was even more powerful than it had been in 1956. Although President Eisenhower may have lacked confidence about the success of a disarming first strike, President Johnson had in mind only "assured destruction" if such a course was to be taken. Both presidents saw U.S. intervention as leading to world war and the death of millions, not to the liberation of Eastern Europe.

Nor did the Nixon administration act to counter the Soviet air defense of Egypt or tactical air support given to Sudan and Iraq, let alone Soviet assaults against China in 1969. Peking, of course, was a bitter antagonist of the United States in 1969, and Soviet military actions against China then as well as those later in support of Arab allies were accepted as having been taken in defense of the territorial integrity of the USSR or Soviet allies. In Eastern Europe, the Kremlin was considered to be acting only to preserve the status quo, since this region had been conceded to the USSR at the end of the Second World War. In crises in Eastern Europe in which the USSR sought to preserve previously made gains, the Kremlin not only held conventional superiority but also appeared ready to go to war; the United States was not.

For its part, Moscow also did not intervene violently to change the status quo, even in Yugoslavia and Rumania after affairs had been allowed to slip too far. Soviet relations with Yugoslavia by 1951 and with Rumania by 1968 had evolved to such an extent that, despite demonstrative uses of Soviet armed forces, actual intervention against these nations might have been viewed by many internationally as actions to change the status quo. The possibility of such intervention caused the Truman and Johnson administrations to raise the prospect, although ambiguously, of U.S. military support for Belgrade and Bucharest, respectively. Even if Moscow was not militarily deterred in these instances by Washington's verbal warnings and small shows of force, U.S. military power might have influenced Soviet decisions, since the Kremlin wanted to avoid drawn-out bloody battles in Yugoslavia and Rumania. Moscow might have counted on a quickly accomplished change of affairs not to lead to conflict between the United States and the Soviet Union; but what the United States might have done in response to a long campaign of suppression was less certain.

Moscow also hesitated in Hungary in 1956. After first intervening, Soviet army units were then withdrawn. The second intervention in Hungary might have taken a different form or, perhaps, not have taken place at all if the British, French, and Israelis had not attacked Egypt and President Eisenhower had not announced in a television statement that the United States would not take military action in Eastern Europe.[11] Although it seemed clear that Prague would not issue a call to battle in 1968, an important reason for this may have been Dubček's certainty that NATO would not intervene and that Czechoslovakia would have to stand alone. U.S. behavior in Hungary twelve years earlier and U.S. diplomacy and the strategic balance in 1968 all supported this conclusion. Bucharest and Belgrade did not count on their ability to defeat Soviet forces but on anxiety in Moscow about the extent of the conflict and where the violence might end.

Moscow was extremely cautious about using armed forces when U.S. military units were already engaged in violence, even if the U.S. target was a Soviet ally. The Soviet Union allowed North Korea to be blockaded and its troops to be thrown out of South Korea by U.S. forces in 1950, and allowed North Vietnam to be bombed without intervening in 1965–68 and again in 1972. In both instances, however, it was the United States that was defending an ally. In 1950, while the West agonized about a possible Soviet attack on Western Europe, Stalin was anxious to avoid conflict between the United States and the USSR. General Douglas MacArthur's drive north of the 38th parallel and the threat to Manchuria and the Soviet Far East in 1950 presented a dangerous situation, however. Moscow might even have worried about an Inchon-type landing on Soviet territory. Fighting between Americans and Russians would have been almost certain if U.S. forces had entered Manchuria and Chinese forces had faltered. Yet rather than widen the conflict into Europe, thus risking a U.S.

11. "Radio and Television Report to the American People on the Developments in Eastern Europe and the Middle East, October 31, 1956," *Public Papers of the Presidents: Dwight D. Eisenhower, 1956* (Government Printing Office, 1958), p. 1060. The important sentence by President Eisenhower is cited in chapter 6.

nuclear strike against the USSR, Stalin might have been content with a holding action in northern China and conceded the Korean peninsula to the West.

The Vietnam War never presented the same risk of superpower conflict as the Korean War did because both Washington and Moscow perceived from the start the necessity for tacit limits on their military activity. Although the United States did not consider Hanoi's actions to be part of a Soviet plan leading to aggression against major U.S. allies elsewhere, care was taken not to invade North Vietnam or engage in all-out conventional bombing of the North until 1972, by which time U.S. ground forces had been withdrawn from South Vietnam and it was obvious that the United States had only limited political objectives. Nor is there evidence that the use of nuclear weapons was ever seriously considered. The Kremlin restricted its support of Hanoi to military matériel and some relatively unadvertised air defense personnel assistance. U.S. policymakers built up to the air war against North Vietnam slowly and tried not to kill Russians. Possibly Moscow would have restrained itself even further if early in the war the United States had secured some North Vietnamese territory just north of the border dividing the two Vietnams. Between 1965 and 1972, however, U.S. political leaders were unwilling to sanction ground intervention north of the 17th parallel and probably would have remained so no matter what defeats were suffered in the South. Presented with imminent disaster, the more appealing option was to bomb the North heavily.

In the late 1940s Moscow was warned that conventional Soviet aggression in Europe or against Japan might lead to a nuclear strike by the United States. But when the USSR began to deploy intercontinental strategic bombers in the mid-1950s this option began losing credibility. When the USSR finally acquired the capability to deploy conventional forces beyond adjacent areas in the late 1960s, the United States was already beginning to think in terms of rough parity in superpower strategic forces. Both countries took great care not to set off events that might end in a launch of nuclear weapons by either superpower.

In a context of nuclear stalemate, which might go back as far as the 1956 Suez conflict, forward and quickly deployable conventional forces have been important determinants of conflict resolution. Since World War II the United States has never maintained forces capable of contesting Soviet land and air power aimed at maintaining authority in Eastern Europe. Similarly, U.S. conventional power directed at Cuba during the missile crisis presented the USSR with such poor options as (1) a suicidal nuclear attack and (2) the issuing of threats to seize West Berlin or attack Western Europe at a time when U.S. leaders appeared willing to use nuclear weapons in defense of these interests. The achievement of strategic parity with the United States gave the Kremlin greater confidence about making forward deployments and threatening military intervention in crises. When Soviet military units were deployed abroad or a threat to do so was made, U.S. policymakers declined to escalate the conflict or were willing to do so only as a screen for diplomatic efforts. This U.S. predicament was glimpsed at the end of the June war; it became clearer during the Soviet air defense of Egypt, and even more so after Brezhnev's threat to intervene at the end of the October war. Although U.S. Sixth Fleet movements in 1967 and the alert in 1973 may have inhibited Moscow from airlifting troops to the Middle East, the United States was probably not prepared to endanger their safe arrival in Syria and Egypt or to join Israel in fighting on Arab soil. Had the 1967 war occurred in 1973, it is possible that Moscow would have threatened a serious interventionary act before Israel seized all of Gaza, Sinai, the Golan Heights, and the West Bank—which is to say that in 1967 U.S. military power was a greater deterrent to Soviet behavior than it was in 1973.

In 1970 the United States did not have much ability to compel Moscow to reverse its decision to provide Egypt with air defense and withdraw its aircraft and missile crews. The circumstances, of course, were radically different from the missile crisis, the only previous occasion in which so many Soviet ground and air combat personnel had been deployed any distance from the USSR. Eight years after the missile crisis the USSR had a powerful strategic capability and a credible counterpart to the Sixth Fleet in the Mediterranean; and it was Egypt that was endangered, not the United States, or even Israel. Conceivably, the Nixon administration could have preempted President Nasser's call for Soviet support or, before Moscow had responded, pressured Israel to end its deep penetration raids. Had the Nixon administration tried to prevent unilateral Soviet military involvement in the 1970 Arab-Israeli conflict, the principal military option of the United States—beyond ship visits—would have been the temporary placement of tactical aircraft in Israel, accompanied by a statement that the deployment was intended to ensure Israel's security. This policy choice was out of the question, however, because Egypt, not Israel, was under attack, because the USSR's proclaimed purpose was defensive, and because the United States sought to curb Tel Aviv and gain favor with the Arabs.

If aircraft piloted by Russians had attacked Ethiopia, Zaire, and Iran to compel these countries to stop supporting the insurgencies in Sudan and Iraq, the United States could have responded with ship or fighter aircraft visits or the dispatch of naval or airborne units for engagement in joint exercises in the hope of pressuring Moscow to desist. Taking such a course would have meant risking exposure of a bluff, however, because the U.S. Congress and the American public probably would not have supported more than these actions, and the executive was unwilling to seriously engage U.S. forces on account of the issues involved in these incidents.

During the October war, U.S. military transport aviation counterbalanced Moscow's use of this instrument by restocking Israel's inventories to such an extent that Egypt and Syria did not obtain an advantage as a result of Soviet shipments. Despite the later Soviet airlifts in support of the MPLA and Ethiopia, the experience during the October war may have persuaded Moscow to hold off from such support if it appeared likely that the United States would act to match Soviet efforts.

In response to a direct provocation or an important third world conflict, U.S. policymakers typically turned first to the navy and ordered to the scene a task force usually including at least one aircraft carrier. The Kremlin's typical reaction to such U.S. moves was to order the appearance of a countering naval force to neutralize the political impact of the presence of U.S. ships. Moscow's timing of deployments, their location, and the activities of Soviet naval vessels generally reflected the Kremlin's caution and efforts to ensure that naval demonstrations constituted only a joint appearance and not preparation for superpower conflict. Since U.S. military intervention in the 1971 Indo-Pakistani war was unlikely, Soviet warships steamed along with the *Enterprise* task force; and after developments that made a U.S. air strike against North Korea also unlikely, Moscow deployed reinforcements to the Sea of Japan after the *Pueblo* was seized.

Soviet naval operations do not seem to have prevented the United States from contemplating violent actions in these instances, although they may have reinforced U.S. caution. Certainly Moscow would have steered clear if U.S. fighter aircraft had arrived on the scene while the *Pueblo* was being taken into custody. Probably the Kremlin would not have reacted militarily to limited U.S. retaliation against North Korea then, in 1969 after the EC-121 shootdown, or after the 1976 murders in Korea's demilitarized zone. In fact, however, once North Korea had done its deeds, U.S. policymakers recognized them as faits accomplis and rejected military retaliation as complicating U.S. objectives and interests, including the distancing of Moscow from Pyongyang.

U.S. policymakers did not worry about provocation by Soviet warships but about setting in motion a series of events that would lead to superpower conflict. The United States came closest to engaging in hostilities in support of Jordan, a close U.S. ally and object of Sixth Fleet support on a number of occasions earlier, when it was in danger of being overrun by Syrian military power in 1970. In this instance, the USSR recognized its adversary's strong motivation, sense of urgency, and yet limited objective, and was prepared to stand clear.

Final Thoughts

Soviet military diplomacy in the future is unlikely to come as a surprise. The United States probably does not need to fear the appearance of Soviet armed forces in otherwise quiescent settings and Moscow's subsequent application of strong military pressure to obtain an advantage for itself or an ally. Soviet political-military operations generally have been mounted in response to instabilities well-known to Western foreign policy directors and to their intelligence services. Military interventions in the past have usually been expected or plausible, based on the observation of an endangered Soviet ally or other interest or on the recognition of an opportunity for easy Soviet entry into a situation of ongoing violence.

Analysts and policymakers need to identify the relatively few instances when the USSR is most likely to resort to the military and to determine the likely character of such interventions. Serious coercive military operations orchestrated by the Kremlin may be forecast to occur only in response to major interstate and civil conflicts—that is, in response to situations of great interest to the United States. In these incidents, the real issue will be how to either preclude Soviet intervention or else respond to it sensibly.

Aside from possible adverse effects a controversy may have on U.S. interests abroad, the successful demonstration of Soviet military power could lead to increased Soviet reliance on military force to secure positions or achieve new objectives abroad. If allowed a clear field, the Kremlin might be more likely to intervene on behalf of clients, or at least intervene at an earlier stage in their conflicts. In addition, the resistance of third parties to Soviet objectives might decline. Nations fearing a Soviet ally or the USSR itself might increase their defense spending and seek more armaments from the United States; however, the United States might have strong reason not to supply the desired weapons and might view their higher defense spending as economically dangerous. Countries in economic trouble might pressure the United States for grant aid or concessionary credits to support increased defense spending. The United States and its industrial allies might also be driven to spend more on defense, thus depriving their citizens of higher standards of living or more stable economies.

In the past, the United States reacted to crises distant from the Soviet Union by alerting or deploying forces, confident that the USSR would not respond militarily. Almost always the crises involved a threat to a regime in power or to a nation having close relations with the United States. U.S. decisionmakers were more motivated than Soviet leaders and able to rely on unchallenged U.S. conventional military capability in crisis areas and a strategic imbalance favorable to the United States. Even during its period of greatest relative strength, the United States rarely attempted to use military units to unseat a Soviet ally or to deny the sovereignty of a Soviet friend. Such U.S. military action is now more dangerous than ever because the USSR can now use credible military force locally and is strongly motivated to prevent U.S. military power from causing the downfall of a friend. In addition, the United States may feel pressure to stand by and watch helplessly if an ally, having gone too far in attacking a Soviet ally, finds itself coerced and its armed forces subjected to violence by Soviet military power. Although Washington may have little sympathy for its ally's position in such circumstances, the United States would stand to lose credibility, and the image of Soviet power would probably be enhanced.

Using U.S. armed forces symbolically when U.S. policymakers are unwilling to resort to violence makes little sense if it gives Moscow an opportunity to engage in counter military measures that can be perceived as a deterrent to U.S. military action. For example, in response to an attack by a Soviet friend against a U.S. ally or on a U.S. military unit or group of civilians, American policymakers might feel impelled to respond militarily and yet avoid violent retaliation. Their inclination probably would be to call on naval units to establish a threatening presence. A naval task group, after all, can be easily withdrawn, does not depend on the permission of third parties, and can draw close to the territory of many nations. But if a naval operation is only symbolic and incapable of defending itself well and projecting power ashore in the face of opposition, it is likely to be perceived as an expression of uncertainty and weakness rather than as a warning of retribution by a great power. If the opposition is a Soviet naval force, the impression might be not only that the United States is divided or unwilling to become embroiled in a local conflict, even when provoked, but also that the United States is more fearful of the USSR than the USSR is of the United States.

To appear powerful at sea in the face of Soviet warships probably requires the use of at least two aircraft carrier task groups. The dispatch of one carrier task group in response to a serious crisis often constitutes in today's world only a gesture, indicative of interest and concern but not of a commitment to use force—if necessary—to achieve a particular outcome. The coupling of strong language with the deployment of a single carrier group may only ensure widespread attention to the fact that the naval presence has been ignored. Carrier task groups are best used to show off U.S. military power and commitment in situations that do not involve crises or when the prospect of U.S. military action (including use of firepower) is very real. In the latter circumstance U.S. policymakers can couple a large naval presence with language strong enough to caution Moscow to stand back and avoid a superpower confrontation at sea. In a crisis in which a Soviet ally is suffering, U.S. warships might also be deployed near Soviet vessels if it is clear that Moscow intends no violence. A prudently timed U.S. appearance of this sort might point up to a Soviet client as well as to others the limited utility of alliance with the USSR.

When a U.S. ally is subjected to a brief burst of violence or fait accompli and a U.S. military response is desired, the airlift of armaments or the forward deployment of tactical aircraft might be sensible. These discrete political-military moves would be less likely to elicit similar moves from the USSR since Moscow would wish to avoid a commitment to an aggressor when the United States appeared willing to become militarily involved. Of course, it does not make much sense to use land-based aircraft in the face of opposition by intermediary nations on which U.S. overflight or landing depends, especially when U.S. policymakers cannot ignore or easily work around such objection.

Extensive U.S. military intervention including the use of firepower has been contemplated most seriously when a valued friend has been attacked by a Soviet ally or subjected to severe domestic violence traceable to Moscow or to a nation having close ties with the USSR. Recognizing the commitment of U.S. policymakers, the Kremlin has been unwilling to seriously engage in a superpower confrontation in such instances. The prospect of gaining a new advantage has not outweighed the risks of escalating a crisis to a level that could lead to war with the United States. Moscow may be particularly responsive to the early U.S. use of force and to clear verbal signals given by U.S. leaders when such moves confirm Soviet expectations—that is, before the Kremlin or its ally commits itself to escalation.

Moscow has not emulated American restraint when that restraint has reflected unwillingness to become militarily involved rather than a wish to avoid unnecessary confrontation with the USSR. If the United States hesitates to give military support to an ally endangered by a Soviet ally, Moscow itself may refrain from military activity. The prudent course, after all, is to have a U.S. ally defeated by a Soviet ally without risking a superpower military confrontation. But the Kremlin also has an interest in being on the scene and appearing at least partly responsible for the triumph of its friends. If the United States is perceived as being unwilling to countenance violent conflict, it is more likely that the USSR will give military support to an ally on the offensive.

In future conflicts, many Americans will probably think that local circumstances do not warrant coercive U.S. diplomacy, let alone violent intervention. Conflict between Congress and the President about the merit of the political use of the military or military intervention in particular situations may also occur. The record of Soviet political-military behavior indicates keen sensitivity to U.S. discord, uncertainty, and temerity about coercive diplomacy. Although it might be sensible for the United States to stay out of foreign conflicts in which important U.S. interests are not directly at stake, signals to this effect—including the nuance that U.S. military intervention will not be provoked by Soviet military involvement —might strengthen the argument of those in the Kremlin who would resort to military means and might dissuade those opposed to the use of force. Moreover, a favorable experience for the Russians, in which the United States did not become involved, might increase the confidence of Soviet interventionists later, when U.S. policymakers might appear similarly inhibited.

If the unilateral use of force by Moscow could be associated with outcomes not harmful to U.S. interests, the United States could stand aside and relax. However, American interests have been harmed by Soviet political-military operations. Sometimes U.S. interests have not suffered very much, but on other occasions they were seriously harmed—for example, by Moscow's gaining access to foreign military facilities, by the doubt cast on American readiness to firmly support allies and other friends, and by the restriction of economic and cultural relations between the United States and nations dependent on the USSR and its allies. Soviet actions have also reinforced arguments for increased U.S. defense spending, led to U.S. shows of force to reassure anxious allies, and affected a broad spectrum of relations between the United States and the Soviet Union. "Linkage" may or may not be preferred as a policy strategy, but in many ways it is a political reality. The distrust occasioned by Soviet military interventions affects the conduct of U.S. negotiations with the USSR, votes in the Congress on foreign policy and on defense issues to which Soviet behavior may be related, and relations between the United States and other nations of interest to the USSR. Although it is difficult to identify the precise effects of such distrust, it is not difficult to see that the Soviet use of force in the 1973 Middle East war, the Angolan civil war, and the Ethiopian-Somalian conflict, as well as smaller and less noticed Soviet political-military operations, had an individual and cumulative negative effect on U.S. relations with the Soviet Union in the late 1970s.

When major U.S. interests do not appear immediately at risk, the political use of the military, to be effective, must be based on a persuasive, clear explanation of international relationships dictating that action to be essential. Potential criticism at home must be preempted by sound argument, and adversaries must be convinced about the strength of American motivation. But even then, in addition to the danger of military confrontation with the USSR, the use of U.S. armed forces may be mistaken; for although Moscow might be locally deterred, U.S. military diplomacy might occasion an adverse impact on American interests equal to or greater than the effects of the unilateral use of force by the USSR. The political use of U.S. armed forces is not necessarily preferable to such unilateral Soviet behavior.

Threats of U.S. military diplomacy, arms transfers, and covert action are obvious instruments that might be used to counter discrete Soviet political-military operations. In some instances these instruments may seem sensible, but in some they may be politically unfeasible or counterproductive to U.S. interests. Even when these tools may seem necessary, they may be insufficient. Moreover, while it does not make sense to allow the USSR and its allies to believe that the United States will refrain from forceful intervention and that they can engage in military diplomacy unilaterally, it is also wise to use other than military means to constrain the Kremlin's use of the military to obtain its objectives. If a crisis begins to loom in the third world, for example, the United States could (1) support regional political solutions and peacekeeping actions; (2) offer verbal commitments of U.S. nonintervention contingent on similar Soviet restraint, and declarations to withhold support from U.S. allies who might intervene if Soviet allies do not become involved; (3) make clear to U.S. allies and others who might turn to the United States that they might not receive U.S. support if they engage in aggression; and (4) draw attention to potential violations by the USSR of sovereignty and other international norms if the Kremlin was dependent on certain air and even sea routes.

The utility of such actions could be enhanced by using them as part of a long-term strategy. The United States could offer third world nations a choice between respect for their regional autonomy, territorial integrity, and an orientation of nonalignment or Soviet and possibly U.S. intervention and interference in their affairs and those close to them. In addition to supporting regional political solutions and peacekeeping efforts, delimitations on alliance support, declarations of conditional nonintervention, and the building of mutual interest in respect for the sovereignty of airspace and innocent passage at sea, the United States also might attempt to reduce the dependency of Soviet allies on the USSR. Moscow certainly ought to be able to understand that Soviet military behavior in the third world does influence U.S. global alliance policy and defense spending, as well as negotiations and other cooperative superpower interactions.

Appendixes

The Incidents

THE 190 incidents in which Soviet armed forces were used as a political instrument between June 1944 and August 1979 are listed in this appendix. The incidents are identified by a phrase describing the political context in which Soviet military units were used and the month and year the action was initiated.

1. Accession of parts of Finland to USSR — June 1944
2. Accession of eastern Poland to USSR — June 1944
3. Political future of Poland — July 1944
4. Accession of northern Bukovina and Bessarabia to USSR — August 1944
5. Political future of Rumania — August 1944
6. Political future of Bulgaria — September 1944
7. Political future of Hungary — October 1944
8. Accession of Sub-Carpathian Ruthenia to USSR. — October 1944
9. Political future of Czechoslovakia — January 1945
10. Accession of East Prussia to USSR — January 1945
11. Political future of Germany — January 1945
12. Political future of Austria — March 1945
13. Accession of southern Sakhalin and Kurile Islands to USSR — August 1945
14. Political future of China — August 1945
15. Acquisition of special rights in Port Arthur and Dairen — August 1945
16. Political future of Korea — August 1945
17. Economic influence sought in Manchuria — November 1945
18. Political future of Bornholm Island — November 1945
19. Communist regime established in northern Iran — December 1945
20. Withdrawal from Czechoslovakia — December 1945
21. Maintenance of security of Port Arthur and Dairen — February 1946

22. Dispute over Turkish provinces and Dardanelles   March 1946
23. Withdrawal from China   March 1946
24. Withdrawal from Bornholm Island   March 1946
25. Sovietization of North Korea   July 1946
26. Occupation of Haiyang Island   March 1947
27. Relations with Iran   August 1947
28. Sovietization of Hungary   September 1947
29. Sovietization of Poland   September 1947
30. Sovietization of Rumania   September 1947
31. Future of West Germany and Berlin   January 1948
32. Communist coup in Czechoslovakia   February 1948
33. Future of West Germany and Berlin   March 1948
34. Future of West Germany and Berlin   June 1948
35. Relations with Denmark   September 1948
36. Withdrawal from North Korea   October 1948
37. Civil war in China   October 1948
38. Relations with Iran   October 1948
39. Maintenance of security of North Korea   ? 1949
40. Relations with Iran   May 1949
41. Relations with Yugoslavia   August 1949
42. Rearmament of West Germany   January 1950
43. Seizure of West Berlin territory   September 1950
44. Maintenance of security of China   October 1950
45. Maintenance of security of North Korea   ? 1951
46. Seizure of West Berlin territory   January 1951
47. Maintenance of security of regime in
    Czechoslovakia   February 1951
48. Maintenance of security of regime in Albania   March 1951
49. Political crisis in Iran   June 1951
50. Rearmament of West Germany   August 1951
51. Yugoslavia's relations with the West   September 1951
52. Rearmament of West Germany   January 1952
53. Japan-U.S. relationship   June 1952
54. Relations with Sweden   June 1952
55. Yugoslavia's relations with the West   July 1952
56. Rearmament of West Germany   October 1952
57. Rearmament of West Germany   March 1953
58. Soviet relaxation of controls in Austria   June 1953
59. Peace offensive: Great Britain   June 1953
60. Demonstrations in East Berlin   June 1953
61. Maintenance of security of Bulgaria   October 1953
62. Relations with Albania   May 1954
63. Restoration of controls in Austria   June 1954
64. Relations with Sweden   July 1954
65. Austria State Treaty   May 1955
66. Withdrawal from Port Arthur and Dairen   May 1955

67. Withdrawal from Porkkala (Finland)	October 1955
68. Relations with Great Britain	October 1955
69. Security of regime in East Germany	December 1955
70. Relations with Japan	January 1956
71. Relations with Yugoslavia	May 1956
72. Relations with China	June 1956
73. Political demonstrations in Poland	June 1956
74. Government change in Poland	October 1956
75. Crisis in Hungary	October 1956
76. Maintenance of security of regime in Rumania	October 1956
77. Maintenance of security of regime in East Germany	October 1956
78. Crisis in Hungary	November 1956
79. Maintenance of security of regime in Poland	November 1956
80. Maintenance of security of regime in Bulgaria	November 1956
81. Western presence in Berlin	November 1956
82. Maintenance of security of regime in Hungary	March 1957
83. Maintenance of security of regime in Syria	September 1957
84. Maintenance of security of regime in Syria	October 1957
85. Western presence in Berlin	October 1957
86. Western presence in Berlin	January 1958
87. Relations with Poland	May 1958
88. Withdrawal from Rumania	May 1958
89. U.S. intervention in Lebanon	July 1958
90. Western presence in Berlin	November 1958
91. Western presence in Berlin	February 1959
92. Relations with Iran	March 1959
93. Insurgency in Indonesia	November 1959
94. Crisis in the Congo	July 1960
95. Crisis in the Congo	September 1960
96. Western presence in Berlin	September 1960
97. Crisis in Laos	December 1960
98. Western presence in Berlin	July 1961
99. Indonesia-Netherlands conflict over West Irian	? 1962
100. Crisis in Laos	January 1962
101. Western presence in Berlin	February 1962
102. Emplacement of missiles in Cuba	July 1962
103. Cuban missile crisis	October 1962
104. Civil war in North Yemen	December 1962
105. Relations with Laos	December 1962
106. Western presence in Berlin	April 1963
107. Western presence in Berlin	October 1963
108. Cyprus crisis	June 1964
109. Insurgency in the Congo	December 1964
110. Border dispute with China	? 1965
111. Bundestag meeting in West Berlin	April 1965
112. Relations with France	October 1966

113. Border dispute with China   February 1967
114. Egypt-Israel political crisis   May 1967
115. Arab-Israeli war   June 1967
116. Arab-Israeli postwar hostilities   June 1967
117. Relations with Sweden   August 1967
118. Relations with Spain   October 1967
119. Sinking of Israeli ship *Eilat*   October 1967
120. Insurgency in North Yemen   November 1967
121. Seizure of U.S.S. *Pueblo* by North Korea   January 1968
122. Relations with Czechoslovakia   March 1968
123. Relations with Czechoslovakia   May 1968
124. Insurgency in South Yemen   June 1968
125. Relations with Czechoslovakia   July 1968
126. Invasion of Czechoslovakia   August 1968
127. Relations with Rumania   August 1968
128. Maintenance of security of regime in Czechoslovakia   October 1968
129. Seizure of Soviet trawlers by Ghana   February 1969
130. West Germany federal election in West Berlin   March 1969
131. Border dispute with China   March 1969
132. Relations with Czechoslovakia   March 1969
133. Shooting down of U.S. EC-121 aircraft by North
     Korea   April 1969
134. Maintenance of security of Cuba   July 1969
135. Relations with Cambodia   December 1969
136. Maintenance of security of regime in Somalia   December 1969
137. Insurgency in Sudan   ? 1970
138. Maintenance of security of Egypt   February 1970
139. Maintenance of security of regime in Somalia   April 1970
140. Relations with France   May 1970
141. Cease-fire in Middle East   Autumn 1970
142. Jordan–Palestine Liberation Organization–Syria
     conflict   September 1970
143. U.S. reaction to USSR submarine tender in Cuba   September 1970
144. Relations with Yugoslavia   October 1970
145. West Germany–USSR treaty   October 1970
146. Demonstrations in Poland   December 1970
147. Maintenance of security of Guinea   December 1970
148. West German political visits to Berlin   January 1971
149. Insurgency in Sri Lanka   April 1971
150. Maintenance of security of regime in Sierra Leone   May 1971
151. Relations with France   June 1971
152. Relations with Rumania   June 1971
153. India-Pakistan war   December 1971
154. Maintenance of security of regime in Somalia   January 1972
155. Relations with Bangladesh   April 1972
156. Relations with Egypt   May 1972

157. U.S. response to North Vietnam's Easter offensive   May 1972
158. Dhofar rebellion in Oman   ? 1973
159. Relations with Iran   January 1973
160. Assassination of PAIGC (Portuguese-Guinean
     insurgents) leader   January 1973
161. Arab-Israeli conflict   April 1973
162. Iraq-Kuwait dispute   April 1973
163. "Cod war" between Great Britain and Iceland   May 1973
164. Arab-Israeli war (1)   October 1973
165. Arab-Israeli war (2)   October 1973
166. Relations with Italy   October 1973
167. Kurdish problem in Iraq   ? 1974
168. Cyprus conflict   July 1974
169. Clearing of Suez Canal   July 1974
170. Relations with Yugoslavia   September 1974
171. Syria-Israel conflict   November 1974
172. Border dispute with China   November 1974
173. Conflict in Angola   March 1975
174. Relations with United States   May 1975
175. Barents Sea dispute with Norway   September 1975
176. Conflict in Angola   November 1975
177. Algeria-Morocco-Polisario dispute   January 1976
178. Conflict in Lebanon: U.S. evacuation   June 1976
179. Relations with Italy   September 1976
180. Ethiopia-Somalia war   November 1977
181. Western presence in Berlin   January 1978
182. Maintenance of security of Cuba   February 1978
183. Relations with China   April 1978
184. Relations with China   May 1978
185. China-Vietnam conflict   June 1978
186. Relations with Japan   June 1978
187. China-Vietnam conflict   August 1978
188. Relations with Japan   ? 1979
189. Civil war in Afghanistan   ? 1979
190. China-Vietnam war   February 1979

Bibliographical Sources for Incidents and Soviet Military Behavior

Books

Abel, Elie. *The Missiles of October: The Story of the Cuban Missile Crisis, 1962*. London: MacGibbon, 1969.

Acheson, Dean. *Present at the Creation*. New York: Norton, 1969.

Adams, Sherman. *Firsthand Report: The Story of the Eisenhower Administration*. New York: Harper and Brothers, 1961.

Agung, Ide Anak. *Twenty Years: Indonesian Foreign Policy, 1945–1963*. Paris: Mouton, 1973.

Allison, Graham T. *Essence of Decision: Explaining the Cuban Missile Crisis*. Boston: Little, Brown, 1971.

Appleman, Roy E. *South to the Naktong, North to the Yalu*. Washington, D.C.: U.S. Department of the Army, 1961.

Armstrong, Hamilton F. *Tito and Goliath*. New York: Macmillan, 1951.

Aspaturian, Vernon. *Process and Power in Soviet Foreign Policy*. Boston: Little, Brown, 1971.

Barker, A. J. *Suez, The Seven-Day War*. London: Faber and Faber, 1964.

Barnet, Richard J. *The Giants: Russia and America*. New York: Simon and Schuster, 1977.

Barnett, A. Doak. *China on the Eve of Communist Takeover*. New York: Praeger, 1963.

Barraclough, Geoffrey. *Survey of International Affairs, 1956–1958*. London: Oxford University Press, 1962.

———. *Survey of International Affairs, 1959–1960*. London: Oxford University Press, 1964.

Barraclough, Geoffrey, and Rachel F. Wall. *Survey of International Affairs, 1955–1956*. London: Oxford University Press, 1960.

Bell, Coral. *Survey of International Affairs, 1954*. London: Oxford University Press, 1957.

Beloff, Max. *Soviet Policy in the Far East, 1944–1951*. London: Oxford University Press, 1953.

Berliner, Joseph S. *Soviet Economic Aid: The New Aid and Trade Policy in Underdeveloped Countries*. New York: Praeger for the Council on Foreign Relations, 1958.

Berman, Robert P. *Soviet Air Power in Transition*. Washington, D.C.: Brookings Institution, 1978.

Berner, Wolfgang, and others, eds. *The Soviet Union, 1973: Domestic Policy, Economics, Foreign Policy*. London: Hurst, 1975.

Bethell, Nicholas. *Gomulka: His Poland, His Communism*. New York: Holt, Rinehart and Winston, 1969.

Betts, Reginald R., ed. *Central and South East Europe, 1945–1948*. London: Royal Institute of International Affairs, 1950.

Binder, Leonard, ed. *Politics in Lebanon*. New York: John Wiley, 1966.

Bishop, Donald G., ed. *Soviet Foreign Relations: Documents and Readings*. Syracuse: Syracuse University Press, 1952.

Bishop, Robert, and E. S. Crayfield. *Russia Astride the Balkans*. New York: Robert M. McBride, 1948.

Black, Cyril Edwin, ed. *Challenge in Eastern Europe*. New Brunswick: Rutgers University Press, 1954.

Black, C. E., and E. C. Helmreich, eds. *Twentieth Century Europe: A History*. 2d ed., rev. New York: Knopf, 1963.

Blechman, Barry M. *The Changing Soviet Navy*. Washington, D.C.: Brookings Institution, 1973.

Blechman, Barry M., and Robert P. Berman, eds. *Guide to the Navies of the Far East*. Annapolis, Md.: U.S. Naval Institute, 1978.

Blechman, Barry M., and Stephen S. Kaplan. *Force without War: U.S. Armed Forces as a Political Instrument*. Washington, D.C.: Brookings Institution, 1978; and report to U.S. Department of Defense, 1976.

Bohlen, Charles E. *Witness to History, 1929–1969*. New York: Norton, 1973.

Bolt, Beranek and Newman, Inc. *The Control of Local Conflict: Case Studies*. 4 vols. Waltham, Mass.: Bolt, Beranek and Newman, Browne and Shaw International Studies Division, 1969.

Bonsal, Philip W. *Cuba, Castro and the United States*. Pittsburgh: University of Pittsburgh Press, 1971.

Booth, Ken. *The Military Instrument in Soviet Foreign Policy, 1917–1972*. London: United Services Institute for Defense Studies, 1973.

Borisov, Boris A. *The Soviet Army*. Moscow: Foreign Languages Publishing House, 1962.

Borisov, Oleg, and B. T. Koloskov. *Soviet-Chinese Relations, 1945–1970*. Bloomington: Indiana University Press, 1975.

Bowie, Robert R. *Suez 1956: International Crisis and the Role of Law*. New York: Oxford University Press, 1974.

Bowles, Chester. *Promises to Keep: My Years in Public Life, 1941–1969*. New York: Harper and Row, 1971.

Brandt, Conrad. *Stalin's Failure in China, 1924–1927*. Cambridge: Harvard University Press, 1958.

Brecher, Michael. *Decisions in Israel's Foreign Policy*. New York: Oxford University Press, 1974.

Breyer, Siegfried. *A Guide to the Soviet Navy*. Annapolis, Md.: U.S. Naval Institute, 1970.

Brezhnev, Leonid I. *On the Policy of the Soviet Union and the International Situation*. New York: Doubleday, 1973.

Bromke, Adam. *Poland's Politics: Idealism vs. Realism*. Cambridge: Harvard University Press, 1967.

Bromke, Adam, ed. *The Communist States at the Crossroads: Between Moscow and Peking*. New York: Praeger, 1965.

Bromke, Adam, and Philip E. Uren, eds. *The Communist States and the West*. New York: Praeger, 1967.

Bromke, Adam, and Teresa Rakowska-Harmstone, eds. *The Communist States in Disarray, 1965–1971*. Minneapolis: University of Minnesota, 1972.

Brown, James F. *The New Eastern Europe: The Khrushchev Era and After*. New York: Praeger, 1966.

Brzezinski, Zbigniew K. *The Soviet Bloc: Unity and Conflict*. Rev. ed. New York: Praeger, 1961.

―――. *Alternative to Partition*. New York: McGraw-Hill, 1965.

Bulloch, John. *The Making of a War: The Middle East From 1967 to 1973*. London: Longman Group, 1974.

Buscaren, Anthony. *Imperial Communism*. Washington, D.C.: Public Affairs Press, 1953.

Byely, Colonel B., and others. *Marxism-Leninism on War and Army*. Washington, D.C.: Government Printing Office, 1972.

Byrnes, James F. *Speaking Frankly*. New York: Harper and Brothers, 1947.

―――. *All in One Lifetime*. New York: Harper and Brothers, 1958.

Byrnes, Robert F., ed. *East-Central Europe under the Communists: Yugoslavia*. New York: Praeger, 1957.

Cable, James F. *Gunboat Diplomacy: Political Applications of Limited Naval Force*. New York: Praeger, 1971.

Cady, Richard H. *U.S. Naval Operations in Low Level Warfare*. BSR 2453. Detroit: Bendix Corp., December 1968.

Calvocoressi, Peter. *Survey of International Affairs, 1947–1948*. London: Oxford University Press, 1952.

―――. *Survey of International Affairs, 1949–1950*. London: Oxford University Press, 1953.

―――. *Survey of International Affairs, 1951*. London: Oxford University Press, 1954.

―――. *Survey of International Affairs, 1952*. London: Oxford University Press, 1955.

————. *Survey of International Affairs, 1953*. London: Oxford University Press, 1956.

Campbell, John C. *Tito's Separate Road: America and Yugoslavia in World Politics*. New York: Harper and Row for the Council on Foreign Relations, 1967.

Carrere D'Encausse, Helene. *La Politique Sovietique au Moyen-Orient, 1955–1975*. Paris: National Political Science Foundation, 1975.

Center for Strategic and International Studies. *Nato After Czechoslovakia*. Special Report Series 9. Washington, D.C.: Georgetown University, 1969.

————. *Soviet Sea Power*. Special Report Series 10. Washington, D.C.: Georgetown University, 1969.

Centre de Récherche et d'Information Socio-Politique. *Congo 1964: Political Documents of a Developing Nation*. Princeton: Princeton University Press, 1966.

Chang, Carsun. *The Third Force in China*. New York: Bookman Associates, 1952.

Churchill, Winston S. *The Second World War: Triumph and Tragedy*. Boston: Houghton Mifflin, 1953.

Clay, Lucius D. *Decision in Germany*. New York: Doubleday, 1950.

Clissold, Stephen, ed. *Yugoslavia and the Soviet Union, 1939–1973: A Documentary Survey*. London: Oxford University Press, 1975.

Clubb, Oliver E. *20th Century China*. New York: Columbia University Press, 1965.

Cohn, Helen Desfosses. *Soviet Policy Toward Black Africa: The Focus on National Integration*. New York: Praeger, 1972.

Colby, William, and Peter Forbath. *Honorable Men: My Life in the CIA*. New York: Simon and Schuster, 1978.

Collier, David S., and Kurt Glaser, eds. *Western Policy and Eastern Europe*. Chicago: Henry Regnery, 1966.

————. *Elements of Change in Eastern Europe: Prospects for Freedom*. Chicago: Henry Regnery, 1968.

Confino, Michael, and Shimon Shamir, eds. *The USSR and the Middle East*. John Wiley, 1973.

Crankshaw, Edward. *The New Cold War: Moscow v. Peking*. Hammondsworth, England: Penguin, 1963.

Crozier, Brian. *The Struggle for the Third World*. Chester Springs, Pa.: Dufour Editions, 1966.

Current History Review of 1959. New York: Rand McNally, 1962.

Dallin, Alexander, ed. *Soviet Conduct in World Affairs*. New York: Columbia University Press, 1960.

Dallin, Alexander, and Thomas B. Larson, eds. *Soviet Politics Since Khrushchev*. Englewood Cliffs, N.J.: Prentice-Hall, 1968.

Dallin, David J. *Soviet Foreign Policy After Stalin*. New York: Lippincott, 1961.

Daniel, Hawthorne. *The Ordeal of the Captive Nations*. New York: Doubleday, 1958.

Dann, Uriel. *Iraq Under Qassem: A Political History, 1958–1963.* New York: Praeger, 1969.

Davison, Walter Phillips. *The Berlin Blockade: A Study in Cold War Politics.* Princeton: Princeton University Press, 1958.

Dayan, Moshe. *Diary of the Sinai Campaign.* London: Weidenfeld and Nicolson, 1966.

Decalo, Samuel. *Coups and Army Rule in Africa: Studies in Military Style.* New Haven: Yale University Press, 1976.

Dedijer, Vladimir. *Tito.* New York: Simon and Schuster, 1953.

————. *The Battle Stalin Lost: Memories of Yugoslavia 1948–1953.* New York: Viking, 1976.

de Huszar, George Bernard, ed. *Soviet Power and Policy.* New York: Thomas Y. Crowell, 1955.

Dellin, L. A. D., ed. *Bulgaria.* New York: Praeger, 1957.

Deutscher, Issac. *Russia, China, and the West, 1953–1966.* Middlesex, England: Penguin, 1976.

Dinerstein, Herbert S. *War and the Soviet Union: Nuclear Weapons and the Revolution in Soviet Military and Political Thinking.* New York: Praeger, 1959.

————. *Intervention Against Communism.* Baltimore: Johns Hopkins Press, 1967.

————. *The Making of a Missile Crisis: October 1962.* Baltimore: Johns Hopkins University Press, 1976.

Dismukes, Bradford, and James McConnell, eds. *Soviet Naval Diplomacy.* New York: Pergamon, 1979.

Djilas, Milovan. *Conversations with Stalin.* New York: Harcourt, Brace and World, 1962.

————. *Memoir of a Revolutionary.* New York: Harcourt Brace Jovanovich, 1973.

Donaldson, Robert H. *Soviet Policy Toward India: Ideology and Strategy.* Cambridge: Harvard University Press, 1974.

Donovan, John, ed. *U.S. and Soviet Policy in the Middle East, 1945–56.* New York: Facts on File, 1972.

Donovan, Robert J. *Conflict and Crisis: The Presidency of Harry S. Truman, 1945–1948.* New York: Norton, 1977.

Duffield, Daniel M., Jr. *United States Security Interests in Eastern Europe: The Case of Poland.* Washington, D.C.: National Defense University, 1977.

Dulles, John Foster. *War or Peace.* New York: Macmillan, 1950.

Duncan, W. Raymond, ed. *Soviet Policy in Developing Countries.* Waltham, Mass.: Ginn, 1970.

Dupuy, Trevor N. *Elusive Victory: The Arab-Israeli Wars, 1947–1974.* New York: Harper and Row, 1978.

Dupuy, Trevor N., and Wendell Blanchard. *The Almanac of World Military Power.* 2d ed. New York: R. R. Bowker, 1972.

Eagleton, William, Jr. *The Kurdish Republic of 1946.* New York: Oxford University Press, 1963.

Ebon, Martin. *Malenkov: Stalin's Successor.* New York: McGraw-Hill, 1953.

Eden, Anthony. *Full Circle.* Boston: Houghton Mifflin, 1960.

Edmonds, Robin. *Soviet Foreign Policy, 1962–1973: The Paradox of Super Power.* London: Oxford University Press, 1975.

Eisenhower, Dwight D. *The White House Years: Mandate for Change, 1953–1956.* New York: Doubleday, 1963.

———. *The White House Years: Waging Peace, 1956–1961.* Garden City, N.Y.: Doubleday, 1965.

Eller, Ernest M. *The Soviet Sea Challenge.* New York: Cowles, 1971

Embree, George D. *The Soviet Union Between the Nineteenth and Twentieth Party Congress, 1952–1956.* The Hague: Martinus Nijhoff, 1959.

Erickson, John. *Soviet Military Power.* Washington, D.C.: U.S. Strategic Institute, 1973.

Fainsod, Merle. *How Russia Is Ruled.* Rev. ed. Cambridge: Harvard University Press, 1964.

Feis, Herbert. *Between War and Peace: The Potsdam Conference.* Princeton: Princeton University Press, 1960.

Fejtö, François. *Behind the Rape of Hungary.* New York: David McKay, 1957.

———. *A History of the People's Democracies: Eastern Europe Since Stalin.* New York: Praeger, 1971.

Finer, Herman. *Dulles over Suez: The Theory and Practice of His Diplomacy.* Chicago: Quadrangle, 1964.

First, Ruth. *Power in Africa.* New York: Pantheon, 1970.

Fleming, Denna Frank. *The Cold War and Its Origins, 1917–1960.* Vol. 2. New York: Doubleday, 1961.

Franck, Thomas M., and Edward Weisband. *Word Politics: Verbal Strategy Among the Superpowers.* London: Oxford University Press, 1972.

Freedman, Robert O. *Soviet Policy Toward the Middle East Since 1970.* New York: Praeger, 1975.

Freund, Gerald. *Germany Between Two Worlds.* New York: Harcourt, Brace and World, 1961.

Freymond, Jacques. *SAAR Conflict 1945–1955.* New York: Praeger, 1960.

Frye, Richard N. *Iran.* New York: Henry Holt, 1953.

Gaddis, John L. *The United States and the Origins of the Cold War, 1941–1947.* New York: Columbia University Press, 1972.

Garthoff, Raymond L. *Soviet Military Policy.* New York: Praeger, 1966.

———., ed. *Sino-Soviet Military Relations.* New York: Praeger, 1966.

George, Alexander L., and Richard Smoke. *Deterrence in American Foreign Policy: Theory and Practice.* New York: Columbia University Press, 1974.

George, Alexander, and others. *The Limits of Coercive Diplomacy.* Boston: Little, Brown, 1971.

Geyelin, Philip. *Lyndon B. Johnson and the World.* New York: Praeger, 1966.

Gittings, John. *The Role of the Chinese Army.* London: Oxford University Press, 1967.

————. *The World and China, 1922–1972.* New York: Harper and Row, 1974.

Glassman, Jon. *Arms for the Arabs.* Baltimore: Johns Hopkins University Press, 1975.

Glubb, John B. *Britain and the Arabs: A Study of Fifty Years, 1908–1958.* London: Hodder and Stoughton, 1959.

Gluckstein, Ygael. *Stalin's Satellites in Europe.* Boston: Beacon Press, 1952.

Golan, Galia. *The Czechoslovak Reform Movement: Communism in Crisis, 1962–1968.* London: Cambridge University Press, 1971.

————. *Yom Kippur and After: The Soviet Union and the Middle East Crisis.* London: Cambridge University Press, 1977.

Golan, Matti. *The Secret Conversations of Henry Kissinger: Step-by-Step Diplomacy in the Middle East.* New York: Bantam Books, 1976.

Goldhamer, Herbert. *The Foreign Powers in Latin America.* Princeton: Princeton University Press, 1972.

Gorshkov, Sergei G. *Red Star Rising at Sea.* Translated by Theodore A. Neely, Jr., from a series of articles originally published in *Morskoi Sbornik.* Annapolis, Md.: U.S. Naval Institute, 1974.

————. *Sea Power and the State.* New York: Pergamon, 1979.

Grechko, A. A. *On Guard for Peace and the Building of Communism.* JPRS 54602. Arlington, Va.: Joint Publications Research Service, 1971.

————. *The Armed Forces of the Soviet State.* Washington, D.C.: Government Printing Office, 1975.

Grechko, A. A., and others. *Selected Soviet Military Writings, 1970–1975.* Washington, D.C.: Government Printing Office, 1977.

Griffith, William E. *The Sino-Soviet Rift.* Cambridge: MIT Press, 1964.

————. *Sino-Soviet Relations, 1964–1965.* Cambridge: MIT Press, 1965.

————., ed. *The World and the Great Power Triangles.* Cambridge: MIT Press, 1975.

Gromyko, Andrei. *The International Situation and Soviet Foreign Policy.* Moscow: Novosti Press Agency, 1968.

Gruliow, Leo, ed. *Current Soviet Policies II: The Documentary Record of the 20th Communist Party Congress and Its Aftermath.* New York: Praeger, 1956.

————, ed. *Current Soviet Policies III: The Documentary Record of the Extraordinary 21st Congress of the Communist Party of the Soviet Union.* New York: Columbia University Press, 1960.

Haas, Ernest B., and others. *Conflict Management by International Organizations.* Morristown, N.J.: General Learning Press, 1972.

Halle, Louis J. *The Cold War as History.* New York: Harper and Row, 1967.

Halperin, Morton H. *The 1958 Taiwan Straits Crisis: A Documented History.* RM-4900-ISA. Santa Monica, Calif.: Rand Corp., December 1966.

Hamm, Harry. *Albania: China's Beachhead in Europe.* Translated by Victor Andersen. New York: Praeger, 1963.

Hammond, Thomas T., ed. *The Anatomy of Communist Takeovers.* New Haven: Yale University Press, 1975.

Hanak, H. *Soviet Foreign Policy Since the Death of Stalin.* London: Routledge and Kegan Paul, 1972.

Harriman, W. Averell, and Elie Abel. *Special Envoy to Churchill and Stalin, 1941–1946.* New York: Random House, 1975.

Hasan, K. Sarwar, and Khalida Qureshi, eds. *China, India, Pakistan.* Karachi: Pakistan Institute of International Affairs, 1966.

Heidelmeyer, Wolfgang, and Guenter Hindrichs, eds. *Documents on Berlin, 1943–1963.* Munich: R. Oldenbourg Verlag, 1963.

Heikal, Mohamed. *The Cairo Documents.* New York: Doubleday, 1973.

——. *Road to Ramadan.* New York: Ballantine Books, 1975.

——. *The Sphinx and the Commissar: The Rise and Fall of Soviet Influence in the Middle East.* New York: Harper and Row, 1978.

Hejzlar, Zdenek, and Vladimir V. Kusin. *Czechoslovakia, 1968–1969: Chronology, Bibliography, Annotation.* New York: Garland, 1975.

Heller, Deane, and David Heller. *The Berlin Wall.* New York: Walker, 1962.

Helmreich, Ernest Christian, ed. *Hungary.* New York: Praeger, 1957.

Hilsman, Roger. *To Move a Nation: The Politics of Foreign Policy in the Administration of John F. Kennedy.* New York: Doubleday, 1967.

Hilsman, Roger, and Robert C. Good, eds. *Foreign Policy in the Sixties: The Issues and the Instruments.* Baltimore: Johns Hopkins Press, 1965.

Hindus, Maurice Gershon. *Crisis in the Kremlin.* New York: Doubleday, 1953.

Hinton, Harold C. *The Bear at the Gate: Chinese Policymaking Under Soviet Pressure.* Washington, D.C.: American Enterprise Institute, 1971.

Hiscocks, Richard. *Poland: Bridge for the Abyss.* London: Oxford University Press, 1963.

Hoffman, Erik P., and Frederic J. Fleron, Jr., eds. *The Conduct of Soviet Foreign Policy.* Chicago: Aldine, Atherton, 1971.

Hoffman, George W., and Fred W. Neal. *Yugoslavia and the New Communism.* New York: Twentieth Century Fund, 1962.

Hohenberg, John. *New Era in the Pacific: An Adventure in Public Diplomacy.* New York: Simon and Schuster, 1972.

Horelick, Arnold L., and Myron Rush. *Strategic Power and Soviet Foreign Policy.* Chicago: University of Chicago Press, 1966.

Horne, Alistair. *Return to Power: A Report on the New Germany.* New York: Praeger, 1956.

Hoskyns, Cathryn. *The Congo Since Independence: January 1960–December 1961.* London: Oxford University Press, 1965.

Howe, Jonathan Trumball. *Multicrises, Sea Power and Global Politics in the Missile Age.* Cambridge: MIT Press, 1971.

Hubatsch, Walther. *The German Question: A Documentary.* Translated by Salvator Attanasio. New York: Herder and Herder, 1967.

Hurewitz, J. C. *Middle East Politics: The Military Dimension.* New York: Praeger for the Council on Foreign Relations, 1969.

Hyland, William, and Richard W. Shryock. *The Fall of Khrushchev.* New York: Funk and Wagnalls, 1968.

Ignotus, Paul. *Hungary*. London: Ernest Benn, 1972.

Ionescu, Ghita. *Communism in Rumania, 1944–1962*. London: Oxford University Press, 1964.

———. *The Breakup of the Soviet Empire in Eastern Europe*. Middlesex, England: Penguin, 1965.

Jain, Jagdish. *Soviet Policy Towards Pakistan and Bangladesh*. New Delhi: Radiant Publishers, 1974.

Jakobson, Max. *Finnish Neutrality: A Study of Finnish Foreign Policy Since the Second World War*. New York: Praeger, 1968.

James, Robert Rhodes, ed. *The Czechoslovak Crisis, 1968*. London: Weidenfeld and Nicolson, 1969.

Johnson, Lyndon B. *The Vantage Point: Perspectives of the Presidency, 1963–1969*. New York: Holt, Rinehart and Winston, 1971.

Joynt, C. B., and Oles M. Smolansky. *Soviet Naval Policy in the Mediterranean*. Bethlehem, Pa.: Lehigh University Press, 1972.

Kalb, Marvin, and Bernard Kalb. *Kissinger*. Boston: Little, Brown, 1974.

Kanet, Roger E., ed. *The Soviet Union and the Developing Nations*. Baltimore: Johns Hopkins University Press, 1974.

Kanet, Roger E., and Donna Bahry, eds. *Soviet Economic and Political Relations with the Developing World*. New York: Praeger, 1975.

Kanshik, Devendra. *Soviet Relations with India and Pakistan*. New York: Barnes and Noble, 1971.

Kaplan, Morton A. *Macropolitics: Essays on the Philosophy and Science of Politics*. Chicago: Aldine, 1969.

———. *The Life and Death of the Cold War: Selected Studies in Postwar Statecraft*. Chicago: Nelson Hall, 1976.

Kapur, Harish. *The Soviet Union and the Emerging Nations: A Case Study of Soviet Policy toward India*. Geneva: Graduate Institute of International Studies, 1972.

Kennan, George F. *Russia and the West Under Lenin and Stalin*. Boston: Little, Brown, 1960.

———. *Memoirs, 1925–1950*. Boston: Little, Brown, 1967.

Kennedy, Robert F. *Thirteen Days: A Memoir of the Cuban Missile Crisis*. New York: Norton, 1969.

Kerr, Malcolm H. *The Arab Cold War*. 3d ed. London: Oxford University Press, 1971.

Kertesz, Stephen D. *Diplomacy in a Whirlpool: Hungary Between Nazi Germany and Soviet Russia*. Notre Dame, Ind.: University of Notre Dame Press, 1953.

Khadduri, Majid. *Independent Iraq, 1932–1958: A Study in Iraqi Politics*. London: Oxford University Press, 1960.

Khrushchev, Nikita S. *For Victory in Peaceful Competition with Capitalism*. New York: Dutton, 1960.

———. *Khrushchev Remembers*. Translated by Strobe Talbott. Boston: Little, Brown, 1971.

————. *Khrushchev Remembers: The Last Testament*. Translated by Strobe Talbott. Boston: Little, Brown, 1974.

Kilson, Martin Luther. *Political Change in a West African State: A Study of the Modernization Process in Sierra Leone*. Cambridge: Harvard University Press, 1966.

Kimball, Lorenzo Kent. *The Changing Pattern of Political Power in Iraq, 1958 to 1971*. New York: Speller, 1972.

Kintner, William R., and Wolfgang Klaiber. *Eastern Europe and European Security*. New York: Dunellen, 1971.

Kintner, William R., and H. F. Scott, eds. *The Nuclear Revolution in Soviet Military Affairs*. Norman: University of Oklahoma Press, 1968.

Kirk, George Edward. *Survey of International Affairs: The Middle East, 1945–1950*. London: Oxford University Press, 1954.

Kissinger, Henry A. *Nuclear Weapons and Foreign Policy*. New York: Harper and Brothers, 1957.

————. *White House Years*. Boston: Little, Brown, 1979.

Klaiber, Wolfgang, and others. *Era of Negotiations: European Security and Force Reductions*. Lexington, Mass: Heath, 1973.

Klieman, Aaron S. *Soviet Russia and the Middle East*. Baltimore: Johns Hopkins Press, 1970.

Kohler, Foy D., and others. *Soviet Strategy for the Seventies: From Cold War to Peaceful Coexistence*. Miami: University of Miami Press, 1973.

————. *The Soviet Union and the October 1973 Middle East War: The Implications for Detente*. Miami: University of Miami Press, 1974.

Korionov, Vitaly. *The Policy of Peaceful Coexistence in Action*. Moscow: Progress Publishers, 1975.

Krammer, Arnold. *The Forgotten Friendship: Israel and the Soviet Bloc, 1947–1953*. Chicago: University of Illinois Press, 1974.

Kuhn, Delia, and Ferdinand Kuhn. *Borderlands*. New York: Knopf, 1962.

Kulish, V. M. *Military Force and International Relations*. JPRS 58947. Arlington, Va.: Joint Publications Research Service, 1973.

Kulski, Wladyslaw Wszebór. *Peaceful Coexistence: An Analysis of Soviet Foreign Policy*. Chicago: Henry Regnery, 1959.

Laqueur, Walter Ze'ev. *The Soviet Union and the Middle East*. New York: Praeger, 1959.

————. *The Road to Jerusalem: The Origins of the Arab-Israeli Conflict, 1967*. New York: Macmillan, 1968.

————. *The Struggle for the Middle East: The Soviet Union in the Mediterranean, 1958–1968*. New York: Macmillan, 1969.

Larson, Arthur D. *National Security Affairs: A Guide to Information Sources*. Detroit: Gale Research, 1973.

Larson, David L., ed. *The Cuban Crisis of 1962: Selected Documents and Chronology*. New York: Houghton Mifflin, 1963.

Lattimore, Owen. *Studies in Frontier History: Collected Papers, 1928–1958*. London: Oxford University Press, 1962.

Lederer, Ivo John, and W. S. Vucinich, eds. *The Soviet Union and the Middle East: The Post–World War II Era.* Stanford: Hoover Institution Press, 1974.

Lefever, Ernest W., and Wynfred Joshua. *United Nations Peacekeeping in the Congo, 1960–1964: An Analysis of Political, Executive, and Military Control.* Washington, D.C.: Brookings Institution for the U.S. Arms Control and Disarmament Agency, 1966.

Legum, Colin. *Congo Disaster.* Baltimore: Penguin, 1961.

Legvold, Robert. *Soviet Policy in West Africa.* Cambridge: Harvard University Press, 1970.

Lehrman, Harold A. *Russia's Europe.* New York: Appleton-Century, 1947.

Lenczowski, George. *The Middle East in World Affairs.* 3d ed. New York: Cornell University Press, 1962.

―――. *Russia and the West in Iran, 1918–1948: A Study in Big Power Rivalry.* Westport, Conn.: Greenwood Press, 1968.

―――. *Soviet Advances in the Middle East.* Washington, D.C.: American Enterprise Institute, 1972.

Lensen, George Alexander. *Russia's Eastward Expansion.* Englewood Cliffs, N.J.: Prentice-Hall, 1964.

Leonhard, Wolfgang. *Child of the Revolution.* Chicago: Henry Regnery, 1958.

Levesque, Jacques. *Le Conflit Sino-Sovietique et L'Europe de L'Est.* Montreal: University of Montreal Press, 1972.

Lewis, Flora. *The Polish Volcano: A Case History of Hope.* London: Secker and Warburg, 1959.

Lewis, Geoffrey. *Turkey.* New York: Praeger, 1955.

―――. *Modern Turkey.* New York: Praeger, 1974.

Libois, J. Gerard, and Benoit Verhaegen. *Congo, 1960.* 2 vols. Brussels: Centre de Récherche et d'Information Socio-Politique, 1961.

Liddell Hart, Basil Henry. *The Soviet Army.* London: Weidenfeld and Nicolson, 1956.

Lieuwen, Edwin. *Arms and Politics in Latin America.* New York: Praeger, 1961.

Linden, Carl A. *Khrushchev and the Soviet Leadership, 1957–1964.* Baltimore: Johns Hopkins Press, 1966.

London, Kurt, ed. *Eastern Europe in Transition.* Baltimore: Johns Hopkins Press, 1966.

―――. *The Soviet Union: A Half-Century of Communism.* Baltimore: Johns Hopkins Press, 1968.

Love, Kennett. *Suez: The Twice Fought War.* New York: McGraw-Hill, 1969.

Low, Francis. *Struggle for Asia.* London: Frederick Mueller, 1955.

Luard, David Evan Trant, ed. *The Cold War: A Reappraisal.* New York: Praeger, 1964.

Mackintosh, John M. *Strategy and Tactics of Soviet Foreign Policy.* London: Oxford University Press, 1963.

————. *Juggernaut: A History of the Soviet Armed Forces.* New York: Macmillan, 1967.

Macmillan, Harold. *Tides of Fortune, 1945–1955.* New York: Harper and Row, 1969.

————. *Riding the Storm, 1956–1959.* New York: Macmillan, 1971.

————. *Pointing the Way, 1959–1961.* New York: Harper and Row, 1972.

Malinovsky, R. Ya. *Vigilantly Stand Over the Peace.* JPRS 19127. Arlington, Va.: Joint Publications Research Service, 1963.

Mamatey, Victor S. *Soviet Russian Imperialism.* New York: Van Nostrand, 1964.

Mansfield, Peter, ed. *The Middle East: A Political and Economic Survey.* 4th ed. London: Oxford University Press, 1973.

Markham, Reuben Henry. *Tito's Imperial Communism.* Chapel Hill: University of North Carolina Press, 1947.

————. *Rumania Under the Soviet Yoke.* Boston: Meador, 1949.

MccGwire, Michael, ed. *Soviet Naval Developments: Capability and Context.* New York: Praeger, 1973.

MccGwire, Michael, and John McDonnell, eds. *Soviet Naval Influence: Domestic and Foreign Dimensions.* New York: Praeger, 1977.

MccGwire, Michael, Ken Booth, and John McDonnell, eds. *Soviet Naval Policy: Objectives and Constraints.* New York: Praeger, 1975.

McKay, Vernon. *Africa in World Politics.* New York: Harper and Row, 1963.

McLane, Charles Bancroft. *Soviet Strategies in Southeast Asia: An Exploration of Eastern Policy under Lenin and Stalin.* Princeton: Princeton University Press, 1966.

————. *Soviet–Middle East Relations.* Vol. 1. New York: Columbia University Press, 1973.

McLaurin, R. D. *The Middle East in Soviet Policy.* Lexington, Mass.: Heath, 1974.

McNeill, William Hardy. *Survey of International Affairs, 1939–1946: America, Britain, and Russia: Their Cooperation and Conflict, 1941–1946.* London: Oxford University Press, 1953.

Méray, Tibor. *Thirteen Days that Shook the Kremlin.* Translated by Howard L. Katzander. London: Thames, 1959.

Merlin, Samuel. *The Search for Peace in the Middle East: The Story of Pres. Bourguiba's Campaign for a Negotiated Peace between Israel and the Arab States.* London: Thomas Yoseloff, 1968.

Merriam, Alan P. *Congo: Background of Conflict.* Evanston, Ill.: Northwestern University Press, 1961.

The Middle East and North Africa, 1967–1968. London: Europa Publications, 1967.

The Middle East and North Africa, 1969–1970. London: Europa Publications, 1969.

The Middle East and North Africa, 1976–1977. London: Europa Publications, 1976.

Middleton, Drew. *The Struggle for Germany.* New York: Bobbs-Merrill, 1949.

Mikolajczyk, Stanislaw. *The Pattern of Soviet Domination.* London: Sampson Low, Marston, 1948.

———. *The Rape of Poland: Pattern of Soviet Aggression.* New York: McGraw-Hill, 1948.

Milestones of Soviet Foreign Policy, 1917–1967. Moscow: Progress Publishers, 1967.

Millis, Walter, ed. *The Forrestal Diaries.* New York: Viking, 1951.

Mitchell, Donald William. *A History of Russian and Soviet Sea Power.* New York: Macmillan, 1974.

Mosely, Philip E. *The Kremlin and World Politics.* New York: Vintage, 1960.

———., ed. *The Soviet Union, 1922–1962.* New York: Praeger, 1963.

Murphy, George Gregory Stanislaus. *Soviet Mongolia: A Study of the Oldest Political Satellite.* Berkeley: University of California Press, 1966.

Murphy, Robert Daniel. *Diplomat Among Warriors.* New York: Doubleday, 1964.

Nagai, Yonosuke, and Akira Iriye, eds. *The Origins of the Cold War in Asia.* New York: Columbia University Press, 1977.

Nagy, Ernest A. *Crisis Decision Setting and Response: The Hungarian Revolution.* Washington, D.C.: National Defense University, 1978.

Nagy, Ferenc. *The Struggle Behind the Iron Curtain.* Translated by Stephen K. Smith. New York: Macmillan, 1948.

Naik, J. *Soviet Policy Towards India from Stalin to Brezhnev.* New Delhi: Vikas Publications, 1970.

Nettl, John Peter. *The Eastern Zone and Soviet Policy in Germany, 1945–50.* London: Oxford University Press, 1951.

Neustadt, Richard E. *Alliance Politics.* New York: Columbia University Press, 1976.

Nixon, Richard M. *Six Crises.* Garden City, N.Y.: Doubleday, 1962.

———. *RN: The Memoirs of Richard Nixon.* New York: Grosset and Dunlap, 1978.

Nollau, Günther, and H. J. Wiehe. *Russia's South Flank: Soviet Operations in Iran, Turkey and Afghanistan.* Translated by Victor Andersen. New York: Praeger, 1963.

Nutting, Anthony. *No End of a Lesson: The Story of Suez.* London: Potter, 1967.

———. *Nasser.* London: Constable, 1972.

O'Brien, Conor Cruise. *To Katanga and Back: A UN Case History.* New York: Simon and Schuster, 1962.

Pahlavi, Mohammed Reza. *Mission for My Country.* London: Hutchinson, 1960.

Pajak, Roger F. *Soviet Arms Aid in the Middle East.* Washington, D.C.: Georgetown University, 1976.

Parkinson, F. *Latin America, the Cold War, and the World Powers 1945–1973.* Beverly Hills, Calif.: Sage, 1974.

Parmet, Herbert S. *Eisenhower and the American Crusades*. New York: Macmillan, 1972.

The Pentagon Papers: The Defense Department History of United States Decisionmaking on Vietnam. 4 vols. Senator Gravel ed. Boston: Beacon Press, 1971.

Pethybridge, Roger, ed. *The Development of the Communist Bloc*. Boston: Heath, 1965.

Petrov, Vladimir. *U.S.-Soviet Detente: Past and Future*. Washington, D.C.: American Enterprise Institute, 1975.

The Policy of the Soviet Union in the Arab World. Moscow: Progress Publishers, 1975.

Ponomaryov, B., and others. *History of Soviet Foreign Policy, 1945–1970*. Moscow: Progress Publishers, 1973.

Porter, Gareth. *A Peace Denied: The United States, Vietnam, and the Paris Agreement*. Bloomington: Indiana University Press, 1975.

Quandt, William B. *Soviet Policy in the October 1973 War*. R-1864-ISA. Santa Monica, Calif.: Rand Corp., 1976.

———. *Decade of Decisions: American Policy Toward the Arab-Israeli Conflict, 1967–1976*. Berkeley: University of California Press, 1977.

Ra'anan, Uri. *The USSR Arms the Third World: Case Studies in Soviet Foreign Policy*. Cambridge: MIT Press, 1969.

Rabinovich, Itamar. *Syria Under the Ba'th, 1963–1966: The Army-Party Symbiosis*. Jerusalem: Israel University Press, 1972.

Ravenal, Earl C., ed. *Peace With China? U.S. Decisions for Asia*. New York: Liveright, 1971.

Remington, Robin Alison. *The Warsaw Pact: Case Studies in Communist Conflict Resolution*. Cambridge: MIT Press, 1971.

———., ed. *Winter in Prague*. Cambridge: MIT Press, 1969.

Roberts, Adam. *Nations in Arms*. New York: Praeger, 1976.

Royal Institute of International Affairs. *The Soviet-Yugoslav Dispute*. London: Royal Institute of International Affairs, 1948.

Rubinstein, Alvin Z. *Red Star on the Nile: The Soviet-Egyptian Influence Relationship Since the June War*. Princeton, N.J.: Princeton University Press, 1977.

———., ed. *The Foreign Policy of the Soviet Union*. 2d ed. New York: Random House, 1966.

———. *Soviet and Chinese Influence in the Third World*. New York: Praeger, 1975.

Rush, Myron, ed. *The International Situation and Soviet Foreign Policy*. Columbus, Ohio: Charles E. Merrill, 1970.

Rusinow, Dennison. *The Yugoslav Experiment, 1948–1974*. Berkeley: University of California Press, 1971.

Sachar, Howard M. *Europe Leaves the Middle East, 1936–1954*. London: Allen Lane, 1974.

Sadat, Anwar. *In Search of Identity: An Autobiography*. New York: Harper and Row, 1977.

Salomon, Michael. *Prague: La Revolution Entranglee, Janvier-Aout, 1968.* Paris: Robert Laffont, 1968.

――――. *Prague Notebook.* Boston: Little, Brown, 1976.

Saunders, Malcolm G., ed. *The Soviet Navy.* New York: Praeger, 1958.

Schandler, Herbert Y. *The Unmaking of a President: Lyndon Johnson and Vietnam.* Princeton: Princeton University Press, 1977.

Schick, Jack M. *The Berlin Crisis, 1958–1962.* Philadelphia: University of Pennsylvania Press, 1971.

Schlesinger, Arthur M., Jr. *A Thousand Days: John F. Kennedy in the White House.* Boston: Houghton Mifflin, 1965.

Schuettinger, Robert L., ed. *South Africa: The Vital Link.* Washington, D.C.: Council on American Affairs, 1976.

Schwartz, Harry. *Prague's 200 Days: The Struggle for Democracy in Czechoslovakia.* New York: Praeger, 1969.

――――. *Eastern Europe in the Soviet Shadow.* New York: John Day, 1973.

Schwarz, Urs. *Confrontation and Intervention in the Modern World.* New York: Oceana Publications, 1970.

Seale, Patrick. *The Struggle for Syria: A Study of Post-War Arab Politics, 1945–1958.* New York: Oxford University Press, 1965.

Seaton, Albert. *Stalin as Warlord.* London: B. T. Batsford, 1976.

Seton-Watson, Hugh. *The East European Revolution.* New York: Praeger, 1951.

Shanor, Donald R. *Soviet Europe.* New York: Harper and Row, 1975.

Shulman, Marshall. *Stalin's Foreign Policy Reappraised.* New York: Atheneum, 1965.

――――. *Beyond the Cold War.* New Haven: Yale University Press, 1966.

Simmons, Robert R. *The Strained Alliance: Peking, Pyongyang, Moscow and the Politics of the Korean Civil War.* New York: Free Press, 1975.

Sinanian, Sylva, Istvan Deak, and Peter C. Ludz, eds. *Eastern Europe in the 1970's.* New York: Praeger, 1972.

Singleton, Frederick B. *Background to Eastern Europe.* London: Pergamon, 1965.

Skendi, Stavro. *Albania.* New York: Praeger, 1956.

――――., ed. *East-Central Europe Under the Communists: Albania.* New York: Praeger, 1958.

Skilling, Harold Gordon. *Czechoslovakia's Interrupted Revolution.* Princeton: Princeton University Press, 1976.

Slusser, Robert M. *The Berlin Crisis of 1961.* Baltimore: Johns Hopkins University Press, 1973.

Smith, Jean Edward. *The Defense of Berlin.* Baltimore: Johns Hopkins Press, 1963.

Smith, Walter Bedell. *My Three Years in Moscow.* Toronto: Longmans, 1950.

Smolansky, Oles H. *The Soviet Union and the Arab East Under Khrushchev.* Lewisburg, Pa.: Bucknell University Press, 1974.

Social Science Research Institute. *Challenge and Response in Internal Conflict.* 2 vols. Washington, D.C.: American University, 1967.

Sokolovskiy, V. D. *Soviet Military Strategy*. 3d ed. New York: Crane, Russak, 1968.

Spector, Ivar. *The Soviet Union and the Muslim World, 1917–1958*. Seattle: University of Washington Press, 1958.

Speier, Hans, and W. P. Davidson, eds. *West German Leadership and Foreign Policy*. Evanston, Ill.: Row, Peterson, 1957.

Stearman, William Lloyd. *The Soviet Union and the Occupation of Austria: An Analysis of Soviet Policy in Austria, 1945–1955*. Bonn: Siegler, 1961.

Stephens, Robert M. *Nasser: A Political Biography*. New York: Simon and Schuster, 1972.

Stern, Ellen P. *The Limits of Military Intervention*. Beverly Hills, Calif.: Sage, 1977.

Stern, Laurence. *The Wrong Horse: The Politics of Intervention and the Failure of American Diplomacy*. New York: Times Books, 1977.

Stockwell, John. *In Search of Enemies: A CIA Story*. New York: Norton, 1978.

Stoessinger, John George. *Why Nations Go to War*. New York: St. Martin's Press, 1974.

Suarez, Andres. *Cuba: Castroism and Communism, 1959–1966*. Cambridge: MIT Press, 1967.

Suh, Dae-Sook. *The Korean Communist Movement, 1918–1948*. Princeton: Princeton University Press, 1967.

Syrop, Konrad. *Spring in October: The Story of the Polish Revolution*. New York: Praeger, 1957.

Szulc, Tad. *Czechoslovakia Since World War II*. New York: Grosset and Dunlap, 1972.

Tarabrin, E. A. *The New Scramble for Africa*. Moscow: Progress Publishers, 1974.

Tatu, Michel. *Power in the Kremlin: From Khrushchev to Kosygin*. Translated by Helen Katel. New York: Viking, 1967.

Taylor, Maxwell D. *Swords and Plowshares*. New York: Norton, 1972.

Thiam, Doudon. *The Foreign Policy of African States: Ideological Bases, Present Realities, Future Prospects*. New York: Praeger, 1965.

Thomas, Hugh. *Cuba: The Pursuit of Freedom*. New York: Harper and Row, 1971.

Torrey, Gordon H. *Syrian Politics and the Military: 1945–1958*. Columbus: Ohio State University Press, 1964.

Treadgold, Donald. *Twentieth Century Russia*. 2d ed. Chicago: Rand McNally, 1964.

Trevelyan, Humphrey. *The Middle East in Revolution*. Boston: Gambit, 1970.

Triska, Jan F., and David D. Finley. *Soviet Foreign Policy*. New York: Macmillan, 1968.

Truman, Harry S. *Memoirs*. Vol. 1: *Year of Decisions*. New York: Doubleday, 1955.

————. *Memoirs*. Vol. 2: *Years of Trial and Hope*. New York: Doubleday, 1956.

Truman, Margaret. *Harry S. Truman*. New York: William Morrow, 1973.

Udovitch, A. L. *The Middle East: Oil, Conflict, and Hope*. Lexington, Mass.: Heath, 1976.

Ulam, Adam B. *The Rivals: America and Russia Since World War II*. New York: Viking, 1971.

————. *Expansion and Coexistence: Soviet Foreign Policy, 1917–1973*. 2d ed. New York: Praeger, 1974.

U.S. Congress. House. Committee on Armed Services. "Inquiry Into the *U.S.S. Pueblo* and EC-121 Plane Incidents." Hearings before the Special House Subcommittee on the *U.S.S. Pueblo*. 91 Cong. 1 sess. Washington, D.C.: Government Printing Office, 1969.

————. Senate-House Joint Subcommittee on Armed Services. *CVAN-70 Aircraft Carrier*. 91 Cong. 2 sess. Washington, D.C.: Government Printing Office, 1970.

————. Senate. Committee on Commerce. *Soviet Oceans Development*. 94 Cong. 2 sess. Washington, D.C.: Government Printing Office, 1976.

U.S. Department of State. *Foreign Relations of the United States, 1946*. Vol. 5: *The British Commonwealth, Western and Central Europe*. Washington, D.C.: Government Printing Office, 1969.

————. *Foreign Relations of the United States, 1946*. Vol. 6: *Eastern Europe; The Soviet Union*. Washington, D.C.: Government Printing Office, 1969.

————. *Foreign Relations of the United States, 1946*. Vol. 7: *The Near East and Africa*. Washington, D.C.: Government Printing Office, 1969.

————. *Foreign Relations of the United States, 1946*. Vol. 8: *The Far East*. Washington, D.C.: Government Printing Office, 1971.

————. *Foreign Relations of the United States, 1946*. Vol. 9: *The Far East: China*. Washington, D.C.: Government Printing Office, 1972.

————. *Foreign Relations of the United States, 1946*. Vol. 10: *The Far East: China*. Washington, D.C.: Government Printing Office, 1972.

————. *Foreign Relations of the United States, 1947*. Vol. 4: *Eastern Europe; The Soviet Union*. Washington, D.C.: Government Printing Office, 1972.

————. *Foreign Relations of the United States, 1947*. Vol. 5: *The Near East and Africa*. Washington, D.C.: Government Printing Office, 1971.

————. *Foreign Relations of the United States, 1947*. Vol. 6: *The Far East*. Washington, D.C.: Government Printing Office, 1972.

————. *Foreign Relations of the United States, 1947*. Vol. 7: *The Far East: China*. Washington, D.C.: Government Printing Office, 1972.

————. *Foreign Relations of the United States, 1948*. Vol. 2: *Germany and Austria*. Washington, D.C.: Government Printing Office, 1973.

————. *Foreign Relations of the United States, 1948*. Vol. 4: *Eastern Europe; The Soviet Union*. Washington, D.C.: Government Printing Office, 1974.

————. *Foreign Relations of the United States, 1948*. Vol. 5, part 1: *The Near East, South Asia, and Africa*. Washington, D.C.: Government Printing Office, 1975.

————. *Foreign Relations of the United States, 1948*. Vol. 6: *The Far East and Australasia*. Washington, D.C.: Government Printing Office, 1974.

————. *Foreign Relations of the United States, 1948.* Vol. 7: *The Far East: China.* Washington, D.C.: Government Printing Office, 1973.

————. *Foreign Relations of the United States, 1949.* Vol. 5: *Eastern Europe; The Soviet Union.* Washington, D.C.: Government Printing Office, 1976.

————. *Foreign Relations of the United States, 1949.* Vol. 6: *The Near East, South Asia, and Africa.* Washington, D.C.: Government Printing Office, 1977.

————. *Foreign Relations of the United States, 1949.* Vol. 7, part 1: *The Far East and Australasia.* Washington, D.C.: Government Printing Office, 1975.

————. *Foreign Relations of the United States, 1949.* Vol. 7, part 2: *The Far East and Australasia.* Washington, D.C.: Government Printing Office, 1976.

————. *Foreign Relations of the United States, 1950.* Vol. 3: *Western Europe.* Washington, D.C.: Government Printing Office, 1977.

————. *Foreign Relations of the United States, 1950.* Vol. 5: *The Near East, South Asia, and Africa.* Washington, D.C.: Government Printing Office, 1978.

————. *Foreign Relations of the United States, 1950.* Vol. 6: *East Asia and the Pacific.* Washington, D.C.: Government Printing Office, 1976.

————. *Foreign Relations of the United States, 1950.* Vol. 7: *Korea.* Washington, D.C.: Government Printing Office, 1976.

————. *Foreign Relations of the United States, 1951.* Vol. 6, part 1: *Asia and the Pacific.* Washington, D.C.: Government Printing Office, 1977.

————. *Germany, 1947–1949: The Story in Documents.* Washington, D.C.: Government Printing Office, 1950.

Urban, George. *Nineteen Days: A Broadcaster's Account of the Hungarian Revolution.* London: William Heinemann, 1957.

Urquhart, Brian. *Hammarskjold.* New York: Knopf, 1972.

Váli, Ferenc Albert. *Rift and Revolt in Hungary.* Cambridge: Harvard University Press, 1961.

————. *Politics of the Indian Ocean Region: The Balances of Power.* New York: Free Press, 1976.

Vandenbosch, Amry. *South Africa and the World: The Foreign Policy of Apartheid.* Lexington: University Press of Kentucky, 1970.

Vatikiotis, P. J. *Conflict in the Middle East.* London: George Allen and Unwin, 1971.

Verhaegen, Benoit. *Congo, 1961.* Brussels: Centre de Récherche et d'Information Socio-Politique, 1962.

————. *Rebellions au Congo.* Brussels: Centre de Récherche et d'Information Socio-Politique, 1966.

Warth, Robert Douglas. *Soviet Russia in World Politics.* New York: Twayne, 1963.

Watt, D. C. *Survey of International Affairs, 1961.* London: Oxford University Press, 1965.

————. *Survey of International Affairs, 1962.* London: Oxford University Press, 1970.

————. *Survey of International Affairs, 1963.* London: Oxford University Press, 1977.

Weinstein, Martin E. *Japan's Postwar Defense Policy, 1947–1968.* New York: Columbia University Press, 1971.

Weisband, Edward. *Turkish Foreign Policy, 1943–1945: Small State Diplomacy and the Great Power Politics.* Princeton: Princeton University Press, 1973.

Werth, Alexander. *Russia at War, 1941–1945.* New York: Dutton, 1964.

Wesson, Robert G. *Soviet Foreign Policy in Perspective.* Homewood, Ill.: Dorsey Press, 1969.

Whetten, Lawrence L. *The Canal War: Four-Power Conflict in the Middle East.* Cambridge: MIT Press, 1974.

White Book on Aggressive Activities by the Governments of the USSR, Poland, Czechoslovakia, Hungary, Rumania, Bulgaria and Albania Towards Yugoslavia. Belgrade: Ministry of Foreign Affairs of the People's Republic of Yugoslavia, 1951.

Whiting, Allen Suess. *China Crosses the Yalu: The Decision to Enter the Korean War.* New York: Macmillan, 1960.

Whiting, Allen Suess, and Sheng Shih-ts'ai. *Sinkiang: Pawn or Pivot?* East Lansing: Michigan State University Press, 1958.

Windsor, Philip, and Adam Roberts. *Czechoslovakia 1968: Reform, Repression, and Resistance.* New York: Columbia University Press for the Institute for Strategic Studies, 1969.

Wolfe, Thomas W. *Soviet Power and Europe, 1945–1970.* Baltimore: Johns Hopkins Press, 1970.

Zagoria, Donald. *The Sino-Soviet Conflict, 1956–1961.* Princeton: Princeton University Press, 1962.

————. *Vietnam Triangle: Moscow, Peking, Hanoi.* Indianapolis: Pegasus, 1967.

Zhukov, Y. *The Third World: Problems and Prospects.* Moscow: Progress Publishers, 1970.

Zhurkin, V. V., and Ye. M. Primakov. *International Conflicts.* JPRS 58443. Arlington, Va.: Joint Publications Research Service, 1973.

Zimmerman, William. *Soviet Perspectives on International Relations, 1956–1967.* Princeton: Princeton University Press, 1969.

Zinner, Paul E., ed. *National Communism and Popular Revolt in Eastern Europe.* New York: Columbia University Press, 1956.

Zumwalt, Elmo R., Jr. *On Watch: A Memoir.* New York: Quadrangle, 1976.

Articles and Papers

Abrahamian, Ervand. "Communism and Communalism in Iran: The Tudeh and the Firqah-i Dimukrat," *International Journal of Middle East Studies,* vol. 1 (October 1970).

Adomeit, Hannes. "Soviet Risk-Taking and Crisis Behavior: From Confrontation to Coexistence?" Adelphi Paper 101. London: International Institute for Strategic Studies, 1973.

Blechman, Barry M., and Robert G. Weinland. "Why Coaling Stations are Necessary in the Nuclear Age," *International Security,* vol. 2 (Summer 1977).

Boyd, J. Huntly, Jr. "Nimrod Spar: Clearing the Suez Canal," *U.S. Naval Institute Proceedings,* vol. 102 (February 1976).

Burt, Richard, and Geoffrey Kemp. "Congressional Hearings on American Defense Policy, 1947–1971: An Annotated Bibliography." Lawrence, Kans.: University Press of Kansas, 1974.

Buzan, Barry. "The Status and Future of the Montreux Convention," *Survival,* vol. 18 (November/December 1976).

Caldwell, Dan. "Soviet-American Crisis Interaction: The Cuban Missile Crisis and the October War." Palo Alto, Calif.: Stanford University Press, 1977.

Dragnich, George S. "The Soviet Union's Quest for Access to Naval Facilities in Egypt prior to the June War of 1967." Professional Paper 127. Arlington, Va.: Center for Naval Analyses, 1974.

Durch, William J. "Revolution from A.F.A.R.—The Cuban Armed Forces in Africa and the Middle East." Professional Paper 199. Arlington, Va.: Center for Naval Analyses, 1977.

———. "The Cuban Military in Africa and the Middle East: From Algeria to Angola." Professional Paper 201. Arlington, Va.: Center for Naval Analyses, 1977.

"Evolution de la Crise Congolaise de Septembre 1960 à Avril 1961," *Chronique de Politique Etrangère,* vol. 14 (September–November 1961).

Horelick, Arnold. "The Cuban Missile Crisis: An Analysis of Soviet Calculations and Behavior," *World Politics,* vol. 16 (April 1964).

Hudson, George. "Soviet Naval Doctrine and Soviet Politics, 1953–1975," *World Politics,* vol. 29 (October 1976).

Hurewitz, J. C. "Russia and the Turkish Straits: A Revaluation of the Origins of the Problem," *World Politics,* vol. 14 (July 1962).

Jones, Christopher. "Soviet Hegemony in Eastern Europe: The Dynamics of Political Autonomy and Military Intervention," *World Politics,* vol. 29 (January 1977).

Jukes, Geoffrey. "The Indian Ocean in Soviet Naval Policy." Adelphi Paper 87. London: International Institute for Strategic Studies, 1972.

Kassing, David. "Changes in Soviet Naval Forces." Professional Paper 183. Arlington, Va.: Center for Naval Analyses, 1976.

Kelly, Anne M. "The Soviet Naval Presence During the Iraq-Kuwait Border Dispute: March/April 1973." Professional Paper 122. Arlington, Va.: Center for Naval Analyses, 1974.

———. "Port Visits and the 'Internationalist Mission' of the Soviet Navy." Professional Paper 145. Arlington, Va.: Center for Naval Analyses, 1976.

Kidd, Isaac C., Jr. "View from the Bridge of the Sixth Fleet Flagship," *U.S. Naval Institute Proceedings,* vol. 98 (February 1972).

Kolodziej, Edward A. "French Military Policy: The Politics of Weakness," *International Affairs,* vol. 47 (July 1971).

McConnell, James M. "The Soviet Navy in the Indian Ocean." Professional Paper 77. Arlington, Va.: Center for Naval Analyses, 1971.

McConnell, James M., and Anne M. Kelly. "Superpower Naval Diplomacy in the Indo-Pakistani Crisis." Professional Paper 108. Arlington, Va.: Center for Naval Analyses, 1973.

Pajak, Roger. "Soviet Arms and Egypt," *Survival,* vol. 17 (July/August 1975).

Petersen, Charles C. "The Soviet Port-Clearing Operation in Bangladesh, March 1972–December 1973." Professional Paper 123. Arlington, Va.: Center for Naval Analyses, 1974.

————. "The Soviet Union and the Re-Opening of the Suez Canal: Mine-clearing Operations in the Gulf of Suez." Professional Paper 137. Arlington, Va.: Center for Naval Analyses, 1975.

Phillips, Heidi. "Host Press Coverage of Soviet Naval Visits to Islamic Countries 1968–1973." CRC 283. Arlington, Va.: Center for Naval Analyses, 1976.

Robinson, Thomas W. "The Sino-Soviet Border Dispute: Background, Development, and the March 1969 Clashes," *American Political Science Review,* vol. 66 (December 1972).

Shulsky, Abram N. "The Soviet Air Force: Silence About Its Interventionary and Political Uses." Memorandum 76-0217. Arlington, Va.: Center for Naval Analyses, 1976.

U.S. Department of State. Bureau of Intelligence and Research. "North Korea: A Case Study in the Techniques of Takeover." Far Eastern Series 103, no. 7118. Washington, D.C.: Government Printing Office, 1961.

————. "Indo-Pakistani Crisis—Chronology of Key Events." Washington, D.C.: Government Printing Office, 1972.

Vincent, R. J. "Military Power and Political Influence: The Soviet Union and Western Europe." Adelphi Paper 119. London: International Institute for Strategic Studies, 1975.

Weinland, Robert G. "The Changing Mission Structure of the Soviet Navy." Professional Paper 80. Arlington, Va.: Center for Naval Analyses, 1971.

————. "Soviet Transits of the Turkish Straits, 1945–1970: An Historical Note on the Establishment and Dimensions of the Soviet Naval Presence in the Mediterranean." Professional Paper 94. Arlington, Va.: Center for Naval Analyses, 1972.

————. "Soviet Naval Operations—Ten Years of Change." Professional Paper 125. Arlington, Va.: Center for Naval Analyses, 1974.

————. "A Potentially Important Indicator of Expansion in the Internationalist Functions of the Soviet Armed Forces." Working Paper 892-74. Arlington, Va.: Center for Naval Analyses, 1974.

————. "Superpower Naval Diplomacy in the October 1973 Arab-Israeli War." Professional Paper 221. Arlington, Va.: Center for Naval Analyses, 1978.

Wells, Anthony R. "The 1967 June War: Soviet Naval Diplomacy and the Sixth Fleet—A Reappraisal." Professional Paper 204. Arlington, Va.: Center for Naval Analyses, 1977.

Chronologies

Africa Confidential (biweekly), 1960–1977.
Africa Contemporary Record (annual), 1968–1977.
Africa Diary (weekly), 1961–1977.
Africa Report (monthly). "News in Brief," 1957–1978.
Africa Research Bulletin (monthly). "Chronology," 1964–1977.
Annual Register of World Events, 1961–1977.
Asian Recorder (weekly), 1955–1977.
Cahiers de L'Orient Contemporain (quarterly). "Le Moyen Orient et en Politique Internationale," 1945–1969.
The China Quarterly. "Chronicle and Documentation," 1960–1977.
Chronique de Politique Etrangère (bimonthly), 1951–1973.
Current Digest of the Soviet Press (weekly), 1949–1977.
Current History (monthly). "Chronology," 1948–1977.
"Current News" (U.S. Department of Defense, daily), 1965–1979.
Documents on International Affairs (annual), 1947–1962.
Institute for the Study of the U.S.S.R. Bulletin (monthly). "Chronology of Events," 1954–1971.
International Affairs, Moscow (monthly), 1955–1977.
Keesing's Contemporary Archives (annual), 1945–1977.
Middle East Journal (quarterly). "Chronology," 1947–1977.
Middle East Record (annual), 1960–1968.
New Times (weekly). "World Events," 1955–1959.
New York Times Index (annual, selected subheadings), 1945–1978.
Soviet Survey (quarterly), 1957–1976.
Strategic Survey (annual), 1969–1977.
Studies on the Soviet Union (quarterly), 1961–1971.
U.S. Department of Navy. Naval Historical Center. Operational Archives. "A Chronology of Naval Events, 1960–1977." Compiled by Barbara Gilmore.
U.S. Naval Institute Proceedings (annual *Naval Review* issue). "Chronology," 1964–1977.

Index

Acheson, Dean, 317, 322
Ackley, Richard T., 522n, 523n
Adane, Bitwoded, 613
Adenauer, Konrad, 120
Administrative statements. *See* Policy instruments
Adomeit, Hannes, 347n
Afghanistan, 32, 40, 146–47, 152
African Party for the Independence of Guinea and Cape Verde (PAIGC), 520, 539, 542–45, 547–49, 555, 564–65
Agreement on Measures to Reduce the Risk of Outbreak of Nuclear War, 134
Air forces: activities, 10–13, 37–38, 41, 44, 199; ally maintenance incidents, 36–38; Angolan civil war, 199, 557, 587, 589–90; Anyanya insurgency, 493, 495, 498; Czechoslovak crisis of *1968*, 229, 230; development of, 8–10, 165, 199; EC-121 crisis, 106, 382–83; Egyptian air defense crisis, 469, 474, 479–80; Ethiopian-Somalian conflict, 199, 620–21, 626, 627; expansionary incidents, 35; incident participation, 35–37, 40, 44, 45, 49; Korean War, 326, 331–32; Kurdish rebellion, 504–05, 507; October war, 441, 447, 449, 450, 452–53, 462; peacetime use, 191–92; poplar tree incident, 398, 399; *Pueblo* crisis, 360–62, 370, 376–77; security incidents, 40–41; third world incidents, 44–45; utility of, 671–73; Vietnam War, 336–37, 346
Albania, 29, 38, 66–67, 84, 88, 163
Algeria, 199, 451
Alla, Malumud Ata, 491n

Allison, Graham T., 54n, 131n
Allon, Yigal, 169n
Ally maintenance: China, 92–96; Cuba, 96–97, 106–07; Czechoslovakia, 80–83; defense against China, 107–13; defense against external threats, 87–107; defense of Eastern Europe, 87–88, 103; disloyalty, 72–86; East Germany, 72–73; Hungary, 78–80; incident characteristics, 35–38; interventionist policy, 85–86; North Korea, 90–92, 106; North Vietnam, 98–105, 107–13; Poland, 73–74, 77–78; Rumania, 83–85; Yugoslavia, 75–77
Alvor Accord, 580, 593
Amin, Hafizullah, 147
Amin, Idi, 497, 576, 597
Anderson, Jack, 184n, 366
Andropov, Yuri, 220–21, 246, 337
Angolan civil war: Angolan behavior, 573–74, 587, 597, 603–05; armed forces used, 587, 588; Cuban behavior, 195–99, 578–79, 583–90, 593–96, 598–605; history, 580–90; military activities, 556, 557, 583–85, 587–90, 593–95; objectives, 577–78, 589–90; outcomes, 599–605, 658, 661, 663, 665–66; policy instruments, 591–92, 595; Soviet behavior, 591–96; third-party behavior, 195–96, 574–80, 597–99; U.S. behavior, 195, 197–98, 573, 576–77, 581, 584–89, 591, 594, 596, 598–99, 602–05, 665
Ankrah, Joseph A., 536
Ansar insurrection, 494–95
Antonov, G. I., 64n
Anyanya insurgency: armed forces used,

717